PARALEGAL LITIGATION AND PRACTICE TITLES FROM WILEY LAW PUBLICATIONS

ADMINISTRATIVE LAW GUIDE FOR PARALEGALS
Wendy Van Duyne

BANKRUPTCY LAW AND PROCEDURE: A GUIDE FOR PARALEGALS (THIRD EDITION)
Steven N. Berger, J. Daria Westland, and Thomas J. Salerno

BUSINESS FORMS FOR PARALEGALS (DISK EDITION)
Charles P. Nemeth

CHILD SUPPORT FORMS AND PROCEDURES
James B. Hardin, Jr.

CONSTRUCTION LITIGATION FOR PARALEGALS: CLAIMS PREPARATION AND MANAGEMENT
Dianne D. Zalewski and Cheryl D. Evans

DEPOSITION MANUAL FOR PARALEGALS (SECOND EDITION)
Christine Bergren Greene

ESTATE PLANNING AND ADMINISTRATION FOR PARALEGALS
Charles P. Nemeth

EVIDENCE HANDBOOK FOR PARALEGALS
Charles P. Nemeth

LITIGATION GUIDE FOR PARALEGALS: RESEARCH AND DRAFTING (SECOND EDITION)
Cynthia Monteiro Osborne

LITIGATION ORGANIZATION AND MANAGEMENT FOR PARALEGALS
Lynn M. Randall

LITIGATION PARALEGAL (SECOND EDITION)
Phillip J. Signey

MEDICAL RECORDS REVIEW (SECOND EDITION)
Kristyn S. Appleby and Joanne Tarver

PARALEGAL BOOK OF LETTERS
Wiley Law Publications

PARALEGAL CAREER GUIDE
Chere B. Estrin

PARALEGAL DISCOVERY: ORGANIZATION AND MANAGEMENT
Joyce Samson and Dianne Zalewski

PARALEGAL DISCOVERY: PROCEDURES AND FORMS (SECOND EDITION)
Pat Medina

PARALEGAL DRAFTING GUIDE
Dorien S. McClellan

PARALEGAL GUIDE TO INTELLECTUAL PROPERTY
Valerie J. Atkinson

PARALEGAL LETTERS DISK
Wiley Law Publications

PARALEGAL LITIGATION: FORMS AND PROCEDURE (SECOND EDITION)
Marcy Davis Fawcett

PARALEGAL LITIGATION: FORMS AND PROCEDURE (SECOND EDITION) (DISK EDITION)
Marcy Davis Fawcett

PARALEGAL MANAGEMENT HANDBOOK
Maureen Brophy and Patsy Pressley

PARALEGAL TRIAL HANDBOOK (SECOND EDITION)
Beverly K. Hutson

PERSONAL INJURY PARALEGAL (SECOND EDITION)
Sharon Atwood

PERSONAL INJURY PARALEGAL: FORMS AND PROCEDURES
Joyce Walden

PERSONAL INJURY PARALEGAL: FORMS AND PROCEDURES (DISK EDITION)
Joyce Walden

REAL ESTATE FORECLOSURE: PARALEGAL PRACTICE AND PROCEDURE
Charles P. Nemeth and Grayson P. Van Horn

STARTING AND MANAGING YOUR OWN BUSINESS: A FREELANCING GUIDE FOR PARALEGALS
Dorothy Secol

ESTRIN SERIES

COMPUTERIZED LITIGATION SUPPORT
Despina C. Kartson and Norman F. Strizek

CORPORATE FORMATION: A PRIMER FOR LEGAL ASSISTANTS
Patricia A. Dris

HANDLING THE AUTO ACCIDENT CASE: A GUIDE FOR THE PARALEGAL
Jimmie Murvin

HOW TO SURVIVE IN A LAW FIRM: CLIENT RELATIONS
Dana Graves, Jill Levin, and Nancy Pulsifer

MEDICAL MALPRACTICE GUIDE FOR PARALEGALS
Stephanie A. Danelson

THE PARALEGAL'S ROLE AT TRIAL
Kerri W. Feeney

SMART LITIGATING WITH COMPUTERS
Patricia S. Eyres

PARALEGAL TRIAL HANDBOOK

SECOND EDITION

SUBSCRIPTION NOTICE

This Wiley product is updated on a periodic basis with supplements to reflect important changes in the subject matter. If you purchased this product directly from John Wiley & Sons, Inc., we have already recorded your subscription for this update service.

If, however, you purchased this product from a bookstore and wish to receive (1) the current update at no additional charge, and (2) future updates and revised or related volumes billed separately with a 30-day examination review, please send your name, company name (if applicable), address and the title of the product to:

Supplement Department
John Wiley & Sons, Inc.
One Wiley Drive
Somerset, NJ 08875
1-800-225-5945

For customers outside the United States, please contact the Wiley office nearest you.

Professional and Reference Division
John Wiley & Sons Canada, Ltd.
22 Worcester Road
Rexdale, Ontario M9W 1L1
CANADA
(416) 675-3580
1-800-567-4797
Fax: (416) 675-6599

John Wiley & Sons, Ltd.
Baffins Lane
Chichester
West Sussex, PO19 1UD
UNITED KINGDOM
Phone: (44) (243) 779777

Jacaranda Wiley Ltd
PRT Division
P.O. Box 174
North Ryde, NSW 2113
AUSTRALIA
Phone: (02) 805-1100
Fax: (02) 805-1597

John Wiley & Sons (SEA) Pte. Ltd.
37 Jalan Pemimpin
Block B # 05-04
Union Industrial Building
SINGAPORE 2057
Phone: (65) 258-1157

PARALEGAL TRIAL HANDBOOK SECOND EDITION

BEVERLY K. HUTSON

Brouse & McDowell
Akron, Ohio

Wiley Law Publications

JOHN WILEY & SONS, INC.

New York • Chichester • Brisbane • Toronto • Singapore

This text is printed on acid-free paper.

Library of Congress Cataloging-in-Publication Data

ISBN 0-471-12167-3

Printed in the United States of America

10 9 8 7 6 5 4

To my beloved husband, David, who generously and unselfishly supplied the love, support, and encouragement which made it possible for me to write this book. You are the best.

PREFACE

Whether you are a paralegal in a private law firm, a corporate legal department, a government office, or freelance business, preparing a case for trial and assisting the attorney during trial require thorough organization and management skills. *Paralegal Trial Handbook* (2d edition) is a dynamic and useful resource work that offers hundreds of specific practical methods and techniques to help paralegals expertly assist attorneys in all aspects of trial work, from investigation and file organization through the courtroom presentation, and beyond the trial into appeals and other posttrial activities. *Paralegal Trial Handbook* provides a fresh approach to defining and resolving the multiple problems you will encounter in trial preparation work and offers tips for preparing a case from both the plaintiff's and the defendant's perspectives. *Paralegal Trial Handbook* discusses the importance of visual media in courtroom presentations and offers tips on designing and developing good trial visuals. This book contains practical advice for paralegals and legal assistants at all levels of experience, from novice through advanced, in all types of civil cases at all court levels. *Paralegal Trial Handbook* offers many tips and techniques that can be adapted for use in courtroom or administrative tribunal appearances of any type, including alternate dispute resolution techniques. In addition, the second edition contains updated and expanded information on using the computer as a tool in trial work, using practical, non-technical language to explain word processing, databases, and automated document management procedures. *Paralegal Trial Handbook* contains hundreds of model questions, samples, forms, logs, worksheets, checklists, and practice tips to help you organize your cases. This book will give you valuable information on

Working with trial attorneys

Building master reference notebooks

Managing time and resources

Budgeting for case preparation

Organizing files and materials for trial

Planning and implementing a document management plan

Indexing and color-coding

Preparing clients and trial witnesses

Working with expert witnesses

Preparing visual aids and demonstrative exhibits

Assembling, preparing, and managing documentary exhibits

Handling nondocument exhibits

Organizing the trial war room

Preparing and serving trial subpoenas

Assisting in voir dire

Processing posttrial motions and appeals

Applying computer technology to trial work

and many other tasks that are critical for the trial paralegal. The comprehensive outlines, master lists, and forms in *Paralegal Trial Handbook* will help you organize time, people, and materials for trial. *Paralegal Trial Handbook* is a complete source book and reference manual for paralegals and legal assistants involved in litigation and trial work. Written by an author with over 20 years' experience in preparing cases and assisting at trial, this book will tell you what is important for a trial paralegal, from understanding the issues to assembling courtroom tools and supplies. You are sure to find many practical, time-saving tips and ideas that you can put to work right away to help you streamline your trial preparation practice.

Akron, Ohio
February 1995

BEVERLY K. HUTSON

ACKNOWLEDGMENTS

I would not consider this project complete without expressing my gratitude and appreciation to the many friends and colleagues who have encouraged and inspired me. I wish to recognize and thank the following persons for their contributions: my friend and mentor, Robert E. Kerper, Jr., Esq., a true believer in attorney-paralegal teamwork, who has given me so many opportunities to gain courtroom experience over the years; my cherished friend, Elaine L. Williams, PLS, for her constant vigilance, common sense, and professional insight; my sister, Layne Elizabeth Kilgore, for her unfailing support; my dear friend, LeAnna Shaffer Burdett, for her patience and cheerful assistance in designing many of the forms and worksheets in this book; my mother, Dr. Patricia Hilton, who understands the effort that goes into writing well; my favorite librarian, Connie L. Pecimon, for helping me keep things together during the birth of this project; legal illustrator, Kathleen Young, for sharing her expertise on visual aids and demonstrative evidence; my first mentor, Michael A. Thompson, Esq., for making me sit down and study the Civil Rules so many years ago; my special friend, Thomas E. Barnes, Esq., for believing in me; my loyal paralegal colleagues, Melanie Misitigh, Lisa Vargo, Jennifer Sybyl, and Carolyn Clark Felton for their friendship, enthusiasm, and support; and Glenn, John, Dale, and Sid, for their esteem, respect, and confidence in my abilities.

B.K.H.

ABOUT THE AUTHOR

Beverly K. Hutson is a senior litigation paralegal with the firm of Brouse & McDowell in Akron, Ohio. With over 20 years' experience in the legal field, Ms. Hutson provides paralegal support to attorneys in all phases of the litigation process. In addition to preparing cases for trial and assisting attorneys in the courtroom, Ms. Hutson's professional responsibilities include advising attorneys on litigation support issues and techniques, computer training, and managing a central forms bank for all departments in the firm. She also does independent consulting, teaching, and seminar speaking on paralegal and litigation support issues.

Ms. Hutson's professional credentials include serving as president of the Northeastern Ohio Paralegal Association (NOPA), directing the 1994 Ohio Statewide Forum, and appointment to the President's Advisory Committee on paralegal issues for the Association of Trial Lawyers of America (ATLA). Ms. Hutson's other professional affiliations include membership in the National Association of Legal Assistants (NALA), the Ohio State Bar Association (OSBA), the American Bar Association (ABA), the Akron Bar Association, National Association of Female Executives (NAFE), and Akron Women's Network.

Ms. Hutson enjoys hearing from readers and welcomes your ideas and comments. If you have suggestions for areas that could be expanded or ideas for new topics you would like to see addressed in future supplements, you may write to her at 500 First National Tower, Akron, Ohio 44308, or call her at (216) 535-5711.

SUMMARY CONTENTS

DETAILED CONTENTS

CHAPTER 1

WORKING WITH THE TRIAL ATTORNEY

§ 1.1 Defining Your Role in the Trial Scenario

Successful trial preparation culminates in having the trial materials, exhibits, and witnesses ready for trial, and then bringing them all together in the proper order, at the right place, and at the right time. As a trial paralegal, you become an extension of the attorney's time, energy, and abilities to ensure the best trial presentation possible. Trial work, perhaps more than any other aspect of law practice, provides an excellent forum for the trial paralegal to demonstrate the true value of legal assisting skills. Trial attorneys can benefit from paralegal assistance in any size or type of case. During trial preparation, the attorney must focus on the legal issues, evidentiary requirements, and witness examinations involved in the case. Even in a relatively simple case, thorough trial preparation demands attention to many different aspects of the case. It is difficult for a trial attorney to manage everything; he or she can always use some help in attending to the myriad peripheral details involved in the trial preparation and courtroom presentation. The purpose of this book is to explore and discuss the wide variety of ways in which you, the trial paralegal, can assist and enhance the attorney and make his or her efforts more productive in preparing cases for trial and successfully presenting them in the courtroom.

§ 1.2 Providing Organization, Structure, and Continuity

Cases that ultimately go to trial often exist for many months, and sometimes several years, between inception and the actual trial date. I think of this as the "life span" of the case. Many significant changes may affect the case during the extended span of the litigation. These could include things such as:

- The case may be "handed off" from one attorney to another within your office
- The opposing parties may change attorneys
- Additional claims or counts may be added to the initial complaint, or new parties may be joined or added as third-party defendants
- Witnesses may move away from the area, making them difficult to locate by the time the trial arrives
- The volume of the file materials or discovery documents may increase to far exceed the amount of documents originally anticipated.

Ideally, a litigation case file will be assigned to one paralegal who can control and monitor the accumulation of the case materials from the very beginning of the case, organizing and structuring the file to facilitate trial preparation as the end result (see §§ **2.4–2.5**). When you are the assigned paralegal throughout the life of the case, you can be invaluable to the attorney by:

- Organizing and building the case files and materials as new documents are added
- Keeping track of changes in the case over time
- Acting as the central records manager for key information pertaining to the development of the case
- Coordinating the litigation support activity, either in-house or through litigation support vendors
- Keeping in touch with the clients and witnesses
- Compiling the materials designated specifically for use at trial
- Documenting the trial planning and strategy sessions
- Developing demonstrative evidence for courtroom use
- Facilitating the trial preparation efforts by being able to quickly locate and retrieve information from the files.

Monitoring the development of a trial case over a life span of several years involves a lot of hard work and carries with it a high level of responsibility for you as the trial paralegal. An important part of that responsibility is preparing for the eventuality that you will not be around to see the case through at trial. This is not a pleasant thought, but a responsible trial paralegal realizes that accidents do happen! Therefore, when you are preparing a case for trial, aim at being organized enough so that someone else could pick up the work if necessary. Try to document the progress of the case in such a manner so that if something happened to you, another paralegal could make sense of how the file was organized, what had been done so far, what else needed to be done, and so forth. Using the forms and checklists presented throughout this book to collect and record case information in a manner that someone else can readily understand will ensure that you leave an "organizational trail" as you prepare cases for trial.

§ 1.3 Understanding the Legal and Evidentiary Issues

Comprehending all the possible ramifications and subtleties of the legal doctrines and theories involved in the case is mainly the trial attorney's responsibility. However, having some degree of familiarity with the basic legal concepts underlying the causes of action in your case will help you to understand the key elements you need to prove or refute at trial. The more you do understand about the legal concepts, the better you will be able to assist the trial attorney. You also need to have a basic understanding of the rules of evidence and how they apply to the dispute in your case. The evidence rules provide guidelines for:

- What evidence is required to prove various elements of a case
- What is or is not permitted to be offered as evidence
- Admissibility requirements for various types of evidence.

Within the framework of the legal doctrines and the applicable rules of evidence, you can then assist the attorney in lining up the factual evidence that supports your claims if you are the plaintiff or that refutes the claims if you are the defendant. You will also need to understand the issues surrounding the attorney-client privilege and work product doctrine in order to deal effectively with discovery and document productions in the case. You need to be familiar with federal and state rules of civil procedure and keep up with changes and amendments to those rules. The mandatory initial disclosure provisions in the Federal Rules of Civil Procedure (FRCP) that became effective in December 1993, are bound to affect the way we conduct discovery, develop cases, and prepare for trial. Refer to §§ **2.23–2.32** for a discussion of the 1993 FRCP amendments.

§ 1.4 Developing Factual Investigation and Research

Virtually any subject matter imaginable can be involved in a lawsuit. In order to adequately develop and try a case involving any profession, product, process, industry, or technical area, the trial team must gain an understanding of the fundamental principles of the subject matter. As a result, legal trial professionals have to become knowledgeable in many diverse subject areas. This variety keeps trial work interesting even after many years of practice. In the trial setting, the attorney will have to communicate information, often complex and technical in nature, to the judge and jury to aid them in making judgments based upon a proper understanding of the subject matter. As a trial paralegal, you can be invaluable to the attorney in developing the case for trial by:

- Using computers and current technology to thoroughly research the subject
- Compiling information and background materials related to the subject matter
- Applying your knowledge and understanding of the subject to the facts of the case at hand.

Refer to § **1.57** for suggestions and techniques for developing your skills in performing factual research.

§ 1.5 Providing a Layperson's Viewpoint

Trial attorneys sometimes become so immersed in the legal issues that they lose sight of the potential effect upon the jury of the information to be presented. The attorney may find it very helpful to try out various ideas and strategic approaches on you for constructive feedback before incorporating them into the trial presentation. Remember that in trial work, there are no stupid questions. If something in the planned trial presentation is not clear to you, it will probably not be clear to the jury members, either. You can help the attorney to simplify complex materials or information for easy assimilation by the judge or jury. Your questions may point out to the attorney some aspect of the case that needs clarification or greater attention to detail in presenting the information in court. You may be able to add ideas that didn't occur to the attorney. You can also assist the attorney by polishing the written documents and pleadings the attorney produces. In order to do this, you need to develop excellent written communication skills and a grasp of grammar and syntax rules. One attorney I work with likes to draft correspondence, pleadings, or memoranda and then give them to me to improve and polish. He has been known to say that his writing is always so much better when I get finished with it, proving that this is a way for me to be a valuable assistant to him in producing his work product.

§ 1.6 Communicating with the Client

Attorneys who handle heavy trial schedules sometimes forget that, to the client, taking a case to trial is a mysterious and anxiety-producing experience. A certain amount of "hand holding" is necessary, even with very sophisticated clients (see § **3.17**). A paralegal who is familiar with the case and with trial procedures can be invaluable in keeping the client informed. Clients rarely complain about having too much communication from their trial attorneys! One of the most effective ways you can assist the attorney as the case progresses toward trial is to help keep the client informed through letters, telephone calls, and personal conferences, about what is happening and why. This lightens the attorney's load during trial preparation and helps to provide the client with timely and accurate feedback on the status of the case. If the attorney has properly introduced you to the client and indicated that you are a **member** of the trial team, the client will feel comfortable and satisfied with communications that you initiate or relay.

Client communication works both ways. The paralegal serves as an alternate contact through which the client can direct information, concerns, or questions related to the trial proceedings in the event the trial attorney is not available. Once the trial begins, the paralegal who has had previous contact with the client is a friendly face in the courtroom. The paralegal can be very supportive to the client by providing reassurances and explanations as the trial progresses. In situations in which a client has special needs, for example, when the client is handicapped, elderly, or extremely ill, the paralegal can be invaluable to the trial attorney by attending to the details involved in dealing with these special problems (see § **3.17**).

§ 1.7 Linking the Attorney to the "Outside World"

An important function of a trial paralegal is to facilitate communication between the attorney and the various other persons that are involved with the case in one way or another. These persons include:

- Clients
- Witnesses
- Expert witnesses
- Office staff
- Judges and their assistants (bailiff, secretary)
- Opposing counsel
- Courthouse personnel
- Court stenographers
- Deposition court reporters/videotape technicians
- Illustrators and photographers
- Investigator and process servers
- Litigation support vendors
- Personnel from other support companies, such as couriers and copy services.

When the attorney is in "trial mode," he or she will be totally immersed in study and mental preparation for the trial. It can be a great help to have you run interference by handling some of the necessary communications with these persons, thus freeing the attorney to concentrate on his or her individual preparation tasks.

§ 1.8 Applying Technology to Trial Work

More law offices have computers now than ever before. Computer products continue to improve, and decreasing prices make computer technology readily available to any size of law office. Attorneys and paralegals are finding that they have to become computer literate in order to keep up with developments in technology and information processing. Computers have had and will continue to have a profound effect on the way we do our work. Paralegals can provide a valuable service to attorneys by taking the lead in learning and embracing the new technology, and discovering new ways to apply automation techniques to trial preparation and courtroom presentation. **Chapter 8** discusses the new technology and provides some information and ideas on ways you can apply it in your work.

§ 1.9 Working in the Law Office

Successfully working with lawyers requires the trial paralegal to develop certain interpersonal skills. You must be able to communicate well with attorneys and other persons in the law office and to understand the dynamics that affect how trial attorneys approach their work. This section deals with survival skills and attitudes you will need to develop to succeed in trial work.

§ 1.10 Learning to Work with Trial Attorneys

I have always enjoyed my work as a litigation paralegal. After 20 years in the legal field, I can attest that the attorneys with whom I have had the good fortune to work are, almost without exception, a truly fine group. Attorneys are among the most intelligent, talented, dedicated, and hard-working professionals I have encountered. They can also be stubborn, moody, arrogant, and impossibly demanding. Working with them can be exhausting and sometimes frustrating, but it is also challenging, interesting, and ultimately (on balance) very rewarding. These are some common sense observations and theories I have formulated over the years that may help you begin to understand the attorneys with whom you work:

- Each trial attorney has his or her own style and approach to trial preparation. In order to be a successful trial paralegal, you must first figure out the attorney's individual work style and habits, and then adapt your work patterns to complement the attorney's preferences and priorities.
- You must earn an attorney's trust and confidence. Attorneys are trained to be skeptical and to question everything. The attorney will not automatically

believe that a capable paralegal assistant is the best thing to happen to trial practice! Be prepared to demonstrate your professional skills and prove your value in preparing a case for trial. Once you have proved yourself, the attorney who believes in you and trusts your judgment and your abilities can be your most loyal supporter.

- You do not have to particularly like the attorney's personality in order to work with him or her professionally. It is very nice when you do happen to like the attorney you work with, but it is not essential. A truly professional trial paralegal must be flexible, gracious, and accommodating toward a broad range of attorney personality types. Learn to set your personal feelings aside and to concentrate on the work at hand.
- It is perhaps one of the greatest ironies in legal work that, although attorneys depend on their communication skills for their livelihoods, they are often such poor communicators with the people who work for them. You will often have to initiate communication and take responsibility for following through in order to get the information you need from the trial attorney.
- Attorneys are generally precise and highly accurate in their work, but they are human, and therefore they do occasionally make mistakes. When you discover an error, you have an ethical responsibility to bring it to the attorney's attention. However, you must be very diplomatic and tactful about pointing out errors because attorneys are trained to be sure of themselves and they hate to admit it when they are wrong.

§ 1.11 Getting the Attorney to Give You Responsibility

If you are new at the job, or if you haven't yet established a good working relationship with the trial attorney in your office, you should be aware of some fundamental truths about most trial attorneys:

- Law schools generally do not teach courses on the effective use of paralegals, so you may have to convince the attorney that there are many ways you can help in trial preparation.
- Attorneys often appear to procrastinate about beginning trial preparation. Realize that things are not always what they seem to be (see § **1.12,** Dealing with Attorney Procrastination).
- Attorneys often think they don't *need* any help in preparing for trial. (This is usually wrong, of course!)
- Busy trial attorneys often don't want to take the time to train or teach their assistants, so you may have to learn some things on your own, through seminars, or from a paralegal mentor.

- Attorneys often have trouble delegating work. Effective delegation requires skills that some attorneys simply have not developed. It may take some effort on your part to overcome the attorney's resistance to sharing the trial preparation work.
- Some attorneys simply will never learn to use paralegals properly in trial work. Reconcile yourself to accepting what you cannot change. Trial attorneys who do not make use of paralegals just do not know what they are missing!

You will find that after you have established a working relationship with the trial attorney that is based upon trust and confidence in your abilities, you will not have to beg for responsibility. Experienced trial paralegals will tell you that, once the attorney is accustomed to delegating trial preparation work, you will have all the responsibility you can handle. These are some suggestions and strategies for getting the attorney's attention and encouraging him or her to give you trial preparation assignments.

Be assertive. Ask the attorney directly if you can help with the trial. (Wise attorneys don't turn down offers of good help, because they know how hectic trials can get!) Let the attorney know you are interested, willing, and available for trial work. Figure out which aspects of the trial preparation the attorney places the highest priority on and offer to help get those jobs completed. Also, volunteer to tackle jobs that you know must be done, but which the attorney may not particularly like to do. You can perform a great service during a busy trial preparation by taking these jobs off the attorney's hands.

Offer help early. Offer your assistance early enough in the trial preparation schedule so the attorney has time to reflect on what you might be able to do to help. He or she may initially refuse your offer, but later reconsider and ask you to help when things get really hectic. Begin working on the case early as possible, so that you will have accumulated considerable knowledge about the case by the time the trial date arrives. However, realize that you can be of some assistance to the attorney regardless of when you are brought in on the case or what segments you are asked to handle. Watch the office docket or calendar for trials that are coming up. Ask the attorney in charge of the case how you can help in the trial preparation.

Do whatever needs to be done. You won't always get the glamour jobs, especially at the entry level. Be willing to do the grunt work. For the first few cases you work on, you may have to "pay your dues" by being the office anchorperson while the attorneys go to trial. Your willingness to take on a supporting role will pay off later in terms of gaining experience and projecting a professional attitude to the trial attorneys.

Be willing to learn. Express your willingness to learn to do tasks the way the attorney likes to have them done. If the attorney is willing to teach you about trial work, take every opportunity to learn from him or her. Go to seminars and report what you have learned to the attorney. Or, if you get a chance to attend a seminar with the attorney, ask questions about the seminar topics. As you gain experience, you can contribute your ideas and suggestions for new ways to do things, but always remember that the attorney is the boss and that he or she makes the judgment calls on strategy and techniques, even if you don't agree with the decision.

Let them know what you know. Take the initiative to suggest ways in which you can help in the trial preparation. Demonstrate your knowledge of the basic elements needed for trial: preparing exhibits, interviewing witnesses, issuing subpoenas, creating demonstrative evidence, and so forth, and ask the attorney if you can assist in these areas.

Keep the attorney informed. When the attorney gives you tasks to do, keep him or her informed of your progress on a regular basis. This does not mean you have to report to the attorney at every step of the way, but establish a habit of meeting regularly to discuss the work and any questions you may have. (See § **2.9** *et seq.*, on initiating the trial preparation agenda meetings.)

Be flexible. Demonstrate scheduling flexibility and availability. Be willing to arrive early, stay late, and skip lunch if necessary, in order to get the job done. The attorney must be able to depend on you to be there when you are needed.

Communicate. Once you are "in" on the case, insist on frequent, substantive communication with the attorney about the progress of the trial work. You have the right to get the answers to your questions. (The attorney can't REALLY expect you to be a mindreader.) Whenever possible, however, save several small questions for one trial agenda session, rather than interrupting the attorney each time a little problem comes up. Learn to take the assignment as far as you can without supervision.

Be the "Keeper of the Keys." Keep good records and documentation of the trial preparation work as tasks are completed. Keep the various indexes, worksheets, and file keys current and updated. Develop a filing system that makes it easy for the attorney to find the needed materials in the files.

Keep a positive attitude. Learn to respond positively to constructive criticism. Being overly defensive or sensitive every time the attorney asks you to revise or correct something is not the way to gain the attorney's confidence and respect.

Stay cool under pressure. If you fall apart, the attorney will not feel comfortable asking you to assist on the next trial. Keep your composure at all times (see § **6.5** on coping with trial stress).

Be enthusiastic. It's okay to reveal you are excited about the trial. Adrenaline is natural, and it helps keep you alert. Your enthusiasm may even help a jaded attorney take a fresh look at trial work.

Be observant. Take note of any publicity or journalism related to issues or entities in the case. Look for TV or radio coverage of topics related to the trial. Watch for mention in the newspapers or legal periodicals of rulings or developments in similar issues or cases. Clip out any related articles and give them to the attorney. Keep a scrapbook of clippings or publicity in a high-profile case. The attorney will be impressed with your interest and grasp of the issues.

Go to the courtroom. Once you have worked on the background trial preparation, it is a logical step to ask if you can attend the trial. It can be very frustrating to work in the background and never have an opportunity to see the results of your work. However, even if the attorney does not permit you to accompany him or her to the courtroom, remain interested and enthusiastic about the outcome of the case. Remember that there is always another trial, and perhaps you can go to the courtroom the next time.

Thank the attorney. After the trial, let the attorney know that you enjoyed the opportunity to work on it, whatever part you took. The attorney may remember this the next time he or she begins to prepare for trial. Apply the lessons you learned in one case to the next trial you get to work on. Trial work is a cumulative learning experience, and your skills will improve with each trial you handle. Use the skills inventory in § **1.26** as a basis for discussions with the attorney for new skills you may wish to develop. Review your skills every so often to see where you may need additional training, and seek opportunities to gain knowledge and practice in new areas.

§ 1.12 —Dealing with Attorney Procrastination

One of the most prevalent complaints among trial paralegals is the attorney who puts off the trial preparation work until the last possible moment, and then expects all the work to be done immediately, resulting in a mad rush to complete everything before the trial date. The attorney who waits until the eleventh hour to begin preparing for trial usually ends up making exorbitant demands on the time and work schedules of the paralegal, the staff, and everyone else directly or indirectly involved with the trial. This creates a tense and stressful situation for the responsible trial paralegal who wants to do a good job.

If you asked them, most attorneys would concede that the last-minute rush approach is not the best way to prepare for a trial. However, it the nature of the business that certain tasks in trial preparation simply cannot be done until the last few days before trial. The most successful trial attorneys, especially those who have the advantage of paralegal assistance, do not wait until the eve of trial before starting to prepare. In fact, they recognize that really thorough trial preparation begins at the very start of the case (see § **2.4** *et seq.*). Unfortunately, even many very good trial attorneys have not actually incorporated this concept into their everyday practice, and so they still tend to procrastinate about starting serious trial preparation.

Indeed, the reality is that some trial attorneys will never change, so trial paralegals must learn to cope with the demands of "eleventh-hour syndrome" attorneys. This may be a little easier if you understand some of the reasons why attorneys procrastinate about getting into the full swing of "trial mode" preparation. Note that these are not EXCUSES for attorney procrastination, but rather are some possible REASONS for it. In fact, what appears to you to be procrastination on the part of the attorney may not really be when you know the whole situation. Before judging the procrastinator too harshly, consider whether any of the following reasons apply, or whether there may be other contributing factors of which you are unaware. This list is not meant to be all-inclusive, nor does every reason apply in every situation. The following reasons for attorney procrastination are roughly grouped into three categories:

1. Circumstances beyond the attorney's control
2. Strategy and practical considerations
3. Work habits and personality quirks.

1. Circumstances Beyond the Attorney's Control.

- Time Considerations: The attorney may have other cases or projects with inflexible deadlines involving highly demanding work that must be completed before beginning trial preparation on the current case. The attorney may have simply been unable to free himself or herself from other work any earlier.
- Unexpected Trial Responsibility: The attorney, especially if he or she is an associate or junior partner, may have suddenly "inherited" the case from a senior attorney who, for whatever reason, decided to delegate the responsibility of handling the impending trial to the younger lawyer. The junior attorney is hardly in a position to refuse the assignment, and so must prepare for trial under the pressure of a very limited time frame.

- Unexpected Complications: The case may have yielded unexpected problems or complications the attorney could not reasonably have foreseen, putting the attorney under pressure to accommodate tight scheduling for the trial preparation.
- Pending Court Rulings: The attorney may be awaiting rulings on outstanding motions that are before the court in order to determine the proper approach toward full-scale trial preparation.
- Court Scheduling: The attorney believes that the anticipated trial date may be "bumped" by another case on the court's calendar that must be given scheduling priority (for example, a criminal case that must be heard before a civil trial).
- Opposing Counsel's Request for Continuance: The attorney may perceive a lack of readiness of the opposing counsel to take the case to trial on the scheduled date, or the opposing counsel may even have indicated a specific reason that would prompt them to seek a continuance of the trial date.

2. Strategy and Practical Considerations.

- Fear of "Peaking" Too Early: The attorney may simply be pacing himself or herself in conducting the trial preparation. Attorneys generally think of trials as the "fun" part of litigation when the adrenaline is pumping and they are gearing up for the actual confrontation in the courtroom. Just as an actor or an athlete paces himself or herself in order to give the best performance, the attorney wants to be at his or her best for the courtroom activities, and so may delay focusing on the trial preparation too early in the interest of avoiding trial "burnout."
- Possibility of Settlement: The attorney may have had settlement discussions or negotiations with the opposing counsel and believes that there is the possibility of an acceptable settlement offer.
- Pending Completion of Discovery: The attorney may need to obtain the results of certain discovery proceedings to determine the likelihood of a favorable verdict at trial. There may also be key discovery (such as the deposition of an expert witness) that has not yet been completed because of scheduling conflicts, and without which the attorney cannot formulate a valid trial strategy.
- Cost Considerations: Not every case justifies a trial "team," and the attorney does not want to spend the client's money unnecessarily on trial preparation costs if the case is likely to be settled or continued.

3. Work Habits and Personality Quirks.

- Underestimating Time Requirements: The attorney (especially one with limited trial experience) may not fully realize the time required to adequately prepare for trial.

- Resistance to "Focusing": A good trial attorney knows that in order to do a good job, once the trial preparation has begun in earnest he or she must literally become immersed in the case and concentrate exclusively on the trial preparation process. This type of focusing requires an enormous amount of energy and discipline, and the attorney may delay beginning the exercise until he or she intuitively feels that it is the right time to do so.
- Resistance to Teamwork: In law school, attorneys are trained in adversarial thinking and independent analysis. They learn to dispute and debate every issue, and to view every situation from a contentious standpoint. This type of training teaches the attorney to construct a strong argument supporting his or her chosen position on almost any issue. Unfortunately, it does very little to foster the concept of teamwork. Most attorneys learn the value of the team effort only after they have been in practice for a number of years, and some of them never learn it! The attorney who thinks he or she does not need any help and can handle the trial preparation all alone is likely to be one of the worst offenders about procrastinating.
- Lack of Organization: Effective trial preparation requires organization and delegation skills that do not come naturally to most attorneys, and the result may be procrastination in beginning trial preparation.
- Preference for Pressure: Some attorneys simply work best under the motivation of tight deadlines. They know that they perform best under pressure, and therefore they wait until time is short to "gear up" for trial preparation. Unfortunately, this way of operating subjects the persons who work with trial attorneys to an inordinate amount of pressure and stress, but the wise paralegal will learn to expect and adjust to this behavior.
- Overwhelming Personal Problems: It may appear that the attorney is procrastinating when in reality he or she is struggling with serious personal or family problems that distract him or her from directing energy toward the trial preparation.
- Laziness or Irresponsible Behavior: Unfortunately, a few attorneys simply do not take their responsibilities seriously. These "bad apples" think they can just "wing it" at trial, and therefore they do not put much time or forethought into trial preparation. This is nearly always a mistake. If it were possible to compile reliable statistics on the wins and losses of this small minority of attorneys, I'd be willing to bet that they lose most of the time. If you work for an attorney who exhibits this type of behavior, you should seriously consider looking for another job.

§ 1.13 —Coping Strategies for Trial Paralegals

The effects of trial attorney procrastination are felt most acutely by the people who fall under the direction of that attorney. Resentment and tension may also arise among the support staff when those persons must work under pressure. As a trial paralegal, you are sure to encounter attorney procrastination in your work. These are some suggestions for ways to cope:

- Understand that the nature of trial work is fast-paced and demanding. Recognize that some trial preparation tasks simply cannot be done until just before the trial, when you are sure that the case is going forward. No matter how far in advance you have started the preparations, there will always be some last minute work that must be completed. Learn to expect this and handle it calmly.
- Investigate to find whether any of the reasons for procrastination in § **1.12** apply to your situation. Try to open lines of communication with the attorney to find out what he or she is thinking in connection with the trial preparation.
- Realize that the attorney probably has been thinking about the trial strategy, but hasn't yet taken the time to discuss it with you. Schedule a short meeting (no more than 15 minutes) with the attorney. Ask what you can be doing on your own to begin the trial preparation. Attorneys often share the work of pulling a large trial together, so sometimes another attorney on the team can give you some insight about the status of the case or guidance about trial preparation that needs to be done.
- Do whatever can be done ahead of time as early as possible, even if the attorney has not yet officially switched into "trial mode." This will put you a little ahead of the game when the attorney is finally able to fully concentrate on the trial preparation efforts.
- Present the attorney with a calendar or reminder timeline (whichever works the best for you) as a graphic representation of how many actual preparation days are available before the trial. This can be instrumental in encouraging the attorney to get moving on trial preparation.
- Stake out a "war room" (see § **5.3**) for the trial preparation materials. This gives the project visibility and may encourage the attorney to get started a little sooner.
- Be enthusiastic and project a professional attitude. Enthusiasm is contagious. Your initial efforts to get things organized may make it a little easier for the attorney to get to work on the trial preparation project.
- Realize that the attorney will not procrastinate forever. He or she must eventually switch into "trial mode," and when this happens, you will probably have more meaningful communication with the attorney than you ever wished for!

There is new hope for paralegals who work with chronic procrastinators. If attorneys follow the new disclosure procedures in the recently amended federal civil rules, much of the discovery and pretrial "gameplaying" should be eliminated. Attorneys will have to negotiate a joint discovery plan with opposing counsel. They will have to agree to a discovery and disclosure agenda or explain to the judge the reasons they haven't been able to agree on a plan. Once the attorneys agree on a plan, they will be more likely to follow it, potentially making litigation scheduling and trial preparation agendas somewhat more predictable for trial paralegals.

It is important for trial paralegals to develop rapport with the attorneys for whom they work. Try to talk to the attorney every day, even if only briefly, about some aspect of the trial preparation. Mingle with the attorneys when they are socializing or having a cup of coffee. Listening to the attorneys' casual conversations can provide clues about various aspects of the trial. Don't be afraid to ask questions about what the attorneys are trying to accomplish with the case. Strive to project a pleasant and approachable demeanor so that attorneys will want to talk to you about the case. One of the keys to dealing with difficult attorneys is keeping your perspective and sense of humor in tense situations. Be sensitive to the attorney's agenda. Notice what appears to be important to him or her. Observe and assess the attorney's demeanor. Make eye contact and ask specific questions about what the attorney expects of you.

You do not have to put up with harassment or abuse from attorneys or anyone else you work with. Occasionally, when you are working with attorneys in a high-pressure environment, something may really get to you, and you feel you have to remark on the situation. Simply speaking up can make you feel much better, but don't just brashly react to the situation. Take a deep breath and think before you speak. Use restraint. Lower your voice rather than raising it when you address the attorney. Don't swear, even if the attorney does. The most successful trial paralegals strive to provide a calm counterbalance to an irate or stressed attorney. Remember: It's better to rue something you didn't say than something you did.

§ 1.14 Coordinating the Efforts of Multiple Attorneys

Preparing for trial in a case where the trial team includes more than one attorney poses some special problems for the trial paralegal. Keeping the lines of communication open takes on added importance, although it becomes more difficult, as more people are added to the trial team.

Advantages and Disadvantages of Multiple Attorneys

For the sake of simplicity, the following observations and comments assume there are two attorneys on the case. However, the same concerns would apply in a situation with more than two attorneys.

Disadvantages.

- When there are multiple attorneys on a case, you have to learn to deal with two or more egos, personalities, and work styles. If one attorney takes a "laid-back" approach to trial preparation and the other attorney is a "hyper" type, some tension may arise between the attorneys and you may be caught in the middle.
- In some cases, your workload of trial preparation tasks may increase because you now have two attorneys giving you assignments to complete.
- Situations are likely to occur in which the attorneys give you conflicting instructions for handling an assignment or indicate differing priorities about which project should be completed first. If this problem arises, you will need to confront both attorneys with the discrepancy in their instructions and ask THEM to decide how you should proceed. While you should be flexible and attempt to please both attorneys wherever possible, you also want to avoid being caught in the middle. Unfortunately, this is sometimes unavoidable.
- The attorneys may have different ideas about how to run the case. You may have to help to iron out a compromise by suggesting a third method or a combination of techniques that suits both attorneys.
- Do not be surprised if the attorneys decide things together and then forget to tell you. This is not usually a deliberate attempt to confuse you. One attorney may just assume that the other attorney informed you, and the second attorney may assume the first one did. Be alert to changes in the trial strategy and ask about any aspect that seems inconsistent with what you thought had been decided. The key is to keep a constant stream of communication open as the trial preparation progresses.
- Communication becomes even more important when you have multiple attorneys on the trial team. It is imperative that each person's duties and responsibilities be clarified in the trial preparation agenda meetings. The attorneys must decide such things as:

  Who will draft the trial pleadings

  Who will handle the voir dire questioning

  Who will give the opening and closing statements

  How the witness examinations will be split, that is, who will question which witnesses.

Advantages.

- In some ways, working with multiple attorneys is easier for the trial paralegal. You have more than one person to ask if you have questions about your trial preparation assignments or if you need an attorney's approval or signature on something, and therefore gaining access to attorney attention becomes easier.
- Scheduling witness preparation conferences is somewhat easier when there are two attorneys because more time slots are available to accommodate the calendar and work schedules of the trial witnesses.
- Each attorney will have less work and stress to deal with because the trial duties will be split.
- Unless the attorneys happen to share the same secretary, there will be more secretarial support available to help prepare the trial documents and materials.
- Because each attorney contributes his or her unique abilities and perspective to the trial preparation process, the trial team can benefit from the combined diversity of experience when deciding upon the appropriate strategy and approach to presenting the case. A second attorney on the case also becomes an alternate source of intelligence on the strategy and status of the trial preparation.
- Working on a trial team with multiple attorneys gives you, as the trial paralegal, an opportunity to reinforce the benefits of the team approach and a chance to prove your abilities to more than one attorney at a time.

§ 1.15 —Working with Corporate Co-Counsel

Large corporations often have an in-house legal staff to handle routine legal problems on behalf of the company. However, the corporation may seek trial counsel from an outside law firm that specializes in litigation. In this instance, the trial team may include an attorney from the client's corporate staff who will work with attorneys from your firm to prepare the case for trial. As the trial paralegal, you should be aware of some special considerations and techniques that may apply in this situation.

- The attorney from the corporate legal department will bring specific knowledge of the technical aspects of his or her company's product or service, as well as background on the company's management policies, goals, and desired public relations image. The successful trial team will incorporate the in-house attorney's knowledge into the overall trial strategy and make sure that the trial presentation is consistent with the management's corporate policies.

- The corporate attorney has the added responsibility of reporting to management on the status of the litigation, so it is very important, as it is with any client, to keep the staff attorney well-informed about the progress of the trial preparation.
- Respect the corporate attorney's workload and other commitments when you are scheduling trial conferences. Try to accommodate the corporate attorney's busy calendar whenever possible.
- Let the corporate attorney know your firm is conscious of the high costs associated with trial preparation. Take care not to incur any unnecessary expenses simply because the client is a corporation that is in a position to pay large legal fees.
- Look for a contact at the client's company who is at an organizational level similar to yours. Ideally, this person will be a corporate paralegal, but such a contact could also include the local office manager, administrative assistant, executive secretary, or aide. This person can be a valuable conduit for information between the attorney and the client. He or she may be privy to key information through internal organizational contacts to which you ordinarily would not have access. Let the client contact help to provide specialized information wherever possible, for example, diagrams, specifications, and organizational brochures. This reinforces the teamwork concept and also provides a backup liaison for relaying information. By communicating with personnel on the lower levels, you will be able to do a better job for the trial team, your client will be happier, and your contact's influence may result in additional business for your firm in the future.

§ 1.16 —Working with Out-of-Town Co-Counsel

If the trial is to take place in your jurisdiction and the out-of-town attorney is not familiar with your court's local rules and procedures, you should provide the attorney with a copy of the pertinent local rules for your court. Some jurisdictions have a printed pamphlet or brochure guide for jurors that shows the layout of the courthouse and the location of various court-related facilities, as well as other useful information about local practices and rules. If your court has such a brochure, send the co-counsel attorney a copy, along with a map of the area and any other information that may be appropriate to familiarize the attorney with the customs in your local jurisdiction.

When one co-counsel attorney is from out of town, the local attorney usually takes the lead in managing the case and the other attorney assists and supplements as needed in conducting the preparation and trial. If possible, discuss the anticipated strategy and approach to this aspect of the case with your attorney before the co-counsel arrives so that you are clear on what your boss expects. Observe the same appropriate professional etiquette for out-of-town counsel as you would for any other guests of your office, such as clients or expert witnesses. You may be expected to attend some lunches or dinners to keep the out-of-town counsel company. Have a company credit card or expense account preapproved through your office so you have operating cash or credit.

If the co-counsel is from another state and is to take an active part in the actual trial proceedings, he or she must be properly admitted to practice before the bar in your local jurisdiction. The usual procedure for accomplishing this is for the local attorney to apply to the judge of the local court to admit the out-of-state attorney to practice pro hac vice, a Latin term which means that the attorney is admitted to practice in a certain jurisdiction for this particular case only. Check with your supervising attorney on the requirements for admission pro hac vice in your jurisdiction. You may be asked to prepare the appropriate application (or motion) and order for this procedure. The motion should state the reasons the out-of-state attorney should be admitted to practice for this case and a brief recitation of the attorney's credentials and affiliations. (See **§ 1.17,** Sample Motion and Order for Admission Pro Hac Vice.) Some jurisdictions require you to furnish a current certificate of good standing (available from the state bar association) for the out-of-state attorney. Check your local rules to ascertain the correct procedures for pro hac vice admission.

§ 1.17 —Motion and Order for Admission Pro Hac Vice

FORM 1–1
SAMPLE MOTION ADMISSION PRO HAC VICE

IN THE COURT OF COMMON PLEAS
[county name] COUNTY, [state's name]

JAMES A. FOSTER,	:	CASE NO. [case number]
	:	
Plaintiff,	:	JUDGE [judge's name]
	:	
vs.	:	
	:	
UNITED INDEPENDENT	:	
LABORATORY,	:	<u>MOTION FOR ADMISSION</u>
	:	<u>PRO HAC VICE</u>
Defendant.	:	

Jane P. Local, an attorney duly admitted to the Bar of the State of [state's name] and authorized to practice before this Court, hereby moves this Court, pursuant to Rule I, Section 9(D) of the Supreme Court Rules for the Government of the Bar of [name of state], for the admission of Douglas J. Williams, Esq., pro hac vice as co-counsel for Defendant, United Independent Laboratory, in the above-captioned case. Mr. Williams is a graduate of Ball State University and the University of Chicago Law School (1974). He is a member in good standing of the Bars of the State of Illinois (since 1975), the United States District Court for the Central District of Illinois (since 1976), and the United States Court of Appeals for the Seventh Circuit (since 1979). Mr. Williams is a member of the Bar Associations of Logan County (Illinois) and the State of Illinois.

Mr. Williams is a partner in the firm of Smith & Jones, L.P.A. Smith & Jones has been retained by the Defendant, United Independent Laboratory, to serve as its general outside counsel. Smith & Jones has been retained by United Independent Laboratory to represent it in this litigation, and Mr. Williams is the member of that firm selected to be chief trial counsel in this case. He will participate in all phases of discovery and will be chief trial counsel for Defendant, United Independent Laboratory, when this case is called to trial in December [year]. Jane P. Local will be associated with Mr. Williams at all times in the representation and defense of United Independent Laboratory in this case.

For all of the foregoing reasons, Attorney Jane P. Local respectfully moves this Court to enter an Order admitting Douglas J. Williams pro hac vice in the captioned case.

____
Jane P. Local
(address)
(telephone)
Attorneys for Defendant,
United Independent Laboratory

CERTIFICATE OF SERVICE

A copy of the foregoing Motion for Admission Pro Hac Vice was served by mail this [day] day of [month] [year] upon all counsel of record in this case.

____
Jane P. Local

FORM 1–2
SAMPLE ORDER FOR ADMISSION PRO HAC VICE

IN THE COURT OF COMMON PLEAS
[county's name] COUNTY, [state's name]

JAMES A. FOSTER,	:	CASE NO. [case number]
Plaintiff,	:	JUDGE [judge's name]
vs.	:	
UNITED INDEPENDENT LABORATORY,	:	
Defendant.	:	ORDER

This Court having considered the Motion of Jane P. Local for Douglas J. Williams to be admitted pro hac vice and to participate in the above-captioned case, the Court finds that Motion to be well taken.

IT IS HEREBY ORDERED, ADJUDGED, and DECREED that the Motion for Admission Pro Hac Vice is granted and Attorney Douglas J. Williams is hereby admitted pro hac vice to appear and participate as counsel for the Defendant, United Independent Laboratory in this case.

____
Judge ____________

Dated: [date], [year]

§ 1.18 —Practicing in Out-of-Town Courts

If your supervising attorney is the one who will be traveling to another jurisdiction for the trial, make sure that the correct procedures are followed to admit him or her to practice in the foreign jurisdiction. (See **§ 1.16** on admission to practice pro hac vice.) When your trial is in an unfamiliar city, take advantage of the opportunity to broaden your experience by learning about the customs and procedures followed in other courts and by other judges. If possible, contact a local attorney or paralegal who is not associated with your case to obtain information on the local court procedures. Contact the foreign city's bar association or paralegal organization to ascertain the applicable local court rules and procedures so that you can accommodate any specific local customs in your trial preparation. Find out if the judge in the foreign jurisdiction has any preferences, special guidelines, and so forth for the format of the trial briefs. (See § **5.33** on preparing trial briefs.)

If you are lucky enough to get to travel with the attorney to the trial, make the most of the opportunity to see another city. You may have to spend most of your evenings working with witnesses or clients to prepare for the next day's testimony, but if you have some free time, try to experience some of the "local color." If your trial will be held in a large city, write to the Chamber of Commerce (or the equivalent) for information on local sightseeing attractions, a city map, a calendar of events, and so on. At the very least, knowing what is happening on the local scene will give you some neutral topics for small talk with clients, witnesses, or local counsel. If your case takes you to an overseas or international locale, be sure to arrange the necessary passports, visas, and inoculations for yourself and the trial attorneys.

When you are working on a trial in another city, it is especially important to have your trial materials highly organized and to have someone to act as your "anchor" back at your home office in the event you need to have materials delivered to you at the trial site. You will also want to have a portable notebook or laptop computer with modem capability to enable you to communicate with the office computer. While staying in a hotel in another city during the trial, you may need to arrange use of business-oriented services offered by that establishment. At your earliest convenience, check with the hotel concierge or business manager on the availability of the following:

- Conference or meeting rooms, for client or witness preparation
- Photocopy machines or services
- Telecopier (or fax) equipment
- Access to computer equipment and modem linkup
- Local courier or delivery services
- Temporary secretarial support.

Keep meticulous records and be sure to get receipts for all the business-related expenses that are chargeable to your office or to the client. Keep time zone differences in mind when you are making telephone calls or telecopier transmissions.

§ 1.19 —Working with Inexperienced Attorneys

As an experienced trial paralegal, you will undoubtedly encounter situations in which you are expected to assist a relatively inexperienced attorney in preparing a case for trial. The definitions of an "inexperienced" attorney could include the following:

- A recent law school graduate without much practical experience in trying cases
- An attorney from another practice area who is gradually working into the litigation area, and is therefore new to trial work
- A lateral hire from another office or another state or an attorney who is otherwise new to your office or your jurisdiction and who is unfamiliar with the local court practices and procedures
- An attorney who is not accustomed to using paralegals in trial work.

Inexperienced attorneys often gain trial exposure by sitting "second chair" to a veteran trial attorney. When you are faced with this situation, do not feel that your position on the trial team is in danger of being usurped by the novice attorney. Even in a relatively small case, there is always more than enough trial preparation work to go around. Instead, view this situation as an opportunity to teach, demonstrate, and reinforce the concept of teamwork in trial preparation.

If you have been fortunate enough to work extensively on past trials with the veteran attorney and the two of you have established a good working relationship, you may be able to discuss the situation candidly with the veteran attorney early in the trial preparation in order to set the tone for teamwork and constructive communication. Younger attorneys will generally take their cues from the more experienced attorney and adopt his or her attitude toward your role as part of the trial team. If possible, have the veteran attorney suggest to the novice ways that you can assist in the trial preparation. Again, this is a good place to focus on the teamwork approach to trial preparation. Early in the case, establish the habit of holding regular trial agenda planning meetings to update trial team members on the status of the trial preparation. (See § **2.9** *et seq.*, Conducting the Initial Trial Preparation Meeting.)

Do not be surprised if the younger attorney at first does some of the tasks you are accustomed to doing for the veteran attorney. Be patient and tolerant of this situation if it happens. Remember that the younger attorney must learn, too. Try to head off such problems by making it clear in your trial agenda meetings who is responsible for completing which tasks. (See § **2.9** *et seq.*, on conducting trial preparation agenda meetings.)

If you are experienced in trial work but the attorney is not, he or she may be reluctant to delegate work to you. Counter this behavior by simply being conscientious and professional with the portions of the trial preparation for which you are responsible. Don't take personal offense. Remember that the new attorney may someday be the head litigator. The best approach is to offer assistance when it is needed, but avoid being pushy. New attorneys have to gain confidence in themselves before they can learn to delegate well to others. They know they are ultimately responsible for the handling of the case. The younger attorney will probably want to do things his or her own way, so be selective with your advice about how things were done in past cases. If you can prevent the attorney from having to reinvent the wheel, you should try, but be tactful about offering suggestions based on how something was done in a previous trial. If the attorney is interested in how you have done things before, be prepared to produce examples of how you solved a similar problem in a previous case.

Be cautious about going over the attorney's head if you see a big problem developing in a case. Try to communicate your concern to the novice attorney first before resorting to other measures. Help the attorney save face, if possible. Ultimately, however, the client's interests should be your overriding concern. This is an ethical dilemma in which you have to strike a balance between what is best for your future relationship with the attorney and your responsibility to serve the client's best interests.

Here are some miscellaneous tips on dealing with the inexperienced trial attorney:

- Realize that the novice attorney may secretly be relieved to have your support, especially if he or she is the only attorney on the case.
- Remember that attorneys often have "touchy" egos. Pave the way for cooperation and teamwork by letting the novice attorney know that you understand that he or she is the boss and you won't undermine his or her authority.
- Be encouraging and supportive. Keep a positive attitude. Provide honest feedback without being overly critical.
- Remember that the attorney is under stress, too. Don't add to the problem by behaving unprofessionally.
- Be available to help in case an emergency arises. Be especially conscientious about informing the attorney of where you can be reached after hours.
- For an attorney who is unfamiliar with your local court's procedures and practices, provide
  —pertinent current local court rules;
  —any inside information about judge you may have;
  —directions to court offices, if necessary.
- If the young attorney is really "green" and you know of in-house training tapes or seminar materials that might help, tactfully suggest these.
- Keep your own record clear. Do your part to keep the attorney informed. Document your work with memos. Be conscientious about your responsibilities and do your part of the job correctly so that an insecure young attorney (or a spiteful older one) has no basis to pin the blame on you if things go wrong during the trial presentation.

§ 1.20 Working with Other Paralegals

The following are things other paralegals can do to help you when you are in trial (or preparing for trial):

- Help you record and document the discussions at the trial preparation agenda meetings. (See § **2.9** *et seq.*)
- Receive and return telephone calls from witnesses to coordinate scheduling for preparation conferences and courtroom testimony.
- Prepare last-minute boards or visual aids for closing argument; help with preparing other exhibits.
- Supervise errand clerks to make sure deliveries and connections are made.
- Perform research needed to prepare jury instructions.
- Keep track of file materials left back in the "war room" at the office and deliver materials to you at the courthouse as needed.
- Cover or handle jobs in your other cases.
- Meet and greet experts, witnesses, or clients arriving from out of town and escort them to the office or courtroom.
- Serve subpoenas on trial witnesses and file returns with the court clerk.
- Perform last-minute factual research. (See § **1.57.**)
- Fill in for you (on a short-term basis) in the courtroom if you absolutely must be elsewhere.

§ 1.21 Working with Other Law Office Personnel

There is always a certain amount of office politics involved for a paralegal in establishing your place on the trial team. In dealing with the office support staff, a trial paralegal must be assertive and authoritative in order to get the job done, while at the same time being diplomatic and tactful in dealing with the support staff in order to gain their trust and cooperation. This section offers some tips to help you achieve this "balancing act" in your relationships with the office support staff.

§ 1.22 —Working with Legal Secretaries

The paralegal profession has existed for a relatively short time compared to that of the legal secretary. Some paralegals have encountered jealousy, resentment, and even outright hostility from seasoned legal secretaries who are not accustomed to working with and for paralegals. In the case of a secretary who has worked for the trial attorney for many years, this enmity may arise from the secretary's fear that you are trying to usurp her position with her boss. It is incumbent upon you to overcome this attitude by maintaining your professional manner and by stressing the teamwork approach to trial preparation. Make it clear from the outset that you value the secretary's skills and that she plays an important role in the work of the trial team.

Early in the trial preparation, discuss with the attorney whether you are at liberty to ask the attorney's secretary to assist you with work for that attorney's trial. If you encounter problems in getting the secretary to cooperate with you, ask the attorney in charge to make it clear to the secretary that you are part of the trial team, that she is to keep you informed of new developments, and that she may expect requests for assistance from you. Word from the attorney will carry more weight with the secretary than if you approach her on your own. You should realize that some experienced legal secretaries are quite capable of doing paralegal-level work, and many of them have been doing so for years. While you will each have your own tasks to complete in the trial preparation, there is nothing to lose and much to gain for both you and the secretary if you cooperate and learn from each other.

Regardless of the secretary's behavior, be careful to demonstrate your professionalism at all times. Above all, do not gloat over the fact that you get to attend the trial and the secretary does not. This is a sure way to make enemies in the office! Remember that when the secretary has been very involved in the trial preparation, it can be very frustrating for her never to see the end product of all that work. In fact, you might even suggest to the trial attorney that the secretary be allowed to come and watch part of the trial, in order to see her boss (and you) in action.

§ 1.23 —Dealing with Other Office Support Staff

In dealing with the other members of the support staff, adopt a policy of never asking anyone to work harder than you yourself are willing to work. If this means making copies or collating trial briefs so that the job gets done on time, you will earn the staff's respect by pitching in and helping right along with them.

- Give as much lead time as you can when you are delegating projects to office personnel. Remember how you feel when the attorney puts you under pressure because he or she is disorganized, and try to avoid doing the same to others. Don't say it is a rush job if it isn't. If the attorney puts you in the middle by asking the impossible at the last minute, handle the situation as diplomatically as possible without betraying your loyalty to the attorney.

- Be considerate and fair to the staff people and treat them with respect. Give clear, concise instructions and keep up your end of the communication flow. Prepare written instructions when the delegated task involves several steps. Let them know where they can reach you if a problem or question arises.
- Put your errand clerks (or the equivalent persons in your office) on notice well ahead of time that you will need them to assist you in transporting equipment to the courthouse on the first or second day of trial.
- Consult the person in charge of the office supply room to make sure you have the proper supplies in stock (binders and dividers for trial notebooks, art supplies for visual aids, and so forth). Do this far enough in advance to allow time for the supply person to order the supplies you need.
- Talk to the supervisor in charge of personnel to arrange for weekend or overtime secretarial support during the last phase of the trial preparation.
- Let the office receptionist know when the trial team will be at the courthouse (or out of town) all day during the trial.
- Always remember to express your appreciation to any support staff member who has gone to extra trouble to help you during trial. Thank each person and let him or her know they made a valuable contribution.

§ 1.24 —Selecting a Key Office Contact

When you get the chance to accompany the attorney to the courtroom, it is important to have at least one dependable key "anchor" person back at the office who knows something about the file for the trial you are working on. Choose someone you know will be available during the time you are out of the office. This can be invaluable if once you get to the courthouse you realize that you have forgotten an important document or list. You may need to call your key contact and ask him or her to bring you a document or file or make arrangements to have it delivered to you.

I always make sure my secretary has a copy of the list of telephone numbers for the trial witnesses. If there is a development in the trial that necessitates rescheduling the times for witness testimony, I can let her know whom to call and what to tell them, and she can begin making the calls. (Because you can't always reach someone on the first try, this can be very helpful.) Likewise, you may have certain standby witnesses ready for rebuttal testimony, and you will need assistance letting them know when they are to appear, or if the attorney has decided not to use their testimony.

Even if you do not have the luxury of having an "anchor" back at the office, do make sure that the receptionist or whoever answers your telephone is aware that you are in trial and that there may be certain important telephone messages that come in while you are away.

§ 1.25 —Enlisting Your Family's Help

Just as you need to let your coworkers know that you will be involved in trial, you need to inform your family and others outside your work life. Explain to them that you may have to work some long days and late nights. Ask family members to help out at home by taking on a few extra household chores. If you have children, let them know that this is an important responsibility for you so they will be prepared when you are not able to spend as much time with them as usual. Line up a backup sitter or companion if you are responsible for the care of children or elderly relatives. When you must work very late hours at the office, check in periodically by telephone with your loved ones so that they will not worry about you.

§ 1.26 Paralegal Skills Inventory

Trial work requires a wide range of interrelated skills: some are skills that can be applied in any office situation; others are related to legal work generally; and still others are unique to courtroom work. In order to be a successful trial paralegal, you must acquire these skills, then learn to combine and apply them to the challenges of trial work. It would be difficult to isolate any single area of skills as being most important, because in trial work they overlap and interact in a variety of ways. The sections that follow discuss some of the general business-type skills you will need in litigation and trial work. More specific discussions of skills you will want to develop for the courtroom may be found elsewhere in this book, as indicated by the referenced sections in the following checklist. Use the checklist as a guide to determine: (1) skills you have already mastered; (2) skills you have that could use refinement; and (3) new skills you need to learn.

§ 1.27 —Skills Inventory for the Trial Paralegal

The following is a checklist of skills for the trial paralegal.

____ 1. Effective Time Management (§ **1.40**)

- ____ Planning ahead
- ____ Setting priorities
- ____ Coordinating schedules
- ____ Calendaring dates and events
- ____ Establishing reliable tickler/reminder systems
- ____ Employing time-saving techniques

____ Timekeeping (tracking billable hours)
____ Holding productive meetings (§ **1.32**)

____ 2. Organization (Paperwork and Systems)
____ Developing organized systems (**Chapter 2**)
____ Indexing, labeling, filing, and retrieval (§ **2.75**)
____ Designing and using standard forms
____ Integrating your firm's systems and procedures
____ Using available equipment and technology
____ Becoming computer literate (**Chapter 8**)

____ 3. Interpersonal Skills
____ Promoting the teamwork concept (§ **2.7**)
____ Understanding attorneys (§§ **1.9–1.11**)
____ Employing diplomacy and consideration
____ Handling client contact
____ Delegating effectively
____ Working with other paralegals (§ **1.20**)
____ Communicating with persons outside the office
____ Building a network of professional contacts

____ 4. Communications (Oral and Written)
____ Using effective telephone skills
____ Developing writing skills
____ Learning to use reference materials (§ **1.57**)
____ Using correct grammar
____ Developing powers of observation and analysis
____ Listening intelligently
____ Documenting activities (keeping notes and records)

____ 5. Problem Solving
____ Employing common sense and logic
____ Keeping an open mind
____ Learning the applicable rules and boundaries
____ Working within the case budget (§ **1.34**)
____ Designing inexpensive alternatives

____ 6. Imagination and Creativity
____ Developing artistic and creative abilities
____ Converting abstract ideas to concrete themes
____ Adapting established ideas to new situations
____ Improvising with the materials available

____ 7. Investigation and Research

- ____ Conducting effective factual research (§ **1.57**)
- ____ Paying attention to detail
- ____ Reading for understanding
- ____ Learning on your own

____ 8. Personal Aspects—Physical and Mental Preparation

- ____ Demonstrating professional conduct and ethics
- ____ Developing good judgment
- ____ Observing applicable business etiquette
- ____ Maintaining an assertive profile
- ____ Dressing appropriately
- ____ Building self-confidence
- ____ Knowing when to ask for help
- ____ Accepting constructive criticism
- ____ Pursuing standards of excellence

____ 9. Courtroom Skills

- ____ Planning and organizing the presentation
- ____ Developing a sense of dramatic impact
- ____ Anticipating the attorney's needs
- ____ Handling courtroom logistics (§ **6.12**)
- ____ Thinking "on your feet"
- ____ Preparing for contingencies
- ____ Handling emergencies calmly

____ 10. Archiving—Learning and Improving

- ____ Building master reference files (§ **1.61**)
- ____ Reviewing and analyzing results (§ **7.58**)
- ____ Learning from experience
- ____ Retaining examples for future reference

§ 1.28 Developing Trial Management Skills

It is important for trial paralegals to understand the important distinction between trial *preparation* and trial *management.* Many training materials and seminars focus on a case's early stages and on trial preparation, which includes all the case activities leading up to trial. Good trial preparation, however, is only part of the picture. Even exemplary trial preparation is of little value to the trial team unless they can do something effective with it—that is, pull it all together into a convincing, seamless courtroom presentation. *Trial management* means maintaining the organization and strategies developed during the investigation, discovery, and trial preparation phases of the case throughout the trial. A trial paralegal must not only analyze the case and determine the best way to organize it, but also figure out ways to ensure that the case stays organized during the trial.

Trial work is part of the business of lawfirms, so it is important to look at the tasks and skills involved in trial management from a businesslike viewpoint. The skills needed to manage trials successfully are by no means limited to legal concepts. Much of what trial paralegals do requires common sense problem solving and solid managerial skills. The variety of skills needed in trial work is proof that trial paralegals are indeed case managers or administrators. If you have any experience in trial work, you have applied administrative skills whether you realized it or not. For example, if you have ever coordinated the appearance of trial witnesses, you were performing administrative tasks (for example, *conducting* the witness preparation sessions, *supervising* the issuance and service of trial subpoenas, and *directing* the flow of witnesses in the courtroom). These are all managerial-type functions.

Anticipating Trial Management Problems

Paralegals can apply management skills and techniques in any size or type of case. Supporting the attorney at trial means integrating all the elements of the case: having the right persons with the right information and the right documents in the right place at the right time (and within the budget). Coordinating all these elements is a major undertaking even in a small case, but in a case that has a high potential for numerous glitches and logistical problems, you have to apply good management skills. Paralegals in small firms must be particularly creative and inventive in applying administrative techniques to solve the problems that more involved cases present. In other words, paralegals in small firms have to be able to do more with less to compete with larger firms. The administrative-thinking paralegal anticipates trial management problems and devises solutions; that is, you

- Set goals for the results you want
- Determine what tasks need to be done to reach the objectives
- Determine the time available to accomplish the work
- Assess the resources available
- Plan how to apply the resources to the problem and use them to their best advantage
- Communicate with the appropriate people
- Provide instructions and training when necessary
- Supervise to see that the plans are executed properly and completely.

This means taking a proactive rather than a reactive approach to trial activities. Don't wait for tasks to become crises or problems. Try to look ahead and anticipate what at least some of the problems will be and plan for handling them, so that they won't ever get to crisis proportions.

Knowing what to expect and putting plans in place to handle the known aspects of the trial will enable you to devote your time and attention to the unique requirements of a specific case. Of course, no two trials are ever *exactly* alike, even when the issues are similar. Each trial you work on will present some new problem or twist that has never come up before, so you can never anticipate all the nuances of a particular case. But you can anticipate and plan for most of them because all cases have certain elements in common (subpoenas, witnesses, exhibits, and so forth). While no single technique is guaranteed to work equally well in all cases, you will find that some techniques and procedures do work in nearly every case (perhaps with only slight variations). These procedures and systems are the core controls that you can use to manage the routine elements of a case. Study what you have done in other cases that worked and incorporate those techniques into your repertoire of trial skills.

In addition, you will be called upon to design creative solutions to organizational and logistical problems in each case. These will be unique problems that require imagination and creativity to fashion solutions tailored to the needs of the individual case. Sound planning for the expected elements allows you to focus your attention on handling these unexpected surprises.

§ 1.29 —Developing "Smart Questioning" Skills

How do you begin to determine the potential case problems? How do you go about assessing your resources? The answer lies partly in your ability to communicate with the trial attorney and elicit the information you need. For a trial paralegal, effective communication means asking the right questions. In her book, *Smart Questions: A New Strategy for Successful Managers* (McGraw-Hill, 1987), management consultant Dorothy Leeds addresses turning "an ordinary conversational skill—the art of asking questions—into a formidable business tool." Leeds observes that the best leaders and managers invariably employ effective questions in various situations to gain information, clarify instructions, and define problems. She recommends using *open* questions that stimulate thought and encourage continued conversation; or, in other words, questions that lead to an exchange of ideas and invite further exploration of the subject at hand.

In trial work, you have to organize and define the problems before you can plan the solutions. You must ask good questions designed to make the attorney think about what he or she hopes to accomplish. The precise focus of your questions for a particular case will depend three factors: (1) How far the case has progressed before you are brought in; (2) How much you already know about the case background; and (3) How well you know the attorney's work style. (Ideally, the attorney will assign a paralegal to a case at the outset, but realistic trial paralegals know this isn't the way it usually happens.) Assuming you are assigned to a case at some point during the discovery phase and before the trial, these are some smart general questions you can almost always ask the attorney to open up the discussion:

- What has to be done?
- What key results are we looking for?
- Can you explain further?
- How do you plan to handle (whatever)?
- When do you need this?
- What are the priorities here?
- What do you see as the next step?
- Is there anything else I should know?

Communication with the attorney and other trial team members is critical to the success of any trial management plan. You will often have to take the initiative for scheduling meetings with the attorney to determine the priorities in the case. **Chapter 2** discusses the trial team approach and the details of organizing a trial preparation agenda meeting. (See § **2.9** *et seq.*)

§ 1.30 —Assessing Resources: People, Paper, Time, and Money

The management, administrative, and organizational problems in trial work revolve around four main components: people, paper, time, and money. These elements interact in different combinations and shifting priorities as the case progresses through its various stages (see below). These four main "ingredients," combined with communication, information, and management skills, are also the resources and tools you have to work with to put the case presentation together. When you organize your "smart questions" to the trial attorney around these categories, you are bound to hit on at least the primary factors that will affect how you manage the case preparation. The following are some suggestions for the types of questions that can help you to ascertain the potential problems and resources in each category.

•PEOPLE Who are the clients? Who are the attorneys on the trial team? What support staff will be working on the case? Who are the witnesses and where are they located? Are there any expert witnesses? Will the clients testify? Will we use any outside vendors or consultants? Who is the judge? Who will serve the subpoenas? What juror characteristics would be desirable?

•PAPER What discovery has been done so far? What remains to be done before trial? How will litigation support be handled? What documents and exhibits exist? Where are the files stored? Will demonstrative evidence be needed, and if so, what kind? What subpoenas must be issued? Will we need exhibit notebooks?

•TIME When is the trial date? How long is the trial expected to take? How much time will we need to present our case? What filing dates, due dates, or other deadlines must be met before trial? Will there be a pretrial hearing? What is the timetable for trial preparation?

•MONEY What is the budget for this case? How much money do we have to work with to prepare for trial? What cost is allocated to litigation support? Will we be paying retainers to expert witnesses? How much should be allocated to demonstrative evidence? What is the arrangement for billing and paying trial expenses? Can we get advance authorization for expenses to avoid red tape later when time deadlines are critical?

Note to Paralegal Managers and Administrators

If you are an administrator or office manager or if you aspire to be one (and especially if your experience is in an area other than litigation), you need to understand how the trial process works and what firm resources the trial team might require (for example, additional personnel, equipment, space, or supplies). The office manager or administrator should work with the trial team to expedite solutions to those requests. The administrator must be aware of the case budget parameters and the procedures for billing and paying case expenses. He or she also must be sensitive to office security, confidentiality, and ethical concerns. The administrator and the paralegals need to understand one another and work together to support the trial attorneys.

§ 1.31 —Skills for Managing Successful Trials

This checklist recaps the skills that a successful trial paralegal must master. Other "general" managerial skills that are important to trial paralegals, such as holding productive meetings and preparing a trial budget, are discussed in the following sections.

____ 1. Approach every case with trial in mind. (See §§ **2.4–2.5.**) Start anticipating problems and planning solutions as soon as you get in on the case.

____ 2. Communicate with the trial attorney and build a network of people and contacts you can call on for support and assistance.

(See §§ **1.9–1.25; 2.7** *et seq.*) Coordinate resource needs with the office administrator.

____ 3. Learn to hold productive meetings, delegate effectively, and ask smart questions. (See §§ **1.28–1.33.**)

____ 4. Determine a case budget and the procedures for handling case expenses. (See § **1.34.**)

____ 5. Learn to set priorities, plan, and schedule. Make use of calendars and timelines. (See § **1.40** *et seq.*) Use computer calendaring and scheduling programs.

____ 6. Use computer power to work efficiently. Learn to use basic word processing, database, spreadsheet, and utility programs. (See **Chapter 8**).

____ 7. Develop efficient ways to organize the paper and documents. (See § **2.62** *et seq.*)

____ 8. Know where to look things up. Collect pertinent reference materials and expand your network of resources and suppliers. (See §§ **1.57–1.64.**)

____ 9. Keep good records. Document your work, meetings, and contacts to track the progress of the case.

____ 10. Observe what works and build on it. (See §§ **7.40–7.58.**)

§ 1.32 Holding Productive Meetings

The most skillful paralegals know that promoting communication among the various entities in the case is a key element in the success of the trial process. Learning to hold effective meetings is an important administrative skill for trial paralegals. Meetings bring people together for a particular purpose, for example, to discuss a trial preparation agenda with the attorneys or to review testimony with a trial witness. As a legal professional, you will be responsible for coordinating various meetings. Meetings are a fact of our everyday business lives and, unfortunately, all of us have been to meetings that were a waste of time. In fact, nationwide surveys of top executives have revealed that meetings accounted for the greatest amount of *unproductive* time, topping phone calls, paperwork, travel, and office gossip. Everyone's time is at a premium (especially during trial preparation), so it is important to make the best use of meeting time while you have the attention of the attorneys, witnesses, or other persons involved. However, good, productive meetings don't just happen by chance. They must be organized and conducted effectively. The checklist in § **1.33** contains some strategies to help you make your professional meetings more efficient and productive. These suggestions are applicable to any meetings you may hold, whether they are large or small, formal or informal. (See also § **2.9** *et seq.,* for tips on handling trial agenda meetings with the trial team.)

§ 1.33 —Strategies for Effective Meetings

1. Define a clear objective for the meeting. First, make sure you really need a meeting and that the objectives can't be met by other means. Then, when you have decided that face-to-face interaction is required to get something done, determine exactly what you want to accomplish during the meeting. One example of an important meeting is the trial preparation agenda meeting discussed in § **2.9** *et seq.* Organizing and preparing for this meeting will help your communications with the trial attorneys while you have their attention.

2. Determine who should be at the meeting. Who should attend is a function of the objective of the meeting. A general rule is that the more specific the objective of the meeting, the fewer the necessary participants. Small groups invite candor and are more likely to get real results. When a meeting is comprised of more than ten participants, it is much more difficult to obtain productive results. (You know how difficult it can be to get any three attorneys to agree on anything—imagine having 10!)

3. Decide when to schedule the meeting. Coordinating the calendars of multiple attorneys and other professionals can be a real challenge, as any paralegal who has scheduled multiparty depositions is well aware. You will have to take responsibility for checking everyone's schedule and securing a satisfactory date and time for the meeting to take place.

4. Arrange the meeting place. Where is the best place to meet? Most of your professional meetings will be held in a conference room or large office with a table. Check the physical layout of the room ahead of time. Are there enough chairs? Is the table clean? Have you arranged for someone to bring in coffee? Do you need a chalkboard or dry-erase board? You also need to decide where to sit yourself. If you are conducting the meeting, choose the "power" position, which is the seat at the end of a rectangular table farthest from the entrance to the room. If you are not the leader of the meeting, the second best spot is the seat just to the right of the head of the table, and the third best is across the table from the leader. How do you get the seat of your choice? Get there first.

5. Notify the meeting participants so they can prepare. Give the meeting participants advance notice of what will be discussed so they can be thinking about it before the meeting. For an internal meeting involving persons from within the office, send a memo confirming the date, time, and place. State clearly the time the meeting will start and when it will end. Briefly state the objective or purpose of the meeting. For example: "We will meet to establish a timetable and determine a preparation agenda for the upcoming case." If the meeting will include persons outside the office (for example, clients, witnesses, vendors, and so forth), confirm this information in a formal letter. Keep the reminder memo or letter brief (no more than one page).

If you want the participants to bring certain materials with them to the meeting, tell them in the confirming memo or letter. It is a good idea to ask participants to bring their calendars to the meeting, as this makes it easier for everyone to schedule another meeting (see #10 on follow-up procedures). After everyone has received notice of the meeting, contact them again to remind them and get confirmation that they are planning to come.

6. Prepare an agenda for the meeting. It is good practice to have an outline of questions for the meeting to help everyone focus their ideas and clarify the issues to be discussed. During the meeting the agenda serves as a guide and a reference. After the meeting, it is a reminder of what was decided and a basis for checking on follow-up actions. Keep the agenda as short as possible, but include specific topics to help you get the information you need. Jot questions on your copy in advance.

7. Conduct the meeting. Direct the discussion. Once the participants arrive at the meeting, don't waste their time. Start on time. Set a time limit in advance and stick to it. How long you allow depends on what project or case you intend to discuss. State the objective, that is, why you called this meeting. To keep a meeting on track, use the prepared agenda as a guide and try to discuss only one question at a time. If the discussion gets off the subject, refer back to the agenda items to help you focus on the objectives for the meeting. In the example above, the trial attorney will probably take the lead in the trial preparation agenda meeting, but you can help to keep the discussions on track by asking questions that return to the agenda.

8. Stop the meeting on time. Learn how to read your "audience" and know when to table things for further discussion. Summarize the discussion and decisions that have been made. Restate assignments that have been made and the follow-up actions required. This is particularly important in the trial preparation meeting, because you will need to produce a work plan that details everyone's responsibilities (see **§ 2.9**). Clarify questions to the extent possible. Don't expect to resolve everything in one meeting.

9. Document the meeting. Write up your notes from the meeting right away, while they are fresh in your mind. If appropriate, develop this into a written follow-up memo and distribute it to the meeting participants. The memo you prepare after the trial preparation agenda meeting becomes the work plan for the trial team (see § **2.9**), or a handy "to do" list for yourself in other types of meetings. Using a simple checklist format for follow-up memos makes it easy for the meeting participants to see critical information and reinforces in writing their oral agreement to complete certain tasks.

10. Schedule additional meetings and follow-up as needed. The timing of the next meeting depends on what was accomplished from the original agenda and what is left to be decided. The closer you are to trial or some other big event, the more often you need to meet to coordinate the details. Subsequent meetings can also be shorter ones. People won't mind attending meetings that you organize because they will soon recognize that you have learned the skills of running efficient and successful meetings.

§ 1.34 Managing the Case Budget

An important administrative skill you will need as a trial paralegal is the ability to manage the trial preparation activities within the constraints of the case budget. This means keeping out-of-pocket expenses under control, tracking case expenses as you incur them, and making sure all the case-related bills are paid (see § **7.35**). In order to do this, you must have some idea of how attorneys determine the budget for the case. A case budget usually encompasses two separate but related segments: (1) pretrial activities (research, investigation, discovery) and (2) trial-related expenses (litigation support, experts, demonstrative evidence). The investigation and discovery process is crucial to any case, because you have to do a thorough job of compiling all the relevant facts and evidence in order to adequately prepare for trial. Developing a case budget involves identifying the pretrial and trial activities that the attorney anticipates will be needed, and then estimating the professional time (and cost) associated with each activity.

Budget planning forces the attorney to begin early in the case to outline strategy, identify areas that will require factual investigation, anticipate discovery activities, and assess internal staffing needs. The approach to trial preparation and management will be influenced to some extent by the resources available to the lawfirm or through the client. Determining the case resources generally includes assessing the people, paper, time, and money components discussed in § **1.28.** For example, the attorney may need to determine what portion of the case budget should be designated for litigation support (building an automated document database, see **Chapter 8**). The amount of documents (paper) is usually the biggest indicator of expense in the case. Consider these potential areas of expense and the related resources:

- Estimated volume of documents (paper)
- Computer equipment costs and maintenance (money)
- Staffing and project personnel (people)
- Outside services (copiers, couriers) (people and money)
- Estimated hours required for coding input (time)
- Costs of outside vendor services, selection of vendor (money, people)
- Attorney hours for privilege review (people, time)
- Paralegal hours for logging, coding, and retrieving (people, time)
- Storage arrangements and cost for the document repository (paper, money)

Attorneys must also consider the client's budget in deciding on methods for handling documents, discovery, expert witnesses, visual aids for trial, and so forth. Does the client have in-house resources (computers, in-house experts) that can be used in developing the case? Clients contemplating litigation will be interested in the probable cost. There are several reasons for getting the client involved in planning the litigation budget:

- The attorney can begin to educate the client about the steps involved in each stage of the litigation and trial.
- The client feels more involved in the case preparation plans.
- The client forms realistic expectations about what to expect when the case goes to trial.
- The client will be aware of the added expenses of going to trial, and can make an informed decision on settlement offers compared to the potential costs of the litigation.

Follow these steps to determine the case budget parameters:

1. Discuss the budget with the attorney. Chances are that the budget will have been determined (at least in preliminary form) by the time you are called in on the case. If the case budget has already been established, ask the attorney about it to get a perspective on the costs of the case and a realistic idea of what budget is available to you to manage the case. You may not have very much control over this aspect, but you need to find out what you can about the value of the case and the anticipated expenses. If you find that an official budget has not been laid out, the attorney may request your help in preparing one. Talk to the attorney about the legal issues and the complexity of the facts in the case. See if you can determine approximately how many parties and potential witnesses will be involved.

2. Check the records (make realistic estimates). In law office budget matters, people's time equates to money (in hourly billing) and can be difficult to estimate. If the case is similar to ones you have done before, you might be able to check back into old records to see how much time a particular task took. Even if this is possible, however, you still can only make an estimate based on a different case.

If the case has already progressed pretty far along by the time you are called in to assist, you should be aware of the time and costs already expended as you work through the file. Check the files for fee agreements with clients, retainer agreements with experts, or other agreements with outside consultants. Determine what retainers have been paid to experts, for example, or what deposition costs have been advanced. You need to get some idea of the amount of money you have to work with to prepare the trial presentation. It may help to look at the billing summary records on the case for a list of billable time and expenditures to date.

3. Track the costs. No matter when you come in on the case, keep track of the costs for which you are responsible (see Trial Expenses Form in § **7.37**). Keeping track of expenses in this way makes finalizing the account a lot easier at the end of the case. You need to have a general idea of the budget for a case, because some situations involve a tradeoff of time versus money. For example, if you are really short on time before trial, you may have to pay expedited transcript fees to a court reporter for really quick (sometimes overnight) turnaround time. You need to know enough about the case budget to determine whether the case can bear this expense.

4. Calculate trial expenses. If the case does go to trial, there will be an additional set of expenditures related directly to the trial preparation. One of the main areas of trial-related expenses will be demonstrative evidence (see § **4.4**). Whenever possible, open office accounts at art supply and office supply stores, copier services, and Federal Express (or other overnight delivery services) to facilitate payment of expenses. Planning ahead for demonstrative evidence can help to keep the costs under control. You need to know that it won't cause a major panic if you have to pay for expedited services in order to produce results at trial.

§ 1.35 Improving Your Professional Skills

Some paralegals find themselves in the awkward position of working with a trial attorney who refuses to take the time to train or teach them about trial work. In this situation, the paralegal must take the initiative to learn and acquire the necessary techniques, procedures, and skills required of a top-notch trial paralegal (see **§ 1.26**). The following sections contain some suggestions for ways you can learn trial skills on your own.

§ 1.36 —Reading Trade Literature

Most law offices subscribe to at least a few trade periodicals in order to keep up to date on new trends and topics in the ever-changing field of law. These publications include numerous magazines, journals, newsletters, bulletins, reports, and so on, in circulation on the national, state, and local levels. Many of these publications contain articles of general interest to legal professionals. Others are geared to a specific practice area, such as trial practice. They offer how-to articles containing tips and practical information on trial techniques and strategies for handling various aspects of trial work. Many articles also give you a behind-the-scenes look at actual trials and the problems and solutions worked out by the trial team. Although most of these publications are generally written by and for attorneys, a trial paralegal can cull much useful information about trial work from them. Read materials written by and for practitioners on both the attorney and legal assistant levels (see reference checklist of legal periodicals). Some of the literature written for attorneys may be too advanced for entry-level paralegals, but chances are you can still learn something that will add to your understanding of the trial process. Find out which legal periodicals are available in your office and local law library, and take advantage of the opportunity to read these magazines regularly. Save copies of articles that offer advice and good ideas for handling trial logistics. Discuss these ideas with your supervising attorney and try to find ways to apply the new information to the trial work you handle.

If your office does not subscribe to any of these publications, check to see if any of them are available through your local law library. If your local law library puts out a newsletter or a column announcing new acquisitions, watch for mentions of new articles and publications that you could read to pick up tips on trial work.

§ 1.37 —National Legal Periodicals

The following is a partial reference listing of some of the major national legal periodicals that are good sources for trial practice tips and techniques.

1. *ABA Journal* (magazine/monthly)
   American Bar Association
   750 N. Lake Shore Drive
   Chicago, Illinois 60601
   (312) 988-5555

2. *ATLA Advocate* (newsletter/10 times per year)
   Association of Trial Lawyers of America (ATLA)
   1050 31st St. N.W.
   Washington, D.C. 20007-4499
   (800) 424-2727
3. *The Brief* (magazine/quarterly)
   Tort & Insurance Practice Section of ABA
   American Bar Association
   750 N. Lake Shore Drive
   Chicago, Illinois 60601
   (312) 988-5555
4. *Criminal Justice* (magazine/quarterly)
   ABA Press for the Section on Criminal Justice
   American Bar Association
   750 N. Lake Shore Drive
   Chicago, Illinois 60601
   (312) 988-6077 or 988-6076
5. *The Docket* (magazine/quarterly)
   National Institute for Trial Advocacy
   Notre Dame Law School
   Notre Dame, Indiana 46556
   (800) 225-6482
6. *Federal Bar News & Journal* (magazine/10 times per year)
   Federal Bar Association
   1815 H Street N.W., Suite 408
   Washington, D.C. 20006-3697
   (202) 638-0252
7. *Legal Assistant Today* (magazine/6 times per year)
   James Publishing Company
   3520 Cadillac Ave., Ste. E
   Costa Mesa, California 92626
   (714) 755-5450
8. *Litigation* (magazine/quarterly)
   ABA Section on Litigation Practice
   American Bar Association
   750 N. Lake Shore Drive
   Chicago, Illinois 60601
9. *National Law Journal* (weekly)
   The New York Law Publishing Company
   111 Eighth Avenue
   New York, New York 10011
   (212) 741-8300

10. *The Practical Lawyer*
    The American Law Institute-American Bar Association Committee on Professional Education (ALI-ABA)
    4025 Chestnut Street
    Philadelphia, Pennsylvania 19104
    (215) 243-1640
11. *Trial*
    Association of Trial Lawyers of America (ATLA)
    1050 31st St. N.W.
    Washington, D.C. 20007-4499
    (202) 965-3500
12. *Trial Diplomacy Journal*
    John Wiley & Sons, Inc.
    7222 Commerce Center Dr., Suite 240
    Colorado Springs, CO 80918
    (800) 879-4539
13. *ACCA DOCKET*
    American Corporate Counsel Association
    1225 Connecticut Avenue, N.W., Suite 302
    Washington, D.C. 20036
    (202) 296-4522
14. *ALA NEWS*
    Association of Legal Administrators
    175 E. Hawthorne Parkway, Suite 325
    Vernon Hills, Illinois 60061-1428
    (708) 816-1212
15. *AMERICAN ASSOCIATION OF LAW LIBRARIES NEWSLETTER*
    American Association of Law Libraries
    53 West Jackson Blvd., Suite 940
    Chicago, Illinois 60606
    (312) 939-0476
16. *THE LAMA MANAGER*
    Legal Assistant Management Association
    P.O. Box 40129
    Overland Park, Kansas 66204
    (913) 381-4458
17. *LAW OFFICE COMPUTING*
    James Publishing Company
    3520 Cadillac Ave., Suite E
    Costa Mesa, California 92626
    (714) 755-5450

18. *NBA MAGAZINE*
National Bar Association
1225 - 11th Street, N.W.
Washington, D.C. 20001-4217
(202) 842-3900

19. *NATIONAL PARALEGAL REPORTER*
National Federation of Paralegal Associations, Inc.
104 Wilmot Road, Suite 201
Deerfield, Illinois 60015-5195
(708) 940-8800

20. *NATIONAL TRIAL LAWYER* (magazine/bimonthly)
Trial Lawyer Publications, Inc.
P.O. Box 1217
Millville, New Jersey 08332-8217
(609) 825-5959

§ 1.38 —Attending CLE Seminars and Workshops

Mandatory continuing legal education (CLE) requirements for attorneys in many states have given rise to a plethora of CLE courses sponsored by bar associations, law schools, and other legal professional organizations on both the local and national levels. Many paralegal associations and schools also offer worthwhile training seminars and workshops in various practice areas. If you are new to trial work, the subject matter in some advanced seminars may be over your head, but you can almost always pick up a tip or two for improving your trial skills. Even when you don't understand everything that is presented, you can at least become familiar with some of the terminology, techniques, and current issues affecting your area of trial practice. Seminar materials often yield pattern forms or useful checklists that you can adapt and include as part of your reference materials. Locally sponsored seminars are especially good sources for tips on local court practices, customs, and the particular procedures followed in your community.

Determine your office's policy on paying for seminars and CLE for paralegals, and take advantage of any such benefits. Seminars are often available to paralegals at reduced rates, especially if you are an associate member of the local or state bar association that sponsors the seminar. In addition to live presentations, many good training seminars are also available on either audio or videotape. If you are a freelance paralegal or you work in an office with a very limited budget for outside seminars, check your local law library for instructional and training tapes that you can borrow free of charge.

§ 1.39 —Networking

Take every opportunity to talk to other trial paralegals in your office and in other lawfirms, especially those paralegals who have more experience than you do. Other trial paralegals may be willing to share ideas, forms, and resources. Ask them about the various types of trials they have handled and the different kinds of problems they have encountered in their work. Join the local paralegal or legal assistant organization in your city or area. Become a member of the local bar association if associate membership is open to paralegals in your community. Volunteer to serve on committees dealing with local court rules and procedures. Cultivate a network of professional contacts within your legal and business community. Exchange business cards with these counterpart professionals, and call on them for assistance when you need help with ideas or problem-solving techniques. Get your name on mailing lists for local bar association and court-related activities, such as "settlement weeks" sponsored by the court.

§ 1.40 Improving Time Management Skills

One of the most difficult aspects of trial preparation is finding enough time to get everything done. I have never worked on a trial that did not involve a multitude of last-minute details to attend to. There will always be unexpected problems and hitches—that is the nature of trial work. As a trial paralegal, you must learn ways to efficiently manage the time available during the trial preparation phase and during the actual trial. This section will discuss some strategies and ideas to help you make the most of your time as you prepare a case for trial.

§ 1.41 Planning for Time Organization

A key element in time management is planning. Careful planning early in the process will give you a head start on managing your time and staying organized during the trial preparation rush and the actual in-court days. This process involves two elements: planning your time and planning the work.

§ 1.42 —Organize Your Calendar

When you first learn of the trial date in your case, enter that date on your personal calendar (also on the automated calendar on your computer system, if you have one). Use a highlighter or brightly colored pen to frame the trial date so that it stands out on your paper calendar. Also enter any filing deadlines, cutoff dates, and pretrial dates the court may have assigned (see **§ 2.16**). Make a note (in pencil) on your personal calendar of the five to seven days immediately before the trial date. Also mark the days you anticipate actually being in trial. If you don't know how long the trial is expected to last, check the pretrial scheduling orders or ask your supervising attorney. This becomes a "cushion zone" on your calendar to help you avoid scheduling anything you don't absolutely have to schedule during the trial period.

Remove or Reschedule Activities

Look at the items on your calendar that are not related to the trial. See if there is anything you can eliminate entirely, such as social engagements, personal appointments, optional luncheon meetings, or similar nonessential dates. Naturally, if you happen to be holding expensive concert tickets for a date during the week before the trial, you will want to keep that on your calendar and plan your trial preparation work around that date so you can use the tickets. If the event is a conference or appointment that can be rescheduled without causing a great deal of inconvenience (or costing money), arrange an earlier time or postpone it until after the trial. If the rescheduling involves a client, check with the attorney in charge to make sure he or she knows about and approves of the change.

Delegate Tasks

If possible, delegate some tasks to another person in your office. If the person taking on the work is not familiar with that type of project, outline the steps you would take and give complete instructions. Schedule a date to review the work to make sure it is progressing satisfactorily. Enter that date on your calendar so you won't forget. If there is another paralegal in your office who is qualified to do the work, ask him or her to do a portion of the project. Be considerate of the other person's schedule. Depending on the nature of the project, check with the attorney in charge and let him or her know that someone else will be handling the work in your absence. In my office we have nearly always had more than one litigation paralegal, as well as several others who can help out. It has been my good fortune to have a willing and cooperative litigation paralegal (who is also a good friend) to assist me by "trading off" jobs and holding the fort while I am in trial. Even if the other paralegals in your office do not routinely handle litigation, call on them for help in covering a job. Be prepared to return the favor at some later date when that person is involved in a trial or is otherwise really strapped for time. If you are really in a pinch, talk to the attorney who gave you the project and explain the time constraints you are facing. See if the project deadline can be pushed back until the completion of your trial. The attorney may offer a solution or alternate plan, or may even agree to take the job back. Take the initiative to alert the attorney to the possibility that you may not be able to complete the work before the original deadline. This is better than turning in a poorly executed project or, worse yet, forgetting it entirely. The attorney will appreciate the fact that you were responsible enough to anticipate a problem, and in most instances will be quite flexible and understanding about a change in schedule. Keep the attorney informed about the progress of the project and complete it as soon as possible after your trial is finished.

Be careful not to let clients in your other cases feel neglected while you are involved in the trial. Return any telephone calls as promptly as you can and tactfully explain what you are working on so that the client knows you are not trying to avoid him or her. This type of candid communication can have positive results, for example, the client believes that if you are so attentive to your current trial you are likely to give his or her case just as much attention and priority when the time comes to go to trial.

Work Ahead

You may be responsible for some deadlines or tasks that cannot be delegated or rescheduled. Look at the task ahead of time and see if you can do all or part of it before the actual trial work gets going in earnest. For example, you may have a statute of limitations date for a personal injury case that falls during the week your trial is scheduled. You have been asked to prepare a complaint to be filed before the statute date, a task that could take several hours. Don't procrastinate! Get the file out now and prepare at least a rough draft for the attorney's review. You will find that it is much easier to get started on this job before the trial, when you can concentrate and devote your full attention to it, than to do the same work during trial preparation week when things are really crazy and interruptions are inevitable. If the attorney is the same one handling the trial you are working on, he or she will be more likely to have time to review your draft, make suggestions, and perhaps even approve the final draft without the distraction of the trial proceedings. There may be a reason the attorney wants to wait until just before the statute date to file the complaint, but if not, go ahead and file the complaint, and then check this conflicting deadline off your list of "other" things to be handled during the time you will be busy at trial. In any event, take the project or assignment as far as you can as early as you can, even if this means coming in to the office an hour early or staying late. When trial week comes and you are swamped with the demands of keeping the trial running smoothly, you will be glad you had the foresight to work ahead. Add reminders or tickler notes as a backup for critical due dates and deadlines during the trial preparation period. It never hurts to have an extra reminder to ensure that you don't miss a critical date. If your office has a docket system for reminders, send one to yourself, your secretary, your supervising attorney, and the attorney's secretary so that even if you should forget or something should happen to you, someone else would get a notice of the important date, deadline, or event.

Plan to Handle Unavoidable Conflicts

Even after rescheduling, delegating, and working ahead, there may still be a few items on your calendar that you will have to take care of during trial week. Be sure these deadlines are clearly marked on your daily calendar so you won't inadvertently forget them because you are so busy with the trial.

§ 1.43 —Develop a Work Plan for Trial Preparation

Make a long-range timeline plan for the weeks between now and trial. Then break it down into weekly plans, listing more specific jobs that need to be done. (Refer to the Comprehensive Timeline/Checklist in **§ 2.6** as a starting point to help you determine what needs to be done.) Check your progress at the end of each week, and update your weekly plan for the next week. Define your trial preparation goals for the next week, and then list the specific actions needed to complete these projects. You may find it helpful to prepare a full-page calendar showing the month containing the trial date (see **Form 1–3,** Calendar Blank) and the two or three months just before that (depending on how much time you have before the trial date). Mark the trial date in bold letters and work backward from there in scheduling witness preparation conferences and other meetings and activities related to the trial. Consider distributing copies of this calendar to trial team members at the initial trial preparation meeting.

Plan as far ahead as possible so you can control the pace of the work. Don't set up an impossible schedule for yourself. Recognize that there are only 168 hours in a week and be realistic about what you can accomplish. It is important to control the number of obligations you have, both at work and at home, so that you can focus your attention on the trial. The trial will be stressful enough without an overload of unrelated responsibilities. Anticipate the rush of trial preparation tasks and plan ahead to accommodate them in stride.

Everyone tends to overestimate what they can accomplish in a given amount of time, so you need to build some flexibility into the trial preparation schedule. You can plan to work extra hours, but only up to a point. By having a plan for how to apply your time, you can catch scheduling problems early in the week and shift priorities if necessary before it is too late to explore other options. Plan consistently every week. You may need to revise the original plan, moving some tasks into the next day or next week. You could also delegate some tasks. Look for ways to simplify and streamline tasks to do them more efficiently.

FORM 1–3
CALENDAR BLANK

SUNDAY	MONDAY	TUESDAY	WEDNESDAY	THURSDAY	FRIDAY	SATURDAY

Time management experts recommend studying your daily diary to spot patterns and trends, such as how often you are interrupted or how much of your time is controlled by your boss. A particular problem for trial paralegals is that a large portion of the time you have to spend is determined by the agenda and whims of the attorney you are supporting. Planning your time becomes increasingly important as you take on higher levels of responsibility in trial preparation. It is virtually impossible to manage all of the elements involved in a trial preparation without careful planning. Count on these three things:

1. Things are usually more complicated than you think they will be.
2. Everything will take longer than you think it should.
3. Anything that can go wrong probably will go wrong.

Try teamwork time planning with the trial team members. When you work on a trial as part of a team, you need to coordinate your plans and goals with the plans and goals of the other members of the team. At regular intervals (perhaps at one of your trial agenda meetings), compare your calendars and look for the connecting points. Discuss how to coordinate activities with the other team members and revise your plans as necessary.

§ 1.44 Using Timesaving Techniques and Shortcuts

One consistent characteristic of trial work is having to accomplish multiple tasks within a very short period of time as the case gets closer to trial. This means that you must make the most of not only your own time, but also that of the trial attorney and the office support staff who are assisting with the trial preparation. Timesavers can be any tool or technique that helps you do something more efficiently.

§ 1.45 —Develop a Good Filing System for Case Materials

Some paralegals mistakenly think they should not spend time on "busywork" tasks, like setting up filing systems, indexing, and labeling. But you will find that in most cases instances a relatively small amount of time and effort early in the case yields a proportionately large return on the time investment. Good filing starts with a broad general inventory of types or sources of material into broad categories, then further details and classifies each component. (See **Chapter 2.**) For example, the initial work of preparing a comprehensive diagram inventory of the trial file (see **§ 2.36**) or designing an efficient indexing and retrieval system (see **§§ 2.75–2.92**) can pay great dividends later in the case. You design the system, then recruit others to help you maintain it. The initial work you do to inventory and catalog the materials pays off by making it easy for you and others to quickly locate and retrieve information throughout the rest of the case. If you manage the paper, then you have gone a long way toward managing the case. A solid file organization system saves time (and therefore, money) over and over as the case progresses for a couple of reasons:

1. You don't have to spend time searching for "lost" information; and
2. Other people who use the file can find what they need *and* put it back where it belongs. One sign of a good filing system is that other people can figure out not only where to find materials, but also *where to return items in the file,* even if you are not right there. Give others the keys to your system. Believe it or not, if you make it easy enough, even the attorneys will put files back where they belong. A good design makes it easy for you to delegate the physical filing tasks to others. They will use it if it's easy enough to figure out.

§ 1.46 —Consolidate and Standardize Tasks

Whenever you have to pick up or deliver materials to various places within your office or outside the office, try to plan your route so that you can accomplish multiple items on one trip instead of making several individual trips. Make more than one telephone call at a session. Set aside a time to make several calls. Enter in your Rolodex™ or telephone/address book any name, telephone number, or address you have to look up more than twice. Jot down any questions that occur during the course of your work so that when you get the attorney's attention, you can ask several questions at the same time.

Standardizing repetitive tasks saves time for both you and your secretary. Write instruction sheets for common procedures, such as preparing and serving trial subpoenas. Keep a notebook of standard form letters, pleadings, and forms for your secretary to use as a guide. Any technique that lets you avoid writing the same information over and over will save you time. Wherever possible, use forms and checklists to collect and enter case information uniformly. You are much more likely to record and retain complete information when a space is provided on a standardized form than if the notes or information are scribbled on various bits and scraps of paper that get scattered throughout the file. These forms can be commercially available preprinted forms, or they may be forms you have designed yourself or adapted to suit the needs of your particular office. Make "task sheet" form memos for instructions to your secretary on often-requested tasks. Checking a box is faster than writing down the instructions. Use no-carbon speed memos to record a short message and reply without having to make a trip to the copy machine. Use mailing label sheets or matrices for often-typed addresses. Learn to use the automated functions and features of your computer software so you can save time when it really counts. (See **Chapter 8** on using the computer in trial preparation.)

§ 1.47 —Use Work Plan Lists

I am a great believer in writing lists, especially in trial preparation work where you have to keep track of so many details at once. Put every item you have to do on a list, keep the list with you at all times, and cross through each task as it is completed. This way you will get to most of the most important tasks. The trick is to consistently write them down and to keep referring to the list. Transfer any scattered notes you may have made to a main central list as soon as possible. This way, even if something happened to you, someone else could see what you had mapped out to do and how much of it you got done. Keep a master list file that should contain a copy of every list you make related to the trial preparation. Include your daily "TO DO" sheets, preprinted forms, witness lists, telephone lists, and so forth.

Lists are also useful for tracking time and billing charges. Sometimes you are so busy doing things in trial preparation that you don't have time to write them down for billing. Reviewing your work list from that day will refresh your recollection as to all the little details you took care of today. Little details add up. Eventually you will know approximately how long it takes to do a certain chore, and you can factor this into your planning. (See § **1.53** on keeping time records during trial.)

§ 1.48 —Make Use of Your Office Systems

Office systems are highly individual to each office, but every office has established procedures for getting the paperwork done. Get to know the office procedures, policies, and systems that apply in your office. Learn how to cut through red tape, and make the office systems work for you in order accomplish everything you need to do for trial. The office procedures you are likely to need for trial work include

- Check or petty cash requisition
- Long distance telephone charges
- Conference room reservation and scheduling
- Advances to the client's account

- Errand clerks/support staff
- Bulk copying
- Computer staff/capabilities
- Travel arrangements
- Seminar requests

Make sure you know how to do these procedures ahead of time. Enlist the aid of your secretary, office manager, or other administrative personnel who can teach you what you need to know.

§ 1.49 —Use Small Bits of Time

The nature of trial preparation work is usually pretty hectic. You rarely have the luxury of a large block of time in which to complete a project. However, you will find you can accomplish much by making use of small bits of time as they become available. For example, you could use the time you are on "hold" on the telephone or otherwise waiting for a piece of information to review and update your lists and indexes of trial-related information. These are some other things you can do in five minutes or less:

- Look up a telephone number or address
- Write a timeslip
- Make a photocopy
- Write a Rolodex™ card
- Call a court reporter to schedule a deposition or confirm arrangements for playing a video at trial
- Locate a form (for example, a subpoena form)
- Fill out a sheet of exhibit labels

§ 1.50 Using the Telephone as a Timesaving Tool

Trial preparation is always chaotic, and it becomes especially so in the last few days before trial. A trial paralegal is often responsible for making numerous last-minute contacts, arrangements, and deliveries very quickly. This can be a daunting task when many things must be accomplished simultaneously and within a very short time. It only makes good sense to take advantage of all the equipment and services available to help you do your job as efficiently as possible. The modern law office and modern attorneys could not function without Mr. Bell's miraculous invention, the telephone. Possibly no other single invention has had such a profound effect on the way lawyers practice as the good old telephone. Modern telephone service is not only reliable and fast, but it is also a bargain in the legal world where time is money. The telephone is such a common fixture in any office that most of us take it for granted. Of course, on those busy, hectic days when the telephone rings incessantly, constantly interrupting your train of thought, you have undoubtedly considered it a real nuisance! But a successful trial paralegal regards the telephone as an important tool to be used in getting things done as efficiently as possible. Besides the availability of the telephone for traditional uses, advanced technology has made the ubiquitous telephone an indispensable tool in conducting the communications that are so important to trial preparation work. Here are some ideas and suggestions for ways you can make the telephone work for you.

§ 1.51 —Traditional Uses

Use the telephone instead of in-person conferences when you can. This eliminates travel time from one office to another, waiting for elevators, chatting with people you meet along the way. If you call someone who is not in, try to leave your message on voice mail. Let clients and coworkers know when you prefer to receive calls in the office. Plan an agenda for each call so that you don't waste time digressing. Be polite, but let the caller know that the case is too important to waste time chatting about unrelated matters. For long-winded callers, put a time limit on the conversation. If you only have five minutes, tell the caller.

Keeping Clients Informed

A telephone call is an easy and quick way for you to assist the trial attorney to update your client on the status of the trial preparations or to convey other important information. A telephone call takes less time than writing a letter. (Note: Some things should also be covered or confirmed in a letter, but an immediate telephone call usually satisfies the client.)

Returning and Documenting Calls

How many times have you left your office for just a moment, and that turns out to be precisely the time the important call from your key expert witness in another state finally comes through? Then, when you try to return the call, the person is on another line, in a meeting, or otherwise unavailable. This is known as playing "telephone tag," and it can be a real headache, but it is an inevitable part of legal work. Make it a habit to return incoming telephone call messages as soon as possible. As you speak, use the Telephone Conference Record (see **Form 1–4**) to record notes on the conversation and jot down any necessary follow-up steps or questions that need to be resolved. Keep these telephone conference forms as a permanent record in the file to document information received or transmitted in the course of the telephone conversation. Be sure to note the date and time the call took place and the length of the conversation on the telephone conference form. This may assist you in reconstructing your timeslips for one of those hectic trial days when you are so busy you don't have time to write everything down. (See § **1.53** on keeping accurate time records.) If the person you are calling is unavailable and you must speak with a secretary or assistant, be sure to get the name of the person with whom you spoke. This may give you easier access for future calls. If you try a call and the line is busy or there is no answer, note the time of day of each attempted call on the telephone conference form so that you have a record of how many times you tried to call.

Obtaining Travel Directions

If you or the attorney will be traveling to a courtroom or office in an unfamiliar area or city, telephone in advance (or have your secretary call) to get clear directions for the best route to follow in order to save travel time. You might also inquire about the availability of parking facilities at or near your destination. Ask your secretary to type up the directions in memo form, and include a map of the area if one is available. Be sure to include the telephone number of the destination office so that you or the attorney can easily call for clarification of the directions in the event you take a wrong turn and get lost. If the directions to this location will be needed again (by your client, an expert witness, or someone from your office), keep a copy of them in the case file. Also, if the directions are to a place such as the federal court building in the state capital, put a copy in your Master Reference Notebook for future reference.

Getting Information Quickly

Sometimes a telephone call (for example, to the reference desk at your public library) can be a quicker way to obtain a piece of information than writing for it or dispatching an errand clerk to get it. Most libraries keep telephone directories for major cities and can provide telephone numbers and street addresses for witnesses or organizations in distant cities. Some libraries have telecopier capability and can transmit copies of brief articles or documents. (Caution: Fax copies are often not high quality reproductions and the glossy paper used in some systems tends to deteriorate when stored in case files. As a safeguard, make regular photocopies of any important documents you

FORM 1–4
SAMPLE TELEPHONE CONFERENCE RECORD

TELEPHONE CONFERENCE RECORD		
CLIENT	FILE No.	DATE
INCOMING CALL [ ] OUTGOING CALL [ ]	START TIME ___A.M. ___P.M.	END TIME ___A.M. ___P.M.
NUMBER(s) CALLED:		
TELEPHONE CONFERENCE WITH OF		
NOTES ON SUBJECT DISCUSSED:		
FOLLOWUP ACTION TO BE TAKEN/THINGS TO DO:		

receive via telecopier transmission.) Keep a list of any important "hotline" or "clearinghouse" numbers that are central repositories for specialized information, for example, legislative or judicial information services on both the state and federal levels. Many numbers are toll-free and some services are accessible 24 hours a day. Don't overlook your client (especially a corporation or other large organization) as a source for obtaining direct telephone numbers for key executives to whom you would not ordinarily have access.

Knowing Where to Call

Keep your Rolodex™ or telephone book up to date so that you have the most current numbers for clients, witnesses, public offices, and so on. Record any number changes immediately. Indicate any telephone numbers that are direct personal lines or unlisted residence numbers so that you do not inadvertently reveal a confidential number.

- Record client or witness telecopier numbers when available.
- Keep a reference list of client codes or file numbers (or the equivalent in your office) close to your telephone for long distance calls that must be charged to the client's account.
- Get an extra copy of the local telephone directory for your area. Cut out the "blue pages" or the equivalent section that lists government offices and agencies. Three-hole punch these pages and insert them in your Master Reference Notebook. This information is free of charge and can be easily updated each year as new telephone books are issued.
- Obtain copies of telephone directories for the major metropolitan areas and surrounding counties in your state. Keep these yourself if you have the shelf space, or deposit them with your secretary, receptionist, or in-house librarian so that you will have ready access to key telephone numbers for persons outside your immediate area.

§ 1.52 —High Tech Uses

Advanced technology has provided modern telephone systems with a variety of special features that can save time for a busy trial paralegal. You need to know how to operate any special features offered by your office telephone system to make the most efficient use of your telephone time. Such features might include the following:

- Learn how to program your "auto dial" function for frequently called numbers, such as, major clients and court clerks.

- Automatic long distance billing to the client number.
- Use the "hands-free" or speakerphone for conference calls.

Note: This function is available on many office telephone systems, but the sound quality is often very poor. I find it very annoying when someone on the other end of the line is using the speakerphone because it is like talking into an echo chamber. Avoid using this feature except for attorney conference calls, or when there is a really good reason to use the "hands-free" mode. Some attorneys, especially those in cities distant from one another, may even hold pretrial hearings or settlement conferences via telephone conferencing.

- Answering machine and voice mail functions can come in really handy for both sending and receiving messages when you must be away from your desk or office, for example, when you are preparing witnesses or exhibits in the war room. The caller may not like talking to a machine, but it is better than missing an important call related to some detail of the trial preparation.
- Call forwarding
- Night pickup line for incoming calls after regular business hours.
- Modem access via telephone lines to computerized databases and research services (LEXIS and Westlaw for legal research and Dialog or InfoNet for factual research).

§ 1.53 Keeping Time Records During Trial

The expression "time is money" is nowhere more true than in the legal profession. You have a responsibility to your employer to keep an accurate record of the work you do on the trial preparation and during the trial so that it can be billed properly to the client and generate income for your company. You have a responsibility to the client to adequately describe the work you perform in your time records so the client can determine precisely what services have been rendered. Of course, this is easier said than done.

Most trials are pretty exciting and some are even glamorous, but make no mistake—the pace of trial preparation days, not to mention the *actual* court days, can be truly hectic. It is difficult enough just to keep your wits about you when the "trial mode" goes into high gear, without worrying about something as mundane as keeping time records.

The exact procedures for transferring individual time records into the billing system vary greatly among law offices. Some firms require daily entry of time records, while others allow time to be entered less frequently. If possible, set up and learn to use a computerized timekeeping program to help you account for your time accurately. Keep your office's operating procedures in mind as you consider the following suggestions for tracking your time during trial.

§ 1.54 —Use a Calendar, Diary, or Daily Time Log

You should already have some type of daily calendar or diary on which you record appointments, planned activities, and your time for billing purposes. Some paralegals like to use a large notebook-style calendar that stays on the desk and has plenty of space in which to record notes on daily tasks completed. Other paralegals prefer a smaller calendar or appointment book that can be easily carried in a pocket or briefcase. The choice of a daily diary is a highly personal one, so use the type you prefer and which works best in your practice.

I find that a daily log sheet covering the 12-hour period from 7:00 A.M. to 7:00 P.M. is suitable for recording my time on most busy trial preparation days. The sample daily time log divides each hour into 12-minute intervals, but you might prefer one that indicates tenths of an hour (six-minute intervals). (See **Form 1–5,** Daily Time Log.) Note the task on which you are working directly across from the time you start it, then mark the time the task is completed (or interrupted). You can easily calculate how much time to bill for that task by bracketing the time between the beginning and ending marks, minus any time spent on interruptions.

The sample Daily Time Log also provides space for notes on any incoming or outgoing telephone calls, as well as other reminders and notes that may occur to you during the busy day. Use these notes as a way to follow up on the numerous details to which you must attend during trial preparation.

§ 1.55 —Reconstruct Your Day

Successful timekeeping depends upon using your calendar consistently to record your work throughout the day, and then reviewing and recapping at the end of every day. Recording your time is fairly easy on days when you are working at your desk all day. But what about those days when you are on the run, working in the war room or in the courtroom all day? Try fastening your daily log sheet on a small clipboard and carrying it with you when you go outside your office.

Of course, some trial days are so incredibly busy that you barely have time to take a restroom break, much less write timeslips! Timekeeping becomes even more complicated if you are working on more than one trial preparation at the same time. Any paralegal who has assisted in a few trials will tell you that it is not unusual to find yourself at the end of the day with absolutely nothing written on your calendar, even though you have been working constantly

FORM 1–5
DAILY TIME LOG

	REMINDERS	TIME		CLIENT	DESCRIPTION
1			00		
2			12		
3		7	24		
4			36		
5			48		
6			00		
7			12		
8		8	24		
9			36		
10			48		
11			00		
12			12		
13		9	24		
14			36		
15			48		
16			00		
17			12		
18		10	24		
19			36		
20			48		
21			00		
22			12		
23		11	24		
24			36		
25			48		
26			00		
27			12		
28		12	24		
29			36		
30			48		
TELEPHONE CALLS			00		
1			12		
2		1	24		
3			36		
4			48		
5			00		
6			12		
7		2	24		
8			36		
9			48		
10			00		
11			12		
12		3	24		
13			36		
14			48		
15			00		
16			12		
17		4	24		
18			36		
19			48		
20			00		
21			12		
22		5	24		
23			36		
24			48		
25			00		
26			12		
27		6	24		
28			36		
29			48		

NOTES:____

since the crack of dawn. If this happens to you, try to reconstruct the day's events as soon as possible. Use the suggestions on the checklist in § **1.56** to jog your memory about tasks you completed.

§ 1.56 —Reconstructing Your Daily Time Records

The checklist is helpful in reconstructing your daily tasks. (See also **Form 1–5.**)

____ 1. Review the notes and papers generated by the day's activities, including the following:

- ____ Telephone message slips
- ____ Telephone conference records
- ____ Miscellaneous notes on self-adhesive tags or other slips of paper
- ____ Current "to do" lists
- ____ Schedule for witness preparation conferences
- ____ Scheduling and planning block sheet (see **Chapter 6**)

____ 2. Look for any papers bearing that day's date stamp.

____ 3. Ask your secretary to make a list of the documents she has processed for you that day.

____ 4. Check the index of pleadings and other indexes in the case to see what may have been filed with the court clerk on that day.

____ 5. Review notes you have taken in client or witness conferences.

____ 6. Mentally visualize the day's events. Recall where you had lunch (if you did) and with whom.

____ 7. If your office receptionist keeps a log of clients or guests who visit the office, check this for clues to names of persons you have talked to that day.

____ 8. Check the office telecopier log to determine whether you received any fax mail.

____ 9. Check your record of expenses advanced to the client's account for clues.

____ 10. Check your copies of any instruction sheets you have given to your secretary or your office errand clerks.

____ 11. Check your computer file storage log to see if you created any computer documents.

§ 1.57 Conducting Factual Research for Trial Preparation

Factual research is an important aspect of trial preparation that is often the trial paralegal's responsibility. Our country's system of statutes, laws, and cases determines the issues, doctrines, and legal theories upon which legal causes of action are based. Within this legal framework, courts and juries render their judgments on the basis of the *facts* presented at trial. It is vitally important for the trial team to help the jury make informed decisions by providing sufficient factual data about the subject matter involved in the lawsuit.

Conducting factual research for trial does not necessarily require legal training. It does, however, require you to use the library skills and study habits you learned in school, together with some standard investigative techniques, a healthy curiosity, persistence and attention to detail, a dash of creativity and imagination, and a good dose of common sense. Fortunately for busy trial paralegals, on-line research services like LEXIS, Westlaw, and others, make it possible to conduct thorough research in a fraction of the time it once took. A computer with a modem can connect you to on-line databases that make factual research easy and interesting. You can have quick access to volumes of information on almost any subject with the touch of a few keys. Ask your local LEXIS or Westlaw representatives about training sessions on these services.

Whether you research manually or electronically, approach your factual research project with confidence, no matter what subject area your trial involves. Do not be intimidated by complex technology or scientific processes. You can learn about any subject if you organize your research approach and keep a positive attitude. The better you understand the subject, the better you will be able to support the trial attorney in developing the facts of the case for trial. The checklist in § **1.58** contains some suggestions and research techniques to get you started.

§ 1.58 —Techniques for Factual Trial Research

This checklist provides a way for organizing your research.

____ 1. Start with an outline of the main issues and subjects involved in your case. Then apply the journalistic approach, asking basic questions (Who? What? When? Where? Why? How?) to develop a plan for the specific information you need to acquire.

____ 2. Work from the general to the specific. One general reference source may lead you to other sources that "zero in" on the exact subject you are researching.

____ 3. Trace the historical development of the product, process, industry, or profession. Certain landmark dates may be significant when viewed from an historical perspective. This information could form the basis for an effective timeline or chronology that could ultimately be demonstrative evidence at trial. (See §§ **4.1–4.3** for tips on demonstrative evidence and visual aids.)

____ 4. Investigate all potential sources of information, including:

- ____ Encyclopedic works and treatises
- ____ Textbooks and training materials
- ____ Books, tapes, microfilm
- ____ General periodicals (*Newsweek, Time, U.S. News & World Report, Forbes,* and so forth)
- ____ Legal periodicals (see § **1.37**)
- ____ Medical journals and reference works (if injuries, health care, or other medical issues are involved in your case)
- ____ Trade journals and newsletters for the business or industry
- ____ Newspapers
- ____ Museum archives
- ____ Professional associations
- ____ Offbeat sources such as collectors, newsletters, fan clubs, support groups
- ____ Computerized on-line databases (see **Chapter 8**)
- ____ Reference information that may be in your client's files and records

____ 5. If any governmental or regulatory agency is involved, track down the address and telephone number of the agency headquarters (ask your librarian for help). Contact the office to find out what printed materials are available. Many such agencies can provide copious amounts of data at no charge or at a very low cost.

____ 6. Document your sources carefully, as this could have a bearing on issues of authenticity and admissibility at trial. Make sure you know where you found statistics, survey results, quotations, and so forth that the attorney may rely on to support the client's case. Always record the dates of your sources and make sure that any data you rely on is current and has not been superseded.

____ 7. Be alert to current events and media information related to the particular product, business, science, or technology you are researching.

____ 8. Don't overlook television as a source of information. Use a VCR to tape a documentary or investigative news program dealing with your subject matter. Some programs (such as public television broadcasts) offer transcripts of the programs by mail for a small fee.

____ 9. Locate the regulations or written rules that govern the profession, product, process, industry, or technical area involved in your case. Almost every discipline will have some type of written

- ____ Guidelines
- ____ Protocols
- ____ Standards
- ____ Regulations
- ____ Specifications
- ____ Codes
- ____ Articles or Bylaws
- ____ Qualifications
- ____ Accreditation criteria
- ____ Licensure requirements

The American National Standards Institute (ANSI), 1430 Broadway, New York, NY 10018 is an organization that publishes and approves test procedures, guidelines, and standards for all sorts of professional and technical areas.

____ 10. Use the expertise and knowledge of expert witnesses or consultants who are familiar with the field or subject you are researching. Ask for their recommendations on authoritative background texts or literature on the subject. Find out if there are any learned treatises that experts consider authoritative works on the subject. (See § **3.35** *et seq.* on working with experts to prepare for trial.)

§ 1.59 Handling Factual Data

The attorney's job at trial is to present information about the subject in a way that is understandable, educational, and interesting to the judge and jury. You can help in this process by summarizing the objective data and relevant background information into an easily digestible format that the attorney can use at trial. Your job is to translate complicated information into everyday terms and language that the average juror can understand. This is especially important in cases involving highly complex or technologically sophisticated products, processes, industries, or professions. Depending on the case and the nature of the information, you may find it useful to

- Break the process down into steps.
- Identify the key components.

- Make a "flow chart" of the process or procedure.
- Locate or create a picture, drawing, illustration, or diagram, and label key parts or processes.
- Prepare a glossary containing definitions of key words or terms (especially in any field that uses complex technical jargon).

You will find many ways to apply the factual information you gather in your research. The exact way in which you use the information at trial will vary from case to case. A solid grounding in the background of the subject area will enable you to ask intelligent questions and help you to fully understand the disputed matters in the case based upon the factual data. By investigating and learning about the profession, product, process, industry, or technical area, and then applying your knowledge to your particular case, you may also be able to

- Discern some pattern of activity or technical nuance that is significant to your case.
- Assist the trial attorney in formulating a strategy or tactical approach to some point in the case.
- Point out a discrepancy or weakness in the opposing side's case.
- Compare the industry standards or requirements to what actually transpired to illustrate deficiencies or compliance with the rules (depending on which side of the case you represent).
- Compile statistical data to support your case or refute the opposing party's allegations.
- Design a chart or visual aid for use at trial.
- Help to formulate a line of questioning for an expert witness.
- Supply published information to support a point on rebuttal.

As you locate research on topics relevant to your case, make photocopies or obtain printouts of the information. Index and compile these materials in a file or binder so the attorney can easily review and assimilate the data.

§ 1.60 —Examples: Factual Research in Specific Trials

The following are examples of some of the factual research areas I have developed in my trial experience.

1. National tire manufacturer alleged RICO violations against a local chain of service stations that were franchised distributors of the tires.

Charges included fraud and conspiracy related to falsifying rebate vouchers for tires supposedly returned by consumers under warranty. The distributor/dealers were "reimbursed" by the manufacturer for thousands of fraudulent warranty claims before the scheme was detected.
Factual areas:

- Tires: franchise and distributor agreements
- Warranty, guarantee, and rebate claim procedures
- Internal accounting procedures of both the manufacturer and the distributors
- Handwriting analysis: to detect falsified rebate claims and forged signatures

2. Construction case involving client who built a parking deck that subsequently deteriorated, resulting in costly repairs and lost revenue from parking fees.
Factual areas:

- Construction standards for covered parking decks
- Types of concrete and steel support structures
- Types and grades of materials used in construction

3. Product liability and personal injury case involving driver who was injured when his car was rammed by a city-owned steamroller that had accidentally rolled down an embankment.
Factual areas:

- Steamroller safety design standards
- Required warnings and cautions
- Training requirements for equipment operators

4. Negligence and wrongful death action involving a nursing home that failed to provide adequate care and supervision to an elderly resident, resulting in an accidental fall and subsequent death of the patient.
Factual areas:

- Definitions and standards for various classifications of long-term care facilities
- Federal requirements for inspection, reporting, and Medicaid/Medicare qualification

- State certification and licensing requirements and procedures
- Recordkeeping protocol standards for nursing care facilities

5. Contract dispute involving a claim against a manufacturer-supplier of plastic components of bathroom fixtures for failure to supply parts manufactured to the correct design specifications.
   Factual areas:

   - Plastic injection mold processes
   - Equipment design tolerances and specifications
   - Industry standards for injection molding

6. Personal injury and pharmacy malpractice case involving a drinking driver who was also taking Valium™. Neither the doctor who prescribed the drug nor the pharmacy that filled the prescription warned the driver that he should not mix the drug with alcohol, or that the drug could affect his alertness and driving ability.
   Factual areas:

   - Toxicology: effects of Valium and Valium combined with alcohol
   - Pharmacy standards (for warning labels)

7. Patent and copyright infringement action involving alleged theft of "recipes" for trade secret rubber and polymer compounds.
   Factual areas:

   - Rubber compounding methods and equipment
   - Action of various chemicals and ingredients on compounds
   - Rubber manufacturing procedures and protocols
   - Patent and copyright registration procedures and requirements

8. Personal injury case involving suit against municipality for failure to properly maintain the roadway and erect proper guardrails and warning signs. Passenger in the automobile crash survived but suffered extensive brain damage that rendered him incapable of leading a normal life.
   Factual areas:

   - Brain injury and neurological damage
   - Roadway design defects and standards
   - Roadway repair and maintenance requirements

9. Environmental pollution and damages action involving a petroleum product storage facility sued by a neighboring chrome-plating facility for allegedly leaking pollutants into the groundwater, adversely affecting the chrome-plating business that used the groundwater in its processing.

   Factual areas:

   - Petroleum storage facilities: construction standards, monitoring, and safety inspection requirements
   - Chrome-plating process: chemicals involved and procedures for monitoring waste disposal
   - Groundwater pollution: EPA standards, regulations, and inspection procedures; complaint investigation and reporting procedures
   - Underground aquifers and water tables
   - Geological factors affecting direction and amount of underground water pollution
   - Laboratory testing procedures for various pollutants

10. Medical malpractice case involving claims against a hospital emergency room and a physician who failed to diagnose a heart attack, resulting in the patient having to undergo life-threatening emergency open heart surgery.

    Factual areas:

    - Various types of heart disease and malfunctions
    - Hospital emergency room protocols
    - Standards of care in diagnosing and treating heart disease
    - Statistical probabilities and survival rates associated with various heart conditions

§ 1.61 Building a Master Reference Notebook

You will find that you routinely need some of the same information each time you prepare a case for trial. The master reference notebook, to which you can add new and updated information you learn as you handle each trial, can be an indispensable timesaver during hectic trial preparation days by providing instant access to many important facts. Unlike a trial notebook that you create for a specific trial, this customized reference notebook is a central repository for information and lists of people, resources, forms, and so forth that you need to have at your fingertips during trial preparation. This notebook is a personalized reference tool, and its contents should include reference information tailored to your area, your office, and the type of trials you handle most often. If you use a personal computer in your work, take advantage of its word processing and database functions to store and index some of this key reference information. The power and flexibility of the computer will enhance your ability to quickly retrieve and update this information with each trial. (See **Chapter 8** on using computer applications in trial preparation.) The following checklist suggests some of the reference lists and resource information you may want to include in your master reference notebook.

§ 1.62 —Information for a Master Reference Notebook

The following checklist contains a number of items that should be included in a master reference notebook.

____ 1. Client file and billing numbers

____ 2. Westlaw and Lexis access codes or passwords

____ 3. List of coworkers' home telephone numbers for emergencies (supervising attorney, other paralegals, key support staff)

____ 4. Building directory or telephone list (security, management office, after-hours deliveries, etc.)

____ 5. Outside vendors (copiers, enlargers, subpoena services)

  ____ Account numbers

  ____ Hours of operation

  ____ Price lists, quotes

____ 6. Travel agency telephone and information

____ 7. Private investigators

____ 8. Local court reporters; services such as SetDepo and DepoNet to locate court reporters in distant cities

____ 9. Courier and delivery services

____ 10. Libraries (public, law, specialized)

____ 11. Directory of court personnel and telephone numbers

____ 12. Court costs lists (local and foreign jurisdictions)

____ 13. Subpoena forms; witness fee and mileage requirements

____ 14. Tables of mileage between major cities (to calculate witness fees)

____ 15. Court rules for your local court and surrounding counties

____ 16. Index of expert witnesses (see § **3.21**)

____ 17. Secretary of State (or equivalent) for other states (for checking corporate information)

____ 18. Basic witness instructions or reminder sheets

____ 19. Map or diagram of courthouse location and layout

____ 20. Map of adjacent public buildings (for example, county offices annex) and parking facilities

____ 21. Written directions to courthouse, to your office from out-of-town highways

____ 22. Masters of trial-related forms (to be photocopied as needed for individual trial "kits")

____ 23. Forms and instructions for out-of-town courts (for example, subpoena forms, special directions with fee schedules)

____ 24. Requirements for ordering accident photographs from police reporting agencies (§ **4.31**)

____ 25. Index of computer file names for standard trial-related documents and forms

____ 26. Index of previous work product, examples of trial pleadings, etc.

____ 27. Equipment inventory, maintenance records, and related information

____ 28. Notations of settings or special instructions for sizing enlargements or reduces copies on your photocopy machine (see § **4.10**).

§ 1.63 Collecting Personal Reference Works

English lexicographer Samuel Johnson said, "The next best thing to knowing something is knowing where to find it." In other words, you are not expected to know every fact you will need in trial preparation work, but you should have some idea of where to look up various types of information. A trial paralegal often functions as a kind of librarian, that is, a collector and user of (sometimes obscure) reference information. No single reference book has all the answers to the endless variety of questions you will encounter in trial work, but an assortment of reference books, manuals, handbooks, directories, and so forth will enable you to locate information on a wide range of topics right on your office bookshelf. Use the list in § **1.64** for ideas on reference books and materials you may want to collect to help you in your trial work. (See also § **1.61** on the master reference notebook; § **1.57** on performing factual research.)

§ 1.64 —Useful Reference Works for Trial Paralegals

The following is a list of useful reference materials.

1. Dictionary

2. Law dictionary

3. Latin dictionary
4. Thesaurus
5. *Harvard Bluebook Citations* (see § **5.47**)
6. Gregg manual
7. Modern english handbook
8. Legal secretarial handbook
9. Legal secretary's encyclopedic dictionary
10. *Elements of Style,* Strunk & White
11. *Government Printing Office Style Manual*
12. Medical dictionary
13. Medical encyclopedia
14. *Physician's Desk Reference* (PDR)
15. *U.S. Pharmacopeia*
16. Products liability resource directory
17. *Federal Rules of Court* (West)
18. Rules of court (your state)
19. Court rules (local and surrounding counties)
20. Telephone directories (Local and surrounding counties and major metropolitan areas)
21. City directory
22. Criss-cross directory
23. National directory of business addresses
24. Toll-free number directory
25. Zip code reference

Legal Directories:

26. *Martindale-Hubbell* (in-house library)
27. *American Bar Reference Handbook*
28. Statewide legal directory
29. Local bar association directory

Professional Association Directories:

30. National paralegal associations (NFPA and NALA)
31. Local paralegal association directory

Maps:

32. World atlas
33. Downtown maps for major cities

34. County map atlas—local and adjacent counties
35. United States road atlas
36. World time zones
37. Folding highway maps

Other miscellaneous reference materials:

- Paralegal manuals and handbooks (many)
- Pleading form books
- Textbooks (various sources)
- Business writing manuals
- Time management books
- Law office management books
- Automated litigation support literature
- Office supply catalogs
- Office personnel manual
- Seminar materials
- Articles from legal periodicals ("How to. . ."; methods; trial practice techniques and procedures)

CHAPTER 2

ORGANIZING CASE MATERIALS

§ 2.1 The Initial Approach to Trial Organization: Considering the Variables

Preparing for trial is not an exact science because no two cases are ever exactly alike, even when they involve similar issues. There is no "perfect" way to organize a case, and no specific trial technique works equally well in all cases. But regardless of the nature of the case, one thing is always true: Preparation appropriate to the unique features of the case is critical to a successful trial. Even the simplest case requires organization, thorough planning, and meticulous preparation to ensure that the trial presentation flows smoothly. As a trial paralegal, a large part of your work will involve analyzing the case and determining the best way to organize it for trial. You will also be responsible for coordinating and marshaling the efforts and energies of the attorneys, support staff members, and others involved in the trial to achieve the best results in the courtroom. This chapter will focus on ideas and methods to help you in communicating with the trial team and organizing the case files and materials.

§ 2.2 —Factors Affecting Trial Organization

A number of related variables can increase the complexity of the case and affect the way you organize the case for trial. The following list outlines some of these factors and how they will influence your approach to trial preparation.

Type of Action. The first consideration is the type of case, that is, the cause of action which resulted in the lawsuit. Different procedural and evidentiary rules apply in various types of cases. The type of action will, to some extent, determine which court has jurisdiction over the case and the techniques required to develop the case and present it at trial.

Court Level. The trial court in most federal cases is the United Stages District Court. The federal system divides the 50 states into 94 districts, each of which has its own federal district court. Federal courts are courts of limited jurisdiction. They hear only actions involving (1) questions of federal law, (2) the United States as a party, and (3) diversity of citizenship cases where the amount in controversy is over $50,000. The federal courts operate according to relatively uniform procedures across the country. In addition to the federal court system, each of the 50 states has a separate trial court system, resulting in a variety of court structures and procedures from state to state. In the state court systems, there is usually one trial court for each county within the state. In different states the trial courts are variously called "county," "common pleas," "circuit," "superior," "district," and "supreme" court. These courts handle both civil and criminal matters, and often have separate subdivisions that handle criminal, juvenile, domestic relations, and probate matters. State courts hear many more types of cases than federal courts, and for this reason you are likely to work on more trials in your state court system than in federal court. The stringent requirements many federal court judges impose (see § **2.16**) may make federal court trial preparation somewhat more complicated than on the state court level. Learn as much as you can about the rules and regulations that control trial practice in both your federal district court and your local state courts.

Scope and Complexity of the Issues. The trial preparation in a case with multiple issues or counts (for example, a RICO action) or one with a combination of issues (products liability and personal injury) will be more complicated than a case with narrower issues. Also, a case that deals with volatile issues, rapidly emerging technology, or controversial legislation (for example, environmental violations, computer-related fraud, intellectual property disputes) is likely to result in a complex trial presentation.

Persons and Entities Involved. Trial preparation becomes more complicated whenever a large number of parties, attorneys, or witnesses are involved in the case. A related factor is the type of parties, for example, when the litigants are public figures or celebrities, complex corporate/commercial entities, or government agencies, as opposed to private individuals.

Time Factors. The span of time covered by the events at issue in the case affects the level of complexity. For example, a case involving an automobile accident usually has only one major, significant event, the date of the accident. By contrast, a case involving a series of fraudulent sales transactions occurring over a period of several years will be more complicated. There will be multiple significant dates, numerous material witnesses (employees, managers, sales representatives, accountants), and many more exhibits (several years worth of sales documentation, receipts, ledgers, computer printouts, banking records, and so forth). These factors will influence the way you prepare the exhibits and courtroom files (see § **6.66**).

In addition, the length of time the case has been pending and the time available before trial can significantly affect the trial preparation. A case that has been in existence for several years will have accumulated massive amounts of papers, documents, and other materials, many of which may be duplicative and redundant. Trial preparation in such a case will be complicated even if the case materials *have* been kept organized, but if the case materials are in chaos, the trial preparation will be a real challenge for the trial team.

Value of Case and Resources Available. The approach to trial preparation will be controlled in part by considerations of the amount of money at stake. Obviously, a case worth millions of dollars will require more sophisticated techniques than one worth only a few hundred dollars. The client's budget must always be a consideration when deciding on visual aids, expert witnesses, and so forth. The approach to trial preparation will also be influenced by the resources available to the lawfirm or through the client, for example, support personnel, outside vendors, and computer equipment and support.

Logistical Factors. Other practical and logistical considerations that will affect the trial preparation include the following:

- Jury trial vs. bench trial
- Distance from courthouse
- Physical courtroom layout and storage space available (see §§ **6.12, 6.68** *et seq.*)
- Amount of technical information involved
- Client needs and special problems (see §§ **3.17, 6.12**)
- Number of documents or other exhibits (see § **5.65**).

§ 2.3 Considering the Defense Perspective

Most of the advice and information in this handbook on paring and organizing for trial is equally applicable to both plaintiffs and defendants. However, some aspects of trial preparation unique to the defendant's perspective of a case should be emphasized.

One advantage of representing the defendant in a trial is that you get the chance to hear the plaintiff's case in its entirety before you present your case. To some degree, this allows you to refine and tailor your case to refute, deflect, and dilute points made by the plaintiff and focus on points most favorable to your client's position in the case. The plaintiff who made the allegations has the burden of proving the truth of those allegations to the judge or jury. The parameters of your case are basically set by the plaintiff's case. If you can determine where the plaintiff makes mistakes or fails to prove his or her case, then your plan of defense becomes clearer. In civil cases, the defendant has only to show the plaintiff failed to prove by a preponderance of the evidence the elements he or she set out to prove.

This is not to suggest, however, that defendants should simply react to the claims and strategies of the plaintiff. It is important to develop an "offensive" strategy for the defense as well, much the same way you would develop a theme or strategy for a plaintiff's case. You need to formulate a cohesive theme for your case and try to figure out how to put the plaintiffs on the "defensive." Defending cases successfully means taking an active role, not a passive one.

From a practical standpoint in the courtroom, the defendants get a chance to observe the judge's habits and preferences, the courtroom layout, and the typical daily routine before presenting their case. Getting to go second with the trial presentation buys you a little additional preparation time. For example, you probably will not have to have your witnesses ready on the first day of trial. However, you still have to be prepared for voir dire, opening statements, and cross-examination of the plaintiff's witnesses. In some trials, the defendant's attorney is allowed to postpone the opening statement until the conclusion of the plaintiff's case. If a defendant's motion for dismissal or for a directed verdict at the close of plaintiff's case is successful, the defense may not even present its case.

In some instances, the defendant may get a certain amount of sympathy from the jury as the "victim" of the lawsuit. During voir dire, the trial team should attempt to eliminate any prospective jurors who believe there is automatically a valid cause of action simply because someone filed a lawsuit.

With respect to trial exhibits, the fact that the plaintiff goes first in introducing exhibits may effectively reduce the actual number of exhibits you have to deal with. There is usually no point in duplicating the documents plaintiff has already introduced, so the defense will generally add only what is needed to support their portion of the case. The defense also gets to see what the plaintiff has prepared for demonstrative evidence and, if necessary, can prepare the appropriate counterevidence in response.

When you represent the defendant, it may be more difficult to schedule trial witnesses, because you cannot calculate exactly when the plaintiff's case will conclude. If there is a scheduling conflict (for example, if your expert is going to be out of the country and unavailable during the second week of trial) you may have to put a witness on the stand out of order, during the plaintiff's case. This can be done only with the court's permission and for good cause. This can be turned into an advantage, however, as long as it is made clear to the jury that the expert is a defense witness. See § **6.64** on scheduling trial witnesses.

§ 2.4 Beginning Trial Preparation at the Start of the Case

Successful presentation of any case depends on two key factors: (1) You must be prepared; and (2) You must be organized. While it is possible to organize a case for trial when it has been in existence for several months or years, it is much easier and more desirable to begin organizing for trial at the very beginning of a case. As the case progresses through its various stages, your role as a trial paralegal is to assist the attorney in building the case that you will present in the courtroom. Treat each case as if it were going to be tried before a jury, even when you believe a case will be resolved or settled before trial. Prepare the case information just as if you were actually getting ready for trial. Experienced trial attorneys and paralegals will tell you that many cases have settled because they were fully organized and prepared to proceed to trial, and the opposition knew it.

§ 2.5 Approaching Every Case with Trial in Mind

As soon as you are assigned to a case, set up a notebook or folder of trial-related forms on which to collect case information. Include the checklists and forms that you find useful in helping you to record and organize information about your cases. You may want to include many of the forms and checklists in this book, as well as others you have created or adapted for your specific purposes. No two trials are ever exactly the same, but a standard set of forms will guide you in any case as you begin to compile the core information needed for trial. Enter the trial date on your calendar and begin developing a work plan for the actions that must completed before the trial (see **§ 1.40**).

The trial attorney may not switch into "trial mode" until very near the trial date (see **§ 1.11** on procrastination), but it's a sure bet that he or she will be delighted that you have most of the important details of the file information under control. Preparing the other trial-related materials (see **Chapter 5**) will be much easier if you have a solid, organized fact base to work from.

If you have access to a computer, look for ways throughout the trial preparation that you can apply the computer's power to help you organize information. See **Chapter 8** for more on applying automation technology to your work. Most offices use a combination of manual and automated methods to record and store information. Use the mix of techniques that works the best for your situation.

Whether you are organizing a new case or one that has been around for awhile, you will find it helpful to record the pertinent case information on a master form such as the Litigation Case Log (see **Form 2–1**). Place this form in the front of your case notebook or inside the cover of your working file. Use it to track the progress of the case as you receive assignments. If you work on several different cases, consider keeping a log for each case arranged in alphabetical order in a looseleaf notebook as a master reference. This will help you track and manage the many tasks and priorities involved in preparing multiple cases for trial.

If the case involves numerous parties, create a Party & Counsel Log (see **Form 2–2**) to record and update the names and addresses of the parties and their attorneys. This is a good quick reference to telephone numbers and addresses for those occasions when you have to arrange a meeting of all the counsel involved in the case. The information on this form can also serve as a basis for your pleadings service list.

Use the forms that work best for the kind of trials you handle, and use them consistently to record pertinent information during the development of the case. A basic address and telephone list form appears in **Form 2–3.** Update the forms and refer to them often as the trial date approaches. Try to capture and record details on the case when you first encounter the information so you won't have to spend time later searching the file for information.

FORM 2–1
LITIGATION CASE LOG

LITIGATION CASE LOG

CLIENT:	FILE No.:
ATTORNEYS:	DATE LOG OPENED:
CASE TYPE:	STATUTE OF LIMITATIONS DATE:
COURT: JUDGE:	DATE COMPLAINT FILED:
CASE No.:	TRIAL DATE:

ADVERSE PARTY INFORMATION

PARTY	SERVICE	ANSWER	ATTORNEY

ORIGINAL ASSIGNMENT:

DATE RECEIVED:

NOTES ON WORK DONE

DATE	STATUS

LITIGATION CASE LOG (continued)

CLIENT: Page ___

DATE	STATUS

FORM 2–2
PARTY & COUNSEL LOG

PARTY & COUNSEL LOG	
CASE NAME:	
COURT:	CASE NO.:
JUDGE:	FILE NO.:

PARTY	COUNSEL

FORM 2–3
ADDRESS AND TELEPHONE LIST

ADDRESS AND TELEPHONE

CASE: ______________________________

NAME & COMPANY	ADDRESS	PHONE/FAX
		HOME:
		WORK:
		FAX:
		HOME:
		WORK:
		FAX:
		HOME:
		WORK:
		FAX:
		HOME:
		WORK:
		FAX:
		HOME:
		WORK:
		FAX:
		HOME:
		WORK:
		FAX:
		HOME:
		WORK:
		FAX:
		HOME:
		WORK:
		FAX:
		HOME:
		WORK:
		FAX:

These forms will then become the core of your master trial notebook (see **Chapter 5**). You will come to recognize which forms are the most useful to you after you have done this on a few trials. Then, in preparation for future trials, you can make up a "kit" of your most-used forms as soon as you begin working on a trial preparation.

The forms technique works equally well whether you record the information manually or convert it to an automated system. If you use a computer, keep a list of your computer storage file names containing case information and a description of their contents (see **Chapter 8**). If you have case management software, use it consistently to update information and ensure complete data. See **Chapter 8** on using computers in trial preparation work. Even if the attorney settles the case, the pertinent information you compile will be handy for settlement negotiations. You will get experience in organizing information for trial, and, if settlement negotiations fall through, you will be ready to try the case.

In order for everything to come together for a cohesive trial presentation, you will have to complete many individual preparatory tasks (see **§ 2.6,** Comprehensive Trial Preparation Timeline/Checklist). Complete the tasks you *know* will have to be done and get them out of the way as early as possible. This will leave you more time during the busy days just before trial to concentrate on the final trial preparations.

The following checklist gives some suggestions for useful forms you may want to include in your trial preparation kit, along with references to the sections where these forms are discussed.

Checklist: Useful Forms for Collecting Trial Information

____ 1. General information—Litigation Case Log (§ **2.5**)
____ 2. File "Diagram" Index (§ **2.43**)
____ 3. "To Do" List (§ **5.83**)
____ 4. Trial Preparation Agenda (§ **2.14**)
____ 5. Calendar Blanks (§ **1.40**)
____ 6. Trial Scheduling and Planning Form (§ **6.64**)
____ 7. Name/Address/Telephone/Fax List (see **Forms 2–2** and **2–3**)
  ____ Attorneys
  ____ Clients
  ____ Parties
  ____ Witnesses
  ____ Key court personnel
____ 8. Expert witness information
  ____ Records Release Log (§ **3.29**)

____ 9. Witness Examination Sheets (§ **5.83**)
  ____ Witness Index (§ **3.2**)

____ 10. Lists of Exhibits/Documents
  ____ Document Index: Witness Testimony (§ **3.7**)
  ____ Original Documents Log (§ **2.60**)
  ____ Deposition Exhibit Index (§ **5.51**)
  ____ Trial Exhibit Worksheet (§ **5.61**)

____ 11. Correspondence Index (§ **2.46**)

____ 12. Discovery Index (§ **2.49**)

____ 13. Deposition Master Index (§ **5.49**)

____ 14. Pleadings Index (§ **2.47**)

____ 15. Research Index (§ **2.48**)

____ 16. Summary Records Index (§ **2.61**)

____ 17. Juror Profile Worksheet (§ **6.20**)

____ 18. Medical Expenses Worksheet (§ **2.67**)

____ 19. Expenses, Receipts, Invoices (§ **7.37**)

____ 20. Trial Witness Subpoena Index (§ **5.32**)

§ 2.6 Comprehensive Trial Preparation Timeline/Checklist

The comprehensive timeline/checklist gives an overview of the multitude of tasks involved in trial preparation, along with references to other sections of this book where you will find more detailed information about specific topics. This checklist outlines a preparation time frame from approximately three months before the trial date to a week before the trial. These time frames are only approximate guidelines as to when the various tasks should be completed. You will need to expand or compress the schedule if you have a longer or shorter time to prepare for the trial in your case. See § **6.1** and the checklists in §§ **6.2–6.4** for details on final trial preparation matters. Of course, all of the items listed will not apply in every case. Each trial will have individual priorities and a unique sequence of tasks to be completed. If your trial is in federal court, refer to the court's scheduling order or case management order for the exact filing requirements and deadlines for your case (see § **2.16**). In addition, always check your local court rules and consult your supervising attorney about any special filing requirements or deadlines that apply in your jurisdiction.

The following checklist includes some tasks the supervising attorney will probably do in most cases, although an advanced trial paralegal can complete many of them. Some items will require cooperative efforts from the trial team members, and you may be responsible for coordinating these. See § **2.9** on conducting trial preparation agenda meetings to coordinate teamwork and update team members on the status of the case.

Use this checklist as a starting point and adapt it to add specific assignments and tasks required for your case. As the case gets closer to trial, shift uncompleted tasks from the earlier time frame to the next list. This helps to ensure that you do not inadvertently overlook any details. For example, anything that was not accomplished in the "Three Months Before" time period should be added to the "Two Months Before" list, and so on. Notice that the tasks on the checklist get more specific as the trial preparation progresses. If you have managed the case from the beginning, you may have already completed many of the items that appear in the first section of the list. The more items you can complete early in the process, the better you will be able to handle those pesky last-minute items that always crop up when you are crunched for time during the last few days before trial.

Comprehensive Trial Preparation Timeline/Checklist
Case ID: ______________________________
Trial Date: ____________________ **Judge:** ____________________

3 Months Before (or as soon as trial date notice is received)

____ 1. Plan "cushion" time for trial preparation and clear your calendar (see § **1.40**)

- ____ Remove nonessential activities
- ____ Reschedule dates
- ____ Delegate tasks where possible
- ____ Work ahead

____ 2. Schedule initial trial preparation agenda meeting for trial team (see § **2.9**)

____ 3. Docket all applicable discovery and motion cutoff dates, filing deadlines, pretrial hearings, and so forth

Note: For federal court cases, consult the court's scheduling order or case management order for trial preparation requirements and deadlines (see § **2.16**)

____ 4. Assemble trial "Forms Kit" (see § **2.5**)

____ 5. Determine value of the case and available budget for trial preparation expenses (see §§ **1.26, 2.1, 4.4**)

____ 6. For cases in a foreign jurisdiction, obtain the applicable local court rules and judge's rules (see § **6.8**)

____ 7. Review and organize the file materials, as needed (see §§ **2.33–2.61**)

____ Prepare "Diagram" Index of the file contents or update index (see §§ **2.34, 2.43**)

____ Prepare or update indexes of various subfile materials (see §§ **2.45, 2.75, 2.76**)

____ Index, tab, and bind medical records, if applicable (see § **2.62**)

____ Prepare translations of medical records, if applicable (see § **2.70**)

____ 8. Update pleadings indexes (see § **2.47**)

____ Locate latest amendments of complaint, answers, cross-claims and counterclaims (see § **5.80**)

____ Review substantive pleadings to outline trial issues (see §§ **2.16, 5.46, 5.91**)

____ 9. Begin compiling materials for the attorney's trial notebook (see § **5.77**)

____ 10. Determine what case information is on computer, if any, and consider what could feasibly be put on computer for use at trial (see **Chapter 8**)

____ 11. Review all discovery in the case to date (see §§ **2.49, 5.5, 5.42**)

____ Prepare discovery index (see § **2.49**)

____ Determine if there are any discovery responses outstanding from opposing party; include documents promised in depositions (see § **5.5**)

____ Prepare "cleanup" interrogatories and discovery requests, as needed (see § **5.5**)

____ Determine whether you need to supplement any discovery responses; prepare responses, as needed (see § **5.5**)

____ 12. Draft Requests for Admissions, if applicable (see § **5.7**)

____ 13. Prepare Deposition Master Index (see § **2.50**)

____ Review depositions for any promised documents or materials outstanding (see §§ **5.5, 5.42**)

____ Index deposition exhibits (see § **5.51**)

____ Summarize depositions, if needed (see § **5.42** *et seq.*)

____ Prepare transcript objection indexes (see § **6.11**)

____ Notify court reporter or video service if videotaped depositions are to be played at trial (see § **5.56**)

____ Request transcripts of any videotape depositions (see §§ **3.40, 5.56**)

____ 14. Notify expert witnesses of trial date (see § **3.35**)

____ Forward materials to expert for review (see §§ **3.29, 3.35**)

____ Obtain any additional materials needed from expert (see § **3.35**)

____ Arrange depositions of opposing party's experts, if not already completed

____ Review and organize individual expert files (see §§ **2.57, 3.27**)

____ 15. Collect preliminary set of trial exhibits (see §§ **5.58–5.61**)

____ Prepare trial exhibit worksheet (see § **5.67**)

____ Check on physical evidence (see §§ **5.64, 6.81**)

____ 16. Begin considering demonstrative evidence to determine what visual aids, illustrations, and so forth would be useful at trial (see **Chapter 4**)

____ Retain photographer, if necessary (see §§ **4.29, 4.35**)

____ Retain graphic artist or illustrator, if necessary (see § **4.57**)

____ Plan summary or work product exhibits (see § **5.58**)

____ 17. Prepare preliminary witness index (see § **3.2**)

____ Assemble statements or conduct interviews with all lay witnesses, as needed (see §§ **3.2, 3.3**)

____ Contact clients and key witnesses to confirm their availability for trial (see §§ **3.1–3.5**)

____ List witnesses for which subpoenas will be needed (see § **5.30**)

____ List documents for which subpoenas duces tecum must be issued (see § **5.10** *et seq.*)

____ 18. Perform factual research or investigation as needed (see § **1.57**)

____ 19. Plan for trial files or binders (see §§ **5.8, 5.42, 5.58**)

____ 20. Incorporate discovery materials received from opposing parties into files, as needed

2 Months Before

____ 1. Hold trial preparation agenda meeting with trial team members (see § **2.9**)

____ Assign preparation tasks (see § **2.9**)

____ Prepare master trial preparation agenda (see § **2.12**)

____ Schedule follow-up preparation meetings (see § **2.15**)

____ Review status of potential settlement negotiations

____ 2. Update witness list to include any additional witnesses; notify opposing counsel

____ 3. Schedule and conduct remaining discovery depositions, if any, of opponent's experts or lay witnesses

____ 4. Confirm availability of expert witnesses for trial date (see § **3.35**)

____ 5. If expert witness is located out of town, have secretary check on flights, hotel accommodations, and so forth; see if discounts can be arranged for early booking; check on penalties for cancellation (see §§ **2.57, 3.35**)

____ 6. Serve Requests for Admission on opposing parties (see § **5.7**)

____ 7. Update preliminary worksheet list of trial exhibits (see § **5.58** *et seq.*)

  ____ Begin assembling exhibit files (see §§ **5.42, 6.65**)

  ____ Consider possible solutions to unusual exhibit storage or transportation problems (see §§ **6.66, 6.78**)

____ 8. Order supplies (for example, looseleaf binders, dividers, tabs, and so forth) for exhibit notebooks (see § **5.74**) and trial notebooks (see §§ **5.77, 5.88**)

____ 9. Continue work on visual aids and demonstrative evidence (see **Chapter 4**)

  ____ Consult with illustrator or graphic artist and expert witness as needed on development of special exhibits (see § **4.57**)

____ 10. Update discovery files to incorporate supplemental discovery responses given and received (see § **5.5**)

____ 11. Continue to summarize depositions, if not already done (see § **5.42** *et seq.*)

  ____ Determine which depositions need to be filed with the court

  ____ Prepare Notice of Filing for deposition transcripts (see § **5.52**)

  ____ Confirm dates with video service for videotape playback at trial (see § **5.56**)

____ 12. Prepare glossary of terminology, if applicable (see §§ **1.40, 2.71, 3.30, 3.44**)

____ 13. Prepare updated summary of medical expenses and booklet of medical expenses documentation, if applicable (see § **2.67**)

____ 14. Prepare outline of issues and elements of proof (see §§ **2.16, 5.34, 5.40, 5.85**)

____ 15. Supervise or conduct necessary research

____ 16. Begin drafting motions in limine to limit issues at trial, obtain preliminary rulings on evidence, and so forth (see § **5.9**)

____ 17. Check requirements for admission pro hac vice; prepare and file motion and order, if necessary (see § **1.17**)

____ 18. Plan mock trial or focus group proceedings (see § **5.2**)

1 Month Before

____ 1. Book conference room or "war room" (see § **5.3**)

____ 2. Hold follow-up preparation agenda meeting(s) with trial team (see §§ **2.9, 2.15**)

  ____ Confirm trial materials needed (see §§ **5.1–5.2**)

  ____ Prepare and distribute updated trial preparation agenda (see § **2.14**)

____ 3. File deposition transcripts with court (see § **5.52**)

  ____ Prepare and serve notice on opposing counsel (see § **5.55**)

____ 4. Determine portions of depositions to be offered into evidence and prepare accordingly (see §§ **2.16, 5.51**)

____ 5. Submit transcripts of video depositions to court with motion for ruling on objections, if necessary (see § **5.56**)

____ 6. Prepare and file motion to compel if opponent has not answered all discovery requests

____ 7. Prepare blank trial notebook for attorney's use (see § **5.34**)

____ 8. Obtain certifications of records or government documents and hospital records, as needed (see § **2.74**)

____ 9. Refine and update witness list (see §§ **3.2, 5.8, 5.31, 5.38, 5.83**)

____ 10. Update witnesses on status of trial date (see §§ **3.7, 5.33**)

____ 11. File Motion and Order Designating Persons to Serve Subpoenas, if needed (see §§ **5.10, 5.26**)

____ 12. Obtain supply of subpoena forms from court clerk (see § **5.13**)

____ 13. Analyze case for voir dire questions (see § **6.16** *et seq.*)

  ____ Formulate juror profile characteristics (see § **6.18**)

  ____ Begin drafting voir dire questions (see § **6.26**)

____ 14. Discuss client and witness preparation with attorney (see §§ **3.8–3.10**)

  ____ Forward previous discovery materials to client for review (see § **3.10**)

  ____ Plan and schedule preparation conferences for clients and witnesses (see § **3.11**)

  ____ Arrange current medical examination by treating physician for client/plaintiff in a personal injury case (see § **3.44**)

____ 15. Further consider visual aids and demonstrative evidence needed; consult with artist or expert as necessary (see **Chapter 4**)

____ 16. Continue to compile and organize trial exhibits (see §§ **5.58** *et seq.*, **6.65** *et seq.*)

____ 17. Finalize mock trial or focus group arrangements (see § **5.2**)

____ 18. Draft motions in limine (see § **5.9**)

____ 19. Prepare materials as needed for final pretrial (see § **2.16**)

3 Weeks Before

____ 1. Hold preparation agenda meeting with trial team members (see § **2.9**)

____ 2. Schedule client and witness preparation conferences (see § **3.10**)

____ 3. Assemble witness preparation files (see § **3.7**)

    ____ Prepare marked copies of exhibits for trial witness (see § **3.15**)

    ____ Prepare courthouse diagram and witness reminders, if necessary (see § **3.14**)

____ 4. Investigate credentials of opponent's expert (see § **3.24**)

____ 5. Confirm trial date with video service for playback of videotape depositions at trial (see § **5.56**)

____ 6. Forward court's rulings on objections to video service for editing tape (see § **5.56**)

____ 7. Continue developing voir dire questions (see § **6.26**)

____ 8. Draft motions in limine (see § **5.9**)

____ 9. Begin drafting trial brief (see § **5.34** *et seq.*)

____ 10. Continue compiling trial exhibits; update exhibit worksheet (see § **5.58** *et seq.*)

____ 11. Visit courtroom and plan organization of exhibits (see §§ **6.12, 6.66–6.74**)

____ 12. Contact judge's bailiff or court administrator about special arrangements for exhibit storage, if needed (see §§ **6.12, 6.66–6.74**)

____ 13. Prepare stipulations with opposing counsel on exhibits and other trial issues

____ 14. Arrange copying of exhibit documents for binders (see § **5.64**)

____ 15. Review demonstrative evidence for foundation requirements (see §§ **4.30, 4.46, 4.54**)

____ 16. Confirm travel and lodging arrangements

____ 17. Research particulars about judge, if necessary (see § **6.9**)

2 Weeks Before

____ 1. Hold trial preparation agenda meeting with trial team (see § **2.9**)

____ 2. Confirm schedule for witness and client preparation conferences (see § **3.10**)

____ 3. Prepare trial witness subpoenas; have issued by court clerk, if required (see §§ **5.13, 5.19**)

  ____ Calculate witness fees (see § **5.28**)

  ____ Order checks for witness fees

____ 4. Confirm preparation conference arrangements with expert witnesses (see § **3.35**)

____ 5. Begin assembling trial notebook (see § **5.77** *et seq.*)

____ 6. Work on draft of trial brief (see § **5.34** *et seq.*)

____ 7. Prepare and file motions in limine (see § **5.9**)

____ 8. Determine voir dire procedure to be used (see § **6.16**)

  ____ Obtain jury pool list, if possible (see § **6.20**)

  ____ Conduct juror investigation (see § **6.19**)

  ____ Revise juror profile sheet (see § **6.18**)

  ____ Draft voir dire questions (see § **6.26**)

____ 9. Assemble equipment (easels, and so forth) in the war room (see § **4.63, 4.65, 5.3**)

____ 10. Plan courtroom logistics for equipment and materials (see § **6.12**)

____ 11. Confer with artist or illustrator on status of demonstrative evidence (see § **4.57**)

____ 12. Order document enlargements, if applicable (see § **4.6** *et seq.*)

____ 13. Hold mock trial or focus group proceedings (see § **5.2**)

____ 14. Have hair cut and styled (see § **6.5**)

1 Week Before

____ 1. Conduct trial preparation agenda meeting (see § **2.9**)

  ____ Schedule daily meetings for last week before trial (see § **2.15**)

____ 2. Analyze results of mock trial or focus group (see § **5.2**)

____ 3. Double-check on calendar obligations that have been delegated or rescheduled (see § **1.40**)

____ 4. Review everything in the file

____ 5. Update pleadings file and index (see § **2.47**)

____ 6. Obtain jury pool list, if not done (see § **6.19**)

  ____ Conduct juror investigation (see § **6.19**)

  ____ Prepare juror information grid (see § **6.25**)

- ____ Finalize draft voir dire questions (see § **6.26**)

____ 7. Serve subpoenas on trial witnesses (see § **5.10** *et seq.*)

____ 8. Decide tentative order for witnesses (see § **6.61**)

- ____ Prepare scheduling sheet diagram (see § **6.61**)

____ 9. Hold witness trial preparation conferences (see § **3.8** *et seq.*)

____ 10. Prepare witness sheets (see § **5.83**)

____ 11. Prepare attorney's trial notebook (see § **5.77** *et seq.*)

____ 12. Mount document enlargements, if needed (see § **4.12**)

____ 13. Assemble all trial materials in the war room (see § **5.3**)

____ 14. Prepare trial exhibit indexes (see § **5.71**)

____ 15. Prepare trial exhibit notebooks to exchange (see § **5.74**)

____ 16. Confirm arrangements for office contact to take phone messages, coordinate deliveries, and so forth during trial (see § **1.24**)

- ____ Notify key persons (at home and at the office) about hours you will be in trial (see §§ **1.24, 1.25**)

____ 17. Hold expert witness preparation conference (see §§ **3.37, 3.44**)

____ 18. Arrange help to transport equipment and materials to the courtroom (see § **6.2**)

____ 19. Polish the trial brief (see § **5.34**)

____ 20. Plan your clothes for at least the first week of trial (see § **6.5**)

See §§ **6.2–6.4** for Final Countdown Checklists.

§ 2.7 Establishing a Teamwork Approach to Trial Preparation

The most successful trial preparation results from the combined efforts of the attorney or attorneys, the paralegal, and various key support staff personnel. These persons make up what I refer to as the "trial team." When you are preparing a case for presentation at trial, it is important for each trial team member to understand the trial preparation goals and what tasks he or she is responsible for completing. It is imperative that the trial team members communicate and keep one another informed about the progress of the trial preparations.

§ 2.8 —Defining the "Trial Team"

The "trial team" in a small case may consist of just one attorney and one paralegal (you), making communication relatively simple. Naturally, the difficulty in sustaining communication increases when more members are added to the team. In cases in which more than one attorney is on the trial team, one attorney (often the a partner or senior trial attorney) is designated as the "lead" attorney or the one in charge of overseeing the case and directing the other team members in the trial preparation. Each team member must keep the rest of the team informed of developments, and therefore frequent, meaningful communication among trial team members throughout the preparation phase is crucial to the success of any trial presentation.

The likelihood of continued productive communication is greatly enhanced when the trial team members attend a series of organized meetings where they can discuss ideas and coordinate plans for completing trial preparation tasks. Ideally, you should schedule an initial planning meeting several weeks before the trial date, followed by a series of update or "status check" meetings at regular intervals as you get closer to the trial date. It may be necessary to have daily meetings during the week before the trial. The timing and frequency of the trial team meetings will depend on several variable factors:

- The size of the case
- The length of time the case has been pending
- The number of persons on the trial team
- The amount of time available until the trial date
- Scheduling conflicts due to other trials or commitments
- How much the attorney procrastinates.

§ 2.9 Scheduling the Initial Trial Preparation Meeting

The initial trial preparation meeting signals the "gearing up" from the discovery phase into "trial mode" thinking. The purpose of the initial meeting is to assess, define, and assign the remaining trial preparation tasks that must be done. It also provides a forum for clarifying questions and identifying problems pertinent to the particular case. The initial meeting will be a planning, strategy, and brainstorming session, so it is important for the entire trial team to be present. By discussing ideas for the best strategic approach to various issues and problems in the case, the trial team can begin to formulate a "game plan" for the trial presentation.

Ideally, the initial meeting should occur approximately three months (90 days) before the trial date to allow adequate time for thorough trial preparation. Realistically, however, you may not be able to schedule this meeting until four to six weeks (or even less) before the trial date. Of course, if the attorney in charge of the case procrastinates until just two or three weeks before the trial, the work has to be compressed into a shorter period of time, making the job much more difficult. It is wise to allow a minimum of two hours for the initial meeting, although this will vary depending on the nature and complexity of the case.

Discuss the need for this type of initial planning meeting with the lead attorney in charge of the case. Stress the importance of the initial meeting to organization and thorough trial preparation. If multiple attorneys are involved in the case, enlist the lead attorney's support in encouraging or directing the other attorneys on the trial team to attend.

§ 2.10 —Things to Accomplish at the Initial Meeting

The following material identifies some goals of the initial trial preparation meeting.

Establish a Trial Preparation Agenda. The trial team must assess the status of the case, decide what tasks need to be done to get the case ready for trial, and assign priorities according to the importance of the individual tasks. The exact agenda will vary with each individual case, but the major categories that should be discussed in most cases are outlined on the checklist for the preliminary master trial preparation agenda (see § **2.12**).

Decide How the Work Will Be Distributed. As each item on the agenda is discussed, the task should be assigned to a specific team member. Each person on the trial team needs to know what is expected of him or her, take responsibility for completing that portion of the trial work, and communicate their progress to the other team members. This is especially true in a trial team comprised of more than one attorney. Making clear assignments of various portions of the trial preparation work helps to avoid misunderstandings and oversights and ensures that tasks are completed in an orderly fashion.

Establish a Timetable for Trial Preparation. The trial team needs to know when there are important deadlines that must be met for completion of the various trial preparation tasks. Mark important deadlines on the trial preparation calendar to emphasize to the trial team members the exact amount of time available to complete the trial preparation work. This is also the point at which you should discuss and decide upon a schedule for followup meetings as the trial preparation progresses.

§ 2.11 —Getting the Most from the Initial Meeting

You can help to keep the meeting on track and get the vital information you need by preparing a preliminary agenda of the topics to discuss. For most trials, the following checklist covers the main subject areas that the team should discuss at the initial trial preparation meeting. Use the checklist in § **2.12** as a guide, tailoring your preliminary agenda to accommodate the issues and items involved in your case. The more case-specific items you can fill in under each heading, the better organized and efficient your meeting will be. Leave room to add items under each category.

§ 2.12 —Preliminary Master Agenda

A suggested preliminary agenda is contained in the following checklist.

Initial Trial Preparation Meeting

____ 1. Outstanding motions still before the court (awaiting ruling) that would determine the approach or strategy of other trial preparations

____ 2. Decisions on legal issues: how to proceed, what position to take, issues to concede or dismiss

____ 3. Discovery still to be completed or supplemented

____ 4. Filing deadlines before trial (either those imposed by court's trial order or agreed upon with opposing counsel)

- ____ Filing of Depositions
- ____ Exchange of Witness Lists
- ____ Exchange of Exhibit Books
- ____ Filing of Motions
- ____ Filing of Jury Instructions

____ 5. Witnesses: decide who will testify; schedule preparation conferences; prepare cross-examination questions

- ____ Clients
- ____ Lay Witnesses—Friendly/Hostile
- ____ Expert Witnesses
- ____ Expected Witnesses for Opposing Parties

____ 6. Exhibits: existing documents and materials to be compiled, labeled, indexed, and copied

____ 7. Demonstrative exhibits or visual aids needed

____ 8. Additional research to be done

- ____ Legal
- ____ Factual

____ 9. Trial pleadings and motions to be prepared

Current location of all the file materials:

____ Filing Cabinets
____ Attorney office(s)
____ Paralegal's office
____ With client
____ With expert witness
____ With opposing counsel
____ With litigation support vendor
____ Other

Add other items, issues, or specific problems as required by your particular case.

§ 2.13 —Documenting the Initial Meeting

At the initial meeting, the trial team will discuss most of the major things that still need to be done before trial. It is important to take thorough notes at this meeting so that you can properly prepare the trial preparation agenda, that will outline and list the tasks to be done and the person responsible for completing each. Use a copy of your preliminary agenda as a guide and fill in or add information as various items are mentioned or discussed by the trial team members.

Even if you provide the lead attorney with a preliminary outline for the initial meeting, the discussion will naturally jump around among various subjects and types of tasks. The difficulty of capturing all the items and ideas put forth will increase in direct proportion to the number of persons on the trial team, so you may need help to document the discussion. If possible, have another person present to assist in either taking notes or outlining the items on a board as they are discussed. This person could be another paralegal; a secretary (preferably one who takes shorthand); or, if you happen to have anyone on your staff who does court stenography, see if he or she can sit in. Failing that, or even in addition to that, take a dictaphone or other small recording device as an audio backup to help you catch all the details of the discussion.

As the attorneys mention items to be done, take detailed notes, or use a dry-erase board, chalkboard, or easel pad to list the ideas, preferably in a place that won't be erased until you are ready. These ideas and items will make up the master trial preparation agenda, an outline of the work needed to prepare the case for trial. As each task is mentioned, ask and note who is to be responsible for completing it.

Educate Yourself by Listening and Asking Questions. If you have been working on the case all along, you will probably already be familiar with the main issues, problems, and types of proof required. If you have just been assigned to the case to help with the trial preparation, ask the attorneys about the witnesses and exhibits they expect to use. Listen carefully to the discussion in order to pick up on the main concepts and learn as much about the case as possible, and most importantly, to understand exactly what is expected of you as the trial paralegal.

This is your chance to ask the trial team attorneys about matters that are not clear to you. Do not hesitate to ask questions for fear of looking foolish. When it comes to trial preparation, there are no stupid questions. The attorney may assume you understand something, but if you are not sure about it, the initial meeting is the time to ask for clarification.

Contribute Your Ideas. If you have suggestions or ideas on how something can be accomplished, speak up! The purpose of the initial meeting is to generate ideas, and yours might be just the solution the team was looking for. Remember, this meeting is a chance to have the undivided attention of the trial team attorneys and you should take advantage of the opportunity to communicate and exchange ideas.

Don't Expect to Resolve Everything in One Meeting. There will be discussion of items that must be put on hold pending receipt of additional information or completion of some other sequence of tasks. You will not be able to resolve all the questions and issues in the initial meeting, but you should carefully note open-ended questions and include them on the agenda for further discussion at subsequent meetings.

§ 2.14 —Drafting the Trial Preparation Agenda

The following procedural steps will help you sort out your notes and organize your ideas to prepare the official Trial Preparation Agenda for the trial team.

1. Prepare the Rough Draft. Immediately after the initial trial preparation meeting, while the discussion is still fresh in your mind, go back to your office and dictate a draft memorandum from your notes, in roughly the order in which items were actually discussed at the meeting. If someone else has assisted you in taking notes, ask that person to transcribe their notes as quickly as possible. Using a computer with word processing capability would be a great help here! See **§ 8.14** on word processing applications in trial work. Type up your notes in checklist fashion, listing the initials of the person to whom the task was assigned. Print out these rough notes.

2. Categorize the Tasks. Review the draft notes and group the various tasks into the following categories:

- Things to decide
- Things to research
- Things to review
- Trial pleadings to prepare
- Additional discovery to be done
- Witnesses
- Exhibits
- Arrangements to be made
- Miscellaneous

3. Revise and Reprint the Document. After you have grouped the items according to the above categories, revise your document and put it into checklist form. At the top of the revised checklist, add the case identification, the trial date, the current date, and the initials of each trial team member. It is also a good idea to note the date of the next trial preparation meeting in a prominent place on the agenda. The resulting document should look similar to the following sample (see **Form 2–4**).

FORM 2–4
SAMPLE TRIAL PREPARATION AGENDA

Trial Preparation Agenda

Case ID: Smith v. Laboratory
Trial Date: November 23, 199__
Initial Trial Preparation Meeting 9/1/9__
Attendees: KER, FJ, BKH
Next Meeting: 9/18/9__

I. THINGS TO DECIDE

____ Decide on issue of Fraud Claim vs. Laboratory—How do we want to proceed? Do we want to bifurcate trial?

____ WITNESSES—Decide whom to call
Determine order of witnesses, scheduling
Decide who is to question each (KER/FJ)
Decide thrust of questioning for each (KER/FJ)

____ VOIR DIRE: Decide how to split between KER & FJ

____ Additional Discovery that needs to be done
? Depose Laboratory employees

II. PLEADINGS TO PREPARE

____ Review pleadings; amend or supplement if necessary (FJ)

____ Review Plaintiff's discovery responses; Supplement as necessary (KER)

____ Request Supplementation of Defts' discovery responses (BKH)

____ Prepare Witness & exhibit lists for opposing counsel (BKH)

____ Trial Brief (FJ)

____ Jury Instructions (KER)

____ Jury Interrogatories (?)

____ Motions in Limine (FJ)

III. THINGS TO RESEARCH

____ Evidentiary issues: (FJ)
—Conversations with Bill Smith (hearsay?)
—Dr. Jones—Friendly witness? Move to exclude testimony?

____ Research defendants' experts (previous trials, and so forth) (BKH)

____ Research to locate dissertations on KER's "case theme" (BKH)

____ Locate Supreme Court case re: no requirement to show HOW LONG plaintiff would have survived (FJ)

IV. THINGS TO REVIEW

____ Get transcript of Dr. Martin's deposition to the Judge for review and ruling on objections

____ Review deposition transcripts of Adams, Graber, Mueller re additional materials they promised to produce

____ Review discovery requests for any outstanding responses due

____ Review expert witness testimony to make sure all materials that formed basis for their respective opinions are in evidence

—Dr. Cook (FJ/BKH to review videotape of Cook deposition)
—Dr. Martin (fact witness) (videotape) BKH
—Dr. Bates
—Samuel Shoup

V. WITNESSES

____ Prepare witness list (BKH)

____ Prepare/issue/serve witness subpoenas (BKH)

____ Schedule witness preparation conferences (BKH)

____ File transcripts of all depositions of Defense witnesses with court (BKH)

VI. EXHIBITS

____ List Exhibits; Index for trial (BKH)

____ Talk to Karen Nishino/Dr. Bates re demonstrative charts

____ Get pathology slides back from Defendant's counsel

____ Ask client for family photographs; pictures

____ Exhibit: Chart from Dr. Cook's article

____ Prepare Jury Book of trial exhibits; ? definitions of medical terminology

VII. MISCELLANEOUS

____ Reserve conference room for trial preparation period through Nov. 23 (BKH)

____ Schedule video service to play depo. at trial (BKH)

____ Coordinate arrangements for "mock trial" on Nov. 17; use office personnel as "jury" (BKH)

4. Make Copies and Highlight Individual Tasks. Make a copy of the revised agenda for each person on the trial team, plus one for your master file or notebook. If you want the agenda to really stand out from other documents and papers, have it copied onto colored paper. On each copy, have your secretary highlight the tasks for which each person is responsible. (For example, on Keith E. Rose's copy, you would highlight all the tasks for which KER is indicated as the responsible team member.) This will help ensure that the assigned tasks for each individual stand out and that nothing is inadvertently overlooked.

5. Distribute to Team Members. Distribute the revised agenda as soon as possible after the meeting. This will reinforce the discussion in the minds of the team members and will give them a good "To Do" list of all the tasks for which they are responsible.

§ 2.15 —Subsequent Trial Preparation Meetings

The closer you get to the trial date and other crucial pretrial deadlines, the more frequently the trial team should meet. Depending upon how far in advance of trial the initial meeting was held, and upon how much work is still left to do, subsequent meetings should be held at least weekly, then every other day, then daily as the trial date approaches. At each followup meeting, follow the same procedure as you did for the initial meeting to update the agenda:

- Take notes at the meeting;
- Use the agenda formulated at the initial meeting;
- Add items, check off, delete, and so forth as required;
- Whenever there are substantial additions or deletions, revise the document, print and distribute an updated agenda to each member of the trial team.

When there are multiple attorneys on the trial team, scheduling meeting times becomes more difficult. Group meetings with the whole trial team are preferable, but this is not always possible. As an alternative, you may have to schedule individual meetings with each attorney to discuss progress on the trial preparation. You will then need to update the agenda and see that each trial team member is informed of additional tasks assigned to him or her. The following are some key points to remember in planning for the subsequent trial preparation meetings:

- If you have trouble getting in to see an attorney, and if it is an attorney whose secretary schedules appointments for him or her, go through the secretary to block out a definite time for an appointment. Treat it (and encourage the attorney to treat it) with the same respect as a client appointment.
- Bring your calendar with you to each meeting; remind the attorneys to bring theirs.

- Set a firm date and time for the next meeting at the end of each meeting. The day before the next meeting, have your secretary send a brief memo to each trial team member reminding them of the date and time for the meeting.
- Each follow-up meeting need not take long. Much can be accomplished in 15–30 minutes with a clear preparation agenda. Frequent updates are essential!
- Discuss preparing the lay witnesses for trial; decide who will contact and interview them (see § **3.5**).
- Discuss the client and witness preparation conferences to determine how the attorney wants to schedule these and what materials will be needed (see § **3.9**).
- Consider the proposed sequence in which the trial witnesses will testify; discuss the strategies and objectives in presenting the case (see §§ **5.62, 6.64**).
- Discuss the development of visual aids and demonstrative exhibits (see §§ **4.2–4.4**).
- Ask the attorney to review the preliminary exhibit worksheet to give you some direction on preparing the exhibit documents. See § **5.62** on getting the attorney's input on trial exhibits.
- Find out whether there are specific labeling and numbering requirements for the trial exhibits (see § **5.63**) and how many sets of exhibit copies you will need to prepare (see § **5.65**).

§ 2.16 Preparing for Trial in Federal Court

Federal judges are extremely busy and they work very hard to keep the cases on their dockets moving steadily toward resolution and disposition, either through settlement or trial. Federal judges hate to have their time wasted. They expect the trial attorneys to resolve most issues among themselves with a minimum of judicial intervention and to assume a high level of responsibility for the efficient management and preparation of cases for trial. Recent amendments to the Federal Rules of Civil Procedure seem to reinforce this trend of encouraging the attorneys for the parties to work out resolutions to disputed issues without intervention by the court (see § **2.23**). This section will examine many of the requirements for conducting cases in federal courts. Always check your local rules for variations in the rules and specific procedural requirements that apply to your cases.

§ 2.17 Examining the Court's Standing Trial Order

Many federal judges have developed written procedures and rules for trial preparation which they require the trial attorneys to follow. The judges have the authority to impose penalties on attorneys who fail to comply. The judge generally informs the attorneys of the specific trial preparation procedures in his or her court by issuing a document entitled "Standing Trial Order" or "Standing Order for Trial Preparation." For federal districts that have opted to follow the amended rules, the court's case management order or scheduling order will be based on the proposed discovery plan filed by the attorneys under amended Rule 26 (see **§ 2.29**). Variations in timing and other requirements according to local rules. The court's scheduling order may be quite lengthy. It sets out detailed instructions pertaining to various aspects of trial preparation, including:

- Timing for disclosures under Rule 26(a)
- Timing for supplemental disclosures and discovery responses
- Time limits, cutoff dates, and filing deadlines
- Rules on extensions and continuances
- Requirements for pretrials and attorney conferences
- Format and content of motions, stipulations, pretrial statements, trial briefs, and other required pretrial pleadings
- Proposed voir dire questions and jury instructions
- Identification of trial witnesses
- Identification of expert witnesses
- Marking, exchanging, and submitting trial exhibits
- Preparing deposition testimony to be used at trial
- Filing of discovery materials to be used at trial

Form 2–5 is a sample condensed version of a typical Standing Trial Order issued by a federal court judge. If your case is in federal court, find out whether the judge has issued a similar standing order. If so, obtain a copy from your supervising attorney or from the judge's clerk. Study the order carefully, taking particular note of the instructions regarding the preparation of witness lists, exhibit lists and notebooks, and deposition testimony for trial. The trial attorney will appreciate your help preparing these materials in compliance with the judge's instructions. Use the sample timetable planning sheet as a guide to calendaring the applicable dates and deadlines in your case.

FORM 2–5
SAMPLE FEDERAL COURT STANDING ORDER FOR TRIAL PREPARATION

UNITED STATES DISTRICT COURT
NORTHERN DISTRICT OF OHIO
EASTERN DIVISION

	)	CASE NO.
______________________	)	JUDGE
__________________________	)	STANDING ORDER FOR TRIAL PREPARATION
	)	
	)	Effective __________, 199__

This Standing Order, which shall apply to all cases assigned to this Court, sets forth procedures for the efficient management and preparation of your case for settlement or trial. Failure of counsel to comply with the provisions of this Order may result in dismissal, default judgment, or the imposition of sanctions, as may be deemed appropriate by this Court.

I. CUT-OFF DATES

Discovery

All discovery shall be completed in this case within five (5) months after the complaint is filed, unless the Court orders a shorter or longer discovery period. The filing of a motion for a protective order or a motion to compel discovery does not extend the time period for the completion of discovery on the remaining matters.

Dispositive Motions

Motions designed to dispose of the case, e.g., Motions to Dismiss or Motions for Summary Judgment, shall be filed within thirty (30) days after completion of discovery unless otherwise ordered by the Court. Every such motion shall be accompanied by a supporting brief containing the necessary factual statements and citations of legal authority, with appended copies of any unreported cases cited.

II. SCHEDULING OF TRIAL DATE

The Court will assign the trial date and notify the attorneys and parties at least sixty (60) days before trial. The trial will start on the scheduled date. Motions for continuance will be considered only upon a showing of good cause. At the time the trial date is assigned, counsel shall immediately notify the

Court of any scheduled conflicting trial dates, giving complete details on the conflict, including the court posing the conflict, the names of the parties, the number of the case, and the name of the presiding judge. Failure of counsel to comply will constitute a waiver of priority.

III. PRETRIAL CONFERENCES

There will be at least one pretrial conference after the completion of discovery and a final pretrial conference. Counsel may request the Court to set additional pretrials or the Court itself may set additional pretrials as needed to facilitate preparation of the case for trial. Notice of all pretrial conferences will be given to counsel at least ten (10) days before a pretrial conference.

A Final Pretrial attended by attorneys and their clients will be held at least five (5) days before trial. Clients must attend the Final Pretrial unless authorization in writing is given to the attorney to settle or otherwise dispose of the case.

IV. ATTORNEY CONFERENCES

To ensure that pretrials scheduled with the Court are meaningful, the attorneys shall meet and confer in person before each pretrial in order to make a good faith attempt to reach agreement on as many issues as possible. Attorneys are encouraged to have as many meetings as necessary to expedite preparation of the case for settlement or trial.

At least twenty-five (25) days before the Final Pretrial, the attorneys shall meet to discuss and concur on as many of the items to be contained in the Final Pretrial Statement as possible. Plaintiff's counsel is responsible for initiating this conference by giving the opposing counsel a minimum of twenty (20) days' notice, and it is opposing counsel's duty to respond affirmatively. Issues that cannot be resolved shall be presented by motion to the Court for resolution.

V. FINAL PRETRIAL STATEMENT

At least five (5) days before the date set for the Final Pretrial, counsel shall jointly prepare and file a Final Pretrial Statement containing all the information required by the Court in the form set forth in this Standing Order. The Final Pretrial Statement, with all required attachments, is to be filed in triplicate with the Deputy Clerk of this Court. Where there are disputed matters upon which counsel cannot agree to a joint statement, each party may submit a separate attachment setting forth the areas of disagreement and their respective positions. The Final Pretrial Statement, as approved by the Court, will be adopted as the Court's Trial Order.

VI. PREPARATION FOR TRIAL

Statement of the Case

Counsel shall meet and prepare a concise joint statement of all uncontested facts in the case for the Court to read to the jury at the beginning of voir dire. This impartial statement, which shall be organized in a logical order and use easily understandable language, shall be submitted in triplicate along with the Final Pretrial Statement. Where the parties are unable to agree on the contents of a case statement, separate statements shall be submitted in triplicate by each party along with the Final Pretrial Statement.

Voir Dire Questions and Jury Instructions

The Court will conduct the voir dire examination and will ask all questions in all cases tried to a jury. Counsel are encouraged to submit special voir dire questions. The Court will ask the jury panel all relevant questions submitted by counsel. Counsel are to submit only those proposed jury instructions relevant to the issues and law in the present case, together with the applicable citations of authority. Plaintiff's counsel shall prepare and serve a copy of its proposed voir dire questions and jury instructions on opposing counsel at least ten (10) days before the attorney conference preceding the Final Pretrial. Counsel shall then confer and attempt to agree on a complete set of voir dire questions and jury instructions which counsel shall jointly submit in triplicate with the Final Pretrial Statement. Where there are disputed voir dire questions and jury instructions, counsel shall submit separate proposed questions in triplicate with the Final Pretrial Statement.

Expert Witnesses

Counsel shall disclose to opposing counsel the names and addresses of any expert witnesses they intend to use. The time period for completing discovery of expert witnesses shall be the same as that set forth above for other discovery. Counsel shall submit, as part of the Final Pretrial Statement, a resume of the qualifications of each expert witness.

Witness List

Counsel shall exchange lists of potential witnesses on or before the date of the attorney conference which is to be at least twenty-five (25) days before the Final Pretrial. As part of the Final Pretrial Statement, counsel shall list the witness names and addresses, and brief summaries of the expected testimony. Any witness not on the list shall not be permitted to testify at trial. The order in which the witnesses are listed shall be deemed to be the order in which they will be called unless counsel submits to the Court a revised order of appearance at least twenty-four (24) hours before such appearance.

Exhibits

At the attorney conference which is to be at least twenty-five (25) days before the Final Pretrial, counsel shall examine, mark, and list all exhibits which they intend to introduce at trial. Proposed trial exhibits shall be submitted with the Final Pretrial Statement as follows:

1. Each party shall submit to the Court one (1) original set and two (2) sets of copies of all exhibits, each set bound in a notebook containing a table of contents or index. Each exhibit shall bear a numbered or lettered exhibit sticker and a corresponding tab extending beyond either the right side or the bottom of the binder.

2. Exhibits shall be marked in the following manner:
   - All exhibit stickers shall bear the assigned case number.
   - Plaintiff's exhibit stickers shall bear the prefix "P" followed by Arabic numerals (e.g., P1, P2, P3).
   - Defendant's exhibit stickers shall bear the prefix "D" followed by capital letters (e.g., DA, DB, DC). In the alternative, in any case where Defendant's exhibits number more than twenty-six (26), Defendant's exhibit stickers shall bear the prefix "D" followed by arabic numerals beginning with the number 5000 (e.g., D5000, D5001, D5002).
   - Where there are multiple Plaintiffs or Defendants, the exhibits shall be designated as described above, but with the addition of the last name of the individual Plaintiff or Defendant (e.g., P1 Smith, P2 Smith; P1 Jones, P2 Jones, P3 Jones; DA Brown, DB Brown; DA Adams, DB Adams).

Deposition Testimony

Where all or any part of deposition testimony is to be offered into evidence at trial, the party intending to use such deposition testimony shall advise opposing counsel that all or part of the deposition testimony will be read as evidence and shall submit it to opposing counsel at least ten (10) days before the attorney conference prior to the Final Pretrial. So that the Court may rule on objections in order to facilitate the use of deposition testimony at trial, counsel shall follow these procedures:

- If a party desires to use the entire deposition transcript, that party shall so advise the opposing counsel. Opposing counsel shall then underline in RED any objectionable portions.

- If a party intends to use only portions of a deposition transcript, those segments shall be indicated by underlining in BLUE. The opposing counsel will underline any objectionable portions in RED. If the opponent wishes to use any additional segments of the deposition, he or she shall so indicate by underlining the additional segments in GREEN. The original proponent shall then underline any objectionable portions in ORANGE.

A party who objects to the reading of any portion of a deposition shall prepare a memorandum referencing the page and line of the objectionable portion, giving reasons and citing legal authority for the objection. The other party may respond by memorandum. The deposition transcript, marked pursuant to the above instructions, together with any memoranda, shall be submitted with the Final Pretrial Statement and copies served on opposing counsel at least five (5) days before the Final Pretrial. The Court will notify counsel of rulings on all written objections filed before the use of the depositions at trial.

Proposed Findings of Fact and Conclusions of Law

At least ten (10) days before the attorney conference preceding the Final Pretrial, counsel shall prepare and serve upon opposing counsel Proposed Findings of Fact and Conclusions of Law, each of which shall be set out in separate consecutively numbered paragraphs. Thereafter, each party shall prepare a review and criticism of the opposing party's Findings of Fact and Conclusions of Law, setting forth the areas of disagreement. Each party shall submit their proposed Findings of Fact and Conclusions of Law, together with the opposing party's review and criticism, in triplicate, with the Final Pretrial Statement.

§ 2.18 Calendaring Federal Court Trial Requirements

Make a working copy of the court's trial preparation order. Review the document and highlight the deadlines and due dates for the various pretrial hearings and trial materials. The following chart shows a detailed overview in checklist form of federal court filing requirements based on the sample standing trial order in **§ 2.17.**

Prepare a summary timetable sheet (see **Form 2–6**) for the various due dates in your case. Work backward from the assigned trial date in your case to calculate the dates for pretrial conferences and the deadlines for preparing trial pleadings and materials in your case. Distribute copies of this summary timetable to the trial team members as a guide to setting priorities and assigning tasks in your trial preparation agenda meetings. See **§ 2.9** *et seq.* You could also use a calendar or docket management program on your personal computer to set up a summary timetable for the pretrial activities and due dates.

FORM 2–6
SAMPLE TIMETABLE PLANNING SHEET FOR TRIAL PREPARATION

	Due Date
Discovery Cutoff— 5 months after Complaint Filed	______
Dispositive Motions— 30 days after Discovery Cutoff	______

==

Trial Date—Set by Court	______
Final Pretrial— At least 5 days before Trial	______
Final Pretrial Statement— At least 5 days before Final Pretrial (10 days before Trial)	______
Final Attorney Conference— At least 25 days before Final Pretrial (30 days before Trial)	______
Trial Materials to be Exchanged— At least 35 days before Final Pretrial (10 days before Final Attorney Conference) (40 days before Trial)	______

==

Materials to be prepared:	Deadline:
• Statement of the Case • Voir Dire Questions and Jury Instructions • Hypothetical Questions for Expert Witnesses • Deposition Testimony (marked transcripts) • Proposed Findings of Fact and Conclusions of Law	35 days before Final Pretrial- at least 10 days before final attorney conference
• Witness List • Names and qualifications of Expert Witnesses • Exhibit lists and copies	Final attorney conference—at least 25 days before Final Pretrial

Final Pretrial Statement following format set by Court	At least 5 days before Final Pretrial

§ 2.19 Alternative Dispute Resolution (ADR)

Only about 5 percent of the cases filed actually go to trial. The other 95 percent are settled or dismissed. Lawyers and judges are finding that it makes sense to devote resources toward efficiently resolving the vast majority of cases that never go to trial. Clients know that trials are expensive and time-consuming. Many clients are "risk averse," that is, they really don't want to go through the emotional investment that trial requires. Clients are willing to consider alternative methods to resolve their disputes in a faster, cheaper, and less stressful manner than going through a trial.

In 1990, Congress responded to the growing concern over excessive delay and costs of civil litigation in the United States by passing the Judicial Improvements Act. Title One of that Act was the Civil Justice Reform Act (CJRA), which charged each federal district court to develop a program by December 1, 1993 for reducing cost and delay in civil litigation procedures. The changes to the Federal Rules of Civil Procedure discussed in **§ 2.23** grew out of the CJRA movement. Another result of that movement is the concept of Alternative Dispute Resolution (ADR), which encompasses several techniques to provide cost-effective and time-saving alternatives to conventional trial litigation. ADR supports and complements the cost and delay reduction programs mandated by the CJRA.

Some courts sponsor or manage programs to help counsel and their clients arrive at satisfactory resolutions of their disputes through means other than trial. These "court-annexed" ADR mechanisms include negotiation, mediation, and arbitration. These alternative procedures can be employed any time for cases that are amenable (some cases are not suitable for settlement). Judges can select cases for ADR techniques on their own initiative or in response to a motion by one of the parties, or the parties can stipulate to the use of ADR.

ADR fosters reallocation of time and efforts for more efficient, quicker, and less expensive resolutions of cases without trial. In contrast to a mock trial (see **§ 5.2**) that one side to a dispute might conduct, ADR techniques involve representatives from both sides who agree to accept help in reaching an acceptable agreement or solution. The various ADR techniques have these factors in common:

- They are less formal than traditional trials.
- They operate under relaxed rules of evidence.

- The procedures are usually voluntary and nonbinding.
- Most are court approved or sponsored.

§ 2.20 —Types of ADR Proceedings

The following is a brief description of various ADR techniques from least formal to most formal.

Negotiation is the least formal ADR process in which the parties and their respective attorneys work out a compromise on their own. Some studies indicate that attorneys spend 85 percent of their time negotiating. The negotiators, called "neutrals," receive training in negotiating skills. The goal of negotiations is partly to move the parties from "what I want" to "why I need it" for a better understanding of their respective positions. Neutrals must be sensitive to clients' emotional attachments to property or money, and be able to figure out what they really value and appreciate in order to reach a compromise.

Early Neutral Evaluation (E.N.E.) involves a neutral evaluator who meets with the parties early in the litigation to help them define the issues, plan discovery, expedite trial preparation, and if possible, settle all or part of the case. The clients have direct input into the process, making them feel more involved and responsible for reaching a compromise.

Mediation is an informal, nonbinding process in which an objective and unbiased third person, called a mediator, guides the parties through a structured discussion of the dispute. The mediator listens to all the parties and helps them evaluate their options for reaching a mutually acceptable agreement.

Arbitration is a slightly more structured procedure where a neutral panel listens to each side and then actually makes a decision about the rights and obligations of each party in the case. Arbitration is an old process that has its roots in the labor movement. Arbitration may be voluntary or mandatory, binding or nonbinding. When the arbitration is mandatory, the parties are usually entitled to an automatic trial de novo.

Summary Jury Trial can be a time-saving procedure, but it is not necessarily an inexpensive process. The concept was invented in Ohio by Judge Thomas D. Lambros in an effort to move cases toward settlement. In a summary jury trial, the parties do not actually call witnesses. Instead, the attorneys for each side present a summary of the testimony and evidence to the jury panel. The evidence may include documents, photographs, videotape, and expert reports. The parties agree on the formula for submitting their respective positions to an advisory jury. A referee or magistrate may give the advisory jury the appropriate instructions on how to evaluate elements in the case. The jurors deliberate and render an advisory verdict. Sometimes the jury is divided into two panels who deliberate separately and reach separate advisory verdicts, often with opposite results. The process is nonbinding, but by giving the parties a gauge on their cases, it encourages settlement negotiations. An advisory jury gives the parties a realistic evaluation of the likelihood of succeeding at trial.

A variation on the summary jury trial is the summary bench trial in which the attorneys make a summary presentation to a judicial officer other than the judge assigned to the case. The judicial officer renders an advisory verdict that can assist the parties in settling the dispute.

§ 2.21 —Court Settlement Weeks

In addition to supporting ADR proceedings, many courts are now scheduling special settlement weeks once or twice a year in an effort to channel resources toward more efficient, quicker, and less expensive dispute resolutions. During settlement weeks, the courts cut back their civil dockets as much as possible, virtually shutting down their regular activities, in effect declaring a litigation truce. Some courts schedule their settlement week during judicial conferences when the judges are absent, in order to take advantage of what would otherwise be downtime for the courts. The courtrooms are used for settlement week conferences conducive to resolving disputes.

Attorneys who practice in the court's jurisdiction can nominate cases for settlement week by submitting a form to the settlement week coordinator. The intake form briefly describes the nature of the case, the parties involved, and the disputes at issue. The settlement week coordinators and/or the judges screen the nominated cases and classify them according to the age of the case, the type of dispute, and other factors. The cases accepted for settlement week must fit certain criteria:

- All or most of the discovery is completed;
- The liability factor is pretty well determined; and
- The parties are in the right frame of mind—amenable to compromise and potential settlement. Of course, this process doesn't work for every case.

The settlement week coordinator's staff schedules the cases into time slots during settlement week and then sends notices to the attorneys involved. As in any ADR technique, the client's voluntary participation in the settlement week process is an important factor in its success. It is important for the attorneys to properly prepare their clients for the settlement week conference. Some courts provide flyers or brochures that attorneys can give to clients to help them understand the settlement week purpose and procedures.

The court generally issues a standing order that applies to all settlement week conferences, covering the rules for preparation and conduct of the settlement week discussions. The discovery should be complete enough to allow the attorneys and mediator to "professionally evaluate the liability, causation, and damages aspects of the case, and make good faith demands and offers of settlement" (from a Southern District of Ohio Settlement Week Standing Order). This does not mean that the attorneys have to do full-scale trial preparation, but they do have to decide how to present the main facts and issues in the case succinctly to the mediator during the short time period scheduled for the conference.

Settlement week mediators are usually local volunteer attorneys who have taken required training in basic mediation techniques. The training is in diplomacy, tact, negotiation, and listening skills. Courts generally hold training seminars to teach the basics of mediation techniques.

The clients must appear at the settlement week session with their attorneys, except in specific limited circumstances, such as medical incapacity or out-of-state residence. The goal is to have persons with decision-making authority about offering or accepting settlement present at the settlement week conference. In some cases, this would include an insurance company representative. All of the parties sit around a conference table. The mediator leads them through a discussion about the facts of the dispute and listens to what each party wants. The mediator controls the process of reaching a settlement agreement, but does not determine the outcome.

If appropriate to the case, mediators can also hold a caucus session with one side only to discuss the strengths and weaknesses of that party's position. The mediator explores the interests and goals of the party. These discussions are confidential and the information revealed is inadmissible in court if the case later goes to trial. As a neutral listener, the mediator can sometimes persuade stubborn or uncooperative clients to view their positions more realistically, thus putting a "reality check" on the client's expectations.

Of course, not all cases can be settled. Several things may happen to the cases that do not settle during settlement week or under other ADR procedures. They may be referred to later follow-up mediation after the parties complete additional discovery. At the very least, the case can be set for trial sooner and the parties will be more prepared.

§ 2.22 Learning from ADR

Although the rules are more relaxed than at a formal trial, the attorney still has to organize the case and present evidence in condensed form. Many of the trial preparation techniques discussed in this book can also apply to preparing for ADR proceedings. Observe as much as possible about the process. Participating in any form of ADR will give you an opportunity to interact with the clients and get to know them better. Assist the attorney in distilling and summarizing the facts and evidence that will be presented to the mediator or other neutral person. The issues will be clearer, as will the strengths and weaknesses of both sides of the case. You will get a feel for what additional technical explanations might be needed to educate a jury at trial.

You can learn from previous ADR files in a case you are preparing for trial. Review any materials that were previously prepared in ADR proceedings for lists of witnesses, document summaries, and investigations or inspections previously undertaken.

§ 2.23 1993 Amendments to the Federal Rules of Civil Procedure

The Federal Rules of Civil Procedure were originally adopted in 1938 in an attempt to simplify and standardize civil litigation practice in the federal courts. These rules outline instructions for conducting cases, from the initial filing through trial and appeal, for the 94 federal district courts in the United States.

The 1993 amendments to the Federal Rules of Civil Procedure went into effect on December 1, 1993, for cases filed after that date. There was much controversy about the recent changes to the rules, which were adopted over the protests of many distinguished scholars, attorneys, and judges throughout the country. The goal of the changes was to reduce the time and cost of litigation by streamlining discovery procedures. Whether the practice under the amended rules will actually result in either cost savings or increased efficiency remains to be seen. It will take some time to assimilate the new procedures and put them into practice.

The revised rules shift the burden from the courts to the attorneys and parties, requiring them to actively participate in *managing* cases in order to resolve them as efficiently and inexpensively as possible. As discussed in **Chapter 1,** managing cases means planning, setting goals, and following up to make sure activities are carried out in a timely manner. The amended rules tend to support the management concept. Rule 1 states, "These rules . . . shall be construed *and administered* to secure the just, speedy, and inexpensive determination of every action." [emphasis added]. The small addition of the words "and administered" to this rule sets the tone for the 1993 amendments, emphasizing the court's duty to ensure that civil litigation is resolved without undue cost or delay.

NOTE TO *Paralegal Trial Handbook* READERS: The following sections contain a general discussion highlighting some of the major changes in the Federal Rules of Civil Procedure along with my comments and predictions on how the changes are likely to affect the ways in which we prepare for and conduct trials. This is merely a guide to the most significant changes, and is NOT, by any means, an exhaustive treatment of the provisions in the 1993 amendments. The interpretations and applications of the provisions in the amended rules are still developing. As with any new set of guidelines, there will no doubt be differing opinions as to how the new rules should be applied. READ THE FULL TEXT OF THESE RULES before putting them into practice. You are responsible for checking the local rules for the district in which the case is filed and for keeping up with future changes and developments. Be aware that federal districts can adopt local rules to "opt out" of these requirements if they choose. This means that the amended rules may not apply in your jurisdiction. Always check your local court rules and discuss questions on the civil rules with your supervising attorney.

Complex actions may involve cases in multiple federal court districts. Do not assume that the local rules are the same from district to district. The local rules may vary not only with each jurisdiction (there is not even a uniform numbering system from district to district), but may also vary from the federal rules themselves. For example, local rules may permit filing by facsimile, they may allow a different number of interrogatories under Rule 34, or they may require that any motion filed be accompanied by a written brief. Determine the applicable local rules for each district involved in your case.

§ 2.24 —Rule 4. Summons

The plaintiff in a federal court case is responsible for serving the defendants within 120 days after the complaint is filed. A new feature of amended Federal Rule 4(d)(2) provides a cost-saving method to accomplish service by allowing a cooperative defendant to voluntarily accept service and waive formal service of a summons. Rule 4 states that a defendant has a "**duty** to avoid unnecessary costs of serving the summons" (emphasis added). A defendant who insists on more expensive formal service methods can be required to pay the costs connected with that service. By agreeing to the waiver procedure, the defendant waives ONLY the official service of the summons and does not waive any other objections, such as jurisdiction or venue.

Generally, you can use this procedure to serve all the defendants in a case, EXCEPT for the following types of defendants: infants or incompetent persons; the United States government; foreign states or their political subdivisions; and states, municipal corporations, or other governmental organizations.

Amended Rule 4(d)(2) provides two new forms for sending notice to and requesting a waiver from the defendant:

- **Form 2–7**—*Notice of Lawsuit and Request for Waiver of Service of Summons* describes the potential consequences when the defendant complies or fails to comply with the waiver request.

- **Form 2–8**—*Waiver of Service of Summons* is the waiver the defendant signs and returns. It must include the "Duty to Avoid Costs of Service of Summons" language at either the bottom or on the reverse side of the waiver form.

§ 2.25 —Steps for Obtaining Service by Waiver

You must follow these steps for obtaining waiver of service by a defendant in a federal court case:

____ 1. Fill in the court district, case number, case caption, and defendant's name in the appropriate blanks on **Forms 2–7** and **2–8.** If the defendant is a corporation, address the notice and request to the person authorized to accept service on behalf of that entity (such as, a statutory agent for a corporation). Include the person's title in the blank provided.

____ 2. Have the attorney sign the request form and fill in the **date the request was sent** on the front of BOTH FORMS. This is important because you use the date you sent the request to calculate both the date the waiver form is due back from the defendant and the answer date for the defendant.

____ 3. Send the following to the defendant by first-class mail (keep copies of everything for your file):

  ____ A time-stamped copy of the complaint;

  ____ Two copies of **Form 2–7**—Notice of Lawsuit and Request for Waiver (signed by the attorney and dated);

  ____ Two copies of **Form 2–8**—Waiver of Service of Summons (also dated), one for the defendant to sign and return, the second for the defendant's records (Rule 4(g)); and

  ____ A return address envelope (with sufficient postage affixed) in which the defendant can return the waiver form.

____ 4. Allow the defendant at least 30 days to return the waiver (60 days for a defendant outside the United States). Calculate the time for return of the waiver from the date you put on the request and waiver forms (see Step 3, above). When you receive the signed waiver form back from the defendant, make a copy and file the original with the court. The signed waiver replaces the usual proof of service for that defendant, and the case then proceeds as if the defendant had been formally served.

Note: If the defendant does not return the waiver:

____ You will have to prepare a summons, have it issued by the court, and serve it with the complaint on the defendant by the conventional methods (usually certified mail or personal service).

____ The court can charge the cost of serving the summons and complaint by other methods to the defendant.

____ 5. Calculate the due date for the defendant's answer; enter this date into your office's docketing system and your personal calendar. Note: A defendant who waives service does not have to file an answer to the complaint until 60 days after the Request for Waiver of Service form was sent (90 days for a defendant located in a foreign country). The waiver procedure gives the defendant more time to file an answer than the 20 days usually allowed under conventional service rules, and this may be an incentive for defendants to agree to the waiver procedure.

FORM 2–7
NOTICE OF LAWSUIT AND REQUEST FOR WAIVER OF SERVICE OF SUMMONS

NOTICE OF LAWSUIT AND REQUEST FOR WAIVER OF SERVICE OF SUMMONS

FORM 1A - Rule 4 - Federal Rules of Civil Procedure

TO: ______________________________
Name of individual defendant (or name of officer or agent of corporate defendant)

as ______________________________
Title, or other relationship of individual to corporate defendant

of ______________________________
Name of corporate defendant, if any

A lawsuit has been commenced against you (or the entity on whose behalf you are addressed). A copy of the complaint is attached to this Notice. It has been filed in the United States District Court for the __________ District of _________ and has been assigned docket number _________.

This is not a formal summons or notification from the court, but rather my request that you sign and return the enclosed waiver of service in order to save the cost of serving you with a judicial summons and an additional copy of the complaint. The cost of service will be avoided if I receive a signed copy of the waiver within _____[(1)] days after the date designated below as the date on which

[(1)]*Addressee must be given at least 30 days (60 days if located in foreign country) in which to return Waiver.*

this Notice and Request is sent. I enclose a stamped and addressed envelope (or other means of cost-free return) for your use. An extra copy of the Waiver is also attached for your records.

If you comply with this request and return the signed Waiver, it will be filed with the court and no summons will be served on you. The action will then proceed as if you had been served on the date the Waiver is filed, except that you will not be obligated to answer the complaint before 60 days from the date designated below as the date on which this Notice is sent (or before 90 days from that date if your address is not in any judicial district of the United States).

If you do not return the signed Waiver within the time indicated, I will take appropriate steps to effect formal service in a manner authorized by the Federal Rules of Civil Procedure and will then, to the extent authorized by those Rules, ask the court to require you (or the party on whose behalf you are addressed) to pay the full costs of such service. In that connection, please read the statement concerning the duty of parties to waive the service of the summons, which is set forth on the reverse side of the Waiver form.

I affirm that this Request is being sent to you on behalf of the plaintiff, this _____ day of __________, 19___.

____
Signature of Plaintiff's Attorney
or Unrepresented Plaintiff

FORM 2–8
WAIVER OF SERVICE OF SUMMONS

WAIVER OF SERVICE OF SUMMONS

FORM 1B - Rule 4 - Federal Rules of Civil Procedure

TO: ____
(Name of Plaintiff's Attorney or Unrepresented Plaintiff)

I acknowledge receipt of your request that I waive service of a summons in the action of

____
(Case Caption)

which is case number ___________ in the United States District Court for the _________ District of __________. I have also received a copy of the complaint in the action, two copies of this instrument, and a means by which I can return the signed Waiver to you without cost to me.

I agree to save the cost of service of a summons and an additional copy of the complaint in this lawsuit by not requiring that I (or the entity on whose behalf I am acting) be served with judicial process in the manner provided by Rule 4.

I (or the entity on whose behalf I am acting) will retain all defenses of objections to the lawsuit or to the jurisdiction or venue of the court except for objections based on a defect in the summons or in the service of the summons.

I understand that a judgment may be entered against me (or the entity on whose behalf I am acting) if an answer or motion under Rule 12 is not served upon you within 60 days after _________ (date request was sent), or within 90 days after that date if the request was sent outside the United States.

Date _______________ Signature: ______________________________
Printed/typed name: ______________________
As ______________________________
of ______________________________

Duty to Avoid Unnecessary Costs of Service of Summons

Rule 4 of the Federal Rules of Civil Procedure requires certain parties to cooperate in saving unnecessary costs of service of the summons and complaint. A defendant located in the United States, who, after being notified of an action and asked by a plaintiff located in the United States to waive service of a summons, fails to do so will be required to bear the cost of such service unless good cause be shown for its failure to sign and return the waiver.

It is not good cause for a failure to waive service that a party believes that the complaint is unfounded, or that the action has been brought in an improper place or in a court that lacks jurisdiction over the subject matter of the action or over its person or property. A party who waives service of the summons retains all defenses and objections (except any relating to the summons or to the service of the summons), and may later object to the jurisdiction of the court or to the place where the action has been brought.

A defendant who waives service must, within the time specified on the waiver form, serve on the plaintiff's attorney (or unrepresented plaintiff) a response to the complaint and must also file a signed copy of the response with the court. If the answer or motion is not served within this time, a default judgment may be taken against that defendant. By waiving service, a defendant is allowed more time to answer than if the summons had been actually served when the request for waiver of service was received.

§ 2.26 —Rule 5. Service and Filing of Pleadings and Other Papers

Amended Federal Rule 5(e) permits courts to accept filings by facsimile, if local rules allow. This is a sign of the times! Check to see whether your local court will accept filings by fax or other electronic means. See **Chapter 8** for more on using fax technology in your work.

§ 2.27 —Rule 11. Signing of Pleadings, Motions, and Other Papers; Representations to Court; Sanctions

Rule 11 was almost completely rewritten with the 1993 amendments. The revised Rule 11 broadens the scope of an attorney's duty to behave honestly and professionally in dealing with the court and sets out the penalties that the court can impose on an attorney whose conduct prevents the "just, speedy, and inexpensive" resolution of the action called for in Rule 1. The highlights of amended Rule 11 are:

- The attorney's signature, address, and telephone number must appear on any pleadings, motions, and other papers submitted to the court. The court can strike unsigned papers unless the attorney promptly corrects the omission of the signature (Rule 11(a)).
- An attorney's signature represents to the court that the attorney believes the information contained in a filed document is not frivolous and that it is complete and correct as of the time it is filed. The attorney must amend or withdraw allegations that later prove incorrect or unfounded (Rule 11(b)). Note the similarity to Rule 26(g) on signing disclosures and discovery requests and responses (see § **2.29**).

A motion for Rule 11 sanctions must be separate from any other pleading and it must specify the nature of the infraction. The moving party must give the person in violation a chance to correct the mistake without action by the court. (This is sometimes referred to as the "safe harbor" provision.) The motion is served on the attorney to notify him or her of the violation, but is not filed with the court. If the attorney fails to correct the error within 21 days, the motion can then be filed with the court. The court can also act on its own initiative to impose sanctions on an attorney whose conduct violates the standards. Rule 11 sanctions apply only to matters contained in papers filed with the court, not to disclosures or other discovery. Rule 26(g)(3) governs sanctions connected with discovery issues.

Rule 11(c) sets out the penalties the court can impose for violations of the standards in Rule 11. The penalty can be monetary (such as ordering a fine payable to the court) or nonmonetary, which could include things such as:

- striking the filing;
- issuing an admonition, reprimand, or censure;
- making the attorney attend seminars or CLE programs; or
- referring the matter to disciplinary authorities.

Note: If the court determines that an attorney or an attorney's employee has violated the rule, the court can also hold a lawfirm jointly responsible for the actions of the individual attorney or employee.

§ 2.28 —Rule 16. Pretrial Conferences; Scheduling; Management

Rule 16 provides for conferences with the court to monitor the progress of discovery and trial preparation. The 1993 amendments modify Rule 16 to focus more on control and management of cases, ensuring the court's early involvement in helping the attorneys to set deadlines, resolve discovery issues, and keep the case moving forward toward settlement or trial.

Amended Rule 16(b) Scheduling and Planning requires the court to confer with the attorneys and issue a detailed scheduling order (sometimes called a Case Management Order) mapping out a plan for managing the case. Whether the judge calls an actual scheduling conference or confers with the attorneys by telephone or letter, this activity takes place only **after the court receives the proposed discovery plan report from the parties under Rule 26(f).** The parties should have already made the initial disclosures required by Rule 26(a) before the scheduling conference. This gives the court the opportunity to review the proposed discovery plan and the attorneys already know enough about the case that they can effectively discuss potential time requirements and other issues associated with discovery and trial preparation.

The court's scheduling order typically includes deadlines for completion of the various phases of discovery, due dates for dispositive motions, dates for pretrial conferences, and the trial date, but it may also include substantial details about managing other aspects of the case, such as bifurcation of the issues or special discovery that the parties want to conduct. The judge has wide discretion to tailor the scheduling order to the needs of a particular case. For example, if the case warrants, the court can modify the required timing and content on the initial, expert, and pretrial disclosures required under revised Rule 26 (see § **2.29**). The resulting scheduling order is a detailed plan for the practical aspects of a case and it generally controls the schedule for the remainder of the case. Most federal judges are very strict about compliance with scheduling orders and rarely allow changes to them except for compelling reasons.

Pretrials

In addition to the initial scheduling conference, the court may call other pretrials as needed to resolve disputes and expedite the handling of the case. Rule 16(c) lists a number of items that the judge may consider and discuss at a pretrial, such as simplification of the issues, disposition of pending motions, and adoption of special procedures for complex cases. Amended Rule 16(c) adds some new topics to the list of possible pretrial considerations, as follows:

- limitations or restrictions on expert testimony under Rule 702 of the Federal Rules of Evidence;
- possibility of summary judgment under Rule 56 in matters when the facts are not really in dispute;
- use of special procedures to assist in resolving the dispute;
- scheduling of disclosures under Rule 26 and other discovery under Rules 29 through 37;
- ordering a separate trial on a specific claim or issue, counterclaim, cross-claim, or third-party claim;
- directing the parties to present evidence that could lead to a judgment as a matter of law under Rule 50(a) or a judgment on partial findings under Rule 52(c);
- limits on the time allowed to present trial evidence or on the number of witnesses or documents that may be presented at trial; and
- any other matters that may facilitate the fair, speedy, and inexpensive disposition of the action.

The court usually issues a pretrial order documenting actions taken, questions raised, decisions made, stipulations entered, admissions made, and the possibility of settlement discussed at the pretrial conference. Always read the court's scheduling order, pretrial orders, and final pretrial order (especially if you are called in to work on a case at the last minute) to understand the court's directions and decisions about how the trial is to be conducted.

Rule 16(d) directs the court to hold a final pretrial conference "as close to the time of trial as reasonable under the circumstances." At the final pretrial, the attorneys will formulate a plan for trial, including streamlining procedures for the admission of evidence at trial. At least one of the trial attorneys from each side must attend the final pretrial conference. The order following a final pretrial conference directs how the trial will be conducted. It can only be modified "to prevent manifest injustice" (that is, if some last-minute issue arises). Litigants who do not appear at scheduled pretrials or who are unprepared to discuss the case can be subject to sanctions (penalties and fines) under Rule 37.

§ 2.29 —Rule 26. General Provisions Governing Discovery; Duty of Disclosure

Rule 26, which contains some of the most revolutionary changes in the amended rules, covers the general provisions for discovery and introduces the concept of mandatory disclosure. The major objectives of the Rule 26 revisions are to expedite the exchange of basic information and to lessen or eliminate the paperwork involved in requesting that information. The two most significant changes in amended Rule 26 are that the parties have a *duty* to (1) meet and exchange basic information to the other side relatively early in the case; and (2) disclose testifying experts and provide written reports (see **§ 3.19**) without awaiting formal discovery requests. *Basic information* is defined as information that is needed in most cases to prepare for trial or make an informed decision about settlement. Another main idea in Rule 26 is that judges should manage cases based on a discovery plan worked out by the litigants. Remember that federal court districts can adopt local rules to "opt out" of these requirements if they choose. Check the local rules in your jurisdiction to determine whether the requirements under these amendments are will apply to your cases.

Amended Rule 26 may have only a limited effect on the actual trial of a case, except that trials may be scheduled sooner because the discovery process is streamlined and more efficient. The mandatory disclosures could also lead to earlier settlement of cases or referral to arbitration or other alternative dispute resolution methods. However, the amendments to Rule 26 will probably have the most impact on the way we prepare for trial early in the case, especially in cases with large document collections. Under the old rules, document management procedures were often not put into place until discovery requests were received, in the hopes that the case would be settled or that the opposing side would not request extensive discovery. Now, however, the initial disclosure procedure outlined in amended Rule 26 require you to produce an inventory of your documents to your opponents before any other discovery is served or answered. This means that you must consider document organization and control from the very start of the case.

Initial Disclosures (FRCP 26(a)(1))

You must provide the following basic information without waiting for a request from the other parties:

Persons. Give the names, addresses, and phone numbers of persons who know about facts alleged in the pleadings. List the subjects each person knows about. (FRCP 26(a)(1)(A))

Documents. Provide either a copy of the documents involved or a description by category and location of the documents. (FRCP 26(a)(1)(B))

Damages. Show how you calculated the damages claimed. Describe and make available for copying all nonprivileged documents that support the calculations. (FRCP 26(a)(1)(C))

Insurance. Reveal any insurance policies that could be used to satisfy a judgment. (FRCP 26(a)(1)(D))

The court can require parties to disclose additional information (beyond the witnesses, documents, damages calculations, and insurance coverage) without formal discovery requests. The court can also modify these initial disclosure guidelines if the case warrants.

Timing. Make the initial disclosures at the Attorneys' Discovery Planning Meeting (FRCP 26(f)) or within 10 days after the meeting. See **Form 2–9.** You must reveal all "relevant" information "reasonably available" to you at the time you make the disclosure, whether or not it supports your case. This could lead to disputes about what is "relevant" because what one party considers critical to their claims may not necessarily be considered "relevant" by the opposing party. You have to make the initial disclosures even if you haven't completed your investigation or the other party has not disclosed their information. You must supplement and update your disclosures as more information becomes available to you.

FORM 2–9
SUGGESTED OUTLINE FOR REPORT OF ATTORNEYS' DISCOVERY PLANNING MEETING

SUGGESTED OUTLINE FOR REPORT OF ATTORNEYS' DISCOVERY PLANNING MEETING

[Insert Caption and Names of Parties]

1. Pursuant to Fed.R.Civ.P. 26(f), a meeting was held on __(date)__ at __(place)__ and was attended by: __(attorney name)__ for plaintiff and __(attorney name)__ for defendant.

2. Pre-Discovery Disclosures. The parties have exchanged [or will exchange by __(date)__] the information required by [Fed.R.Civ.P. 26(a)(1)] or [local rule].

3. Discovery Plan. The parties jointly propose to the court the following discovery plan:
   - Discovery will be needed on the following subjects: (brief description of subjects).
   - Discovery to be completed by (date).
     Discovery on __(issue for early discovery)__ to be completed on __(date)__.
     If discovery is complex -
     - Phases of discovery?
     - Limit discovery or focus on particular issues?
     - Need changes to local court rules limiting discovery?
     - Other limitations?
   - Maximum of _____ interrogatories by each party to any other party. Responses due _____ days after service .
   - Maximum of _____ requests for admission by each party to any other party. Responses due _____ days after service.
   - Maximum of _____ depositions by plaintiff(s) and _____ by defendant(s).
   - Each deposition limited to maximum of _____ hours unless extended by agreement of parties.
   - Reports from retained experts under Rule 26(a)(2) due:
     from plaintiff by __(date)__.
     from defendant by __(date)__.
   - Supplementations under Rule 26(e) due __(times or intervals)__.

4. Other Items.
   - The parties [request][do not request] a conference with the court before entry of the scheduling order.
   - The parties request a pretrial conference in __(month and year)__.
   - Plaintiffs allowed until __(date)__ to join additional parties and until __(date)__ to amend the pleadings.
   - Defendants allowed until __(date)__ to join additional parties and until __(date)__ to amend the pleadings.
   - All potentially dispositive motions should be filed by __(date)__.
   - Settlement [is likely] [is unlikely] [may be enhanced by use of the following alternative dispute resolution procedure]: (describe procedure).
   - Final lists of witnesses and exhibits under Rule 26(a)(3) should be due
     from plaintiffs by __(date)__.
     from defendants by __(date)__.
   - Parties should have _____ days after service of final lists of witnesses and exhibits to list objections under Rule 26(a)(3).

- The case should be ready for trial by __(date)__ [and at this time is expected to take approximately (length of time) .

[Other matters tailored to the needs of the particular case.]

Date: _________ Signatures of Attorneys

Disclosure of Expert Testimony (FRCP 26(a)(2))
Expert Information (FRCP 26(a)(2)(A))

In addition to the initial disclosures, you must identify your expert witnesses (provide name, address, and phone number).

Report. (FRCP 26(a)(2)(B)) Provide a report, prepared and signed by the expert, containing:

- The expert's opinions and the reasons for those opinions.
- A description of the information (documents and materials) the expert reviewed in forming the opinions.
- Any exhibits summarizing or supporting the opinions.
- The expert's qualifications, including a list of books, articles, or papers written by the expert in the last 10 years (usually listed on the expert's résumé or curriculum vitae).
- How much the expert is being paid for the review and testimony.
- List of other cases (either trials or depositions) in which the expert has testified for the last four years.

The expert's report is supposed to be comprehensive. See § **3.34**. If you fail "without substantial justification" to disclose information on an expert, you could be prevented from using the expert's testimony at trial or be subject to other sanctions. The requirement of a written report may be waived for certain experts by local rule, order, or written stipulation.

Timing. (FRCP 26(a)(2)(C))
Produce the expert's report

- when the court orders it; or
- when the parties agree to produce it; but
- at least 90 days before trial.

If the evidence is merely rebuttal to the opposing party's expert, produce the expert information within 30 days after the other party discloses their expert information.

Pretrial Disclosures (FRCP 26(a)(3))

Before the trial, you have to provide some information in addition to the initial disclosures and the expert report. (Many courts already have a similar rule.)

Identify the trial witnesses. (FRCP 26(a)(3)(A)) Give names, addresses, and phone numbers, indicating which persons you r definitely plan to call and which you may call if you need them.

Identify testimony you will introduce by deposition. (FRCP 26(a)(3)(B)) Provide transcripts of the portions of the depositions you plan to use, even if the deposition is on videotape.

List your trial exhibits. (FRCP 26(a)(3)(C)) Indicate which exhibits you definitely plan to use and which you may use if you need them.

Timing. Provide the pretrial information at least 30 days before trial when the court orders, when the attorneys agree, or at the final pretrial under Rule 16). Within 14 days after the pretrial disclosures, file **OBJECTIONS** to deposition testimony proposed by other parties or admissibility of the proposed exhibits identified by other parties. If you don't file objections, you waive your right to object.

Form of Disclosures; Filing (FRCP 26(a)(4))

All disclosures (initial, expert, and pretrial) must be:

- in writing;
- signed by the attorney;
- served on opposing counsel; and
- filed with the court.

Methods to Discover Additional Matter (FRCP 26(a)(5))

Parties can obtain additional discovery through:

- depositions
- interrogatories
- requests to produce documents
- requests to inspect property

- physical and mental examinations
- requests for admission.

Discovery Scope and Limits (FRCP 26(b))

Generally, parties can conduct discovery on any relevant, nonprivileged matter related to any claim or defense, including information on documents and materials and the identity of persons who know about any discoverable matters. The information sought must be reasonably calculated to lead to the discovery of admissible evidence. (FRCP 26(b)(1))

Limitations (FRCP 26(b)(2))

Either on its own or in response to a motion, the court can change the number of depositions, interrogatories, and requests allowed and/or limit the length of depositions. The court can also limit the use of discovery methods if it decides that:

- the discovery is repetitive or can be obtained faster and less expensively by some other method;
- the party has already had adequate opportunity to get the information; or
- the expense of the proposed discovery outweighs the benefits, given the circumstances of a particular case.

Trial Preparation: Materials (FRCP 26(b)(3)) (No substantive changes to this rule.)

You cannot discover the other side's materials prepared in anticipation of litigation or trial *unless* you can convince the judge that:

- the information is crucial to your case preparation; *and*
- you cannot get the equivalent information any other way without "undue hardship."

If the court allows discovery of these materials, it must take steps to protect against disclosure of attorney work product.

A party is entitled to a copy of any written, recorded, and/or transcribed statement previously made by that party about the case. A nonparty may request a copy of a previous statement the individual made about the case. If the request is refused, the nonparty may move for a court order. If the motion is granted, the costs of the motion may be assessed to the party or the attorney who refused the request.

Trial Preparation: Experts (FRCP 26(b)(4))

A party has a right to depose any expert identified as a potential trial witness, but not until after the expert's report is provided. (FRCP 26(b)(4)(A))

A party can take a deposition or ask interrogatories of an expert who is NOT a trial witness ONLY under exceptional circumstances. (FRCP 26(b)(4)(B))

The party seeking discovery from another party's expert has to pay a reasonable fee for the expert's time in responding to the discovery. (FRCP 26(b)(4)(C))

Claims of Privilege or Protection of Trial Preparation Materials (FRCP 26(b)(5)) (new rule)

If you withhold information as privileged, you have to provide a description of the information withheld (that is, a Privilege Log), with enough detail to allow the other parties to determine that a privilege claim applies.

Protective Orders (FRCP 26(c))

Attorneys must first meet and try to work out an agreement concerning protection of sensitive information (for example, trade secrets or confidential commercial research). If the attorneys cannot come to an agreement, they can apply to the court for a protective order. The court can make whatever orders are needed (depending on the case) to protect sensitive information. If the motion for protective order is denied, the court can require the party to provide the information and may require that party to pay for the expenses associated with the motion. Courts in some districts already have a similar local rule in place.

Timing and Sequence of Discovery (FRCP 26(d))

- Generally, you cannot file formal discovery requests until the attorneys have held the discovery planning meeting. (Discovery can begin earlier if authorized by local rule, order, or stipulation.)
- You can use the discovery methods (interrogatories, depositions, document requests, requests for inspection or examination, requests for admission) in any sequence.
- Parties can conduct discovery at the same time.

Supplementation of Disclosures and Responses (FRCP 26(e))

Generally, you have to update your initial disclosures and your responses to discovery (interrogatory answers, produced documents, responses to requests for admission) whenever you gain new information and/or learn that your previous response was incomplete or incorrect, unless the parties have already acquired the new information some other way. For expert disclosures, you have to update both the expert's report and deposition information by the time the pretrial disclosures are due.

Meeting of Parties; Planning for Discovery (FRCP 26(f))

Timing. The attorneys must have a discovery planning meeting as soon as it is feasible for them to do so, but **at least** 14 days before the court scheduling conference or scheduling order (Rule 16(b)); about 75 days after the defendants have entered an appearance. NOTE: Local rules in some districts encourage, but do not *require,* the attorneys to meet and discuss discovery issues.

Purposes of Attorneys' Discovery Planning Meeting

- Discuss respective claims and defenses;
- Consider the possibility of settling the case;
- Make the initial disclosures (FRCP 26(a)(1)) or schedule a date to make them; and
- Develop a proposed case discovery plan (and written report).

Proposed Case Discovery Plan. The written report should include:

Initial Disclosures
- Date made or scheduled to be made;
- Changes to timing, form, or other disclosure requirements.

If the attorneys agree and the court approves, disclosure requirements can be tailored to the case needs.

Discovery
- What discovery will be done
- When discovery should be completed
- Specific dates for supplementing disclosures and discovery.

If discovery is complex

- Phases of discovery?
- Limit discovery or focus on particular issues?
- Changes needed to local court rules limiting discovery?
- Other limitations?

Other orders

- Protective Orders (26(c))
- Court Scheduling Order (Rule 16(b))
- Pretrial (Rule 16(c))

(See suggested outline for case discovery plan report.)

Attorneys are responsible for:

- Scheduling and attending discovery planning meeting;
- Attempting to agree on a proposed case discovery plan; and
- Preparing and jointly filing a written discovery plan report within 10 days after the attorney meeting (at least four days before the scheduling conference or order).

Signing of Disclosures, Discovery Requests, Responses, and Objections (FRCP 26(g))

The attorney must sign every initial disclosure or pretrial disclosure. Your standard signature block should always state the attorney's name, [attorney identification number, if required], office address, telephone, and fax numbers. (FRCP 26(g)(1)) By signing, the attorney certifies that the disclosure is complete and correct to the best of his or her knowledge and belief, formed after a reasonable inquiry. Note that this applies to information the attorney knows at the time the disclosure is made. The attorney must supplement or update the information if it changes.

The attorney must also sign all discovery requests, answers and responses, and objections. (FRCP 26(g)(2)) By signing, the attorney certifies that the responses are:

- correct according to the rules;
- not intended to delay or increase the cost unnecessarily; and
- reasonable under the circumstances of the case.

The court can strike an unsigned request, response, or objection unless it is signed promptly after the lack of signature is discovered. (The attorney could

FORM 2–10
CHECKLIST: FEDERAL COURT FILING REQUIREMENTS (UNDER 1993 FRCP AMENDMENTS)

ACTIVITY	GUIDELINES	DATE
COMPLAINT FILED	120 days to serve defendant	
REGULAR SERVICE MADE or REQUEST FOR WAIVER OF SERVICE SENT TO DEFENDANT [Form 1A & 1B] WAIVER OF SERVICE FILED	Defendant has 20 days to answer Allow defendant 30 days to return waiver (60 days if outside U.S.)	
DEFENDANT ENTERS APPEARANCE and/or ANSWERS COMPLAINT	Allow defendant 60 days to answer (90 days if outside U.S.)	
ATTORNEYS' DISCOVERY PLANNING MEETING [Rule 26(f)]	As Soon As Feasible; at least 14 days before Rule 16 Scheduling Conference or Order	
INITIAL DISCLOSURES EXCHANGED	At or within 10 days after Attorneys' Discovery Planning Meeting	
WRITTEN PROPOSED DISCOVERY PLAN REPORT TO COURT	Within 10 days after Attorneys' Discovery Planning Meeting; at least 4 days before Rule 16 Scheduling Conference or Order	
CONVENTIONAL DISCOVERY COMMENCES	After Rule 26(f) Attorneys' Discovery Planning Meeting	
RULE 16 SCHEDULING CONFERENCE and/or ORDER	Within 90 days after defendant files appearance or within 120 days after defendant served AND after Court receives Proposed Discovery Plan	
EXPERT DISCLOSURE/REPORT	At least 90 days before trial	
REBUTTAL TO EXPERT DISCLOSURES	Within 30 days after receipt of Expert Disclosures & Report [Rule 26(a)(2)(C)]	
DEPOSITIONS OF EXPERTS	After Expert Disclosure Report received	
DISCOVERY CUTOFF DATE/ DISPOSITIVE MOTIONS DEADLINE/ OTHER COMPLETION DEADLINES	As court orders at Rule 16 Scheduling Conference, and/or as stipulated by attorneys	
PRETRIAL CONFERENCES	As ordered at Scheduling Conference	
SUPPLEMENTAL EXPERT DISCLOSURES	By the time of the Pretrial	
PRETRIAL DISCLOSURES [26(a)(3)]	At least 30 days before trial	
OBJECTIONS TO PRETRIAL DISCLOSURES	Within 14 days after Pretrial Disclosures	
FINAL PRETRIAL (if needed)	As ordered by court	
TRIAL	As ordered by court	

[TEXT] 26(a)(1)

Rule 26. General Provisions Governing Discovery; Duty of Disclosure

(a) Required Disclosures; 'Methods to Discover Additional Matter.

(1) ***Initial Disclosures.*** Except to the extent otherwise stipulated or directed by order or local rule, a party shall, without awaiting a discovery request, provide to other parties:

(**A**) the name and, if known, the address and telephone number of each individual likely to have discoverable information relevant to disputed facts alleged with particularity in the pleadings, identifying the subjects of the information;

(**B**) a copy of, or a description by category and location of, all documents, data compilations, and tangible things in the possession, custody, or control of the party that are relevant to disputed facts alleged with particularity in the pleadings;

(**C**) a computation of any category of damages claimed by the disclosing party, making available for inspection and copying as under rule 34 the documents or other evidentiary material, not privileged or protected from disclosure, on which such computation is based, including materials bearing on the nature and extent of injuries suffered; and

(**D**) for inspection and copying as under Rule 34 any insurance agreement under which any person carrying on an insurance business may be liable to satisfy part or all of a judgment which may be entered in the action or to indemnify or reimburse for payments made to satisfy the judgment.

Unless otherwise stipulated or directed by the court, these disclosures shall be made at or within 10 days after the meeting of the parties under subdivision (f). A party shall make its initial disclosures based on the information then reasonably available to it and is not excused from making its disclosures because it has not fully completed its investigation of the case or because it challenges the sufficiency of another party's disclosures or because another party has not made its disclosures.

[ANNOTATIONS] 26(a)(1)

Rule 26. GENERAL PROVISIONS GOVERNING DISCOVERY; DUTY OF DISCLOSURE

Initial Disclosures. [26(a)(1)]
You must provide the following basic information **without waiting for a request from the other parties:**

Persons. Names, addresses, and phone numbers of persons who know about facts alleged in the pleadings. List the subjects each person knows about. **[26(a)(1)(A)]**

Documents. Provide either a copy of the documents involved or a description by category and location of the documents. **[26(a)(1)(B)]**

Damages. Show how you calculated the damages claimed. Describe and make available for copying all non-privileged documents that support the calculations. **[26(a)(1)(C)]**

Insurance. Reveal any insurance policies that could be used to satisfy a judgment. **[26(a)(1)(D)]**

The court can require parties to disclose additional information (beyond the witnesses, documents, damages calculations, and insurance coverage) without formal discovery requests. The court can also modify these Initial Disclosure guidelines if the case warrants.

Timing. Make the Initial Disclosures at the Attorney Discovery Planning Meeting [26(f)] or within 10 days after the meeting.

You must reveal all "relevant" information "reasonably available" to you at the time you make the disclosure, whether or not it supports your case. This could lead to disputes about what is "relevant" because what one party considers critical to their claims may not necessarily be considered "relevant" by the opposing party.

You have to make the initial disclosures even if you haven't completed your investigation or the other party has not disclosed their information.
You must supplement and update your disclosures as more information becomes available to you.

[TEXT] 26(a)(2)

(2) ***Disclosure of Expert Testimony.***

(A) In addition to the disclosures required by paragraph (1), a party shall disclose to other parties the identity of any person who may be used at trial to present evidence under Rules 702, 703, or 705 of the Federal Rules of Evidence.

(B) Except as otherwise stipulated or directed by the court, this disclosure shall, with respect to a witness who is retained or specially employed to provide expert testimony in the case or whose duties as an employee of the party regularly involve giving expert testimony, be accompanied by a written report prepared and signed by the witness. The report shall contain a complete statement of all opinions to be expressed and the basis and reasons therefor; the data or other information considered by the witness in forming the opinions; any exhibits to be used as a summary of or support for the opinions; the qualifications of the witness, including a list of all publications authored by the witness within the preceding ten years; the compensation to be paid for the study and testimony; and a listing of any other cases in which the witness has testified as an expert at trial or by deposition within the preceding four years.

(C) These disclosures shall be made at the times and in the sequence directed by the court. In the absence of other directions from the court or stipulation by the parties, the disclosures shall be made at least 90 days before the trial date or the date the case is to be ready for trial or, if the evidence is intended solely to contradict or rebut evidence on the same subject matter identified by another party under paragraph (2)(B), within 30 days after the disclosure made by the other party. The parties shall supplement these disclosures when required under subdivision (e)(1).

[ANNOTATIONS 26(a)(2)]

DISCLOSURE OF EXPERT TESTIMONY. [26(a)(2)]

EXPERT INFORMATION. [26(a)(2)(A)]
In addition to the Initial Disclosures, you must **identify your expert witnesses** (provide name, address, and phone number) [See FRE 702. Testimony by Experts; 703. Bases of Opinion Testimony by Experts; and 705. Disclosure of Facts or Data Underlying Expert Opinions.]

Report. [26(a)(2)(B)]
Provide a report, prepared and signed by the expert, containing:

- The expert's opinions and the reasons for those opinions.
- A description of the information (documents and materials) the expert reviewed in forming the opinions.
- Any exhibits summarizing or supporting the opinions.
- The expert's qualifications, including a list of books, articles, or papers written by the expert in the last ten years (usually listed on the expert's Résumé or Curriculum Vitae).
- How much the expert is being paid for the review and testimony.
- List of other cases (either trials or depositions) in which the expert has testified for the last four years.

The expert's report is supposed to be comprehensive. If you fail "without substantial justification" to disclose the information, you could be prevented from using it at trial or be subject to other sanctions.
[See suggested Outline for Expert Report, §326]

Timing. [26(a)(2)(C)]
Produce the expert's report

- when the court orders it; or
- when the parties agree to produce it; but
- at least 90 days before trial.

If the evidence is merely rebuttal to the opposing party's expert, produce the expert information within 30 days after the other party discloses their expert information.

[TEXT] 26(a)(3)

(3) ***Pretrial Disclosures.*** In addition to the disclosures required in the preceding paragraphs, a party shall provide to other parties the following information regarding the evidence that it may present at trial other than solely for impeachment purposes:

(A) the name and, if not previously provided, the address and telephone number of each witness, separately identifying those whom the party expects to call and those whom the party may call if the need arises;

(B) the designation of those witnesses whose testimony is expected to be presented by means of a deposition and, if not taken stenographically, a transcript of the pertinent portions of the deposition testimony; and

(C) an appropriate identification of each document or other exhibit, including summaries of other evidence, separately identifying those which the party expects to offer and those which the party may offer if the need arises.

Unless otherwise directed by the court, these disclosures shall be made at least 30 days before trial. Within 14 days thereafter, unless a different time is specified by the court, a party may serve and file a list disclosing (i) any objections to the use under Rule 32(a) of a deposition designated by another party under subparagraph (B) and (ii) any objection, together with the grounds therefor, that may be made to the admissibility of materials identified under subparagraph (C). Objections not so disclosed, other than objections under Rules 402 and 403 of the Federal Rules of Evidence, shall be deemed waived unless excused by the court for good cause shown.

[ANNOTATIONS 26(a)(3)]

PRETRIAL DISCLOSURES. [26(a)(3)]
Before the trial, you have to provide some information in addition to the initial disclosures and the expert report. (Many courts already have a similar rule.)

Identify the trial witnesses. [26(a)(3)(A)]
Give names, addresses, and phone numbers, indicating which persons you definitely plan to call and which you may call if you need them.

Identify testimony you will introduce by deposition. [26(a)(3)(B)]
Provide transcripts of the portions of the depositions you plan to use, even if the deposition is on videotape.

List your trial exhibits. [26(a)(3)(C)]
Indicate which exhibits you definitely plan to use and which you may use if you need them.

Timing.
Provide the pretrial information at least 30 days before trial (or when the court orders, when the attorneys agree, or at the Final Pretrial under Rule 16).

Within 14 days after the Pretrial Disclosures, file **OBJECTIONS** to:
(i) deposition testimony proposed by other parties; or
(ii) admissibility of the proposed exhibits identified by other parties. If you don't file objections, you waive your right to object.
[See FRE Rule 402. Relevant Evidence Generally Admissible; Irrelevant Evidence Inadmissible, and Rule 403. Exclusion of Relevant Evidence on Grounds of Prejudice, Confusion, or Waste of Time.]

[TEXT] 26(a)(4) & 26(a)(5)

(4) ***Form of Disclosures; Filing.*** Unless otherwise directed by order or local rule, all disclosures under paragraphs (1) through (3) shall be made in writing, signed, served, and promptly filed with the court.

(5) ***Methods to Discover Additional Matter.*** Parties may obtain discovery by one or more of the following methods: depositions upon oral examination or written questions; written interrogatories; production of documents or things or permission to enter upon land or other property under Rule 34 or 45(a)(1)(C), for inspection and other purposes; physical and mental examinations; and requests for admission.

[ANNOTATIONS 26(a)(4)]

FORM OF DISCLOSURES; FILING.
[26(a)(4)]
All disclosures (initial, expert, and pretrial) must be:
- in writing;
- signed by the attorney;
- served on opposing counsel; and
- filed with the court.

Methods to Discover Additional Matter.
[26(a)(5)]
Parties can obtain additional discovery through:
- depositions;
- interrogatories;
- requests to produce documents;
- requests to inspect property;
- physical and mental examinations;
- requests for admission.

[TEXT] 26(b)

(b) Discovery Scope and Limits.

Unless otherwise limited by order of the court in accordance with these rules, the scope of discovery is as follows:

(1) ***In General.*** Parties may obtain discovery regarding any matter, not privileged, which is relevant to the subject matter involved in the pending action, whether it relates to the claim or defense of the party seeking discovery or to the claim or defense of any other party, including the existence, description, nature, custody, condition, and location of any books, documents, or other tangible things and the identity and location of persons having knowledge of any discoverable matter. The information sought need not be admissible at the trial if the information sought appears reasonably calculated to lead to the discovery of admissible evidence.

(2) ***Limitations.*** By order or by local rule, the court may alter the limits in these rules on the number of depositions and interrogatories and may also limit the length of depositions under Rule 30 and the number of requests under Rule 36. The frequency or extent of use of the discovery methods otherwise permitted under these rules and by any local rule shall be limited by the court if it determines that: (i) the discovery sought is unreasonably cumulative or duplicative, or is obtainable from some other source that is more convenient, less burdensome, or less expensive; (ii) the party seeking discovery has had ample opportunity by discovery in the action to obtain the information sought; or (iii) the burden or expense of the proposed discovery outweighs its likely benefit, taking into account the needs of the case, the amount in controversy, the parties' resources, the importance of the issues at stake in the litigation, and the importance of the proposed discovery in resolving the issues. The court may act upon its own initiative after reasonable notice or pursuant to a motion under subdivision (c).

[ANNOTATIONS 26(b)]

Discovery Scope and Limits. [26(b)]

Generally, parties can conduct discovery on any relevant, non-privileged matter related to any claim or defense, including information on documents and materials and the identity of persons who know about any discoverable matters. The information sought must be reasonably calculated to lead to the discovery of admissible evidence. [26(b)(1)]

Limitations. [26(b)(2)]
The court can change the number of depositions, interrogatories, and requests allowed and limit the length of depositions. The court can also limit the use of discovery methods if it decides that

- the discovery is repetitive or can be obtained faster and less expensively by some other method;
- the party has already had adequate opportunity to get the information; or
- the expense of the proposed discovery outweighs the benefits, given the circumstances of a particular case.

The court can make these orders on its own or in response to a motion.

[TEXT 26(b)(3)]

(3) ***Trial Preparation: Materials.*** Subject to the provisions of subdivision (b)(4) of this rule, a party may obtain discovery of documents and tangible things otherwise discoverable under subdivision (b)(1) of this rule and prepared in anticipation of litigation or for trial or for another party or by or for that other party's representative (including the other party's attorney, consultant, surety, indemnitor, insurer, or agent) only upon a showing that the party seeking discovery has substantial need of the materials in the preparation of the party's case and that the party is unable without undue hardship to obtain the substantial equivalent of the materials by other means. In ordering discovery of such materials when the required showing has been made, the court shall protect against disclosure of the mental impressions, conclusions, opinions, or legal theories of an attorney or other representative of a party concerning the litigation.

A party may obtain without the required showing a statement concerning the action or its subject matter previously made by that party. Upon request, a person not a party may obtain without the required showing a statement concerning the action or its subject matter previously made by that person. If the request is refused, the person may move for a court order. The provisions of Rule 37(a)(4) apply to the award of expenses incurred in relation to the motion. For purposes of this paragraph, a statement previously made is (A) a written statement signed or otherwise adopted or approved by the person making it, or (B) a stenographic, mechanical, electrical, or other recording, or a transcription thereof, which is a substantially verbatim recital of an oral statement by the person making it and contemporaneously recorded.

[ANNOTATIONS][no change to 26(b)(3)]

TRIAL PREPARATION: MATERIALS. [26(b)(3)] (No substantive changes to this rule.)
You cannot discover the other side's materials prepared in anticipation of litigation or trial **unless** you can convince the judge that:

- the information is crucial to your case preparation; **and**
- you cannot get the equivalent information any other way without "undue hardship."

If the court allows discovery of these materials, it must take steps to protect against disclosure of attorney work product.

A party is entitled to a copy of any written, recorded, and/or transcribed statement previously made by that party about the case.

A non-party may request a copy of a previous statement the individual made about the case. If the request is refused, the non-party may move for a court order. If the motion is granted, the costs of the motion may be assessed to the party or the attorney who refused the request.

[TEXT 26(b)(4)]

(4) ***Trial Preparation: Experts.***

(**A**) A party may depose any person who has been identified as an expert whose opinions may be presented at trial. If a report from the expert is required under subdivision (a)(2)(B), the deposition shall not be conducted until after the report is provided.

(**B**) A party may, through interrogatories or by deposition, discover facts known or opinions held by an expert who has been retained or specially employed by another party in anticipation of litigation or preparation for trial and who is not expected to be called as a witness at trial only as provided in Rule 35(b) or upon a showing of exceptional circumstances under which it is impracticable for the party seeking discovery to obtain facts or opinions on the same subject by other means.

(**C**) Unless manifest injustice would result, (i) the court shall require that the party seeking discovery pay the expert a reasonable fee for time spent in responding to discovery under this subdivision; and (ii) with respect to discovery obtained under subdivision (b)(4)(B) of this rule the court shall require the party seeking discovery to pay the other party a fair portion of the fees and expenses reasonably incurred by the latter party in obtaining facts and opinions from the expert.

[ANNOTATIONS 26(b)(4)]

TRIAL PREPARATION: EXPERTS.
[26(b)(4)]

A party has a right to depose any expert identified as a potential trial witness, but not until after the expert's report is provided. [26(b)(4)(A)]

A party can take a deposition or ask interrogatories of an expert who is NOT a trial witness ONLY under exceptional circumstances. [26(b)(4)(B)]

The party seeking discovery from another party's expert has to pay a reasonable fee for the expert's time in responding to the discovery. [26(b)(4)(C)]

[TEXT 26(b)(5)]

(5) ***Claims of Privilege or Protection of Trial Preparation Materials.***
When a party withholds information otherwise discoverable under these rules by claiming that it is privileged or subject to protection as trial preparation material, the party shall make the claim expressly and shall describe the nature of the documents, communications, or things not produced or disclosed in a manner that, without revealing information itself privileged or protected, will enable other parties to assess the applicability of the privilege or protection.

[ANNOTATIONS 26(b)(5)]
CLAIMS OF PRIVILEGE OR PROTECTION OF TRIAL PREPARATION MATERIALS.
[26(b)(5) (new rule)]

If you withhold information as privileged, you have to provide a description of the information withheld (i.e., a PRIVILEGE LOG), with enough detail to allow the other parties to determine that a privilege claim applies (see §150).

[TEXT] 26(c)

(c) **Protective Orders.**
Upon motion by a party or by the person from whom discovery is sought, accompanied by a certification that the movant has in good faith conferred or attempted to confer with other affected parties in an effort to resolve the dispute without court action, and for good cause shown, the court in which the action is pending or alternatively, on matters relating to a deposition, the court in the district where the deposition is to be taken may make any order which justice requires to protect a party or person from annoyance, embarrassment, oppression, or undue burden or expense, including one or more of the following:
(1) that the disclosure or discovery not be had;
(2) that the disclosure or discovery may be had only on specified terms and conditions, including a designation of the time or place;
(3) that the discovery may be had only by a method of discovery other than that selected by the party seeking discovery;
(4) that certain matters not be inquired into, or that the scope of the disclosure or discovery be limited to certain matters;
(5) that discovery be conducted with no one present except persons designated by the court;
(6) that a deposition, after being sealed, be opened only by order of the court;
(7) that a trade secret or other confidential research, development, or commercial information not be revealed or be revealed only in a designated way; and
(8) that the parties simultaneously file specified documents or information enclosed in sealed envelopes to be opened as directed by the court.

If a motion for a protective order is denied in whole or in part, the court may, on such terms and conditions as are just, order that any party or other person provide or permit discovery. The provisions of Rule 37(a)(4) apply to the award of expenses incurred in relation to the motion.

[ANNOTATION RULE 26(c)]

Protective Orders. 26(c)
Attorneys must first meet and try to work out an agreement concerning protection of sensitive information (e.g., trade secrets or confidential commercial research).

If the attorneys cannot come to an agreement, they can apply to the court for a protective order. The court can make whatever orders are needed (depending on the case) to protect sensitive information.

If the motion for protective order is denied, the court can require the party to provide the information and may require that party to pay for the expenses associated with the motion.

[TEXT] 26(d)

(d) Timing and Sequence of Discovery.
Except when authorized under these rules or by local rule, order, or agreement of the parties, a party may not seek discovery from any source before the parties have met and conferred as required by subdivision (f). Unless the court upon motion, for the convenience of parties and witnesses and in the interests of justice, orders otherwise, methods of discovery may be used in any sequence, and the fact that a party is conducting discovery, whether by deposition or otherwise, shall not operate to delay any other party's discovery.

[ANNOTATIONS: Rule 26(d)]

TIMING AND SEQUENCE OF DISCOVERY. [26(d)]

- Generally, you cannot file discovery requests until the attorneys have held the Discovery Planning meeting.
- You can use the discovery methods (interrogatories, depositions, document requests, requests for inspection or examination, requests for admission) in any sequence.
- Parties can conduct discovery at the same time.

[TEXT] 26(e)

(e) Supplementation of Disclosures and Responses.
A party who has made a disclosure under subdivision (a) or responded to a request for discovery with a disclosure or response is under a duty to supplement or correct the disclosure or response to include information thereafter acquired if ordered by the court or in the following circumstances:
(1) A party is under a duty to supplement at appropriate intervals its disclosures under subdivision (a) if the party learns that in some material respect the information disclosed is incomplete or incorrect and if the additional or corrective information has not otherwise been made known to the other parties during the discovery process or in writing. With respect to testimony of an expert from whom a report is required under subdivision (a)(2)(B) the duty extends both to information contained in the report and to information provided through a deposition of the expert, and any additions or other changes to this information shall be disclosed by the time the party's disclosures under Rule 26(a)(3) are due.

(2) A party is under a duty seasonably to amend a prior response to an interrogatory, request for production, or request for admission if the party learns that the response is in some material respect incomplete or incorrect and if the additional or corrective information has not otherwise been made known to the other parties during the discovery process or in writing.

SUPPLEMENTATION OF DISCLOSURES AND RESPONSES [26(e)]

Generally, you have to update your initial disclosures and your responses to discovery (interrogatory answers, produced documents, responses to requests for admission) whenever you gain new information and/or learn that your previous response was incomplete or incorrect, unless the parties have already acquired the new information some other way.

For expert disclosures, you have to update both the expert's report and deposition information by the time the Pretrial Disclosures are due.

[TEXT] 26(f)

(f) **Meeting of Parties; Planning for Discovery.**
Except in actions exempted by local rule or when otherwise ordered, the parties shall, as soon as practicable and in any event at least 14 days before a scheduling conference is held or a scheduling order is due under Rule 16(b), meet to discuss the nature and basis of their claims and defenses and the possibilities for a prompt settlement or resolution of the case, to make or arrange for the disclosures required by subdivision (a)(1), and to develop a proposed discovery plan. The plan shall indicate the parties' views and proposals concerning:
(1) what changes should be made in the timing, form, or requirement for disclosures under subdivision (a) or local rule, including a statement as to when disclosures under subdivision (a)(1) were made or will be made;
(2) the subjects on which discovery may be needed, when discovery should be completed, and whether discovery should be conducted in phases or be limited to or focused upon particular issues;
(3) what changes should be made in the limitations on discovery imposed under these rules or by local rule, and what other limitations should be imposed; and
(4) any other orders that should be entered by the court under subdivision (c) or under Rule 16(b) and (c).

The attorneys of record and all unrepresented parties that have appeared in the case are jointly responsible for arranging and being present or represented at the meeting, for attempting in good faith to agree on the proposed discovery plan, and for submitting to the court within 10 days after the meeting a written report outlining the plan.

[ANNOTATIONS: Rule 26(f)]

MEETING OF PARTIES; PLANNING FOR DISCOVERY. [26(f)]

TIMING. The attorneys must have a discovery planning meeting as soon as it is feasible for them to do so, but **at least** 14 days before the court Scheduling Conference or Scheduling Order [Rule 16(b)]; about 75 days after the defendants have entered an appearance.

PURPOSES OF PLANNING MEETING
• Discuss respective claims and defenses;
• Consider the possibility of settling the case;
• Make the Initial Disclosures [26(a)(1)] or schedule a date to make them; and
• Develop a proposed case Discovery Plan (and Written Report).

CASE DISCOVERY PLAN - WRITTEN REPORT includes:
Initial Disclosures
• Date made or scheduled to be made;
• Changes to timing, form, or other disclosure requirements. If the attorneys agree and the court approves, disclosure requirements can be tailored to the case needs.

Discovery
• What discovery will be done
• When discovery should be completed
If discovery is complex -
• Phases of discovery?
• Limit discovery or focus on particular issues?
• Changes needed to local court rules limiting discovery?
• Other limitations?

Other orders
• Protective Orders [26(c)]
• Court Scheduling Order [Rule 16(b)]
• Pretrial [Rule 16(c)]
(See §___, suggested outline for case discovery plan report.)

Attorneys are responsible for:
• Scheduling and attending Discovery Planning meeting;
• Attempting to agree on a proposed case discovery plan; and
• Preparing and jointly filing a written discovery plan report **within 10 days after the attorney meeting (at least four days before the scheduling conference or order).**

[TEXT] 26(g)

(g) Signing of Disclosures, Discovery Requests, Responses, and Objections.

(1) Every disclosure made pursuant to subdivision (a)(1) or subdivision (a)(3) shall be signed by at least one attorney of record in the attorney's individual name, whose address shall be stated. An unrepresented party shall sign the disclosure and state the party's address. The signature of the attorney or party constitutes a certification that to the best of the signer's knowledge, information, and belief, formed after a reasonable inquiry, the disclosure is complete and correct as of the time it is made.

(2) Every discovery request, response, or objection made by a party represented by an attorney shall be signed by at least one attorney of record in the attorney's individual name, whose address shall be stated. An unrepresented party shall sign the request, response, or objection and state the party's address. The signature of the attorney or party constitutes a certification that to the best of the signer's knowledge, information, and belief, formed after a reasonable inquiry, the request, response, or objection is:

(A) consistent with these rules and warranted by existing law or a good faith argument for the extension, modification, or reversal of existing law;

(B) not interposed for any improper purpose, such as to harass or to cause unnecessary delay or needless increase in the cost of the litigation; and

(C) not unreasonable or unduly burdensome or expensive, given the needs of the case, the amount in controversy, and the importance of the issues at stake in the litigation.

If a request, response, or objection is not signed, it shall be stricken unless it is signed promptly after the omission is called to the attention of the party making the request, response, or objection, and a party shall not be obligated to take any action with respect to it until it is signed.

(3) If without substantial justification a certification is made in violation of the rule, the court, upon motion or upon its own initiative, shall impose upon the person who made the certification, the party on whose behalf the disclosure, request, response, or objection is made, or both, an appropriate sanction, which may include an order to pay the amount of the reasonable expenses incurred because of the violation, including a reasonable attorney's fee. [Amended notes omitted.]

[ANNOTATION RULE 26(g)

SIGNING OF DISCLOSURES, DISCOVERY REQUESTS, RESPONSES, AND OBJECTIONS. [26(g)]

The attorney must sign every initial disclosure or pretrial disclosure. Your standard signature block should always state the attorney's name, [atty. ID number, if required], office address, telephone and fax numbers. [26(g)(1)]

By signing, the attorney certifies that the disclosure is complete and correct to the best of his or her knowledge and belief, formed after a reasonable inquiry. Note that this applies to information the attorney knows at the time the disclosure is made. The attorney must supplement or update the information if it changes.

The attorney must also sign all Discovery Requests, Answers and Responses, and Objections. [26(g)(2)]
By signing, the attorney certifies that they are:

- correct according to the rules;
- not intended to delay or increase the cost unnecessarily; and
- reasonable under the circumstances of the case.

The court can strike an unsigned request, response, or objection unless it is signed promptly after the lack of signature is discovered. (The attorney could have inadvertently missed the signature line on one page.) The opposing party does not have to take any action in response to the item until it is signed.

SANCTIONS. [26(g)(3)]

If an attorney signs a certification that does not meet these criteria, the court can impose fines or other appropriate sanctions.

have inadvertently missed the signature line on one page. There is no harm done so long as the attorney signs the page right away.) The opposing party does not have to take any action in response to the item until it is signed.

Sanctions (FRCP 26(g)(3))

If an attorney signs a certification that does not meet these criteria, the court can impose fines or other appropriate sanctions.

§ 2.30 —Rule 29. Stipulations Regarding Discovery Procedure

Amended Rule 29 encourages the attorneys to work out as much as possible on their own and to prepare written stipulations reflecting the agreed terms for discovery matters. For example, the attorneys can agree to allow more than 25 interrogatories or to allow more than 30 days to answer interrogatories, as long as they stay within the time parameters of the court's scheduling order. The attorneys can ordinarily agree to modify the disclosure and discovery provisions without the court's permission. However, a court can direct that the attorneys obtain approval for certain types of stipulations, and they must have court approval if an agreed time extension would interfere with the completion dates in the court's scheduling order.

§ 2.31 —Rule 30, 31, and 32 Depositions

Rule 30 limits depositions to 10 per side, unless the attorneys stipulate otherwise or the court orders a different number. (Some courts already have local rules in place limiting the number of depositions allowed.) The attorneys can depose each witness only once. This does not apply when a deposition is temporarily adjourned and then continued at a later date. The attorneys should discuss the proposed number, timing, and length of depositions at the discovery planning meeting, and they have an obligation to develop an efficient and cost-effective plan for taking depositions in the case.

The court can limit the length of depositions, if appropriate. For example, the court might put a time limit on depositions that occur close to the trial date so the parties can focus on trial preparation. The parties cannot take depositions until after the attorneys' discovery planning meeting, except in extreme circumstances, such as when the witness is preparing to leave the country and would not be available for deposition later on.

The Notice to Take Deposition must state how you plan to record the testimony (stenography, videotape, and so forth). You don't need special permission for an audiotape or videotape deposition, but you must be prepared to produce a written transcript of a taped deposition if you plan to offer the deposition as evidence at trial. You have to give a deponent "reasonable" notice (defined as at least 11 days) of the deposition date. At the deposition, attorneys must state objections concisely and avoid prolonged argument or discourse.

§ 2.32 —Other Discovery Methods

Under Rule 33, Interrogatories to Parties, parties are limited to 25 interrogatories, unless the attorneys stipulate otherwise or the court orders a different number (local rules often do allow more). Subparts of interrogatories count as separate questions in this context. You can't serve interrogatories until after the attorneys' discovery planning meeting. Theoretically, you should need fewer interrogatories than before because you can expect to receive the basic information (which you would normally ask for via interrogatories under the old rules) through the initial disclosures.

Under Rule 34, requests for production of documents or for inspection of premises cannot be served until after the attorneys' discovery planning meeting. Response time is 30 days, unless the attorneys stipulate otherwise.

Under Rule 36, requests for admission cannot be served until after the attorneys' discovery planning meeting. Response time is 30 days, unless the attorneys stipulate otherwise.

§ 2.33 Organizing Case Files and Materials for Trial

A large part of your job as a trial paralegal will involve organizing and managing the papers, documents, and other materials in the litigation file. One of a trial paralegal's most important skills is the ability to organize a file so that any document or piece of written information can be located, retrieved, and refiled correctly and efficiently. Ideally, you will work on the case from its inception, and you can control and "build" the organization of the file materials by developing indexes and logs throughout the course of the case. This is the best case scenario. The worst case scenario is when you are brought in on a case at the last minute by a panicked attorney who has suddenly realized he or she is about to go to trial and who needs to have the file organized quickly. This may even be a file that was "inherited" from another law office, so the attorney does not know what the file contains. In reality, of course, most of the time you will be brought into the case at some midpoint in the development of the case before trial.

The approach you use toward organizing the case materials will vary depending on (1) how large the case is; (2) how much time you have to prepare before trial; (3) the specific task you are asked to do; and (4) how the materials were previously organized, if at all.

While no two cases are ever exactly alike, most litigation files include similar general categories of information and materials. This section discusses organization with the assumption that you are asked to organize the entire trial file and all of the accumulated materials. If your task is to organize only part of a file, use the specific suggestions that apply to the type of material you have. You can use many of the ideas for specific types of materials no matter when you are brought in on a case. To become familiar with the case file as quickly as possible, you must determine three things: (1) what types of materials this file contains; (2) what materials are the really important ones; and (3) what materials will be needed at trial. So, where do you start? The guidelines in the following section should help you organize the material in a case and keep it organized.

§ 2.34 A Ten-Step Procedure for Organizing Case Materials

The process for organizing a case containing diverse files and materials can be broken down into the steps that are outlined below and described in the following sections. Exactly where you start will depend on how familiar you are with your case and how the materials are presently organized. For example, if you are starting from scratch to completely reorganize a large case, begin at Step 1. But if you already know the case background information, begin with Step 2, and so on.

Step 1: Get some background information on the case (see § **2.35**).

Step 2: Make an overview survey of the file contents (see § **2.36**).

Step 3: Confer with the attorney (see § **2.37**).

Step 4: Separate the materials into stacks (see § **2.38**).

Step 5: Review and organize the individual stacks (see § **2.39**).

Step 6: Decide how to best contain the materials in each stack (see § **2.40**).

Step 7: Consult the attorney again (see § **2.41**).

Step 8: Make fresh labels, folders, binders, and files (see § **2.42**).

Step 9: Prepare a comprehensive "diagram" index of the main sections and subfiles (see § **2.43**).

Step 10: Index materials within the individual subfiles as needed (see § **2.44**).

§ 2.35 —Get Background Information on the Case

When you receive the initial assignment from the attorney, ask for a brief synopsis of the issues and entities involved in the case. Jot down the names of companies or individuals the attorney mentions, particular contracts or agreements that may be in dispute, and specific events, dates, or time ranges that may be at issue. The details the attorney mentions in a quick outline of the case will give you an indication of where you should concentrate your efforts as you plan the organization of the file. Ask the attorney about any pending deadlines for preparation or production of materials, so that you can plan how to best spend your time. See **Form 2–10** for a checklist of federal court filing requirements.

Ask questions, if necessary, to clarify your understanding of the nature of the case. A good question to ask an attorney who wants the file organized but cannot tell you exactly what he or she wants is, "What types of documents does this case involve?" The type of documents the attorney mentions in answer to this question will very likely be the key documents to that you need to pay particular attention when you organize the case. It may also be helpful to talk with any other attorneys or paralegals who have previously worked on the case to find out additional background information from their understanding of the issues of the case.

§ 2.36 —Make an Overview Survey of the File Contents

First—without rearranging anything—glance through the file materials quickly to get a general idea of what types of materials are in the file and how they have been organized up to this point. Someone, be it an attorney, another paralegal, a secretary, or a file clerk, may have been responsible for the maintenance of this file in the past. You may be able to determine a logical scheme for organizing the file by observing how someone else has previously classified the materials. If possible, try to build on the organization that has already been done instead of starting completely from scratch. However, remember that if the person did not organize the file with trial in mind, you may have to adapt the file organization to develop it for trial use. If you know who previously maintained the file and if that person is still around, ask him or her to explain or clarify any ambiguous labels or headings you encounter in the file.

See if there are any labeled folders, envelopes, or packets of materials in the file. Pay close attention to what is attached to what. When materials are clipped together in a file, there is usually a reason for it. In addition to typed labels, there will usually be at least a few files containing handwritten notations that will give you general clues on how the file contents or subject matter is classified. List the existing file labels, just as they appear on the files.

Use the File Diagramming Worksheet to record this information if you do the list manually (see **Form 2–11**). If you have access to a computer or word processing system, enter the preliminary list on computer so the items can easily be rearranged and embellished later (see § **8.14**).

As you look quickly through the file, note the different kinds of documents and materials contained in the file. See **Form 2–12** Sample: Preliminary Listing of Existing Files. For example, note whether there are:

- any bound documents, such as deposition transcripts or financial reports
- large packets of documents, such as hospital records, medical bills, or tax returns
- loose documents that do not seem to belong to a specific file. (Not everything will automatically fit into a clear-cut category.)

Do this preliminary survey quickly and do not take the time to review individual documents in detail at this point. Use self-adhesive tags to flag any files that appear to hold substantive information that you think will merit further review later on. Do not physically rearrange anything yet.

Practice Tip: If you are pulled in on the case at the absolute last minute and you must "come up to speed" on the file very quickly, be on the lookout for summary documents that will give you a quick overview of details and issues involved in the case. Look for any documents with titles including words such as "Summary," "Abstract," "Digest," "Index," "Analysis," "Overview," and so on.

§ 2.37 —Confer with the Attorney

Have a conference with your attorney at this point to discuss any questions you have about arranging the file materials. The items you noted in your quick review of the file will suggest some questions you need to ask of the attorney. Find out if the attorney expects to receive large amounts of additional documents or materials from opposing counsel. Try to determine whether you have all the materials related to this file or if the attorney has other materials "stashed" or filed separately elsewhere in the office. If there are additional materials, collect them and add their descriptions to the preliminary listing you started in Step 2.

FORM 2–11
FILE DIAGRAMMING WORKSHEET

FILE DIAGRAMMING WORKSHEET	
(Step 2) PRELIMINARY - EXISTING FILES	(Step 4) GENERAL CATEGORIES

FORM 2–12
SAMPLE PRELIMINARY LISTING: EXISTING FILES (STEP 2)

Pleadings—Case #89-CV-012754

Correspondence 1985-1988

Correspondence 1989-1991

Loose correspondence

Pleadings—Foreclosure on 5th St. property

Client interview notes

Mrs. Parker's Diary & Calendar

Deposition: Mrs. Parker

Parker Companies—Financial Statements (bound)

Mr. and Mrs. Parker—Income Tax Returns

Memoranda

Research

Interrogatories to Defendant

Medical Bills & Expenses

Duplicate & Draft pleadings

Attorney Notes

Newspaper clippings—articles on merger

Records on Rental Properties

Real Estate Appraisals (Notebook)

Documents from Parker Family Trust

Sheridan & Company—Accountants' documents

Hospital Records—City General Hospital (envelope)

Newburn Investigations, Inc.

C.P. Johnson, Ph.D.—Economist (Expert)

§ 2.38 —Separate the Materials into Stacks

If you are starting from scratch with a voluminous file, and the subfiles are not clearly labeled or different types of documents are mixed together, put all the materials into a large folder (small case) or a box (medium case), or multiple boxes or bins (large case). Find a large table or other large horizontal work surface where you have plenty of room to take the file apart and spread out the materials. If possible, use a conference room or workroom where the files will not be disturbed if you have to leave them overnight.

At this point, refer to the preliminary list you prepared in Step 2 and indicate the general category into which each file or packet appears to belong (for example, correspondence, discovery, legal research, and so on). Do not be too concerned if every piece of material in the file doesn't fit neatly into a classification. You may initially assign one category, and then later decide the material fits better into another category. Remember that these are only general subject classifications for the file information, so you have some flexibility in assigning categories. This list, plus any additions you make in Step 5, will be a guide for making up new file labels (see Step 8) and it will become the basis for the main section headings in your diagram index (see Step 9). Use the file diagramming worksheet to record the general headings (or add these to your word processing document if you are using a computer). You are then ready to rearrange the materials into new stacks.

Sort the materials into stacks according to general categories and types of documents, putting like documents together. Where there are multiple files with similar labels, ("notes" or "research") consolidate these into one stack. Put all the pleadings and court papers together, all the deposition transcripts together, and so on. As you come across a new kind of material for which you do not already have a stack, place it in a stack by itself and label it as to the type of material. Self-adhesive tags work well for this type of temporary labeling, especially if you use a color such as pink or blue that will stand out against the white paper of the files. If you are not immediately sure to which general category something belongs, put it aside temporarily and come back to it later. You may turn up other similar documents as you go through the remaining file materials.

Put each "general category" stack into a temporary box or folder, or simply place a large rubber band or binder clip around the material. It does not matter what kind of folders, binders, or envelopes you use for this preliminary grouping. This is a good way to recycle old manila file folders, but you don't have to use folders at all. Just use a bold marker to print the category or document type in large letters on blank sheets of paper and lay the paper on top of the stack which it describes.

If your list is on a computer or word processor, rearrange the subfiles so that they are grouped under the general headings you have assigned to each (see **Forms 2–13** and **2–14**). By revising your list into groupings, you will begin to see the shape of the file contents. (See Step 9 for more on this.) At this point, you can also begin to plan a tentative sequence for the various file divisions. Follow these general tips to logically organize your files:

- Put the active, dynamic files that occur in every case in the first group (correspondence, pleadings, discovery documents);
- Put the "reference" group next (background, research, client documents);
- Then add case-specific materials, putting related case-specific groups adjacent to one another (for example, financials next to accounting information).

FORM 2–13
SAMPLE PRELIMINARY FILE LISTING: GENERAL CATEGORIES (STEP 4A)

LISTING	CATEGORY
Pleadings—Case #89-CV-012754	PLEADINGS
Correspondence 1985-1988	CORRESPONDENCE
Correspondence 1989-1991	CORRESPONDENCE
Loose correspondence	CORRESPONDENCE
Pleadings—Foreclosure on 5th St. property	PLEADINGS
Client interview notes	BACKGROUND INFO
Mrs. Parker's Diary & Calendar	CLIENT DOCUMENTS
Deposition: Mrs. Parker	DISCOVERY
Parker Companies—Financial Statements (bound)	FINANCIAL INFO
Mr. and Mrs. Parker—Income Tax Returns	CLIENT DOCUMENTS
Memoranda	NOTES/INTERNAL MEMOS
Research	RESEARCH
Interrogatories to Defendant	DISCOVERY
Medical Bills & Expenses	MEDICAL RECORDS
Duplicate & Draft pleadings	PLEADINGS
Attorney Notes	NOTES/INTERNAL MEMOS
Newspaper clippings—articles on merger	BACKGROUND INFO
Records on Rental Properties	REAL ESTATE INFO
Real Estate Appraisals (Notebook)	REAL ESTATE INFO
Documents from Parker Family Trust	CLIENT DOCUMENTS
Sheridan & Company—Accountants' documents	FINANCIAL INFO
Hospital Records—General Hospital (envelope)	MEDICAL RECORDS
Newburn Investigations, Inc.	BACKGROUND INFO
C.P. Johnson, Ph.D.—Economist (Expert)	EXPERT WITNESS

FORM 2–14
SAMPLE PRELIMINARY FILE LISTING:
GROUPED CATEGORIES (STEP 4B)

LISTING	CATEGORY
Pleadings—Case #89-CV-012754	PLEADINGS
Pleadings—Foreclosure on 5th St. property	PLEADINGS
Duplicate & Draft pleadings	PLEADINGS
Correspondence 1985-1988	CORRESPONDENCE
Correspondence 1989-1991	CORRESPONDENCE
Loose correspondence	CORRESPONDENCE
Client interview notes	BACKGROUND INFO
Newspaper clippings—articles on merger	BACKGROUND INFO
Newburn Investigations, Inc.	BACKGROUND INFO
Mrs. Parker's Diary & Calendar	CLIENT DOCUMENTS
Mr. and Mrs. Parker—Income Tax Returns	CLIENT DOCUMENTS
Documents from Parker Family Trust	CLIENT DOCUMENTS
Deposition: Mrs. Parker	DISCOVERY
Interrogatories to Defendant	DISCOVERY
Memoranda	NOTES/INTERNAL MEMOS
Attorney Notes	NOTES/INTERNAL MEMOS
Research	RESEARCH
Medical Bills & Expenses	MEDICAL RECORDS
Hospital Records—General Hospital (envelope)	MEDICAL RECORDS
Records on Rental Properties	REAL ESTATE INFO
Real Estate Appraisals (Notebook)	REAL ESTATE INFO
Parker Companies—Financial Statements (bound)	FINANCIAL INFO
Sheridan & Company—Accountants' documents	FINANCIAL INFO
C.P. Johnson, Ph.D.—Economist (Expert)	EXPERT WITNESS

§ 2.39 —Review and Organize the Individual Stacks

Review each of the "general category" stacks one at a time and look closely at the materials. It may be necessary to break these general files into smaller, more specific subject headings or subfiles in order to adequately reflect the file contents, particularly when the materials have outgrown their original folder, envelope, or file jacket. Add to the list you prepared in Step 2 and Step 4 (or to your computerized list) any additional subfiles you need to contain finer subdivisions of materials within each general category. Again, use self-adhesive tags to temporarily label the new subfiles as you review them.

The subdivisions under each general category will be a guide for making up new file labels (see Step 8) and will become the basis for the second and third level subheadings in your "diagram" index (see Step 9). At this point, you should also begin to plan any color-coding scheme you wish to use for the file. See § **2.85** on color-coding.

§ 2.40 —Decide How to Best Contain the Materials

Once you have examined the materials in each general category and its corresponding subsections, you can decide the best kind of folders, envelopes, or binders to contain them. See § **2.45** *et seq.*, for suggestions on organizing specific types of materials. As you select containers appropriate to the size and use of the materials, remember to allow room for expansion to accommodate new and additional materials as the case develops.

Your office probably has various types and sizes of file folders in stock. The supplies you use can be very simple or more elaborate, depending on the budget and the type of supplies available in your office. You can improvise with folders you have in stock, or, if time and budget permit, you can order new filing supplies. Look through any office supply store catalog for dozens of ideas on filing supplies and systems. These are some suggestions for filing supplies you might use:

- Standard manila folders (letter or legal size)
- Expanding "red" files (file "buckets") These come in several sizes with gussets for expansion and they hold multiple standard manila folders.
- Multileaf folders (letter or legal size with a pronged fastener at the top or side of each page)
- Manila file "jacket" envelopes
- Large-size manila envelopes with fasteners
- Looseleaf binders (various sizes and coverings) and prepunched index dividers or pockets
- Elastic or ribbon-tie "pouch-type" folders, with or without internal dividers.

In a large file you are likely to find stacks of loose documents and papers that seem to belong together in a group, but there is no apparent logical way to organize them, or you have no time to examine them thoroughly at this point, or they may be originals that you do not want to punch, staple, or otherwise deface (see also **§ 2.60,** Preserving Original Documents). Here are some suggestions for quick and inexpensive (temporary) methods for keeping these groups of papers together without harming them, even when the papers are of various sizes:

- Put them in a labeled manila envelope or pocket folder.
- Fasten the stack with a large spring-type binder clip.
- Rubber band the stack and back it with cardboard so the papers will not crinkle or roll up. (This is a good way to recycle the cardboard backings from legal pads.)

§ 2.41 —Consult the Attorney Again

Once you have had a chance to examine the various materials contained in the file, you will surely have some specific questions to ask the attorney about the relevance or relative importance of various items. Schedule a brief conference with the attorney to discuss the case specifically from the standpoint of organizing for trial, both to refresh the attorney's memory about the file and to determine how you can best use the time available before trial. The attorney may have forgotten about or lost track of some of the file materials and will welcome your efforts to organize the file thoroughly with pending trial preparation in mind. These are some items you may want to cover at this follow-up meeting with the attorney:

Determine the attorney's priorities. Find out which segments of the file he or she thinks are the most important to get organized. Ask the attorney for guidance on specific projects upon which you should focus your attention. This is especially important if you have very limited time for preparing the case for trial.

Find out if the attorney expects to receive a large amount of additional materials or documents in any particular category. If you discussed this in your previous conference, get an update on the status of additions to the file. Incorporate this into your plan for containing and labeling the file materials to allow for expansion as the additional documents are received.

Ask the attorney about any preferences he or she may have for filing or labeling supplies. Most attorneys do not care what type of files or labels you use to contain the materials, so long as the information is clearly labeled and easy to locate. However, some attorneys are very particular about these things, right down to the color of the folders and labels used. If you are not familiar with the attorney's style, ask about his or her preferences.

Suggest setting up a new file division devoted strictly to trial preparation materials. See **Chapter 5,** Preparing Materials for Trial. Try to enlist the attorney's cooperation in building the file of materials meant specifically for use at trial. Let the attorney know that you are anticipating the trial and beginning to prepare for it. This may encourage her or him to begin working with you on the trial preparation earlier than usual. See **§ 1.10** for more on coping with attorney procrastination.

Ask specific questions about the particular files in your case. Remember, no two cases are ever exactly alike, so these questions will vary with each case.

§ 2.42 —Make Fresh Labels, Folders, Binders, and Files

When you have decided on the appropriate folders, envelopes, or binders to contain the file materials (see Step 6), have your secretary prepare clean, neatly typed labels to identify the contents of each main file division and its corresponding subsections. Fresh labels help you be visually organized because you can clearly see what materials you have and it is easy for the attorney or other trial team members to locate specific information within the file. New labels should accurately reflect each file's contents or purpose, with general headings assigned to the main file divisions and more specific labels assigned to smaller divisions or subfiles. Use the cumulative list of file headings you created in Step 2 and embellished in Steps 4 and 5 as a guide for typing the label text (see **Form 2–15** Sample: Revised File Listing). If you have planned a color-coding scheme for the file, give your typist clear directions on which colors to use for each category of labels (see **§ 2.85**).

Follow the conventions used in your office for including the necessary identifying information, such as your client file number or the case number on the labels. For large files that exceed the capacity of a single expanding folder or box, the label on each folder or box division should indicate "File 1 of 6, File 2 of 6, File 3 of 6," and so forth so you can always tell whether you have the complete set of files.

Use the type of label stock appropriate to the binder or folder you are labeling, and in the proper size to accommodate the amount of information you need to put on the label. If your secretary uses a regular typewriter to type sheets or strips of standard file labels, have her make a photocopy of the label sheet after the labels are typed and before they are affixed to the files. If your secretary has an automatic typewriter that can store the label text, ask her to print out a copy of the file labels on a plain sheet of paper to give you an instant list of the subfiles you have created. Use the list of file labels as a basis for your comprehensive diagram index to the files, as described in Step 9.

If your file index is on computer, you may be able to automatically generate file labels on your printer (see § **8.14**). This same information can easily be formatted into the comprehensive diagram index.

If the cost of supplies is a consideration, it is not necessary to use brand new folders, although you should replace any folders that are torn or dog-eared. You can recycle used manila folders that are still in good condition, or at least put new labels on existing folders. See § **2.92** for more ideas and tips on labeling and tabbing.

FORM 2–15
SAMPLE REVISED FILE LISTING (STEP 8)

PLEADINGS
- Pleadings—Case #89-CV-012754
- Pleadings—Foreclosure on 5th St. property
- Duplicate & Draft pleadings

CORRESPONDENCE
- Correspondence 1985-1988
- Correspondence 1989-1991
- Loose correspondence

BACKGROUND INFO
- Client interview notes
- Newspaper clippings—articles on merger
- Newburn Investigations, Inc.

CLIENT DOCUMENTS
- Mrs. Parker's Diary & Calendar
- Mr. and Mrs. Parker—Income Tax Returns
- Documents from Parker Family Trust

DISCOVERY
- Deposition: Mrs. Parker
- Interrogatories to Defendant

NOTES/INTERNAL MEMOS
- Memoranda
- Attorney Notes

RESEARCH
- Research

MEDICAL RECORDS
- Medical Bills & Expenses (envelope)
- Hospital Records—General Hospital

REAL ESTATE INFO
    Records on Rental Properties
    Real Estate Appraisals (Notebook)

FINANCIAL INFO
    Parker Companies—Financial Statements (bound)
    Sheridan & Company—Accountants' documents

EXPERT WITNESS
    C.P. Johnson, Ph.D.—Economist (Expert)

§ 2.43 —Prepare a Comprehensive "Diagram" Index

You will need a concise overview of the file headings so you can see at a glance how the file is organized and where specific materials are located. Using the cumulative list you prepared in Steps 2, 4, and 5, prepare a "diagram" file index, listing the various subfiles according to the fresh label text you assigned in Step 8 within each main section or division. Place the main section headings at the left margin, then indent the text to indicate descending levels of subfiles. Add a note describing the physical appearance of each file if it is other than a standard red file or manila folder. For example, you may have an envelope or a notebook or binder that merits a separate label. See **Form 2–16,** Sample File Diagram Index. This diagram index should also be coordinated to any color-coding system you have devised (see § **2.85**). Place a copy of the diagram index in your master trial notebook (see § **5.88**), attach a copy to the front of the first main file, and post a copy near the file storage cabinets or drawers. This will assist anyone using the file to locate, retrieve, and refile materials easily. The diagram index is also useful later on when you are preparing the file closing inventory at the conclusion of the case.

FORM 2–16
SAMPLE FILE "DIAGRAM" INDEX (STEP 9)

PLEADINGS
    Pleadings—Case #89-CV-012754
    Duplicate & Draft pleadings
    Pleadings—Foreclosure on 5th St. property

CORRESPONDENCE
    Correspondence 1985-1988
    Correspondence 1989-1991
    Miscellaneous correspondence

BACKGROUND INFO
- Client interview notes
- Newspaper clippings—articles on merger
- Newburn Investigations, Inc.

CLIENT DOCUMENTS
- Mrs. Parker's Diary & Calendar
- Mr. and Mrs. Parker—Income Tax Returns
- Documents from Parker Family Trust

DISCOVERY
- Deposition: Mrs. Parker
- Interrogatories to Defendant

NOTES/INTERNAL MEMOS
- Memoranda
- Attorney Notes

RESEARCH
- Research

MEDICAL RECORDS
- Medical Bills & Expenses
- Hospital Records—General Hospital (envelope)

REAL ESTATE INFO
- Records on Rental Properties
- Real Estate Appraisals (Notebook)

FINANCIAL INFO
- Parker Companies—Financial Statements (bound)
- Sheridan & Company—Accountants' documents

EXPERT WITNESS
- C.P. Johnson, Ph.D.—Economist (Expert)

§ 2.44 —Index Materials Within Individual Subfiles

You may need to give detailed attention to the individual subfile materials, depending on what your file contains. Index and document the contents of each subfile, organizing it to make information retrieval as easy as possible (see **§ 2.76** on indexing). Some materials will not require extensive sorting and handling at this point. Use the priorities you discussed with the attorney (see Step 7) as a guide to how much time and attention you should devote to various sections of the file.

Use the ideas and suggestions in § **2.45** along with the various indexing logs and forms as needed to organize specific materials (see also § **2.76** on indexing). Remember to be on the lookout for materials and potential exhibit documents that will be used at trial and begin collecting these. See § **5.58** *et seq.* for more on collecting exhibit documents.

§ 2.45 Organizing Specific Types of Materials

This section contains suggestions and guidelines for organizing some specific types of materials you are likely to encounter in the typical litigation or trial file. Typical categories of materials include the following:

- Correspondence (see § **2.46**)
- Pleadings (see § **2.47**)
- Research (see § **2.48**)
  —Legal
  —Medical/Factual/Reference
- Discovery (see § **2.49**)
  —Depositions
  —Interrogatories
  —Document Productions
  —Requests for Admissions
  —Miscellaneous
- Attorney Notes and Internal Memoranda (see § **2.50**)
- Client Documents and Photographs (see § **2.51**)
- Background Information and Investigation (see § **2.52**)
- Expert Witness Materials (see § **2.53**)
- Corporate and Financial Information (see § **2.54**)
- Expenses, Receipts, and Invoices (see § **2.55**)
- Original Documents (see § **2.56**)
- Miscellaneous Records (see § **2.57**)

Note: Organization of Medical Records and Reports is covered separately in § **2.62** *et seq.*

§ 2.46 —Correspondence

A well-organized correspondence file can assist you in locating important information that might otherwise be inadvertently "buried" in a voluminous correspondence file. If you are lucky, the correspondence from the case will at least be collected in one folder or file. If not, gather all the correspondence you find scattered throughout the case materials into one stack and proceed as follows:

1. If the file is very thick, sort the correspondence into two piles, one for substantive letters (for example, expert witness opinion letters or reports, agreements to produce discovery documents, medical reports) and the other for nonessential "junk" such as transmittal letters, cover letters, and express mail receipts.
2. Pay close attention to any enclosures or exhibits attached to the correspondence. If the cover letter is merely a transmittal letter, carefully disassemble it from the exhibits, attachments, or enclosures and put the letter in date order in the correspondence file. Write a notation on the bottom of the letter indicating what documents were attached and where they may be found in the file. On the top of each attachment document, note the date and the writer of the letter to which it was attached. In this way you can handle the attachment documents separately without the clutter of the transmittal letter, but you could reconstruct the entire piece of correspondence if necessary.
3. Put the correspondence in date order from the oldest on the bottom to the most recent on top.
4. Two-hole punch the letters at the top and fasten them securely into a manila folder with a two-prong fastener or three-hole punch them and place into a looseleaf binder.
5. If the correspondence covers a span of several years, insert tabbed dividers indicating the yearly divisions. This will make it easier to locate a letter from a certain date more quickly. These dividers can be preprinted tabbed pages but they need not be any more elaborate than sheets of colored paper with a self-stick tab attached either along the side or at the bottom of the sheets. If the file is really voluminous, put the correspondence for each year into a separate manila folder or binder and label them accordingly.
6. It may help you to assemble a master correspondence file that contains the original or a copy of ALL the correspondence, forming a complete chronological record of all the activity in a case. Then have copies made of the substantive materials and place the copies in their respective files.

(expert witness reports go into the expert witness file, agreements to produce documents go into the appropriate discovery file, medical reports go into the medical records file, and so forth.) Naturally, if a document applies in some way to more than one subfile, make two copies and place one copy in each file. In this way the attorney or the next person seeking the information is more likely to locate it no matter which file he or she starts with. This technique also helps to build complete subfiles so that all the materials pertaining to a particular subject are in one place.

Have your secretary prepare the divider tabs or folders. Jot down a list of the tabs or labels you need and let her type them up and affix them to the divider sheets. She can also make the copies of the subfile documents. Put a self-adhesive tag on the document indicating how many copies you need if the document pertains to more than one subfile.

As the file develops, you may have a subfile of key correspondence that has become very significant in the case. You may find it helpful to use the Correspondence Index form to list these important pieces of correspondence. See **Form 2–17:** Correspondence Index.

§ 2.47 —Pleadings

A litigation file will always contain pleadings. There are at least three schools of thought on the best method for organizing pleadings. The first method involves including and indexing EVERY pleading into a master pleading index that then resembles the court's file on a case.

The second method involves separating out the substantive pleadings from the procedural ones and making a separate index for each. Thus, the substantive pleadings such as the complaint, the answer, the counterclaim or cross-claim, major discovery requests, and any substantive motions would go into one file while such things as stipulations for extension of time, notices of filing discovery, and notices of hearing dates would go into a second file.

The third method uses a completely separate file or binder and index for discovery requests and responses. These are often quite voluminous, especially in document-intensive cases, so they would be too thick and bulky to insert in the actual pleadings index. Number the discovery pleadings in sequence with the regular pleadings, but include the first page only of the discovery document in the pleadings index. Indicate this on the index along with a notation of where the whole discovery response can be found. This makes it easy to tell at a glance if all outstanding requests have been answered and keep track of supplemental and second-wave responses. See **§ 2.49** on organizing discovery subfiles. Check with your supervising attorney to see which

FORM 2–17
CORRESPONDENCE INDEX

CORRESPONDENCE INDEX

#	DATE	SENDER	RECIPIENT	CC	SUBJECT	ATTACHMENTS

method he or she prefers, then proceed as follows. (Note: You can have your secretary do steps 2 through 6.)

1. Arrange the pleadings in order by date, oldest to most recent. Place the newest ones on top if you are using Acco binders; reverse that if you use binders. If you notice a large gap in time during which nothing was filed, you may want to obtain a copy of the court docket of pleadings filed with the court in the case. This will give you an outline of pleadings so that you can make sure you have a complete set of substantive pleadings. If some are missing and you cannot locate them in your files, you can obtain copies of these pleadings from the court file.
2. If any pleadings do not show a date upon which they were stamp-filed, look at the date of the certificate of service that indicates when the pleading was served on opposing counsel. Write this date in at the top right corner of the pleading beneath the case number and use this to determine the date order in which the pleading belongs.
3. Two-hole punch the pleadings at the top and fasten them in place in a top fastening, two-prong folder or three-hole punch and place in loose-leaf notebooks.
4. Give each pleading a number, starting with number 1 for the oldest (probably the original complaint or petition). Write the number in pencil at the bottom right corner of the pleading.
5. Affix corresponding number tabs directly onto the right-hand edge of the pleadings in a graduated fashion. This permanently marks the first page of the pleading with a number tab so that it can be easily put back in the proper order if it is removed for copying.
6. Use the "pleadings index" form (see **Form 2–18**) to develop an index by number of each pleading filed. The index can be either handwritten or typed, and it should contain the pleading number, the date it was filed or received, and the title of the pleading. Use abbreviations for Plaintiff (PLTF) and Defendant (DEFT) and last names only of the parties to save time and space. This index can be kept manually or it can be easily converted to a computer word processing document if you have access to that equipment. Keep the pleadings file up to date, adding number tabs and entries to the index as new pleadings are filed or received from opposing counsel. Punch the index and place it on top of the pleadings in the file or folder you choose. Attach clear plastic reinforcements on both sides of the pleadings index sheet so the punched holes will stand up to repeated use.

FORM 2–18
PLEADINGS INDEX

PLEADINGS INDEX

ITEM No.	DATE FILED	DESCRIPTION

§ 2.48 —Research and Reference Materials

The trial materials will include research and reference materials, most of which typically fall into two general categories: (1) legal research and (2) factual research (including medical research and reference materials). If yours is a small file, you may want to organize both legal and factual/reference materials in the same folder. If there is very much of either type of material, however, it is usually easier to separate them into research subfiles:

1. Legal research materials. These are copies of cases, statutes, judicial opinions on similar cases or issues, legal memoranda summarizing issue-specific research, legal periodicals and sections from finding aids such as American Jurisprudence and Corpus Juris Secundum. This would also include materials from computer research services, such as ATLA Exchange, JVR, LEXIS, Westlaw, and other on-line services.
2. Factual research materials. Some cases will contain factual or reference materials that the attorney uses for background information to learn about and understand the subject matter of the case. These may be items that you, the attorney, or the expert witness has come across that, for whatever reason, you thought would be helpful in understanding some factual aspect of the case. For example, in a personal injury case there may be information pertaining to the type of injury involved and the corresponding medical treatment and terminology. In a products liability action you might expect to find technical articles or treatises regarding the safety standards of the particular piece of equipment or product involved. Factual reference documents could include statistical studies, government reports, articles or clippings from journals, newspapers, and magazines, statistical tables or studies, and a wide variety of other background and reference materials. This may also include materials from computerized research services (LEXIS, Westlaw, or Dialog) or other on-line services.

Whether or not you prepare a detailed index of these materials will depend upon your supervising attorney's particular requirements. Generally, it will suffice to file the research and reference materials in clearly labeled folders until such time as the attorney wishes to use the research in preparation for trial.

§ 2.49 —Discovery

For a small file with only one or two depositions and a small amount of discovery documents, you may be able to comfortably fit all the discovery into one folder. Use the condensed "Discovery Index" (**Form 2–19**) to keep a record of what discovery has been conducted. See § **2.47** on separating discovery pleadings from substantive pleadings. However, if more than two kinds of discovery appear in the case materials, separate them into the following categories, as appropriate for your case:

- Depositions
- Interrogatories
- Requests for Admissions
- Requests for Production of Documents
- Miscellaneous Discovery

If the file is large and there are multiple parties, all of whom have propounded discovery to the others, the job of sorting out the discovery becomes more complicated. You may want to divide the material pretty finely, making a "Discovery Directed To" and a "Discovery Propounded By" file for each party.

§ 2.50 —Depositions

If your file has a small number of depositions (fewer than 10), put them all together in a red expanding folder. Arrange them logically to suit your case. See § **5.42** *et seq.* on preparing depositions for trial. Make a set of "working copies" of the transcripts. If you have access to document binding equipment, have each transcript copy bound in a separate booklet. Place the transcripts in separate report folders or all together in a three-ring notebook. Or, use the technique described in § **5.50** to store transcripts in magazine storage boxes. If you use a notebook, have your secretary make divider tabs indicating the name of the deponent and the date of the deposition. Use the "Deposition Master Index" chart (see § **5.49**) to log in each deposition as you receive the transcript. As you prepare summaries of the deposition transcripts, place a copy of each summary in a separate three-ring binder, arranged according to the same index number you assigned to the transcript booklet. Place a copy of the Deposition Master Index in the front of this notebook. If you use a computer to summarize the transcripts, be sure to note the computer file name under which each summary is stored. See **Chapter 8** on computer applications for trial.

FORM 2–19
DISCOVERY INDEX

DISCOVERY INDEX		
CLIENT	FILE	ATTY.
vs.		PLAINTIFF DEFENDANT
COURT	CASE No.	

DEPOSITIONS					
#	Deponent	Called by	Date	Place	Filed

INTERROGATORIES					
#	Directed To	Served By	Date	Ans. Due	Ans. Filed

REQUEST FOR PRODUCTION OF DOCUMENTS					
#	Directed To	Served By	Date	Response Due	Served

REQUEST FOR ADMISSIONS					
#	Directed To	Served By	Date	Response Due	Served

§ 2.51 —Interrogatories

For each set of interrogatories propounded, make a separate file that will contain the following:

- The original interrogatories
- Answers to the interrogatories
- Any documents produced in conjunction with the interrogatory answers
- Any supplemental answers provided.

§ 2.52 —Requests for Admissions

Make a separate file for each set of requests. Include the following:

- The original request
- Any formal responses or objections.

§ 2.53 —Requests for Production of Documents

Make a separate file for each production request. Include the following in each file:

- The original request
- Any formal responses, including descriptions of privileged documents that are identified but not produced
- Copies of any documents produced in response to the request
- Any supplemental responses or documents produced.

Be sure to designate which documents answer which requests, and keep track of who has received copies of each document.

§ 2.54 —Attorney Notes and Internal Memoranda

You can often glean important information about the case from reviewing the handwritten notes and internal memoranda generated on a trial file. Attorney notes will often capture ideas for an approach to the case or observations that the attorney made at a particular time, and these can easily be forgotten if no one ever takes the trouble to look at the notes again. If your supervising attorney has handwriting that is difficult to read, consider asking his or her secretary to transcribe the rough notes so you can read them more easily. Ideally, the attorney follows the good practice of writing the date at the top of the page of notes. If not, however, you may have to estimate the date the notes were taken.

§ 2.55 —Client Documents and Photographs

These will be documents and materials provided by your client. Take particular care with special documents that would be difficult or impossible to replace, such as marriage, birth, and death certificates, diplomas, or other awards or merit certificates. Protect these documents by inserting them into a plastic page protector. If the documents are already in a binder, it is best to keep them in the original container until you decide on the specific use for the documents. Note the date upon which documents were received from the client, and keep a careful listing of these because you will need to return the materials to the client at the conclusion of the case. See § **2.60** on preserving original documents.

In addition to the one-of-a-kind documents mentioned above, you might find the following in a file of client documents:

- Insurance policies (automobile, property loss, and health/medical)
- Photographs (see § **4.29**)
- Diaries, calendars, or chronologies kept by client
- Tax returns or financial statements (**Note:** These may require a separate file if they are extensive, particularly where one or more corporate entities are involved.)

§ 2.56 —Background Information and Investigation

This could include the following materials:

- Client interview sheets or questionnaires
- Private investigator's reports
- Factual research, newspaper clippings, articles (these may overlap with research materials)
- Materials from other cases that treat similar issues

§ 2.57 —Expert Witness Materials

Set up a separate file for each expert witness to contain copies of any correspondence between the expert and the attorney regarding theories of the case, the retainer agreement, and memoranda on the subjects the expert was asked to evaluate. Other items that should be placed in this file are:

- Résumé or curriculum vitae, or other information on the expert's qualifications and credentials;
- Copies of any books, articles, or lists of publications authored by the expert;
- Written reports prepared by the expert and any supplemental reports or documentation (see §§ **2.29, 3.34**);
- An index of the materials supplied to the expert for information or background on the case (see § **3.29** on documents released to experts);
- A copy of the expert's deposition, if one has been taken;
- Any background materials the expert has provided to you. See also § **3.27**, Assembling the Expert Reference Folder.

§ 2.58 —Corporate and Financial Information

If your case concerns issues involving tax returns or the financial status of a corporation, there may be a large volume of financial and accounting-related materials in the files. Put these materials in chronological order in a separate file.

§ 2.59 —Expenses, Receipts, and Invoices

During the course of case development and trial, you will need to keep track of all the case advances for such things as depositions, court reporter fees, copy charges, research services materials, medical records, expert retainers, outside visual aids, court costs, investigator costs, travel costs, and mileage. Collecting all the documentation of these advances into one folder in the file can be a big help at the end of the case when you are trying to summarize the advances to the client's account.

§ 2.60 —Preserving Original Documents

Litigation and trial case files contain many different types of documents. Some of these will be original documents that may come from a number of sources:

- Your client may provide items such as insurance policies, photographs, original medical bills, or tax returns. See § **2.59.**
- An expert witness may supply original materials for your review, such as government statistics or tables, brochures, articles, and pamphlets that support the expert's opinions (see § **2.57**). A medical expert will often provide a written report setting forth his or her opinions.
- Many times the original documents will be certified copies of records that you obtain on behalf of your client. These include certified copies of court documents, birth or death certificates, certified medical records (see § **2.62**), good standing certificates for a corporation (or other certified records obtained from the Secretary of State), and notarized or verified affidavits or witness statements.

It is important to keep original documents from being wrinkled, torn, marked on, or otherwise defaced. Never write anything on your original except a document control number (see § **2.80** on document numbering). Make a working copy to use if you want to highlight some information or to indicate distribution or production to opposing counsel.

Preserving the integrity of the original is particularly important if you plan to use an enlargement, or "blowup," of the document for demonstrative purposes at trial. The enlargement will show in magnified detail every mark, wrinkle, or speck (including marks from photocopy equipment). Copy quality deteriorates as copies are recopied. Because the original document is usually clearer and cleaner than a photocopy (especially third or fourth generation copies), have any enlargements made from a clean first copy taken directly from the original for the best results. See §§ **4.7–4.8** on preparing documents for enlargement.

Always make at least one set of working copies from the originals for actual handling in the case. Put the originals away until they are needed at trial. Some types of paper become brittle with age, so certain documents may be very fragile. Be very careful with the originals when you are making the set of working copies so that the originals do not get jammed in the copy machine. When the originals are on thin onionskin paper or very slick, shiny paper, do not use the automatic feed device on your copier. Instead, be prudent and hand-feed the originals through the copy machine. Multiple photocopies are usually needed in trial cases for exchange with opposing counsel, exhibits to depositions, and support for motions. Use the working copies of the documents to make additional photocopies for these purposes to reduce the amount of handling of the originals. If a particular document is used extensively in discovery, you may find it helpful to use removable tags to indicate this on the original document, for example, Plaintiff's Exhibit 1 in Williams deposition, Defendant's Exhibit B in Smith deposition. If something should happen to one of the working copies, you can always make additional copies from the original document (see **§ 5.64** on copying trial exhibit documents).

Put each original document into a plastic page-protector sleeve. This designates the document as an original and protects it from being defaced. These page protectors come in top-loading and side-loading styles with punched edges to insert in ring binders. This makes it easy to fasten the original documents into a notebook without punching holes in the document. This is also a handy way to contain documents smaller than 8 1/2 by 11 inches so they do not fall out of the file and get lost.

Keep these original documents in their plastic page protectors all together in a looseleaf notebook where they will be contained and protected but can be easily removed if you need to make additional copies. Keep a list in the front of the notebook to log the description of the document, the date it was received, and from whom it was received. See **Form 2–20,** Original Documents Log. This set of original documents is likely to be the nucleus for your set of trial exhibits (see **§ 5.61**). If the document, such as a lengthy financial statement or business prospectus, is too thick to fit into a plastic page protector, put it in a larger folder of a different color from the other manila folders in the files. Label the folder clearly to indicate that it contains an original document. If you have several thick documents or bound documents of the same type, use a slightly larger expanding folder and put them together in one folder. Prepare a list indicating each document contained in the folder and attach the list permanently to the outside of the folder with transparent plastic tape. Store the original documents in a safe place, preferably in a locked file cabinet under your control. This allows you to keep a complete set of the original documents intact until they are needed at trial.

§ 2.61 —Summary Records Index

When the supervising attorney asked you to review and organize the file, he or she may have mentioned specific documents or categories of documents that will be significant in the case, either as exhibits or as background information. When you make your survey and review of the file materials, you can begin collecting these documents. Use the Summary Records Index form as a guide to list the documents the attorney mentions, check them off as you find them, and indicate their location in the file. This guide will also help you

FORM 2–20
ORIGINAL DOCUMENTS LOG

ORIGINAL DOCUMENTS LOG			
DOC.#	DESCRIPTION	DATE RECEIVED	SOURCE

determine if certain documents the attorney mentions are missing from the file so you can take steps to locate or obtain these documents. This will be a starting reference list when you begin to compile the preliminary set of trial exhibits. See § **5.61.**

Form 2–21 is tailored to the type of records you would normally find in a personal injury or automobile accident case. **Form 2–22** can be used for records in any type of case.

§ 2.62 Organizing Medical Records and Reports

The case files in personal injury, wrongful death, and medical malpractice actions will include various types of records and documents related to the client's injuries and medical treatment. The quantity of the records to be organized will depend upon the severity of the injuries, the length of the hospitalization, and the number of medical practitioners involved in the patient's treatment.

There is no need to feel intimidated by a thick packet of hospital records. Once you become familiar with the components of the typical hospital record, you will understand how to organize them logically.

§ 2.63 Organizing the Hospital Admission Chart

The compilation of all the records pertaining to a hospital admission is collectively known as the patient chart. The chart consists of records from various departments which are kept daily by hospital personnel. The hospital chart is usually organized according to type of record, although sometimes it is assembled in chronological order, mixing records from different departments.

When you receive a certified copy of a patient's hospital chart, the copies may be either single- or double-sided, and the pages may or may not be sequentially numbered. Keep the original set of the hospital records intact, together with the original certifications prepared by the records custodian for use at trial (see § **2.73**). Do not mark on or punch any holes in the originals.

If the hospital records are very voluminous and will be reviewed extensively, have a working copy set made and insert the copy in a looseleaf notebook or binder. If the originals are double-sided, make sure to copy both sides. Clearly label this volume as the working copy set and use it for noting or highlighting significant portions of the records. If you have records from multiple hospital admissions at the same or different hospitals, insert looseleaf dividers and label each admission clearly.

In order to make the chart more manageable, it is helpful to index the various types of records found in the hospital chart. If the pages have been numbered by the hospital records custodian, index them in the order they appear.

FORM 2–21
SUMMARY RECORD INDEX 1
(ACCIDENT/PERSONAL INJURY CASE)

SUMMARY RECORD INDEX 1 (ACCIDENT/PERSONAL INJURY CASE)				
NEED	ITEM	REQUEST	REC'D.	LOCATION
	Accident Report			
	Photographs			
HOSPITAL RECORDS				
	1.			
	2.			
	3.			
	4.			
DOCTOR REPORT(s)				
	1.			
	2.			
	3.			
	4.			
EXPENSES DOCUMENTATION				
	1. Medical Bills			
	2. Prescription Receipts			
	3. Towing Bill			
	4. Repair Estimates			
	5. Auto Rental Receipts			
	6.			
	7.			
OTHER RECORDS/DOCUMENTS				
	1. Wage Loss Verification			
	2. Insurance Policy			
	3. Driving Record			
	4. Expert's Report			
	5. Investigator's Report			
	6.			
	7.			
	8.			
	9.			

FORM 2–22
SUMMARY RECORD INDEX 2
(GENERAL CASE)

SUMMARY RECORD INDEX 2 (GENERAL CASE)				
NEED	ITEM	REQUEST	REC'D.	LOCATION
TYPE OF RECORDS:				
	1.			
	2.			
	3.			
	4.			
	5.			
TYPE OF RECORDS:				
	1.			
	2.			
	3.			
	4.			
	5.			
TYPE OF RECORDS:				
	1.			
	2.			
	3.			
	4.			
	5.			
MISCELLANEOUS RECORDS/DOCUMENTS				
	1.			
	2.			
	3.			
	4.			
	5.			
	6.			
	7.			
	8.			
	9.			
	10.			

If the pages are not already numbered, you may want to resort them according to the type of records, then into chronological order within each category. Then add page numbers yourself and prepare an index keyed to the page numbers to facilitate locating specific records (see **Form 2–23,** Sample Hospital Chart Index).

The following are descriptions of the various types of records generally found in hospital charts, in the approximate order you could expect to find them in a typical hospital chart. The actual forms used will vary widely among hospitals across the country, but similar records will be found in every hospital chart where there was an admission. You may find additional specialized records, depending upon the treatment rendered and the procedures performed.

FORM 2–23
SAMPLE HOSPITAL CHART INDEX

DAVID R. WILLIAMSON—INDEX TO HOSPITAL CHART

CITY GENERAL HOSPITAL - Admission 8/2/94 to 8/16/94

	PAGE
Certification of copies	i
Admission Face Sheet	1
Patient Discharge Summary	2
Patient Data Sheet	3
Financial Responsibility, Waiver, etc.	4
Emergency Room Record	5
History & Physical	6–9
Social History	10
Clinical Sheets	11–37
Admission Nursing Assessment	38–40
Radiology/X-ray Reports	40–44
Surgical Pathology Reports	45–50
Operative Report	51–52
Anesthesia Records	53–54
Consultation Record	55
Surgical Pathology Reports	56–59
Microbiology Report	60
Anesthesia Records	61–62
Operative Report	63–65
Cytology Reports	66–67
Laboratory Reports	68–71
Laboratory Slips	72–80
EKG Chart	81
TPR Charts	82–85

Admission Record, Face Sheet, or Summary Sheet

This is usually the first page of the chart. It includes

- Patient identification information
- Admitting physician's name
- Patient's next of kin
- Employment and insurance information.

This sheet indicates the date and time of admission, the hospital patient reference number, and usually an initial diagnosis. The bottom part of the page may also be used for the patient discharge information, or the discharge information may be on a separate sheet.

Abstract or Discharge Summary

This is an overall summary, usually dictated by the doctor. It is an important record which briefly reflects the entire hospital course. It contains the following items:

- A summary of the reason for admission
- History of the present illness
- Physical examination findings
- A description of the hospital course of treatment
- Homegoing instructions, if any
- Final diagnosis
- Procedures performed.

Emergency Room Record

This will be part of the records only when the patient was treated in the emergency room. You can obtain much important information from the emergency room record. This will include the following:

- The patient identification information
- Patient's condition upon arrival at the hospital
- The tests administered or ordered
- The initial diagnosis
- Lab or X-ray findings
- The responsible physician's signature.

History and Physical Examination—Admitting Notes

This record, also sometimes labeled "Personal History," is usually a multiple-page form on which the house physician or resident records remarks as he or she conducts the initial examination of the patient. Usually the history portion is completed first by asking questions of the patient (or of a family member if the patient cannot answer). This section may alternatively be called "Social History." The actual physical exam is then conducted by the house staff. A review of the following systems is generally included:

- Endocrine
- Respiratory
- Musculoskeletal
- Neurological
- Cardiovascular
- Gastrointestinal
- Genitourinary

Information on possible allergies to medication will also be included on this form. There may be a separate admitting note which summarizes the history and physical examination findings.

Progress Notes

The physician uses these forms to record significant items about the patient periodically, usually on a daily basis. The doctor indicates changes in symptoms, test results, responses to therapy, and plans for the next treatment step. Each entry should be dated and signed by the physician making it. These entries can often be difficult to read because of the quality of the doctor's handwriting and the numerous abbreviations and symbols used. See **§ 2.72** on translating medical records.

Physician's Orders

The doctor uses this form to specify instructions on the details of the patient's daily treatment, tests or procedures ordered, specific nursing care to be carried out, medications ordered, and discharge orders.

Laboratory Data or Laboratory Reports

This information is generally recorded on specialized lab report forms or slips, and can include a wide variety of forms, depending on the particular laboratory tests required. The initial tests on an adult typically include

- CBC (complete blood count)
- Urinalysis
- Blood clotting and cross-matching for transfusion
- Blood sugar level
- Hematology
- Microbiology
- Blood components
- Blood chemistry profiles.

Later additions could include various X-ray and radiology reports; EKG or ECG, EEG, and pulmonary function testing records; and nuclear medicine examinations. A specialized type of laboratory record would be a pathology report on tissue examination.

Special Treatment Reports

Whenever an operation or surgical procedure is performed in the hospital, typical records would include the following:

- Preoperative checklists
- Pre- and postanesthesia evaluation
- Anesthesia record
- Transfusion record
- Operative report
- Operating room record or checklist

- Preoperative nursing care record
- Recovery room record.

In addition, the chart may include records of respiratory therapy treatments, IV therapy records and monitoring notes, or records of other specifically ordered procedures, each of which would have its own form.

Nurse's Admitting Notes or Nursing Assessment

When a patient is admitted to a hospital ward, the initial interview is generally done by a registered nurse, who records the information on this preprinted chart. The information elicited from the patient includes:

- Details of admission
- Description of illness
- Past hospitalizations
- Medications
- Allergies
- Information on special nursing care
- List of problems to be solved during hospitalization (patient care plan).

There may also be a nutrition assessment chart and diet information, as well as a list of clothing and valuables indicating the disposition of these to relatives or to the hospital safe.

Nurse's Progress Notes

These important forms give a daily record of the patient's symptoms, treatment, and vital signs based upon observations of the nursing staff. Nursing department records may include

- Graphic charts upon which vital signs (temperature, pulse, and respirations) are recorded
- Essay-type written observations by nurses
- Various flow sheets
- Intake/output charts
- Medication records
- Nursing care accountability record
- Traction-circulation flow sheet
- Patient hygiene or care records.

Consultation Report or Consultation Record

These reports are created when other doctors are called in to see a patient. The consulting doctor renders an opinion to the main physician on proposed treatment or therapy to solve the patient's particular problems.

Physical Therapy Evaluation and Reports

If the patient is given physical therapy, there will be a form indicating an initial assessment and daily progress notes on physical therapy treatments and results.

Intensive Care Unit (ICU)

In hospitalizations where the patient is in the intensive care unit, there will be special forms indicating transfer to and from the ICU, as well as other specialized daily records tailored to the patient's treatment.

Home Instructions/Patient Discharge Summary

This record, which may be similar to the abstract described above, gives the physician's final diagnosis and a summary of the operative procedures performed.

Autopsy Report and Death Records

In cases where the patient dies in the hospital, there will be documentation on forms which may include:

- An autopsy report
- Death certificate
- Coroner's report
- Release and removal of body
- Burial information.

Miscellaneous

Other records which may be included in the patient chart are the hospital registration form, patient consent/release forms, financial responsibility information, incident reports, or other records not otherwise classified.

In addition to the hospital records, a typical case involving medical issues could include the following types of records:

- Hospital outpatient treatment records
- Doctor's office records
- Medical opinion reports from physicians, physical therapists, or other medical practitioners
- Medical bills and expenses
- Health insurance or medicare information
- Medical research or reference materials.

§ 2.64 —Outpatient Treatment Records

These will be similar to hospital records, but they will not be as extensive. There will be a sheet similar to the face sheet in the hospital record, giving a summary of the details of the outpatient visit. Other outpatient records may include laboratory and test results, ambulance report, emergency room record, and discharge instructions for the patient. Outpatient records can generally be contained by placing them in a notebook in the same way as the hospital chart records. There should be an individual certification prepared by the hospital records custodian for each set of outpatient treatment records in the file (see § **2.74**).

§ 2.65 —Doctor's Office Records

Keep the original set of any doctor's office records or physical therapist's notes intact. Make a working copy to use for depositions or trial preparation.

§ 2.66 —Medical Opinion Reports

Use plastic page protectors to preserve the originals of doctors' opinion reports.

§ 2.67 —Medical Bills and Expenses

Make a separate file in which to accumulate the bills and invoices related to the client's medical expenses. Since these bills tend to come in a variety of shapes and sizes, it is a good idea to use plastic page protectors, file pockets, or large envelopes to contain undersized bills.

Use the worksheet (see **Form 2–24,** Medical Expenses Worksheet) to keep track of the expenses as bills are received from the client.

§ 2.68 —Health Insurance or Medicare Information

Separate these records, claim forms, and correspondence from the actual medical bills (see above) and keep them in an adjacent file. In this file also keep records on Medicare or other medical insurance documents or benefits statements. Keep a separate or adjacent folder of attorney protection letters and subrogation information. This may overlap with the insurance information.

§ 2.69 —Medical Research or Reference Materials

If a nurse or medical technician has reviewed the medical records and prepared an interpretive report, keep that report and any supporting documents in the same file as the records evaluated. Remember that a report of this type is work product and should be marked accordingly.

§ 2.70 Translating Medical Records

A patient's medical records can be a valuable source of information for the trial team in cases involving personal injury and medical malpractice. The relevant medical records are almost always used as trial exhibits in these cases, and the attorney must have a working knowledge of their contents in order to conduct proper trial examination of the injured party and the medical witnesses, such as the treating physician (see **§ 3.44**). Unfortunately, most hospital records and doctor's office records contain many mysterious symbols, acronyms, and abbreviations which make them difficult for the layperson to read and understand. In fact, some medical records are so peppered with these strange hieroglyphics that they look as if they were written in a foreign language! To add to the readability problem, many medical records consist of handwritten notes by doctors, nurses, and other medical personnel who often have nearly illegible handwriting. Before the attorney can effectively use the contents of the medical records during discovery and at trial, they must be carefully examined and "translated" into a usable form. You can assist the attorney by deciphering the medical records in your case and preparing a glossary containing the various medical terms and references. Learn to use a good medical dictionary, encyclopedia, and other medical-legal reference works which you can find at your law library or medical library.

FORM 2–24
MEDICAL EXPENSES WORKSHEET

MEDICAL EXPENSES WORKSHEET				
DOCTOR or HOSPITAL and ADDRESS	DATE OF SERVICE	HAVE BILL COPY	AMT.	CLIENT PAYMENT/ INSURANCE SUBROGATION
1.			$	Client Paid $ Ins. Paid $ Subrogated $
2.			$	Client Paid $ Ins. Paid $ Subrogated $
3.			$	Client Paid $ Ins. Paid $ Subrogated $
4.			$	Client Paid $ Ins. Paid $ Subrogated $
5.			$	Client Paid $ Ins. Paid $ Subrogated $
6.			$	Client Paid $ Ins. Paid $ Subrogated $
7.			$	Client Paid $ Ins. Paid $ Subrogated $
8.			$	Client Paid $ Ins. Paid $ Subrogated $
9.			$	Client Paid $ Ins. Paid $ Subrogated $
10.			$	Client Paid $ Ins. Paid $ Subrogated $
TOTAL THIS PAGE				

§ 2.71 —Abbreviations in Medical Records

Table 2–1 gives the common translations for a number of abbreviations, acronyms, and symbols which frequently appear in medical records. This table should be used only as a starting point and general guide for decoding your medical records. You may encounter other abbreviations which are not on this list, as well as alternate meanings for some of the listed abbreviations. The common usage for some medical abbreviations varies among medical communities in different parts of the country, so you should always check with the physician or medical expert to confirm your translations.

Table 2–1

Alphabetical Reference to Medical Abbreviations

Abbreviation	Meaning
A	
@	at
abd.	abdomen, abdominal
ABP	arterial blood pressure
abs.	absent
a.c. or a/c	before meals
acc.	accident
ad lib	as desired, as much as desired
adm.	admit, admitted, admission
alb.	albumin
alc., alcho.	alcohol
alt.	alternate
a.m., A.M.	morning
amb.	ambulate, ambulant, ambulatory (up and about)
amp.	amputation
amt.	amount
anes.	anesthesia
ant.	anterior
ante	before
A&P.	auscultation and percussion
approx.	approximately
aq.	water
AROM	active range of motion
art.	artery, arterial
ASAP	as soon as possible (stat)
A-V	arteriovenous
ax.	axillary, axilla
B	
B.	bath
BaEn, BE	barium enema
bas.	basal

Table 2–1
(continued)

B&B	bowel and bladder
b.i.d.	twice a day (bis in diem)
bk.	back
blad.	bladder
bl., bld.	blood
BM	bowel movement
BMR	basal metabolic rate
BP, B/P	blood pressure
BR	bathroom
BRP	bathroom privileges
BS	bowel sounds
Bx	biopsy
C	
c̄	with
C	Centigrade
Ca.	calcium
ca.	about
cal.	calorie, calories
caps	capsules
card.	cardiac
cath.	catheter
Cauc.	Caucasian
CBC	complete blood count
cbl	chronic blood loss
cc, c.c.	cubic centimeter
CC	chief complaint
CCU	cardiac care unit
cf.	compare
ch.	chest
Cl, chlor.	chloride
Cl. liq.	clear liquid
cm.	centimeter
CNS	central nervous system
c/o	complains of
CO_2	carbon dioxide
comb.	combine, combination
comf.	comfortable
comp.	compound, compress
cons.	consultation
cont.	continue, continuous
contrib.	contributory
CPR	cardiopulmonary resuscitation
C&S	culture and sensitivity

C-section .... Cesarean section
CSF .... cerebrospinal fluid
C-V .... cardiovascular
CVA .... cerebrovascular accident (stroke)
CVP .... central venous pressure
Cx .... cervix
cysto .... cystoscopy

D

D/C .... discontinue
D&C .... dilation and curettage
decr. .... decrease, decreased
decub. .... decubitus
dehyd. .... dehydrated
depr. .... depressed
dept. .... department
derm. .... dermatology
dil. .... dilute, diluted
dim. .... diminished
dis. .... disease
dist. .... distilled (water)
disch. .... discharge
DOA .... dead on arrival
Dr. .... doctor
dresg. .... dressing
DT's .... delerium tremens
Dx .... diagnosis

E

EBL .... estimated blood loss
ECG .... electrocardiogram
EEG .... electroencephalogram
EENT .... eye, ear, nose, and throat
EKG .... electrocardiogram
elev. .... elevated
EMG .... electromyogram
En. .... enema
ENT .... ear, nose and throat
EOM .... extraocular movement
epis .... episiotomy
ER .... emergency room
ess. .... essentially
exp. .... expired
ext. .... external
extr. .... extremities, extremity
extens. .... extension

Table 2–1
(continued)

F	
F	Fahrenheit
F.	(in medical history) female or father
FB	foreign body
FBS	fasting blood sugar
Fe	iron
fem.	femoral, femur
F.H.	family history
fl.	fluids
fl. oz.	fluid ounces
ft.	foot or feet
Fx.	fracture
G	
gal.	gallon
GB, G.B.	gallbladder
gen.	general
genit.	genitalia
GI, G.I.	gastrointestinal
gluc.	glucose
gm	gram
gr.	grains (dosage)
GU, G.U.	genitourinary
GYN	gynecology
H	
h.	hour
H.	hypodermic
HCI	hydrochloric acid
H & C	hot and cold
H_2O	water
Hd.	head
HD	heart disease
HEENT	head, eyes, ears, nose, throat
hern.	herniated
Hg	mercury
Hgb	hemoglobin
HR	heart rate
h.s.	at bedtime
ht	height
htn.	hypertension
Hx	history

I

ICU . . . . intensive care unit
I&D . . . . incision and drainage
i.d. . . . . during the day (in diem)
imp. . . . . impression
I.M. . . . . intramuscular
in. . . . . inches
inc. . . . . incomplete
inj. . . . . injury, injured
int. . . . . internal
I&O . . . . intake and output
IQ . . . . intelligence quotient
irreg. . . . . irregular
irrig. . . . . irrigate, irrigation
IT . . . . inhalation therapy
IUD . . . . intrauterine device
IV . . . . intravenous infusion
IVP . . . . intravenous pyelogram
IVU . . . . intravenous urogram

J

jt. . . . . joint

K

K . . . . potassium
KCl . . . . potassium chloride
kg . . . . kilogram
KJ . . . . knee jerk
KUB . . . . kidney, ureter, bladder

L

L . . . . (depending on context) liter, liver, left, lumbar
(L) . . . . left
L&A . . . . light and accommodation (pupil reflexes)
lab. . . . . laboratory
lac. . . . . laceration
lam. . . . . laminectomy
lap. . . . . laparotomy
lat. . . . . lateral
lav. . . . . lavatory
lb. . . . . pound
lg. . . . . large
lig. . . . . ligament
liq. . . . . liquid
LLE . . . . left lower extremity

Table 2–1
(continued)

LLL	left lower lobe (lung)
LLQ	left lower quadrant
LML	left middle lobe
LMP	last menstrual period
LS	low salt
ltd	limited
LUE	left upper extremity
LUL	left upper lobe
LUQ	left upper quadrant
M	
m	murmur
M.	(in medical history) male or mother
max.	maximum or maxillary
mcg, mcgm	microgram
meds	medicines or medication
memb	membranes
mg, mgm	milligram
Mg	magnesium
min.	minimal
MI	myocardial infarction
ml	milliliter
mm	millimeter
mod.	moderate, moderately
MOM	milk of magnesia
mono	monocytes
M.S.	multiple sclerosis
musc.	muscle, muscular
N	
n.	nerve
N_2	nitrogen
N_2O	nitrous oxide
Na	sodium
NA	nurse's aide
NaCl	sodium chloride
N.A.D.	no abnormalities detected
NAD	no acute distress
NB	newborn
NBM	nothing by mouth
neg.	negative
neuro.	neurology
NG	nasogastric
NH	nursing home

noc. . . . . night, nocturnal
norm. . . . . normal
NPO . . . . nothing by mouth
N.S. . . . . nervous system
NSR . . . . normal sinus rhythm

O

"O" . . . . oral
O_2 . . . . oxygen
OB . . . . obstetrics
OBS . . . . organic brain syndrome
occ., occip. . . . . occiput, occipital
occas. . . . . occasional
O.D. . . . . right eye (oculus dexter)
OD . . . . overdose
OOB . . . . out of bed
op. . . . . operation
OPD . . . . outpatient department
OR . . . . operating room
ORIF . . . . open reduction with internal fixation
orth., ortho . . . . orthopedics
os . . . . mouth
O.S. . . . . left eye (oculus sinister)
OT . . . . occupational therapy
O.U. . . . . both eyes
oz. . . . . ounce

P

P . . . . phosphorus
P&A . . . . percussion and auscultation (chest exam)
palp. . . . . palpate, palpated, palpable
PAR . . . . postanesthesia recovery room
p.c., p/c . . . . after meals
pdr. . . . . powder
PE, P.E. . . . . physical examination
Ped . . . . pediatrician
pen. . . . . penicillin
per os . . . . by mouth
PERLA . . . . pupils equal, react to light and accommodation
PERRLA . . . . pupils equal, round, react to light and accommodation
PH . . . . past history or personal history
pharm . . . . pharmacy
phys. . . . . physical
PI . . . . present illness
p.m. . . . . afternoon
PMI . . . . point of maximum impulse

Table 2–1
(continued)

pneu.	pneumonia
PO	by mouth
pos	positive
poss.	possible
post.	posterior
post-op	postoperative
pre-op	preoperative
prev.	previous
prn.	as needed, when needed, as required
PROM	passive range of motion
prox.	proximal
pt.	patient
PT	physical therapy
Pulm.F.	pulmonary function
pulv.	powder
Px.	physical examination
Q	
q.	every
q.d.	every day, daily
q.n.	every night
q.h.	every hour
q_2h	every 2 hours
q_3h	every 3 hours
q_4h	every 4 hours
q.i.d.	four times a day
q.n.s.	quantity not sufficient
q.o.d.	every other day
q.s.	sufficient quantity
qt.	quart
q.v.	as much as desired
R	
R	rectal
(R)	right
rad.	radial
RBC	red blood cells
re	regarding, about, as to
reg.	regular
rehab.	rehabilitation
resp.	respirations, respiratory
Rh	Rh factor of blood
RLE	right lower extremity

RLL . . . . right lower lobe
RLQ . . . . right lower quadrant
RML . . . . right middle lobe
R/O . . . . rule out
ROM . . . . range of motion
ROS . . . . review of systems
rt. . . . . right
RUE . . . . right upper extremity
RUQ . . . . right upper quadrant
Rx . . . . take, treatment

S

$\bar{s}$, s . . . . without (sine)
Sa. . . . . saline
Sc . . . . scapula
sens. . . . . sensory, sensation
serol. . . . . serology
SF . . . . salt free
SH . . . . social history
sibs. . . . . siblings
sig. . . . . take (on prescription)
skel . . . . skeletal
sl. . . . . slight, slightly
SLB . . . . short leg brace
SLWC . . . . short leg walking cast
SNF . . . . skilled nursing facility
SOB . . . . shortness of breath
sol. . . . . solution
S.O.S. . . . . when necessary
sp. . . . . spine, spinal
sp. cd. . . . . spinal cord
sp. fl. . . . . spinal fluid
S/P . . . . status post
spec. . . . . specimen
sp.gr., sp. grav . . . . specific gravity
spon. . . . . spontaneous
ss . . . . half, one-half
ST . . . . speech therapy
staph . . . . staphylococcus
stat . . . . immediately
stom. . . . . stomach
strep . . . . streptococcus
subq . . . . subcutaneous
sup. . . . . superior
surg . . . . surgical, surgery
sys. . . . . system

Table 2–1
(continued)

T	
T.	temperature
T&A	tonsillectomy and adenoidectomy
tab	tablet
talc	talcum
TB	tuberculosis
tbsp	tablespoon
temp	temperature
TIA	transient ischemic attack
t.i.d.	three times a day
TLC	tender loving care
TPR	temperature, pulse, and respirations
trach.	tracheal
tsp	tablespoon
tx	traction
U	
u	unit
u/a	urinalysis
uln	ulnar
ung	ointment
upper GI	upper gastrointestinal
u/o	under observation
u/o	urinary output
URI	upper respiratory infection
urol	urology
UTI	urinary tract infection
V	
vag.	vagina or vaginal
VD	venereal disease
vent.	ventral
VNA	Visiting Nurses' Association
vol.	volume
VO	vocal order
VS	vital signs
W	
WB	weight bearing
WBC	white blood count or cells
w/c, wh.ch.	wheelchair
W&D, W/D	warm and dry
w.d.w.n.	well developed, well nourished
wk.	week

w.f., WF .... white female
w.m., WM .... white male
WNL .... within normal limits
wt. .... weight

XYZ
X, x .... times
xs .... excess, excessive
yrs. .... years
YO .... years old
= .... equals

§ 2.72 —Preparing Side-by-Side Reference Translations

The translation will be much easier for the attorney to read and use effectively if it is on the same page with the medical record to which it corresponds. Use the following method to prepare a reference copy of translated medical records for the attorney to use in preparing the medical witnesses or for use at trial.

Make a reduced-size copy of the medical record, turning it sideways on a standard letter-sized sheet. The reduced medical record will cover only one-half of the sheet. In the remaining space, write or type in the deciphered version of the record. Space the translated text in approximately the same format it appears on the original record to make it easy for the attorney to keep his or her place when referring back and forth. Use a highlighter pen to mark any significant portions of the record. This method of preparing translated medical records also leaves plenty of space for any notations or questions the attorney may want to add regarding specific points to cover within the medical records.

§ 2.73 —Admissibility of Hospital Records

Hospital records are generally classified as "business records" under Federal Rule of Evidence 803(6). In order for hospital records to be properly admitted into evidence, they must be authenticated by the records custodian of the hospital or medical care institution. This means that you have to subpoena the hospital's records custodian or librarian to testify in court regarding the authenticity of the records. However, the rules in some states provide for a simplified procedure to qualify hospital records which eliminates the need to call the records custodian as a witness. This procedure involves the preparation and signing of an affidavit by the records custodian certifying the hospital records.

The following sample form complies with Ohio Revised Code § 2317.422. Check your local rules for the exact requirements in your state.

Most hospitals routinely certify copies of a patient's medical records, but some do not unless specifically requested to do so. To avoid delay at trial time, always request a certification affidavit (preferably typed on the hospital's letterhead stationery) from the hospital at the time you order a client's medical records. Preserve the original certification affidavit in a clear plastic page protector to prevent loss or damage and so it will be readily available at trial.

It is possible to have a set of hospital records certified long after they were originally produced, but it is a lot of trouble and there may be an additional charge. You must hand deliver the records to the hospital's records custodian, who will compare the copies with the original records. If the records are voluminous, it may take several days for the records custodian to verify the records. The records custodian must then prepare and sign the certification affidavit.

You must notify opposing counsel of your intention to use the records and the certification affidavit, and deliver a copy of the records to opposing counsel a certain number of days before the trial. (The exact number of days varies from state to state. Check your state and local rules to determine the requirements in your area.) This should not be a problem in most cases because you will have already produced the records to opposing counsel during the discovery phase of the case.

§ 2.74 —Elements of the Certification Affidavit

The following list indicates the necessary elements which should generally be included in a standard certification affidavit for hospital records. See **Form 2–25** for an example of a certification affidavit.

1. The name and title of the person who made the copies or under whose supervision the copies of the records were made.
2. The notarized signature of the person identified in Item #1, above.
3. Identification of the specific patient to whom the records pertain.
4. Identification of the dates covered by the hospital records.
5. Statement that the subject records are a complete and accurate record of the subject hospital admission.
6. Statement that the records were prepared in the usual course of business of the institution at or near the time the recorded events took place.
7. Statement of the manner in which the copies were made.

FORM 2–25
SAMPLE CERTIFICATION AFFIDAVIT
FOR HOSPITAL RECORDS

A F F I D A V I T
CERTIFICATION OF HOSPITAL RECORDS
(Pursuant to Ohio Revised Code Section 2317.422)

STATE OF OHIO, _________ COUNTY, SS:

BEFORE ME, a Notary Public, in and for said County and State, personally appeared _________, who, being duly sworn, deposed and said that he/she is _________ at _________, and that as such, he/she is the Official Custodian of all of the Medical Records therein. Affiant said further that the accompanying photostatic copies of the medical records of _________ are true copies, prepared under his/her supervision from the original medical records, which were made and maintained in the normal course of business by persons authorized by the hospital to do so, and contemporaneously with the events reported therein. Affiant said further that such records form a complete and accurate record of the hospitalization(s) of said patient for the following periods:

Admitted	Discharged

with no exceptions other than noted above. Further, Affiant said naught.

Signature: ______________________________
Title: ______________________________

SWORN TO BEFORE ME AND SIGNED IN MY PRESENCE THIS _____ DAY OF ___________, 19___.

____
Notary Public

§ 2.75 Indexing Effectively for Trial

Trial work requires controlling and managing massive amounts of information, most of which is found on documents and papers. Even with advances in automation technology, our primary means of exchanging information is on paper. For a trial paralegal, "control" means logical organization of and ready access to the vital materials and files in the case. Any handbook or manual about organizing cases for trial (including this book) includes numerous references to indexing. The ability to index file materials effectively is perhaps the most important single skill a trial paralegal needs because proper indexing results in **control** over the case information.

Indexing information involves arranging random materials into a specific order, documenting that order, and keeping the materials in order. To understand the process of indexing, you must first understand WHY you need an index. An effective index is a reference tool that helps you to do the following:

- See at a glance how the materials are organized
- Locate any individual item in the materials quickly
- Document the addition of new materials to the system
- Easily compare the item descriptions to determine common elements among the items
- Create subsets and supplementary lists based upon relationships among various types of materials
- Refile the materials easily.

§ 2.76 Understanding the Mechanics of Indexing

Think about how you actually use an index. You read a list to select the item you want, find the reference number that has been assigned to the item, then locate the corresponding tag, tab, or label on the item itself. If your index is on a computerized system, you may use a search command to locate the desired item and reference code, but otherwise the process is the same for both manual and computerized indexes (see **§ 8.19**). But how do you go about preparing an index? There is no single best way to index, but the following steps will help you get started on any indexing project involving trial files.

1. List the items.

A common synonym for "index" is "list." In the context of trial work, an index is essentially an enhanced list. The first step in indexing is to survey the materials and LIST them, formulating a brief description of each item. The amount of detail you include in the description will depend on the nature of the materials and the intended use for the index. (See the following discussion of descriptive elements in an index.)

2. Assign a reference code to each item on the list.

This reference is usually a number, but it could also be a letter or other alphanumeric code. See **§ 2.80** on numbering techniques. Each item on the list is given a unique reference that becomes its "address," indicating to the user of the index where a specific listed item may be located within a logical sequence of related items.

3. Label the items.

Affix a tag, tab, or label containing the reference code corresponding to the individual listed items (see § **2.92**).

See § **2.34** for a 10-step procedure to indexing trial file materials; see also §§ **5.58–5.74** on preparing exhibits for trial.

§ 2.77 —Planning the Components of the Index

Indexing is a means of describing diverse items of material or information in an abbreviated format, usually arranged into orderly columns and rows. The very simplest type of index contains only two basic columns of information: 1) an item reference number, and 2) a description of each item. More complex indexes contain these same elements, but the information comprising the description is more detailed, and is usually structured into additional data columns. The end result of this type of index is actually a grid composed of rows and columns. The rows are the listed items and the columns designate various discrete pieces of data relative to each item. The number of data columns is generally indicative of the index's complexity and level of detail.

Because we read from left to right, the reference number or code is usually located in the first or left-hand column of the index page. Alternatively, the reference code may be the last or right-hand column, such as in a table of contents where the page number is the reference.

Item descriptions on the index may be either freeform and very brief or more structured and detailed. Designing an index format requires deciding what information to record about the items. It is important to include enough significant detail in the descriptive elements to enable you to identify and distinguish between similar materials. The exact data elements will vary, depending on the specific requirements of the project and the materials.

Trial file indexes often include the following data elements:

1. Date—This may be complete dates (month, day, and year) or partial dates (month and year or year only).
2. Type or Category—This is usually included in indexes when different kinds of documents are mixed together in a set.
3. Source—This is used when it is important to know the origin of a document.
4. Person—This may designate the witness who will testify about a particular document or it may be another name that is significant in

connection with the item, for example, the author or recipient of a piece of correspondence.

5. Subject, Topic, or Issue—This can be used in a variety of ways depending on the complexity of the case.
6. Miscellaneous—It is a good idea to leave an extra column for remarks, comments, or other significant information that does not fit into any of the structured columns.

§ 2.78 —Cross-Referencing

The type of descriptive index discussed above involves the imposition of an arbitrary numerical (or other reference coding) arrangement upon the listed items as an aid to locating the actual materials within the file. Depending on the needs of your case, you may find it useful to prepare one or more cross-reference indexes for your trial materials. A cross-reference index uses the same information as the main index, but arranges the data in a different order, such as, alphabetically or chronologically as opposed to numerically. This assists you in viewing the information from more than one perspective and in locating the materials more easily. See also § **6.79,** Tracking and Cross-Referencing the Opponent's Exhibits.

§ 2.79 —Other Considerations in Indexing

The following is a list of some other suggestions for indexing effectively.

- Set up the columns in the descriptive portion of an index to fit the data elements that occur *most frequently* in the documents or materials. The column headings define common elements among the items on the list. Arrange them left to right, starting with the most general information and progressing to the most specific.
- Indexes that require only a few basic data elements can accommodate wider spaces for each column across the page.
- Use forms to collect index data in an orderly fashion. See § **2.33** *et seq.* for various model log and index forms to control different types of information.
- Allow for expansion and additions to the indexed materials. It is important to keep the index up to date as materials are added to the file. The usefulness of an index is limited if it reflects only part of the file's contents.
- Some indexing projects require totally revamping a referencing system, but if the materials already have numbers or other reference designations

you may not have to start from the very beginning. See if you can arrange the materials in some logical order and build the index from that point.

- If you have access to computer equipment and programs, learn to use their powerful indexing capabilities to update and maintain your indexes. See **Chapter 8** on using computers in trial work.

§ 2.80 Numbering Documents

Document numbering is the first and least expensive step toward gaining control of the information in any set of documents. A sequential numbering stamp, or "Bates" stamp, is a convenient tool to have for applying document index numbers, but it is not essential in cases with fewer than 100 documents. If you do not have a sequential stamp, or if your stamp makes a poor imprint, it is better to use neatly handwritten numbered labels. Label stock comes in a wide variety of shapes and sizes to accommodate almost any indexing job. Labels are inexpensive and readily available from any office supply store. You can get removable labels if the attorney is reluctant to put a permanent label on original documents.

If you decide to use handwritten labels, write the numbers in sequence on the label sheets and make up several sheets at one time. Let the ink dry for a few minutes so that the numbers will not smear, then peel the labels away from the backing sheet and affix them to the individual documents. This helps to ensure that you do not miss any numbers, and you will always know exactly the last number you used. Be sure to use a bold marker pen that is compatible with your label stock and in a color (black or dark blue) that will copy well. Red ink numbers will stand out nicely on the originals, but many copiers will not pick up a red number. If you have any doubts about whether your pen will copy well, experiment with a couple of scrap documents to make sure the numbers will show up when the document is copied.

Traditional methods of applying document control numbers (such as the sequential Bates stamp and handwritten labels described above) may not be feasible in a case involving large numbers of documents. A simple and neat way to number documents is by using preprinted self-adhesive number labels. Several companies can supply these labels (see resource list, § **2.95**), that come in self-adhesive sheets or rolls. The labels are inexpensive (starting at about $10.00 per 1000) and can be printed in any series or with any prefix letters or customized text the case or the court requires. Numbering labels are available in both permanent and removable styles. You can also create computer-generated sequential numerical labels with label software on your own computer. You may want to take advantage of this capability if it is available in your office. See **Chapter 8** on using computers in trial work.

Preprinted labels are nice for a document numbering project because they make a crisp clean number on the document that comes through clearly when the documents are photocopied. Some companies can provide labels printed on a clear backing so that the number label doesn't cover up any printing on the document. Label sheets make it easy to keep track of where the numbering stopped, which number series have been assigned to various sets of source documents, and which numbers have and have not been used.

§ 2.81 —Document Numbering Techniques

These tips apply to manual numbering systems in small to medium sized in-house document cases.

1. Number ORIGINAL documents *before* you make copies. Note: Some attorneys do not agree with the idea of marking the originals. If your attorney is hesitant about stamping a number on an original document, use removable labels for numerical indexing.
2. Stamp the number in the margin at the bottom right corner of the document, perpendicular to the bottom of the page. This placement has two advantages:

- Document numbers are easy to spot when the documents are placed sideways in file folders or jackets.
- The document number clearly stands out as an index number and is not likely to be mistaken for part of the original document.
- You may choose a different placement for the index number, such as the upper right corner or lower left corner of the page. This is fine, as long as you are consistent.

3. Take care not to stamp over any wording or numbers on the document, but do not place the stamped number so close to the edge of the document that it is likely to be cut off when the document is copied.
4. Keep the felt pad of the number stamp well-inked (use black or blue ink) and make sure the numbers are very clear. This is important because the documents may be copied many times. If you have never used a sequential stamp, practice a few times on some scrap paper until you get a feel for how much pressure you have to apply to get a sharp, clear impression. For the clearest imprint on single documents, try placing a tablet or legal pad under the document for "padding."
5. Number every page that contains information. If there are any double-sided documents, number both the front and the back of each double-sided page. (See below for some ideas on alternative numbering schemes.)

6. For numbering purposes, it is usually best to leave the documents in the original order in which you found them in the files, and be sure to return them to their original folders or jackets after stamping the index number.
7. If your documents include any that are on a dark background (for example, microfilm copies of old deeds) or documents (such as photographs) that are printed on glossy paper, the number stamp ink is likely to run or smear. To avoid this problem, stamp the number onto a small white self-adhesive label and attach it to the document. This will ensure that the document number stands out clearly when the document is copied.
8. Keep some paper towels or napkins handy so you can wipe up quickly if the number stamp ink gets on your fingers or your desk. Be very careful not to get the ink on your clothes, because it stains permanently. (Roll up your sleeves!)

§ 2.82 —Alternative Numbering Schemes

In most instances, the best method for thorough document indexing is to number every page of every document, including both sides of double-sided pages. However, this can become quite cumbersome if your originals include many multiple-page or bound documents, such as books, lengthy contracts, or insurance policies. In this case, when the entire document will generally be considered as a whole, you may decide it is more efficient to simply give the large document a single document number, and then indicate on your index the total number of pages included in the document.

A variation on this method is to number only the first page of each document, then use 16A, 16B, 16C, and so forth, for subsequent pages of multiple-page documents, where the contents of individual pages are important. This approach has limited application, however, because if the document is more than 26 pages long, you have to start using 16AA on the 27th page, 16BB on the 28th page, and so on. This can quickly become quite cumbersome and confusing.

Another possibility for multipage documents is to use a single document number and then indicate subsequent pages with decimals (for example, 16.1, 16.2, 16.3, etc.) or hyphens (for example, 16-1, 16-2, 16-3, and so forth).

§ 2.83 —Subject or Source Numerical Coding

When your case involves documents that come from a number of different sources, you can devise a numbering system that automatically incorporates a source "code" prefix into the document index number. To do this, assign a specific series of numbers to each source. For example:

Document Numbers	Source
1000–1999	First Good Deal Banking Co.
2000–2999	Campground Management, Inc.
3000–3999	Smith & Jones Lumber Company
4000–4999	Landscaping Associates

This method takes a little advance planning, but the result is that even if the documents get mixed up later in the case (or at trial), you can quickly determine which source produced the document. In the above example, if you have a document bearing the index number "3028," you can instantly tell that the document was produced by Smith & Jones Lumber Company.

If it makes more sense for the documents in your case to be grouped by subject matter, issue, or type of document rather than according to the document source, you can adapt this technique to incorporate a "subject," "issue," or "type" code. You must first review and sort the documents into categories, and then assign a series of numbers to each type or subject. For example:

Document Numbers	Document Types
1000–1999	Contracts
2000–2999	Letters and Correspondence
3000–3999	Sales and Publicity Brochures
4000–4999	Technical Specifications
5000–5999	Financial Statements & Tax Returns

Document Numbers	Issues or Subjects
1000–1999	Illegal Sales Activity by F. Samuels
2000–2999	Transactions re sales of products
3000–3999	Sales Districts & Customer Lists
4000–4999	Sales Training materials

In order to successfully use this type of numerical coding, you must make a key or master list to keep track of which number series you have assigned, and then be consistent when you add new documents to the indexing system.

§ 2.84 —Planning a Document Numbering Project

When you begin a document-numbering project, determine the following information:

1. Estimate the total ("ballpark") number of documents to decide how many digits to allow in the index number. If an automated system will be used,

remember to use initial zeros so that the computer sort function will work properly (001, 002, 003). See **Chapter 8** on using computers.

2. Find out whether you have all the documents at the outset, or if additional documents will be added to the system.
3. How many types of documents are there? How many sources for documents will there be?
4. Determine whether the documents are presorted, and if so, according to what criteria.
5. Have the documents been screened to remove privileged documents? Are the privileged documents going to be numbered?
6. Are duplicates to be eliminated at the beginning? It may not be possible to weed out all the duplicates until all the documents are indexed. It can sometimes be significant to the case that a duplicate of a certain letter was in more than one person's files.
7. How far has the case progressed? Time limitations may determine how detailed the document numbering and indexing systems will be.
8. Do any documents from other sources already have index numbers? If so, can you build on the existing numbering system, or do you need a separate one?
9. What equipment and personnel are available to work on the project?

§ 2.85 Using Color-Coding to Organize for Trial

During the hectic pace of trial days, it helps to have your files and materials organized so that you can retrieve and refile materials quickly. Color-coding your files and materials can help you get organized and stay organized under pressure.

Developing a color-coding system is a highly subjective process that calls for a somewhat creative approach to file organization. There is no single correct method. There are as many different ways to color-code as there are people, cases, and projects. Color-coding can be used in a variety of imaginative ways, ranging from very simple to quite complex. The size and complexity of the project will determine how complicated the color-coding system needs to be. The key to successfully color-coding any project is setting up a system and then sticking with it as new materials are added to the file. You have to be consistent!

A comprehensive color-coding system for case files and materials is most effective when it is begun early in the file development and carried throughout the life of the case. Color-coding as a last-minute project is less effective, but it can still be put to good use in organizing specific trial files.

§ 2.86 —Benefits of Color-Coding

The following are the benefits of color-coding:

- After the eye and mind are trained in the color system, there is instant recognition of type of material by color, resulting in shortened retrieval time.
- A color-coded system ensures consistency in filing materials by type or subject.
- Color-coding can be quite inexpensive, especially if you use supplies you already have in stock. (If you do have the budget to special order supplies, color-coding still results in saved time and effort.)
- Color-coding helps to avoid misfiling and mistakes. It has the added benefit of making it easier for someone else to help you with filing tasks.
- Color-coding simplifies filing chores so you are not as likely to procrastinate about doing them.
- Color-coded filing has beneficial psychological effects:

  —Colored files look nice and they are cheerful.

  —Color-coding makes your files appear to be organized.

  —Color-coded filing raises spirits. (Manila is boring, and there is always so much of it in law offices!)
- A well-organized color-coding system becomes "insider" information to the trial team during trial, allowing team members to locate the desired materials quickly and easily.

§ 2.87 —Problems with Color-Coding

The following are the problems with color-coding:

- Setting up a color-coding system requires an initial investment in planning time and effort. You have to give the project some thought and plan a system tailored to the needs of the particular case.
- Color-coding cannot really be done properly if time is very limited. It has only limited effectiveness as a last-minute project.
- One person must be in charge of assigning colors and subject areas and adding to the coding key.
- Too many colors can become confusing and defeat the organizational purposes of the original system.
- The person who sets up the color-coding system will have to train the trial attorney and other individuals to use the system. This person will probably have to remind and encourage people to stick with the system as well.

- A member of the trial team who suffers from color blindness may have difficulty using an index or filing system based on color-coding.

§ 2.88 —Designing a Color-Coding System

The principal behind color-coding is simple: You assign a particular color to represent each subject, type of material, or main division in your file. You then use that color for labels, folders, notebooks, and so forth to instantly designate the subject or type of material represented. Use the following list as a guide to designing a color-coding system.

1. Survey your file to determine what kind of materials you have and how to logically group them into divisions. See § **2.33** *et seq.* on organizing file materials; see especially § **2.42.**
2. Consider what filing and labeling supplies are needed for your materials, what is readily available (in stock) in your office, and what supplemental new supplies you can order or purchase for your system.
3. Determine what colors are available, either in stock or readily obtainable (see #2 above).
4. Decide which color to use for each division. Allow for expansion or adding materials to the system.
5. Develop a key to the color-coding system.
6. Use the system consistently.

Considerations in Assigning Colors

1. Check with the supervising attorney and his or her secretary to see if there are any existing preferences for color labeling. The secretary may have already worked out a preliminary color-coding system for preparing file labels in the past. It may be possible to build on the existing system.
2. Use highly contrasting colors for adverse or opposites, similar tones for like or related materials. For example, in a case with one plaintiff and one defendant, the color-code plan can be fairly simple (such as blue for plaintiff, yellow for defendant). In a case with multiple defendants, assign each defendant a separate, but related, color (such as yellow, orange, and brown).
3. Use a basic or neutral color (such as blue or black) for your standard files or for the type of material that comprises the largest division in your file. Do not assign a hard to find color such as pink or lime green to a division that has massive amounts of material. The supplies may be difficult to get and the cumulative effect will be blinding!

4. Save red, orange, or pink for "hot" items, that is, urgent, high-priority, or high-activity materials.
5. Be consistent. Use the same color for all folders, labels, containers, and notebooks for a particular kind of material. For example, if a case involves medical issues, use one color to designate all hospital and medical records, doctor's reports, and so forth.

§ 2.89 —Color-Coding Supplies

A large variety of colored labels, stickers, paper, file folders, and notebooks is available. Check your office supply catalog for dozens of ideas for labeling, filing, and indexing supplies. As in other areas of trial preparation, the supplies you use for color-coding projects can be elaborate or very simple, costly or very inexpensive. The supplies and techniques you use will depend on your budget and access to supplies.

- Use colored pens or highlighters in coordinating colors to color-code plain white stock. (Inexpensive tip)
- File folder labels come in a wide variety of colors, either the whole label is colored or a strip at the top of the label is colored and the remainder is white. Use colored labels to color-code standard manila folders.
- File folders themselves come in numerous bright, distinct colors.
- Three-ring notebook dividers are available with colored tabs or clear tabs with colored inserts.
- Preprinted self-adhesive color-code numbers and letters are sold in rolls, strips, or sheets.
- Use signal dots and shapes to color-code existing manila folders or individual documents.

§ 2.90 —Developing a Key to the Color-Coding Scheme

The color-coding key is a simple index indicating what file divisions the colors represent. If you use more than three colors, you need to make a key. Make several copies of the key. Put one near the front of your master trial notebook. Post copies of the key in conspicuous places near the file materials so people using the files can learn the color system. If you expand the system and add colors during the development of the file, be sure to make the corresponding additions to all copies of the key. Make sure your secretary understands the color-coding system and has a copy of the color-coding key.

§ 2.91 —Simple Ways to Use Color-Coding

The following list contains examples of simple uses of color-coding.

1. Marking depositions:

- Highlight or underline portions of deposition transcripts to be read into the record. See § **2.16** *et seq.*, on federal court's instructions for marking deposition transcripts for trial.
- Mark depositions for reference using a different color for each issue or subject.

2. Use colored underlining to designate between different drafts (additions and deletions) of a document.

3. Switch colors when taking notes at trial to designate switch in speaker or subject. Use red or another contrasting color to emphasize key points. See § **6.53** *et seq.* on taking notes.

4. Exhibit notebooks, especially if numerous exhibits and witnesses have to switch back and forth. Use different colors for plaintiff and defendant to make the notebooks easier to tell apart. Standard black notebooks all tend to look the same. See § **5.74** on assembling exhibit notebooks.

5. Attorney's trial notebook. Use colored divider tabs or colored paper to designate various sections of the notebook. See § **5.77** *et seq.*

6. Use a different color of marker for each witness who adds or marks something on a diagram or map at trial. See §§ **4.47–4.48** on "interactive" testimony.

7. Save time by highlighting issues as you read.

8. Put special documents in colored folders to designate them as originals. See § **2.60** on preserving original documents.

9. Use contrasting colors for plaintiff and defendant exhibit stickers (see § **5.63**).

§ 2.92 Labeling and Tabbing

Labeling is an integral part of proper indexing. Labeling is what makes indexing work. An index shows the overall organization of the materials and the reference code or number corresponding to each item, but indexes are not very helpful in locating materials unless the individual items are clearly marked with corresponding labels or tabs to physically identify them. Accurate labeling allows ready identification and easy access to a specific portion of case materials. Whether they are in files, notebooks, drawers, or boxes, clearly labeled materials are more likely to be refiled in the proper place.

Many types of labels and tabs suitable for trial file indexing are available. Most brands of labels and tabs now come in self-adhesive strips or sheets.

- Most tabs and labels are meant to be permanent, but some styles are removable. Make sure you have the correct product for your indexing needs.
- Use the best labeling and tabbing supplies you can afford.
- Indexing tabs must be able to withstand constant handling. Tabs should extend beyond the edge of the standard 8 1/2-by-11 inch paper and be reinforced or coated for strength and durability.

I make extensive use of preprinted Tabbies™ for my trial file indexing. These durable plastic-coated tabs are printed on both front and back, and they are suitable for either side-tab or bottom-tab indexes. The sticky side of each tab bears position markings to ensure accurate edge placement. These useful little tabs come in standard numeric sheets (1-10, 11-20, 21-30, and so forth) and alphabetic sheets, as well as month names and type-on or write-on blanks. You can also have them custom-printed to your specifications.

Tabbies™
Division of Xertrex International, Inc.
1530 W. Glenlake Avenue
Itasca, IL 60143
(312) 773-4160
1-800-822-2437

Ideas for Index Tabbing Supplies

Preprinted Tabbed Divider Sheets
Advantages:

- Durable coated reinforced tabs
- Good for looseleaf notebooks
- Available in standard numeric or alphabetic formats
- Reusable

Disadvantages:

- Tab is not attached directly to the document
- Extra divider pages add extra bulk
- Some waste involved with broken sets

Divider Sheets with Insert Tabs

- Good for looseleaf notebooks
- Durable plastic-reinforced tabs and punched edges
- Easily customized by using insert cards
- Reusable by replacing insert cards
- Easily color-coded by using colored inserts

"Canvas" Write-on Edge Tabs

- Inexpensive and flexible
- Attach directly to documents
- Not self-adhesive
- Glue may yellow and brittle with age

§ 2.93 —Labeling Trial Materials and Equipment

One of your principal duties during the trial will be keeping track of all the case materials and equipment. It is prudent to affix some type of identification label to every item that is taken outside your office during the trial. In addition to the actual case files and documents, you may be responsible for other items of trial "gear" such as

- Trial briefcases
- Easels and flip-chart pads
- Projector and screen
- VCR and television monitor
- Pointer
- Oversized charts and boards
- Portfolio
- Boxes of documents and exhibits

Permanently mark and identify your firm's trial equipment so that if an item should become separated from your other materials, the court personnel will know to whom it belongs. If the equipment (such as an overhead projector) is borrowed or rented, use a removable label so you can take it off before you return the equipment to its owner.

I have assisted in cases in which we had to change from one courtroom to another several times during the course of the trial. In one such case, we had a number of large charts, three display easels, a vinyl portfolio, several boxes of exhibit documents, and several notebooks of deposition materials, and it was my responsibility to see that everything was successfully moved to the new courtroom. After we were settled in the new courtroom I realized that one of my easels was missing, so I went back to the first courtroom to look for it. The court bailiff had discovered the easel I had inadvertently left behind, but because it was labeled with our firm name, he was holding it for safekeeping in his office. He said he would have called our office if we had not come back to claim the easel before the end of the trial. Labeling your equipment can help prevent loss, theft, and inadvertent misplacement at the courthouse. It is also a good idea to prepare an inventory of the equipment you take to the courtroom so that you can make sure you have everything back in its proper place at the end of the trial. See also § **4.63** on monitoring trial equipment.

§ 2.94 —Labeling Ideas

These are some suggestions and ideas for simple ways to label your equipment and materials for trial.

1. Label both the fronts and backs of file folders (for example, deposition folders, witness preparation files) to make it easier to grab the right folder out of a briefcase, box, or drawer.
2. Some files and folders get pretty rough handling, especially those requiring long-term storage during the life of the case. Self-adhesive folder and file labels tend to become brittle and fall off after a couple of years. To reinforce and protect your labels, use self-adhesive clear plastic label protectors. These not only protect your file labels from dirt and damage, they also give your files a glossy, almost "laminated" look that is very neat and attractive.
3. Have your secretary type up a batch of self-adhesive labels containing the specific case identification, the firm name or the trial attorney's name, and the office telephone number. Attach one of these labels to each piece of equipment you take to trial. If something does get lost, it will be easy for the finder to let you know so you can arrange to retrieve it.
4. In a very large case if the budget allows the expenditure, consider having a quantity of identification labels printed just for use in that case.
5. Tape a case identification label to the back of exhibit charts or visual aids that must be stored with the court reporter or elsewhere at the courthouse during the trial. This will help the court personnel determine to which case the exhibits belong.

6. Any label—even a handwritten one—is better than no label; you don't have to use elaborate printed or typed labels, especially if you are in a hurry or on the run at the courthouse without access to a typewriter or a secretary. Do not leave a piece of equipment unlabeled because you do not have a typed label. Simply print your company's name and telephone number on a piece of paper and tape it to the exhibit or piece of equipment. Or, use a broad-tipped marker and write the information directly onto the back of an exhibit board or onto the end of a box of materials. Do try to write or print as neatly as you can in the interest of preserving a professional appearance.
7. An easy and inexpensive labeling idea is to tape your business card to the back of an exhibit board, to the top and side of the box, or to the bottom of a piece of equipment.
8. Label both the ends and the lids of corrugated cardboard transfer boxes. This makes it easy to identify the box you want from any angle and helps you replace the lids on the correct boxes.
9. To identify your trial briefcases, attach an inexpensive vinyl luggage tag (available in most office supply stores) to the handle of each briefcase. Insert either a business card or a typed label behind the clear window in the tag. If you have several briefcases that all look alike, you may also want to indicate a number on the inside flap or on the tag for each case.
10. Invest in a label-maker machine (such as Click-Tape™, by Dymo Labelmaker) that embosses letters onto a strip of self-adhesive plastic tape, which can then be affixed to almost any surface. The plastic tapes come in a variety of colors, so you could even use a color-coded system. See § **2.85** on color-coding.
11. Use a rubber stamp with the firm name and telephone number to make instant labels or stamp directly onto the back of charts and boards.
12. For expensive equipment like projectors and VCR equipment, attach permanent plastic identification labels or metal nameplates imprinted with the firm's name and telephone number. These labels can be special ordered from industrial supply or office supply companies. One supplier is:

Seton Name Plate Company	Phone:	203-488-8059
P.O. Box RB-1331	Sales:	800-243-6624
New Haven, CN 06505-9970	FAX:	800-345-7819

13. Another way to identify valuable equipment is to use a hand-held electric engraving tool (also available from Seton) that permanently marks metal, wood, plastic, and ceramic.

§ 2.95 Products and Suppliers Resource List

This section contains a listing of sources for various types of office and litigation-related products and supplies. Use this list as a starting point for collecting data on the supplies and products you need in your work. You will find other sources to add to these. Many sources on the list were culled from resource files and periodicals; others were discovered through valuable "junk" mail. Their inclusion on this list does not constitute an endorsement from the author or the publisher as to the products and services represented. These companies will be glad to send you information about their products upon request. Write or call them and ask for their catalogs or product brochures.

ABBOT OFFICE SYSTEMS
Asbury Avenue
Farmingdale, NJ 07727
800/631-2233 or 201/938-6000
- Scheduling kits, boards, project systems

AFAB Computer Solutions
19020 North 73rd Lane
Glendale, AZ 85308
602/561-8447
- Bates numbering software

ALL-STATE LEGAL SUPPLY CO.
One Commerce Drive
Cranford, NJ 07016
800/222-0510 or 201/272-0800 or 609/921-0104
- Legal forms, supplies, and tickler systems

AMERICAN COMPUTER SUPPLY
2828 Forest Lane
Dallas, TX 75234
800/527-0832
- Computer supplies and accessories

AMERICAN NATIONAL STANDARDS INSTITUTE (ANSI)
1430 Broadway
New York, NY 10018
- Consumer and technical information

ANATOMICAL CHART CO.
8221 Kimball Avenue
Skokie, IL 60076
800/621-7500
In IL Call Collect: 708/679-4700
FAX: 708/674-0211
- Medical models and charts; free 248-page general catalog

ANATOMY SYSTEMS
1009 Duke Street
Alexandria, VA 22314
703/739-0400
- Custom medical models, illustrations, and diagrams

ANCOM BUSINESS SYSTEMS
Brunswick, OH
800/845-8261
- Color-coded tabs and labels

ASSOCIATED BAG COMPANY
400 West Boden Street
Milwaukee, WI 53207-7120
800/926-6100
FAX: 800/926-4610
- Vinyl and poly organizers and document protectors; envelopes; shipping and packaging products

ASSOCIATION OF MEDICAL ILLUSTRATORS
1819 Peachtree Street N.E.
Suite 560
Atlanta, GA 30309
404/350-7900
- Information on certified medical illustrators

ASSOCIATION OF RECORDS MANAGERS AND ADMINISTRATORS (ARMA)
4200 Somerset Drive
Suite 2145
Prairie Village, KS 66208
800/422-2762 or 913/341-3808
- Catalog of publications available

AT-A-GLANCE
101 O'Neil Road
Sidney, NY 13838
607/563-9411
- Time management tools; calendars and organizers

AVERY COMMERCIAL PRODUCTS
808 Oak Park Road
Covina, CA 91724
800/541-5507
- Filing, indexing, and labeling supplies

BATES MANUFACTURING COMPANY
Hackettstown, NJ 07845
800/22BATES or 201/852-9300
FAX: 201/852-7837
- Bates automatic numbering machines and supplies

BAUMGARTEN'S
544 Armour Circle
Atlanta, GA 30324
800/247-KLIP
or in GA: 404/874-7675
- Binder clips, prongs, and fasteners

BELL & HOWELL CO.
2202 N. Irving Street
Allentown, PA 18103-9554
- Bar-coding equipment

BIBBERO SYSTEMS, INC.
1300 N. McDowell Blvd.
Petaluma, CA 94954-1180
800/358-8240
or in CA: 800/BIBBERO
FAX: 707/778-0824
- Legal file organizing systems, dividers, folders, tabs, labels, and accessories

BIGELOW RESOURCES INC.
216 First Avenue South
Suite 320
P.O. Box 4266
Seattle, WA 98104
206/682-2059
- Custom-printed litigation labels and stickers

BINDERTEK
P.O. Box 806
2656 Bridgeway
Sausalito, CA 94966-0806
800/456-3453
FAX: 800/765-3299
- LawFiles Trial Notebooks; EuroFiles binder systems; indexing sets and systems

BIO-LEGAL ARTS
5520 E. Second St.
Suite E
Long Beach, CA 90803
800/544-7974 or 213/434-7491
FAX: 213/438-7949
- Medical and anatomical illustrations

BUSINESS & INSTITUTIONAL FURNITURE CO.
611 N. Broadway
Milwaukee, WI 53202
800/558-8662
- Office furniture and equipment

C-LINE PRODUCTS, INC.
1530 E. Birchwood Avenue
Des Plaines, IL 60018
800/999-6361
- Sheet protectors, project folders, report covers, overhead projection supplies

CADDYLAK SYSTEMS
510 Fillmore Avenue
Tonawanda, NY 14150
800/523-8060
FAX: 800/222-1934
- Time management forms; wall planning systems and scheduling charts; organizers; presentation products

CONLEY & HODGE ASSOCIATES, INC.
103 Broad Street
Boston, MA 02110
617/338-6292
- Document control number stickers

CONSUMER INFORMATION CATALOG
The Consumer Information Center
Pueblo, CO 81009
- Free consumer information (Write for catalog)

CONVOY, INC.
P.O. Box 8589
Canton, OH 44711
216/453-8163
FAX: 216/453-8181
- Heavy cardboard storage and filing boxes

CURTIS MANUFACTURING COMPANY, INC.
30 Fitzgerald Drive
Jaffrey, NH 03452
800/548-4900
or 603/532-4123 ext. 94
- Computer supplies and accessories

DAY RUNNER, INC.
3562 Eastham Drive
Culver City, CA 90232
800/232-9786 or 213/837-6900
- Notebook organizers and time planners

DAY-TIMERS, INC.
P.O. Box 2368
Allentown, PA 18001
215/395-5884
- Notebook organizers; time and work planners; time and project management tools

DELL DIRECT SALES
9505 Arboretum Boulevard
Austin, TX 78759-7299
800/568-3158
- IBM-compatible computer sales and leasing; hardware and software

DENNISON MANUFACTURING COMPANY
Framingham, MA 01701
800/DENNISON
- All sorts of labeling, indexing, and filing supplies

DEVOKE DATA PRODUCTS
P.O. Box 58051
Santa Clara, CA 95202-8051
408/980-1347
- Computer supplies, furniture, and accessories

DUO-TANG, INCORPORATED
800/852-0039, ext. 224
- Report and presentation covers

ESSELTE PENDAFLEX CORP.
Clinton Road
Garden City, NY 11530
516/741-3200
- Folders and filing supplies, equipment, and accessories

EXCELSIOR-LEGAL, INC.
Corporate Headquarters
62 White Street
New York, NY 10013
800/232-0411
- Legal exhibit tabs, indexes, and closing sets; specially printed index sets; litigation-related products

EXECUTIVE SCANCARD SYSTEM
The Executive Gallery, Inc.
380 Dublin Avenue
Columbus, OH 43215
800/447-5552 or 614/469-3100
- Appointment, time, and project card management tools and notebooks

FELLOWES MANUFACTURING CO.
1789 Norwood Ave.
Itasca, IL 60143
312/893-1600
- Filing and storage equipment and supplies

FILOFAX, INC.
500 West Avenue
Stamford, CT 06902-6325
800/345-6798 or 203/353-9777
- Date planners; information and project organizers

FRANKLIN DAY PLANNER
Franklin International Institute, Inc.
P.O. Box 25127
Salt Lake City, UT 84125-0127
800/654-1776 or 801/975-1776
- Date planner binders; information organizers

GBS FILING SYSTEMS
P.O. Box 308
Malvern, OH 44644
800/873-4427
- Filing products, color coding and bar coding supplies

GLOBAL COMPUTER SUPPLIES
2249 Windsor Ct., Dept.41
Addison, IL 60101
800/8GLOBAL or 800/845-6225
In IL: 708/627-8800
FAX: 708/627-1742
- Computer supplies, furniture, and accessories

GLOBAL BUSINESS FURNITURE
63 Hemlock Drive
Hempstead, NY 11550
800/645-1232
- Office furniture and equipment

HAMILTON SORTER CO., INC.
3158 Production Drive
P. O. Box 8
Fairfield, OH 45014
800/543-1605
or in OH: 513/870-4400
- Office furniture and equipment

IDL CORPORATION
730 Garden Street
Carlstadt, NJ 07072
201/933-5774
FAX: 201/933-3577
- Custom self-inking stamps

INMAC
2465 Augustine Drive
Santa Clara, CA 95054
800/547-5444 (Product hotline)
- Computer furniture, accessories, and supplies

INNOLOG, INC.
P.O. Box 93967
Los Angeles, CA 90093
213/851-6215
- Master binder clips

JETER SYSTEMS
1560 Firestone Parkway
Akron, OH 44301
800/321-8261
- Color-coded tabs and labels

KOH-I-NOR RAPIDOGRAPH, INC.
100 North Street
Bloomsbury, NJ 08804
201/479-4124
- Presentation graphics, overhead, and plotter supplies

LEGAL DIMENSIONS
P.O. Box 1132
Laguna Beach, CA 92652
800/535-7753
or in CA: 714/778-2460
- Trial notebook tabs and file organizers and supplies

LEGAL TABS CO.
Basalt, CO
800/322-3022
- Preprinted tabs and labels

LIGHT IMPRESSIONS
431 Monroe Avenue
Rochester, NY 14607-3717
800/828-6216
or in NY: 800/828-9629
- Storage for photographs, slides, and negatives

LITIGATION VISUALS, INC.
39 Essex Circle
Hudson, OH 44236
216/656-3810
- Custom charts and illustrations for all types of litigation

MAGNA VISUAL, INC.
9400 Watson Road
St. Louis, MO 63126
800/843-3399 or 314/843-9000
- Magnetic visual control boards and accessories

MARKHAM ANATOMICAL
211 Atlantic Street
P.O. Box 950
Stamford, CT 06901
800/242-2449
or in CT: 203/324-5959
FAX: 203/975-7748
- Medical models and charts; free catalog

MARUZEN INTERNATIONAL CO., LTD.
917D North Plum Brove Road
Schaumburg, IL 60173
708/697-4400
FAX: 708/697-4406
- Heavy duty holepunching equipment

MAX BUSINESS MACHINES CORP.
585 Commercial Avenue
Garden City, NY 11530
800/223-4293
or in NY: 516-222-2184
FAX: 516/222-1046
- Electronic lettering machines and systems

MEDICAL LEGAL ILLUSTRATIONS, INC.
1899 Powers Ferry Road, Suite 460
Marietta, GA 30067
800/338-5954 or 404/980-1899
FAX: 404/955-3088
- Medical-legal illustrations, animations and presentations

MEDICAL PLASTICS LABORATORY
Professional Health Educators
P. O. Box 38
Gatesville, TX 76528
800/433-5539
or in TX: 817/722-8525
FAX: 817/865-8011
- Medical models and charts; free catalog

MEMINDEX, INC.
149 Carter Street
Rochester, NY 14601
800/828-5885
or in NY: 716/342-7890
- Executive desk tools and accessories; planner guides

METALCRAFT
P.O. Box 1468
Mason City, Iowa 50401
800/437-4283 or 515/423-9460
- Nameplates and identification tags and labels

MICROCOMPUTER ACCESSORIES, INC.
P. O. Box 66911
Los Angeles, CA 90066-0911
800/521-8270
or in CA 213/301-9400
- Office and computer furniture, accessories, and supplies

MICRO WAREHOUSE
1720 Oak Street
P.O. Box 3014
Lakewood, NJ 08701-3014
800/367-7080
FAX: 908/905-5245
- Personal computer software, hardware, and peripherals

MISCO COMPUTER SUPPLIES AND ACCESSORIES
One MISCO Plaza
Holmdel, NJ 07733
800/US-MISCO
800/876-4726
or in NJ: 908/264-1000
FAX: 908/264-5955
- Computer products, furniture, accessories, and supplies

MOORE COMPUTER SUPPLIES & FORMS CATALOG
Moore Business Products Division
701 Woodlands Parkway
Vernon Hills, IL 60061
- Computer forms, supplies and accessories

MULTI-MEDIA EXHIBIT SYSTEMS
1603 Old York Road
Abington, PA 19001
800/33BOARD
- Reusable professional litigation exhibit boards and kits

MULTIPLEX DISPLAY FIXTURE COMPANY
1555 Larkin Williams Road
Fenton, MO 63026
- System 4000 slide cabinets

NATIONAL BUSINESS FURNITURE, INC.
222 E. Michigan Street
Milwaukee, WI 53202-9956
800/558-1010 in WI 800/242-0030
- Business and office furniture and supplies

NEUMADE PRODUCTS CORP.
P.O. Box 5001
Norwalk, CT 06856
203/866-7600
- Storage for photographs, slides, and negatives

NORWOOD PRODUCTS CO.
1012-N Thompson Lane
Nashville, TN 37211-2627
- Memogenda and Zipagenda project tracking organizer systems

OBLIQUE FILING SYSTEMS
P.O. Box 5735
Columbia, SC 29250
800/845-7068
- Filing and indexing equipment

PERSONAL RESOURCE SYSTEMS, INC.
P.O. Box 2529
Del Mar, CA 92014
800/542-8488
or in CA: 800/255-9018
- Notebook organizer systems

PLANIT BOARD SYSTEMS, INC.
515 S. 25th Street
Colorado Springs, CO 80904
800/222-7539
- Dry marker boards and charts

PLANNER PADS®, INC.
5088 S. 107th Street
P.O. Box 27187
Omaha, NE 68127-0187
402/592-0666
FAX: 402/592-1906
- Weekly appointment and task planners; Executive desk books, calendars, diaries, planning pads

QUEBLO IMAGES
131 Heartland Blvd.
Brentwood, NY 11707-0698
800/523-9080 or 516/254-2010
FAX: 516/254-2019
- Specialty papers, card stock, transparencies

QUILL CORPORATION
100 Schelter Road
Lincolnshire, IL 60069-9585
708/634-4800
- Office and filing system supplies

QUO VADIS
120 Elmview Avenue
Hamburg, NY 14075-3770
800/535-5656 or 716/648-2602
- Business planners

RAND MATERIALS HANDLING EQUIPMENT CO.
P.O. Box 3003
515 Narragansett Park Drive
Pawtucket, RI 02861
800/366-2300
FAX: 800-755-RAND
- Stackable bins, boxes, totes and racks; storage cabinets and shelving; packaging products

RELIABLE HOME OFFICE
1001 W. Van Buren
Chicago, IL 60607
800/621-4344 or 312/666-1800
- Office furniture and desk accessories

RELIABLE OFFICE SUPPLY
P.O. Box 1502
Ottawa, IL 61350-9914
800/735-4000
FAX: 800/326/3233
- Discount office supplies

REMARKABLE PRODUCTS
245 Pegasus Avenue
Northvale, NJ 07647
201/784-0900
- Organizing charts, boards, forms and supplies

REUSE'IT POSTER BOARD, INC.
6687 Jimmy Carter Boulevard
Norcross, GA 30071
800/826-0343 or 404/263-8893
- Lightweight write-on/wipe-off charts and boards

R.F. YOUNG CO., INC.
P.O. Box 40005 Dept. T
Indianapolis, IN 46240
800/875-1759 or 317/848-1759
FAX: 317/843-0738
- Leather brief bags and trial briefcases

ROL-A-CHART
William A. Steward Company
4708 Oak Hill Road
Placerville, CA 95667
800/824-0212 or 916/622-2437
- Continuous roll visual control charts

ROLODEX CORP.
245 Secaucus Road
Secaucus, NJ 07094-2196
201/348-3939
• Desk accessories and supplies

R.S. RUGGLES & COMPANY, INC.
303 West Crescent Avenue
P.O. Box 213
Allendale, NJ 07401
800/526-0863
or in NJ: 201/934-1230
• Legal exhibit dividers and tabs; custom indexes

RUBBERMAID
Wooster, OH
216/264-6464
• Portable desk supplies and accessories (Call for a store in your area)

SAFECO PRODUCTS COMPANY
9300 West Research Center Road
New Hope, MN 55428
• Storage cabinets and supplies

SAFEGUARD BUSINESS SYSTEMS, INC.
P.O. Box 7501
Fort Washington, PA 19034
800/523-2422
• Project organizer products and forms

SBS SOUTHERN BINDING & SUPPLY
P.O. Box F
Hot Springs, AR 71902
800/331-5295
or in AR: 501/525-0133
FAX: 501/525-1527
• Binding equipment & supplies; transparencies; custom tabs and binders; laminating products

SETON NAME PLATE COMPANY
P.O. Box BB-1331
New Haven, CT 06505-9970
800/243-6624 or 203/488-8059
FAX: 800/345-7819
• Identification tags, labels, and tools

SMEAD PRODUCTS
Hasting, MN
612/437-4111
• All types of filing, indexing and labeling supplies

SUCCESS CALENDARS
1827 Powers Ferry Road, Bldg. 23
Marietta, GA 30067
800/558-0466 or 404/988-9955
• Appointment books and desk calendars

SUPLEE ENVELOPE COMPANY
P.O. Box 449
Upper Darby, PA 19082
800/523-0192 or 215/352-2900
FAX: 215/626-7440
• File folders and jackets; stationery and office paper supplies

TAB PRODUCTS CO.
Palo Alto, CA
800/672-3109 ext. 3304 or in
CA: 800/742-0099 ext. 3304
- Color-coded tabs, filing equipment and accessories

TABBIES, Division of
Xertrex International, Inc.
1530 W. Glenlake Avenue
Itasca, IL 60143-1171
708/773-4160
- Legal kits, indexes and tabs, labels; color-coded labels

TENNSCO
P.O. Box 606
Dickson, TN 36055-0606
800/251-8184
- Filing systems and equipment

3M PRESENTATION PRODUCTS
c/o USI, Inc.
P.O. Box 644
Branford, CT 06405
800/243-4565
FAX: 203/481-7508
- Office and audio-visual supplies and presentation products; free catalogs

TIME/DESIGN MANAGEMENT SYSTEM
11835 W. Olympic Boulevard
Suite 450
Los Angeles, CA 90064-5005
800/637-9942 or 213/312-0288
- Planning and project organizers

20th CENTURY PLASTICS
P. O. Box 30022
Los Angeles, CA 90030
800/767-0777
FAX: 800/786-7939
- Photo, slide, and negative pages and albums; organizers, folders, pockets, and jackets

VISIBLE
1750 Wallace Avenue
St. Charles, IL 60174
800/323-0628
FAX: 800/233-2016
- Discount office products; computer supplies and accessories

VISUAL HORIZONS
180 Metro Park
Rochester, NY 14623
716/424-5300
FAX: 716/424-5313
- Various photographic and presentation supplies

WESTINGHOUSE FURNITURE SYSTEMS
4300 36th Street, S.E.
Grand Rapids, MI 49508
800/445-5045
- Business furniture and equipment

WHITE OFFICE SYSTEMS
50 Bright Avenue
Kenilworth, NJ 07033
201/272-8888
FAX: 201/272-7081
- Records storage and management systems

WILSON JONES
800/952-4637
- Binders and notebook supplies

CHAPTER 3

PREPARING TRIAL WITNESSES

§ 3.1 Preparing Lay Witnesses for Trial

There are two basic categories of trial witnesses: lay witnesses and expert witnesses. (See **§ 3.19** *et seq.*, for more on expert witnesses.) The lay witnesses are the persons who were directly or indirectly involved in the events or actions that are the subject of the lawsuit. For example, the list of lay witnesses could include your clients, the officers of a company that is being sued, an eyewitness to an accident, or other individuals who have some factual knowledge related to the activities at issue in the case.

§ 3.2 Listing the Potential Trial Witnesses

As soon as you are assigned to a case that is likely to go to trial, you need to become familiar with names of the "players" in the case. As you review the case materials, begin listing the names of potential witnesses. Note the names of your clients, the named parties in the lawsuit, other persons involved in the transaction or incident, coworkers, family members, eyewitnesses, and so on. Record the names identified in discovery depositions and interrogatory answers, as well as those your client may have mentioned. All of these are potential trial witnesses.

Use the Preliminary Witness Index (see **Form 3–1**) to record the names of various potential witnesses and indicate where you found their names. As the trial date approaches, you may find it helpful to divide the list of potential witnesses into categories, such as liability witnesses, damage witnesses, medical witnesses, and so on. But to begin with, just record all the names you come across and indicate where you heard or read them. You should also record the person's address and telephone number, if available, for future use.

Of course, it is always best for trial preparation purposes if you are on the case from the beginning so that you can develop a list of potential witnesses as the case develops. But the witness index is a most useful tool if you are brought in on the middle of a case, after most of the discovery has been done and before the trial preparation has started in earnest. Keep it handy as you work through the case materials and during your trial preparation conferences with the attorney. Identifying potential trial witnesses will help bring you up to speed on the case and you may even be able to discover the name of a useful witness which was inadvertently lost in the shuffle.

§ 3.3 Evaluating the Trial Witnesses

Use the preliminary witness index as a reference list for discussion at your trial preparation agenda meetings (see **§ 2.9**). The trial team must carefully evaluate a number of factors in selecting the individual trial witnesses and the attorney may ultimately choose only a few key persons from the preliminary list to testify at the trial. Each case will have some unique factors that must be weighed, but the following checklist is a guide to some general criteria the trial team should consider in selecting the trial witnesses.

§ 3.4 —Twelve Basic Questions for Evaluating Lay Witnesses

The following questions are a good starting point for interviewing lay witnesses:

FORM 3–1
PRELIMINARY WITNESS INDEX

PRELIMINARY WITNESS INDEX							
#	NAME	ADDRESS	PHONE	CAPACITY	SUBPOENA	FEE	

1. Will this person's testimony add something to the case?
2. Does the person have personal knowledge of significant facts which you need to establish at trial?
3. Will this person make a good impression on the jurors?
4. Is this person sufficiently articulate and poised to competently relate what he or she saw or what he or she knows on the witness stand?
5. Will this person stick to his or her story or can he or she be persuaded to change it by a skillful interrogator?
6. Does this person come across as honest and truthful?
7. Is the person related in any way to your clients or to any other party involved in the lawsuit?
8. Are there any other factors which would prejudice his or her interest in the outcome of the case?
9. Is there anything in the person's background (a felony conviction, a history of drug use, involvement in previous lawsuits) which the opposition could exploit to impeach his or her credibility?
10. Is this person healthy and physically capable of giving courtroom testimony?
11. Is this person cooperative and willing to testify in your case? (You can usually subpoena a reluctant witness, but the results at trial will be better if the witness is willing to be there.)
12. If the answers to any of the above questions are negative, is there anyone else who can testify to the necessary facts, or is there an alternate way to introduce the witness's testimony into evidence?

§ 3.5 Conducting Pretrial Interviews with Lay Witnesses

The pretrial interview with a potential lay witness to evaluate his or her suitability as a trial witness is somewhat different from the investigative interview which normally occurs during the preliminary investigation phase of the case. In civil cases, it is not unusual for the pretrial interview to take place months or even years after the initial interview because of the length of time it takes for a case to come to trial. The trial paralegal can do the following to assist the supervising attorney in the pretrial evaluation interview:

- Contact the lay witness and renew communication with him or her;
- Inform the lay witness of the case status and the forthcoming trial date;
- Refresh the recollection of the lay witness about previous testimony;

- Observe the lay witness and provide feedback on his or her suitability as a trial witness;
- Enlist the witness's cooperation in testifying at trial.

Locating the lay witness can sometimes be a problem if the witness has moved since the date of the initial interview. Of course, you would have asked the witness at that time to keep you informed of any change in address, but witnesses tend to forget those little details when so much time has passed. Do not assume that the witness you interviewed two years ago during the case investigation will still be living in the same place and employed at the same job. You may have to do a bit of detective work to determine his or her whereabouts. (See § **6.22** for tips on locating persons through a search of public records.) Once you have tracked down the witness, do not assume that he or she will be overjoyed to see you after all this time. Remember that although the case has been a high priority to you, the witness may well have put the matter out of mind and forgotten about it.

The lay witness who is not a client or a party generally has no real stake in the outcome of the case. While he or she may have been flattered by the attention and willing to talk at length when the events were fresh, the witness may now seem indifferent and appear reluctant to get involved in the actual trial. He or she will probably recall talking to you or someone from your office way back then, but his or her recollection of the details may have faded.

In setting up the pretrial interview, be very courteous and accommodate the lay witness's schedule as much as possible. Try to establish a rapport with the witness and prepare him or her for the possibility of testifying under oath in front of a jury. The attorney will conduct the final trial preparation conference if he or she decides to use the testimony of the lay witness, but you can begin the process of preparing the witness in the pretrial interview.

You will have an understanding from your meetings with the trial attorney of how the lay witness's testimony fits into the overall plan for the trial presentation. It is a good idea to explain this to the witness when you are attempting to enlist his or her cooperation, but be cautious about revealing too much detail about the trial strategy. Discuss with the attorney the specific areas you should cover with the witness.

By the time of the pretrial interview you will be familiar with the discovery that has taken place and have a better grasp of the issues in the case than you did at the investigative interview. In the first interview you may have simply asked open-ended questions and let the witness ramble as a means of eliciting the maximum usable information. At this point, however, you will be able to narrow your questions to focus on precisely what is needed from the witness at trial.

§ 3.6 —Conducting the Pretrial Interview

Use the following suggestions as guidelines in conducting pretrial interviews with lay witnesses.

1. Update the lay witness on the status of the case and the approaching trial date.
2. Frame concise questions to the lay witness based upon your knowledge of what the witness knew or saw, but be careful not to lead the witness.
3. Use documents, photographs, copies of previous statements, and so forth to refresh the witness on the facts and events about which he or she previously testified.
4. Refresh your memory as to the witness's appearance, demeanor, speech, and so forth, and consider how these would affect his or her suitability as a trial witness.
5. If you did not conduct the initial interview, it may be your first opportunity to observe the witness in person. Compare your observations to those documented by the original interviewer.
6. Compare the witness's current recollection with previous statements; note and explore any discrepancies.
7. If you were the first party to obtain a statement from the witness, try to find out if he or she was subsequently contacted by opposing counsel.
8. Update your file data on the witness's current situation, for example, residence, employment, lifestyle, children, and so on.
9. Give the lay witness an idea of what to expect as far as the trial procedures.
10. Determine the best time and place to contact the lay witness to schedule the final trial preparation conference.
11. If the witness is really uncooperative, inform the witness that you have the power to subpoena him or her to testify in court. This leverage should be threatened only as a last resort.
12. Report back to your supervising attorney on the results of your interview and your impressions of the witness.

§ 3.7 Assembling Witness Examination Files

In preparing for examination of a trial witness, the attorney needs to review all the pertinent information from the file relating to that witness. Assist the attorney by assembling these materials into a witness preparation file. Make a separate folder labeled with the witness's name for each potential trial witness. In this folder, place copies of all of the following materials which are available in your case files:

- A copy of the deposition transcript and the deposition abstract or summary, together with copies of any exhibits introduced or discussed in the deposition;
- Any discovery responses which mention or relate to the witness (for example, answers to interrogatories, responses to request for production of documents, responses to requests for admissions);
- Copies of any substantive correspondence or other privileged communications between the attorney and the witness;
- Any documents, records, photographs, or other materials produced by the witness or about which the witness has knowledge and can testify;
- Any notes made by trial team members regarding the anticipated testimony of this witness. This includes previous interviews, deposition preparation notes, telephone conference notes, and so forth;
- Fact sheet or questionnaire containing biographical data or background information about the witness;
- Excerpts from any other depositions in which the witness is mentioned;
- Copies of any documentary exhibits the witness will be called upon to authenticate or identify at trial;
- An outline or index of any additional physical evidence (nondocument exhibits) about which the witness will testify;
- Drafts or copies of any charts or other demonstrative evidence which will be used with the witness;
- Copies of any previous affidavits or statements provided by the witness to anyone relative to this case;
- Copies of any certified records or reports (for example, hospital records, birth certificate, driver record, school grade transcripts) pertaining to the witness;
- Any memoranda the attorney or another trial team member has prepared outlining elements of proof and the corresponding points which should be covered with the witness in trial testimony;
- Outline of any anticipated cross-examination questions by the opposing parties;
- Copies of any written reports prepared by an expert witness on issues pertaining to the witness;
- Witness information packet or reminder sheet, including directions to the courthouse, parking information, and a diagram or map, if necessary;
- Any other background materials or documents related to the witness.

Prepare an index listing the documents pertaining to each witness (see **Form 3–2**). After the attorney has reviewed the materials and used them to prepare the witness testimony, use these document indexes to help you compile the courtroom witness files and the trial exhibit worksheet (see **Chapter 5**).

§ 3.8 Preparing Clients to Testify at Trial

As part of the trial preparation, the attorney will want to meet with the client shortly before the trial date. The purposes of this meeting are: (1) to refresh the client's memory about the accident or other event that gave rise to the lawsuit; (2) to review the substance of the client's testimony regarding those events; and (3) to explain to the client what he or she can expect to happen in the courtroom. As part of the trial team, you should be present at the trial preparation conferences. You may be asked to schedule and coordinate the trial preparation conferences for one or more clients. You can be of great assistance to the attorney in this portion of the trial preparation.

§ 3.9 Arranging the Client Preparation Conference

Schedule the client preparation meeting as close to the trial date as possible, preferably during the week just before the trial, but not more than two weeks before the trial date. Discuss the client preparation conferences with the attorney during your trial planning meeting approximately one month before the trial date (see § **2.7** *et seq.*)

1. Ask the attorney which clients and witnesses you should bring in for preparation conferences and make a list of those persons.
2. Ask the attorney to check his or her calendar and give you some specific dates and times available for client meetings during the week before trial. Use a calendar blank and block in the times when the attorney is free.
3. Contact each client by telephone to discuss the most convenient time for the conference. In setting up the client conferences, try to accommodate the client's work or school schedule as much as possible. This may mean holding the conference very early in the morning, in the early evening hours after the regular workday, or on a weekend, depending upon the attorney's availability.
4. Once you have agreed upon a date convenient to the client and the attorney, follow up with a letter to the client confirming the date and time he or she is to be at your offices and enclosing any materials you want the client to review. (See **Form 3–3** in § **3.10.**)

FORM 3–2
DOCUMENT INDEX—WITNESS TESTIMONY

DOCUMENT INDEX - WITNESS TESTIMONY

CASE ID ____________________ **WITNESS NAME** ______________________________

DOC.#	DESCRIPTION	DATE	PAGES	REMARKS

5. If the attorney likes to hold these meetings in a conference room instead of his or her private office, remember to book a conference room with the person in your office who is in charge of conference room scheduling.

§ 3.10 Reviewing the Client's Previous Testimony

Very often the trial date is two years or more from the date of the accident or other event. Discovery in the form of interrogatories, depositions, document production, and requests for admissions will have been issued and answered in the case many months before the case comes to trial. Arrange for the client to review his or her previous testimony or statements in the case before the preparation conference.

1. Review the file and compile a set of materials for each client related to any previous testimony or information supplied by the client. These materials might include any or all of the following: interrogatory answers, transcript of deposition testimony, statements or affidavits, photographs, as well as any personal records, notes, or diaries the client may have kept. (See **§ 3.7** on preparing witness examination materials.)
2. In addition, assemble copies of all the documents written by, addressed to, or involving the client, and about which he may be asked to testify at the trial. Include any documents produced by opposing counsel in his discovery responses.
3. Prepare an index list of the documents pertaining to each client/witness (see **§ 3.7**). Add to the list any other documents that the attorney discusses with the client at the preparation conference.
4. Forward photocopies of these materials to the client so that he or she will have a chance to review them before the trial preparation conference (see the sample letter, **Form 3–3**).

FORM 3–3
SAMPLE LETTER ENCLOSING TESTIMONY MATERIALS

(Date)

Mr. Client
Street Address
City State Zip

RE: Trial Preparation Conference

Dear Client:

This will confirm our telephone discussion of this date concerning scheduling an appointment for your trial preparation conference with Attorney [attorney's name] for Tuesday, May 16, 199_ at 10:00 A.M.

I am enclosing a photocopy of the Answers to Interrogatories which were filed on April 9, 199_ together with the transcript of your deposition which was taken on July 6, 199_ in this case. Please take time to read these materials to refresh your recollection before to your meeting with [attorney's name]. As you review these documents, please jot down any questions you may have about them or about the case and bring your questions with you to the trial preparation conference.

If you should have a conflict which would prevent you from attending the meeting on May 16, please let us know as soon as possible so that we can reschedule. Otherwise, we will plan on seeing you in our offices on that date.

Very truly yours,
[Paralegal]

Enclosures

§ 3.11 Conducting the Trial Preparation Conference

If you have not already met the clients, the preparation conference is your opportunity to get acquainted with them. The attorney should introduce you to the clients and explain to them that you will be assisting in the courtroom. If you have been involved in the case and have already met the clients, this meeting is a chance for you to reassure and encourage the clients about the events to come. Clients who are anxious or nervous about the trial will feel more comfortable when they know that you will be a familiar and friendly face in the courtroom.

§ 3.12 —Taking Notes at the Trial Preparation Conference

The attorney will probably want to review the subjects to be covered by the client's testimony. He or she will also go over questions that are likely to be posed in the opposing counsel's cross-examination so that the client will know the kinds of questions he or she might expect at the trial. If you have not been in on the case from the beginning, listen carefully and take notes of the main points the attorney discusses with the client. This will give you an outline of the substance of this client's testimony.

If you have been in on the case from the beginning, one of your duties in the trial preparation may have been to prepare an outline of the points to cover with this witness. If you have such an outline, follow it while the attorney is speaking with the client and check off each important point as it is covered. If the attorney fails to mention something on the list, remind him or her to bring it up with the client. Also, if an area is discussed which is not on your list, jot down a note and add this question to your outline.

§ 3.13 —Dealing with Inconsistencies or Changes in Testimony

As the attorney reviews the client's testimony, listen carefully for any answers or statements which are inconsistent with the client's previous testimony or statements. Opposing counsel may try to discredit your client's testimony by showing that an answer to a question on the witness stand is different from the answer that person gave during a deposition. If your client does give an answer which is inconsistent with previous testimony, bring that fact to the attorney's attention so that he or she can determine why the answer is different now. Has the client reviewed some document which refreshed his or her memory? Was the client's original statement made in error? Has the client been influenced by other testimony in the case? Is the client confused about what is being asked? Alert the attorney to any discrepancy so that he or she can address the issue directly with the client. Review the errata sheets from the client's deposition transcript to make sure the client is clear on the correct answers he or she gave in deposition (see § **5.51**).

§ 3.14 Reviewing Exhibits and Documents with the Client

If any trial potential exhibits were prepared by, addressed to, or in any other way involve your client, be sure to have the client review a copy of the document at the preparation conference. The attorney should explain to the client the process of authenticating a document so that it may be admitted into evidence; that is, in the courtroom, the attorney will ask if he or she has ever seen the document before, and if so, to describe it, tell the court what it says, and, more importantly, what it means. If the document is work product which is an abstract or summary of information compiled from various sources, have the client review it carefully to ensure that the client can identify the document on the stand and testify truthfully that it is an accurate summary of the underlying information.

If the client's testimony will include information that is on a chart or diagram, have him or her study the chart to make sure he or she understands it and can verify the information shown on it. Likewise, if the attorney will be using any sort of mock-up or model to illustrate the testimony, the client should practice answering those questions while showing how the model works. (See also § **4.47** and § **4.48** on preparing for interactive testimony.)

§ 3.15 Explaining Courtroom Procedures

You can help the attorney explain to the clients what they may expect to happen in the courtroom. Briefly review the sequence of events which will occur at the trial: voir dire, opening statements, plaintiff's case (direct and cross-examination), defendant's case (direct and cross-examination), rebuttal, closing statements, jury deliberation, and so forth. You will also want to make sure that either you or the attorney explains to the client about sidebar conferences and objections by counsel during questioning. Depending on the client, you may want to remind him or her about some or all of the specific items in the following checklist to help polish his or her testimony.

Gear your explanation to the level of sophistication of the client. A corporate executive may have had some experience with trials, but most clients have never been in a courtroom before. They know only what they have seen on television. If the client is anxious or nervous, reassure him or her that these emotions are natural, and that one of the purposes of this conference is to provide information about what to expect so he or she will be more comfortable at the trial.

A task which often falls to a paralegal is instructing the client on what to wear in the courtroom. Again, remember the level of sophistication of your client, but do not just assume that the client knows what is proper courtroom attire.

§ 3.16 Client Trial Reminders

The following is a list of important points to discuss with the client prior to trial.

1. Always tell the truth; don't guess at an answer.

2. Avoid hearsay. Testify only about what you yourself actually saw, heard, or felt.

3. If you honestly can't remember something, it is okay to say so.

4. Pause after each question is asked and before you answer to make sure you understand the question. If you do not understand, say "I don't understand" and ask for clarification by the questioner until you do understand the question.

5. If opposing counsel asks you whether you discussed your testimony with your attorney, it is okay to tell them you did. There is nothing wrong with this; in fact, it would be foolish not to meet with your attorney before the trial. If opposing counsel asks you what your attorney told you to say, say that he or she told you to tell the truth.
6. If a question can be answered "Yes" or "No," give the appropriate answer and then stop. Wait for a follow-up question before you give further information.
7. If a question cannot be answered with a simple "Yes" or "No" answer, say so and ask for a chance to explain your answer. However, do not volunteer information that is not responsive to the question at hand.
8. Never argue with opposing counsel, even if he or she makes you angry or says something you dislike. Remember at all times that you are being watched by the judge and the jury, who will be weighing your credibility as a witness.

§ 3.17 Considering the Client's Needs

Remember that most clients never have been through a courtroom trial and probably are not as familiar with the procedure as you are. Be sensitive to the fact that the family sees the trial as an ordeal and that it may be causing some emotional stress. Try to convey to the family members that you understand that they are on unfamiliar ground. When several members of the same family are involved, consolidate their pretrial instruction conferences into one group preparation meeting. This saves time for everyone.

If your clients are really uneasy about the prospect of appearing in the courtroom, consider taking them to the courthouse during the week before trial so that they can view in advance the venue where the trial will take place. During a regular weekday, you may even be able to sit in for a few minutes on another trial in progress that is open to the public. This will serve both to familiarize your clients with how to get to the courthouse and to let them know more about what they can expect when they get there.

Make sure your clients know where and when they are supposed to appear on the first day of trial. You may want to have the clients come to your office and then proceed to the courthouse together, or it may be more convenient for the clients to meet you in the lobby of the courthouse or just outside the courtroom. If your client has never been in the courthouse, prepare a simple map or diagram of the courthouse layout with instructions on where to park and how to get to the courtroom. Again, tailor this information to the level of sophistication of your clients.

If you are involved in a large number of trials and you find yourself giving routine explanations repeatedly, you may want to develop an instruction sheet for your clients and witnesses by compiling a checklist of information and reminders about the courtroom.

Do whatever you can to reassure the clients and make them feel comfortable and confident about appearing in the courtroom. As you work with the clients before the trial, be observant and aware of clients who have special needs. For example, an elderly client may need a chair cushion in order to sit comfortably in the courtroom. If the client takes regular medication (such as high blood pressure medication or insulin for a diabetic) remind the client to bring it to court on trial days. If the client is confined to a wheelchair, help him or her locate the handicap access ramps and facilities at the courthouse. You can greatly assist the trial attorney by attending to these details. (See also § **6.12** on courtroom logistics and special problems.)

§ 3.18 Returning to the Site of the Incident

In some cases it is beneficial for the client to return to the scene of the accident or incident to refresh his or her memory as to distances, heights, and so forth. If the attorney thinks this is needed in your case, make arrangements for the clients to return to the site. The attorney may also ask you to accompany the client. If the case involves an accident on a public roadway, ask the client to simply drive by that portion of the roadway and take another look. However, if your case involves an industrial accident at a factory, you will probably have to secure permission from the company for your client to view the site. Ask your attorney whom you should contact to obtain such permission. If the client, for whatever reason, is unable to drive, you may have to act as chauffeur.

§ 3.19 Working with Expert Witnesses

Some cases involve areas of medical, scientific, or technical information that are not common knowledge to the average judge or jury. It is the duty of the trial team to educate the judge and jury on those scientific or technical matters during the presentation of the case. One way to accomplish this is through the use of an expert witness. Just what is an *expert* witness? Rule 702 of the Federal Rules of Evidence (FRE) provides:

> RULE 702. TESTIMONY BY EXPERTS
>
> If scientific, technical, or other specialized knowledge will assist the trier of fact to understand the evidence or to determine a fact in issue, a witness qualified as an expert by knowledge, skill, experience, training, or education, may testify thereto in the form of an opinion or otherwise.

Expert witnesses are persons with particular expertise in some field or discipline who are selected by the trial team to evaluate the factual evidence, assist in preparing the case for trial, explain complex information to the jurors, and render opinions based on the facts combined with their specialized knowledge of the subject area. In trials involving highly technical matters, expert testimony is usually essential to give the jurors enough knowledge to make informed decisions about the case. One of the most obvious examples of an expert that attorneys call on is the physician or medical expert (in trials involving personal injury), but there are virtually hundreds of other types of experts who can assist the trial team in successful preparation and presentation of the case. Professors, specialists, consultants, and others who are proficient and have special skill or knowledge in a specific area are potential expert witnesses.

There are two main differences between expert witnesses and fact witnesses:

1. The expert witness does not need to have been involved in the events that gave rise to the lawsuit; and
2. Fact witness are limited in the type of opinion testimony they may give (see FRE 701), but the expert witness can give opinions based upon a review of the facts and evidence combined with his or her knowledge, training, and experience with the subject matter. Experts usually have advanced degrees and experience in a specific scientific or technical area.

Occasionally, however, attorneys are unable to locate anyone with a Ph.D. in the exact area that needs to be explained to the jury. In that event, the attorney may opt to consult a person who, although he or she does not have the formal education, does have many years of practical experience in the area. This can actually help the trial presentation, because an expert by experience may be able to explain a piece of machinery or a manufacturing process in nontechnical, everyday language that the jury can easily understand.

§ 3.20 Locating Expert Witnesses

Once the attorney has decided to use an expert witness on the case, he or she may assign you the task of finding someone qualified. This may be a difficult assignment, depending on the field of expertise you are looking for. Where do you start looking to locate the appropriate person? It is usually economical to use experts who live or work in nearby communities, but you can't always find the expertise you need that close to home. The following checklist contains some suggestions for places you can start your search to locate potential expert witnesses.

§ 3.21 —Information Sources for Expert Witnesses

The following list identifies good sources for locating expert witnesses.

1. Technical Advisory Service for Attorneys (TASA)
1166 DeKalb Pike
Blue Bell, Pennsylvania
1-800-523-2319; (215) 275-8272

2. Technical Assistance Bureau (TAB)
P.O. Box 2908
Reston, Virginia 22090
(703) 471-5026

Both of these organizations specialize in providing attorneys with names of consultants and expert witnesses in all fields of medicine, science, and engineering nationwide. They can provide a comprehensive listing of expert witnesses in many technical and scientific fields, including accident reconstruction, environmental issues, engineering, forensic identification and analysis, science disciplines including agriculture, biology, chemistry, geography, geology, mathematics, and many areas of medicine, health, and psychology. Call or write them for information.

3. Universities and Colleges

Check any local universities or colleges that have departments dealing with the subject matter in your case. Professors and teachers often have the experience that qualifies them to testify as experts. If you don't know the departments of a particular school, go to the registrar's office and ask for a catalog of courses. You can find out how the college is set up and what divisions it includes, as well as the names of the staff and the department heads. Contact the head of the appropriate department by telephone or letter and give that person a brief description of the type of expert you are seeking. Even if that particular school does not have the right person, the personnel there may be able to give you a referral or a lead to an associate at another college or educational institution.

4. Libraries

Law libraries and university libraries as well as public libraries can be sources of information on experts in various fields. Ask the librarian to assist you in locating directories of professional and technical experts. Peruse the card catalog and *Readers' Guide to Periodical Literature* under your subject matter for leads to authors who have expertise in the area. Many libraries now have computerized catalogues and other on-line search aids to help you locate literature on your subject matter. Review the literature and recent periodicals for names of persons who may qualify as experts. Even if you locate the name of an expert, you can compile a selection of background materials for the attorney to study to become familiar with a particular subject. (See § **1.57** on conducting factual research for trial.)

5. Professional Associations

Many professional fields have one or more organizations or associations to which their members belong. Your public library should have an address for the headquarters of any established professional organization. Many national, state, and local professional associations publish directories listing their members, often indicating areas of specialization or particular expertise. Contact them for referrals to experts in the field.

6. Classified Advertisements

Legal publications and trade journals carry classified advertisements for expert consultants and witnesses in many fields. Check the ads in several publications. (See § **1.37** for a reference list of legal publications.)

7. Research Services

Research services like the Association of Trial Lawyers of America (ATLA) can help plaintiffs' lawyers identify potential sources of expert assistance. For a small fee, an ATLA member can send in a brief factual description of the case and get back the results of a computer search listing numerous cases dealing with the same or a closely related subject, complete with the names of attorneys involved in the cases and the amounts of verdicts or settlements reached. By contacting these attorneys, you may be able to locate an expert in the field involved in your case.

The ATLA Exchange
1050 31st Street, N.W.
Washington, D.C. 20007
(800) 424-2725

8. On-line Databases

If you have access to computerized information databases, such as Westlaw or the LEXIS/NEXIS network, a search of these resources by subject matter can yield information on names and extensive background information on experts in a variety of disciplines.

9. Referrals

If you have used experts in past trials who were qualified in the subject area, it is logical to call on them again, either to testify themselves or to obtain a referral to a colleague in their field. Ask attorneys and paralegals from other firms for referrals to experts with whom they have worked successfully.

10. Client Resources

If yours is a corporate client with a research and development department, there may be someone on the corporate staff who has the necessary expertise to serve as an expert witness. This person would have the advantage of knowing the internal corporate structure of your client's company. Ask your client (check with your supervising attorney first) or the corporate counsel for recommendations. Even if no one in the company possesses the necessary qualifications, they may be able to give you a referral or a lead to a person outside the company who has the requisite knowledge and experience.

§ 3.22 Evaluating the Potential Expert Witness

Before you engage an expert in any area, the attorney must first determine that the particular expert is the right one for your case. You can assist the trial attorney by obtaining a current resume or curriculum vitae from the expert. The attorney will want to have a face-to-face meeting with the expert early enough in the case to allow time to find an alternate, if necessary. At the initial meeting, you can help the attorney evaluate the expert by considering the following points:

- Is the expert poised and articulate?
- Does the expert understand your case?
- Does the expert understand the function of his or her potential trial testimony in the proper context?
- Is the expert in good health and up to the demands of courtroom examination and cross-examination?
- Will the expert have the time to devote to trial preparation and testimony?

One of the most important factors in determining the right expert for your case is the extent of experience and exposure he or she has had as an expert witness. The following checklist suggests some areas of inquiry to familiarize you with the expert's previous witness experience.

§ 3.23 —Evaluating the Expert's Experience

These are suggested questions for help in evaluating your potential expert's experience.

1. How many times has the expert acted as a consultant to attorneys in cases involving the expert's field or area of specialization?
2. In how many cases has the expert actually testified, either by deposition or at trial?
3. Were the issues in those cases similar to the issues in your case?
4. Has the expert ever been employed by the opposing counsel and if so, what type of opinions did the expert render?

5. What percentage of the expert's previous trial work was done on behalf of plaintiffs' cases and what percentage was on behalf of defendants' cases?
6. What recordkeeping method does the expert use to ensure against conflict of interest problems, such as inadvertently working for parties on opposite sides of the same case?
7. Has the expert written or published any articles, papers, or treatises concerning the subject matter involved in your case?

There are both advantages and disadvantages to using an experienced expert witness. The experienced expert who knows the routine of deposition and trial may be expected to be fairly comfortable with it, whereas an expert in his or her very first trial may be quite nervous. You will need to spend less preparation time on the fundamentals of testifying and courtroom procedure with the experienced expert than you will for someone who is doing it for the first time. However, the experienced expert may be so busy with other cases that accessibility to the expert's time is limited and scheduling becomes a problem. Experts who are involved in many cases sometimes tend to confuse the information from different cases and find it difficult to focus on your case. This is less likely to be a problem with the expert who is working solely on your case.

The fact that the expert has previously done work for the opposing counsel does not necessarily disqualify him or her for your case. If the other side hired the expert, it shows it respects his or her work and there should be no doubts as to the expert's qualifications and credibility. However, if in the previous work for opposing counsel the expert supplied information that is contradictory to that required in your case, or if he or she supplied similar opinions and the opponent lost the case, the attorney will want to carefully consider whether this expert is the best person for the job in the current case.

If the expert has worked for both plaintiffs and defendants, it may indicate an ability to render impartial opinions based purely upon the facts of the case. Conversely, it may also mean that the expert can manipulate statistics to prove anything you need him or her to say. The honesty and integrity of the expert witness are of utmost importance. Steer clear of the "expert for hire" who will say anything you want for a fee.

§ 3.24 —Investigating the Opposition's Expert

Just as your side can employ an expert, so can the other side. When both experts are equally qualified, yet they render opposing opinions in a trial, the balance may be tipped in the minds of the jurors by testimony that tends to discredit or impeach the opposing expert's qualifications. The attorney may ask you to conduct some investigation into the credentials of the opposing expert. Review a copy of the expert's resume or curriculum vitae and consider the following:

- Verify any graduate or postgraduate degrees listed by checking with the college or institution indicated.
- Check with the issuing board or organization to verify any special honors or awards indicated on the CV.
- If the expert has published any books or articles on the subjects involved in your case, review these materials for any opinions or information that contradict the expert's testimony in the current case.
- Obtain and review transcripts of the expert's testimony in other cases to see if the expert's testimony in some other case is inconsistent with his or her opinions in the current case. (You can do this only if you have plenty of time and if money is no object.)

§ 3.25 Engaging the Expert Witness

The attorney usually makes the initial contact with the expert, often by telephone, to outline briefly the case and determine whether the expert is qualified and willing to work on the case. In the initial conversation, the attorney and the expert will generally discuss the theories or evidence the attorney needs to prove or support and the information the expert can provide.

If the attorney and the expert agree on objectives for the case at hand, the attorney may ask you to prepare documentation (usually in letter form) of the terms for engaging the expert. The letter should describe the understanding between your office and the expert regarding the purpose for which the expert is being retained and the arrangements for paying the expert's fee. If your office has a standard format for the expert engagement letter, follow the customary procedures for its preparation. The following checklist contains a number of items that the attorney may want wish to include in the expert witness engagement letter.

§ 3.26 —Elements of the Expert Witness Engagement Letter

Letters engaging the services of an expert witness may include the following items:

1. Identification of the case the expert will work on.

2. A brief statement of the reasons you are retaining the expert on behalf of your client. This will be tailored to each individual case. Caution: Consult your supervising attorney concerning the level of detail that should be included in the letter to the expert.
3. The date the Expert Disclosure Report is due (according to FRCP 26(a)(2); see § **2.29**).
4. The date the trial is scheduled, if you know it.
5. Fee arrangements:

   - Whether the expert will charge a retainer, and if so, the amount and the manner in which it will be applied. Terms will vary depending on the field the expert comes from.
   - A clear statement of the hourly fee the expert will charge. There may be different amounts for consultation, research, deposition time, and trial testimony. Include a statement indicating that these are the expert's usual and customary fees for this type of services.
   - How the fee is to be billed (at the end of the expert's work on the case, monthly, or other terms).
   - Whether there will be additional fees if the attorney requests expedited work.
   - How the expert should handle expenses and advances. If the expert will need to travel, specify how the travel arrangements and expenses are to be handled.

6. Whether the expert is authorized to contact the client directly for information.
7. Description of any materials being forwarded to the expert for review, or a statement that these will be sent separately at a later date. (See § **3.29** on releasing records to the expert witness.) It will be important to keep track of this for the FRCP Rule 26 disclosure report. See § **2.29.**
8. Documents or materials the expert agrees to provide to the attorney.
9. When the expert will provide a written report of his or her findings and opinions under FRCP 26. This may be left for determination at a later date. (See § **3.34** on requesting the expert's report.)
10. Confidentiality and privileged information clause. This would be warranted specifically in cases dealing with competitive trade secrets or similar highly sensitive data.
11. Names of other persons in your office the expert may contact (a paralegal, another attorney) for additional information and questions on the case.

12. An acknowledgement for the expert to sign and return indicating that the agreement set forth in the letter comports with his or her understanding of the engagement terms.

§ 3.27 —Assembling the Expert Witness Reference Folder

Begin a separate folder or file for personal, biographical, and contractual information related to each expert witness you engage in the case. (See also § **2.67** on organizing expert witness materials.) At the conclusion of the case, you can place your notes from this folder in your master reference notebook (see § **1.61**) in the event you need to use the expert's services again on some future case. The reference folder should include the following items:

- The expert's proper name, title, and business address. This could be simply the expert's business card affixed to the inside cover of the folder.
- Information on how to reach the expert by telephone, especially if the expert maintains more than one office. Include a home telephone number and a fax number, if possible. Also include the name of the expert's secretary or assistant, if there is one. (See § **3.30** on communicating with the expert's staff.)
- Engagement letter (see § **3.25**).
- Copy of retainer checks or vouchers on fees paid.
- Copies of airline tickets, hotel reservations, and other receipts related to travel expenses incurred by the expert.
- Resume or curriculum vitae.
- List of articles or publications written by the expert.
- Records Release Log (see § **3.29**).
- Copies of receipts for any materials that must be returned to the expert at the conclusion of the case.
- Copies of any correspondence with the expert.
- Notes on the initial consultation.
- Notations of dates of contact with the expert as the case progresses.

Cross-examination questions at deposition and trial will always cover when the expert was retained and what objectives he or she was asked to evaluate. Ascertain the date of the attorney's initial contact with the expert and note it so that you can refresh the attorney's memory during trial preparation. You also need to track the dates of subsequent meetings and consultations with the expert as the case develops. The attorney should know how many times he or she met with the expert and the specific materials the expert reviewed in forming his or her opinions. If you have not been working on the case from the beginning and no one has kept careful records, you may have to search the file to reconstruct the dates and contents of meetings with the expert during the development of the case.

§ 3.28 —Engaging Experts as Consultants Only

An expert may be retained and employed early in the case as a consultant rather than as a trial witness to assist the attorney in formulating and developing theories and strategy on the case. The trial team may also call on the consultant to do the following:

- Provide background materials and information
- Develop discovery questions and responses
- Develop cross-examination questions for the opposing party's expert witness
- Investigate the opposing expert's credentials
- Suggest leads to help locate possible witness experts in the same or related fields
- Assist in general trial preparation
- Assist in developing visual aids for trial

The Federal Rules of Civil Procedure permit a much narrower scope of discovery from the consultant expert than from the witness expert. FRCP 26(b)(4)(B) provides:

> A party may, *through interrogatories or by deposition,* discover facts known or opinions held by an expert who has been retained or specially employed by another party in anticipation of litigation or preparation for trial and who is *not* expected to be called as a witness at trial, *only* as provided in Rule 35(b) or upon a showing of exceptional circumstances under which it is impracticable for the party seeking discovery to obtain facts or opinions on the same subject by other means.

Rule 35(b) allows discovery of a nonwitness expert's opinions only if the expert performed a physical examination of a party. In most cases, you are not even required to disclose the consultant's name to the opposing counsel if the consultant will not be a trial witness. Generally, a consulting expert's written report is not discoverable unless it has been reviewed and used as a basis for the opinions of another expert who will testify at trial. You should be aware of this on any case where you engage a expert consultant.

§ 3.29 Preparing Information for the Expert Witness

The expert witness must know the factual background and understand the attorney's theory of the case before he or she can conduct a valid analysis and formulate opinions. In order to facilitate this, you must provide the expert with sufficient materials and information related to the case. The expert needs to be aware of both the strengths and weaknesses of your case to form an accurate assessment. The specific materials you supply to the expert will vary depending on the nature of the case and the type of analysis desired. Refer to the later sections in this chapter for guidelines on materials to provide to specific types of experts. The basic information you provide to any expert should include the following:

1. Factual Statement.
   This should be a narrative case background statement that clearly and objectively states the known, provable facts of the case, the persons involved, and the timing and sequence of events leading up to the occurrence of the incident that is the subject of the lawsuit. The facts contained in this statement must be the same ones that will be offered into evidence at the trial (see **§ 5.37**).
2. Legal Issues Statement.
   This will include a brief discussion of the legal theories, issues, and elements of proof involved in the case. This will give the expert an idea of how his or her analysis will help support your client's case.
3. Investigation.
   This could include witness statements, interviews, or reports provided by a private investigator. Caution: Witness statements and other reports of information obtained by a private investigator could be classified as attorney work product, and as such would ordinarily be protected from discovery by the opposing counsel. However, if such reports are released to the expert, the expert uses them as a basis in forming an opinion, and the expert testifies as a witness, the documents could then become discoverable. The attorney must decide whether to release this type of material to the expert witness.
4. Discovery.
   This would include any relevant testimony or information gathered through discovery in the case, including documents, interrogatory answers, and deposition transcripts. You may wish to provide only certain portions of lengthy deposition transcripts so that the expert does not have to waste valuable time reviewing a lot of irrelevant pages. Be careful, however, about statements taken out of context that could be misinterpreted by the expert. If you provide only excerpts of transcripts,

make sure that they are clearly marked as such and that the expert knows they are taken out of context. Note on your Records Release Log (see **Form 3–4**) the exact page numbers of the deposition transcript given to the expert. Remember that opposing counsel has access to the whole transcript, and could impeach the witness by locating contradictory statements elsewhere in the transcript. If you decide to give the expert the entire transcript, highlight or underline the specific portions of the transcript to which the attorney indicates the expert should direct attention.

It is important to keep track of which materials and records are released to an expert witness throughout the case, because the expert will rely on these in forming opinions. As you prepare materials to send to the expert, use the Records Release Log to keep a permanent and comprehensive record of the information being sent. (See **Form 3–4,** Records Release Log.)

§ 3.30 Communicating with the Expert Witness

Expert witnesses often lead busy professional lives, just as trial attorneys do. You can help to ensure that the trial attorney makes the most of his or her contacts with the expert witness by facilitating communications between them. One aspect of this involves compiling background information for the attorney in the expert's area or discipline. The suggestions in this section will assist you in perfecting your role as a liaison between the attorney and the expert witness.

§ 3.31 —Researching the Expert's Subject Area

Read the relevant literature in the field for background information that will help you understand the facts of your case. Regardless of the field of expertise, the expert witness should be able to provide you with a bibliography of authoritative books, texts, treatises, and articles related to the subject matter. Ask the expert to indicate two or three that he or she considers the most authoritative works in the field. As the trial paralegal, you can proceed to:

- Locate and obtain copies of as many of the recommended books or articles as are available. (See § **1.57** on performing factual research.)
- Obtain the publications, books, or articles written or co-authored by your expert on the subject pertaining to your case.
- Read and analyze the materials for their relevance to the subject matter involved in the current trial.

FORM 3–4
RECORDS RELEASE LOG

RECORDS RELEASE LOG

CASE ID ______________ EXPERT NAME __________________________

DATE	DESCRIPTION OF DOCUMENTS AND MATERIALS	HOW SENT	INITIALS
	#		

- Compile either a manual reference file or a computerized database of information related to the subject matter. (See § **8.19** on computer database applications.)

The trial attorney may ask you to research and summarize the important literature to extract the most important and relevant background information. Or the attorney may wish to read all the background materials, depending on the subject matter, the volume of material, and the time available. Based on your review and understanding of the literature, you will be able to consider the facts of your case and record any questions the attorney would like the expert to answer.

§ 3.32 —Preparing a Glossary of Relevant Terms

In order to effectively communicate with the expert and understand what you hear and read, you need to gain at least a basic understanding of the terms that occur most frequently in relation to the subject matter. Most professions have a specialized language or jargon pertaining to technical terms within the discipline, which includes shortened forms, slang, abbreviations, and acronyms. These "terms of art" become incorporated into the everyday language of experts who converse daily with others in the same field. You need to become familiar with the terminology used by the expert and others in the field in order to assist the expert's communication with the trial team.

Depending on the field of expertise, these technical terms may include everything from polysyllabic words to slang terms to standardized acronyms that occur repeatedly in the literature and the conversation of the expert. You may find it helpful to begin an informal reference glossary of these commonly occurring technical terms. As you find definitions or examples of usage in the technical literature, add this information to your informal glossary (arranged alphabetically) for easy reference. This will help you and the attorney to understand the frame of reference of the expert's field. Medical terminology is an obvious example, but the same concept applies in every field of expertise (for example, economics, banking, or geology) Use your computerized word processing and database functions to create a flexible and accessible glossary of relevant terms (see §§ **8.14; 8.19.**)

An important part of your job as the trial paralegal is to make sure the expert can be understood by a jury composed of average citizens. Whenever possible, ask the expert to explain a complex term or concept in lay terms, that is, plain, everyday language. You can help to alert the trial attorney to terms that may require explanation for the jury to understand. The items in your cumulative reference glossary will serve as a checkpoint for terms and concepts that need to be carefully explained to a jury at trial.

Caution: Do not clutter up the trial presentation with definitions of peripheral terms, but make sure that the core terms and concepts are explained by either the attorney or by the expert.

§ 3.33 —Strategies for Effectively Communicating with the Expert Witness

The following items are suggestions for some additional ways you can help to facilitate communications between the trial attorneys and the expert witness as you prepare the case for trial.

1. Befriend the expert's staff.
Most busy professionals, especially those who hold important positions at universities or research facilities, have one or more staff members who are assigned to act as buffers from intrusions from the outside world for these brilliant minds and incredibly busy schedules. This person (often a trusted aide or executive secretary) relays messages, handles correspondence, and schedules appointments for the expert. Address this person with the utmost respect. Get to know her or his name and use it. It is likely that you will conduct most of your business with the expert's assistant over the telephone, so adopt a courteous tone of voice in your conversations, and be cooperative and friendly in coordinating scheduling problems, answering questions, and providing materials. Let the assistant know that you understand how it is to work for a busy boss. If you can befriend the person who looks out for the expert, your chances of successfully gaining access to the expert's time and attention will be greatly enhanced. An additional bonus is that you will already have an office contact in the expert's office if you use this particular expert again in a future trial.

2. Pay the expert's fee promptly.
Experts and their assistants or office managers tend to give preferential attention to those clients who have already paid a substantial retainer or consulting fee. Pay any outstanding invoices or statements as quickly as possible, according to terms of the retention letter and agreement. (See § **3.25** *et seq.*, on the terms of engagement of the expert witness.)

3. Make yourself known to the expert.
Send your business card along with any early correspondence in the case to make it easy for the expert's secretary or assistant to file your name and telephone number in the office records. Identify yourself, your office, and the case name whenever you contact the expert's office by telephone.

4. **Keep track of communications with the expert.**
   Keep a log or special file of your communications (via telephone or correspondence) with the expert or the secretary or assistant so you know exactly when your last communication occurred. Return telephone calls or messages requesting information as quickly as possible. Use the telecopier to speed vital communications. Record the fax number of the expert's office or facility for quick reference.
5. **Keep the expert informed about the case.**
   Be sure to relay any change of status of the case (a change in arrangements for deposition, continuation of the trial date, settlement of the case, and so forth) to the expert immediately. Let the expert know the trial date (new or rescheduled) as early as possible. Try to accommodate the expert's schedule and conflicting commitments whenever possible. Check with the expert's calendar before scheduling meetings, depositions, or preparation conferences. Honor any longstanding commitments that may already be on the expert's calendar.
6. **Don't waste the expert's valuable time.**
   Make the best use of the expert's time. Do not expect the expert to have to translate or struggle to make sense of the materials you have sent him or her. Index your materials clearly, and indicate the reason you have included them. Transcribe or decipher any handwritten notes and records, especially if the handwriting is difficult to read. Send the expert clear, legible copies of documents and materials.

§ 3.34 Requesting the Expert Witness Report

In many cases the expert may communicate his or her findings orally to the trial attorney. Such discussions are generally considered privileged communications and are therefore not subject to discovery by the opposing party. Note: The expert's opinions are discoverable, but the expert's oral conversations with the attorney are not.

The expert may or may not provide a written report setting forth his or her conclusions and opinions. The 1993 Amendments to the Federal Rules of Civil Procedure (FRCP 26(a)(2)(B)) require an Expert Disclosure Report. Rule 26(a)(2)(C) specifies the timing for producing the expert's report:

- When the court orders it; or
- When the parties agree to produce it; but
- At least 90 days before trial.

If the evidence is merely rebuttal to the opposing party's expert, produce the expert information within 30 days after the other party discloses his or her expert information. An outline of the information required in the expert disclosure report is set out in the example below.

Your expert's written report may contain tables, calculations, diagrams or other information that could be the basis for a visual aid to be used at trial. (See **§ 3.39** on working with the expert witness to develop demonstrative evidence for trial.)

Be very careful to protect any written reports produced by your expert witness, including any updates or supplementation to an original report. Check with the supervising attorney and get clear instructions before releasing any part of an expert's written report to anyone. **Form 3–5** is a sample outline for an expert witness disclosure report.

FORM 3–5
SAMPLE OUTLINE FOR EXPERT DISCLOSURE REPORT
(FRCP 26(a)(2)(B))

[CASE CAPTION]
[TITLE]
Expert Disclosure Report

This Disclosure is made pursuant to FRCP 26(a)(2)(B) as amended effective December 1, 1993.

I. Identify the expert
  Name
  Address
  Telephone

II. Statement of expert's opinions and bases for opinions

III. Statement of information considered by the expert witness in forming the opinions

  (Describe documents reviewed, interviews, or research conducted, and so forth)

III. Statement of exhibits to be used to summarize or support the opinions

IV. Statement of qualifications of the expert witness

- Occupation; credentials; experience (Attach résumé)
- List all publications written by the expert in the last 10 years
- List other cases in which the witness has testified as an expert at trial or by deposition within the preceding four years.
- Compensation the expert is to be paid for the study and testimony

V. Signature of expert

VI. Certification by attorney

§ 3.35 Preparing the Expert Witness for Trial

Notify the expert of the trial date by letter or telephone as soon as you receive it from the court. This procedure will confirm that the expert will be available for trial and will allow you to head off and resolve any potential scheduling conflicts. Ask the expert to check his or her calendar and advise you as soon as possible of any prior commitments that would conflict with the trial date. For example, the expert may have been subpoenaed to testify in another trial on the same date as your case, or perhaps the expert is scheduled to attend an important professional conference abroad during the week your trial is set. If the expert indicates a bona fide reason that he or she cannot be available on the designated date, the trial attorney may wish to file a request for continuance of the trial date in your case. Remember to keep the expert informed of any continuance in the trial date by other parties or for other reasons so that the expert can keep his or her calendar up-to-date.

An alternative in the event the expert cannot be available on the trial date is to take a videotape *de bene esse* deposition of the expert at some time before the actual trial. (See **§ 3.40;** see also **§§ 5.50; 5.52; 6.11.**) Always check with your supervising attorney for precise instruction before contacting the expert.

§ 3.36 —Preparing Notification Letter to Expert Witness

Use this list as a guide for information to include in the notification letter to the expert witness (see also **Form 3–6,** Sample Notification Letter.)

1. Clearly identify the case for the expert's reference.
2. State the actual date set for the trial.
3. State how long the trial is expected to last.
4. Indicate approximately when you anticipate the expert's testimony will be needed during the trial.
5. Advise that you will need time for a preparation conference before the expert testifies.
6. Request that the expert check his or her calendar and advise you immediately of any conflicts in scheduling.
7. Enclose documents for the expert to review to prepare ahead of time.
8. Request any additional information or materials owed to you by the expert, if applicable.
9. Thank the expert for his or her assistance and remind the expert that you will expect to hear from him or her to confirm the trial date.

10. List any enclosures right on the face of the letter for a quick reference to exactly what documents you sent to the expert.

FORM 3–6
SAMPLE NOTIFICATION LETTER

(date)

Expert Witness, Ph.D.
Inside Address
Realtown, Ohio 44308

Re: Johnson vs. Extra-Accurate Calculator Company
Grand County Common Pleas Court Case No.

Dear Dr. Expert:

We have received notice from the Court that the trial date on the above-referenced case has been set for Monday, March 18, 199__. We anticipate that the trial will last at least the entire week of March 18th, and it possibly may carry over into the following week. We would like to offer your testimony early in the trial presentation, so it is likely that we would need you to testify either in the afternoon session on March 19, 199__, or during the morning session on Wednesday, March 20, 199__. We also need to schedule some time before your court testimony to review the case with you and prepare you to testify.

Please check your calendar for the week of March 18, 199__, and advise us immediately if you foresee any conflicts in scheduling that would prevent you from being available to testify during the time frame outlined above.

To assist you in preparing for this trial, I am enclosing a copy of the transcript of the deposition you gave in this case on September 7, 199__, so that you can review it at your convenience.

In reviewing my file I find that I have not yet received the reference articles you agreed to send me on this matter when we last discussed the case in October. Please see if you can locate those materials and forward them to me at your earliest convenience.

Again, thank you for your assistance to our trial team in preparing this case for trial. I shall look forward to hearing from you soon to confirm your availability for the trial.

Very truly yours,

Enclosures: (list documents)

§ 3.37 Scheduling the Trial Preparation Conference

Give the expert as much notice as possible when you are arranging the trial preparation conference. Schedule the preparation conference as close to the trial date as you can, preferably within three to five days before the expert is to testify. You may have to work with the expert's secretary or assistant to schedule a time that is convenient to both the expert and the trial attorney. Naturally, you will want to accommodate the expert's schedule to the extent you can. It is very important to arrange adequate trial preparation time with the expert witness, especially if the expert is working on many other cases besides yours. One of the purposes of the trial preparation session is to refresh the expert's memory and focus his or her attention on the facts of your particular case. The exact amount of time you will need for the trial preparation conference will vary from case to case. Ask the trial attorney for guidance on how much time to allow for the preparation conference. Some of the following factors could affect the time needed.

The extent of the expert's experience in trial testimony. If the expert has never testified before, the trial team will need time to explain the trial procedure, what is expected of the expert witness, and so on. The trial attorney may wish to use a videocassette training tape to help prepare the expert for what will occur at trial. On the other hand, if the expert has had sufficient previous trial experience, the attorney may not think it is necessary spend time on an extensive review of rudimentary courtroom procedures.

The complexity of the information involved and the expert's function in your case. The attorney may need extra preparation time with an expert who will testify about complex technical or highly specialized matters, or with an expert whose services will include assisting the trial attorney in preparing the cross-examination of the opposing party's expert.

Where the expert witness is located. If the expert witness resides or works in or near your city, the attorney may have several occasions to meet with him or her to discuss various aspects of the case as the trial preparation progresses. However, if the expert must travel from out of town or out of state for the trial, you may not be able to schedule a preparation conference until shortly before the expert is to testify. Depending on the expert's schedule and the available travel arrangements, the trial preparation conference may have to be condensed into whatever time is available on the day before the expert's testimony.

When an expert must travel from out of town, the trial paralegal is often put in charge of coordinating the travel and lodging arrangements. Although you may delegate tasks such as booking airline flights and making hotel reservations to your secretary, you should always follow up to make sure the details are confirmed and that the expert is advised of the arrangements.

§ 3.38 —Preparing the Expert Witness for Trial

These suggestions will assist you in preparing the expert for trial.

Before the Preparation Conference:

1. Notify the expert of the anticipated time frame for trial (see **Form 3–6,** Sample Notification Letter).
2. If you have not already done so, send the expert a copy of the transcript of his or her deposition, if applicable, to allow the expert to review previous testimony before the preparation conference.
3. Provide copies of any other relevant documents or materials that the expert has not yet seen, if any, pertaining to the subjects about which the expert will testify.
4. Discuss with the attorney the need for issuing a trial subpoena to the expert witness. Prepare the subpoena if one is necessary (see **§ 5.10** *et seq.* on preparing trial subpoenas).
5. Discuss how the attorney will establish the expert's qualifications as an expert witness on direct examination at trial. If you do not have a current resume or curriculum vitae, ask the expert to provide one.
6. Review the contents of the expert's file to see if the expert agreed or promised to provide any materials that you have not yet received. Remind the expert in the notification letter about any outstanding materials.

During the Preparation Conference:

7. If you have not previously determined whether the expert has ever been retained by the opposing counsel in past cases, be sure to ask the expert about this.
8. Discuss the questions the attorney could ask to bring out the type of services the expert routinely provides, such as examples of the type of calculations, opinions, and so forth that the expert is qualified to give and why.
9. Refresh the expert's memory about when the expert was first contacted about the case and the dates of subsequent communications between the expert and the attorney.

10. Discuss what materials the expert received and reviewed (documents, photographs, depositions, and so forth) and what additional investigation, if any, he did.
11. Review your log of documents released to the expert (see § **3.29**) or produced by the expert. Check with the attorney to make sure that everything the expert relied upon in forming his or her opinions will be introduced into evidence at some point during the case.
12. Clarify whether the expert is to bring any files, materials, notes, or other items to the courtroom, and, if so, determine the exact materials that are to be brought.
13. Outline for the expert the order in which you plan to present your evidence at trial, so that the expert can see how his or her testimony fits in with the planned presentation. Discuss your strategy in determining the order of witnesses, so that the expert's testimony is presented to the best effect to support your client's case.
14. The expert can assist the attorney in outlining the direct examination. The questions should follow a logical progression to clarify any technical terms and lay the proper foundation for the expert's opinions.
15. Discuss the formulation of a line of questioning that allows the expert to explain the general methods used to evaluate a matter (whatever it is the expert specializes in), then detail specifically how those methods were applied to the facts in this particular case.
16. Discuss and develop any hypothetical questions the attorney plans to use in direct examination. Refine the details of the hypothetical question that asks the expert to assume certain facts and give his or her opinion based upon those facts. This is to ensure that the expert is comfortable with the hypothetical and that the expert's honest answer will enhance or support your case.
17. Test the visual aids you will use with the expert to make sure they are clear and can been seen across a room. The expert should have a chance to practice his or her testimony with the demonstrative evidence before actually using it in the courtroom.
18. Observe the expert as he or she interacts with the attorney during this practice run of the testimony. If necessary, remind the expert to speak slowly and clearly. The expert must also be careful to define and explain technical terms in language that will be readily comprehensible to the jury. Experts who are also teachers are usually very good at this kind of explanatory, teaching answer.
19. Discuss the anticipated cross-examination by the opposing counsel. An expert who has been deposed may already have a feel for the opposing

counsel's approach to the cross-examination. If he or she has not been deposed, the attorney must supply his or her best estimate of how the opposition will attack the expert's testimony.

20. The expert can help the trial team prepare for the examination of the opposing party's expert. Review the known facts and any discovery testimony of the opposing expert with your expert and incorporate his or her suggestions or insights into weaknesses he or she perceives in the opposing expert's statements. This can take the steam out of the opposition expert's testimony.

§ 3.39 Working with the Expert to Develop Visual Aids

The expert witness can often assist you in developing ideas for visual aids. The extent to which the expert can help you with this aspect of trial preparation depends on the area of expertise and how well the expert's testimony lends itself to illustration or graphic representations. Analyze the expert's testimony and think about what type of visual aids would best complement the testimony. Early in the course of your contact with the expert, ask the expert for input or ideas for visual aids that would be useful in explaining or illustrating his or her testimony. This gives you the maximum time to plan and prepare the visual aids.

The background materials the expert provides to you may suggest an appropriate chart or graph to illustrate or support points in his or her testimony. Check the attachments or exhibits to the expert's formal report, if there are any, for possible sources of ideas for visual aids. These could range from very simple visuals (a blowup of a document or photograph), to charts, graphs, or diagrams compiled specifically for the purpose of this case, to complex (a working model or miniature, an illustration or photograph with overlays) and so on. (See also **Chapter 4** for more information and tips on preparing visual aids and demonstrative evidence for trial.)

Suggestions for Visual Aids from Various Experts

1. Doctors (see § **3.43** *et seq.;* see also § **4.53** *et seq.*)

- Medical or anatomical models
- Anatomical diagrams or charts
- Specific pages from medical or hospital records
- Custom-painted medical illustrations—The doctor may need to work with a graphic artist or medical illustrator to develop complex

illustrations, for example, showing "normal" versus "damaged" body part or system.

2. Accident Reconstruction Expert (see § **3.51**)

- Diagram of accident scene
- Photographs of vehicles
- Illustration of road design standards

3. Economist (see § **3.47**)

- Chart showing elements of damages
- Easel and pad for economist to perform calculations and write them on the pad in the courtroom

4. Engineer (see § **3.50**)

- Schematic diagram
- Blueprints or construction plans
- Working model or miniature

Caution: Always make sure that any foundation documents or materials for the visual aid are put into evidence as part of the trial exhibits.

§ 3.40 Videotaping Expert Depositions

As a general rule, it is preferable to have expert witnesses appear in person in the courtroom. Live testimony keeps the jurors interested in the trial proceedings and permits them a firsthand opportunity to evaluate the appearance and demeanor of the witnesses. However, sometimes circumstances prevent the witness from appearing in the courtroom. The Federal Rules of Civil Procedure provide a remedy to this problem by allowing the use of de bene esse deposition testimony in lieu of live testimony when the circumstances warrant (see § **5.53** for further discussion).

Advances in the quality and availability of videotape technology and equipment, together with general acceptance by the legal community, have made videotaped testimony a commonplace occurrence in today's courtroom. Trial attorneys have found the videotaped deposition to be a viable and useful alternative to the expert's live trial testimony, particularly in the case of busy professional expert witnesses, such as physicians. Certainly, videotaped testimony is more interesting to the jury than listening to the tediously dry reading of deposition transcripts.

The following are reasons you might use a videotape deposition:

- A busy professional, such as the treating physician, is reluctant to appear live at trial. (See § **3.43** for more on using the physician as a medical expert at trial.)
- An expert witness cannot resolve a bona fide scheduling conflict that would prevent the witness from appearing in person at the trial.
- To preserve the testimony of an expert witness who is elderly or very ill, for use in the event the witness is not available at the time of trial.
- The expert resides in a remote location and the attorney feels it would be a logistical impossibility for the expert to appear live in the courtroom.
- In the attorney's estimation, the expert simply would not come across well in the courtroom. The expert could be highly qualified and very intelligent but have a debilitating fear of testifying before a judge and jury. The expert might be more effective and more comfortable testifying in a familiar setting in the presence of only the attorneys and the court reporter.

§ 3.41 —Pros and Cons of Using Videotaped Depositions at Trial

Review the items on the following checklist to help you evaluate the benefits of videotaping the expert's deposition in lieu of live testimony at trial.

1. Scheduling.
   The video deposition allows great flexibility in scheduling the date for the deposition, both for the expert and for counsel for all parties. However, it can be very difficult to arrange a mutually convenient date if several parties and counsel are involved.
2. Comfort and Convenience.
   The video deposition generally takes place in the office of the expert or in a conference room at the office of the attorney calling the deposition. In either case, the surroundings tend to be less formal than the courtroom setting, which usually means it is more comfortable and convenient for all concerned. However, either location is more prone to outside noise and telephone interruptions than the courtroom. Also, if the office of the expert is located some distance from those of the attorneys, someone must travel to the deposition site, necessitating travel time and expense.

3. Cost.
The costs associated with the court reporter or qualified video technician in recording the videotape deposition are relatively high in comparison to traditional court reporting methods. Besides the initial cost for taking the video deposition, additional costs may include the following:

- Transcribing the tape onto a paper transcript
- Providing an audio cassette tape backup (usually available)
- Creating a duplicate videotape for reference and review by counsel
- Editing the tape for court presentation after rulings on objections; and
- Travel costs and service time of the video technician for courtroom playback of the videotape.

However, these costs must be weighed against the cost of scheduling an afternoon of trial testimony for an expert who charges a very high hourly fee, especially because there is always a chance that the expert will end up waiting in the hallway at the courthouse until you are ready for him or her to testify.

4. Impact on the Jury.
As mentioned above, live witnesses are generally the most interesting to jurors. However, because everyone is used to watching television, the novelty of the videotaped deposition may serve as a change of pace in an otherwise monotonous trial.

The judge will instruct the jurors that they are to give the same weight and consideration to the testimony they hear via videotape as they do to the live testimony, but I have often wondered whether jurors are really able to do that. The appearance of the witness on television as opposed to in person could lessen the dramatic impact of the testimony on the jurors. From a defense perspective, this could be an advantage if the plaintiff presents key testimony via videotape because the defense counsel may be able to downplay subtly or at least offset the significance of the video testimony.

5. Impact of Visual Aids.
Visual aids may not be as effective when viewed on a television monitor as they could be when used by a live witness. However, if the visual aids used with the videotaped expert witness are offered as exhibits, they will be available in the jury room for the jurors to examine at close range.

6. Judge's Preference.
While the judge may be required by law to permit the use of videotaped testimony, this does not mean he or she has to like it. Some

judges simply have not fully accepted the use of videotape in their courtrooms. If you have a judge who has this attitude, consider whether the benefits of using videotape outweigh the possibility of annoying the judge. (See § **6.9** on learning about the judge's attitudes and preferences.)

7. Advance Knowledge.
The attorney who presents the videotaped testimony of an expert will know the exact content of the expert's testimony in advance of the trial. The objections raised by counsel in the deposition will already have been ruled upon (see § **6.11**), and the attorney will know how the expert's video testimony will sound to the jurors. However, the opposing counsel has the same advantage.

8. Presentation Flexibility.
The presenting attorney can introduce the taped testimony at the point in the trial he or she thinks is the most suitable. He or she will know exactly the amount of time it will take for the playback of the deposition tape, which can be very useful in planning the order of witnesses and in determining the strategy for the presentation (see § **6.61**). The attorney also has flexibility to play the videotape in the event the other witness testimony does not take as long as expected and the attorney needs to fill a gap in time before the next witness arrives to testify. However, the attorney or the trial paralegal must notify the video technician and allow time for the technician to reach the courthouse and set up the equipment for the playback. (See § **5.57** on playing the videotape deposition at trial.)

§ 3.42 —Preparing the Notice of Videotape Deposition

If you plan to videotape the expert's deposition for use at trial, you must clearly state this in the notice to the opposing counsel. The form is basically similar to a regular deposition notice, but it specifies that the deposition will be recorded by videotape and is for use at trial. The sample notice in **Form 3–7** illustrates the necessary information that should be included in the videotape deposition notice.

FORM 3–7
SAMPLE NOTICE OF DEPOSITION BY VIDEOTAPE

IN THE COURT OF COMMON PLEAS
________ COUNTY, OHIO

CHARLES SELBY,	:	CASE NO. ________
Plaintiff,	:	JUDGE __________
vs.	:	
GENERAL AUTO PARTS, et al.,	:	NOTICE TO TAKE DEPOSITION BY VIDEO TAPE (DE BENE ESSE)
Defendants.	:	

TO: Paul N. Kelly, Attorney for Defendant
7101 Northside Plaza
Akron, Ohio 44308

PLEASE TAKE NOTICE that, pursuant to Rule 30, Ohio Rules of Civil Procedure, Counsel for the Plaintiff will take the DE BENE ESSE deposition of Dr. Andrew H. Thomason as a trial witness on behalf of the Plaintiffs in the above captioned case on Thursday, December 6, 199__, at 2:00 P.M. at the offices of Dr. Thomason at the City Clinic Hospital, 1500 Everett Avenue, Cleveland, Ohio.

The deposition will be upon oral examination and will be recorded by videotape before a certified court reporter from the court reporting firm of Video Court Services of Stow, Ohio. Said videotape deposition shall be recorded, preserved and filed pursuant to Rule 12 of the Rules of Superintendence for the Courts of Common Pleas of Ohio. The oral examination will continue from day to day until completed. You are invited to attend and cross-examine.

____
[attorney]
[address]
[telephone]
Attorneys for Plaintiff,
Charles Selby

CERTIFICATE OF SERVICE

A copy of the foregoing Notice to Take Deposition By Videotape (De Bene Esse) was served by mail this ____ day of November, 199__, upon all counsel of record in this case.

____
[attorney]

§ 3.43 Using Doctors and Other Medical Experts in Trial Work

In cases involving bodily injury, medical testimony is used to support the injured party's claim for damages. An injured person's treatment may involve several types of medical personnel, depending on the care required. There is a wide variance among physicians and other medical personnel in their willingness to cooperate with the trial attorney. This section discusses a number of ways the trial paralegal can assist the trial attorney in communicating with medical personnel and obtaining their cooperation as trial witnesses.

§ 3.44 —Working with the Physician

The doctor's function in personal injury litigation is to establish the nature and extent of the injuries suffered by the patient and to substantiate the causal connection between the tort and those injuries. In the context of personal injury litigation, there are basically three categories of physicians:

1. Treating Physician. The treating physician is usually the first doctor to treat the patient after the trauma. He or she may have been the patient's personal doctor before the accident, or he or she may have become familiar with the patient's history in the course of treating the patient for the specific injury. In the trial context, the treating physician is the doctor who has been primarily responsible for directing and overseeing the patient's medical care and treatment in connection with the injuries resulting from the accident at issue.

2. Follow-up Physician. The follow-up physician is usually a specialist to whom the patient is referred by the treating physician, who determines a need for consultation services in a specific area of expertise, (a plastic surgeon, an orthopaedic specialist, a neurologist, and so on). Depending upon the importance of the specialized treatment to the overall picture of the patient's injuries, the attorney may wish to use the testimony of the follow-up physician instead of or in addition to that of the treating physician.

3. Reviewing Physician. The reviewing physician is not directly involved in the patient's treatment. The reviewing physician is usually a specialist who reviews the patient's medical records and the treating physician's medical report, and then examines the patient for the purpose of rendering an opinion as to the nature and extent of the patient's injuries. This category often applies to a doctor (hired by the defendant or the defendant's insurance company) who conducts the defense examination ("independent medical examination") of the plaintiff.

The physician's contribution to the case before trial may consist of the following:

- Providing copies of office records pertaining to the patient's treatment;
- Suggesting appropriate articles and medical texts to which the attorney can refer for background reading in order to fully understand the patient's injuries;
- Rendering a written medical report detailing the patient's injuries, the course of treatment, and the prognosis;
- Consultation with the attorney to discuss the details of the injury, treatment, and prognosis for purposes of settlement.

Most doctors are fairly cooperative with attorneys in the preliminary stages of the case. However, problems may arise when the attorney needs the physician to testify as a medical expert at the trial. Many doctors are reluctant to do this, mainly because of the time involved and the resulting cost in lost patient fees. In a medical malpractice case, where the physician would be called upon to testify against a colleague, he or she may also be afraid of damage to his or her professional reputation among the members of the medical community.

The trial paralegal can assist the attorney and facilitate successful interaction with the physician by laying the proper groundwork for gaining the doctor's cooperation. The following are some good ways to accomplish this:

1. Extend all of the same professional courtesies and considerations extended to any other expert witness. This means giving the physician reasonable notice of trial dates and compensating the physician for his or her time on the case. (See §§ **3.20–3.40** on working with expert witnesses.)
2. Suggest taking the physician's de bene esse deposition on videotape for use at trial if he is reluctant to make a live appearance at trial. (See § **3.40** for a discussion of videotaping expert depositions.)
3. Compile, review, and summarize the notes and materials from any previous meetings between the attorney and the physician. Include the physician's medical report, if any, as well as other hospital records, outpatient records, and so on. This will save time for both the doctor and the attorney when they meet again to prepare the doctor for trial or deposition testimony.
4. Schedule a face-to-face conference between the attorney and the doctor if they have not met previously. Schedule this meeting at the doctor's convenience. Doctors usually prefer to have the attorney come to the hospital or medical office rather than have to waste the travel time to go to the attorney's office. Work with the doctor's secretary, nurse, or

receptionist to determine the best time and place for a meeting between the attorney and the doctor. Arrange the meeting as far ahead of time as possible in order to accommodate the doctor's calendar. Inquire into the doctor's policy on fees for consultation and trial testimony and arrange to have the consultation fee paid well before the conference, if possible.

5. Arrange for the client/patient to visit the doctor within a few weeks before the doctor will be expected to testify so that the doctor can give his or her opinions of the person's medical condition based upon recent examination findings. Ask the trial attorney whether it is necessary or desirable to obtain an updated medical report from the physician.

6. Help the attorney make efficient use of the doctor's time at the trial preparation conference.

—Prepare a packet containing copies of any background medical research in your file for the attorney to review before he or she goes to the conference so that he or she can become familiar with the nature of the client's injuries.

—Prepare the patient's medical records for the attorney's review ahead of time, highlighting important entries. If necessary, prepare a glossary of medical terminology for the attorney's reference.

—Make sure the attorney has a copy of any previous report or opinion rendered by the physician readily available so that he or she can discuss it with the doctor.

—Prepare an outline of questions and points for the attorney to discuss with the physician in preparing trial or deposition testimony. Use the following checklist as a starting guide for areas to discuss with the doctor, and then tailor the outline to include specific questions pertaining to your specific trial.

—If possible, accompany the attorney to the doctor's preparation conference so you can assist with the documentation, take notes, and help the attorney make sure all the important points are covered in the discussion.

§ 3.45 —Subjects for Attorney-Physician Conference

These subjects should be covered during the attorney's conference with the doctor.

I. Establish the Physician's Qualifications and Credentials as an Expert:

1. Schools attended

2. Degrees conferred

3. Licenses and certifications earned
4. Experience, especially in the areas related to the type of services rendered to the patient
5. Hospitals where doctor has staff privileges
6. Professional associations or organizations of which the physician is a member
7. Books, articles, or treatises written and/or published
8. Teaching or lecturing experience
9. Obtain a current curriculum vitae or professional résumé

Note: In some instances you will find it prudent to check up on the physician's credentials as represented to the attorney. (See § **3.23** *et seq.* on investigating and evaluating the expert's qualifications.)

II. Regarding the Patient/Client:

10. Circumstances under which physician came to know and treat the patient
11. Overview of the past history of the patient
12. Description and explanation of the exact injuries the patient sustained in the accident
13. Causal connection between the subject injuries and the accident at issue
14. Review the pertinent hospital or other medical records to gain an understanding of the patient's treatment, medications, and details of any surgical procedures performed
15. Discuss any excerpts from the hospital or medical records which the attorney feels would make effective visual aids (using blowups) at trial.
16. Diagnostic tests performed to evaluate the extent of the injuries and the results of those tests
17. Patient's current medical condition
18. Relationship of the injury to the present medical condition
19. Explain aggravation of preexisting condition, if applicable
20. Prognosis and outlook for the patient's future medical status (permanency, degree of disability, how patient's lifestyle will be affected)
21. Increased susceptibility to future problems due to this injury, if applicable
22. Expected future treatment, if any
23. Estimated expense of future medical treatment
24. Medical expenses incurred by the patient are fair and reasonable for the services rendered (Show the doctor the summary of medical expenses that you will present as an exhibit at trial.)

III. Possible Visual Aids to Illustrate Injuries to the Jury (See also § **3.39** on working with experts to prepare visual aids; § **4.53** *et seq.* on using visual aids in medical testimony.)

25. X-rays (to provide a clear picture of fracture)
26. Medical photographs
27. Anatomical drawings
28. Medical models
29. Brace, prosthesis, steel pins, orthotic devices, TENS unit, and so forth (to show the jury what the patient had to endure as a result of this injury)
30. Graphs or charts drawn from objective diagnostic test results

IV. Cover Probable Cross-examination Questions from Opposing Counsel; Prepare for Cross-examination of the Opposition's Medical Expert:

31. Disclose the amount being paid to the doctor for court or deposition appearance
32. Amount paid by the patient to the doctor for medical services rendered
33. Doctor's testimony in other cases, if applicable
34. Review report or opinion rendered by opposition's own medical expert

V. Miscellaneous: Any other questions or areas which are particularly pertinent to the injuries at issue, tailored to the individual case

§ 3.46 Working with Other Types of Experts

You will have the opportunity to work with experts other than physicians and medical personnel. The function of some experts, such as photographers (see § **4.35**) and illustrators (see § **4.57**), is to help prepare demonstrative evidence for trial. Other experts serve as consultants to educate and assist the trial team (see § **3.28** and § **6.50**). In some cases, the expert witness is called upon to analyze the case to support theories of liability or negligence (see §§ **3.50–3.51**). Many other experts are employed to offer analyses and opinions on factual aspects of the case directly or indirectly related to the assessment of damages. Damage experts are often considered plaintiff's witnesses, but defense trial teams should be aware that these experts can assist in either proving or disproving damage theories, depending on which side of the question you represent.

This section will examine some of the specialized types of experts you may encounter in your trial work. Combine the suggestions presented here with the general information on working with experts in §§ **3.19–3.40.**

§ 3.47 Working with the Forensic Economist

The economist is a special type of expert witness often used by trial attorneys to assist in assessing and proving damages at trial. The economist, who is usually a Ph.D., generally has education and training in the fields of economics, statistics, accounting, and business concepts. This broad base of knowledge enables him or her to measure and evaluate the economically significant aspects of a case involving damages. The services which the forensic economist can provide to the trial team could include the following:

- Evaluating the economic impact of injury or disability on an individual's future earning capacity and quality of life.
- Evaluating the economic impact of disability on the family members of the injured person.
- Providing statistics to support a claim for monetary loss as a result of injuries.
- Assessing the value of intellectual property in a case where this is an issue.

In order to evaluate the person's earning capacity (had he or she not been injured) and work life expectancy (the average number of years the person would have been able to work had he or she not been injured), the economist must be provided with enough information to allow him or her to get a picture of the person's general lifestyle and any specific factors which would affect the calculations. You may be asked to work with the client and the economist to obtain and forward this data.

§ 3.48 Information to Provide to the Expert Economist

(Note that some items may be records and documents; others may be summary or narrative information you compile.)

1. Personal and Family Statistics

   - Name, date of birth, date of injury (or death), race
   - Names, dates of birth of all immediate family members

2. General Information

   - Health of the individual, both before and after the injury (medical records and doctors' reports may be appropriate for specific information on injuries)

- General information on health, life span of parents, grandparents (possible significant hereditary factors)
- Personal habits (smoking, hobbies, sports, activities)
- Personal consumption—Information on how the family spends its money (for housing, automobiles, recreation, savings, and so forth)
- Description of the injured person's contribution to the family household, chores, and so forth

3. Education

- Level of education attained by individual, parents, other family members
- School records/grades for education obtained to date
- Educational goals the injured person may have had (plans to go to college, chances for a scholarship)
- Job or career expectations or vocational plans the injured person may have had

4. Occupation and Wage Earning History

- Job description, title, classification
- Employer(s) names, dates of hire
- Wage history—Salary or hourly wage rates for past 5 to 10 years, with effective dates for each
- Description of hours worked per week, regular and overtime
- Information on any other method of compensation for work performed, as applicable (commission, bonus)
- Documentation of Income for the past 5 to 10 years (for example, W-2 forms, federal income tax returns)
- Any other information pertinent to an individual's work life, such as physical agility or strength requirements of the job

5. Fringe Benefits

- Employer's contribution for medical plans, pension plans, stock plans, bonuses, profit-sharing, and so forth
- Booklets or brochures describing benefits, if available

6. Business Records (if the injured person owned a business)

- Description of the type of business, date of inception, number of employees, product made or service provided

- Financial reports, statements, or pro formas
- Corporate tax returns
- Market surveys/analyses/projections
- Information on subsidiaries or affiliated companies

7. Special Expenses

- Information and documentation on expenses incurred as a result of the injury
- Medical bills and expenses
- Medication or prescription expenses
- Special equipment purchased (wheelchair, special mattress, ramps, hand controls for automobile, and so forth)
- Special modifications to house or residence to accommodate injury (for example, wheelchair access); may even have had to move residence (for example, to a one-story house or apartment)
- Special therapy (for example, nursing care, physical therapy, rehabilitation or occupational therapy)
- Cost of institutional care, special schooling
- Projections or data on cost of future care or future medical expenses (for example, inevitable future operation), including the estimated length of time the care will be needed and approximate current cost of the care

8. Miscellaneous

- Any other data specifically pertinent to this individual (case-specific)
- Prospective inheritance

§ 3.49 Working with the Vocational Assessment Expert

Another type of expert witness which the trial attorney may employ to assist in proving economic damages is the vocational assessment expert. The vocational assessment expert has many things in common with the forensic economist. (See **§ 3.47.**) The vocational assessment expert (sometimes called a vocational rehabilitation specialist) usually holds a master's or a doctorate degree and has a background in career counseling. In personal injury cases, the vocational assessment expert evaluates the injured client to determine that person's future work capability, based on age, education, previous work experience, and a review of the medical evidence. This type of professional can provide expert witness testimony at trial regarding the claimant's reduced capacity for doing his or her regular work due to the physical injuries suffered. The vocational assessment expert's opinion is based upon a comparison of the person's present capabilities to projections of what the person could have done had he or she not been injured. The following checklist outlines the usual procedures involved in working with the vocational assessment expert.

The following steps should be taken to obtain the vocational expert's opinion:

1. The trial attorney (or the paralegal) provides materials for background and review to the vocational assessment expert. (See the following list of materials.)
2. The expert may request the client's treating physician to provide specific information on the nature and severity of the client's physical impairment and limitations. This data may be requested in a letter or in the form of a questionnaire upon which the physician indicates the physical activities and working conditions that are medically contraindicated because of the client's physical impairment.
3. The vocational assessment expert then interviews the client and administers a battery of tests designed to measure physical and mental capabilities and limitations.
4. The vocational expert analyzes the test results and interview data in conjunction with the background materials.
5. The expert can then formulate an opinion and, if requested, provide a report stating his or her opinion as to the claimant's earning capacity and future prospects relative to earning power.

The following is a list of materials for the vocational expert (see also **§ 3.47,** Information to Provide to the Expert Economist):

1. Medical records—include the most recent medical data, especially doctors' reports
2. W-2 forms or income tax returns (last 4–5 years) to establish a "stream of earnings" or "stream of income" for the client prior to the injury
3. Employer and work records—include information on the time the client was off work due to the injuries, the date he or she returned to work, any limitations placed upon work
4. Lost wage statement from the employer
5. Work history—note particularly if the client was ever turned down for a job due to physical limitations caused by the injuries
6. School records—high school grades, SAT/ACT scores; transcript of college grades, if any

7. Records of medical expenses incurred due to the injuries
8. Family data—names and dates of birth of client and immediate family members
9. Comments on any changes in lifestyle experienced by the client due to the injuries

§ 3.50 Working with Engineers and Design Experts

In a products liability case or in an accident case involving an industrial machine defect or malfunction, the trial attorney may need to consult an engineer or design expert in order to fully understand the mechanism and the defect which caused the accident. There is someone who understands the applicable design standards for virtually any type of product or machine which could conceivably be involved in a lawsuit. (See § **3.20** on locating expert witnesses.)

The engineer or design expert may also be helpful to the trial preparation team by

- Providing sources for relevant background and technical information;
- Suggesting lines of further questioning;
- Pointing out the specific information needed in order to formulate an opinion;
- Indicating specific documents which should be requested through discovery procedures;
- Giving suggestions for applicable theories of liability;
- Furnishing an opinion, based upon factual evidence, regarding the subject hazard or defect.

Just as with any other expert, it is important to provide documentation of all the known facts to the engineering or design expert. This package of information should include only those facts of which the trial team is absolutely certain, and which can be proved without dispute at trial. As the trial paralegal, you may be asked to assist in the factual investigation and assembly of the materials package for the engineering or design expert. (See § **1.57** on conducting factual research.)

The following is a list of materials for the engineering or design expert:

1. Client's name, address, and telephone
2. Date and time of accident
3. Narrative description of how the accident occurred
4. Description of the injuries sustained
5. Employer's name, address, and telephone
6. Manufacturer's name, address, and telephone

7. Seller or distributor name and address
8. Name of the owner of the machine on the date of accident
9. Installer of the machine at employer's premises
10. Any available information identifying the type, model, serial number, and so forth of the machine
11. Any documentation available regarding the date of purchase (for example, an invoice or shipping order)
12. Any warranty, guaranty, service contract, service records, repair records, which would indicate who was responsible for maintaining or servicing the machine
13. Employer's "First Report of Accident" form or Incident Report
14. Names and telephone numbers of any witnesses to the accident
15. Written or recorded statements of any witnesses
16. Report of any physical inspections of the premises
17. Police department report, if any
18. Records or evidence of any changes, upgrades, or alterations made since the machine was manufactured or installed
19. Description of the exact conditions on the accident date and any changes made to those conditions after the accident date
20. Photographs or schematic drawings
21. Operating manual, handbook, or instructions
22. Copies of any posted warnings or caution signs
23. Reports of any previous or subsequent accidents related to the same product or machine
24. Technical drawings or specifications
25. American National Standards Institute (ANSI) Standards
26. National Safety Council (NSC) Industrial Data Sheets
27. Accident Prevention Manual, if any

§ 3.51 Working with an Accident Reconstruction Expert

In a motor vehicle accident case, the attorney may use the services of an expert who is specially trained in traffic accident analysis and reconstruction. The accident reconstruction specialist can assist in the following ways:

- Analyze the case for specific factors
- Help prepare the case for trial
- Testify as an expert witness at trial.

By scientifically analyzing specific factors of the accident and applying the proper mathematical calculations, the reconstruction expert can provide support for your case by rendering opinions on such things as:

- The preimpact direction of movement and speed of the vehicles involved in the accident
- The amount of reaction time the driver had
- The probable cause of the accident
- Whether the collision could have been avoided.

The accident reconstruction expert may be retained only for consultation to assist the attorney in preparing the case for trial. The expert may be able to supply calculations the attorney didn't know were possible or may not have thought of. The expert may be able to assist in developing your approach to the case and provide some ideas for how to go about proving your case. The expert can help the trial team determine whether a witness's version of the facts is plausible in light of the physical evidence.

The accident reconstruction expert may also be used to provide expert testimony at trial. The scope of the expert's involvement depends in part on whether the expert can render opinions which support the case and the client's testimony about the events. The testimony of an accident reconstruction expert who also has training in traffic and highway engineering could be used to support a claim involving highway design defects or deficiencies as contributing causative factors in a particular accident. Such design deficiencies might include:

- A road that is improperly signed and marked for its design
- A roadway that is improperly maintained
- A road that lacks proper guardrails or warning signals.

(See also § **3.20** on Locating an Expert Witness; § **3.23** on Evaluating the Expert's Experience; and § **3.25** on Engaging an Expert.)

§ 3.52 —Supplying Information to the Accident Reconstruction Expert

As with any other expert witness, you must supply the accident reconstruction expert with sufficient information and materials on the case for him or her to perform calculations. In addition to the information you provide, the expert may conduct his or her own investigation, including a personal visit to the accident site to view it and make measurements, notes, and so forth. You may have to accompany the expert to the site to point out various objects. He or she may also rely upon information such as published standards (ASHTO

Standards) for road design, government publications, engineering publications, textbooks, and articles to supplement the base of information.

It is important to keep track of the materials and records you release to the accident analysis expert, and what he or she refers to or relies upon in forming opinions in the case. Use the Records Release Log discussed in § **3.29** to catalog the materials you send to the accident expert. Generally, the more information you can give the expert, the better he or she can assist you in developing calculations to support your case. The following is a list of materials and information which you could provide to the accident reconstruction expert.

1. Accident report prepared by the investigating law enforcement officer
2. Photographs of the vehicles involved in the collision (either exterior or interior views), or of the roadway or the accident scene
3. Documentation of the length and location of skid marks or gouges in the road surface made by the vehicles involved in the accident
4. Description and/or photographs of any fixed object(s) struck or damaged by the vehicles. (See § **4.29** *et seq.*, on using photographs.)
5. Evidence of drugs or alcohol consumed by either driver. Check the accident report and hospital records for evidence of any tests for alcohol or drugs
6. Detail on road construction. Check your state Department of Transportation for maps of interstate highways, possibly engineering drawings
7. Composition of roadway surface (for example, asphalt, gravel, or concrete)
8. Diagrams or maps of the accident area
9. Type and location of traffic controls (stop signs, traffic lights) or road signs
10. Legal and/or posted speed limits
11. Weather conditions at the time of the accident
12. Description of the vehicles involved in the accident, including model, make, year, and condition of vehicles
13. Dimensions and weights of vehicles
14. Weight of motorcycle
15. Weights of individuals. This may not be of particular significance with a car, but would be a significant fraction of motorcycle weight

The accident reconstruction expert may or may not provide a written report setting forth his or her conclusions and opinions, depending upon the attorney's instructions. A written report by the accident expert may contain one or more diagrams of the accident site showing the preimpact and post-impact locations of various objects, measurements taken, and so on. In many accident cases, this type of diagram can serve as the basis for a visual aid to be used at trial. Work with the expert on developing an accurate diagram representing the accident scene, which the expert can use to illustrate as he or she testifies. (See § **3.39** on working with the expert witness to prepare visual aids; see also § **4.50** on preparing site diagrams.)

§ 3.53 Working with Translators and Interpreters

An increasing number of United States lawfirms have expanded into international practice, largely due to the proliferation of foreign-owned businesses in the last few decades. This expansion has created a growing need in trial work for the services of interpreters (for oral communication) or translators (for written materials). As a trial paralegal in today's litigious society, it is likely that at some time you will be asked to assist in a case which requires the expertise of a qualified person familiar with not only the oral and written language, but also with the culture and traditions of a foreign country.

Some examples of situations where you might need an interpreter or translator include the following:

- The key documentary evidence to support your case is written in a foreign language and must be translated into English to be usable.
- You have retained an internationally acclaimed expert in some discipline as a consultant on your case, but the expert is of foreign nationality and does not speak any English.
- The trial attorney must communicate with certain principals from your client's overseas subsidiary, and the company people primarily speak only their native language and do not understand English well.

The rates charged by interpreters and translators will depend on the scope of the project, the length and complexity of the job, and the amount of specialization required (such as highly technical terminology). Oral interpreters may charge an hourly fee or a daily flat rate.

Translations from major Western languages (French, German, Spanish) into English are generally somewhat less expensive than translations from English into those languages, or from and to more exotic languages. Remember that there may be additional charges for such things as

- Expedited service (requiring immediate turnaround)
- Overnight delivery
- Weekend or holiday work
- Translation from difficult-to-read materials (such as old handwritten manuscripts).

§ 3.54 —Locating Translators and Interpreters

If you are in charge of locating a translator or interpreter for your case, two sources you may wish to contact are The American Translators Association (ATA) and Berlitz Translation Services (BTS).

The American Translators Association, a national not-for-profit organization, was established in 1959 and is now the largest professional society of translators and interpreters in the United States. The ATA seeks to promote the recognition of translation as a profession, maintain standards of competence, and improve the standards and quality of translation. In 1963, the ATA established an Accreditation Committee which formulated a program, first implemented in 1972, to objectively define and measure a translator's skills in a given language combination. By passing an accreditation examination, an applicant may qualify for a certificate of accreditation issued by the ATA. An accredited translator has objective proof of possessing the basic skills and training necessary to function as a professional in the field.

The ATA offers a variety of services and can assist businesses, institutions, and lawfirms in locating competent translators and interpreters. The ATA has a number of local chapters and divisions throughout the United States, most of which publish a directory of members listing language combinations, areas of specialization, and indication of accreditation by the ATA. A list of ATA chapters, divisions, and cooperating groups is available from ATA Headquarters in Ossining, New York. Their office hours are 9:00 AM to 5:00 PM, Eastern Time, Monday through Friday.

American Translators Association (ATA)
109 Croton Avenue
Ossining, New York 10562
Telephone: (914) 941-1500
Fax: (914) 941-1330

Berlitz Translation Services (BTS) is a division of Berlitz International, Inc., the well-known language instruction organization. BTS specializes in translation and interpretation services and offers a full range of audio-visual services for foreign language adaptations. Through its worldwide network of language specialists, BTS provides services to the legal profession in the form of translators, interpreters, and language consultants in a wide variety of technical and commercial areas.

BTS operates a Business Document Center in Washington, D.C., that specializes in translating short documents from any language into English in a short turnaround time at competitive prices. For more information, contact:

Berlitz Translation Services
257 Park Avenue South, 17th Floor
New York, New York 10010
Telephone: (212) 598-2422; (800) 221-5504
Fax: (212) 505-9975.

CHAPTER 4

PREPARING VISUAL AIDS AND DEMONSTRATIVE EVIDENCE

§ 4.1 Planning Demonstrative Evidence

The attorney's job in the courtroom is to communicate clearly and effectively the facts of the case to the judge and jury. Communication in the courtroom can be verbal or nonverbal. The lawyers' words, the witnesses' testimony, and the judge's comments are all forms of verbal communication. But the appearance of the trial participants, the documents used as exhibits, and the visual aids all convey nonverbal information that is just as important to the jurors' understanding of the case as the verbal communication. The attorney uses demonstrative evidence to illustrate, demonstrate, or recreate an object or event for the jury. Demonstrative evidence:

- adds interest, variety, and persuasiveness to witness examinations;
- makes witness testimony easier to understand; and
- can help to focus the jurors' attention on specific issues.

Planning and creating visual aids is an interesting and creative aspect of trial work. It is challenging to translate a concept from abstract terms into a concrete visual picture. Creating effective visual aids to enhance the trial testimony is one of the most important ways you can assist the attorney with the courtroom presentation.

§ 4.2 Determining the Purpose of the Visual Aid

When a case involves complex facts or highly technical information, the attorney must educate the judge and jury to help them make an informed decision. Visual aids are powerful nonverbal tools that the attorney uses to help the jury understand and remember key information. A visual aid can truly be worth a thousand words when it comes to reinforcing key information. For example, visual aids can be used to summarize graphically massive amounts of data or statistics, making the potentially confusing numerical information easier for the witness to explain and for the jury to comprehend. Visual aids also help to reinforce the spoken testimony. Studies have shown that jurors are much more likely to remember facts conveyed by both visual and verbal testimony than through either method alone. Almost every case can use some kind of visual aid. The determination of whether the visual aid should be a photograph, a map, diagram, graph, chart, model, or some other type of demonstrative evidence depends on the type of information the attorney wishes to convey.

Some cases require more than one type of visual aid to adequately explain or illustrate the information.

Visual aids range from simple to elaborate, depending on the nature of the information, the time available to prepare them, and the budget available to produce them (see § **4.4**).

The techniques and materials range from very inexpensive to very expensive and from low-tech to sophisticated high-tech. Whatever form of visual aid you choose to illustrate the information, plan and execute it carefully. The inexpensive projects should be crafted just as carefully as the expensive ones. Careful planning, layout, and attention to detail can make even a very inexpensive chart an effective visual aid. Sloppy or careless charts may not cause you to lose the case, but they won't enhance your presentation, either. Visual aids can add dramatic impact to a trial presentation, but they must be accurate and not misleading. A chart that is inaccurate or distorts the information can damage the credibility of the trial presentation.

Include discussions to determine the attorney's objectives for demonstrative exhibits on the agenda for your trial preparation meetings (see § **2.9**). Ask the attorney to discuss the type of visual aids he or she plans to use in the case. Chances are the attorney has some preliminary ideas for possible visual aids. If he or she has not thought about it, this discussion may encourage him or her to start. There may be some document, map, chart, or table among the file documents that could serve as the basis for a visual aid, or you may be able to abstract key information from an existing document that could be easily be converted to demonstrative evidence to illustrate an important point.

As with all trial preparation tasks, the earlier you begin to plan and prepare the demonstrative evidence, the better. Early planning for visual aids has these advantages:

- It allows you the time to obtain the necessary art supplies if you do not have them on hand.
- You can do an unhurried and thorough job in preparing the visual aids.
- It allows you to commission specialized work from a professional illustrator or graphic artist, if needed. See § **4.57** on working with a professional medical illustrator to produce visuals.
- The attorney will be able to use the demonstrative exhibits before trial in the witness preparation conferences.
- The attorney can practice explaining charts and graphs and plan how to best incorporate the visual aids into the overall trial presentation.

Try to capture the attorney's initial thoughts on possible demonstrative evidence and visual aids at one of the first trial preparation meetings. Find out what key points the attorney wants the jury to remember. If the data could be conveyed in a chart or graph, prepare a rough layout to see if it would be effective in presenting the information. Review the draft chart with the attorney at your next meeting and discuss whether it accurately reflects the information the attorney wants the jury to understand. You can then refine the chart before you make up the final version. Go through this process whether you will do the artwork or have an outside firm or artist produce it. You must have a thorough understanding of the attorney's objectives if you are to convey the ideas to the artist and work with him or her to develop the final product.

§ 4.3 —Deciding Which Type of Visual Aid to Use

Naturally, the type of visual aid you use will depend on the nature of the case, the client's budget (see § **4.4**), and the time available. The attorney must also keep in mind the potential objections to admissibility that could be raised by the opposing parties. Not all types of visuals would be equally appropriate in every case.

If you are starting from "scratch" in thinking about possible visual aids, be creative! Do some brainstorming with the attorney and consider any idea that comes up. It costs nothing to generate ideas, and the result could be an original and attractive visual aid that is very valuable to the presentation of the case.

§ 4.4 —Considerations in Creating Visual Aids

Use the following smart questions list to help you stimulate discussions and ideas for visual aids.

1. What visual information would help to support or explain witness testimony? Think about the witnesses you have and the elements of the case you need to prove.
2. Are there any existing photographs? Could accurate, relevant photographs be taken, and if so, would they add to the presentation? If the case involves an accident site or an industrial facility not accessible through a jury view, photographs might be essential. If the case involves a land dispute, an aerial photograph may be the only way to give an adequate visual overview. See § **4.29.**
3. Are there any key documents or key phrases that could be excerpted from a contract and enlarged to focus the juror attention on the important language? See § **4.6.**
4. Could a map or diagram help to explain the circumstances or facts of the case? For example, you could prepare a composite map to depict the various property claims in a land dispute? See § **4.45.**

5. Is the case statistic-laden? Will the numbers be difficult for the jury to understand without some sort of visual illustration? Perhaps a chart showing a table of information or a graph would be appropriate. See **§ 4.16.**
6. Does the expert witness need to convey technical information that could be presented lecture-style, with the aid of transparencies shown on an overhead projector? See **§ 4.65.**
7. Do the facts lend themselves to being charted or graphed? Perhaps a bar graph or a line graph would be effective in comparing two or more sets of data. See **§ 4.19.**
8. Does the case involve a question of equitable division of an estate among various heirs or of the assets in a divorce? Consider using a pie chart to show the relative size of each person's portion. See **§ 4.19.**
9. Does the case involve a series of events that occurred over a period of time? Perhaps a timeline or chronology would be appropriate. See **§ 4.26.**
10. Does the case involve a complicated piece of machinery or other technically complex information? Perhaps a scale model or a detailed schematic diagram is in order. See **§ 4.61** and **§ 4.45.**
11. Does the case involve severe bodily injuries that can be adequately explained only through expert medical testimony? A detailed anatomical drawing or model comparing the normal tissue to the damaged area could be used. See **§ 4.53.**
12. Does the case involve data summarized or compiled from a large number of slips, vouchers, or invoices? Perhaps you could use a simplified chart supporting the bottom-line numbers on a computer printout. See **§ 4.16.**
13. Is there a question or dispute over the authenticity of a signature? Perhaps a blowup comparing the genuine and the forged signatures, side by side, could prove useful. See **§ 4.6.**
14. Does the case involve amounts of money, such as commissions or bonuses? Perhaps a simple chart showing the calculations could be useful. A second chart showing alternative calculations might also be in order. See **§ 4.16.**
15. Is there a complex set of relationships among individuals or corporate entities in your case? Perhaps a flow chart or organizational chart could be prepared to illustrate and clarify the various relationships. See **§ 4.28.**
16. Will you have an expert witness (such as an accountant or an economist) who will testify about various financial calculations? Either a flipchart or a prepared chart of the relevant numbers could help to illustrate the testimony. See **§ 4.16.**

17. Does the case involve allegations that could be proved or disproved by scientific testing? Perhaps a courtroom experiment or demonstration would provide a dramatic illustration to the jury. See § **4.59.**
18. Does the case involve sophisticated equipment or technology that could not be adequately conveyed by conventional graphics? Perhaps a videotaped recreation or computer animation would solve the problem. See **Chapter 8.**

§ 4.5 Weighing Cost Factors of Demonstrative Evidence

Most trial attorneys like the idea of using demonstrative evidence, but they are concerned about the cost. They think that all demonstrative evidence is expensive and should be used only in large cases. However, demonstrative evidence is a powerful tool in courtroom communication and persuasion, and successful trial teams recognize that some form of demonstrative evidence is appropriate in almost every case. The trial team has a responsibility to keep the cost of the demonstrative evidence in proper proportion to the value of the case and the client's budget. The cost of producing demonstrative evidence must be a consideration in planning the visual aids for your case. A number of variables can affect the cost considerations surrounding demonstrative evidence. See **Form 4–1,** Cost Continuum.

Amount of Time Available to Prepare for Trial. The illustrator, graphic artist, or media technician who has a reasonable amount of time to prepare visual aids can charge normal rates for the services involved. Requests for expedited service or immediate turnaround inevitably result in additional fees, and a rushed production schedule can lead to errors that could have been avoided with adequate preparation and testing time. Execution of very complicated or high-tech visuals may not be feasible at all if the preparation time is extremely limited.

Complexity of Subject Matter in the Case. A case concerning highly technical information or complicated processes generally involves more work and higher costs to produce the visual aids than a case with relatively simple information that can be conveyed by less expensive methods. As the amount of technical detail involved in the project increases, the more difficult and expensive the visual aid will be to produce. The high cost of demonstrative evidence may certainly prove to be justified in cases where it helps the jury understand very complex information or where it makes an otherwise dry and boring subject come to life for the jury.

FORM 4–1
COST CONTINUUM
DEMONSTRATIVE EVIDENCE TECHNIQUES

Cost Continuum
Demonstrative Evidence Techniques

Lowest Cost
Conventional
Simple to Prepare

Chalkboard
Easel Pad
Dry-Erase Board

Document Enlargements

Overhead Transparencies
Photographs
Photographic Slides

Static Graphs
(2-D tables, charts,
maps, and diagrams)

Standard Commercial Charts
(e.g., anatomical charts)
Customized Medical Illustrations)

Standard 3-Dimensional Models
Custom-built Models

Aerial Photography
Micro-photography
Infrared photography

Scientific Testing or Experiments

Videotape Recreations
Motion Pictures

Computer-Generated Reconstructions
Computer Animation/Graphics

Expensive
High-Tech
Innovative

Level of Sophistication Needed to Adequately Convey the Visual Information. This factor is also related to the degree of complexity of the subject matter—the more innovative the visual technique, the more expensive it is likely to be. The trial team must consider how sophisticated the demonstrative evidence needs to be to explain the subject and get the point across to the jury. Jurors today are constantly bombarded by vivid visual images from television and print media. Some cases may require a high level of mental stimulation that can be achieved only through sophisticated state of the art demonstrative evidence. The trial team must consider whether the cost of producing high-tech visuals is justified by the result. Sometimes the simplest visual aid is also the most effective. The jury may identify more readily with a relatively informal visual presentation of the information than it would with a dazzling high-tech method. In fact, an overly sophisticated presentation can confuse the jury and arouse their suspicions about the veracity of the innovative visual presentation technique.

Type of Background Information and Resources the Client Can Provide. The client may be able to provide research materials (drawings or photographs), equipment (computer data processing) and personnel (engineers, technicians, or support staff), resulting in lower costs to produce the demonstrative evidence. In a case involving personal injury or death, the client and family members may be able to provide photographs, diaries, awards, or other personal mementos that can be used very effectively as demonstrative evidence at little or no cost.

Availability of Expert Witness or Consultant to Assist in Developing Demonstrative Evidence. Experts can be of great assistance in developing accurately detailed visuals. Indeed, the expert's advice and input are essential in cases involving highly technical information. However, such extra involvement and demands on the expert's time will add to the overall costs of the demonstrative evidence.

Whether Demonstrative Exhibits are Produced In-house or by an Outside Illustrator or Technician. If your firm has the necessary equipment, supplies, and expertise in-house, it may be possible to produce high-quality conventional types of visual aids very economically. However, certain demonstrative evidence techniques (video animation, aerial photographs, detailed medical illustrations) require hiring outside help, resulting in additional expense to produce the visuals. Here again, the trial team must determine whether the cost of outside help is justified given the parameters of a specific case.

Nature and Extent of Changes During Preparation. Meticulous advance planning is important to cost-effective demonstrative evidence. Requests for numerous or extensive modifications to the visual aid made after the design work is in progress will result in higher costs. Also, any special or additional features that may be required to tailor or customize the visual aid (acrylic overlays, removable adhesive add-ons) will add to the cost.

Whether All or Part of the Demonstrative Evidence is Reusable in Future Cases. A generic anatomical chart or model illustrating a normal joint or organ may be reused in future cases involving similar bodily injuries. Customized models or drawings are expensive and generally cannot be used again, but the expense may be warranted in many cases.

§ 4.6 Using Document Enlargements

Document enlargements, or "blowups," are commonly used as demonstrative evidence in the courtroom because they are inexpensive, easy to prepare, and usually very effective. Most cases involve one or more key documents that contain significant information about the contract, transaction, or event at issue. The attorney may question witnesses about the documents during direct and cross-examination. Using an enlarged photocopy is an effective way to direct the jurors' attention to a key document as the witness is testifying about it. Reading the document as well as hearing testimony about it helps jurors remember important information. The blowup allows everyone in the courtroom to read the document at the same time, thus keeping the witness examination flowing smoothly. During closing argument, the attorney may reinforce key points of the testimony by underlining or highlighting a key phrase on the enlargement in front of the jury. Examples of routine uses for document enlargements during a trial might include:

- A copy of a letter may be proof that something was discussed or promised;
- An invoice, purchase order, or receipt may be of particular significance to monetary issues;
- A signed and dated contract or agreement may be proof of who agreed to the contract terms and upon what date they did so;
- An accident report can show that the driver was cited by police at the scene for a driving violation.

A more dramatic use of an enlargement would be to support of testimony of a handwriting analysis expert. An enlargement makes it easy for the expert to explain to the jury the handwriting characteristics he has determined.

Comparison of an authentic signature with an example of the forged signature could be very effective in a forgery case.

§ 4.7 Getting the Best Enlargement

Use the best original you have to copy for enlargement. Sometimes you will have the actual original document. If so, use it to make a sharp, clean photocopy on your office's best copy machine. If necessary, use the appropriate setting on your copier to darken the copy quality slightly so that the image is sharp. You may also have several copies of the same document from different sources in response to discovery requests. Assuming they are all identical, pick the cleanest copy for enlargement. If the copies are not identical, ask your supervising attorney which version you should use. Never send your original document out of the office to be photocopied and enlarged. An exception is the original vellum of a blueprint (see § **4.15**).

§ 4.8 Cleaning up the Copy for Enlargement

The blowup can be only as good as the copy from which it is made. An enlargement magnifies any flaws on the surface of the paper, such as staple marks or wrinkles. Tiny specks can become large blots on the blowup. Many times the first original you receive in the case will be a second- or third-generation photocopy of poor quality (very light characters, not straight on the page, or marks transferred from the glass surface of the photocopy machine). These marks may distract attention from the text of the document, so it is best to clean up the copy as much as possible before having it enlarged. Any special treatment of this type by a copy center or photo lab will cost extra.

You can clean up incidental marks and blemishes on a copy without changing the content of the document. Dab over any incidental specks with correction fluid. Use the formula made specially for copies to keep from smearing the photocopy toner. If the flawed area is large, consider trimming a copy or using extra wide correction tape to cover the spots. If the copy is not straight on the page, trim the margins and place the trimmed sheet straight on a clean paper backing. Then make another clean photocopy to send out for enlargement.

§ 4.9 Deciding What Size You Need

How large is large enough? This depends on how the attorney plans to use the document in the courtroom. For some uses, you may be able to use your office copier to enlarge a document. For enlargements over 11 by 17 inches, you will probably need to send the work out to a firm which specializes in making enlargements. Documents can usually be enlarged to 24 by 36 inches, 30 by 40 inches, or even 40 by 60 inches. The 30 by 40-inch size is the most versatile. The document is large enough to read across a regular size courtroom, yet it is still small enough to transport and store manageably.

§ 4.10 Making Enlargements on Your Office Copier

If your office copier has an enlargement feature, learn how to use it. If no one in your firm knows how to use the enlargement feature, borrow a copy of the operator's manual for that machine and read the instructions yourself. Then experiment, following the instructions carefully, until you discover the right combination of settings with which you can produce quick enlargements. When you do find the right settings, make a note of them in your master reference notebook (see **§ 2.9**) so you can reset the machine quickly when you must produce enlargements. You may want to do this under the supervision of the key operator, copy monitor, or the equivalent person in your office. Get whatever permission is necessary to learn how to access the full capabilities of the copy equipment. Make sure that you have 11 by 17 inch paper in stock. This is usually the maximum size copy regular office machines can handle.

§ 4.11 Sending Documents Out for Enlargement

For blowups larger than 11 by 17 inches, scout out the best local copy services in your area. Many copy centers have the equipment to enlarge an 8 1/2 by 11 inch page to 30 by 40 inches or larger. Try blueprint or graphics businesses specializing in enlargements or with equipment specifically devoted to enlarging. Copy centers usually use a two-step process in which they make one enlargement, then copy the enlarged document, again enlarging, so that the end product is from 30 by 40 inches to as large as 40 by 60 inches.

For documents with mostly alphanumeric characters, such as typed letters, the 30 by 40-inch size works best. It is large enough to see, but still fits on a standard 30 by 40-inch sheet of foam-core board. This size is still small enough to allow you to handle the boards easily for transportation and storage.

§ 4.12 Mounting Enlargements

You can have the enlarged documents mounted on backing boards by outside services, usually the same companies that do the enlarging, but this can be quite costly. If you are on a tight budget, you may want to mount the enlargements yourself. There is a very simple and neat way to do this. You will need the following supplies: a piece of 1/4-inch foam-core board slightly larger than the blowup, scissors, a ruler, a light pencil, and a can of spray adhesive (available at any office supply or art supply store). It is also helpful to have a damp cloth and a dry cloth to remove any excess adhesive from your fingers.

Lay the document out on the board before you apply the spray adhesive. Trim off any excess white margin if the document is slightly larger than the backing board. Center the document on the board. If the margins are uneven, measure a strip down the wider margin and cut it off. Cut as cleanly as you can. If you are mounting more than one document, do all the trimming and measuring on the boards before you spray any adhesive. Center and straighten the copy on the board, and mark very lightly in pencil each corner of the copy so you can place it precisely on the board once you have sprayed the adhesive. Leave a slightly larger margin at the bottom of the document so that no important text is hidden when you display the board on an easel. Before you spray the adhesive:

1. Choose a well-ventilated room in which to work. The fumes from the spray adhesive are highly toxic.
2. Protect your table or work surface with newsprint, brown parcel wrapping paper, or oilcloth before you spray the adhesive. Use one end of the table to spray the adhesive and the other end for smoothing the enlargement onto the backing board.
3. If possible, have someone help you with the final placement. Two pairs of hands are better when handling large sticky documents.
4. Shake the can of adhesive well.

Take the first board and lay it on the table, away from the area where you will be spraying the adhesive. Turn the document enlargement face down on the other end of the table (protected by newsprint, brown wrapping paper, or oilcloth). Starting at one corner of the back of the enlarged document, spray a light, even film of the adhesive over the entire surface of the back of the enlargement, concentrating slightly more adhesive at each corner of the paper. Have your helper take the top corners of the document while you take the bottom corners and hold the document face up (adhesive side down) over the backing board. If you are working alone, fold the bottom corners up to the top corners, adhesive side out (just like strips of wallpaper) and carry it over to the board. Be careful not to crease the fold into the paper.

Place the two top corners of the document along the pencil guide marks you made earlier on the backing board and press lightly into place. Hold the bottom of the page up away from the board. Then, working quickly, gradually smooth the paper down onto the board from the top with your fingers, gently working out any wrinkles or air bubbles. Press very lightly until you check to see if the document is straight on the board. If it is crooked, GENTLY lift the paper up from the bottom and adjust carefully, then smooth it back down toward the bottom. Once you are satisfied with the placement, smooth over the page with your fingers again, using a little more pressure to set the adhesive. Make sure the corners lie flat and are securely glued. You may need to spray just a bit more adhesive under each corner to make sure it is securely attached. Set the board up against a wall or cabinet and let the adhesive dry completely. The spray adhesive dries very quickly, so this will only take a few minutes.

§ 4.13 Mounting a Multipage Document

If your enlarged document consists of more than one page, such as a two-page letter or a multipage agreement, you can mount all the pages on the same board. Glue only the last page down onto the background board with the spray adhesive. Fasten the remaining pages at the top with brass brads, available at any office supply store. Leave these pages loose at the bottom so that they can be flipped over the board to reveal subsequent pages.

When you have a multipage document, lay out the pages against the backing board and trim them as described in **§ 4.12,** except make sure the pages are all the same size. Take the last page of the document and use the spray adhesive to mount it on the board as described above. Then measure the top of the board and make four or five equidistant marks to mark the place where the brads will be inserted. Lay the enlarged pages on the board and, using a utility knife or razor blade, cut a small slit through all the layers of paper and through the backing board. Keep this slit very small (about 1/4 inch will do), just big enough to slip the brad through to the back of the board. Insert the brad through the papers and the board and bring it out on the back side of the board. Bend the "legs" of the brad down flat so that the papers are fastened tightly against the backing board. When the brads are in place, use a strong plastic tape to cover the legs of the brad on the back of the board. This holds the fastener tightly in place and protects the fingers of anyone handling the board so they don't get stabbed by the ends of the brads. If the chart will get a lot of use or if the papers begin to tear away from the board where the brads are inserted, apply clear plastic hole reinforcements (the kind you use for three-ring notebook pages) around the slits on each layer of the paper to add strength and durability.

§ 4.14 Copying Oversized Documents

In some cases you will encounter documents which start out oversized, such as plat maps and engineering drawings. To mount these large documents, use the suggestions and techniques in **§ 4.12** and **§ 4.13.** For duplicates of oversized documents (to include in a notebook of trial exhibits), you will need to locate a commercial graphics firm or blueprint company which has the equipment to accommodate large-size document copying.

§ 4.15 Working with Blueprints

Duplicating architectural blueprints poses a particular problem, because the blue lines will not transfer to the copy on standard reproduction equipment. Blueprints ARE copies of the original plans drawn in black on a heavyweight white vellum sheet. Unless you happen to have the original vellum, the commercial graphics lab will have to make a sheet called an autopositive which replicates the original vellum before it can be copied. This is a time-consuming and very expensive process. Contact your local graphics firm for details.

§ 4.16 Developing Tables, Charts, and Graphs for Trial

Remember that the purpose of a visual aid is to simplify information. Trying to show too much information on one chart can result in a very cluttered and confusing visual aid. It is better to have two simple charts than one cluttered and confusing one. Where you must show several phases or versions of additional activity related to a specific chart, consider using acetate overlays.

Plan the chart layout carefully on paper first, before doing anything with the chart board. Discuss with the attorney what must be included and what could be omitted on the final version of the chart. If the chart looks confusing or cluttered on the paper plan, it probably will on the large board also. When planning the chart layout, allow space for the top title, which should be the largest size lettering on the board. The best placement for the title is usually centered, although occasionally it looks better to place it off-center. Allow adequate side margins, especially if you will use descriptive labels or a legend on the chart. Make the bottom margin at least one inch so that the bottom of the chart is visible when it is sitting on an easel bar.

Simplify the wording on a chart as much as possible, while still including all the essential information. Use common acronyms or company letters to save space where possible. Decide on the exact wording to be included on the chart before planning the layout. Count the number of letters in each line of lettering and determine the center letter. Adjust to allow a bit extra width for wide letters and a little less for narrow ones. When working with stencils or vinyl adhesive letters, start from the center and work out toward the edges of the chart. (Be sure everything is spelled correctly!) If your office has an automatic lettering machine, use it to print out the needed label strips and plan the layout with these before permanently sticking anything down on the chart board. Use chart tape to make lines and borders on charts. It will make crisp neat lines that will look sharper than lines drawn with ink or markers.

§ 4.17 Working with Foam-Core Board

The best all-purpose board for professional looking courtroom visual aids is 1/4-inch foam-core board. This board is composed of a thin sheet of styrofoam in the center, bonded on both sides to smooth, white, opaque posterboard. It comes in sheets of standard sizes (20 by 30 inches; 30 by 40 inches; 40 by 60 inches) but you can easily cut it to any size you need. (See the following checklist.) I prefer this board for courtroom visuals because:

1. It is lightweight, durable, easy to work with, and stiff enough to stand by itself on an easel. Thinner poster board will be "floppy" and thicker board will be heavy and brittle.
2. It will not wrinkle, warp, or bleed through when heavy pens and markers are used, and both sides can be used.
3. It takes glue, ink, line tape, adhesive letters, and acetate overlays equally well.
4. Pencil guide marks erase easily with an art eraser.
5. You can easily bore through it to attach a brad or other type of fastener.
6. It is strong enough to withstand repeated removal of "add-on" pieces fastened with Velcro™.

The best way to store foam-core board is to lay it flat, either on the floor or in oversized drawers such as the ones used by architects to store large blueprints. Alternatively, foam-core sheets can be stored standing on edge in a cabinet fitted with narrow slots or flush against the wall in a cupboard or storage room. Foam-core board does have a tendency to warp or bow if it is not stored completely flat.

Cutting Foam Core Board

When you need to cut a sheet of foam core board to size, follow this easy procedure to get a clean, straight cut.

1. Measure from the edge of the foam-core sheet to mark the desired size using a yardstick, T-square, or ruler. (Remember to allow for a margin around all four sides of your chart.)
2. With a No. 3 pencil lightly make several hash marks to indicate the line where you want to cut. Place a yardstick along the hash marks and draw a very light guideline all the way across the board.
3. Lay the board on a large table or other flat surface. Using your pencil guidemarks, place a yardstick or straightedge along the line. With a sharp blade utility knife held at a slight angle against the edge of the yardstick, cut carefully on the marked line, cutting only part way through the top paper layer and the styrofoam core, (scoring) the board. Exert light but steady pressure to keep the knife steady against the straightedge. It is very helpful to have someone else hold the yardstick in place on the board while you cut.
4. Stand the board up on its edge. Take one edge in each hand and gently fold the two halves away from the scored line, until the foam core snaps along the scored line. The foam will break cleanly along the cut, but the two pieces will still be held together by the paper bonded to the uncut side.
5. Turn the board over to the uncut side. Use the point of the utility blade to cut carefully through the paper down the length of the fold, using the fold as a guide for the blade. Be careful when you get to the bottom of the cut not to gouge the table or surface underneath.

See **§ 4.12** and **§ 4.13** on mounting enlarged documents onto foam-core board.

§ 4.18 Using Tables as Demonstrative Exhibits

Whenever you can reinforce a point in your case by using information arranged in columns or a columnar listing of related data items, a simple table can be a very effective visual aid to assist the attorney or the witness. Use tables to contrast and compare simple sets of information, or to concisely summarize complex numerical information found elsewhere in the case documents and exhibits. A table can convey complex information by neatly organizing it the data into labeled rows and columns, making it easier for the jury to comprehend multiple items of data simultaneously. Tables that illustrate calculations resulting in a bottom-line amount can be equally effective, especially when the figures represent significant sums of money.

Use your computer's spreadsheet program to help decide the layout for tabular charts (see **Chapter 8**). Always double-check the accuracy of the underlying numbers and calculations on a tabular chart. Never consider a tabular chart finished until you have run a calculator tape to proof the numbers. You can use colored letters and numbers for emphasis on tabular charts, but plan this carefully (especially with numbers representing money values) so that the chart is not misleading. For example, red numbers tend to indicate negative figures ("in the red") so it is best to use black, brown, green, or blue for values, unless you want to draw attention to a negative value.

Example: Suppose your case concerns the annual sales figures for the years 1985 through 1991 for the fictitious Kilgore Manufacturing Company, which has two divisions, the East Plant and the West Plant. An important aspect of the case is the amount each plant contributed to the annual sales over the subject time period. Another important point in the case hinges on the comparison of the company's actual total sales to the accountant's projected sales figures for the same time period. Your task is to create a visual aid chart illustrating all this financial data in an easy-to-understand fashion. You first review numerous financial statements, accounting records, and other related documents to obtain the correct figures. Then you organize the figures into a set of rows and columns and make a chart similar to the one shown here as **Table 4–1. Table 4–1** summarizes each plant's sales, the actual total sales, and the projected sales for each year in the time period from 1985 through 1991.

Table 4–1

Kilgore Manufacturing Company Sales 1985–1991

Year	East Plant	West Plant	Total Sales	Projected Sales
1985	$24,581,932	$11,194,310	$35,776,242	$35,000,000
1986	$25,172,127	$13,590,877	$38,763,004	$37,500,000
1987	$19,486,100	$14,732,850	$34,218,950	$39,000,000
1988	$22,490,168	$19,308,720	$41,798,888	$41,500,000
1989	$26,903,765	$22,159,380	$49,063,145	$44,000,000
1990	$30,654,820	$24,190,555	$54,845,375	$47,000,000
1991	$32,610,460	$25,455,250	$58,065,710	$50,000,000

Example: Another aspect of the case involving Kilgore Manufacturing Company is the amount of 1991 sales attributed to the top three sales representatives for the purpose of calculating a percentage bonus distribution. You want to make a chart to illustrate that these three top sales representatives far exceeded any of the other representatives in the proportion of sales for which they were responsible. You prepare a table such as the one in **Table 4–2.** See also **§ 4.23** for pie graphs that graphically illustrate the sales distribution and percentages.

Table 4–2

Kilgore Manufacturing Company
Top Sales Representatives 1991
(Bonus Distribution Calculation)

Sales Rep Name	Amount
R. Keith	$23,450,000
H. Glenn	$17,505,000
K. Adams	$12,065,000
Other	$5,045,710
Total	$58,065,710

§ 4.19 Using Graphs as Demonstrative Exhibits

If you can illustrate information in table format, with labels across the top and down the side, you can probably show the same data in a graph. The most effective kind of graph for your project will depend on the nature of the data and the particular point you want to illustrate. Graphs can be used to display different types of information: Money, in hundreds, thousands, or millions of dollars; weight or volume, in ounces, pounds, or tons; time, in increments of days, months, or years, and so on. The following sections briefly discuss some of the various types of graphs you might use for visual aids in the courtroom.

§ 4.20 —Bar Graphs

Bar graphs are effective when you want to compare two sets of similar information. The height (in vertical bar graphs) or width (in horizontal bar graphs) of the bars represent the values on the graph. Bar graphs can also show contrasts or differences between data items. When you need to illustrate only one type of value, a single-range or simple bar graph compares values within a set to each other (see **Figure 4–1,** Sample Simple Bar Graph). A multiple-range bar graph displays bars of varying heights, indicating comparable values from two sets of data at the same time. Complex bar graphs can use various shadings or colors to identify the bars representing each type of data (see **Figure 4–2,** Sample Complex Bar Graph).

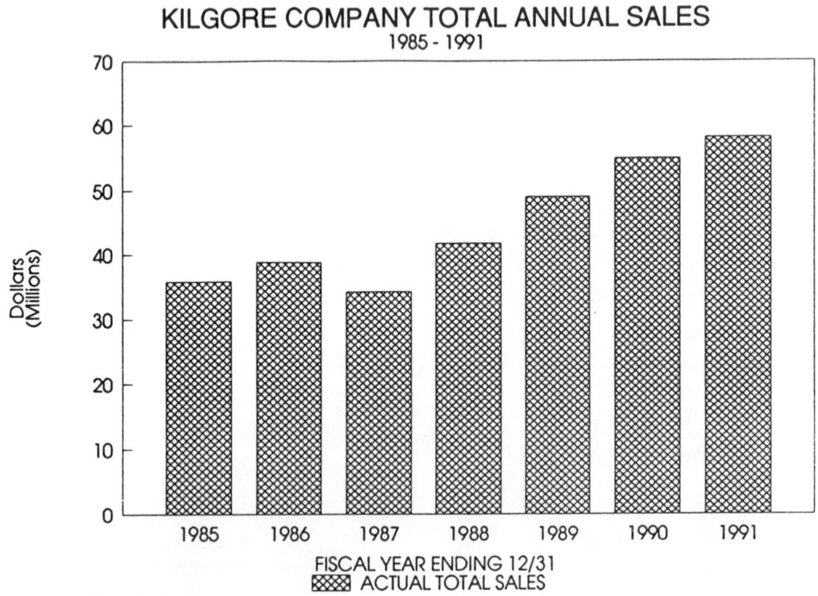

Figure 4-1. Sample simple bar graph.

Example: Suppose you wanted to graphically illustrate the fluctuation in the Kilgore Manufacturing Company's total sales for the period from 1985 through 1991 using the figures from **Table 4–1** in **§ 4.18.** A vertical bar graph showing the values in the Total Actual Income column in **Table 4–1** might look like the one in the sample simple bar graph.

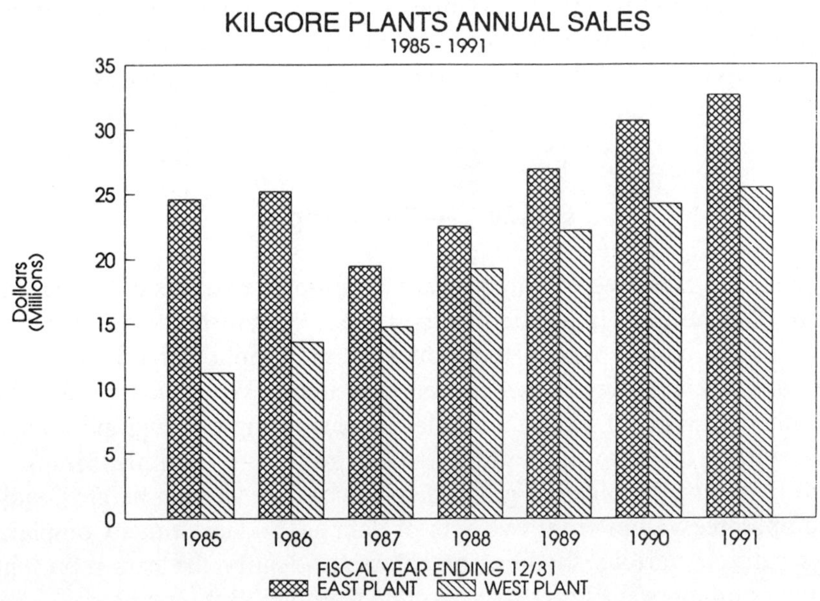

Figure 4–2. Sample complex bar graph.

If you wanted to compare the sales from the East Plant to the sales from the West Plant for each year during the time period, your graph might be similar to the complex bar graph in the second sample. Note the use of shading and a legend or key to differentiate the profits from each plant division.

§ 4.21 —Stacked-Bar Graphs

A variation of the bar graph is the stacked-bar graph, which you would use to compare different sets of information while at the same time illustrating the component parts and the total of each set. The totals are shown by stacking the bars representing the individual components one on top of another.

Example: The sample stacked-bar graph illustrates the company's total sales for the six-year period, but it also gives a breakdown of how much each plant contributed to the total sales. Here again, notice how the shading is used to distinguish the bars representing the East and West plants. The complex bar graph in **§ 4.20** is more effective if you want to compare the earnings of the two plants. The stacked-bar graph shown here would be more effective if the *combined* total sales is the point you want to illustrate. See **Figure 4–3** for a sample stacked-bar graph.

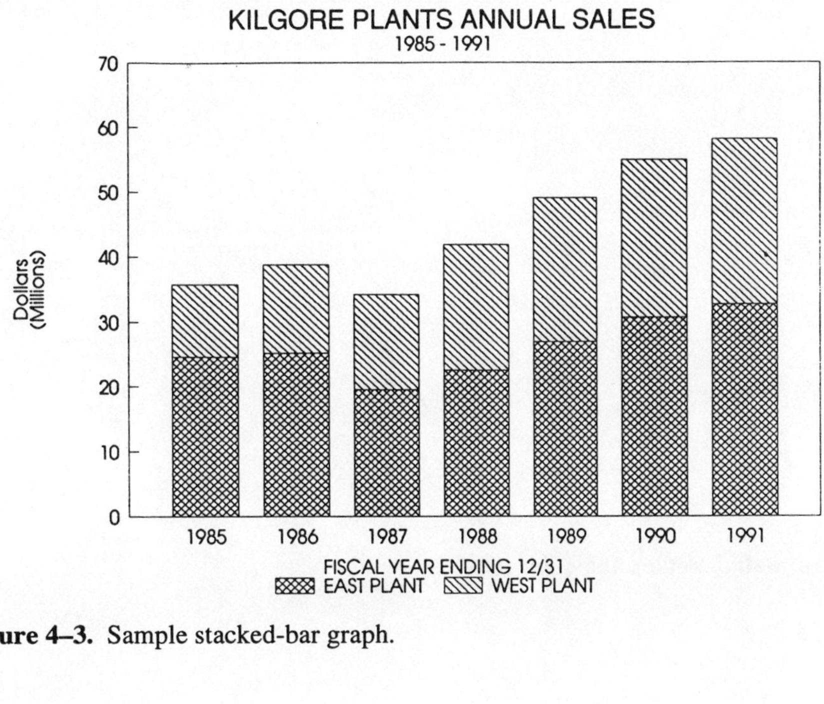

Figure 4–3. Sample stacked-bar graph.

§ 4.22 —Line Graphs

Line graphs are particularly effective for indicating changes in information over time, although they are not limited to that use. Each value in a line graph is represented by a point placed at an appropriate distance above the horizontal (X) axis of the graph. A line connects the points to show the increase or decrease in value. The line graph in the **Figure 4–4** illustrates the same values as the simple bar graph in § **4.20.** Notice that the rise and fall of the sales figures is easier to read by looking at the angles on the line graph. You might use the line graph if you wanted to point out the up-and-down fluctuation of the company's annual sales for the six-year period rather than just charting the dollar values.

A complex line graph may use multiple lines on the same graph to compare changes in one set of data to changes in another set of data. For example, the sample graph shown charts the comparison of the company's actual sales to the projected sales over the subject time period (see **Figure 4–5,** Sample Complex Line Graph). This line graph makes it easy to visualize how the company's actual sales exceeded the projected sales figures for every year after 1987.

Figure 4–4. Sample simple line graph.

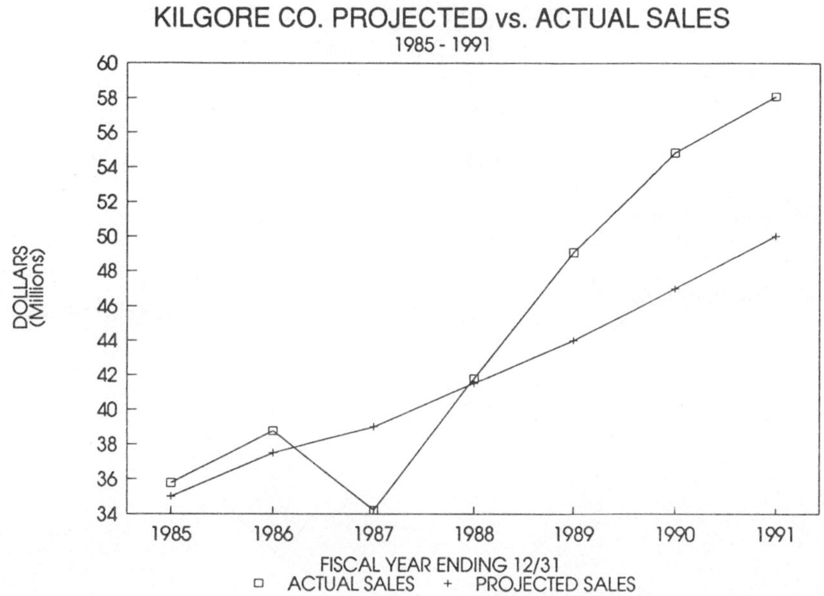

Figure 4–5. Sample complex line graph.

§ 4.23 —Pie Graphs

A pie graph uses a circle divided into slices to compare individual parts to the whole and illustrate relationships among components of a single set of data items. Each value is represented by a wedge or slice of the pie, and the sum of the slices represents the entire pie, or 100 percent. You can add various shadings or colors to make it easier to distinguish the various pie wedges.

Example: Suppose one question of proof at trial hinged on the proportional share of sales bonuses earned by the top three sales representatives of Kilgore Manufacturing Company. The information from a simple table chart (see **§ 4.18, Table 4–2**) shows the information, but it is difficult to visually compare the amounts. The pie graph (see **Figure 4–6**), based on the figures in **Table 4-2,** makes it much easier to visualize the proportional share attributed to the top three Kilgore sales representatives. The segments on the pie graph can be enhanced by coloring or shading to make the graph easier to read or for emphasis on a particular segment, if desired (see **Figure 4–7,** Sample Shaded Pie Graph).

A variation of the pie graph "explodes" one or more wedges to emphasize a particular value or values. This segment is set apart slightly from the rest of the pie chart. For example, if you wanted to emphasize the sales attributed to representative R. Keith, you could explode that segment so that it stands out from the remainder of the pie (see **Figure 4–8**).

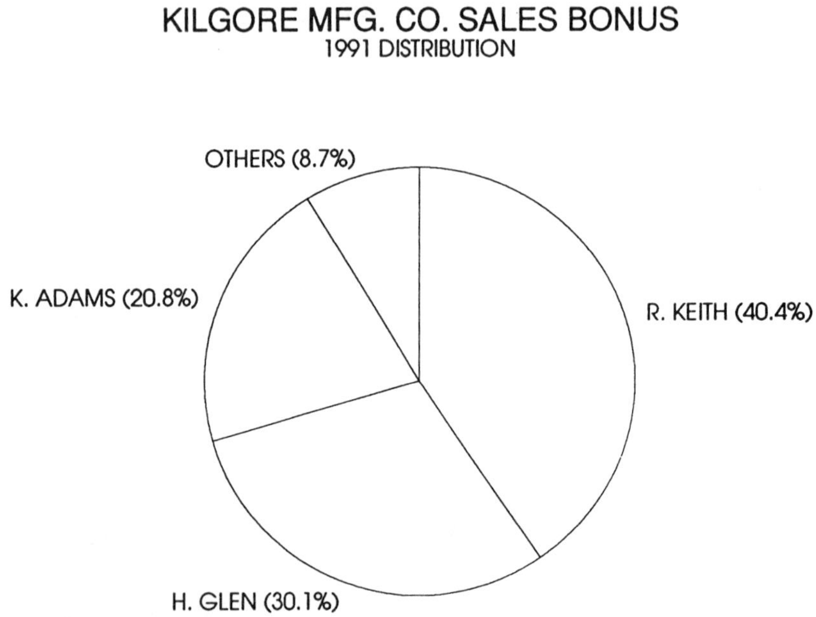

Figure 4–6. Sample unshaded pie graph.

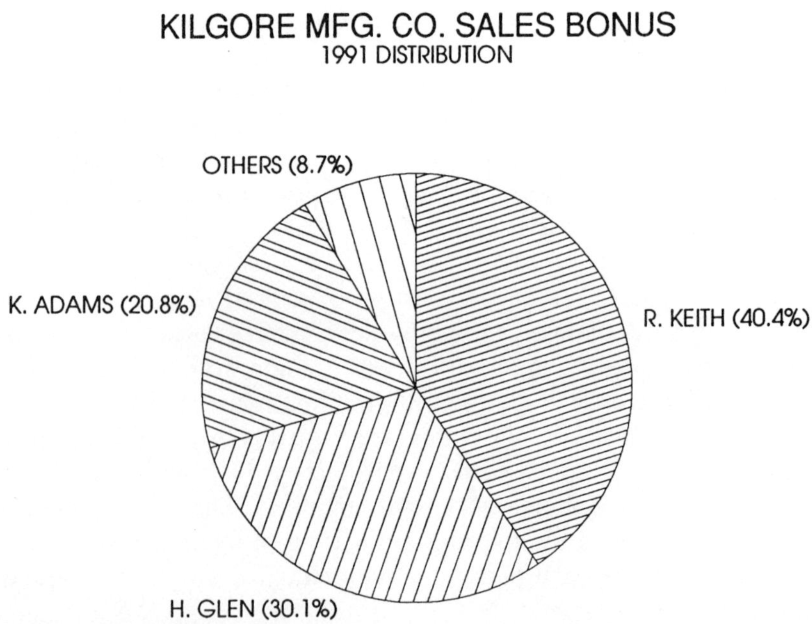

Figure 4–7. Sample shaded pie graph.

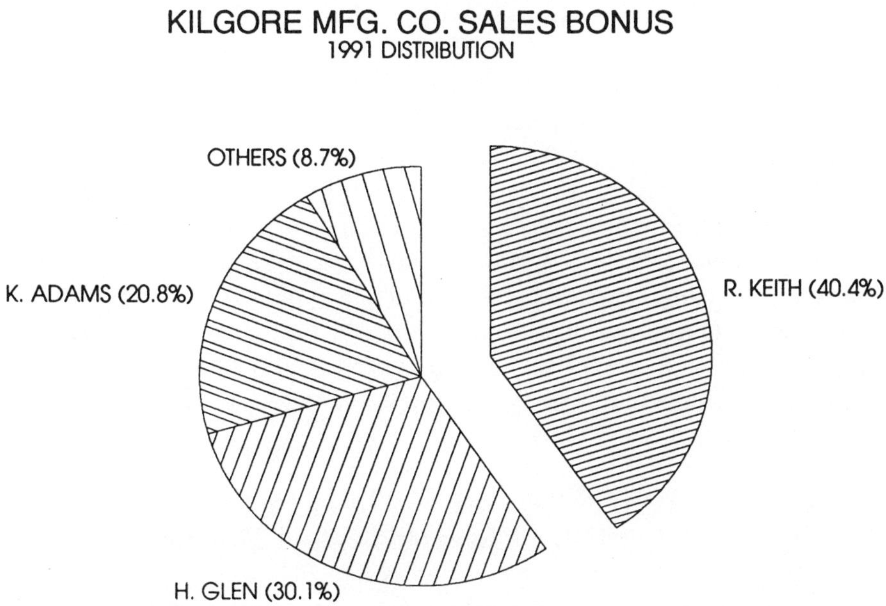

Figure 4–8. Sample exploded pie graph.

§ 4.24 Tips for Creating Good Graphs

If one axis of a graph indicates the time covered by the activity on the graph, the beginning of the activity rests at one end of the scale and the ending of the activity extends to the other end of the same scale. Amounts or numbers range from zero at one end of the scale to the highest value involved in the specific set of facts at the other end of the scale.

You can add horizontal or vertical grids (or both) to make numerical data easier to read, but this also tends to clutter the graph unnecessarily and may actually detract from the clarity of the graph. Whether or not you decide to darken the grid, measure the grid squares and lightly draw the grid lines in with a very light pencil to ensure accuracy when you actually plot the graph points or values. Make sure you have enough squares to accommodate the amount of data you want to show.

Use shading or crosshatching to distinguish one set of data from another when you have multiple data sets on a graph. If you have more than one graph showing the same information in different ways, use consistent coloring or shading for that type of information on each graph. Make a simple legend or key to correspond to shading or colors used to represent values for different entities. Keep the lettering and labeling as simple as possible (see **§ 4.16**) so that it will not detract from the effectiveness of the graph itself.

§ 4.25 —Using Computer-Generated Graphs

You can plot graphs manually on graph paper. However, if you have access to Lotus 1-2-3®, Excel®, or another spreadsheet type of program with graphics capability, experiment with the graph function and produce the same data on several different types of graphs to see which yields the most effective illustration of the information for the purposes of your case. Use the computer-generated graph to help you plan the layout of your visual aid graph. See **Chapter 8** on using spreadsheet and graphics applications. If your printer is capable of printing high-quality graphics, you may even be able to use the computer-generated graph itself by enlarging it and enhancing it. See **§ 4.11** on document enlargements or by copying it onto a transparency to use with an overhead projector (see **§ 4.61**).

§ 4.26 Using Chronologies and Timelines

Many cases involve issues surrounding the date upon which something happened, the order in which certain events occurred, or the frequency with which events occurred over a specified period of time. In such cases it is often useful to illustrate graphically the spatial or linear relationship between the dates of the events in question by means of a chronology or timeline.

Chronologies and timelines perform similar illustrative functions as demonstrative exhibits. The timeline is usually oriented horizontally, while a chronology is generally used in a vertically-oriented representation of the sequence of a selected set of events. The chronology will be similar to a tabular format (see **§ 4.18**), set up in two columns, one for the date and the second for a description of the activity which occurred on that date. Use the functions on your computer software to arrange the significant events in date order to determine whether a chronology would be useful (see **Chapter 8**).

If the particular sequence or pattern of events is important to the foundation of the case, consider using a timeline as a sort of linear calendar to orient the jury as to the amount of time between events or the pattern of occurrence or frequency of some activity. A timeline is an efficient way to condense many years' or months' worth of events into an easily digestible chart highlighting key events or transactions.

§ 4.27 —Planning a Timeline

Use the following tips to help you plan a timeline.

1. Decide what units of time you need to illustrate.

   Consider the first date and the last date that must be included and determine the total length of the time span in days, months, weeks, or years. The dates you want to depict may not fall neatly into calendar years. You do not necessarily have to waste chart space by starting with January if the first significant date did not occur until June. As long as the years and monthly increments are labeled clearly, indicating the correct spatial relationships in the span of time from the first event to the last with even increments in between, the timeline will not be misleading.

2. Decide the scale of the timeline.

   It is important to draw the timeline to scale so the information will not be distorted. How fine do the divisions need to be? Is showing the month an event occurred precise enough, or is there some significance to the number of days elapsed between events? Discuss this with the attorney so you know how much detail to include.

3. Determine the shape of the timeline.

   Make a rough drawing of the significant dates on paper to determine where the approximate center of the timeline will fall on the timeline continuum.

4. Prepare the board for the timeline chart.

   Measure the dimensions of the chart board on which you plan to lay out the timeline. (The following examples use a 30 by 40-inch board with the 40-inch side turned horizontally.) Measure and lightly mark a 2-inch a margin on each edge of the board. On a 40-inch board, this leaves 36 inches of horizontal center space for the timeline. Measuring from the edge of the board, lightly mark the center of the horizontal space with a light pencil.

5. Calculate the size of the time increments.

   The general rule is that the longer the time span you need to illustrate, the smaller the individual increments will be (note the examples at the end of this section). Decide how much space you can allocate to each time increment, based on the total inches of usable horizontal space available after you have subtracted the margin (see Step 4).

Note: When the timeline covers a very long time period and you have a number of events to emphasize, you may have to use a double-length board. This increases the amount of horizontal space so the timeline won't look so crowded, but it also makes the exhibit bulkier and more difficult to handle. Consider using a hinged board with two horizontal strips laid end to end to increase the illustration space available. Place the seam at a strategic place in the timeline where there is no critical information. Use binder clips on the top and bottom to keep the ends in place when the hinge is unfolded. See § **4.17** for tips on working with foam-core board.

6. Decide how to label the timeline.

   In a timeline that covers several years, labeling every month could result in a very cluttered and confusing chart. Clearly label each year, but use just capital-letter abbreviations for the month names within each year: JFMAMJJASOND. When labeling individual dates on the timeline, use simple phrases and economize on words as much as possible.

Use the following examples to help you plan the correct incremental measures to suit the time span on your timeline.

Example 1: Suppose you want to show monthly occurrences over a period of three years. Measure 6 inches in each direction from the center line mark, dividing the board (exclusive of margins) into three equal sections of 12 inches each. Make long hash marks to show the main yearly divisions. Then, if you want to indicate particular months within the year, divide the line into 12 one-inch segments, one for each month. Use smaller hash marks to indicate monthly divisions.

Example 2: You want to illustrate monthly increments for a time span of one year. Divide the 36-inch space into 12 three-inch segments, one for each month of the year.

Example 3: You need to show monthly increments over a period of two years. Measure the 36-inch space into 1.5 inch increments, resulting in 24 months.

Example 4: You need to show the days in one month. Measure the 36-inch space into segments of approximately 1.2 inches for each daily increment.

You can borrow a technique from construction project scheduling charts to produce a special type of timeline chart to illustrate concurrent events overlapping series of events, or the simultaneous activities of multiple entities. Prepare a background grid indicating the appropriate weekly or monthly intervals, then superimpose strips of color across the linear space to show the overlap.

§ 4.28 Flow Charts and Organizational Charts

Flow charts and organizational charts can be used at trial to illustrate complex processes or relationships among companies or entities. A flow chart is most useful for graphically representing sequential steps or stages, such as a complex manufacturing process. A chart breaking the process down into simple steps, diagramming the various production steps and adding directional arrows can be a great visual aid for an expert witness in helping the jury to understand a complex manufacturing process.

Organizational charts can be effective to illustrate and clarify complex relationships among interrelated entities or companies, such as corporate subsidiaries. These are similar to the charts which large companies use to diagram their internal network of authority (the "chain of command").

§ 4.29 Preparing and Using Photographs in Trial Work

Photographs are often used as visual aids in trial work because they are easy to obtain and widely accepted as evidence. Whether taken in conjunction with the incident involved in the lawsuit or taken specifically for use at trial, a picture that accurately depicts a location, person, or object conveys a powerful message to a jury in a realistic way. Key photographs can enhance witnesses' verbal descriptions and help to familiarize the jurors with locations, persons, or objects discussed in the testimony. Indeed, a picture may be the only way to portray a person who is unable to be in the courtroom.

The most commonly used type of photographs are still photographs, either in color or in black and white. These may be in the form of prints or slides. However, other types of photography are useful in trial work, such as X-rays, motion pictures, videotape, and specialized types of photography such as aerial and infrared photography and photomicrography.

§ 4.30 —Admissibility Issues for Photographs

Photographs are defined in Rule 1001 of the Federal Rules of Evidence (FRE) which reads as follows:

ARTICLE X. CONTENTS OF WRITINGS, RECORDINGS, AND PHOTOGRAPHS
RULE 1001. DEFINITIONS

For purposes of this article the following definitions are applicable:

(1) **Writings and Recordings.** "Writings" and "recordings" consist of letters, words, or numbers, or their equivalent, set down by handwriting, typewriting, printing, photostating, photographing, magnetic impulse, mechanical or electronic recording, or other form of data compilation.

(2) **Photographs.** "Photographs" include still photographs, X-ray films, video tapes, and motion pictures.

(3) **Original.** An "original" of a writing or recording is the writing or recording itself or any counterpart intended to have the same effect by a person executing or issuing it. An "original" of a photograph includes the negative or any print therefrom. If data are stored in a computer or similar device, any printout or other output readable by sight, shown to reflect the data accurately, is an "original."

(4) **Duplicate.** A "duplicate" is a counterpart produced by the same impression as the original, or from the same matrix, or by means of photography, including enlargements and miniatures, or by mechanical or electronic re-recording, or by chemical reproduction, or by other equivalent techniques which accurately reproduces the original.

Rule 901(a) of the Federal Rules of Evidence governs the test for admissibility of photographs:

RULE 901. REQUIREMENT OF AUTHENTICATION OR IDENTIFICATION

(a) General Provision. The requirement of authentication or identification as a condition precedent to admissibility is satisfied by evidence sufficient to support a finding that the matter in question is what its proponent claims.

You must be aware of the admissibility issues applicable to photographs if you plan to use them in your trial presentation. Before it can be properly admitted into evidence a photograph must meet these basic criteria:

1. The photograph must be relevant and material to the factual issues in the case.
2. The photograph must assist the jury in understanding some aspect of the facts.
3. The photograph must be qualified through supporting witness testimony.

The testimony must establish that the photograph fairly and accurately portrays the subject matter and that it is what the offering party claims it is, according to the provisions of FRE 901(a). A photograph may be verified by the testimony of the photographer who actually took the picture or another person with personal knowledge of the items depicted who can state that the photograph accurately represents the objects, injuries, accident scene, and so on.

The purpose for which the photograph is used at trial determines the extent of the witness testimony needed to properly authenticate it. When a photograph is used simply as a general reference to aid the testimony of a witness, basic identification and verification by a witness are usually sufficient to qualify it. However, when a photograph is introduced as evidence to illustrate specific details such as spatial relationships, distance, or height, the testimony attesting to the accuracy of the photograph must be more extensive. The trial judge determines whether the supporting testimony offered is adequate to verify the photograph.

Photographic Enlargements. See also § **4.39.**

Photographic enlargements are considered "duplicates" under the definition in FRE 1001(4). The person who actually created the enlargement does not have to testify, but the basic criteria for the admissibility of photographs must still be met:

- The enlargement must be properly identified and verified by the testimony of a knowledgeable witness.
- The items or scene depicted must be material to the issues in the case.
- The enlargement must not confuse or mislead the jury.

Changes in Conditions. A problem with admissibility may arise when photographs are taken months or years after an event occurred and certain conditions have changed since the date of the occurrence. If there has been a substantial change in conditions which are relevant to the issues in the case, the photograph may not be admissible. However, the photograph may be admissible even with the changes, provided the changed conditions are not material to the facts at issue in the case. The party offering the photograph must be able to meet the opposing counsel's objection to admissibility of the photograph by:

- Identifying precisely what conditions changed
- Fully explaining the changes
- Explaining what portions of the photograph should be disregarded because of the changes
- Satisfying the judge that the photograph will not confuse or mislead the jury.

§ 4.31 Obtaining Official or Police Photographs

If your case involves a motor vehicle accident, especially one which resulted in severe damage or injuries to one or more of the drivers or passengers, check to see if any photographs were taken by the law enforcement officer who investigated and reported on the accident. Because police photographs are taken at the accident scene shortly after the accident occurred, they can reliably illustrate such things as damage to the vehicles, the angle of impact, skidmarks or gouges in the road surface, and stop signs or other traffic controls. Of course, the quality of the pictures will depend to some degree on the photographic skill of the police officer, but police training includes instruction on taking documentary photographs for accident reporting. An advantage to using police photos is that they are representations of the actual scene, taken in the course of official business, and thus they can be readily authenticated by the reporting officer. See § **4.30** on authentication of photographs.

Check the official accident report filled out by the investigating officer to find out whether police pictures were taken in your case. The accident report forms may vary somewhat in design among various law enforcement organizations (local police, county sheriff, state highway patrol), but somewhere on the form (frequently at the top right-hand corner) there will be a box or blank for the officer to check indicating whether pictures were taken. A photo reference number may also be indicated. If there is a separate photo reference number, be sure to include it when you request copies of the photographs from the reporting agency.

The procedure for obtaining police photographs will vary depending on the particular agency involved. You may be able to order copies of the photographs from your local police department in person or over the telephone by calling the records department and arranging for payment of a small fee. Local records departments may require you to fill out a short form giving identifying information about the case to assist them in locating the photographs. See **Form 4–2,** Sample Photo Request Form.

Call the reporting agency to find out how you can obtain copies of the photographs. As you determine the requirements for ordering photographs from various law enforcement agencies, keep notes in your master reference information notebook for future reference. See § **2.9** on building a reference resource notebook.

FORM 4–2
SAMPLE PHOTO REQUEST FORM

LOCAL POLICE DEPARTMENT

PHOTO REQUEST

Accident Report No.: ____________________ Photo Ref. No.:______

Names of Driver(s): ______________________________________

Location: ____________________ Accident Date: __________

Photographs: ( ) sets 4 x 6 @ $3.00 ____________

( ) sets 8 x 10 @ $5.00 ____________

MAKE CHECKS PAYABLE TO: Local Police Department

Company: ____________ Signature: ____________

Address: ____________ Telephone: ____________

Most county and state law enforcement agencies require a written request, on either a preprinted form or a letter, and advance payment of a small fee (usually less than $10.00) directed to the appropriate records custodian. The reporting agency then prints the photographs from the negatives and forwards them to you by return mail. If there is no request form for the agency involved in your case, put the relevant information in a letter. Be sure to include enough information about the case so that the photographs can be located easily by the records custodian. Enclose a self-addressed, stamped envelope for the return postage. See **Form 4–3,** Sample Letter Requesting Photographs.

The usual size for photographs from state and county agencies is $3\,1/2 \times 5$ inches, but many local police departments can provide other sizes (4×6 or 8×10 inches). If there is a choice, specify the size you want when you make your request. Naturally, the larger the prints, the more they will cost. Unless money is no object, it is wise to request the smaller size prints first to see what the photos contain before spending the money for the larger ones. If you know you will need to send copies of the pictures to an expert witness or opposing counsel, order two sets at the same time, so that you can keep a complete set intact for your file.

FORM 4–3
SAMPLE LETTER REQUESTING PHOTOGRAPHS

May 12, 199__

County Sheriff's Office
Attn: Records Department
1234 Main Street
Anytown, Ohio 00000
Re: Accident Report No. GS-127
Photo Reference No. 127-90-4
Accident Date: April 19, 1995
Location: Intersection of Seventh Street and Maple,
Anytown, Ohio

Dear Sir or Madam:

Please send me a duplicate set of the photographs taken by the investigating Deputy Sheriff in conjunction with the above-referenced accident. I am enclosing a check in the amount of $10.00 to cover your fee for duplicating these photographs in the 4x6 inch size. Also enclosed is a stamped return envelope for your convenience in returning these photographs to me.

I believe the information above is sufficient for you to locate the desired photographs. However, should you have any questions or need further information, please contact me at (216) 745-0000. Thank you for your assistance.

Very truly yours,

Paralegal

Once you have the official photographs in hand, you will need to index them (see **§ 2.75** *et seq.* on indexing). Examine the photographs to see if they have been prenumbered by the reporting agency. If so, index them according to these numbers. If they are not numbered, first arrange the pictures in some logical order or progression, then assign each photograph a number or letter. Do this by writing the number on the top right-hand corner of the face of the photograph, or on the back, using a pen formulated specially for marking on glossy surfaces. If you have two identical sets of pictures, make sure to number the sets exactly the same to avoid later confusion. Then, for each photograph, write a brief description telling what is shown in each picture. Keep the descriptions simple, but include enough information so that you can match the pictures to their descriptions. See **Form 4–4,** Sample Descriptive Index of Photographs.

FORM 4–4
SAMPLE DESCRIPTIVE INDEX OF PHOTOGRAPHS

1. Head-on view of front-end damage to client's 1985 Toyota Corolla.
2. Close-up view of front-end damage to client's 1985 Toyota Corolla.
3. Front view of damage to client's 1985 Toyota Corolla, showing indentation in windshield resulting from internal impact of client's head against windshield.
4. Side close-up view of windshield showing indentation in windshield resulting from impact of client's head.
5. View of client's car from front right angle showing front-end damage.

6. View from front-left angle of impact damage to other driver's 1989 Chrysler LeBaron.

7. View from rear left angle of damage to other driver's 1989 Chrysler LeBaron.

8. View of roadway looking west on Rte. 66 (direction our client was traveling at time of impact). Cones denote skid marks from client's swerving to the left in an attempt to avoid the collision.

9. View of westbound Rte. 66, showing green road sign (only partially visible) in the upper right of the picture, marks side road where the other driver was sitting prior to pulling out into the path of our client's car.

10. View looking southbound across Rte. 66 from side road, where other driver was sitting before he pulled out.

11. Close-up of skid marks at intersection.

12. View of side road from the south side of Rte. 66. Cone marks position where client's car came to a stop after skidding across roadway after collision.

You may want to enter the photo descriptions on a separate Descriptive Index (see **Form 4–5**). Use the "Remarks" column to record notes on further use of particular photographs, such as when you forward them to an expert witness or when you decide to offer them at trial. See § **3.29** on releasing documents to experts.

§ 4.32 Taking Your Own Photographs

Although you may not be on hand to photograph the actual scene at the time of the accident, you may be asked to take some photographs later in a case in preparation for trial. Discuss with the attorney the specific purpose for the photographs so you know what subject matter you should concentrate on. Talk about what you need to show to prove your point.

While taking photographs is a task you can do, know your limitations as an amateur photographer. If the request to take photos comes up often in your cases and you are not sure of your skills in handling a camera, consider taking some courses at a local college or university to learn photographic and investigative techniques.

Caution: Remember that if your pictures are offered as evidence at trial, you may have to testify regarding the circumstances under which they were taken. See § **4.30** regarding admissibility of photographs.

FORM 4–5
DESCRIPTIVE INDEX OF PHOTOGRAPHS

DESCRIPTIVE INDEX OF PHOTOGRAPHS

CASE ID: TAKEN BY: DATE:

ID#	DESCRIPTION	REMARKS

Practical Tips for Taking Good Pictures

1. Have a camera you know how to use. This may be your own camera or it may belong to your employer. The best all-purpose type of camera is a 35mm SLR (single-lens reflex) with a built-in flash attachment. This type of camera has fully adjustable exposure settings to accommodate a wide variety of lighting conditions. The addition of specialized lenses can allow you to take close-ups, long shots (telephoto), or to shoot in low-light situations.
2. Whatever type of camera you use, learn how to maintain it, load it, and adjust the exposure settings for the best results.
3. Store the camera equipment in a safe place so that it will be ready when you need it.
4. Use the correct film for the best results. Always have a spare roll of film on hand. Label each roll of film as it is exposed. It is not advisable to use Polaroid® film for trial evidence photographs because there are no negatives from which to reprint. Copies of Polaroid pictures are possible, but the process is expensive and the results can be less than ideal. See § **4.39** on photo enlargements.
5. Take your time and work carefully. Take extra photos in case one does not come out. Film is relatively inexpensive, so take lots of pictures.
6. Take photos from several different angles, being sure to include important signposts, benchmarks, and so forth.
7. Get close enough to your subject to show sufficient detail. Measure your distance away from a fixed object and note this on your picture log.
8. In cases in which a precise measurement or distance is important, have someone hold a ruler, yardstick, or tape measure against the object or distance to be measured and include the measuring rule in the photograph. Get close enough to show the amount of detail needed, but far enough away to show perspective.
9. If you are asked to photograph an intersection or roadway where an accident occurred, do this as soon as possible after the accident (although you may not be in on the case until months after the accident occurred) because things change: streets get repaved, skid marks wear off, and bent sign posts or street lights get replaced. See § **4.30** on admissibility of photographs when conditions have changed.
10. If there are any skidmarks or scrapes on the road surface caused by the accident in your case, be sure to get close-ups of these.

§ 4.33 Photographing an Accident Vehicle

You may be asked to take pictures of the damaged car your client was driving in the accident. You may have to make special arrangements to see the car if it is stored at a garage or towing yard. Call ahead and talk to the person in charge so that they will be expecting you. If the vehicle is stored at a facility in an undesirable neighborhood, take someone with you. Do not put yourself in danger by going alone. If the vehicle is stored in a dark garage or warehouse, you will need a flash attachment to provide sufficient light. It is best to photograph the accident vehicle during daylight hours, but if that is not possible, direct as much light as you can onto the vehicle when you photograph it.

Make certain you have the correct vehicle. Include photographs of the car head-on, from the rear, and views from each side. If the windshield is broken, take a photograph of the interior from the driver's seat, if possible. If the inside of the car is crushed or bent, open the door, if possible, or put the camera in through the window to get shots of the interior damage. Be sure to photograph all dents, scrapes, bent chrome trim, and broken lights or glass. Include at least one shot showing the license plate of the vehicle.

§ 4.34 Photographing the Client's Injuries

In a personal injury case, it is important to document photographically the client's injuries. Photographs of the client's injuries can provide graphic, convincing evidence to present to a jury. It may be two years or more before the case goes to trial. Bruises, scrapes, and lacerations will heal and disappear eventually, probably before trial, so you need to capture the client's injuries on film as early as possible in the case. This is a type of photographic task which is well-suited to a paralegal's skills. You may already have accompanied the client to a physical examination, so you already have a more intimate acquaintance with the client than the attorney does. If the attorney is a male and the client is female, or vice versa, the client will no doubt be more comfortable with a same-sex photographer.

Depending on the type and location of the injury, submitting to photographs may be very uncomfortable or embarrassing for a modest client. You may need to take photographs on several different dates to document the various stages of healing. Avoid embarrassing the client as much as possible. Fully explain to the client the reason you need to take such pictures, and accommodate the client's schedule when you are arranging the photo session.

These photographs can be very effective simply because they are natural snapshots showing the person in his or her home surroundings. Get pictures of the client in a wheelchair, in a cast, wearing an orthopaedic appliance, or using a walker if this applies in your case.

Always record the date, time, and place the photos are taken for later reference. Keep a log of the shots taken or formulate a checklist ahead of time and check off items as you take the pictures. See **Form 4–6,** Photo Log/Checklist form. To use the form as a checklist, jot down ideas for the shots you plan to get in the "Details of Shot Desired or Attempted." Use the "Notes" column to record any special camera settings and to note any problems or other technical details regarding the shot.

If the client will not agree to let you take pictures, give the client directions on taking the necessary photographs to document the injuries. See § **4.40** on using the client's photographs.

§ 4.35 Working with a Professional Photographer

In cases where the case budget and time allow it, the attorney may wish to use the expertise of a professional photographer to take certain photographs specifically for use at trial. As a trial paralegal, you will act as a liaison between the attorney and the photographer, thus extending the attorney's abilities in the case. Your responsibilities in this process could include

- Locating a qualified photographer
- Initiating contact with the photographer
- Following through to communicate the needs of the case to the photographer.

Trial attorneys often wait until the last minute to engage a professional photographer because they want to avoid incurring the expense if the case settles. However, in some cases, you may have to act very early in the case preparation in order to get relevant photographs of sites or scenery which could change long before the case goes to trial. Also, photographic evidence can often be instrumental in leading to settlement. Therefore, it is important to engage the photographer as early as feasible in your case so that he or she can do a thorough job.

§ 4.36 —Locating a Professional Photographer

It is essential to select a qualified photographer with experience and expertise in preparing photographic materials for use in court. The reliability of the photographer is important for purposes of admissibility of the photographic evidence at trial. The photographer may have to testify about where and when the pictures were made in order to authenticate them. Make sure the photographer understands this and agrees to be available to testify at trial if this is necessary.

FORM 4–6
PHOTO LOG/CHECKLIST

PHOTO LOG/CHECKLIST						
CASE ID		PHOTGRAPHER		CAMERA/EQUIPMENT USED		
#	DATE	TIME	PLACE	DETAILS OF SHOT DESIRED/ATTEMPTED	NOTES	✓

To locate a professional photographer, use the same procedures you would use to locate any other expert. See § **3.20** on locating expert witnesses. You may be able to get a recommendation from other attorneys or paralegals who have used photographers on other cases. If your client is a large corporation, check with its public relations or advertising department personnel to see if they have a photographer on their staff. These are some other places to check for qualified photographers:

- Newspaper photography departments
- Private investigation services
- Local university fine arts department
- Classified advertisements in legal publications
- Computer research services

§ 4.37 —Briefing the Photographer

You and the attorney must work closely as a team with the photographer to get the most effective results. Even a highly skilled photographer cannot perform properly without the cooperation of the trial team. Plan an initial consultation conference with the attorney and the photographer at the earliest date possible in the trial preparation. This will give the photographer the maximum time to work and also to assure that the photographs are available early enough for use in preparing witnesses for trial. Remember to extend the same courtesy to photographers for their professional time and scheduling that you would to any other expert consultant on a case.

At the initial meeting, the attorney should brief the photographer on the general background and facts of the case. You can assist the attorney in this by preparing a version of the case summary geared specifically to enlighten the photographer. See § **3.29** on preparing case information for the expert witness. The attorney should also give the photographer an idea of the theory of the case and the approach he or she plans to use so that the photographer will understand what is important to photograph and why. The three of you should discuss the exact types of photos you want to use at trial. The photographer is most likely to produce relevant, useful photographs if you can give clear and specific instructions for what you want. Once the photographer understands the theory of the case, he or she may be able to contribute some ideas for effective photographs which had not occurred to the attorney.

§ 4.38 —Following up with the Photographer

It is important for you to sit in on the consultation meeting and to understand what photographic evidence is needed, because you may be asked to accompany the photographer to the scene or location where the photographs are to be taken. Accuracy is of the utmost concern in court photos. You may need to give instructions on site to assure the relevancy and usefulness of the photographs being taken.

You also need to be available to work with the photographer to review the photographic proofs and decide which ones should be used at trial, and to give instructions on preparing enlargements if you decide to use them. Keep in close touch with the photographer as the trial date nears so that you can contact him or her if it is necessary for him or her to testify at trial. You will need to make sure the final photographs are picked up or delivered to your office before the trial. Also be sure that the photographer's bill is paid promptly and that you thank him or her. If the photographer's work has been satisfactory, keep a business card in your master information notebook for future reference. See **Chapter 1** on building a reference notebook.

§ 4.39 Using Photographic Enlargements or Blowups

As you prepare for trial, the attorney may decide that one or more photographs would be useful to enhance the testimony of a witness and to get certain points across to the jury. If a witness testifies about a small photograph that the jurors cannot see right away, their attention may be diverted and they may not remember the testimony later when they do get a chance to see the photograph. It is usually better to have an enlarged version of the photograph so that everyone can see it at the same time the witness is testifying about it. Using photographic blowups is similar to using document enlargements, except that photographic enlargements tend to be more expensive to prepare. See **§ 4.6** on using document enlargements. Be selective about the photographs you choose to enlarge, because too many photo blowups can result in overkill in the courtroom. Examine the photographs carefully and consider whether an enlargement would be likely to distort the picture's perspective or otherwise mislead the jury. Problems with admissibility can arise at trial if the enlargement tends to confuse or mislead the jurors. See **§ 4.30** on admissibility issues related to photographs.

In order to produce photographic enlargements efficiently, you need to provide a negative of the photo film from which the photographer can work. It is possible for photo laboratories to make enlargements directly from prints, but this is complicated, time-consuming, and expensive. The photographer must first take a picture of the picture in order to get a negative, then use that negative to produce the blowup.

Just as with document enlargements, the photo enlargement can only be as good as the original. If the original photograph is blurred or out of focus, the enlargement will be too. In a typical photographic enlargement made without the original negative, the quality degrades as the photo is enlarged. This sometimes results in a grainy look in the enlargement. Making an enlargement from a print may be necessary if the only key photograph available is a Polaroid snapshot or if the negative cannot be located. However, it is much simpler, faster, and less expensive to have photographic enlargements made if you have the negative of the photo.

If your client provides you with any photographs or snapshots, always ask the client to try to locate the negatives. If the photos were taken with a home camera, the negatives will be in strips. Do not cut the strips apart. Locate the number on the edge of the negative which is closest to the center of the picture you want to have printed and use that number as a reference when you give instructions to the photo lab.

Give specific instructions to the photo lab about the photographs you want to have enlarged and what size you want the enlargements to be. Most photographs can be printed in enlarged sizes up to 30 by 40 inches.

Telephone several local photography labs to determine where you can get the best prices and the fastest turnaround time for enlargements. Keep a copy of your notes on price quotations in your master reference notebook. See § **2.9** on building a reference resource notebook. Be sure to ask about the cost for any special handling, such as mounting, and any extra charges for expedited service. Remember that any special handling you request will add to the cost of the enlargement.

Most photo labs can mount photographic blowups on a stiff backing board, but they will charge extra to do this. If you choose to have the photo enlargements mounted at the lab, allow sufficient time to have the work done to avoid extra charges for expedited service.

You can mount the photo enlargements yourself on foam-core board. The technique is basically the same as for mounting document enlargements. See § **4.12** on mounting document enlargements. However, photographic paper tends to be much heavier than the regular copy stock used for document blowups, so a very large photograph may be too heavy for the spray adhesive alone to hold. You can reinforce the mounting on a large photo by using a dab of rubber cement under each corner to secure the photo to the board. The heavy photographic paper has the advantage of not wrinkling as easily as copy stock, so rubber cement is quite effective for this type of mounting.

When you use photographic blowups as exhibits, place a small-size copy of the photo in the trial notebook or exhibit notebook, indicating that the actual exhibit is the enlargement. See § **5.74** on preparing exhibit notebooks.

§ 4.40 Using the Client's Photographs

Your client may be a source for photographs which can be incorporated into the evidence presented at trial. Indeed, in some cases the only pictures available may be photographs or snapshots supplied by your client. In accident or personal injury cases involving individual clients, consider the following checklist of ways in which you could use the client's photographs.

Checklist: Using the Client's Photographs

____ 1. Show the differences in the client "before" and "after" the accident, particularly if the client is in a wheelchair or a cast. If the injury was disfiguring to the client, it may be especially important to show a "before" photograph. Larger sized formal studio portraits (8 by 10 inches or larger) can often be used "as is" for this purpose.

____ 2. Show the client's family members, especially if any key persons are deceased or otherwise unable to be present.

____ 3. Show different occasions in the person's life, or things he or she was capable of before the accident, such as the person performing some sports activity before the accident.

____ 4. Illustrate damage to vehicles or property. The client may have taken pictures of his car at the towing yard or repair garage before repairs were performed. If two vehicles were involved and both were towed to the same place, the client may also have pictures of the damage to the other car.

Your clients in other types of cases (products liability, contract, patent infringement, real estate dispute, property damage) may be able to provide photographs which could be helpful at trial. A company or corporate client may have pictures of equipment or machinery, or stages in a manufacturing process, or the various type of products they produce. These may be photographs produced in conjunction with promotional or marketing literature. Historical or archival photographs may be available, for example, pictures of a very old building in its original form before architectural changes. A large company may even have its own photography personnel (perhaps within the public relations department). Real estate developers, insurance companies, or appraisers may have pictures of land or buildings taken for sales or appraisal purposes.

You must be aware of the evidentiary requirements for admissibility when you decide to use a client's photographs. See § **4.30** on admissibility issues relating to photographs. Make sure you have a client/witness who can testify from personal knowledge about what is pictured in the photographs to authenticate them as evidence. This is not usually a problem when an individual client provides family vacation, holiday, sports, or home photographs. For example, even if the client's visiting Uncle Frank took the snapshots, the client and his or her family members would be familiar with the persons and activities pictured. However, locating an authenticating witness may be somewhat more difficult if you use photographs provided by a company or corporate client such as the ones mentioned above. You may need to add a witness for the sole purpose of providing testimony to authenticate these pictures (the company president or owner, a long-time employee, or a photographer from the client's advertising department).

§ 4.41 —Advantages of Using Client Photographs

These are the advantages to using client photographs:

1. They are personal and they lend authenticity. "Real home photos" can be powerful illustrations of the effects of an accident on the lives of real people. Because they are often pictures taken in home surroundings or with family members, instead of posed for effect, they may help appeal to the sympathies of the jury.
2. They are inexpensive trial exhibits. This is especially important for the client who is on a tight budget.
3. They can be prepared as exhibits for trial at the last minute, if necessary.
4. They can be readily identified and authenticated by the client, a family member, or an employee.

§ 4.42 —Disadvantages of Using Client Photographs

These are the disadvantages of using client photographs:

1. They may not be very good photos; out of focus, too far away, overexposed. This is typical of many home snapshots. The average home photographer taking pictures at a family reunion would not be anticipating that the photos would someday be used in court!
2. The photographs may not be in good condition. They may be damaged, torn, old, yellowed, or cracked.
3. It may not be possible to determine the exact date the photographs were taken, especially if they are several years old.

4. The photographs may be black and white instead of color. (Note: This is not always a drawback. Sometimes black and white photos are better.)
5. Snapshot prints may be several different sizes, depending on the type of film and the developer.
6. If you need an enlargement, the client may not be able to locate the negative.
7. You may only discover the photos or the client may uncover them only days (or hours) before trial.

If a critical or key photograph is very old, damaged, torn, yellowed, or cracked, investigate the possibility of using a photographic restoring service to repair the damage.

Photo restoration is an expensive process, so make sure the picture is important enough to justify the expense. Also, this process will take time, so it can't be done at the last minute. For severely overexposed pictures, it may be possible to have the negative reprinted to adjust the exposure so that more detail shows up.

§ 4.43 Creating a Photo Montage

If your client is able to provide photographs, you must first decide which ones to use as trial exhibits. Because they add a personal touch, the cumulative effect of several small photos can sometimes be better than one large one. An effective way to display several snapshots or photographs is to create a photo montage.

Creating a Photo Montage

1. Decide which pictures to use. Collect all the available pictures and review them with the attorney. Try to avoid duplication of points which could be proved by other evidence in the case. Pick the clearest or the best representative shots, one from each angle. Remember, if a picture doesn't add anything to the presentation, it is better not to use it.

2. Plan the layout. When you have decided which photographs to use, you must plan the layout. Start with a piece of 30 by 40-inch foam-core board. See § **4.17** on working with foam-core board. Lay the photos out on the board. In deciding how to arrange the pictures, think about the point you want to make with them in the context of the trial. Think about arranging the pictures in one of several ways:

- "Before" and "After": Split the layout either vertically for a side-by-side comparison, or horizontally to make top and bottom areas.
- Chronological order
- Reverse chronological order
- Stages or phases of life, development, healing, (personal injury case) or stages in a manufacturing process
- Series of events or activities

If the photos are snapshots, the prints will probably be in various sizes and shapes. Move the pictures around on the board until you arrive at a pleasing layout. Try to balance one large picture with two smaller ones, and so on.

For chronological or serial montages, make sure you have the dates or approximate dates on the backs of the photos. Snapshots may have the date printed in the margin, or the client may have written the date on the back. If possible, find out from your client the approximate date the photos were taken. Then add labels to the montage to indicate the date corresponding to each photograph.

Ask the attorney whether he or she wants a heading or title on the montage (such as, "Stages in the Life of . . ." or "Photos of . . ." or "Before" and "After"). Plan to leave space for any other explanatory lettering, such as dates or names, which will identify individual pictures.

3. Mount the Photos. Once you have arrived at a pleasing layout (remember to leave space for adding labels, if necessary), lightly mark the place of each picture on the board by tracing the corners of each picture with a No. 3 pencil. Buy a package of photo mounting corners—the same kind you would use in a scrapbook or album—which are available at any office or photo supply store. Fit a photomount onto each corner of the photograph, moisten the glue or remove the paper backing from the corners, and press the picture in place on the board, using your pencil marks as guides. These mounting corners will hold the photos securely in place but still allow them to be removed so that they can be returned to the client without being destroyed.

If the photos are very light and would show up better against a dark background, buy a piece of lightweight poster cardboard and lay out the photos against it as described above. This forms a sort of visual frame around the pictures to make the grouping more attractive. Match the background mat color to the intended impact of the picture grouping. For example, use a lively "happy" color like bright blue or red for the "before" pictures, but put the "after" pictures on a dark or somber background, such as black or gray (denoting tragedy and sadness). Use the photomounts to attach the pictures to the cardboard mat, then fasten the cardboard to a piece of foam-core board. See § **4.17** for instructions on fastening to foam-core board.

If the photos are bent or are very large, heavy, or floppy, secure them to the board by placing a small piece of double-sided tape in the center of the back of the photo. This keeps the photos from falling out but doesn't damage or destroy them.

§ 4.44 Using Photographic Slides

If your case could use a series of photographs to illustrate various points, consider having the negatives made up into photographic slides that can be projected through a slide projector onto a screen in the courtroom. This serves the same purpose as an enlargement by allowing the judge and jury to see the pictures at the same time the witness is testifying about them. In addition, the witness can use a pointer to direct the jury's attention to specific things on the slides without turning away from them.

Photographic slides are relatively expensive, but they can be easier to handle in the courtroom than numerous blowups. Using slides makes it easy to show a large number of pictures in a short period of time and to easily flip back and forth from slide to slide. This can be an effective technique to use with an expert witness who can explain technical information "lecture-style" to the jury.

Besides the obvious complication of having to transport the projector and screen to the courtroom, the major disadvantage of using slides is that the slides require special equipment to view them and therefore the jury will not have easy access to the pictures in the jury room.

Store photographic slides carefully to protect them from dust and damage.

- Use a carousel or a rectangular holder with slots designed to hold standard 3 by 3-inch slides. (Check photography or camera supply stores.)
- Plastic sheet designed for a photo album page with slots to display standard slides.
- Photo-mount corners attached to a lightweight cardboard sheet (inexpensive idea)

Using Slides in Trial Presentation

Follow these guidelines if you plan to use slides in the trial presentation:

1. Make arrangements well before the trial date to borrow or rent a projector and screen (if your office does not own this equipment).
2. Check the layout of the courtroom ahead of time and locate the available electrical outlets to decide the best placement for the projector and screen (see § **6.13**).

3. Practice setting up the screen and projector so that you can do it smoothly and quickly in the courtroom.
4. Practice using the slide advancer, and make sure you know how to work the projector controls and focus knobs. If the expert witness is the one who will be advancing the slides, have him or her practice with the projector during the trial preparation conference.
5. Make sure you have an extra bulb which fits the projector and a heavy duty extension cord.
6. Be sure to have a pointer stick available for the witness to use.
7. Make arrangements to have someone bring the equipment to the courtroom at the appropriate time and return it to the office when you are finished with it.
8. Load the slides into the projector slide tray. Arrange the slides in the correct order in which they will be presented. Number the slides and make an index just in case the slide tray gets dumped accidentally.

§ 4.45 Using Maps, Diagrams, and Drawings as Demonstrative Exhibits

Demonstrative evidence often includes maps and diagrams which are used in the courtroom in a manner similar to the way photographs are used for illustrative purposes. "Measurement-oriented" maps and diagrams can be useful, either alone or as a supplement to photographs, to aid the witness in explaining testimony in almost any case in which location and proximity are factors. A map or diagram representation helps the jury to understand exactly what events occurred by showing

- The layout of a certain area
- What objects or persons were in the area
- The exact locations of the objects or persons
- The relative distances of the objects or persons from one another.

§ 4.46 —Admissibility Issues for Maps, Diagrams, and Drawings

The trial judge has the authority to determine the manner in which a map, diagram, or drawing is used at trial and whether it is admitted into evidence. Most courts allow the use of such demonstrative exhibits to illustrate and explain oral testimony, but courts differ in their treatment of these articles as evidence. In some trials, the attorneys and witnesses may use a map or diagrams merely as a general reference during the testimony without officially introducing the item into evidence. If the trial attorney wants the map or diagram to be available for inspection by the jurors in the jury room, he or she must offer it and it must be admitted by the court as an evidentiary exhibit in the case.

The elements of admissibility for maps, diagrams, and drawings at trial are similar to the requirements for photographs (see § **4.30**). In order to be admissible, maps and diagrams must be

- Relevant
- Accurate
- Properly authenticated.

Authentication by a witness who has personal knowledge of the events or conditions depicted is a key element in the admissibility of a map, diagram, or drawing into evidence at trial. A witness may use a diagram or drawing the witness made on some earlier date before the trial if the diagram depicts the actual conditions that existed on that earlier date and the witness can testify about those conditions from personal knowledge.

A map, diagram, or drawing prepared by someone other than the witness is admissible if the judge is satisfied that the witness can sufficiently identify and verify its contents from personal knowledge. If the precise measurements or distances depicted in a diagram are critical to issues in the case, the court will require stricter proof of the witness's knowledge of the area and the distances involved than if the diagram is used simply as a general reference. The witness may have actually made the measurements personally or been present when they were taken. Any supporting notes concerning measurements made by or in the presence of the witness should be available in court.

§ 4.47 —Using Maps, Diagrams, and Drawings with the Witness

The trial attorney may use an "interactive" approach with the demonstrative exhibit by having the expert or lay witness place a mark on a diagram or add something to a map during the testimony in full view of the jurors. In cases involving numerical calculations, an expert witness may write out the figures on a board or easel pad to demonstrate how he or she arrived at a specific number. Having the witness write or draw something "spontaneously" in the courtroom is a useful technique that serves to:

- Keep the jury interested in the proceedings
- Emphasize or highlight specific facts

- Focus attention where the attorney wants it
- Reinforce the contents of both the visual aid and the oral testimony so that the jury understands and retains the information.

It can be effective in some cases to ask the witness on the stand to draw a rough diagram on a chalkboard or easel pad to illustrate or clarify a location or direction about which the witness is testifying. This should be done only when a very precise measurement is not required (for example, the approximate route of a proposed road through a housing development, the rough course of drainage from a waste dumping facility). A similar technique would be to ask the witness to place an attachment (such as a small magnetic model car) in the correct position on a map or diagram. Such interactive methods can backfire if the witness fumbles with the visual aid or otherwise looks awkward in front of the jury. You can help the attorney avoid this problem by properly preparing your witness.

- Explain to the witness ahead of time how the attorney plans to use the interactive technique in the courtroom.
- Have the visual aid prepared far enough in advance so that it is available for the witness preparation conference.
- Remind the attorney during the preparation conference to let the witness practice with the visual aid to become comfortable with it.
- Make sure that the placement of the exhibit in the courtroom facilitates interactive testimony. See § **6.12** on courtroom logistics.
- See that the attorney has the necessary accessories, such as markers or attachments, when needed in the courtroom.

Examples of Interactive Techniques

1. In a trial involving a property line dispute, the witness could show how the shape of a parcel of land would be affected under different scenarios by drawing alternate property lines on a plat map.
2. In an automobile accident case, the witness might indicate his or her recollection of the location of cars, people, trees, buildings, and so forth by attaching small magnetic models to a metal board diagram.
3. In a construction defect case, an expert witness might indicate exactly where a structural support failed by drawing arrows to the stress points on a diagram of the structural beams.
4. In a case involving groundwater pollution from oil storage facilities, the witness might draw a circle on a map to indicate the location of the storage tanks, the waste dump, the water wells, and so forth.

5. In a criminal case, a witness could indicate on a diagram of the floor-plan layout of the building where the crime was committed, or where the suspect was seen.

§ 4.48 Preserving a Record of Interactive Testimony

A logistical problem may arise for the paralegal in keeping a good record of the testimony when one of these interactive techniques is used. It is often important later in the trial to know exactly what each witness indicated on a map or diagram. However, the witness's drawing or addition to a map or diagram is usually not permanent and may be easily removed or erased. Witnesses with conflicting testimony may present different versions of the events and make corresponding marks on a map, resulting in a very confusing visual aid. **Table 4–3** compares the characteristics of several common types of demonstrative exhibit tools. **Section 4.49** addresses some specific problems and solutions for preserving a record of interactive witness testimony.

Table 4–3

Interactive Witness Testimony
Comparison of Spontaneous Write-On Surfaces

Type	Advantages	Disadvantages	Accessories Required
Chalkboard	Most courts have them Large surface Flexible Inexpensive	Easily erased (No record) Ordinary Difficult to read	Chalk White and Colors Eraser
Pad of Newsprint Paper (on easel)	Many courts have them Good size - 30×40 inches Inexpensive Portable Can be saved for record	Paper tears easily Page is larger than normal exhibits Marker ink may "bleed" through on newsprint	Easel and cross-bar attachment Flip chart markers in various colors

Dry-Erase Metal Board	Smooth non-glare surface Portable Reusable	Easily erased (No record) More expensive initially Heavier to transport	Special markers & Eraser Magnetic attachments
Plastic laminate over static graphics	Works on any mounted board Gives some weather protection Non-glare surface Flexible and professional looking	Erasable (No Record) Easily scratched or creased	Special markers

§ 4.49 Interactive Testimony: Problems and Solutions

Problem 1: Anything drawn or written on a chalkboard is not permanent and can be easily changed or erased by another witness or the opposing counsel.

Solution: Copy the figures, arrows, and so forth onto a sheet in your notes as the witness writes. Ask the witness to verify that this is an accurate representation of what he or she wrote on the board. At the very least, you will have a record for your trial notes to refresh the attorney's memory. **Tip:** Use your pocket calculator to quickly check the math on any numerical calculations. You could also take a photograph of the completed board to preserve it for the record.

Problem 2: A witness with a conflicting story changes the positions of the magnetic pieces on an accident diagram.

Solution: Have the first witness use a marker pen to trace the outline of any magnetic models he or she has placed on a map or diagram, and then write his or her initials inside the outline. Or, use two different colored markers to indicate an "X" where each witness placed the models. See § **2.85** on using color-coding.

Problem 3: The witness drew several different versions of a diagram on pages of an oversized easel pad.

Solution: Retain the actual pages from the easel pad so you can refer to exactly what the witness indicated. Number the actual pages used. Photograph the pages or have the oversized pages copied and reduced to a manageable size. If the markings are on a chalkboard, have each witness use a different color chalk, and proceed as in #1, above.

Problem 4: Multiple markings by various witnesses on a single original map make it very confusing and difficult to read.

Solution: Use plastic laminate or acetate overlays (one for each witness) to protect the original map. Have each witness initial and date his or her version. Give each overlay a separate exhibit number or letter designation.

Problem 5: The witness has made some important notations on the surface of an oversized aerial map. The map is the only one of its kind, and it is too large to handle easily with the other exhibits or to attach to the posttrial brief.

Solution: Take a photograph of the completed board and substitute duplicates of the photograph for the actual exhibit in the trial materials.

§ 4.50 Preparing Site Diagrams

A site diagram is a simplified type of map which is used to illustrate the specific layout of an area where an incident or accident occurred. The most effective site diagrams are uncluttered scale maps which clearly indicate the details specifically relevant to the incident or accident. Site diagrams are routinely used in automobile accident cases to show such things as:

- Length and placement of skid marks
- Width of the street
- Angle of the intersection
- Traffic controls (lights, stop signs)
- Street markings
- Fixed objects (trees, utility poles, guardrails).

In order to be effective and admissible, the site diagram must be highly accurate and drawn correctly to scale. An unbiased general diagram may be used by attorneys and witnesses on both sides of a dispute to illustrate conflicting testimony.

Whether you hire a professional artist or an expert (see also **§ 3.39** on working with an expert witness to produce visuals; **§ 3.51** on working with an accident reconstruction expert) or prepare the site diagram yourself, use the following list as a guide to developing this type of visual aid.

Preparing Site Diagrams

1. Decide on the scope of the diagram, that is, what area will be included. Consult with the trial attorney about the parameters of the diagram and the specific objects to be represented.
2. Decide on the proper scale for the drawing based upon the size of area to be depicted and the size needed in the courtroom (for example, 1 inch = 1 foot). Prepare a preliminary small-scale drawing on grid paper (available from your office supplier in a variety of grid sizes) and then convert the measurements to poster size. If you prefer to make the preliminary diagram poster size, first measure and draw very light grid lines on a piece of foam-core board. Make sure the grids are square or the drawing will be distorted!
3. Study all available materials carefully (police report, photographs, etc.) and compare with other known data or testimony. Check against the reconstruction expert's diagram. **Caution:** Police reports sometimes contain inaccuracies.
4. Study a good city map of the accident area (enlarge the map on your office copier, if necessary). For a diagram of an intersection, measure the angle of the intersection on the map with a protractor, then transfer to your drawing. To draw curves accurately, trace the curve from an official map onto an acetate transparency on which you have measured and drawn grid lines. Transfer the curve block by block to the larger poster size.
5. Visit the actual site and make meticulous and careful measurements. Use your preliminary drawing to collect accurate field measurements and take complete and accurate notes. Remember that you may have to testify about the method and manner in which the measurements were made.
6. Double-check the placement and measured distances between traffic signals, signs, road markings, and fixed objects (trees, guardrails, and so forth).
7. Note any obstructions of the view from any angle (hedges or shrubbery, overhanging branches, protruding concrete abutments, and so forth).
8. Eliminate extraneous details to keep the diagram as simple as possible, including the detail necessary to illustrate your points at trial. An uncluttered map helps the jury to focus on the facts and distances significant to the incident.

9. Keep the lettering and labeling simple. Use letters in a size which can be read from a distance (1-inch minimum).
10. Use color and simple shapes (such as a red octagon to represent a stop sign) sparingly for the best effect.
11. Always include an arrow indicating north orientation, preferably at the top of the diagram, as well as a scale and a legend, if necessary.
12. Always have a ruler or yardstick available in the courtroom for measuring scale distances.
13. Check and double-check the accuracy of your measurements and conversions to the diagram scale. A site diagram which is inaccurate or misleading may be ruled inadmissible and can damage the trial team's credibility in the eyes of the jury.

§ 4.51 Obtaining Prepared Maps

In many cases you may be able to use a prepared or commercial map instead of creating one yourself. An official or government map which is properly certified by the appropriate official is considered a self-authenticating document and thus eliminates any questions regarding admissibility. In addition, commercially prepared maps are generally less expensive than custom drawn maps and they can often be reused. The following is a list of sources for prepared maps.

1. Bookstores usually have a variety of maps ranging major metropolitan areas to the entire world.
2. Street atlas maps published by commercial surveyors are available in a booklet format which shows a detail of each sector of the county and usually an enlarged detail of the business district for major cities.
3. Government agencies can often supply maps at very low cost. United States Geological Survey (USGS, Reston, Virginia 22092) topographical maps are available for most areas of the country. Check the revision date to make sure you have the most current version. Your state's highway department may have aerial or other maps available for purchase.
4. Real estate agencies often have excellent maps of a city's residential and commercial business districts.
5. In larger cities a convention center or visitors' information bureau can often provide a simplified map of various features of the city. **Caution:** make sure this type of map is drawn to scale. Some tour guide maps are "stylized" and do not accurately represent spatial relationships.

6. Road maps, available at service stations, are useful for showing highway routes, outlines of large urban/suburban areas, river courses, general reference.
7. Libraries and educational supply companies are excellent sources for a wide variety of maps.
8. Check your county recorder's office and the tax office for current plat and tax maps in your area.
9. Check a United States or world atlas for specialized types of maps: geographical features, demographics, population, topography, rainfall, average temperature, and so forth. Remember that you will need time to obtain reprint permission for any copyrighted material you plan to enlarge.

§ 4.52 Enhancing Existing Maps

These are some suggestions for presenting a map to best effect.

1. Darken the outline of an area with chart tape or heavy marker, or shade in the area of interest with a highlighter pen.
2. Mount the map on a metal board and use magnetic flags, signals or other attachments to indicate specific locations.
3. Cover the map with an acetate overlay and use markers to indicate directions, routes, locations, and so forth.

§ 4.53 Using Visual Aids in Medical Testimony

Physicians and other medical experts employ a variety of tests to help them locate, evaluate, and determine treatment for injuries and abnormalities. Most of these diagnostic tests, which are produced by electronic, mechanical, photographic, or radiological processes, yield some type of permanent visual record of the test results. These records can be valuable and persuasive visual aids in a trial involving bodily injuries when they are used to supplement the testimony of a medical expert who can explain and interpret the significance of the test results.

These types of records are included in FRE Rule 1101, the same rule which covers photographs (see § **4.30**). However, the requirements for admissibility are somewhat different. The following section discusses admissibility requirements for test results frequently found in medical records, such as X-rays which are commonly accepted as reliable demonstrative evidence. More innovative diagnostic techniques require an even higher level of evidentiary proof to make them acceptable for admission as trial evidence.

§ 4.54 Using X-Rays at Trial

The X-ray is probably the most familiar of the visual diagnostic tools used by medical experts. X-rays are commonly used in the courtroom to clarify a physician's testimony concerning medical injuries. As a practical matter, X-rays are sometimes inferior to medical illustrations or other types of medical "photographs" in helping the jury to understand the injuries. X-ray films are usually the best visual aid to illustrate bone fractures, but they do not show muscle, nerve, or soft tissue damage.

Viewing X-ray film requires a shadow box or other special equipment which is not readily available in the courtroom or in the jury room. (You may be able to avoid this problem by obtaining positive prints of the X-rays which can be read without special viewing equipment.) Some courts refuse to permit examination of X-rays during jury deliberations even with the necessary viewing equipment because X-rays are susceptible to misinterpretation by unqualified laymen.

X-rays are included in Article X of the Federal Rules of Evidence under the definition of photographs in Rule 1001(2). See **§ 4.30.** However, the admissibility requirements for X-rays differ somewhat from those applicable to photographs because the X-ray illustrates something which is not ordinarily visible to the naked eye. Because the X-ray image depends upon a scientific process rather than sensory observations, the authentication requirements are covered in FRE 901(b)(9):

> Process or System. Evidence describing a process or system used to produce a result and showing that the process or system produces an accurate result.

In order for an X-ray to be admissible as trial evidence, it must be authenticated by a witness, such as a doctor or radiology technician, who is qualified to describe the X-ray process and affirm that the procedure was correctly used to accurately produce the evidence. Before a medical expert can use X-rays to illustrate his or her trial testimony, the attorney must lay the proper foundation for the admission of the X-rays. The testimony of a qualified witness, usually a physician, must verify and authenticate the X-rays, by addressing the basic points on the following checklist.

Checklist: Testimony to Authenticate X-rays

____ 1. The X-ray does belong to the injured person and does accurately depict the injured area of the body.

____ 2. The injured person's condition was the essentially the same at the time the X-ray was taken as it was at the time of the accident or injury.

____ 3. The person who took the X-ray and processed the film was properly skilled and qualified to make a correct and accurate X-ray.

____ 4. The equipment was dependable and was working properly when the X-ray was taken.

____ 5. Proper procedures were followed in making the X-ray.

§ 4.55 Commercial Medical Charts and Models

Medical charts and anatomical models are often effective demonstrative evidence tools in trials involving medical injuries. Doctors and other medical experts can use charts and models to great advantage

- As visual aids to enhance and support their courtroom testimony;
- To educate the jury about basic anatomy; and
- To explain specific injuries or medical procedures.

The following is a source list for places you may obtain accurate medical charts and models to use in the courtroom.

Sources for Medical Charts and Models

1. Anatomical Chart Co.
Customer Service Department
8221 Kimball Avenue 8:00 A.M. - 5:00 P.M.
Skokie, Illinois 60076 Monday through Friday
Free 248-Page General Catalog
To Order Call Toll-Free: 1-800-621-7500
In Illinois Call Collect: 708-679-4700
FAX: 708-674-0211

2. Markham Anatomical
211 Atlantic Street
P.O. Box 950
Stamford, Connecticut 06901
Free Catalog
Call Toll-Free: 1-800-242-2449
In Connecticut: 203-324-5959
FAX: 203-975-7748

3. Medical Plastics Laboratory
Professional Health Educators
P. O. Box 38
Gatesville, Texas 76528
Free Catalog
To Order Call Toll-Free: 1-800-433-5539
In Texas Call: 817-722-8525
FAX: 1-817-865-8011
Customized medical models

§ 4.56 Customized Medical Illustrations

Customized medical illustrations are used as demonstrative evidence tools to help the jury understand the nature of the specific injuries at issue in the case. Medical illustrations can give a comprehensive picture of the injuries by depicting a wide variety of injuries, such as bone fractures, soft tissue injuries, muscle damage, surgical procedures, and the nature of a functional disability, in a lifelike and readily understandable way. Medical illustrations can supplement X-rays and other diagnostic test results to clarify the physician's trial testimony, with some additional advantages:

- Medical illustrations are complete in themselves and can be viewed without special equipment.
- Lay jurors can easily understand medical illustrations without special interpretation.
- Medical illustrations can be colored or highlighted to emphasize the area of injury and attract the attention of the jury.

§ 4.57 Working with a Medical Illustrator

The first step in planning customized medical illustrations for trial is to locate and retain a qualified medical illustrator. Medical illustration is a highly specialized discipline incorporating artistic talent and training, medical training, and understanding of legal evidentiary requirements. The medical illustrator combines this expertise with meticulous attention to detail and high standards of accuracy to create customized illustrations to assist in the presentation of medical testimony at trial. The medical illustrator is specially trained to convert complex medically-oriented technical information into artwork which communicates to and teaches the jury. The typical medical illustrator must complete a graduate level course curriculum which includes training in areas such as

- Human anatomy and systems
- Effects of trauma on human tissue
- Medical terminology and procedures
- Surgical and anatomical illustration
- Interpretation of medical records
- Three dimensional modeling
- Exhibit design and graphic presentation techniques.

Commissioning a qualified medical illustrator to prepare detailed illustrations is not a task that can be left until the last minute in trial preparation. The medical illustrator should be brought in on the case as soon as possible after the decision to go to trial has been made. If you are assigned the task of locating a qualified medical illustrator, check first with any medical schools, medical libraries, large clinics or teaching hospitals in your area. See § **3.20** on locating experts. Many such institutions have qualified staff illustrators who are available to do freelance work, or who may be able to give you a lead or a referral to a qualified medical illustrator. The treating physician or other medical expert involved in your case may also be able to give you some leads to qualified illustrators. Another source might be The Association of Medical Illustrators (AMI), a professional association which develops and monitors standards for accreditation of medical illustration programs and also publishes a membership directory. For more information, write:

The Association of Medical Illustrators
1819 Peachtree Street N.E. - Suite 560
Atlanta, Georgia, 30309
Phone: (404) 350-7900

Determine the extent of the artist's experience with preparation of materials for trial. Ask to see the illustrator's portfolio if you are not familiar with his or her work. You may also want to obtain references from attorneys for whom the illustrator has done work in the past. Make sure the illustrator understands the need for confidentiality and will be able to complete the necessary work within the trial preparation schedule. Consult your supervising attorney regarding the type of contract or retention letter you should use with the illustrator. See § **3.25** on basic criteria for an expert retention letter.

The cost for the medical illustrator's services will range from $200 on up, depending on the complexity of the project and the time required. The illustrator may be able to give you a cost estimate based upon his or her experience with similar projects. Expect to pay extra for:

- Expedited work
- Travel and research time
- Substantive involvement in the development of the illustration concept
- Numerous changes from the original concept during preparation of the illustration
- Extra services, such as laminating the boards or providing photographs of the finished product for the trial notebooks.

As a trial paralegal you will function as a liaison to establish and coordinate communication among members of the trial team, the expert medical witness, and the illustrator. Extend the same professional consideration to the medical illustrator as you would to any other type of expert witness or consultant. The medical illustrator must have adequate time to review thoroughly the relevant medical and hospital records, ambulance and EMS reports, doctor's notes, photographs, and any other materials pertaining to the injuries. He or she may also need to interview the injured client as well as doctors, nurses, and other medical personnel in order to understand the precise nature and location of the injuries and the medical procedures performed. It is your responsibility to provide the illustrator with the necessary background materials, authorizations, and releases. Use the Records Release Log (see **§ 3.29**) to keep track of the materials you send to the illustrator.

It is imperative that the doctor, the attorney, and the illustrator understand precisely how the illustration will be used to develop the medical testimony at trial. The medical illustrations must be approved by the doctor who will use them well in advance of trial. The doctor must be comfortable with the illustrations and confident of their accuracy, so the illustrator must be able to consult directly with the doctor to ensure technical accuracy in the finished product. You will need to coordinate at least one conference at which the attorney, the illustrator, and the doctor are all present to discuss the purpose and intended use for the medical illustrations.

These are some of the questions and issues which should be discussed with the illustrator.

1. What is the intended purpose for the illustration, and how will it be used at trial?
2. Does the attorney want black and white, natural color, or artificial color?
3. Should the illustration show a normal vs. injured body part? If so, should these both be on one board or on two separate boards?
4. Will the medical witness need to mark or draw on the illustration?
5. Would a storyboard setup or acetate overlays be useful to show the stages of a procedure, the layers of injured tissue, and so forth?

§ 4.58 Using Models as Demonstrative Exhibits

Some cases involve subjects that can only be adequately explained through the use of a three-dimensional model. A model can be a highly effective demonstrative aid in the courtroom because it helps the judge and jury gain a better understanding of the facts than they could get from witness testimony alone. For example, an expert witness's explanation of how a complex piece of machinery malfunctioned could be very confusing to the jury. However, if the jurors were able to look at a working model of the machine at the same time the expert was explaining the problem, it would be much easier for them to understand exactly what happened.

Just as with any other type of demonstrative exhibits, models must meet certain requirements before they can be deemed admissible evidence, and the trial judge has wide discretion to determine whether the admissibility requirements have been met. Models must be properly authenticated by the testimony of a qualified witness who has personal knowledge of the specific facts relevant to the case and the model. In order to establish a proper foundation for the admissibility of a model, the witness must be able to testify regarding the following elements:

- Who created the model.
- When the model was made.
- How the model was made. (**Note:** Any underlying drawings, specifications, measurements, photographs, and so on must also be put into evidence.)
- Whether the model is made to scale. If it is not made to scale, the witness must be able to explain any deviations. The court may rule the model inadmissible if a critical portion is not to scale and lack of scale would be misleading or confusing to the jurors.
- The model is substantially similar in operation and function to the original object.
- The model helps to explain the oral testimony and is needed for a complete understanding of the testimony.
- The model will not confuse or mislead the jury.
- The model is a fair and accurate representation of the original object or subject (except for size).

If there are slight differences from the original, the witness must be able to explain them, and the dissimilarities must be on aspects of the object NOT relevant to the issues in the case. For example, suppose the original piece of machinery was red and the model is painted black. The red color of the original machine had nothing to do with the reason the machine malfunctioned. Although the model is a different color from the original, this difference can be explained and has no bearing on the malfunction issue, so the model would still be admissible assuming the other foundational requirements are met. Even a model with slight inaccuracies may still be admitted if the parties stipulate to it which, of course, they would do only if the inaccuracies were not material to the case issues. If the trial attorney thinks there will be a challenge to the admissibility of a model, he or she may attempt to get a stipulation from the opposing counsel, or alternatively, file a motion in limine to obtain a ruling on admissibility before the trial begins.

In some jurisdictions, a model that is used during testimony may not have to be admitted into evidence, but in that situation the opposing party is entitled to a jury instruction that the model is not evidence. It is generally considered preferable to introduce the model into evidence so that it will be available for the jury to examine during their deliberations.

Models are generally an expensive type of demonstrative exhibit to create, so the trial team should consider carefully whether the model's benefits in presenting the case will justify the cost. Models also have inherent logistical problems for the trial paralegal. For example, a very large model will not only be difficult to transport, it may be too large to fit through the doorway or take up too much space in a small courtroom. Use the following checklist as a guide to some other practical and logistical considerations involved in presenting models as demonstrative exhibits.

§ 4.59 —Using Models in the Courtroom

The following suggestions will assist the attorney using models in the courtroom:

1. Find out when the attorney wants the model in the courtroom. Does the attorney want the jurors to see the model ahead of time? If not, do you need some type of cover to protect or conceal it until the attorney is ready to use it?
2. Will you need any special equipment or furniture (a stand or a large table) on which to display the model?
3. Will the model require special storage space in or near the courtroom?
4. There is always the risk that a model may help your opponent more than it helps you, especially if it doesn't work properly! Have your expert (or whoever will testify about the model) test it to make sure any moving parts work properly.
5. If your expert will use the model in his or her testimony but someone else actually created the model, make sure the expert and the creator of the model work together to develop the model so the expert is familiar with how the model was made, who made it, when it was made, and so on.

6. If more than one witness will use the model to assist in their testimony, make sure each witness is familiar with the model and how it works.
7. Substitute photographs for the three-dimensional model in the trial exhibit notebooks and for the court reporter's record.

§ 4.60 Equipment to Have in the Courtroom: Easel or Tripod

One of the most useful pieces of equipment to have in the courtroom is an easel or tripod upon which to display large charts or illustration boards. Check your office supply catalogue for descriptions of the various types of easels available. The easel I have found the most useful is the three-legged metal type with telescoping legs. This versatile type of easel can be used at three heights: table top, partly extended, or fully extended. These easels are fairly inexpensive, lightweight, and compact. With the addition of a top crossbar piece and a large pad of paper, the easel becomes a flip-chart for the attorney or witness to use for writing key words or calculations. In the courtroom, the easel pad has the advantage over a blackboard and chalk because it cannot be erased. The paper in the large easel pad is often of newsprint quality, and this is usually sufficient for courtroom use, although other types of paper are available if your attorney prefers a higher quality stock.

Have a minimum of two easels and the crossbar attachment available. Use one easel to display charts and large visual aid boards and the other to hold the pad of paper. Always have a second large pad of paper available in case the first one is used up. Also, make sure you have a set of broad felt-tipped marking pens to use on the paper. Check your office supply store or art supply vendor for markers that are specially formulated not to soak through on newsprint. You will want to have basic colors such as black, blue, or brown, as well as red and green for contrast.

Before you actually use the easel in the courtroom, make sure you know how to set it up. Practice with it to make sure that it does operate properly and that you can set it up quickly, quietly, and efficiently. As with all equipment you expect to take outside the office, remember to affix a permanent sticker with your firm's name, address, and telephone number onto the top portion of the easel so that it can be easily returned to you if it is inadvertently left at the courthouse.

§ 4.61 Using the Overhead Projector in the Courtroom

The overhead projector is another demonstrative evidence tool you can use in the courtroom when there is a need for the witness, judge, and jurors to view a chart or diagram simultaneously. The advantages of using an overhead projector and acetate transparencies are similar to those of photographic slides (see § **4.44**). Transparencies are simple to produce and generally less expensive than slides, photographic enlargements, or document blowups. Transparencies are neat and easy to handle, and the actual acetate sheets can be easily marked as trial exhibits (unlike chalkboard illustrations or blowups). You can add color for emphasis or contrast or use overlays with the transparency to illustrate the various stages of a process, steps in a sequence, and so on.

The technique you use to produce transparencies will depend on the nature of the illustration. There are several ways to prepare transparencies:

- Drawing by hand, if you are artistically talented.
- Tracing a diagram or illustration onto the acetate.
- An outside vendor or commercial photocopy shop can prepare transparencies for you, although this adds to the cost.
- Some standard transparency illustrations, such as anatomical diagrams, are available commercially. These are reusable and relatively inexpensive compared to other types of medical illustrations (see §§ **4.55, 4.56**).
- Almost any diagram, drawing, or document on paper can be transferred to a transparency on a standard copy machine.

The acetate transparencies are sold in boxes of 50 sheets. Check with your office supplier to get the type that is compatible with your office copier. Standard acetate transparencies are 8 1/2 × 11 inch size. If the glass "stage" (the horizontal surface upon which the acetate is laid) of your projector is wider than 8 1/2 inches (a typical stage is 10 inches wide), a band of light down each side will be projected onto the screen. Block out this distracting glare by taping strips of white paper to the long edges of your transparencies, or use commercially available cardboard frames that look similar to a picture frame mat. 3M Company makes a neat product for this purpose called a Flip-Frame™ Transparency Protector. This clear plastic sleeve protects the acetate sheet and has pretaped edge strips to give the projected image a professional framed look. The Flip-Frame also has a punched edge that makes it easy to store a series of transparencies in a looseleaf ring binder or notebook. 3M Company also makes a transparency acetate formulated specifically for use on a laser printer. This product allows you to print directly onto acetate from your computer. Contact your office supplier or the 3M company to find out more about these products.

3M Visual Systems Division
3M Center Building 225-3NE-01
St. Paul, Minnesota 55144-1000
Phone: 1-800-328-1371; In Minnesota, call 612-736-1285

§ 4.62 —Using the Overhead Projector at Trial

There are three main components of the overhead projector presentation:

- The projector itself;
- The acetate transparency; and
- The screen.

Follow these guidelines for using them in your trial presentation.

1. Arrange early in the trial preparation to rent or borrow an overhead projector and screen (if your office does not own this equipment). If possible, obtain a wheeled cart or sturdy carrying case for easier transportation of the projector.
2. Make sure the screen you plan to use has an adjustment bracket at the top so that you can slant the screen forward to eliminate any distortion that may occur when the screen is positioned higher than the lens of the projector.
3. Practice setting up the screen and projector so that you can do it smoothly and quickly in the courtroom.
4. Learn how to use the focus control and make a note of the setting that works best to produce a sharp image on the screen. Make sure you can project the image squarely on the screen.
5. Find out how to clean the projector stage to eliminate dust and smudges. Take the necessary cleaning supplies with you to the courtroom.
6. Survey the courtroom in advance to locate the available electrical outlets and decide upon the best placement for the projector and screen. Take a heavy duty extension cord with you to court (see § **6.12** on handling courtroom logistics).
7. Make sure you have a spare bulb for the projector and a pointer stick for the witness to use.
8. If the attorney or the expert witness plans to write or draw on the transparencies (underlining, drawing arrows, and so forth) be sure you have markers in several colors. Get the type of marking pens that are made specifically for writing on glossy acetate transparencies.
9. Have the attorney or witness practice with the transparencies they will use at trial. Remind them to turn the projector lamp off when they change transparencies to avoid glare from the empty screen.
10. Arrange the transparencies in the order in which they will be used during the testimony. Number and index the transparencies so you can put them back in order quickly if they should get out of sequence.

11. Make arrangements to have someone bring the equipment to the courtroom when you need it and return it when you are finished with it.

§ 4.63 Securing Equipment and Supplies for Trial

It is your responsibility as the trial paralegal to see that the necessary equipment and supplies are available and in place when they are needed. The following list contains some suggestions to help you plan ahead for your supply and equipment needs to help make the actual trial preparation go more smoothly.

1. Order the supplies you will need for trial early enough to avoid a last-minute time crunch. Order enough to allow for errors and additions. Check with your office supplier on the return policy for unused merchandise. If you are in charge of ordering and stocking supplies, buy often-used items such as standard black ring binders, exhibit tabs and dividers in quantity wherever possible because they will be less expensive in the long run.
2. Enlist the help of the person in your office who controls the key to the supply storage room, or get access to a key yourself, in case you are working late at night or on weekends and you need supplies from the storage room.
3. Get advance approval for emergency art supply purchases. Have an understanding with your office's management about the reimbursement procedures to be followed if you must make an emergency purchase.
4. Open accounts in the name of your office at your local art and office supply stores. (Check with the office administrator on the proper procedures.) When you are really rushed in trial preparation, a store charge can save you time by not having to get a check or petty cash before you make the purchase.
5. Make arrangements as far ahead as possible for buying, renting, or borrowing special equipment, such as an overhead projector and screen, if your office does not own this equipment.

§ 4.64 Monitoring the Use of Trial Equipment

In firms with a heavy trial practice, there may often be several trials going on simultaneously. When trial teams on the various cases need to use the easels, portfolios, trial briefcases, and other equipment, it can be difficult to keep track of the whereabouts of the equipment. Some large firms have separate audio-visual departments in which a person is assigned the job of keeping tabs on the equipment. However, many small and medium-sized firms have no organized department, and the duty often falls to the trial paralegal to look after the equipment and make sure it is available for trial. If conflicts routinely arise in your office as to who is responsible for the equipment, you may find it necessary to organize a system to reserve and check out various pieces of trial equipment. Use sign-out sheets for each piece of equipment and post these inside the closet or cupboard where the equipment is stored. Also, keep a central notebook or expanding file containing:

- A record of the equipment serial numbers
- User's manual or instructions
- Repair contracts, guarantees, or warranties
- Regular maintenance and repair records
- Source for replacement supplies (for example, bulb on overhead projector).

Checklist: Standard Trial Equipment

The trial equipment which you need to keep tabs on could include the items on the following checklist.

____ 1. Camera, attachments, and accessories (see § **4.32**)
____ 2. Overhead projector and screen (see § **4.61**)
____ 3. Slide projector and screen (see § **4.44**)
____ 4. VCR and television monitor
____ 5. Easels or tripods (see § **4.60**)
____ 6. Easel crossbar attachment (see § **4.60**)
____ 7. Oversized newsprint tablets
____ 8. Pointer
____ 9. Trial "box-sided" briefcases
____ 10. Artist's zippered vinyl portfolio (for charts)

§ 4.65 Stocking Supplies for Demonstrative Exhibits

As a trial paralegal, you need to keep enough versatile, basic supplies on hand to enable you to create a solution to almost any demonstrative exhibit problem. Producing visual aids and demonstrative exhibits is easy if you build up a stock of basic art supplies and a few all-purpose tools. You really don't need a lot of fancy supplies. Many of the items you will use most frequently are standard office supplies and common household utensils to which you apply a little imagination and creativity.

Checklist: Basic Art Supplies and Tools

Use the following checklist as a guide to basic art supplies and materials you can collect to make creating visual aids easy.

____ 1. Cutting Tools
- ____ Heavy duty utility knife (with extra blades)
- ____ Exacto™ Knife (with extra blades)
- ____ Sharp scissors (large and small)
- ____ Paper cutter
- ____ Kitchen knife
- ____ Letter opener

____ 2. Measuring and Drawing Tools
- ____ Metal or cloth retractable tape measure
- ____ Rulers: 12-inch and 18-inch, plastic and metal
- ____ Architect's rule
- ____ Yardstick or meter stock
- ____ T-square
- ____ Protractor
- ____ Compass
- ____ Plastic Templates

____ 3. Fasteners

Stapler and staples, regular and heavyweight
- ____ Staple remover
- ____ Brass brads
- ____ Prong fasteners
- ____ Rubber bands
- ____ Spring-loaded binder clips (assorted sizes)
- ____ Paper clips (large and small)
- ____ Thumb tacks
- ____ Push pins

____ 4. Tape and Adhesives
- ____ Regular cellophane tape
- ____ Self-adhesive tags (for temporary placement)
- ____ Drafting tape
- ____ Double-sticky tape
- ____ Masking tape
- ____ Reinforced strapping tape
- ____ Crepe edging tape
- ____ Plastic mending tape (clear and assorted colors)
- ____ Spray adhesive
- ____ Paper mounting squares
- ____ Glue spots

____ Photo mounting corners (self-adhesive)
____ Rubber cement
____ White liquid glue
____ Glue stick
____ Velcro™

____ 5. Label Stock
____ Preprinted exhibit labels
____ Plain self-adhesive label stock, assorted colors, shapes, and sizes
____ Notebook dividers
___ Oak tag labels with attached string (for nondocument exhibits)
____ Tabbies—numerical/alphabetical/exhibit/blank

____ 6. Chart Supplies
____ Foam-core board (standard sheets)
____ Illustration board, poster board
____ Chartpak™ tapes & borders (Letraset)
____ Vinyl adhesive letters (various styles and sizes)
____ Transfer letters
____ Lettering machine
____ Stencils and templates, assorted sizes
____ Acetate overlay
____ Pantone™ film

____ 7. Erasers and correction supplies
____ Standard felt blackboard eraser
____ Magnetic porcelain-finish board (wipe-off)
____ Art gum; kneaded
____ Pencil stick w/brush
____ Ink
____ Correction products:
____ Cover-up tape, assorted widths
____ Liquid, white or tinted, various formulations

____ 8. Paper
____ Colored/tinted papers
____ Notebook paper with reinforced edges
____ Graph paper/blue grid paper
____ Ledger paper
____ Brown wrapping paper
____ Cardboard

____ 9. Writing Tools
____ Ballpoint and felt-tip pens; various widths, colors
____ Colored pens/pencils/crayons
____ Chalk

- ____ Highlighters
- ____ Heavy markers
- ____ Sharpies™
- ____ Wipe-off markers
- ____ Photograph marking pen

____ 10. Additional Supplies and Tools

- ____ Hole reinforcements
- ____ Signal dots (assorted colors)
- ____ Self-adhesive tags (assorted colors and sizes)
- ____ Tape flags
- ____ Storage boxes with lids
- ____ Storage cabinet or drawers for oversized boards
- ____ Tools/supplies you won't find in the art store:
  - ____ Tweezers
  - ____ Small stiff paintbrush (for whisking eraser squiggles)
  - ____ Small manicure scissors (for trimming edges)
  - ____ Rubber fingertip protectors
  - ____ Nail clippers
  - ____ Orange-wood manicure stick
  - ____ Kitchen knife
  - ____ Screwdrivers, assorted sizes, regular and Phillips
  - ____ Hammer
  - ____ Pliers, regular and needle-nose
- ____ Hole punchers
  - ____ Heavy duty punch
  - ____ Large 3-hole punch—adjustable (extra large holes)
  - ____ 2-hole Acco punch (top fastening)
  - ____ Single hole punch (handheld, portable)
- ____ Binding machines and supplies
  - ____ Spiral bind (comb binder)
  - ____ Heat bind (Velo-bind)
  - ____ Thermal bind
  - ____ Punch/brad binder
- ____ Looseleaf supplies
  - ____ Notebooks/binders/folders
  - ____ Hardback/softcover
  - ____ Various sizes/colors
  - ____ 3-ring

- ____ Acco folders
- ____ Plastic page protector sleeves

____ Stamps

- ____ Date stamper
- ____ Sequential Bates stamp
- ____ Rubber stamps

CHAPTER 5

PREPARING TRIAL MATERIALS

§ 5.1 Preparing Trial Materials

Trial materials are the items you will assemble during the last phase of the trial preparation that specifically relate to different aspects of the courtroom presentation. Some documents are exchanged with the opposing attorneys, some are filed with the court, and others are prepared for the attorney's use in presenting the case. Although these materials are not used until the actual trial, you can start compiling the information needed to prepare them early in the trial preparation process. For example, the contents of the attorney's trial notebook may include information you collected or developed during the case, such as deposition summaries and witness statements.

Like the demonstrative exhibits discussed in **Chapter 4,** many of these materials cannot be completed until the attorney is certain the trial is actually going forward. (If the case settles, the materials will not be needed.) Most of the trial materials are based on discovery information and other documents generated earlier in the case and they correspond to various aspects of the trial, such as:

- Refining the trial presentation and strategy (mock trial)
- Organizing for the courtroom presentation (attorney's trial notebook)
- Securing attendance of trial witnesses (subpoenas)
- Court's filing requirements (trial briefs, etc.)
- "Shaping" the trial proceedings (motions in limine)
- Tracking various trial information (exhibit index)
- Use in the courtroom during trial (exhibits and exhibit notebooks).

The exact materials you prepare and the order in which you prepare them will vary from case to case, depending on the type of case, the court's requirements (see § **2.16**), and what information has already been exchanged with the opposing side. Use the following checklist and the references to other sections of this book as a general guide to the documents, pleadings, indexes, and other materials that you may be asked to prepare specifically for use at trial. Always check your local rules and consult your supervising attorney about the specific materials needed for your case.

Checklist: Materials to Prepare for Trial

____ 1. Final discovery (see § **5.5**)

  ____ Supplemental discovery responses

  ____ "Clean up" interrogatories and document requests

  ____ Request for admissions

____ 2. Motions in limine

  ____ Motion for protective order

  ____ Motion to preclude testimony of expert

  ____ Motion to exclude evidence

  ____ Motion to bifurcate trial issues

  ____ Motion and order for admission pro hac vice (see § **1.17**)

  ____ Motion for jury view (see § **6.15**)

  ____ Pretrial motion ruling chart (see § **6.10**)

____ 3. Witness subpoenas (see § **5.10**)

  ____ Trial witness subpoena index

____ Motion and order appointing persons to serve subpoenas
____ Subpoena duces tecum for documents
____ Return of service of subpoenas

____ 4. Trial brief (see § **5.34**)
____ Introductory information
____ Statements of fact
____ List of anticipated witnesses
____ Summary of testimony
____ List of trial exhibits
____ Issues of law

____ 5. Attorney's trial notebook (see § **5.77**)

____ 6. Paralegal master trial notebook (see § **5.88**)

____ 7. Jury and voir dire materials (see § **6.16**)
____ Juror profile worksheet
____ Juror investigation
____ Composite jury data grid
____ Proposed voir dire questions
____ Jury box diagram

____ 8. Depositions materials (see § **5.42**)
____ Deposition master index
____ Deposition exhibit index
____ Notice of video deposition de bene esse (expert testimony)
____ Notice of filing transcripts
____ Request for ruling on objections
____ Objection transcript index (see § **6.11**)

____ 9. Exhibits (see § **5.58**)
____ Trial exhibit worksheet
____ Exhibit index (public)
____ Master reference index (private)
____ Exhibit notebooks

____ 10. Courtroom files or binders (see § **5.8**)
____ Exhibit files or binders (see § **6.66**)
____ Witness notebooks (see § **3.1**)

____ 11. Visual aids and demonstrative exhibits (see **Chapter 4**)

____ 12. Final trial preparation agenda (see § **2.9**)

§ 5.2 Setting Up a Mock Trial

Your supervising attorneys may want to try out their case theories and techniques by presenting the case in a condensed fashion to a simulated jury, especially if the case deals with complicated legal issues or facts. The mock trial process, which amounts to a dress rehearsal for the trial presentation, lets the attorneys get feedback from impartial individuals not previously involved with the case about the strengths and weaknesses of the case, what particular evidence is most memorable or important, what points need clarification when presented to the actual jury, and how a jury might decide the case. The mock trial process also gives the trial team attorneys a chance to play "devil's advocate" when they have to evaluate and plan for the points the opposing side will make in their case presentation.

These are some guidelines to follow if you are asked to set up this type of experiment in your case.

1. You will need someone to act as a judge-moderator to introduce the case and a panel of persons to listen as pretend jurors. The attorneys can summarize the testimony of the witnesses for each side.
2. Decide how many persons you need to approximate the size of the actual jury. Always plan to have a couple of extra persons as alternates in case one of the original group is unable to sit in at the last minute.
3. Clear the procedure with the managing partner or office manager to allow the staff permission to take time away from their regular duties to serve on the simulated jury.
4. Talk to the office staff and enlist their cooperation in agreeing to serve on the simulated jury. Try to get a fair cross-section of persons, that is, various educational and occupational levels and a mix of men and women. Use nonlawyer personnel to eliminate persons who have extensive legal training. The goal is to approximate the types of persons you would expect to get on a real jury, such as secretaries, bookkeepers, clerks, librarians, students, and so forth. Of course, because these are company employees, they will not be completely unbiased, but emphasize that they should try to set aside any bias or favoritism and attempt to render an impartial decision.
5. Try to schedule the trial simulation on a date just a few days before the real trial so that the case preparation will be nearly completed and the exhibits will be ready.
6. Schedule the trial simulation in a conference room large enough to hold the jurors, the attorneys, and the exhibits. If you can, arrange the furniture in the conference room to approximate the location of the jury box, the attorney's table, and the witness stand in the courtroom you will be using for the real trial.

7. To the extent possible, use the actual exhibits you will present at trial. This helps you determine the approximate sequence for the exhibits and you get a chance to practice setting up equipment such as easels and oversized chart boards.
8. With the help of the trial attorneys, prepare a set of simplified jury instructions and a jury questionnaire, if appropriate, to assist the jurors in calculating a monetary award according to the guidelines that will apply in the actual case.

When you have the attorneys and the simulated jurors assembled on the appointed day, present the case in the same order it would be presented at the actual trial: first, brief opening remarks by the judge-moderator; second, presentation of the plaintiff's case; third, presentation of the defendant's case; fourth, instructions to the jury by the judge-moderator; and finally, deliberation and rendering of a verdict by the simulated jury.

The lawyers present the substance of each side's case to the mock jurors by giving a capsulized, condensed version of the testimony and evidence they expect to introduce at trial. Naturally, it will not be possible to have the actual witnesses present, but the attorneys can review for the jury the highlights of the anticipated testimony and their main arguments in the case.

After the presentation of both sides of the case, the judge-moderator reads the jury instructions to the jury. The trial team and the moderator should then withdraw from the room and leave the jurors to deliberate. If it is possible to do so without their knowledge, arrange to tape record the jurors' discussion or listen to the deliberations via an intercom or speakerphone hookup. You should be available to answer questions or provide answers from the attorneys if the jurors need clarification on some point during their deliberations. After the jury has reached a verdict, the attorneys can ask questions about how they arrived at their decision. You may want to ask the jurors to write a brief memo stating their impressions of the case presentation and any points or evidence that they thought were particularly memorable or impressive.

The mock trial takes time and effort to prepare and present and obviously, the trial team cannot rely too heavily on the verdict reached by such a simulated jury. However, the successful trial simulation has a number of distinctly positive results:

1. It forces the trial team to have the case preparation completed or nearly completed before the actual trial.
2. It forces the trial team to go through the exercise of anticipating the case the opposing side will present. They can then plan how to counter most effectively the opposing party's expected evidence and testimony.
3. Presenting the case to a simulated jury helps to distill and clarify the important issues in a case, and lets the trial team see how others view the weaknesses and strengths of the case.

4. By presenting the case to a simulated jury and observing their reactions, the trial team can polish the actual trial presentation to provide needed clarification on information or evidence and decide what is most important to emphasize to the actual jury.
5. A mock trial can help an inexperienced attorney practice his or her delivery in front of an audience before actually going into the courtroom.
6. Mock trial experiments in my office have had the unexpected positive result of really getting the office staff interested and excited about the case. During the actual trial, we have found that they are very supportive and many have even come to the courthouse to observe the real proceedings. The participating office staff members feel they had a valuable role in assisting the trial team to prepare the case, and so they are very interested in the outcome.
7. The mock trial is valuable from a paralegal's perspective because you learn what evidence and testimony the attorney plans to present and which exhibits, visual aids, and equipment you will need to have ready for the courtroom.

§ 5.3 Preparing the Trial "War Room"

In a very small case, the primary work area may be a stack of boxes in a corner of the lead attorney's office. But trial preparation in even a relatively small case will generate materials in addition to the actual case files, and these can quickly outgrow the capacity of an individual attorney's office. It is advantageous to designate a specific area or room in which you can assemble and keep track of these materials, files, and equipment during the last phase of the trial preparation.

Arranging for specialized work space dedicated to the needs of the case preparation is one of the administrative duties you may be asked to handle as a trial paralegal. The trial team will benefit in several ways by having "war room" space that is designated as a control room or headquarters from which to conduct and coordinate the trial preparation activities. Setting aside a specific area for activities related to the trial preparation sends a clear indication to other persons in the office that the team has switched into "trial mode" and that the members of the team are seriously involved in the business of pulling the case together for trial. Establishing a central location for the war room separates the trial materials from other case files in the offices of the trial team members and provides a place for the trial team to concentrate on the trial preparation without the distractions that inevitably occur in a normal office setting. The war room serves as a central staging area where the trial team can:

- Hold planning and strategy meetings (see § **2.9**)
- Review and organize case files and materials (see **Chapter 2**)
- Store and organize deposition transcripts and corresponding exhibits (see **Chapter 2, § 5.58**)
- Perform document coding, data processing, and other manual and computerized litigation support activities (see **Chapter 8**)
- Prepare witnesses to testify (see §§ **3.1, 3.8** *et seq.*)
- Confer and consult with expert witnesses (see § **3.19** *et seq.*)
- Select, tag, and index trial exhibit documents and prepare exhibit packets or notebooks (see § **5.58**)
- Prepare and store oversized demonstrative exhibits and visual aids (see **Chapter 4**)
- Assemble the supplies and equipment that will actually be taken to the courtroom (see §§ **4.60–4.63, 5.87**)
- Track and manage the daily influx of trial notes, transcripts, and exhibits during a lengthy trial (see § **6.65**).

Exactly how much space you need for the war room will be determined by the same administrative components (people, paper, time, and money) that apply in other aspects of case management:

1. People—the number of attorneys, paralegals, and support personnel working on the case.
2. Paper—the number of documents and the amount and type of paper generated by the case, as well as the methods of litigation support to be employed in processing the paper materials.
3. Time—how long the space will be needed and how much time is left to prepare the case for trial.
4. Money—the monetary resources the firm or the client can afford to devote to space needs (especially in large cases).

The best logistical arrangement for the war room in terms of convenience and accessibility is usually dedicated on-site space within the law office that allows the trial team to remain in close proximity to the office equipment and support facilities necessary to the trial preparation. Many lawfirms have work rooms that are reserved for this type of use, but any small conference room or office in which the trial materials can be spread out for review and stored from day to day without being disturbed will serve the purpose. If possible, select a work area for the war room that is conveniently located in relationship to the lead trial attorney's office. If you plan to commandeer space that is not ordinarily devoted to intensive case work, coordinate this arrangement with your office manager or firm administrator. If your office uses a scheduling sheet for the conference rooms, arrange with the person in charge to book the room for at least the last one to two weeks before the trial date, and be sure that person notes the purpose for which you will be using the room. When you are working in the war room, advise the office receptionist and your secretary of your whereabouts so you can have trial-related telephone calls put through to you there. You may wish to post "Do Not Disturb or Discard" signs in prominent places near the documents and files so that no one inadvertently will disturb or trash the materials.

If there is absolutely no room available in the law office, or if the case is very large and complex, you may find it necessary to rent or lease off-site space. This may involve scouting out appropriate retail loft or second-floor storefront space, especially in crowded urban locales. Another possibility for off-site war room space is converting rooms on the client's premises if the client is a company or corporation with sufficient available office space. There are some inconvenience factors associated with the use of off-site war room facilities. For example, legal personnel have to commute to the off-site work space, and this often means extra trips, extra time involved, and missed messages, which may complicate the work in progress. In addition, someone must be responsible for providing and maintaining the necessary equipment and supplies, coordinating support personnel and resources, and working out security considerations and procedures for gaining access to the site after hours.

§ 5.4 —Features of the "War Room"

The following is a list of desirable features for a war room facility. Many of these items will be readily available if you are using dedicated on-site space within the law office. If you are using off-site space, however, you may have to work out many additional special logistical arrangements to ensure that the trial team has the necessary equipment, supplies, and services to enable them to properly prepare the case efficiently and comfortably.

1. Adequate open work space that is accessible to all the attorneys, paralegals, and support staff working on the case.
2. Large work tables on which to spread out files, documents, and exhibits, and accompanying comfortable chairs.
3. Dry-erase board, chalkboard, or easel pad on which to outline ideas and strategies.
4. Bulletin board or cork board on which to hang charts, maps, timelines and so forth.
5. Boxes, bins, or filing cabinets in which to organize and store various types of trial materials.

6. Adequate shelving for boxes and binders containing working copies of the case documents.
7. Telephone hookups, preferably with conference call capability. Adequate telephone lines are especially important if computer data will be transmitted via modem.
8. Good lighting.
9. Adequate power outlets for all equipment to be used.
10. Small work rooms or private areas for client meetings or witness interviews.
11. Computer hardware, software, and peripherals, including fax hookups, if needed.
12. Photocopier and supplies.
13. Microfilm reader/printers or imaging work stations (when microfilm or imaging technology is used in litigation support).
14. Video cassette recorder and television (for playing videotape depositions and witness training videos).
15. Food service and supplies, such as a coffee machine, small refrigerator, and microwave oven.
16. Adequate water, plumbing, and restroom facilities.
17. Proper heating, ventilation, and air conditioning controls.
18. Janitorial service (trash removal and cleaning).
19. Paper recycling and/or shredding facility for papers containing confidential information.
20. Procedures for tracking billing and paying expenses (for off-site facility).

§ 5.5 Preparing Final Discovery Responses and Requests

Discovery plays an important role in the context of trial preparation. The discovery process allows each party to learn about the other side's case so it can formulate strategies and prepare its case without worrying about surprise tactics from the other side. The mandatory initial disclosure procedures set out in the 1993 amendments to the Federal Rules of Civil Procedure are designed to streamline the discovery process for cases in the districts that adopt these guidelines (see § **2.29**). By the time a case gets to trial, each side should have a good grasp of the opponent's case, because disclosure and discovery have allowed them to:

- Narrow and clarify the disputed issues
- Define the damages claimed (how the damages are determined and calculated)

- Determine which lay witnesses will testify about the factual aspects of the case and what they will say
- Determine which expert witnesses will testify and what opinions they will offer
- Establish the documents, objects, or other physical evidence that will be offered as trial exhibits.

As you begin to prepare the trial materials, review all the discovery in the case, including interrogatories, depositions, admissions, and document productions. If you prepared a Discovery Index (see **Chapter 2**) when you first organized the files, use it as a guide to determine what discovery has been served and answered by both sides. Determine whether there are any missing or incomplete discovery responses, for instance, information or documents you need to provide or which the opposing attorney promised but has not yet delivered or produced.

§ 5.6 —Supplementing Discovery Responses

Parties to a lawsuit sometimes do not have all the information requested when they initially respond to discovery requests. They may serve incomplete responses to interrogatories or document requests, indicating that the answers will be supplemented at a later date when they have completed their investigation or additional information becomes available. Rule 26(e) of the Federal Rules of Civil Procedure (amended effective December 1, 1993) specifies the duty of the parties to supplement incomplete or incorrect disclosures and discovery responses. Each party must make a good faith effort to supplement or update discovery responses in a timely manner if the party finds his or her original answers are incomplete or incorrect. Under the amended rules, the court can levy penalties against parties who fail to properly supplement their disclosures (see **Chapter 2** for a discussion of the provisions in the 1993 rules amendments). You will need to review the discovery files in your case well before the trial for:

1. Interrogatory answers, responses to requests for admission, and responses to requests to produce documents that may need to be updated; and
2. Any missing or incomplete discovery responses from the opposing party.

If you need to supply additional discovery information, you can offer to prepare the supplemental discovery response. You can combine supplemental information on interrogatories, document productions, and so on in the same filing (see **Form 5–1**).

FORM 5–1
SAMPLE SUPPLEMENTAL DISCOVERY RESPONSES

IN THE COURT OF COMMON PLEAS
________ COUNTY, ________

____________,	)	CASE NO.
	:	
Plaintiff,	)	JUDGE
vs.	:	
____________,	)	PLAINTIFF'S
	:	SUPPLEMENTAL
	)	DISCOVERY RESPONSES
Defendant.	:	

Plaintiff, __________, pursuant to Rule 26(e) of the Federal Rules of Civil Procedure, hereby supplements his responses to Defendant's previous discovery requests directed to Plaintiff, as set forth below.

SUPPLEMENTAL RESPONSE to Defendant's Interrogatory No. 4:
[insert the updated information]

SUPPLEMENTAL RESPONSE to Item No. 6 of Defendant's First Request for Production of Documents:

Copies of the documents requested are attached hereto.

[Attorney]
[address]
[telephone]
Attorneys for Plaintiff

If you have not previously served discovery on the opposing party requesting information about trial witnesses, exhibits, and so forth, ask the attorney if you should prepare a set of cleanup interrogatories or requests for production to request this information formally (see **Forms 5–2, 5–3**). Remember that you must serve discovery requests on the opposing party early enough to allow sufficient time (usually 30 days) for them to answer before the trial, so you will need to prepare these requests early in your trial preparation efforts.

Note: The amendments to the Federal Rules of Civil Procedure, effective for cases filed after December 1, 1993, may eventually reduce the need to serve cleanup interrogatories, particularly those concerning expert witnesses. Under the initial disclosure procedures in revised FRCP 26, litigants must provide most of the information on expert witnesses early in the case (see **§ 2.29**).

FORM 5–2
SAMPLE CLEANUP INTERROGATORIES

[Insert your standard caption and introductory remarks.]

Interrogatories:

1. State the name, address, and capacity of the person supplying the information to answer these interrogatories.

2. State the name and address of each person you intend to call as a lay witness to testify on your behalf at the time of trial and the order in which they will testify.

3. For each witness listed in your answer to Interrogatory No. 2, give a brief summary of the expected testimony of that witness.

4. For each witness listed in your answer to Interrogatory No. 2, identify each and every document or exhibit the witness will produce, identify, or authenticate at trial.

5. Identify any persons you have consulted purporting to be experts in any field related to any of the issues or allegations in this case, including any persons you have employed to assist in the preparation of your case for trial.

6. For each person identified in your answer to Interrogatory No. 5, please identify each one you intend to call as an expert witness at the trial of this matter and the order in which they will testify.

7. For each person identified in your answer to Interrogatory No. 6, state the following:

   a. The field of expertise for each such person;
   b. A brief resume of the expert's education and professional background;
   c. The title, publisher, date, and form of all books, articles, or documentary material published or written by each such expert;
   d. The subject matter upon which the expert is expected to testify at trial;
   e. The substance of the facts and opinions to which the expert is expected to testify at trial;
   f. A brief summary of the grounds for each opinion to which the expert is expected to testify at trial;
   g. The date upon which you first contacted the expert;
   h. Identify all reports written or prepared by such experts related to the issues in this case;
   i. Identify all documents and materials that provided a basis for or upon which the expert relied in forming his or her conclusions and opinions;
   j. Identify all documents the expert will produce, identify, or authenticate at trial.

8. For each person identified in your answer to Interrogatory No. 6, state whether that person has ever testified as an expert in the trial of any other lawsuit. If so, please list the following for each such case:

   a. The caption of the case;
   b. The case number;
   c. The type of suit;
   d. The date of trial;
   e. The disposition of the case;
   f. The subject matter about which the expert testified.

9. Identify and describe with specific detail each and every document or item that you intend to mark as an exhibit at the trial of this action.

10. Identify and describe all demonstrative evidence not previously disclosed that you plan to use at trial.

11. State specifically the amount of damages you will claim at the trial of this case, and give a breakdown of the components and the method of calculation of such damages.

FORM 5–3
SAMPLE CLEANUP REQUEST
FOR PRODUCTION OF DOCUMENTS

[Insert your standard caption and introductory remarks.]

1. Copies of all documents not previously disclosed that _________ intends to mark as exhibits at the trial of this matter, including but not limited to those described in _________'s response to Interrogatories No. 9 and 10.

2. Copies of all documents that will be identified or authenticated by any lay witness at the trial of this case.

3. Copies of all documents that will be identified or authenticated by any expert witness at the trial of this case.

4. All documents and materials that _____ agreed to furnish at the deposition of __[witness]__ on __[date]__, 199__, in this case, specifically: [List documents, giving page and line number references from deposition transcript.]

5. All documents and materials that __________ agreed to furnish in correspondence dated _________, 199__, in connection with this matter. [attach correspondence]

§ 5.7 —Handling Requests for Admissions

Although the request for admissions is technically a discovery method under Rule 36 of the Federal Rules of Civil Procedure, it can also be a powerful trial preparation tool. The request for admissions is routinely used early in a case to distinguish existing facts and issues that are then resolved through other types of discovery (such as depositions and interrogatories). However, this valuable technique is sometimes overlooked in the context of trial preparation. The request for admissions is an inexpensive way to expedite trial procedures by

- Narrowing the scope of disputed issues
- Verifying the truth of certain material facts
- Reducing the time required to introduce foundational elements for the admissibility of documents and business records.

Like the cleanup interrogatories and document requests discussed in § **5.6,** you must prepare and serve the request for admissions far enough ahead of the trial to allow the opposing party sufficient time (usually 30 days) to respond by admitting or denying the requests. These are some important points to remember about requests for admissions:

- The request for admissions can be a commanding weapon at trial because, if a timely response is not filed, the facts in the request for admissions are deemed "conclusively established" under the provisions of FRCP 36(b).
- A request answered by an evasive or incomplete denial may also be deemed to be an admission at trial.
- If a party fails to admit a fact set out in a request for admissions and that fact is later proved at trial, the party who failed to admit the fact may be required to pay any costs incurred in making the proof, including reasonable attorney's fees. FRCP 37(c) (See § **7.14.**)
- All admissions are valid for the pending action only and may not be used in any other proceeding.

Your responsibilities as a trial paralegal may include handling the requests for admissions in your case. Carefully review the requests for admission and discuss the responses with the supervising attorney. Promptly enter the due date for responses on your trial preparation calendar and see that the answers are filed and served on time.

§ 5.8 Preparing the Courtroom Files and Notebooks

Prepare a separate set of files or looseleaf binders to contain the refined and condensed trial materials the attorney needs for the courtroom. You may already have created some of these files when you initially organized the case (see §§ **2.30, 2.45**) or at some other point during the trial preparation. On the other hand, if you have been pulled in on the case at the last minute to help with the trial preparation, there may not be any trial-related files, so the files or binders you prepare at this point will constitute the main set of courtroom materials.

Use these files and binders as a repository for materials culled from the main case files that will actually be used in the courtroom. Include in these files a copy of any indexes or lists of materials you previously prepared. You may want to put copies of these indexes in your master trial notebook and in the attorney's trial notebook as well. The exact categories you set up for these files will vary from case to case, as will the number of subfiles or notebook divider tabs needed, depending on the nature of the case and how the remainder of the file is organized. For example, if your information is already organized in notebooks and binders, you may need fewer files. Generally, however, you will need at least one file to accommodate materials from each of the areas described on the checklist in § **5.9.**

Whether you use folders, notebooks, or a combination of both, affix bright, clear labels so that either you or the attorney can easily locate the desired folder or binder. Use large bold letters and label both sides of the folder or divider tabs so they will be readable from either front or back. Label all files, binders, and boxes, that you will transport to the courtroom with the case identification, the attorney's name, and your law office name and telephone number. This will help to ensure that the materials are returned to you if a notebook gets separated from the other materials or is inadvertently left behind in the courtroom.

§ 5.9 —Files and Binders to Prepare for the Courtroom

These files and binders should be taken to court.

____ 1. Trial notes.
This folder will remain empty until the trial begins, at which point you may use it to contain the attorney's daily trial notes. You may decide to include your daily notes as well. (See § **6.46** on taking notes at trial.)

____ 2. Pretrial activities.
Use this file to contain copies of any motions in limine or other pretrial motions, as well as the pretrial motion rulings chart (see § **6.10**) and deposition objection transcript index (see § **6.11**). You may also include notes on the judge, courtroom logistics, and other pretrial activities discussed in § **6.7** *et seq.*

____ 3. Opening statement.
The attorney may wish to place an outline or other materials he or she plans to use in opening statement in this folder or binder section (see §§ **5.82, 6.53**).

____ 4. Voir dire.
Place the juror profile worksheet and proposed voir dire questions in this section. Include the court's prospective juror list and any investigative data, as well as the various forms and materials discussed in § **6.16** *et seq.* Remember to include plenty of paper for notes on the voir dire proceedings.

____ 5. Lay witnesses.
The materials you compiled for the witness examination and trial preparation conferences (see **Chapter 3**) will form the core of the courtroom witness files. You will probably want to make a separate file or binder section for each witness. (You may be able to reuse the ones you previously created.) For each of your witnesses, place in this folder the relevant background materials, discovery, and exhibit documents, as well as the attorney's notes or proposed outline for the witness's testimony in the courtroom. Also include any notes on proposed cross-examination questions of the opposing side's witnesses.

____ 6. Expert witnesses.
Use this file or binder to hold a copy of the expert's curriculum vitae or resume and other credentials, articles, publications, and other background materials previously discussed with the expert. Also include a copy of the expert's report and any proposed hypothetical questions the attorney has prepared for trial. (See § **3.19** *et seq.* on preparing the expert witness for trial.)

____ 7. Trial witness subpoenas.
Use this folder to contain copies of the trial subpoena index, the actual subpoenas and returns of service, copies of the witness fee checks, and any other materials related to issuance and service of the trial subpoenas (see § **5.10** *et seq.*)

____ 8. Trial Exhibits.
The attorney will probably want a separate file folder for each exhibit. You may also want to compile a master exhibit binder containing one copy of each exhibit for easy reference. Place a

copy of the exhibit indexes in this binder, along with notes on any special storage or transportation arrangements for exhibits. Refer to § **5.58** *et seq.* and § **6.65** *et seq.* for details on preparing and managing trial exhibits.

____ 9. Demonstrative Exhibits.
If you have a number of demonstrative exhibits or visual aids, use this folder or notebook section to hold letter-sized copies of large exhibits, plus notations on the planned use and special equipment needed to present them. (See **Chapter 4** on preparing demonstrative evidence.)

____ 10. Depositions/Other Discovery.
In some cases you may need to include only summaries and indexes of the discovery, but in others you will want to take copies of the discovery responses and the deposition transcripts to the courtroom. Condensed versions of the transcripts can reduce the volume of paper in this notebook considerably (see § **5.50**). If you have previously included a copy of the deposition transcript in the individual witness files (see item #5 and #6 above) you may not need to repeat those materials here. (See § **5.42** *et seq.* for a detailed discussion of preparing depositions for use at trial.)

____ 11. Rebuttal Witnesses and Evidence.
Use this folder to contain standby materials related to potential rebuttal testimony and evidence. Consult the attorney about plans for possible rebuttal testimony.

____ 12. Closing Argument.
Use this file to collect documents, notes, and other materials that the attorney wants to include in the summation or closing argument. You will probably add items to this file throughout the trial. (See § **6.59** on preparing for closing argument.)

____ 13. Jury Charge.
Place the proposed jury instructions prepared by both sides in this file where they will be handy for the attorney's reference throughout the trial. When the judge gives the actual jury charge, follow along on your copy of the proposed instructions and take notes on the exact instructions the court gives to the jury panel (see § **5.86**).

____ 14. Miscellaneous.
The characteristics of your particular case will suggest other specific files that you will need for the courtroom. It is always a good idea to have a few extra folders or blank divider tabs for courtroom materials that you could not have anticipated beforehand and that do not fit into any of the other categories.

§ 5.10 Preparing and Serving Trial Subpoenas

The trial paralegal is usually responsible for overseeing the preparation, issuance, and service of subpoenas for the trial witnesses. This section discusses general procedures concerning subpoenas and the recent changes to Rule 45 of the Federal Rules of Civil Procedure governing subpoenas in the federal courts (see **§ 5.13**). Forms and procedures for state court subpoenas vary widely from state to state. Always check your local court rules for specific information on the correct subpoena forms and procedures for your area.

§ 5.11 —Definition: Subpoena

The term "subpoena" is derived from the two Latin words *sub poena,* which mean "under penalty." In modern legal usage, the subpoena is a written order issued by the clerk of the trial court or by the attorney as an officer of the court (see **§ 5.13**), commanding a person to appear at a specific place and time (usually the trial courtroom) to testify about certain matters. A subpoena can also command a person to permit inspection of the premises or to produce records at a certain place and time (see **§ 5.12**). A person who fails to obey the directions of a subpoena may be found in contempt of court.

§ 5.12 —Definition: Subpoena Duces Tecum

Some trial subpoenas may bear the designation *duces tecum,* a Latin term that translates to "bring with you." A subpoena duces tecum includes a description of certain documents, records, or objects that the witness is commanded bring to the trial. Your supervising attorney will give you the details on the specific documents, records, or objects the witness is to produce. You can then insert this description on the subpoena or praecipe form. The federal court subpoena form provides a block for details on the documents or objects to be produced. When you have a lengthy list of items to be produced, the block provided may not provide adequate space for the entire description. You can solve this problem by inserting the following notation in the block:

SEE DOCUMENTS DESCRIBED ON ATTACHED "EXHIBIT A"

Staple a separate sheet containing the document descriptions to the subpoena form.

§ 5.13 Preparing Subpoenas in Federal Court (FRCP 45)

Rule 45 of the Federal Rules of Civil Procedure sets out guidelines for issuing and serving subpoenas in the federal courts. Rule 45 contains significant additions and revisions that became effective on December 1, 1991. The new Rule 45 clarifies and consolidates the provisions of the previous rule and adds certain new provisions related to:

- permitting attorney-issued subpoenas;
- protecting subpoenaed witnesses;
- accessing information from nonparty witnesses;
- facilitating distant district service; and
- compelling attendance of witnesses within the state.

The full text of revised Rule 45 appears below, followed by a discussion of these provisions.

RULE 45. SUBPOENA
[Effective December 1, 1991]

(a) Form; Issuance

(1) Every subpoena shall

(A) state the name of the court from which it is issued; and

(B) state the title of the action, the name of the court in which it is pending, and its civil action number; and

(C) command each person to whom it is directed to attend and give testimony or to produce and permit inspection and copying of designated books, documents, or tangible things in the possession, custody, or control of that person, or to permit inspection of premises, at a time and place therein specified; and

(D) set forth the text of subdivisions (c) and (d) of this rule.

A command to produce evidence or to permit inspection may be joined with a command to appear at trial or hearing or at deposition, or may be issued separately.

(2) A subpoena commanding attendance at a trial or hearing shall issue from the court for the district in which the hearing or trial is to be held. A subpoena for attendance at a deposition shall issue from the court for the district designated by the notice of deposition as the district in which the deposition is to be taken. If separate from a subpoena commanding the attendance of a person, a subpoena for production or inspection shall issue from the court for the district in which the production or inspection is to be made.

(3) The clerk shall issue a subpoena, signed but otherwise in blank, to a party requesting it, who shall complete it before service. An attorney as officer of the court may also issue and sign a subpoena on behalf of

(A) a court in which the attorney is authorized to practice; or

(B) a court for a district in which a deposition or production is compelled by the subpoena, if the deposition or production pertains to an action pending in a court in which the attorney is authorized to practice.

(b) Service

(1) A subpoena may be served by any person who is not a party and is not less than 18 years of age. Service of a subpoena upon a person named therein shall be made by delivering a copy thereof to such person and, if the person's attendance is commanded, by tendering to that person the fees for one day's attendance and the mileage allowed by law. When the subpoena is issued on behalf of the United States or an officer or agency thereof, fees and mileage need not be tendered. Prior notice of any commanded production of documents and things or inspection of premises before trial shall be served on each party in the manner prescribed by Rule 5(b).

(2) Subject to the provisions of clause (ii) of subparagraph (c)(3)(A) of this rule, a subpoena may be served at any place within the district of the court by which it is issued, or at any place without the district that is within 100 miles of the place of the deposition, hearing, trial, production or inspection specified in the subpoena or at any place within the state where a state statute or rule of court permits service of a subpoena issued by a state court of general jurisdiction sitting in the place of the deposition, hearing, trial, production, or inspection specified in the subpoena. When a statute of the United States provides therefor, the court upon proper application and cause shown may authorize the service of a subpoena at any other place. A subpoena directed to a witness in a foreign country who is a national or resident of the United States shall issue under the circumstances and in the manner and be served as provided in Title 28, U.S.C. § 1783.

(3) Proof of service when necessary shall be made by filing with the clerk of the court by which the subpoena issued a statement of the date and manner of service and of the names of the persons served, certified by the person who made the service.

(c) Protection of Persons Subject to Subpoenas

(1) A party or an attorney responsible for the issuance and service of a subpoena shall take reasonable steps to avoid imposing undue burden or expense on a person subject to that subpoena. The court on behalf of which the subpoena was issued shall enforce this duty and impose upon the party or attorney in breach of this duty an appropriate sanction, which may include, but is not limited to, lost earnings and a reasonable attorney's fee.

(2) (A) A person commanded to produce and permit inspection and copying of designated books, papers, documents or tangible things, or inspection of premises need not appear in person at the place of production or inspection unless commanded to appear for deposition, hearing or trial.

(B) Subject to paragraph (d)(2) of this rule, a person commanded to produce and permit inspection and copying may, within 14 days after service of the subpoena or before the time specified for compliance if such time is less than 14 days after service, serve upon the party or attorney designated in the subpoena written objection to inspection or copying of any or all of the designated materials or of the premises. If objection is made, the party serving the subpoena shall not be entitled to inspect and copy the materials or inspect the premises except pursuant to an order of the court by which the subpoena was issued. If objection has been made, the party serving the subpoena may, upon notice to the person commanded to produce, move at any time for an order to compel the production. Such an order to compel production shall protect any person who is not a party or an officer of a party from significant expense resulting from the inspection and copying commanded.

(3) (A) On timely motion, the court by which a subpoena was issued shall quash or modify the subpoena if it

(i) fails to allow reasonable time for compliance;

(ii) requires a person who is not a party or an officer of a party to travel to a place more than 100 miles from the place where that person resides, is employed or regularly transacts business in person, except that, subject to the provisions of clause (c)(3)(B)(iii) of this rule, such a person may in order to attend trial be commanded to travel from any such place within the state in which the trial is held, or

(iii) requires disclosure of privileged or other protected matter and no exception or waiver applies, or

(iv) subjects a person to undue burden.

(B) If a subpoena

(i) requires disclosure of a trade secret or other confidential research, development, or commercial information, or

(ii) requires disclosure of an unretained expert's opinion or information not describing specific events or occurrences in dispute and resulting from the expert's study made not at the request of any party, or

(iii) requires a person who is not a party or an officer of a party to incur substantial expense to travel more than 100 miles to attend trial, the court may, to protect a person subject to or affected by the subpoena, quash or modify the subpoena or, if the party in whose behalf the subpoena is issued shows a substantial need for the testimony or materials that cannot be otherwise met without undue hardship and assures that the person to whom the subpoena is addressed will be reasonably compensated, the court may order appearance or production only upon specified conditions.

(d) Duties in Responding to Subpoena

(1) A person responding to a subpoena to produce documents shall produce them as they are kept in the usual course of business or shall organize and label them to correspond with the categories in the demand.

(2) When information subject to a subpoena is withheld on a claim that it is privileged or subject to protection as trial preparation materials, the claim shall be made expressly and shall be supported by a description of the nature of the documents, communications, or things not produced that is sufficient to enable the demanding party to contest the claim.

(e) Contempt

Failure by any person without adequate excuse to obey a subpoena served upon that person may be deemed a contempt of the court from which the subpoena issued. An adequate cause for failure to obey exists when a subpoena purports to require a non-party to attend or produce at a place not within the limits provided by clause (ii) of subparagraph (c)(3)(A).

§ 5.14 —FRCP 45(a): Form and Issuance of Subpoenas

Section (a) of FRCP Rule 45 covers what must be included in the subpoena, where the subpoena is issued, and who may issue the subpoena. A subpoena commanding a witness to appear at a trial, hearing, or deposition may include a duces tecum (see **§ 5.12**) commanding the witness to produce documents or permit inspection of property. The duces tecum subpoena may be issued separately from the command to appear.

One of the most significant changes to Rule 45 is found in paragraph (a)(3). The new rule omits the language of the previous rule requiring clerks to issue subpoenas under the seal of the court. The revised rule allows an attorney to issue a subpoena "as an officer of the court," and that subpoena carries the same authority as one issued by the trial court clerk. Although it grants the attorney expanded authority in issuing and serving subpoenas, the new Rule 45 also explicitly imposes an increased duty on the trial attorney (and, by extension, the attorney's legal assistant) to guard against abuse or misuse of this power. The attorney-issued subpoena (see **Form 5–4**) must contain the full text of new sections (c) and (d) of Rule 45, which deal with certain rights and protections afforded a witness subject to a subpoena.

FORM 5–4
SUBPOENA IN A CIVIL CASE

AO 88 (Rev. 11/91) Subpoena in a Civi

United States District Court

____________________ DISTRICT OF ____________________

V.

SUBPOENA IN A CIVIL CASE

CASE NUMBER:

TO:

☐ YOU ARE COMMANDED to appear in the United States District Court at the place, date, and time specified below to testify in the above case.

PLACE OF TESTIMONY	COURTROOM
	DATE AND TIME

☐ YOU ARE COMMANDED to appear at the place, date, and time specified below to testify at the taking of a deposition in the above case.

PLACE OF DEPOSITION	DATE AND TIME

☐ YOU ARE COMMANDED to produce and permit inspection and copying of the following documents or objects at the place, date, and time specified below (list documents or objects):

PLACE	DATE AND TIME

☐ YOU ARE COMMANDED to permit inspection of the following premises at the date and time specified below.

PREMISES	DATE AND TIME

Any organization not a party to this suit that is subpoenaed for the taking of a deposition shall designate one or more officers, directors, or managing agents, or other persons who consent to testify on its behalf, and may set forth, for each person designated, the matters on which the person will testify. Federal Rules of Civil Procedure, 30(b) (6).

ISSUING OFFICER SIGNATURE AND TITLE (INDICATE IF ATTORNEY FOR PLAINTIFF OR DEFENDANT)	DATE

ISSUING OFFICER'S NAME, ADDRESS AND PHONE NUMBER

(See Rule 45, Federal Rules of Civil Procedure, Parts C & D on Reverse)

AO 88 (11/91) Subpoena in a Civil Case

PROOF OF SERVICE

	DATE	PLACE
SERVED		

SERVED ON (PRINT NAME)	MANNER OF SERVICE

SERVED BY (PRINT NAME)	TITLE

DECLARATION OF SERVER

I declare under penalty of perjury under the laws of the United States of America that the foregoing information contained in the Proof of Service is true and correct.

Executed on ______________________
DATE

____
SIGNATURE OF SERVER

____
ADDRESS OF SERVER

____

Rule 45, Federal Rules of Civil Procedure, Parts C & D:

(c) PROTECTION OF PERSONS SUBJECT TO SUBPOENAS.

(1) A party or an attorney responsible for the issuance and service of a subpoena shall take reasonable steps to avoid imposing undue burden or expense on a person subject to that subpoena. The court on behalf of which the subpoena was issued shall enforce this duty and impose upon the party or attorney in breach of this duty an appropriate sanction, which may include, but is not limited to, lost earnings and a reasonable attorney's fee.

(2)(A) A person commanded to produce and permit inspection and copying of designated books, papers, documents or tangible things, or inspection of premises need not appear in person at the place of production or inspection unless commanded to appear for deposition, hearing or trial.

(B) Subject to paragraph (d)(2) of this rule, a person commanded to produce and permit inspection and copying may, within 14 days after service of the subpoena or before the time specified for compliance if such time is less than 14 days after service, serve upon the party or attorney designated in the subpoena written objection to inspection or copying of any or all of the designated materials or of the premises. If objection is made, the party serving the subpoena shall not be entitled to inspect and copy the materials or inspect the premises except pursuant to an order of the court by which the subpoena was issued. If objection has been made, the party serving the subpoena may, upon notice to the person commanded to produce, move at any time for an order to compel the production. Such an order to compel production shall protect any person who is not a party or an officer of a party from significant expense resulting from the inspection and copying commanded.

(3) (A) On timely motion, the court by which a subpoena was issued shall quash or modify the subpoena if it

(i) fails to allow reasonable time for compliance;

(ii) requires a person who is not a party or an officer of a party to travel to a place more than 100 miles from the place where that person resides, is employed or regularly transacts business in person, except that, subject to the provisions of clause (c)(3)(B)(iii) of this rule, such a person may in order to attend trial be commanded to travel from any such place within the state in which the trial is held, or

(iii) requires disclosure of privileged or other protected matter and no exception or waiver applies, or

(iv) subjects a person to undue burden.

(B) If a subpoena

(i) requires disclosure of a trade secret or other confidential research, development, or commercial information, or

(ii) requires disclosure of an unretained expert's opinion or information not describing specific events or occurrences in dispute and resulting from the expert's study made not at the request of any party, or

(iii) requires a person who is not a party or an officer of a party to incur substantial expense to travel more than 100 miles to attend trial, the court may, to protect a person subject to or affected by the subpoena, quash or modify the subpoena or, if the party in whose behalf the subpoena is issued shows a substantial need for the testimony or material that cannot be otherwise met without undue hardship and assures that the person to whom the subpoena is addressed will be reasonably compensated, the court may order appearance or production only upon specified conditions.

(d) DUTIES IN RESPONDING TO SUBPOENA.

(1) A person responding to a subpoena to produce documents shall produce them as they are kept in the usual course of business or shall organize and label them to correspond with the categories in the demand.

(2) When information subject to a subpoena is withheld on a claim that it is privileged or subject to protection as trial preparation materials, the claim shall be made expressly and shall be supported by a description of the nature of the documents, communications, or things not produced that is sufficient to enable the demanding party to contest the claim.

§ 5.15 —FRCP 45(b): Service of Subpoenas

FRCP 45(b) addresses service procedures for federal court subpoenas, including:

- Who may serve a subpoena
- How a subpoena may be served
- Where a subpoena may be served
- Contents of the proof of service
- Where the proof of service must be filed.

The new Rule 45(b) omits the language of the previous version regarding service of subpoenas by the United States Marshall and his deputies, probably because the procedure is used so infrequently. Rule 45(b) simplifies the procedures for issuance and service of a subpoena on a witness located in a district distant from the district where the trial is being held. In effect, this section gives any attorney who is admitted to practice in a federal court the same authority as the clerk to issue a subpoena in any other federal court. This provision eliminates some of the administrative problems previously associated with procedures for foreign district service of subpoenas.

§ 5.16 —FRCP 45(c): Rights of Witnesses

FRCP 45 grants certain protections to persons subject to subpoenas. New sections (c) and (d) of Rule 45 define the rights and duties of witnesses in responding to a subpoena. Sections (c) and (d) are addressed to the witness, and Rule 45(a) requires the full text of the these two sections to be printed on the subpoena form (see **Form 5–4**) the witness receives. An important change is that under certain circumstances the court can compel a witness to travel from any location within the state to attend trial, even if local state law does not include this provision. However, the expanded rules provide for reasonable compensation to a witness who must incur substantial travel expense to attend trial and afford certain protective measures to a witness served with an unduly burdensome request. The issuing attorney has a duty to avoid causing unnecessary burden or expense to the person subpoenaed. If the attorney does not uphold this duty, the court can impose appropriate penalties which may include payment of lost earnings and reasonable attorney's fees to the witness.

The subpoena may request production or inspection separately from a command to appear at hearing or trial. A person responding to a subpoena to permit inspection or to produce documents may allow the inspection or provide the documents without appearing in person, unless the subpoena also specifies a date and time the witness must appear to give testimony at a hearing, deposition, or trial.

A person must serve written objections to a subpoena to opposing counsel within 14 days after receipt of the subpoena. If the basis for the objection is a claim of privilege or confidentiality, the witness must describe the documents and the basis for the objection in enough detail to support the claim and allow the opposing party to contest the claim. The issuing party may file a motion to compel the production, and this motion must be served on the witness. If the witness files objections, the issuing party is restrained from conducting the examination or inspection until the court rules on the objections. A court order compelling production by a nonparty witness must include a provision to reimburse the witness for "any significant expense resulting from the inspection and copying commanded" FRCP 45(c)(2)(B).

FRCP 45(c)(3)(A) provides that a court can quash or modify a subpoena to protect the witness if:

1. The witness is not given sufficient notice or a reasonable time period in which to respond to the subpoena.
2. The subpoena requests privileged information and the claim of privilege is upheld by the court.
3. The subpoena is unduly burdensome.
4. The witness is required to travel more than 100 miles to testify. EXCEPTION: The witness may be summoned from anywhere within the state under certain limited conditions.

If the party issuing the subpoena can prove that the requested testimony or information is crucial and cannot be obtained in any other way, the court can order compliance with the subpoena under specific conditions designed to protect the witness, including reasonable compensation to the witness for time and expenses incurred. For example, an order from the court might be necessary to protect confidential information if disclosure would be harmful to the witness or to protect the intellectual property of a nonparty witness, such as an expert who has made a study of the general subject matter (not of the specific matters in dispute) independent of any party's request.

§ 5.17 —FRCP 45(d): Duties of Witnesses

The witness has certain obligations in responding to a subpoena, and these are set out in FRCP 45(d). If the subpoena directs a person to produce documents or records, the witness may either produce the requested documents in the form in which they are kept in the normal course of business, or the witness may organize and label the documents to correspond to the categories described in the subpoena duces tecum.

If privilege or protection claims apply to the requested information, the witness must file a proper objection to the subpoena and adequately support the claims by describing the documents and explaining the basis for the objection claimed. The procedure for objecting to a subpoena is described in Rule 45 (c)(2)(B).

§ 5.18 —FRCP 45(e): Contempt

The court may compel a witness to comply with the subpoena issued by an attorney, and failure to comply may subject the witness to sanctions for contempt of court. The witness may be found in contempt of court unless he or she has an adequate excuse for not obeying. One example of an adequate excuse is being requested to travel an unreasonable distance to testify. The parameters for witness travel are set out in Rule 45(c)(3)(A)(ii).

§ 5.19 Preparing the Subpoena

In federal courts and in most state courts, you can get blank subpoena forms from the court clerk. Court clerks will usually give you a small supply of their forms at no charge, or you may be allowed to use photocopies. All the federal courts use the same basic form (see **Form 5–4**), but most state and local courts will accept only subpoenas prepared on their specific forms. Keep a supply of the trial subpoena forms used by the courts in your area. Some state courts will accept a subpoena that is set up like a pleading (see **Form 5–5**) or typed on a commercial printer's subpoena form blank, as long as all the necessary information is included. You can order subpoena blanks from legal stationers and printing companies that sell other types of legal forms (see § **2.95,** supplier resource list).

FORM 5–5
SAMPLE STATE COURT SUBPOENA FORM—ISSUED BY CLERK

IN THE COURT OF ________
________COUNTY, ________

____________________	)	SUBPOENA
____________________	:	TO WITNESS
	)	
Plaintiff,	:	Case No. ____________________
vs-	)	
____________________	:	Attorney: ____________________
____________________	)	Address: ____________________
	:	____________________
Defendant.	)	Phone: ____________________

TO: ____

ADDRESS: ____
____
____

YOU ARE HEREBY REQUIRED to appear before the ________ Court, at the ________ County Courthouse, ________ , in Courtroom No. ____, ____ Floor, on the ____ day of __________, 19__ at ____ __.M., to testify as a Witness in the trial of the above case on behalf of the Plaintiff/Defendant.

YOU ARE FURTHER REQUIRED to bring with you and produce at the above place and time the following:

____
____
____

Hereof fail not, under penalty of law, and have you then and there this writ.

WITNESS my hand and the seal of this Court this ____ day of ________, 19__

________(Court Clerk)________

By: ____________________

==

RETURN OF SERVICE

I received this writ on the ____ day of ________, 19__ and served the person named therein on the day and in the manner indicated.

Date Served ______________ Personal ___ Residence ___

Fees: ____ Process Server: ____________________
Mileage: ____ ____________________
Total: $____ ____________________

§ 5.20 Praecipe for Subpoena

Some courts require you to fill out a praecipe form before they will issue the subpoena. The *praecipe* is a written request to the court clerk to issue a writ (the subpoena). See **Form 5–6.** The praecipe contains the pertinent information that is needed for the subpoena or subpoena duces tecum. Based on the information in the praecipe, the court clerk then types the actual subpoena form to be served on the witness. **Note:** The praecipe is usually a separate paper, but some courts combine the praecipe and the subpoena on the same form.

FORM 5–6
SAMPLE PRAECIPE FOR SUBPOENA DUCES TECUM

PRAECIPE FOR SUBPOENA
DUCES TECUM

________________	)	__________ Court
	:	
________________	)	
	:	
Plaintiff	)	Case No.________
vs.	:	
	)	
________________	:	
	)	PRAECIPE FOR SUBPOENA
________________	:	DUCES TECUM
	)	
Defendant.	:	

To the Clerk of said Court:

Issue a Subpoena Duces Tecum in the above case for: ________________
____
whose address is ____
to bring with him ____
____
____
and to appear on the ____ day of ____________, 19___, and make said writ returnable according to law.

____

____

Attorney for ________________

§ 5.21 —Filling Out the Subpoena Form

If your court requires you to prepare the subpoena form, have your secretary type the appropriate information in the blanks, as follows:

1. The names of the plaintiff and defendant, the case number, and the name, address, and telephone number of the attorney issuing the subpoena. Local rules may also require the attorney's state supreme court identification number.
2. The name of the witness and the address(es) where the witness may be served. Include complete information on any alternate addresses (such as a business address) where the witness may be located.
3. The date and time the witness is to appear at the trial. If the subpoena form does not contain a preprinted description of the place the witness is to appear, give the location of the courthouse and identify the courtroom where the trial will be held.
4. Include the description of documents or records the witness is to produce at trial, if applicable (see § **5.12**).
5. Indicate the party issuing the subpoena.
6. Leave the "Return of Service" portion of the form blank for now. You will fill this in after the subpoena has been served on the witness.

§ 5.22 —Having the Subpoena Issued by the Court

After you have filled out the subpoena form completely, make three photocopies. Take the original subpoena document along with the three copies to the court clerk, who will affix the date and time stamp, sign and emboss the seal of the court on the original subpoena. This constitutes *issuance* of the subpoena by the clerk. (See § **5.13** on changes to Federal Rule 45 authorizing attorneys to issue subpoenas in federal courts.)

§ 5.23 Arranging for Service of Trial Subpoenas

When you discuss the names of witnesses to be subpoenaed, ask the trial attorney who should serve the subpoenas once they have been issued, and whether the subpoena must be delivered to the witness personally or if it may be left with another person (such as a spouse at the residence of the witness or a secretary at a place of business). Make a note of these and any other special instructions on your Trial Witness Subpoena Index (see **Form 5–7**).

§ 5.24 —Obtaining Service by a Court Officer

To have a subpoena served by the sheriff, bailiff, or other court officer, you must request this service through the court clerk at the time the subpoena is issued. You will usually a have to pay an advance fee that is then charged to the court costs in the case. This fee will generally be higher if the witness is located outside the county where the trial is held. Check your local rules to determine the fees required for service of a subpoena by a court officer, then prepare a check for the proper amount. Present the check with the subpoena form when you file it with the court clerk. When you want the sheriff to serve a subpoena, file the original and two photocopies with the court clerk, who will then forward them to the sheriff for service. Have the third photocopy time-stamped and retain it for reference in a trial witness subpoena file. If the attorney or an appointed server will deliver the subpoena, leave one copy with the clerk and keep the original and remaining copies (see § **5.26**).

Note: Most jurisdictions require you to serve a COPY of the subpoena on the witness and file the ORIGINAL with the completed "Return" or "Proof of Service" with the court clerk. Check your local rules to determine the preferred procedure in your court.

After the sheriff or a deputy has served the subpoena on the witness, he or she will fill out and sign the "Return" or "Proof of Service" section located at the bottom or on the reverse of the subpoena form, attesting to the date and time the subpoena was served, the person upon whom it was served, whether it was served by personal or residence service, and what, if any, fees were incurred. The return is then filed with the court clerk to complete the record of service of the subpoena on the witness. Confirm that the subpoena was successfully served on the witness by checking the docket of the court clerk for a notation indicating the proof of service filing by the sheriff. If you anticipate a problem with service of a particular subpoena, keep in touch by telephone with the sheriff's office so you can monitor their attempts to serve the subpoena and provide additional information if necessary.

A drawback to having the sheriff serve trial subpoenas is that it often takes several days for the paperwork to be processed and for the sheriff to actually complete service of the subpoenas. All jurisdictions require that you give the witness adequate notice (usually a minimum of three days) before the date and time you wish the person to appear at the trial. If you are issuing subpoenas

FORM 5–7
TRIAL WITNESS SUBPOENA INDEX

TRIAL WITNESS SUBPOENA INDEX

CASE IDENTIFICATION NO. ____				TRIAL DATE ____				
NO.	NAME	ADDRESS	PHONE	HOW/BY WHOM SERVED	DATE	RETURN	FEE/ MILEAGE	CHECK NO.

very close to the trial date or if you have a large number of subpoenas to be served, consider having the subpoenas served by someone other than the sheriff.

§ 5.25 —Other Methods of Serving Subpoenas

If the witness is friendly and cooperative and knows he is going to be subpoenaed, he or she may agree to pick up the subpoena at your office, rather than have a sheriff or other court officer show up at his home or place of business. The attorney for the party can always serve a subpoena and in federal court, any person over 18 who is not a party to the case may serve a subpoena. In most state courts, persons other than the court officer or the attorney can serve trial subpoenas only if the court specifically grants the authority to serve subpoenas (see § **5.26**).

§ 5.26 Appointing Subpoena Servers

If your local court rules require it, you must file with the court a Motion Designating Persons to Make Service of Subpoenas, and the trial court judge must sign an order allowing this (see **Form 5–8**). This type of order is not necessary in federal court. When you prepare the motion and order, include your name as well as other paralegals, clerks, or other non-attorney personnel from your firm who might be called upon to serve the subpoena. It is a good idea to also include a catchall phrase, such as "or any other qualified representative of the law firm of Blank & Blank" so that in the event one of the named persons is unable to serve the subpoena, you can substitute someone else or serve it yourself. Not all courts allow this type of blanket order, however, so check your local rules.

Have the order signed by the judge, file it with the court clerk, and get several certified copies of the order. (It may be necessary to show the certified copy to the witness to prove that the person serving the subpoena is authorized to do so.) Mail a time-stamped copy of the motion and order to opposing counsel, just as you would any other pleading filed with the court.

An order designating persons to serve remains effective for the rest of the time the case is active, even if the trial is continued and you have to serve another round of subpoenas later. If you anticipate that you will need to have a subpoena server appointed, you can do this several weeks before trial. This avoids having to do it at the last minute when you are busy attending to a multitude of other details. It also reminds the opposition that you are already preparing for trial. Even if the case settles or the trial is continued to a later date, there is no harm done by filing the motion and order.

FORM 5–8
SAMPLE MOTION AND ORDER
DESIGNATING PERSONS TO SERVE SUBPOENAS

IN THE COURT OF COMMON PLEAS
OF ________ COUNTY, ________

XYZ CORPORATION,	:	CASE NO. _________
	)	
Plaintiff,	:	JUDGE ____________
	)	
vs.	:	
	)	
SUZIE SMITH, et al.,	:	MOTION TO DESIGNATE PERSONS
	)	
Defendants.	:	TO SERVE SUBPOENAS

Now comes John P. Lawyer, attorney for the Plaintiff, XYZ CORPORATION, and respectfully moves this Court to issue an Order designating [insert names of persons who will serve subpoenas], or any other qualified representative of the law firm of Blank & Blank, not parties to this action and each being not less than eighteen (18) years of age, as persons authorized to serve subpoenas in the within action and to make due return of said writs to this Court verified by oath.

____
John P. Lawyer
[Address]
[City, State, Zip]
[Telephone]
ATTORNEY FOR PLAINTIFF,
XYZ CORPORATION

CERTIFICATE OF SERVICE

I hereby certify that a copy of the foregoing Motion to Designate Persons to Serve Subpoenas was served by regular U.S. Mail, postage prepaid, upon [name of opposing counsel], Attorney for [name], at [address], this _______ day of December, 19___.

____
John P. Lawyer
ATTORNEY FOR PLAINTIFF,
XYZ CORPORATION

IN THE COURT OF COMMON PLEAS
OF ________ COUNTY, ________

XYZ CORPORATION,	:	CASE NO. ________
	)	
Plaintiff,	:	JUDGE ________
	)	
vs.	:	
	)	
SUZIE SMITH, et al.,	:	ORDER DESIGNATING PERSONS
	)	
Defendants.	:	TO SERVE SUBPOENAS

Upon motion of John P. Lawyer, attorney for the Plaintiff, XYZ CORPORATION, and for good cause shown, this Court hereby appoints and designates [names of persons who will serve subpoenas], or any other qualified representative of the law firm of Blank & Blank, not parties to this action and each being not less than eighteen (18) years of age, as persons authorized to serve subpoenas in the within action and to make due return of said writs to this Court verified by oath.

Dated: ____________

____
JUDGE

§ 5.27 —Service by Private Investigator or Professional Process Server

When the witness upon whom the subpoena is to be served lives in an undesirable neighborhood, if you think that the witness may try to avoid the subpoena, or if there is any reason to believe that the subpoena server might be put in danger, consider using a private investigator or other professional process server to serve the subpoena. Never send someone from your office out to an unsafe neighborhood and never put yourself in danger to serve a subpoena. Hire a private investigator or professional process server experienced in handling rough situations. This would be especially appropriate when you must serve subpoenas on unfriendly or uncooperative witnesses in criminal trial proceedings.

When you hire an investigator or process server, provide all the information you have available about the location of the witness being subpoenaed. Include any alternate addresses such as relatives or place of employment, or any clubs or businesses the witness is known to frequent. A physical description of the witness is helpful if you have it, as is a description of the car the witness drives.

§ 5.28 Calculating Witness Fees

If the witness lives outside the district or county, you must include with the subpoena a check payable to the witness for one day's attendance in court, plus round-trip mileage from the residence of the witness to the courthouse. This check should be served with the subpoena, that is, given to the witness at the same time he receives the subpoena. Place a copy of the check with your copy of the subpoena in your trial witness subpoena file for reference.

If you do not know the exact mileage from the witness's place of residence to the courthouse, you can usually obtain this information by calling your public library reference desk or your local automobile association. Consult the attorney to make sure you have the jurisdictional power to compel the witness to attend through a subpoena. Check your local rules as to how far you may compel a witness to travel and the amount of the witness fees and mileage.

Example: Calculation of Witness Fees

Assume that the witness fee in your jurisdiction is $20.00 for one day's attendance at trial, and the mileage allowance is 22.5 cents per mile. The witness lives in a city that is 30 miles from the court where the trial will be held. You would calculate the witness fee as follows:

Mileage: 30 miles × 2 (round-trip) = 60 miles

60 miles at 22.5 cents per mile = $13.50 mileage

Fee: $20.00 for one day's attendance

Total: $20.00 attendance plus $13.50 mileage = $33.50

§ 5.29 Filing the Proof or Return of Service

Once the subpoena has been served on the witness, the person serving it fills out the return of service located at the bottom or on the reverse of the original subpoena form. This return states when, how, and upon whom the subpoena was served, and the name of the person who served it. The return must then be filed with the court clerk to complete the proof that the subpoena was properly served on the witness. Filing the return of service protects the party at whose instance the subpoena was issued in the event the witness does not appear at the designated time. The return is proof to the court that you did achieve proper service of the subpoena on the witness, and that the witness was timely and properly notified that he was supposed to appear before at trial.

As each return of service is completed by the server and filed with the court, note this on the trial witness subpoena index (see **Form 5–7**) and place a copy of the completed time-stamped return in your reference file.

§ 5.30 Deciding Which Witnesses to Subpoena

In your trial preparation meetings, the attorney will mention various persons who are potential witnesses. As you take notes at the meetings, keep a running list of these potential witness names. As the trial date nears, review your notes and your preliminary witness index (see § **3.2**). Consult the attorney and review your preliminary list to determine which of the potential witnesses will actually testify at the trial.

Compile a list containing the name, address, and telephone number of each proposed witness. If the case file is not familiar to you, review the file materials to acquire this information. Use the trial witness subpoena index chart to record this information on each witness as you locate it in the file. If you cannot immediately locate the addresses and telephone numbers in the file, check for the following: any correspondence to or from the witness; any interview sheets or background notes; any investigator's reports; and any documents or records that may contain an address for the witness.

Practice Tip: If the witness has previously been deposed and you have the deposition transcript, you can usually find the residence address at the beginning of a deposition transcript. The transcript may also provide information as to the witness's place of employment.

If the witness has moved since your first contact with her early in the case, you may need to do some investigating to determine her current whereabouts. Telephone directories and city directories can be helpful here. (See also § **6.19** *et seq.* on conducting jury investigation.)

§ 5.31 Tracking Numerous Trial Subpoenas

In a large trial, numerous witnesses must be subpoenaed. Use the trial witness subpoena index to help you keep track of all the subpoenas issued, the amount of witness fees expended, and the successful service and filing of the returns. You can also use this chart to record how the witness was served and who performed the service. Place this chart in the front of your trial witness subpoena file so that you can refer to it and update it easily. If you use a computer to track the case information, put the witness subpoena data on a database or spreadsheet for easy updates. (See **Form 5–7:** Trial Witness Subpoena Index.)

§ 5.32 —Trial Witness Subpoena File

Create a file folder (or a section of your trial notebook) to contain information on trial witness subpoenas. Place the following items into this file:

- Trial Witness Subpoena Index
- Copy of the trial scheduling sheet (§ **6.61**)
- Copy of each subpoena
- Return or proof of service
- Witness fee check
- Copy of motion appointing servers
- Certified copies of order appointing servers

§ 5.33 Maintaining Contact with the Witnesses

For friendly and cooperative trial witnesses who have agreed to testify in court, do them the courtesy of calling them to let them know that you will be serving them with a subpoena. Do this also with witnesses from your client's company or cooperative ex-employees who now work for other companies. Let them know that the subpoena is coming, so they won't be surprised or embarrassed when they receive it. Many lay people don't understand subpoenas. When they receive one, they tend to think they have done something wrong. Talk to the witness to find out the best time to serve him and whether he would prefer that you serve the subpoena at work or at home. For cooperative witnesses, residence service left with a spouse or other adult family member is usually sufficient. Check with the attorney if you are not sure of the best way to serve a particular witness.

As a practical matter, you may not be able to tell the witness the exact time he will be needed in the courtroom. This is a good reason for keeping in touch with the witness by telephone as the time for his testimony approaches. If possible, note which witnesses could be at the courthouse with only a few minutes' notice, so that you could call them if an emergency opening in the scheduling arises. When you cannot determine the exact time you will need the witness, type in the date of the first day of trial at 9:00 a.m. on the face of the subpoena, then attach a notice to the subpoena asking the witness to telephone your office when he has received the subpoena to determine the exact time he will be needed. (See also § **6.61** on scheduling trial witnesses.)

Avoid having the witnesses take off work until very close to the time that you need them, but make sure that they are available at least at the beginning of the morning or afternoon session during which the attorney plans to use their testimony. It is better to have witnesses standing by that you don't get to that day than to have the court waiting for you to produce your next witness and when you have no one waiting to testify. Be sure you know the location of a public telephone in the courthouse in case the attorney tells you to call a particular witness right away. Try to confirm a time with the witnesses at least the day before they are to appear so that they understand what is expected of them.

It can be very frustrating when you have all the witnesses lined up waiting to testify, only to have the trial settle. In this case, immediately let every subpoenaed witness know what has happened and that their services will not be needed. Be polite and thank them for their cooperation. Follow up with a letter of appreciation.

§ 5.34 Preparing the Trial Brief

As a trial paralegal, you may be asked to assist in the preparation of the trial brief. The trial brief is a pleading-type document that is prepared after the completion of discovery and before the start of the trial. In some courts it is called the pretrial brief (see § **2.16** on federal court requirements). A party's trial brief sets forth a concise statement of the facts, evidence, and legal issues involved in the case which will be before the court at trial. The main function of the trial brief is to educate the judge about the background and the nature of the case he or she is about to hear. Because the trial brief is essentially a written outline or plan for the case, the exercise of preparing it results in the following additional benefits:

1. Writing the trial brief forces the trial team to think through the strengths and weaknesses of their client's case and to plan the strategy they will use in the trial presentation.
2. The trial brief identifies the witnesses who will testify on various points and outlines their expected testimony.
3. The trial brief identifies the exhibits which will be offered into evidence.
4. When disposition of specific claims or issues has been made in pretrial proceedings, the trial brief defines and clarifies the remaining issues to be decided at trial.
5. The exchange of trial briefs listing witnesses, exhibits, and issues allows opponents in a case to know what to expect and ensures that there will be no unfair surprises from either side at trial.
6. The trial brief consolidates the essential information about the case into a nutshell. If you ever have to fill in for another paralegal on a case with which you are unfamiliar, read the trial brief for a quick overview of the case issues.

The court usually requires the trial brief to be filed from three to seven days before trial (see § **2.16**). As soon as you receive the court's trial order, note the due date for filing the trial brief on your trial preparation calendar. (See § **2.6**, Trial Preparation Timeline Checklist.)

Checklist: Preparing the Trial Brief

The manner in which you assist the attorney in preparing the trial brief will depend on your level of experience and legal writing skills, the extent of your involvement in and knowledge of the case, and the wishes of the individual attorney. Advanced paralegals may be asked to draft entire sections of the trial brief. Typically, however, the attorney will write the main portion of the brief, and you will then perform the "proofing and polishing" necessary to produce the final product. The following checklist suggests some specific tasks you can do to assist the attorney in preparing the trial brief.

____ 1. Review the case file for any pending motions which the court must rule upon before the trial begins. Verify the dates of previous motions and rulings by the court, for example, the granting of a Partial Motion for Summary Judgment, which would affect the issues at trial.

____ 2. Double-check the spelling and accuracy of names, dates, amounts, and other information presented in the factual statement section of the brief. Pay particular attention to the usage of technical or medical terms.

____ 3. Prepare a list of the trial witnesses and a brief outline of the testimony expected from each.

____ 4. Prepare a list of the exhibits to be offered into evidence at trial, preferably in the approximate order you plan to introduce them.

____ 5. Proofread the brief for content to ensure that it states points concisely and that it makes sense.

____ 6. Proofread the brief for format to ensure that the sections, subsections, pages and footnotes are consistently and consecutively numbered.

____ 7. Cite check the cases, statutes, or other legal authorities which are referenced as support for the legal issues (see § **5.40**).

____ 8. Prepare and label any attachments, appendices, or explanatory materials which are referenced in the brief.

____ 9. Supervise the copying, binding, filing with the court, and service of the trial brief upon opposing counsel.

§ 5.35 —Organizing the Trial Brief

The actual format of the trial brief will vary depending on the court, the complexity of the issues, and the instructions of the trial judge as to what must be included. If you are not familiar with the court's preferences for the format of trial briefs, check with the judge's bailiff or secretary to see if there are any written guidelines.

A trial brief for a federal court case may be longer and more formal than for a case in state court, especially when the case involves complex issues, such as the Racketeer Influenced and Corrupt Organizations Act (RICO). Generally, the information in a trial brief can be arranged into four main sections:

- Introductory Information (see § **5.42**)
- Statements of Fact (see § **5.37**)
- Evidence—Witnesses and Exhibits (see §§ **5.38, 5.39**)
- Legal Issues (see § **5.40**)

In addition, depending on the nature of the case and the preference of the court, trial briefs in some jurisdictions may include

- Itemization of Damages
- Proposed Hypothetical Questions to be Used with Expert Witness
- Motions in Limine—a brief discussion of anticipated Motions in Limine which will be filed
- Proposed Jury Instructions

§ 5.36 —Drafting the Introductory Information

The introductory information is placed at the beginning of the brief to identify the various trial participants. This may be stated in a single paragraph or it may be broken out into separately labeled sections:

- Appearances—identifies which attorneys represent which parties.
- Parties—identifies the names of the parties and whether they are plaintiffs or defendants. Also clarifies any cross-claiming, counterclaiming, or third-party relationships among the parties.
- Type of Action—states the relief being sought and basically why the lawsuit was filed.
- Jurisdiction—particularly in federal court, cites the applicable United States Code sections or other statutes under which the case was brought.

- Pending Motions—lists any outstanding motions which have been filed but upon which the court has not yet made a ruling.
- Status of the Case—discusses previous motions and rulings by the court, such as the granting of a Motion for Partial Summary Judgment or a bifurcation of the issues, which will affect the conduct of the trial.

§ 5.37 —Drafting the Statements of Fact

This section of the trial brief should contain a concise recitation of the known facts, describing the events which led to the cause of action. The factual statements are usually arranged in chronological order. The statements of fact may be set out in numbered paragraphs similar to a complaint or they may be written in narrative form. If the case file contains a factual background summary prepared for an expert witness (see § **3.29**), you may be able to use that document as a basis for drafting this portion of the trial brief.

The statements of fact contained in the trial brief are generally the facts which are agreed upon by all parties to the lawsuit. The section may be subdivided into stipulations (agreed facts) and disputed facts, setting out a brief discussion of the points of fact where there is disagreement among the parties.

§ 5.38 —Listing Anticipated Witnesses

This portion of the trial brief lists names and addresses of the witnesses who will be called to testify at trial with a short description of the anticipated testimony of each witness. In cases in which there are several expert witnesses, separate subsections may be provided for expert witnesses and fact witnesses. In addition to the live witnesses, this list should include any testimony which is to be introduced through deposition, either by reading the deposition transcript into the record or by videotape. (See § **3.40** on videotaping expert witness depositions for trial; see also § **5.42** *et seq.* on using depositions at trial.) Depending on the number of witnesses and the format of the trial brief, the witness information may be contained either within the body of the brief or on a separate attachment which is labeled as an appendix to the trial brief.

§ 5.39 —Listing Trial Exhibits

The evidence portion of the trial brief includes a listing of all the exhibits which will be introduced and offered into evidence at the trial. Ideally, the exhibits on the list will bear a number or letter designation which corresponds to the actual exhibit designation to be used at trial. (See § **5.58** *et seq.* on Preparing Exhibits for Trial.) As with the witness list, the exhibit information may either be contained within the body of the trial brief or listed on a separate appendix to the brief.

§ 5.40 —Preparing the Issues of Law

This portion of the trial brief, which may be alternatively labeled "Legal Issues," "Statement of Issues," "Issues of Law," or "Statement of Law," sets out the legal issues which form the basis for the claims or the defenses, together with the supporting statutory and case authorities. The complexity of this segment depends on the number of issues involved in the case and the nature of those issues. If the case involves only two or three major issues, this section will be fairly simple. However, when the case issues are complex, as in a RICO action, the Issues section may be broken down into multiple subsections in order to cover all of the relevant issues.

In most instances, the attorney will write the Issues of Law section, and your job will be to cite check the cases and other legal authorities referenced in the brief. The purpose of cite checking is to make sure that the citation is written in the proper format, and so that someone reading the brief would be able to locate the correct reference source if he or she desired to do so. The purpose of cite-checking cases is to make sure that the cases cited are "good law," that is, that they have not been reversed or overruled, so that they may be correctly used as support in the brief. If you have access to a Westlaw or LEXIS terminal you can use the computer to assist you in these tasks (see **Chapter 8**) or you can use traditional manual methods. It is beyond the scope of this book to give detailed instructions on citation checking. However, the tips in the following checklist will help you get started on a cite-checking project.

§ 5.41 Procedures for Manual Cite Checking

These procedures are suggested for efficient cite checking.

1. Make a working copy of the brief. Read through the Legal Issues section and highlight each citation, including any direct quotations. Number the citations in the order in which they appear in the brief. Be sure to include citations to any statutes, codes, ordinances, treatises, or other works which are referenced to support the legal issues.
2. Copy each citation or statutory reference on a 3 by 5-inch card exactly as it appears in the brief. You can have your secretary do the typing or

copy the brief on your word processing system, extract a table of the citations, and print the cites onto slips of paper. Indicate the number you assigned to the citation (see above) and the page number of the brief on which it appears.

3. If the brief contains any direct quotations from case authorities, indicate this on the index card so you will remember to proofread the quotation. It is not necessary to copy a long quotation, but do make a note of its location so you can check it against your copy of the brief.
4. Arrange the index cards into groups according to the various reporter systems (F.2d, N.E.2d, F. Supp., and so forth). If the brief is on word processing equipment, extract a list of the citations from the brief and use the computer to sort them into reference groups before they are printed out.
5. Take your working copy of the brief and the index cards to the law library and pull the reporter or code volume for each citation. This is where sorting the citations into groups is useful, because you can check all the cites from one set of reporters in one location, rather than bouncing all over the library.
6. Compare the cite information in the reporter with the citation in the brief for accuracy. Check for any typographical errors, transpositions in numbers, accurate spelling of case names and accurate punctuation in abbreviations, and so on. Use a red pen to mark any corrections or changes on the brief and on the card.
7. If you are not sure of the correct citation form, refer to *A Uniform System of Citation,* commonly known as the "Bluebook." This book, published by the Harvard Law Review Association, gives rules for uniform standard citations for a wide variety of reference sources. The Bluebook should be a standard reference book in every legal office.
8. Pay particular attention to any direct quotes from the cases. Compare the quotations as they are typed in the brief with the original text in the case reporter or other source to make sure the quotation is identical to the original. With a very long block quotation, have another person read the passage from the original source while you compare it with the brief, just as you would check a legal description in a deed.
9. After you have verified each citation, make a check mark on both the index card and on the brief itself to indicate that the citation has been checked. Remember to mark any necessary changes or corrections on both the card and the brief as well.
10. Mark any questionable citation references with stick-on notes or removable signal tabs. Discuss these with the attorney before proceeding.

11. Return the brief to the typist to have your corrections incorporated into the brief. Proofread the corrected draft against the cards to make sure the appropriate changes were made.

12. Save the cards to use for cite checking the cases.

§ 5.42 Preparing Depositions for Trial

When you prepare a case for trial, give some consideration to organizing the deposition transcripts that have accumulated in the case. The attorney will need to review the transcripts before the trial and will rely on them extensively in preparing outlines for direct and cross-examination questions. Naturally, if you work on the case from the beginning, you can keep track of the depositions as they occur and as you receive the transcripts. Typically, however, you may not start working on the case until after a number of depositions have taken place. The transcripts may be scattered throughout the case files and materials or tossed into a large box or folder. Your initial objectives in organizing the transcripts should be to:

- Arrange the transcripts in a logical order for storage
- Create a master index of all witnesses deposed in the case
- Track administrative details on each deposition
- Prepare the transcripts for filing with the court
- Keep a record of which transcripts have been summarized and which have been filed with the court.

Use the Deposition Master Index Form described in **§ 5.49** as a log to record the information about each deposition. Don't confuse the master deposition index with summarizing, digesting, or abstracting deposition transcripts. The master index is a reference list to help you to quickly locate and retrieve the transcript of any particular deposition. If you use computer, follow this form to develop a word processing table, a simple database, or a spreadsheet to track the information electronically (see **Chapter 8**).

§ 5.43 —Organizing Transcripts

There is no hard-and-fast rule on the correct way to organize the transcripts. There are many methods of arranging them, and the one you choose will depend on the type of transcripts and the number of transcripts in your case. Gather all the transcripts from the case together and scan the cover pages before you decide on a plan for organizing them (also see § **2.50**). Assign a reference number or letter to each transcript so that it can be easily filed back into the proper order. I like to use bright-colored stickers for this purpose because they are inexpensive, easy to obtain, and the bright square of color is easy to locate and read. Put the sticker on the upper right corner of the front page of the transcript.

A second step in containing the transcripts is to purchase some inexpensive storage boxes like the ones made for storing back issues of magazines (ask your office supplier). Transcript booklets are the perfect size to fit in the magazine storage boxes. When you label the boxes and stand them up on a bookshelf or cabinet, you create an instant library of transcripts that are easy to find and retrieve. The storage boxes help you keep the transcripts in good condition without cluttering up the other case files. If your collection includes any videotaped depositions, the magazine files will also hold video cassettes and keep them close to their transcripts and materials.

Following are descriptions of several ways to organize deposition transcripts on the shelf. You can decide which method best suits the transcripts in your particular case.

§ 5.44 —Chronological Order

Determine the dates of the depositions and put them in chronological order from the earliest to the latest date. If more than one deposition was held on the same day, put them in order according to the time of day they were taken, from earliest to latest. This method is usually the most logical if you have only a small number of depositions. When there is more than one deposition of the same witness, or a deponent's deposition was started on one date and concluded on another, you will have multiple transcripts for the same deponent. Use the same index number you originally assigned to that witness, but label the first transcript 1A, the second 1B, the third 1C, and so forth. This will keep all the transcripts for the same witness together in the file. Do this also when the voluminous exhibits are bound in a separate folder from the main transcript.

§ 5.45 —Alphabetical Order

Put the transcripts in alphabetical order according to the last name of the deponent. This method works well with any number of depositions. Label the spine of the transcript volume in large letters with the name of the witness and the date to make it easy to locate the correct transcript on the shelf.

§ 5.46 —By Deposing Party

You may want to use this method when both sides of the case have taken numerous depositions. Separate the depositions into two groups: those taken by the plaintiff and those taken by the defendant. If there is more than one defendant, subdivide the transcripts into groups for each party. Then put the subgroups into order either chronologically or alphabetically.

§ 5.47 —Liability versus Damages

The depositions taken in many cases, especially personal injury and medical malpractice cases, can logically be divided into two groups: (1) witnesses whose testimony deals with liability issues and (2) witnesses whose testimony is about damages. Some examples of liability witnesses in an automobile accident case would be the police officer who investigated the accident, the other driver, or an eyewitness. Damages witnesses would be doctors, economists, vocational rehabilitation specialists, and family members who testify how the injuries have affected the family or the person.

§ 5.48 —Fact Witnesses versus Expert Witnesses

In a case in which you have several expert witnesses such as doctors, economists, or engineers, separate these transcripts from the transcripts of the lay witnesses or fact witnesses. Expert witnesses are generally handled differently in the courtroom from lay witnesses and the exhibits to their depositions are often more voluminous than those in other depositions. (See **§ 3.35** *et seq.*, Preparing Expert Witnesses for Trial.)

§ 5.49 Preparing a Deposition Master Index

Use the Deposition Master Index form to record basic pertinent data about the deposition transcripts (see **Form 5–9**). This form can be adapted to use in several different ways, depending on the size of your case. If you use database software on your personal computer, use the form as a guide for the layout of your database design (see **Chapter 8**). If your case has only a few depositions, put the information about all of them on the same sheet. Divide the page horizontally into plaintiff's depositions and defendant's depositions. If the case has numerous depositions, use one chart for plaintiff's witnesses and a second copy of it for defendant's witnesses. If there are a number of

FORM 5–9
MASTER INDEX OF DEPOSITIONS

MASTER INDEX OF DEPOSITIONS

CASE NO.__________ FILE NO.__________

ID NO.	DEPONENT	DATE	PLACE	CAPACITY	EXHIBITS INDEXED	TRANSCRIPT INDEXED	DATE FILED

expert witnesses, you may want to list them on a separate sheet from the lay witnesses. First, fill out the top of the form with the appropriate case identifying information. Also indicate any subdivisions you decide to use in grouping transcripts. Then fill out the columns (or "fields") on the form with the following information:

1. The index reference number or letter you assigned to the transcript (see § **5.43**).
2. The name of the deponent or witness. A deposition witness under oath is usually asked to state his or her full formal name. If the name has an unusual spelling or difficult pronunciation, the witness will generally indicate to the court reporter the correct spelling and this will become part of the record. Use this to make sure you have the full formal name and put the name in this form on the index. Even if you know a witness is informally called "Mike," spell out "Michael." The deposition is a good source for information on a residence or business address for a witness. (See § **5.31** on preparing the trial subpoena index.)
3. Indicate whether the witness is a party (plaintiff or defendant), a relative, an employee, an expert witness, and so forth.
4. Record the date the deposition took place. If the witness gave more than one deposition, log the earliest one first. Indicate whether the second deposition was a completely separate one or whether the second date was a continuation of the first one because it could not be completed in one session. (See § **5.43** on organizing deposition transcripts.)
5. The place where the deposition was held. This is usually at the office of the attorney who called the deposition, but not always. In the case of doctors or other expert witnesses, the deposition may be taken in the expert's office. An elderly or infirm witness may give a deposition at home. The place of taking the deposition is particularly important if travel expenses are involved.
6. Indicate which party called the deposition. In simple cases this will be fairly obvious, but in complicated cases with multiple defendants, you need to know which party called which witnesses.
7. Most depositions are discovery cross-examination. However, some depositions are called to make a record that will be used at trial if the witness cannot be available to testify live. Be sure to indicate this. (See § **5.54** on de bene esse depositions.)
8. Indicate if this is a videotape deposition (see § **5.57**; see also § **3.40** on videotaping expert witnesses).
9. Note the name, address, and phone of the court reporter who recorded the deposition. This will be handy if you need to have the reporter transcribe the deposition some time after the date it was taken (see next

item), or if you want to direct the court reporter to file the transcript with the court in anticipation for trial (see § **5.53**). You may also want to note how much you paid for the court reporter's services at the deposition and for the transcript or for a copy of the transcript.

10. Transcript indexed. Once you have the transcript, you will need to summarize it at some point during the trial preparation. Keep track of whether you have done this here. If you use transcripts on computer diskettes with deposition summary software, you may want to indicate that you have the transcript in electronic format (see **Chapter 8**).

11. Exhibits indexed. Many court reporters include an index at the front or back of the transcript indicating the page upon which each exhibit was introduced or discussed. If the transcript does not have this, prepare the index yourself and note here when this is done (see § **5.52**). Indicate if the transcript is more than one volume or if the exhibits are in a separate binder from the main transcript.

12. Note the date when depositions are filed with the court in anticipation for trial. (See § **5.53** on filing transcripts with the court.)

§ 5.50 Using Deposition Transcripts to Prepare for Trial

The time, thought, and effort that go into preparing for and conducting depositions make it essential for trial attorneys and paralegals to use the resulting information as efficiently as possible. Paralegals often spend much valuable time painstakingly preparing traditional deposition digests, only to find that the attorneys never really make good use of the summaries. When you consider the value of all the attorney and paralegal time involved in a deposition (attorney preparation, witness preparation, actual deposition session, and transcript summary preparation), it is clear that traditional deposition digests are much more expensive than most attorneys realize (in the range of $13 to $25 per page for a standard 150-page transcript). Some trial attorneys may still insist that paralegals prepare conventional deposition digests, but a good case can be made for other alternatives.

§ 5.51 —Using Deposition Transcripts

These are suggested uses of deposition transcripts:

1. Prepare a Brief Table of Contents. When you receive the deposition transcript, skim the transcript to get a general idea of the subjects covered. Make a brief table of contents indicating the page ranges for the major subjects discussed. This brief table of contents serves as a preliminary guide to locating pertinent testimony on a selected topic until more detailed indexing can be done.

2. Capture the Attorney's Thoughts: The attorney's thoughts and mental impressions right after the deposition will often prove to be very valuable information in formulating strategies during trial preparation. New data, facts, and inferences the attorney gleans during the deposition testimony are fresh and clear at the end of the deposition, but unless properly recorded and preserved, this information begins to fade within a few hours after the deposition concludes. Therefore, it is important to capture the attorney's thoughts and impressions from the deposition while they are still fresh, if at all possible. One way to do this (if you are in the office at the conclusion of the deposition session) is to encourage the attorney to take just a few minutes right after the deposition to dictate or jot down an "impressions memo" relaying the highlights of what occurred during the deposition. Keep this write-up with the deposition transcript and exhibits. These notes serve as reminders of key testimony or important follow-up work to be done and can be quite useful in developing trial witness examinations. They can also give you guidelines about important issues if you decide to prepare a digest or summary of the transcript later on.

Note: If you are organizing a file containing transcripts that were taken in the past (when you were not present at the conclusion of the deposition to remind the attorney to dictate his or her impressions) you may still find attorney notes that were made either in preparation for the deposition or at the time of the actual deposition testimony. Review these notes for key information or questions, and place the notes with the deposition transcript and exhibits.

3. Get Compressed Transcripts. Make it a practice to obtain compressed transcripts of depositions from your court reporter. The court reporter uses special software to prepare condensed or compressed transcripts in one of several different formats. Essentially what the software does is eliminate the white space, wide margins, and extra lines found on standard transcripts and reduces the type size, making it possible to view from four to six traditional transcript pages on one page. A standard 150-page transcript compresses into about 18 double-sided pages. The compressed transcripts (also called "scrunch," "travelling," or "tote transcripts") are easy to carry, read, and scan. Having your deposition transcripts printed in condensed format allows you to easily assemble all the transcripts from one case into a single notebook. Most court reporters can provide compressed transcripts at very little or no cost. (Expect to pay about $25.00 for a 150-page transcript in compressed format.) The compressed transcript combined with a subject table of contents provides economical low-level control of the deposition testimony, and in some cases may be all you need to control the information.

4. Order Transcript Disks. Get an electronic version of the transcript on a diskette from the court reporter. Nearly all court reporters provide these now at a reasonable cost of about $25 to $30, which is an insignificant portion of the total cost of the deposition. Electronic transcripts are cheap, convenient, and a useful bargain. Using them with a deposition summary software program enables you to search the full text of any transcript for references in seconds as opposed to a time consuming and expensive manual review.

5. Use Deposition Summary Software. A very large case may justify more complex computerized indexing of electronic transcripts using litigation support software designed for the purpose. The cost of computerized indexing is equivalent to that of the traditional transcript digest, but it provides much more reliability, depth, and speed. Computerized indexing can assist you in generating detailed reports of all testimony on a particular topic, lists of people or facts, chronologies or event timelines, or synopses of exhibits and related testimony. Computerized indexing allows you to add annotations to portions of transcript testimony and to track testimony on key topics across the depositions of multiple witnesses (see **Chapter 8**).

6. Prepare Attorney Briefing Files. Even when they are provided with an excellent transcript digest, most trial attorneys are not satisfied with anything less than reading the verbatim transcripts. Try to get the attorney to indicate significant points by tagging portions of transcript text with removable adhesive notes or marking them with a highlighter pen (on a working copy of the transcript that you have provided). If the attorney reads the transcript before you summarize the deposition, these notations will assist you in determining important issues and passages that should be included in a transcript digest. Ask the attorney to indicate which of the deposition exhibits could be potential trial exhibits.

7. Assemble the Deposition Exhibits. As you review each deposition, assemble a complete set of the exhibit documents introduced or discussed at the deposition. Also check to make sure that any documents promised at the deposition have been produced. If some documents have not yet been provided, you will want to include requests for them in your of supplemental discovery requests (see **§ 5.5**). Many court reporters will include an index of the exhibits with the transcript. If the reporter has not provided one, use a deposition exhibit index form to record references to documents and exhibits as you review the transcript. Place a copy of the exhibit index form with the transcript. Use the deposition index form as a check sheet to make sure you have a complete set of exhibit copies. The deposition exhibit indexes can also help you compile a preliminary set of trial exhibit documents. (See § **5.64,** *et seq.*)

8. Transfer Errata Corrections to the Transcript. Fasten any loose errata sheets and signature pages into the back of the transcript booklets. If the witness has noted any changes or corrections on the errata sheet, you will need to incorporate these into the transcript. Mark through the incorrect words and neatly write the correction in the space directly above the line on the transcript page.

9. Prepare Marked Transcripts for the Court. Some courts require attorneys to submit and exchange marked copies of deposition transcripts indicating the portions of the testimony that they intend to read into the record at trial. If your court has this requirement, consult the attorney about which portions of the deposition testimony will be read into evidence. Carefully follow the court's instructions (as to the color of underlining and so forth) and prepare enough uniformly marked transcript copies to file with the court, exchange with opposing counsel, and retain a reference copy in your trial witness file. (See § **2.16** on federal court requirements for exchanging color-coded marked transcripts.)

10. Prepare Blowups of Transcript Excerpts. The attorney may want to enlarge excerpts of key deposition testimony to use as demonstrative aids at trial. When you prepare blowups of transcript pages for the courtroom, be sure to affix a label with the witness name, deposition date, page, and line numbers of the excerpt. (See § **4.6** *et seq.* on preparing document enlargements.)

§ 5.52 Filing Depositions with the Court

Federal Rule of Civil Procedure 30(f) provides for the filing of any deposition that is to be presented as evidence at the trial of a case. Filing the deposition transcript with the court formally enters the testimony into the case record. The most common reason for filing the deposition of a witness is so that the attorney can used it to impeach a witness who gives testimony in the courtroom that contradicts a statement he made in deposition. (See § **3.10** on reviewing previous deposition testimony.)

The deposition of a witness, whether or not a party, may also be used at the trial in certain other situations: if the witness is dead; if the witness is unable to appear in court and testify because of sickness, old age, or imprisonment; if the witness is beyond the subpoena power of the court; or if the witness is an attending physician or medical expert. The filing of the deposition with the court ensures that, in the event the witness is unable to attend the trial, his deposition testimony can be used instead of live testimony.

§ 5.53 De Bene Esse Depositions

In many cases where the testimony of a doctor or other expert witness is required (see **§ 3.40**), the deposition will be designated "de bene esse," which means it is for use at trial. This type of deposition is slightly different from the usual discovery deposition in that there is both direct and cross-examination of the witness. The attorneys ask questions of the witness just as if the witness were actually on the stand in the courtroom. Then at the trial, the deposition is read into the record so that the evidence and testimony are presented to the jury just as if the witness were present.

Doctors usually prefer this technique to testifying live because they can schedule the deposition at a convenient time before the trial (see **§ 3.44**). The doctor then does not have to be "on call" to testify during the trial. Many attorneys prefer this arrangement because they can use the deposition testimony at the best strategic point in the trial without worrying about the doctor's schedule. (See **§ 6.64** on scheduling witness testimony.) Also, when you are estimating the time required for each witness, you can calculate how long it will take to read in the deposition. The de bene esse deposition may also be used as a precautionary measure to record and preserve the testimony if the witness is elderly or very ill and there is concern that the witness might die or be too ill to appear in person at the trial.

§ 5.54 Working with the Court Reporter

Determine which depositions you should arrange to have filed with the court. The transcripts must be filed at least one day before the beginning of the trial. Check your local rules for requirements regarding the filing of depositions. The court reporter who recorded the deposition usually does the actual filing of the deposition transcript, but not all courts require automatic filing of transcripts. The attorney or paralegal must ask the court reporter to file the transcript. Contact the court reporter and request the filing of the deposition. If the reporter has given you the original transcript, you will have to return the original, together with any exhibits, to the reporter when you request that it be filed. Be sure to keep a copy of the entire transcript for your file.

When the court reporter receives a request for filing, he or she will prepare an envelope large enough to contain the transcript and exhibits. On the outside of the envelope the reporter will type the case identification information: the court, the case caption, the name of the judge, the case number and the names of the attorneys. The reporter will also include a designation of the name of the witness and the date of the deposition, such as "Transcript of Deposition of John Jones, taken on May 13, 199__."

The court reporter will place the transcript and exhibits in the envelope and seal it, and then file it with the clerk of courts. The reporter should notify you when the filing is completed so that you can prepare and serve the notification to the opposing parties (see **§ 5.55**).

§ 5.55 Preparing the Notice of Filing

When a party files a deposition transcript with the court, that party must notify the opposing counsel that this was done. This is done through a Notice of Filing Depositions (see **Form 5–10:** Sample Notice). The notice is filed with the court and copies are served on all opposing counsel. If more than one deposition is being filed at the same time, you can place all the notifications in a single notice (see **Form 5–11**).

FORM 5–10
SAMPLE NOTICE OF FILING—SINGLE DEPOSITION

UNITED STATES DISTRICT COURT
________ DISTRICT OF________, ________ DIVISION

THE XYZ PAINT COMPANY,	:	CIVIL ACTION NO. __________
Plaintiff,	:	JUDGE ____________________
vs.	:	
MARY L. LAMB,	:	<u>NOTICE OF FILING DEPOSITION</u>
Defendant.	:	

PLEASE TAKE NOTICE that on the 27th day of May, 19___, the deposition of Mark Clark heretofore taken in the above-entitled action on May 22, 19___, was filed for record with the Clerk of Courts in the above-captioned case.

____
[attorney]
[address]
[city, state, zip]
[telephone]
ATTORNEYS FOR PLAINTIFF,
THE XYZ PAINT COMPANY

CERTIFICATE OF SERVICE

I hereby certify that a copy of the foregoing Notice of Filing Deposition was served by regular U.S. Mail, postage prepaid, upon Alice B. White, Attorney for Defendant, at [address], [city], [state], [zip] this ____ day of May, 19___.

____
[attorney]

FORM 5–11
SAMPLE NOTICE OF FILING—MULTIPLE DEPOSITIONS

UNITED STATES DISTRICT COURT
________ DISTRICT OF________, ________ DIVISION

THE XYZ PAINT COMPANY,	:	CIVIL ACTION NO. ________
	:	
Plaintiff,	:	JUDGE ____________
	)	
vs.	:	
	)	
MARY L. LAMB,	:	NOTICE OF FILING
	)	DEPOSITIONS
	:	
Defendant.	)	

PLEASE TAKE NOTICE that on the 20th day of June, 19___, the following depositions heretofore taken in the above-entitled action were filed for record with the Clerk of Courts in the above-captioned case:

Lisa Vargo, deposition taken May 22, 199__
Melanie Misitigh, deposition taken January 27, 199__
Jennifer Sybyl, deposition taken March 13, 199__

____
[attorney]
[address]
[city, state, zip]
[telephone]
ATTORNEYS FOR PLAINTIFF,
THE XYZ PAINT COMPANY

CERTIFICATE OF SERVICE

I hereby certify that a copy of the foregoing Notice of Filing Deposition was served by regular U.S. Mail, postage prepaid, upon Alice B. White, Attorney for

Defendant, at [address], [city], [state], [zip] this _____ day of May, 19___.

____
Jane P. Smith

§ 5.56 Handling Videotape Depositions

If a doctor or other expert witness cannot testify live, many attorneys record a de bene esse deposition on videotape so that the tape can be viewed by the jury in the courtroom (see **§ 3.40**). This allows the jury to actually see and hear the expert testify by watching the videotape recording. Jurors find this more interesting than listening to a dry reading of the deposition into the record. Another advantage of videotaped depositions is that the attorney can use the deposition at the point where it best fits into the trial presentation.

When you have a video deposition, the court reporter will provide the actual tape of the deposition along with a paper transcript. If there are objections on the recording, the ruling on these must be obtained from the court before the presentation of the video at trial. The reporter can then edit out any objectionable portions of the tape so that the jury does not hear that part of the deposition as evidence. The transcript must be filed with the court together with a request for a ruling on the objections. (See **Form 5–12:** Sample: Notice of Filing and Request for Ruling on Objections.) (See also **§ 6.11** on recording the court's ruling on de bene esse deposition objections.)

FORM 5–12
SAMPLE NOTICE OF FILING AND REQUEST FOR RULING ON OBJECTIONS (VIDEOTAPE DEPOSITION)

IN THE COURT OF COMMON PLEAS
_________ COUNTY, _________

THE XYZ PAINT COMPANY,	:	CIVIL ACTION NO. ___________
	:	
Plaintiff,	:	JUDGE ___________________
	:	
vs.	:	
	:	
MARY L. LAMB,	:	NOTICE OF FILING OF
	:	DEPOSITION AND REQUEST FOR
Defendant.	:	RULING ON OBJECTIONS

Plaintiff, XYZ PAINT COMPANY, hereby gives notice, pursuant to the Rules of Civil Procedure, of the filing for use at trial of the videotape deposition of Lawrence A. Howard, M.D. Further, in accordance with Civil Rule 32 and Rule

12 of the Rules of Superintendence for Courts of Common Pleas, Plaintiff asks that the Court rule on defendant's objections contained therein. A written transcript of the deposition is being submitted herewith for the convenience of the court.

____
[attorney]
[address]
[city, state, zip]
[telephone]
ATTORNEYS FOR PLAINTIFF,
THE XYZ PAINT COMPANY

CERTIFICATE OF SERVICE

[add certificate of service]

§ 5.57 Playing Videotape Depositions at Trial

Stay in touch with the video court reporter or video technician who recorded the depositions that are to be played at trial. Contact the reporter or technician early in the trial preparation and advise him or her of the approximate date and time you will need to have the deposition tape played at trial. (See § **6.64** on trial scheduling.) Update the video technician on the status of the trial periodically as the trial progresses, and give the technician as much notice as possible of the exact time you will need to have the tape played in the courtroom. (This is something you can ask another paralegal or your office contact person to do for you.) Find out how long it will take the video operator to set up the playback equipment so you can inform the attorney of this in order to use the videotape to the best advantage in the courtroom. If possible, schedule the video playback so that the technician can set up the equipment while the jury is absent (on a morning or afternoon break or at lunchtime). Even though most videotape operators can set up their equipment fairly quickly and smoothly and they are used to doing it in front of an audience, do your video operator a favor and try to avoid having the technician set up in front of the jury. Technical problems with setting up the equipment while the jury is watching can have a subliminal effect on the credibility of your case presentation in the minds of the jury.

§ 5.58 Preparing Exhibits for Trial

The word exhibit comes from the Latin verb *exhibere* meaning "to present" or "to show." An *exhibit* can be any document or object presented at trial to substantiate witness testimony and to assist in convincing the judge and jury of the truth of a party's allegations. Exhibits also help the judge and jury to understand the testimony and the background of the case. Trial exhibits in civil cases can range in number from just a few to thousands or even hundreds of thousands in complex litigation. This section discusses the categories of trial exhibits and some general concepts that apply to preparing trial exhibits in any case. The approach you take to organizing and handling trial exhibits will vary somewhat depending on the type of issues, the number of parties involved, and the number of exhibits in your case. Refer to § **6.65** *et seq.* for more on handling exhibits in the courtroom.

§ 5.59 —Main Exhibit Categories

Trial exhibits can generally be classified into one of the following categories:

1. Documents and Objects Collected In Discovery. The vast majority of trial exhibits, especially in civil cases, will be documents. These will include materials your client provides (see § **2.55**) as well as those produced by opposing parties in response to formal or informal requests for production during the course of discovery. The documents used as deposition exhibits or attached to interrogatory answers are likely to become trial exhibits. In this context, the definition of a "document" includes any type of paper or records, whether typed, printed, or handwritten, such as letters, memoranda, telegrams, notes, contracts, forms, minutes, books, magazines, newspapers, pamphlets, brochures, appraisals, reports, charts, lists, and so on. The term "document" is also used to describe photographs, computer data, computer printouts, microfilm or microfiche, tape recordings, video recordings, and other records kept by mechanical or electronic storage means.

In addition to documents, some cases will involve exhibits that are objects, such as machinery, products, tires, tools, laboratory test samples, and so forth. "Objects" can include almost any type of physical evidence that does not fall under the definition of a document. (See § **6.78** for ideas and information on handling nondocument exhibits.)

2. Expert Witness Materials and Reports. The documents and materials an expert witness reviews for information or which in any way form the basis for the expert's opinions are potential trial exhibits. In most cases, part of these materials will be the same documents and objects as those collected during discovery, which are provided by the attorney to the expert for background information or analyses (see § **3.29**). The expert may provide certain additional materials, such as reference works and publications, which support the expert's opinions and are possible trial exhibits. Most expert witnesses will provide a resume or curriculum vitae as well as a written report.

3. Compilations, Abstracts, Analyses, and Summaries. This category refers to any type of analysis prepared by the attorney or the attorney's employees using data or information gleaned from the actual case documents. This type of exhibit, when prepared carefully and accurately, can save much valuable time at the trial. A summary listing or compilation of data may reveal certain patterns of information that were not readily observable from looking at the individual documents. Analyses or summaries of this type may be the basis for charts, graphs, or tables which are presented as demonstrative evidence at trial (see § **4.16**).

In order for the attorney to use the analysis or summary that is based upon data from other documents, the original underlying documents must be introduced into evidence. The attorney's job is easier if the parties have stipulated to authenticity of the underlying documents. The person who prepared the summary or analysis may have to testify as to when and how it was prepared.

4. Demonstrative Evidence and Visual Aids. The fourth category of exhibits is demonstrative evidence; that is, photographs, charts, graphs, diagrams, maps, or models prepared specifically for use at trial. This may be an enlargement of a discovery document or it may be a chart or graph based on information derived from the documents which the attorney will use for illustrative purposes at trial. This type of material may or may not be marked as an actual exhibit at trial. Demonstrative exhibits can also include items other than documents, such as three-dimensional models. (See **Chapter 4** for more on preparing demonstrative evidence and visual aids for trial.)

§ 5.60 —Case-Specific Sample Exhibit Lists

Because no two cases are ever exactly alike, it would be impossible to list the exact exhibits for a particular case. Your case will always have a unique set of exhibits. However, the following sample lists will give you a general idea of the kinds of exhibits you might find in various types of cases.

I. Sample Exhibit List—Contract Dispute

1. Contract or agreement, preferably the signed and dated original
2. Any addenda or modifications to the agreement
3. Correspondence, notes, or memoranda related to performance (or nonperformance) of the contract or to the understanding of the parties as to the terms of the contract
4. Notes or minutes of meetings involving negotiation of the contract terms
5. Invoices, records of payment, delivery slips, and the like related to transactions arising out of the contract

II. Sample Exhibit List—Personal Injury/Automobile Accident

1. Accident report
2. Emergency rescue squad or ambulance report
3. Hospital records, emergency room records
4. Doctors' or therapists' office records
5. Doctors' medical report(s)
6. Medical illustrations or diagrams explaining injuries
7. Photographs—vehicles; injured person or persons
8. Driving record of the driver(s) (obtained from the state bureau of motor vehicles)
9. Medical expenses and bills—summary indicating total expenses, documented by copies of actual bills
10. Property damage estimates, bills for automobile repairs, towing charges, rental car
11. Employer's statement verifying lost wages or time lost from work due to injuries
12. Other expert reports, such as economist or vocational rehabilitation expert
13. Brace, crutches, or other medical appliances used by the injured person
14. Personal recovery diary of injured person

III. Sample Exhibit List—Real Estate Dispute

1. Deeds (warranty, mortgage, Quitclaim)
2. Real estate descriptions
3. Plat maps
4. County tax maps
5. Real estate tax bills and receipts
6. Title guaranty policy
7. Zoning codes and regulations
8. Purchase offer
9. Surveyor's notes and records
10. Inspection Report (for example, termite inspection)

IV. Sample Exhibit List—Products Liability Action

1. Diagrams or schematics of the product
2. Marketing, sales, or promotional brochures
3. Advertisements or catalogues featuring product
4. Manufacturing specifications
5. Product assembly instructions
6. Owner's manual or operator's manual

7. Consumer safety guidelines
8. Warning label requirements
9. Photographs of the product, perhaps showing defective part or inadequate warning label.

§ 5.61 Collecting the Preliminary Set of Exhibits

As you begin to prepare in earnest for the trial, you will need to compile a set of potential exhibits. If you are fortunate enough to have been working on the case from the beginning, you will be familiar with the documents which have accumulated during the development of the case. These are the documents which your client provided, those produced by opposing parties in response to production requests, materials used by expert witnesses, and the documents used as exhibits in the various depositions taken in the case. Of course, you will also have collected copies of these key documents in the appropriate folder or file as the case progressed. Start with these key documents when you begin to collect potential trial exhibits.

If you have been called in to work on a case that has been in the office for some period of time, the job of collecting the initial set of exhibits will be somewhat more difficult, depending upon how well the file materials are organized. If the file is in total chaos, you may need to reorganize it as you attempt to determine which documents are potential exhibits. (See § **2.33** *et seq.* on organizing case files and materials for trial.) As you review and reorganize the case files and materials, check the following for key documents that are potential trial exhibits:

Discovery Files. Wherever you find deposition transcripts, you are likely to find exhibits that were identified in those depositions. Pay particular attention to documents that appear as exhibits in several depositions. Chances are that the documents discussed by several deposition witnesses will be key exhibits in the case. Also check files which contain responses to requests for production of documents or requests for admission, and answers to interrogatories provided by your client or by opposing parties. Many of the key documents will turn up in one or more of these discovery files.

Attachments to Pleadings. Key documents in a case will often be attached as exhibits to the complaint, the answer, or other major substantive pleadings. This is particularly true of contract cases and real estate cases which involve a contract or agreement and subsequent transactions (see § **2.58**).

Labeled Files. Obviously, any files or subfiles bearing labels such as "Documents" or "Records" could hold potential exhibits. (See § **2.36** on surveying existing case files.) In a typical accident case, this type of file might yield the accident report, medical records, official government documents, birth or death certificates, and so on. Of course, these documents might also be mixed in with other materials in the files.

Client's Documents. Be on the lookout for items of a personal or background nature such as diaries, calendars, medical bills, and photographs your client provided as background information. If the client is a company or organization, such documents could include financial statements, tax returns, sales brochures, proposals, promotional materials, and so forth (see § **2.58**).

Research Files. The typical legal research file will contain copies of cases and related reference materials. However, in a case that has generated factual or medical research, the research file may yield anatomical diagrams or illustrations, statistical tables, government reports, articles, clippings and so forth. Some of these may be appropriate for demonstrative exhibits at trial (see § **2.48**).

Expert Witness Files. These may contain the expert's resume or curriculum vitae, the written report prepared by the expert, articles or publications written by the expert, and various other documents and materials used by the expert witness in forming his or her opinions and conclusions. (See § **2.57 Chapter 3**.)

Investigator's Reports. If you have employed a private investigator to conduct interviews or surveillance, there may be photographs, affidavits, schematic diagrams, and other documents which could be included as trial exhibits.

Not all the documents generated in a case will be introduced as evidence. If a document was requested and produced in discovery but turned out to be of no significance to the case, it probably will not be used at trial. Some documents may be duplicative of information that can be found in other exhibits in the case, so the attorney will decide to eliminate them to avoid redundancy. Some of the documents you encounter in the files may have been withheld from production due to a claim of privilege, either on the basis of attorney-client communication or attorney work product. In addition, certain documents may be classified as Confidential because they contain sensitive or secret information, such as a company's product formulas or other proprietary data. Pay particular attention to the status of privileged and confidential documents (see **Chapter 1**).

Once you have gathered a stack of documents which appear to be potential exhibits, use a trial exhibit worksheet to compile a rough preliminary list of the potential exhibits collected so far. This worksheet list can be either handwritten or typed, or you can generate it on computer with a word processing or database program (see **Chapter 8**). Do not be concerned at this point about the order in which the exhibits are listed. Use the columns on a trial exhibit worksheet to record the following for each potential exhibit:

1. A sequential number (so you will know the approximate number of potential exhibits, even if you decide to use an alphabetical exhibit designation later)
2. A brief description of each document or item
3. The date of the document
4. Source (where you found the document in the files)
5. The person (or witness) who could testify about or authenticate the exhibit
6. Use the last column for any comments or remarks about the exhibit, such as a cross-reference to a deposition exhibit number or reference to any other previously assigned sequential number or reference.

If all or part of the relevant case document information is already on computer, you may be able to generate a list of potential exhibits based upon the case-tracking information. However, this type of list will probably not include all the documents which will ultimately be used at trial, so consider it a preliminary listing only. (See **Chapter 8** on using computers in trial work.)

§ 5.62 Obtaining the Attorney's Input on Exhibits

At this point, arrange a meeting with the attorney to review your preliminary list and discuss what other exhibits need to be obtained or prepared for trial. These are some items related to trial exhibits to discuss at a trial preparation meeting with the attorney (see § **2.9**):

Timing. Discuss the court's scheduling order or case management order and confirm when the exhibits are to be exchanged with opposing counsel and whether the court requires that a premarked set of exhibits be filed before the trial (see § **2.16**).

Authentication. Discuss any exhibits where authentication may be a problem. Ask about the possibility of obtaining a stipulation among the parties as to the authenticity of certain documents.

Privilege. Be sure to ask the attorney if you have any questions regarding confidential or privileged documents (see **Chapter 1**).

Additional Exhibits. Note any additional exhibits the attorney mentions which have to be created or located. See if the attorney has any files that contain additional exhibits in his or her office. Also note any exhibits that your client still needs to provide, such as photographs or diaries. Make a note to contact the client to make arrangements to obtain these.

Sequence. Discuss the tentative order of the exhibits. There are many ways to go about organizing exhibits logically for trial, depending on the nature and complexity of the case. In most cases, the best way to arrange exhibits for the courtroom is in the approximate order you expect them to be identified by the witnesses. Before you can do this, you first have to decide with the attorney—at least tentatively—the order in which you will call the various witnesses (see § **6.61**). This can never be an exact procedure, however, because the order of witnesses may change unexpectedly, the opposing party may introduce the same document with a different exhibit designation, or more than one witness may testify about the same document. You should put the exhibits in anticipated rough order before assigning exhibit designations and labeling with exhibit stickers (see § **5.69**).

Labeling. Discuss the court's requirements and instructions regarding labeling exhibits, that is, whether your side is supposed to use numbers, letters, or a combination.

Demonstrative Evidence. The attorney should have some thoughts on demonstrative evidence and visual aids he or she will want to use at trial (see **Chapter 4**).

Rebuttal. Ask which exhibits are likely to be used for rebuttal purposes only.

Exclusions. The attorney may also be able to tell you if certain documents will NOT be used as exhibits so you can eliminate those from your list.

Index. Update your preliminary exhibit worksheet according to the information you get from the attorney on various exhibits.

§ 5.63 Assigning Exhibit Labels

Check the conventions of the courts in your area regarding the labeling of exhibits. Many courts assign a series of numbers to each party (e.g., 0001–1999 for plaintiffs; 2000–2999 for defendants). In smaller cases the trial order may dictate whether your side's exhibits should be numbered (Ex. 1, Ex. 2) or lettered (Ex. A, Ex. B). Or there may be no specific instructions from the court, and the parties will simply agree among themselves on the numbering system to be adopted. (See § **2.16** on federal court trial preparation requirements.)

Alphabetical labeling works fine for cases with only a few exhibits, but in a case with many exhibits, I prefer to use numbers as exhibit designations. The problem with alphabetical labeling is that if you exceed 26 exhibits, you have to start using Ex. AA, Ex. BB, Ex. CC and so forth, so that by the time you get to the eightieth document, your label would be "Ex. BBBB." This becomes cumbersome and confusing when there are numerous exhibits.

Most courts prefer that you use the preprinted exhibit stickers which are available from legal office supply stores. The stickers are usually in contrasting colors indicating Plaintiff's Exhibit (usually yellow) or Defendant's Exhibit (usually blue). If you make up your own exhibit stickers, try to coordinate with opposing counsel to use different colors to facilitate the identification and labeling process at trial. (See § **2.85** for other color-coding tips.)

As in every aspect of trial preparation, numbering and tracking exhibits is slightly more complicated where there are multiple parties to a lawsuit. A confusing problem may occur in identifying exhibits from multiple defendants unless something is done to separately designate each defendant's exhibits. You can avoid this problem by typing the defendant's name on the exhibit stickers before they are affixed to the documents (for example, "Deft. Smith, Ex. 1").

Prenumber or preletter the exhibit stickers on the backing sheet before affixing them to the documents to avoid skipping numbers. Use a felt tip pen to make bold numbers or letters on the exhibit stickers so that they will be easy to read and will show up on the copies. When you attach them to the actual exhibit documents, place the stickers in a uniform place on each document, preferably in the lower right-hand corner. However, if there is not a sufficient margin in the lower right-hand corner, or if the sticker would cover up something important on the document such as a signature or a date, put the sticker elsewhere on the document. Other sticker placement choices are, in order of preference: upper right corner, bottom-center of the page, right-hand margin, top left corner and bottom left corner.

For multipart documents or multiple versions of the same document, consider using 26A, 26B, 261C or K1, K2, K3 instead of assigning separate numbers. Whichever system you decide upon, use it consistently throughout the document numbers. Talk this over with your supervising attorney to decide which method will work best for the exhibits in your case. (See § **2.80** on general document numbering techniques; see also § **5.82** on numbering bulky documents.)

Whatever exhibit labeling system you decide to use, put the identification you assign to each exhibit on the worksheet list beside the exhibit it describes. Assign identification slots to the exhibits and put the labels on before you copy the exhibit documents.

§ 5.64 Arranging Copying for Exhibit Documents

Once you have collected the bulk of the exhibits, you need to make arrangements to have them copied. Depending on the number of documents to be copied and the copying equipment available at your office, you may have the copies made in-house, or you may send all or part of them out to a copy service.

The following steps apply generally to flat paper documents in standard sizes, which can be copied on a standard office copy machine. Tips for special handling of other types of exhibits are in the following sections. (See also § **6.78** on handling nondocument exhibits; §§ **4.6–4.14** on handling enlargements and oversized documents.)

§ 5.65 —Determining the Number of Copies Needed

Discuss with the attorney how many sets of exhibits you will need for trial. Remember to make a complete working set for the attorney, in addition to the loose set of originals. It is a good idea to keep one extra copy of everything in your control, just in case something gets out of order or lost. You may need the following exhibit sets:

- At least one set (possibly two or three) for the court file. Check on any court requirement for exhibits to be filed in duplicate or triplicate
- A reference set for the judge to use in the courtroom
- One set for each opposing counsel
- One set for the witness to use on the stand
- A working set for the attorney
- A set for you to follow and update for the file records
- A master reference set to leave at the office for safekeeping.

Use the chart in § **6.77** to list each party who will need a set of exhibit documents on the chart. (See also § **6.77** on updating exhibit notebooks during trial.)

Practice Tip: If you are not sure how many copies you will need, it usually doesn't hurt to make an extra set anyway (within reason) if you have a batch of fewer than 100 pages. If you have numerous bulky documents, select the ones that are likely to be key trial exhibits and prepare an extra set of those documents to keep on hand for emergencies.

§ 5.66 —Preparing Exhibit Documents for Copying

If you have been using a set of working copies during the discovery phase of the case, they are probably second- or third-generation copies and may have been folded or marked. If necessary, go back to your originals to make a clean copy for the trial exhibit sets. Be very protective of the originals of the exhibit documents (see **Chapter 2**). Handle fragile originals very carefully yourself, and make a working copy to send out for bulk copying. Pay particular attention to documents on slick or very thin paper. They can easily get jammed in an automatic document feeder. It is wise to copy these documents one page at a time, laying the sheet directly on the glass of the copier. Treat your originals with care!

If you do not have the original document, use the best, cleanest, clearest copy available. Carefully remove any staples or brads and use a large paper clip, binder clip, or rubber band to keep the loose document pages together temporarily. (See also § **5.70**).

§ 5.67 —Handling Undersized or Oversized Exhibit Documents

If a document (such as a birth certificate) is on paper smaller than the standard 8 1/2 by 11 inches, place the original document on a clean background sheet before copying it onto standard size copy paper. This will eliminate any markings which might come through on the copy from the machine itself. Insert the original of the undersized document into a plastic page protector with a three-ring punched edge so you can fasten it into a standard looseleaf exhibit notebook with less chance of it falling out or getting lost. (See **Chapter 2** on preserving original documents.)

For documents longer than 11 inches or wider than 8 1/2 inches, use the reduction feature on your photocopier to reduce the copies to 8 1/2 by 11 inches. Or, fold the excess up from the bottom or in from the side so that the copies will fit into your exhibit notebooks. Very large documents such as maps and blueprints will require special handling (see § **4.15**).

§ 5.68 —Supervising the Exhibit Copying Process

Whether you have the copying done in your office or by an outside vendor, supervise the process carefully. List everything you send to the copier and check the materials returned against the list to make sure everything was returned to you. Write out explicit instructions for any reducing, stapling, or punching you want the outside service to do. If the special handling applies to only one document, write it on a note and attach it to the document. Remember that any special handling done by the copy service, such as removing staples, restapling, and drilling holes will add to the cost of the outside service (see § **5.69**).

§ 5.69 —Arranging for Special Handling

If you use looseleaf binders for your exhibit notebooks, the documents will need to be punched so they can be inserted into the binders. If you have an outside vendor do the copying, check into having them drill the holes at the same time. This is usually not very expensive because copy centers have equipment that can punch many sheets at the same time. If you do the copying in-house, you will need to have someone punch the holes with a manual three-hole punch. Use a heavy duty model to make the job go faster. Some devices punch an oval hole to make the pages in a thick notebook easier to turn.

Practice Tip: Whether you run the copies in-house or send them out, this idea will save you a lot of time if you will be using exhibit notebooks instead of files: Have the copies run on paper that is prepunched to fit into three-ring binders. The prepunched paper may be slightly more expensive than regular copy paper, but you eliminate the tedious chore of punching holes in large stacks of documents later. This saves time you can spend on other things!

If you punch the holes yourself after the copies are made, it pays to check a sample page to make sure the punched holes are spaced to correctly fit the exhibit notebooks you will be using. Although most three-ring binders have standard spacing between the rings, there are slight variations among brands and sizes of notebook binders. This may sound elementary, but few things are more exasperating during trial preparation than punching holes in 200 documents, and THEN DISCOVERING the hole spacing pegs were not correctly set. Believe me, it can happen!

§ 5.70 Tips for Obtaining Good Exhibit Copies

Here are some helpful suggestions to obtain good copies:

1. Nothing looks less professional than smudged, crooked, or illegible copies in an exhibit notebook. It is worth a bit of extra effort to start out with the best copy you can get. (See § **4.8** on preparing documents for enlargement.)

2. Make sure all the copies are straight on the page and that they are dark enough to be legible. Pay particular attention to penciled notes in the document margins, as they often do not copy well. If the original is a microfilm copy, adjust the exposure control on your machine to get the best copy. There is nothing wrong with adjusting the photocopier settings to improve the quality of the copy, so long as you do not alter the original document.
3. Be careful not to cut off any of the edges of documents. For documents on which the text runs very close to the left side of the page, use the adjustment on your copier to slightly reduce the copy size. Leave a margin for a hole punch on the left-hand side so that no printing is cut off. Be sure to copy both the front and back of any two-sided original documents.
4. Many of the documents may have been used as exhibits in depositions, and so will bear a sticker or label designating the deposition exhibit number. While it is important to keep track of what documents were used in which depositions, having several exhibit stickers showing on the copy can be very confusing at trial time. For the trial exhibit ONLY, block out any existing deposition exhibit labels to avoid confusion.
5. Learn how to operate and maintain your photocopy equipment. If you work in a very large firm, there may always be copy room staffers around to help you. But if you work in a smaller office, chances are very good that, at some point during the trial preparation, you will be making copies after regular business hours (or even during the wee hours of the morning). You need to know how to load the paper bin, use the enlargement and reduction features, fix a paper jam, add toner to the machine, and so on. Take time to learn these things before you get caught up in a rush trial preparation. (See also **§§ 4.6–4.11** on preparing document enlargements.)

§ 5.71 Preparing Trial Exhibit Indexes

You will need to prepare two main indexes to your set of trial exhibits. The first one is for "public consumption" and the second one is a detailed master reference index for use by you and the trial attorney in tracking the exhibits throughout the trial.

§ 5.72 The Public Index

The first index, which I will call the "Public Index," will be the table of contents for the exhibit notebooks which you exchange with opposing counsel. See

Form 5–13. You may also give copies to the judge, the court reporter, and so forth (see § **5.65;** also see § **5.74** for more on exhibit notebooks). This index will be a simple list of your proposed trial exhibits, including the following:

- Your exhibit designation (identifying number or letter)
- A brief description of the document, including the type of document; the date; author and recipient, for correspondence
- A brief explanation if the item, oversized document, or set of documents is not actually inserted in the notebook. (See § **5.74** on using "marker pages" to represent exhibits that cannot be duplicated for the exhibit notebooks; see also **Chapter 2** on preserving original documents.)

The public index could be in a chart format, which would look similar to the preliminary trial exhibit worksheet discussed in § **5.61,** with the addition of the case caption and other identifying information. You may prefer to prepare the public index on a word processor or from a database. If you have the computer capability to produce such an index, the text can be stored so that it can be quickly and easily updated during the trial (see **Chapter 8**). Apply plastic hole reinforcements to the index pages so they will not tear out when placed in the front of the exhibit notebooks, or have the index printed or copied onto looseleaf paper with a coated reinforcement panel along the edge with the punched holes.

§ 5.73 The Private Master Reference Index

The second exhibit index is a reference tool prepared exclusively for use by the trial team. See **Form 5–14.** You can adapt the master exhibit index form to include any extra notes necessary for you and the attorney to track the exhibits. In addition to the basic exhibit identification and description, the master index could include columns to indicate:

- Cross-reference to opposing party's exhibit designations
- Witness who is expected to testify about the exhibit
- Original source of the exhibit
- Intended use in direct or cross-examination
- Issue or subject to which the exhibit relates
- Notes on related demonstrative evidence (chart or blowup)
- Number-stamp used for reference during discovery, if applicable
- Cross-reference to any depositions where the document was used as an exhibit (name of the deponent, deposition date, deposition exhibit designation).

FORM 5–13
SAMPLE TRIAL EXHIBIT INDEX

IN THE COURT OF COMMON PLEAS
OF SUMMIT COUNTY, OHIO

CAROL C. WILSON, et al.	:	CASE NO. ________________
Plaintiffs,	:	JUDGE ________________
vs.	:	
SAMUEL D. GRANT, et al.,	:	INDEX TO PLAINTIFFS' TRIAL EXHIBITS
Defendants.	:	

EX.#	DESCRIPTION	DATE
1.	Official Accident Report—Salem Police Dept.	9/8/90
2.	Emergency Medical Service Report -	9/8/90
3.	Emergency Room Record—Salem Memorial Hospital -	9/8/90
4.	Hospital Admission Records—Salem Memorial Hospital -	9/8/90 to 9/24/90
5A.	Photograph of Wilson automobile—Salem P.D. -	9/8/90
5B.	Photograph of Wilson automobile—Salem P.D. -	9/8/90
5C.	Photograph of Grant automobile—Salem P.D. -	9/8/90
6.	Summary of Medical Expenses—with copies of bills	
7.	Neuropsychological Evaluation Report on Carol C. Wilson—Michael C. James, Ph.D. -	10/18/90
8.	W-2 forms and IRS Form 1040 for 1990—Carol C. Wilson	
9.	Medical Report by Walter Benson, M.D. -	10/1/90
10.	Back brace worn by Carol C. Wilson [Note: Photograph only in exhibit notebooks. Original is in plaintiff's counsel's possession.]	
11.	Affidavit of Carol C. Wilson's employer -	11/4/90
12.	Copy of ticket issued to Samuel D. Grant by Salem Police Department for Failure to Control -	9/8/90

FORM 5–14
TRIAL EXHIBIT INDEX (BLANK)

IN THE COURT OF ____________
OF ____________________

____________________________	:	CASE NO. ________________
	:	
Plaintiffs,	:	JUDGE ____________________
	:	
vs.	:	
	:	
____________________________	:	INDEX TO ____________'S
	:	TRIAL EXHIBITS
Defendants.	:	

EXHIBIT NO.	DESCRIPTION	DATE
________	________________________________	____________
________	________________________________	____________
________	________________________________	____________
________	________________________________	____________
________	________________________________	____________
________	________________________________	____________
________	________________________________	____________
________	________________________________	____________
________	________________________________	____________
________	________________________________	____________
________	________________________________	____________
________	________________________________	____________
________	________________________________	____________
________	________________________________	____________
________	________________________________	____________
________	________________________________	____________
________	________________________________	____________

§ 5.74 Assembling Trial Exhibit Notebooks

Once you have collected all the exhibits, labeled them, copied them, and prepared an index of them, you may be asked to prepare exhibit notebooks for the judge and opposing counsel. In many courts the trial order requires counsel to exchange sets of marked exhibits from one to three days before the trial (check your local court's requirements). The judge may also require counsel to submit a marked set of exhibits to the court. Find out from your supervising attorney exactly when the exhibits need to be ready to exchange.

The approach you take to containing the sets of trial exhibits will depend on the number and type of exhibits involved in your case. I like to use vinyl three-ring binder notebooks for this purpose, preferably the style with pockets on the inside of the front and back covers. The looseleaf style allows you to insert and remove documents as necessary and the book will lie flat for examining an individual document. The size notebook you use will depend on the number of exhibits you have. Use notebooks with "D-rings," which hold more than round rings to make turning the pages easier. For cases with a very large number of exhibits, you may need to use multiple volumes. Make arrangements ahead of time to stock the proper size notebooks and make sure there are enough available. If the case has numerous exhibits and the witnesses will have to switch back and forth between exhibit notebooks for the plaintiff and defendant, use two different colors for the notebook binders to make it easier for the witness to distinguish which notebook to use. Use good quality notebooks. Make sure the rings match up and the holes are punched large enough and spaced correctly so that pages turn easily (see § **5.69**).

§ 5.75 —Tabbing and Labeling Exhibit Notebooks

Insert a copy of the public exhibit index in the front of the notebooks. If there are numerous documents, you may want to insert divider sheets (use a different color paper) between exhibits or affix side tabs to facilitate locating a particular document. Prepare labels for the front and spine of each volume indicating the case caption, trial date, judge, and the name of the party you represent. (See also **Chapter 2** on tabbing and labeling.)

Check the completed sets of copies against the originals to make sure that all the pages did get copied, that they are legible, and that they are in the correct order in the exhibit notebooks. Consider whether you want to staple multipage documents which will be inserted into the notebooks. This will add bulk to the notebook (see § **5.85**). Use plastic hole reinforcements on the front and back pages so they will not tear out easily.

§ 5.76 —Special Handling for Bulky Exhibits

The following suggestions will help you deal with bulky or lengthy exhibits.

Using Excerpts of Volumes. In most cases, it would not be practical to reproduce a lengthy document, such as a complete book, in its entirety when only a portion of it is relevant as an exhibit. You will, of course, need to have the actual book available as the original trial exhibit, but you may be able to reproduce only the portions relevant to the testimony for the trial notebooks. Copy the front cover of the book and the title page, then the marked excerpts.

Using a Marker Page for Bulky Documents. In cases involving a very large number of separate forms, such as invoices or claim slips, it would be ridiculous and wasteful to copy every one of thousands of slips for the exhibit notebooks. You may have only the original set. Opposing counsel will have had a chance to examine these documents during the discovery process before trial, so you will probably not need to copy them. The parties will often agree to the entering of the slips collectively under one exhibit number in order to simplify handling them at trial. To represent this collection of slips in the exhibit notebooks, have a "marker page" typed up saying the following: "Exhibit No. 6, Standard Claim Forms. (Note: Collective Exhibit—Individual items are not reproduced here due to volume, pursuant to stipulation between the parties dated October 3, 199__.)" Use this same technique for oversized or one-of-a-kind items. For example, suppose you have a large aerial map of property which is in dispute. Obviously, you cannot reproduce this in a notebook. Instead, insert a marker page similar to the one described above, indicating that the aerial photograph will be an exhibit, but is not reproduced because of its size.

In the case of an object, such as a piece of machinery or an orthopaedic appliance used by the injured party, you could use the method above, or you could insert a photograph, drawing, or diagram of the object, together with a brief explanation that since there is only one in existence, it is not actually reproduced in the notebook.

For oversized tax maps, drawings, or blueprints, insert a reduced-size copy, if possible. If the original is too large to make this practical, you can have the oversized documents copied, then fold them to notebook size and insert in clear plastic page protectors which have a three-ring edge attachment. An alternate idea is to clip or staple folded documents into the back of the exhibit notebook. (See § **4.14** on oversized documents.)

When you are using an enlarged version of a document as a visual aid, consult with the attorney on whether to give the enlargements a separate number. Indicate with a marker page that this exhibit is an enlarged version of the exhibit. (See § **5.63** on assigning exhibit designations.)

§ 5.77 Preparing the Attorney's Trial Notebook

The trial notebook is a compilation of all the essential case information, condensed and reduced to its simplest form, which the attorney needs to have readily available at trial. The attorney will use the notebook to record plans, notes, lists, and outlines of key elements for the courtroom presentation. There are no hard-and-fast rules for organizing the attorney's trial notebook. It is a personalized working tool which must be tailored to the requirements of the particular case. Do not be surprised if each trial attorney with whom you work prefers a different way of organizing the trial notebook. (Some attorneys do not use a notebook at all, but instead prefer a set of labeled folders for organizing the key trial materials.) Ask the supervising attorney at one of your early trial preparation meetings for instructions and suggestions on what to include and how to organize the materials, and then arrange the notebook or files to suit the attorney's preferences.

You can begin developing the trial notebook early in the trial preparation. A three-ring looseleaf binder is usually the best trial notebook container. A binder securely holds the notebook contents, but lets you easily insert, remove, and rearrange pages as needed. (You may need to reorganize the materials several times as new information is added during trial preparation, so the notebook must be flexible.) The following checklist contains some helpful suggestions for preparing the trial notebook binder and section dividers.

§ 5.78 —Tips for Preparing the Trial Notebook

The following list are suggestions for preparing the trial notebook.

1. Use high-quality notebook binders in the appropriate size for the volume of materials in the case. Notebooks with D-shaped rings will hold more pages than those with round rings. Make the attorney's notebook a color that is easy to distinguish from other binders in the case.
2. Make sure the ends of the notebook rings line up properly so that the pages will turn easily. The ring mechanism should open and close smoothly and quietly.
3. If the notebook will hold a large volume of material, make sure the binder includes a pair of plastic sheet lifters to assist the attorney in turning pages without tearing them. **Note:** Massive cases may require multiple trial notebooks to adequately accommodate the necessary information.
4. Use sturdy reinforced notebook dividers, with graduated tabs arranged in roughly the same order as the trial stages (see **Form 5–15:** Sample Notebook Index). Label the tabs on both sides so the attorney can easily locate the desired section from either the front or back of the notebook.

5. If you incorporated a color-coding system into the development of the trial file (see § **2.88**), consider using divider tabs in colors corresponding to other color-coded folder labels to designate segments of the trial file (red for witnesses, blue for exhibits, and so forth) Even without a color-coding system, colored tabs (as opposed to all white ones) will make it easier for the attorney to find the desired trial notebook section quickly. Consider using one of the ready-index products that are available at any office supply store to instantly color code the binder sections (see § **2.95,** Resource List).
6. Leave a couple of extra (blank) divider tabs in case the attorney decides to insert a new section or subdivide an existing one. Also include a prepunched envelope pocket to hold small notes and papers.
7. Use your photocopier to reduce any documents longer than 11 inches to letter size for the trial notebook so the attorney will not have to bother with oversized pages.
8. Prepare a table of contents or index listing the main tabbed divisions and place it in the front of the notebook. Apply clear plastic reinforcements to both sides of the punched holes for added strength and durability.
9. Provide plenty of lined paper for notes. Some attorneys like to use yellow or buff foolscap (letter-size and three-hole punched) for notes because the colored paper is easy to distinguish from all the other (white) papers in the notebook.
10. In the courtroom, make sure that any materials removed from the notebook are replaced at the end of the day. The attorney may not have time to do this.

Some trial attorneys will want you to provide only the skeleton of the trial notebook (just the binder and labeled dividers), while others may ask you to prepare many of the notebook materials as well. Your ability to prepare the contents of the trial notebook will depend on your amount of trial experience and your familiarity with the case.

The first order of business in preparing the trial notebook is deciding what materials are to be included. The contents of the trial notebook will be influenced by many of the same factors which affect other aspects of the trial preparation, such as the nature and scope of the case, the number of witnesses, the number of exhibits, and so forth. Review the trial brief as well as your notes on the other materials and activities discussed in your trial preparation meetings for clues to additional sections the attorney may want to add to the trial notebook. The following sample trial notebook index lists the basic sections which would be needed for a typical simple case (see **Form 5–15**). The trial notebook in a more complex case would require additional sections or subdivisions to accommodate more detailed information, such as expert witness hypotheticals, evidentiary memos, legal authorities, and so on (see **Form 5–16**). The attorney may want to include other indexes and reference lists such as the ones shown throughout this book. Suggestions and pointers for preparing basic materials for the attorney's trial notebook may be found in the following subsections.

FORM 5–15
SAMPLE BASIC TRIAL NOTEBOOK INDEX (SIMPLE CASE)

1. Planning/"To Do" List
2. Trial Notes
3. Key Pleadings
4. Pretrial Motions
5. Voir Dire
6. Opening Statement
7. Witnesses
8. Exhibits
9. Closing Argument
10. Jury Instructions

FORM 5–16
SAMPLE DETAILED TRIAL NOTEBOOK INDEX (COMPLEX CASE)

1. Trial Notes
2. Things to Do
3. Trial Preparation Agenda
4. Trial Briefs
5. Pretrial Motions
6. Voir Dire
7. Opening Statement

8. Witness Index
9. Witness Examination Outlines
10. Plaintiff's Testimony
11. Defendant's Testimony
12. Direct Examination
13. Cross-examination
14. Expert Witnesses
15. Hypothetical Questions
16. Exhibits
17. Case Summaries
18. Factual Statements
19. Pleadings
20. Discovery Index
21. Depositions
22. Outline of Liability
23. Outline of Damages
24. Analysis of the Issues
25. Outlines of Proof
26. Law and Evidence Briefs
27. Medical Brief
28. Technical Notes
29. Final Arguments
30. Proposed Jury Instructions

§ 5.79 Pretrial Motions and Matters

The attorney will use the space in this section to list and make notes on motions in limine and other evidentiary motions or procedural questions which must be resolved before the trial begins. Insert a copy of the pretrial motion papers filed by each side. If the case involves a number of motions in limine or other pretrial matters, prepare a chart following the form in **§ 6.10** outlining the various motions in limine or other matters awaiting resolution. Place a copy of the chart in this section of the trial notebook to assist the attorney in tracking the court's ruling on each matter.

§ 5.80 Pleadings

A case with very few pleadings may not warrant a separate section for pleadings in the trial notebook. In cases with large volumes of pleadings, however, you will find it useful to include a copy of at least the master pleadings index. If you have been maintaining a separate index for discovery pleadings (see **§ 2.47**), place copies of both indexes in this section of the trial notebook. Remember to update the trial notebook copy of the pleadings index if any pleadings are filed after the trial commences. The master set of pleadings for the case should be housed in a separate binder, but the attorney may want to place copies of certain key pleadings in the trial notebook as well. These items could include the following:

- Complaint (If the complaint has been amended or supplemented, be sure you have the latest version.)
- Answer for each defendant
- Counterclaims or cross-claims, if any, and the corresponding replies
- Substantive motions filed before or during trial
- Trial brief for each party

In a complex case involving multiple counts, you should prepare a summary sheet briefly setting out the basis for each count in the complaint to help you keep track of the various elements which must be proved in the case.

§ 5.81 Voir Dire

Obviously, you only need to include sections on jury-related matters if the case is a jury trial (as opposed to a bench trial). For convenience at trial time, place the voir dire section near the front of the trial notebook. The attorney may want to reposition the voir dire materials at the back of the trial notebook or remove them entirely at the conclusion of the voir dire process. In this section of the trial notebook, assemble copies of all the available information and forms (see § **6.16**) relating to the jury, including

- Juror Profile Worksheet (§ **6.18**)
- Jury roster or list from court officer (§ **6.20**)
- Background investigation data (§ **6.21**)
- Composite juror data grid (§ **6.25**)
- Outlines of proposed voir dire questions (§ **6.26**)
- Jury Box Diagram (§ **6.49**)
- Extra paper for notes.

§ 5.82 Opening Statement

The trial attorney will almost always prepare the opening statement notes and materials. Some attorneys prepare a written draft of their entire opening statement, just as they would for a formal speech, while others prefer to write down only a few key words to serve as topical reminders. The attorney may not place anything in this section of the trial notebook until the day before the trial when he or she has polished the opening statement materials. Unless the attorney gives you specific directions to the contrary, you will probably only need to insert paper for notes in this section of the trial notebook. Like the voir dire section, the attorney may want to move these materials to the back of the notebook after the opening statements have been delivered.

§ 5.83 Witnesses

This portion of the trial notebook can be handled a variety of different ways, depending on the number and type of trial witnesses. At a minimum, you will need to prepare two indexes of the anticipated trial witnesses. The first index should be an alphabetical listing of all the witnesses, along with the telephone numbers at which they can be reached during the trial. The second index should list the witnesses in the order in which you plan to call them to testify.

After the witness index lists, place a separate witness sheet for each witness, indicating the witness name at the top right-hand corner (see **Form 5–17**). Either you or the attorney can use the witness sheets to outline the key points to be covered with each witness and list the corresponding exhibits to be introduced or discussed. Arrange the individual witness sheets either alphabetically or by order of testimony, depending on which works best for your case. Confer with the trial attorney to determine which method he or she prefers.

FORM 5–17
WITNESS SHEET

WITNESS SHEET

NAME: ______________________________

ADDRESS: ______________________________

PHONE: ______________________________

OUTLINE OF TESTIMONY	EXHIBITS

If the trial involves a large number of witnesses, you may want to enhance this section of the trial notebook by adding labeled divider tabs for individual witnesses or for groups of witnesses (such as direct examination and cross-examination witnesses). Consider preparing a separate tabbed section for a witness who will give extensive or very detailed testimony (such as an economist or a medical expert).

§ 5.84 Exhibit Index

In this section, place a copy of the master index of the trial exhibits (see § **5.79**). Include annotations on usage and special handling (which witness will testify about the exhibit, whether there is an enlargement for demonstrative evidence, and so on). Unless you have a very small number of exhibit documents, you will need to use a separate binder to hold the copies rather than putting them in the trial notebook. Place letter-sized copies of any enlarged documents or oversized charts into this section in the trial notebook. Staple or clip a sheet of extra exhibit stickers into this section just in case the attorney needs to change or add an exhibit designation during the trial.

§ 5.85 Closing Argument

The attorney will use this section to make notes during the trial in preparation for the closing argument or summation to the jury. Insert copies of any documents the attorney mentions during the course of the trial which could be useful in a summary fashion for the closing. (See § **6.59** on preparing for closing arguments.)

§ 5.86 Jury Instructions

At the close of the evidence in a jury trial and after the closing arguments, the judge will give the jury instructions (also known as the charge to the jury) on how they should apply the law to the evidence and testimony they have heard. Each side may submit their proposed jury instructions to the judge at the start of the trial or during the trial, and additional or supplemental instructions may be requested. At the close of the case, the judge decides which instructions from each side are proper for the jury. Insert copies of the proposed jury instructions from each side in this section of the notebook.

§ 5.87 Assembling Your Courtroom Tools and Supplies

In addition to preparing the materials and exhibits which the trial attorney will use in the courtroom, there are some items which you, as the trial paralegal, will need to assemble for your own use in the courtroom.

§ 5.88 Building the Paralegal Master Trial Notebook

As you work through the trial preparation, you need to compile a Paralegal Master Trial Notebook (PMTN). Although it will contain some of the same information as the attorney's trial notebook (see **§ 5.77**), the PMTN should be organized in the manner most logical and helpful to you. This important trial tool is your "command headquarters" for all the key information you will need to have at your fingertips during the trial. As you assemble and organize your PMTN, keep these points in mind:

1. Begin building your PMTN from the beginning of the case or at least from the beginning of the trial preparation, and keep it with you all the time during the trial preparation period.
2. Place a copy of the file diagram index you prepared when you originally organized the file (see **Chapter 2**) in the PMTN to assist you in quickly locating the desired materials in the case file.
3. The PMTN should be a capsulized version of the trial plan and other vital information you need related to coordinating the many details involved in presenting the trial.
4. Organize the key trial information in your PMTN so that someone else could follow it if something happened to you.
5. At the conclusion of the trial, the contents of the PMTN will become the core of the archive record for the case.

The choice of the actual binder or container for your Paralegal Master Trial Notebook is a personal one, just as the attorney's trial notebook is subject to the attorney's personal preference. Choose the type of binder or folder which works the best for you. Remember that the PMTN should be:

- Easy to update (to add or delete materials)
- Lightweight but durable
- Large enough to hold the necessary materials, but small enough to be easily portable

- A standard size to contain 8 1/2 by 11 inch pages
- Easily distinguishable from the other trial materials and notebooks.

Organize the PMTN according to your preferences, and tailor it to the type of trials you work on. Customize it to your specifications by "fitting it out" to hold various types of forms and information as appropriate. Some aids to organizing this notebook could include the following:

- Envelope or pocket for loose items
- Plastic page protectors
- Trial preparation agenda (see § **2.9**)
- Notes and lists of things "To Do"
- Various lists and indexes (witnesses, exhibits, equipment)
- Indexes
- Dividers
- Trial forms
- Scheduling and planning sheet (see § **6.61**)
- Pretrial forms (deposition objection transcript, motion in limine chart)
- Blank paper for notes
- Holder for business cards

Other tips:

- Assemble a set of trial forms to record key information as soon as the trial preparation starts
- Accumulate key information and "To Do" lists
- Rearrange and streamline the contents of the notebook immediately before trial for the best utility
- For sheets or documents larger than 8 1/2 by 11 inch size, use the reduction feature on your copier
- Place just inside the front cover: name/phone/address list of all key persons (opposing counsel, witnesses, video reporting service, and so forth).

§ 5.89 Assembling Your "Traveling Office" Supplies

During the trial you will be spending long days at the courthouse, away from your office and your desk where you have a well-organized supply cabinet or drawer (which you probably take for granted). When you are working in the courtroom all day, you must be equipped to handle those pesky little emergencies (yours, the client's, and the attorney's) that inevitably pop up. Use the suggestions in the following sections to help you prepare the necessary courtroom tools and supplies to handle a variety of these small problems.

§ 5.90 —The Personal Briefcase Kit

You can save the day in the face of minor personal crises by having the foresight to pack the proper emergency supplies in your briefcase. You just never know when someone will need a tissue, get a nasty paper cut, or even lose a jacket button. You can make the trial attorney's day go a lot better when you are able to produce—as if by magic—a couple of aspirin to relieve a headache or a throat lozenge to soothe a persistent cough! A day or two before the trial, take the time to assemble the items on the following checklist into your personal briefcase so you can leave for the courthouse feeling that you are fully prepared to meet any emergency.

Checklist: Personal Briefcase Supply Kit

____ 1. Roll of quarters for telephone calls, copies, newspaper (in case the trial is delayed and the client wants something to read, for example.)

____ 2. Tissues and/or handkerchief

____ 3. Lip balm, comb and brush, other basic grooming items (include a travel-size toothbrush and toothpaste)

____ 4. Travel size eyeglass cleaner or contact lens solution

____ 5. Basic and essential medications:

- Aspirin or non-aspirin pain reliever
- Antacid tablets
- Other medicines (e.g., allergy pills, prescription blood pressure medication)

____ 6. Breath mints

____ 7. Package of cough drops or hard candy

____ 8. Small bandaids (for paper cuts)

____ 9. Nail file or emery board

____ 10. Miniature sewing kit

____ 11. Small packages of raisins, nuts, crackers, and so forth. (If you are too busy for a lunch break, you may need an emergency snack to help you stay energetic and alert throughout the day.)

§ 5.91 —The Emergency Desk Supply Kit

In addition to handling the little personal crises mentioned in § **5.90,** you may have to do some last minute on the spot preparations or repairs to the trial materials. For example, suppose one of your document blowups is damaged in transit from the office to the courthouse. You may have to perform an emergency repair with tape or glue. Or suppose you realize after you get to the courtroom that the copies of one of the main trial exhibit documents were incorrectly collated. You need to quickly remove the staples from the documents, put the pages in the correct order, and restaple them. This could be a problem if you have to borrow a staple remover and stapler from one of the courthouse offices. However, because you are a well-prepared trial paralegal, you can use your own tools to quickly rectify the problem with very little fuss.

The trick, of course, is to pack all the necessary tools and supplies and not end up with a briefcase that weighs a ton. You will have plenty of other trial materials to carry, so your traveling office supplies need to be as compact and lightweight as possible. Pack small quantities and use miniatures and small sizes wherever possible. I like to use a transparent vinyl zippered pouch (the kind you fastened into your notebook when you were in grade school) to contain my essential courtroom desk supplies. Resealable polyvinyl bags (see § **6.80**) are also handy for containing small items.

Of course, you can't anticipate everything that could possibly go wrong at trial, but assembling the items on the following checklist will give you a versatile traveling office supply kit which will enable you to improvise at least a temporary solution to most of the courtroom problems you will encounter.

Checklist: Emergency Desk Supply Kit

____ 1. Small stapler and staple remover, extra staples
____ 2. Assorted sizes of paper clips and binder clips
____ 3. Assorted sizes of rubber bands
____ 4. Hole punch (single)
____ 5. Plastic hole reinforcements
____ 6. Small scissors, pen knife, or pocket cutter
____ 7. Small plastic bottle of white glue
____ 8. Small roll of transparent tape
____ 9. Ruler or small measuring tape
____ 10. Correction tape or liquid
____ 11. Chalk (white and colored)
____ 12. Pens, markers, pencils (assorted colors)
    ____ Highlighter pens
    ____ Heavy marker (for labeling)

- ____ Overhead transparency markers
- ____ Flip-chart markers
- ____ Pen refills (if you have a favorite refillable pen)

____ 13. Self-adhesive tags (assorted sizes)

____ 14. Extra legal pads

____ 15. Clipboard

____ 16. Extra exhibit stickers (both plaintiff and defendant)

____ 17. Extra manila file folders

____ 18. Extra business cards

____ 19. Small pocket calculator (credit card size)

CHAPTER 6

ASSISTING THE ATTORNEY IN THE COURTROOM

§ 6.1 Moving into "Trial Mode" (or, It's Showtime, Folks!)

The attorney-paralegal teamwork that has existed throughout the case development should continue into the courtroom. The wise attorney recognizes the value of having proficient paralegal support in the courtroom during the actual trial. Before the trial, you help the attorney gather, analyze, and summarize evidence, plan strategy, and prepare witness testimony and exhibits to support your client's case. In the courtroom, you can oversee and attend to the many logistical details involved in assembling the witnesses, documents, demonstrative exhibits, and equipment the attorney needs for the actual trial presentation. A paralegal's courtroom role is comparable in many respects to a stage manager's job in a Broadway play. You are in charge of managing the production details, so the attorney is free to concentrate on arguing the motions in limine, giving the opening statement, conducting the witness examinations, and delivering the closing argument or summation to the judge and jury.

Unfortunately, paralegals do not always get the opportunity to sit in on the courtroom proceedings. If your supervising attorney does not ask you to assist in the courtroom, get a firsthand look at the procedure by observing other trials on your own. Most trials are open to the public. By watching these you can learn a lot about how trials are conducted in your local courts. Talk to the assignment commissioner or clerk in charge of scheduling trials to find out when different kinds of cases are scheduled, and then try to sit in on the ones that interest you. Observe the functions of the court reporter, the bailiff, the attorneys, and the witnesses in the courtroom proceedings. Check with paralegals in your local association or in other firms to find out when they will have a trial in progress that you could observe.

The courtroom experience is valuable because you get the opportunity to see the results of all of the background work and preparation—how all the puzzle pieces come together into a cohesive trial presentation. It is educational and satisfying to be involved in the trial process from beginning to end, and your support skills and techniques will improve with each trial. This chapter examines some of the many ways you can support and assist the trial attorney in the courtroom.

§ 6.2 Final Preparation Considerations

If you have done a mock trial exercise (see § **5.2**), you should have a good idea of what to expect in the courtroom. However, it is natural in every trial to have the nagging feeling that you have not had quite enough time to prepare. Of course, there is always a chance the trial will be continued or that the case will settle, although you can never count on this. If the trial is continued, you will have time to do all those things you thought you didn't have time for.

As a practical matter, realize that you will probably have a bit of breathing time after you get to the courthouse. (The trials on television shows always condense the action for dramatic effect. The events in real life trials rarely move that fast.) Most courts start promptly at the appointed time, but others may have delays. The judge may have to handle motions or criminal arraignments before directing attention to your case. Your research on the trial judge may give you some indication of his or her habits on this count (see § **6.8**). Even when things start right on time, there are almost always pretrial matters which the attorneys and the judge will have to resolve outside the presence of the jury. A bench trial will generally be slightly more relaxed because there is no jury "audience."

In a jury trial, the voir dire procedure will take some time. Depending on the court and the case, voir dire can be a lengthy process. Even if you represent the plaintiff, you probably won't start with witnesses the first day.

(Don't assume this, however. Have your first witness ready and standing by on call, just in case.)

While you are sitting in court observing the pretrial motions or voir dire, jot down any thoughts which occur to you about details you still need to handle. Take care of these at the first opportunity. Call back to the office, if necessary, to check on the details you have delegated. Use the following checklist as a guide to checking the status of final preparations on the night before the trial begins. Then, after the trial begins, take things one day at a time and regroup at the end of each trial day (see § **6.3**).

Checklist: The Day (or Night) Before Trial
(Often a Sunday, as many trials begin on Monday)

____ 1. Assemble everything you plan to take with you to court for the first day:

- Pretrial Motions, Trial Brief, Stipulations, and so forth to be filed with the court clerk. **Note:** The court in your jurisdiction may require that such items be filed from one to three days before the first day of trial. Check your local rules and ask the trial attorney about any pertinent deadlines.
- Substantive Pleadings Index
- Deposition Transcripts and Objection Index (see § **6.11** on recording the rulings on deposition objections.)
- Voir dire materials (see § **6.18** *et seq.*)
- Exhibit notebooks (see § **5.58, 5.74** *et seq.*)
- Opening statement materials or equipment needed by the attorney.
- Attorney's trial notebook or file (see § **5.77**)
- Your master trial notebook (see § **5.88**)
- Complete witness files for at least the first one or two witnesses you plan to call.

____ 2. Pack your "traveling office" supply kit and briefcase. (See § **5.89.**)

____ 3. Check the status of service and return of subpoenas for trial witnesses. (See § **5.10** *et seq.*)

____ 4. Double-check on arrangements for transporting trial materials, demonstrative exhibits, equipment, and so forth, to the courtroom. You will have already lined up errand clerks to help you, but you may want to leave them reminder notes.

____ 5. Have a final meeting with the attorney to go over any last minute items and questions.

____ 6. Make sure the clients know when and where they are to meet you on the first day of trial.

____ 7. Make sure your first witnesses are ready in case they are needed for the first day.

____ 8. Double-check your desk and your calendar to make sure activities in your other cases are covered. If necessary, leave reminders or instructions for your secretary (or others who will be helping you cover your workload during the trial.)

____ 9. Check your clothes closet and assemble the outfit you plan to wear for the first day of trial. Remember to plan for inclement weather (umbrella, raincoat, gloves) if applicable.

§ 6.3 The Typical Trial Day

If the trial continues for an extended period, your days will begin to fall into a routine or pattern. The typical trial day can generally be divided into three main parts:

- Before Court: At the office
- At the Courthouse: A.M. Session/Lunch/P.M. Session
- After Court: At the office

Checklist: The Typical Trial Day
Before Court: At the Office

____ 1. Get to the office early so you can take care of any last minute emergencies and still arrive at court on time.

____ 2. Check on arrangements for transporting trial materials, demonstrative exhibits, equipment, and so forth to the courtroom. If you have errand clerks to help you, give them explicit instructions about what is to be delivered, when you need it, and where they should put it at the courthouse.

____ 3. Greet the clients, and go over any last minute instructions or questions. (On subsequent trial days, it may be easier for the clients to go directly to the courthouse and meet you there rather than come to your office first each morning.)

____ 4. Check on the day's planned witnesses. Make any last minute phone calls to confirm the availability of standby witnesses.

____ 5. Remind your coworkers where you will be. Secure your "office anchor" person to be standing by in case you need to phone instructions from the courthouse.

____ 6. Check with your secretary and answer questions or give instructions on matters for other cases which may need your attention.

At the Courthouse: A.M. Session/Lunch/P.M. Session

This outline assumes the trial is being held in your jurisdiction and that your office is within walking distance (or a short drive) to the courthouse. Some adjustments will have to be made for other situations. For example, you will have to allow extra travel time if you are commuting to an out-of-town court. You may also decide to go directly to the courthouse instead of stopping at your office first, in which case you will need to have the day's materials ready the night before.

First day of trial:

If the trial is to be in your local courthouse, you will have already inspected the courthouse facilities and the courtroom layout. (See § **6.13** on surveying the courtroom.) However, if the trial is being held in an unfamiliar locale, you may not have had an opportunity to visit the courthouse before the first day of trial, so you will need to get your bearings.

____ 1. Upon arrival at an unfamiliar courthouse on the first trial day, if you have not already done so, locate the following:

- the courtroom where the trial is to take place.
- the office of the Clerk of Courts (for filing pleadings, pretrial motions, and so forth).
- the offices of the judge, bailiff and court reporter.
- the public telephone nearest the courtroom in case you have to place calls to your office or to witnesses. Or, find out if you are allowed to use the telephone in the judge's or bailiff's office for this type of call.
- the restroom and water fountain facilities, for your own convenience and for that of your clients and witnesses.
- a photocopy machine you can use in case you have to make a few last minute copies.

____ 2. Arrange filing with the court clerk of any pleadings or documents (Motions in Limine; Returns of Service of Subpoenas; and so forth) Update your master pleadings index accordingly to incorporate new documents filed by all parties. (See § **2.47** on the pleadings index.) Make sure the judge and all counsel are properly served with copies of any pleadings you file.

____ 3. Assess the courtroom layout (see § **6.13**) and set up any exhibits or equipment needed for voir dire, opening statements, and/or your first planned witness.

____ 4. Observe, take notes, and assist the attorney as needed in pretrial activities (see § **6.7** *et seq.*)

____ 5. Observe, take notes, and confer with the attorney in jury selection. (See § **6.18** on assisting in voir dire.) **Note:** In some cases voir dire will take more than one day.

____ 6. Observe jurors during opening statements and take notes (see § **6.53** *et seq.*)

Subsequent Trial Days:

____ 7. Survey the courtroom (see § **6.13**) and set up any exhibits or equipment needed for the day's planned witnesses.

____ 8. Take notes during direct and cross-examination of witnesses.

____ 9. Assist the attorney in locating the exhibits to be used with each witness.

____ 10. Keep a daily list of the exhibits introduced or used with each witness.

____ 11. Update all sets of exhibit notebooks, as needed, if exhibits are added to the original set (see § **6.80**).

____ 12. Contact witnesses, as needed, to make sure they are present to testify at the appropriate time.

____ 13. Keep a record of the proceedings as they transpire in the courtroom on your Scheduling and Planning chart (see § **6.64**).

____ 14. Attend to the needs of clients or witnesses, as required, including taking the clients to lunch.

____ 15. Supervise moving your equipment and materials to a different courtroom, if necessary (as with a visiting judge who must use whatever courtroom is available.)

After Court: At the Office

At the end of the first trial day:

____ 1. Meet with the attorney to assess the impact, if any, of the court's pretrial rulings on your planned trial presentation. Revise your scheduling sheet as necessary (see § **6.64** *et seq.* on scheduling trial witnesses).

Subsequent Trial Days:

____ 2. Assess and regroup at the end of each day to gauge how the trial is developing.

____ 3. Reassemble materials used throughout the day into trial briefcases. Reorganize all materials which have gotten out of place in the trial files.

____ 4. Update your exhibit index.

____ 5. Confer with the court reporter regarding exhibits introduced so far to make sure your list is up to date.

____ 6. Make arrangements with the judge's bailiff to store easels, oversized boards, and so forth, overnight at the courthouse, as needed.

____ 7. Fill in any gaps in your notes while the testimony of that day's witnesses is still fresh in your mind. Date all materials you used that day.

____ 8. Collect, date, label, and file any trial notes taken by the attorney.

____ 9. Discuss the day's proceedings with the attorney. Follow up on any additional tasks as they become necessary.

____ 10. Adjust the witness scheduling agenda if you didn't get as far as anticipated or if you got further than you expected to (see § **6.64** on trial witness scheduling).

____ 11. Check the planned agenda for the next day's trial witnesses. Call the witnesses as necessary so that they know when you will need them. Confirm any special transportation arrangements.

____ 12. Go over the plan for next day's witnesses. Line up the exhibits needed for each witness.

____ 13. Hold trial preparation conferences with the next day's witnesses, if necessary.

____ 14. Meet with your expert witness, if necessary.

____ 15. Add to your list or folder anything the attorney has mentioned which should be noted or used in closing argument or in the jury charge.

____ 16. Supervise any additional research which may be needed to prepare the jury instructions.

____ 17. Check your desk or with your secretary for messages, and leave instructions for any items to be completed on your other cases while you are in trial.

§ 6.4 If Your Client Is a Defendant

You will have the same duties discussed in § **6.2** and § **6.3,** except you will not usually present your case on the first day of trial. You will, however, have to be prepared for pretrial activities, voir dire, opening statements, and cross-examination of the plaintiff's witnesses. (See also § **2.3,** The Defendant's Perspective.)

1. Take notes and check off cross-examination questions as the attorney covers points with plaintiff's witnesses.

2. Ascertain what additional witnesses plaintiffs will call. Prepare for cross-examination of those witnesses, if you have not already done so.

3. Try to project when you will start your case. You will have to adjust your schedule based upon how far the plaintiffs get with their case. This will also depend on whether there are multiple defendants, and in which order the defendants will be presenting their respective cases (see § **6.61** on scheduling witnesses).

4. Keep your witnesses informed on the progress of the trial and the approximate time they will be needed to testify.

5. Hold preparation conferences with your witnesses.

6. Keep track of the exhibits introduced by the plaintiffs. Compare and cross-reference with your proposed trial exhibits. Discuss with the attorney and decide whether to use the plaintiff's exhibit designations. (See § **6.79** on cross-referencing the opponent's exhibits.)

7. Confer with your expert witness to develop cross-examination questions for the plaintiff's expert.

8. Begin preparing any motions which will be filed at the end of plaintiff's case (for example, Motion for Dismissal or Motion for Directed Verdict).

§ 6.5 Handling Trial Stress

The final hectic days of trial preparation and the looming prospect of the actual trial proceedings can be substantial sources of stress and anxiety. You have been working long days to complete the items on your extensive trial preparation agenda, plus numerous other jobs the attorney requests at the last minute. The attorney is gearing up for "trial mode" and this is making you more nervous. You will be in charge of keeping track of clients, witnesses, exhibits, and equipment. The attorney is also depending on you to take good notes and handle any last minute emergencies that arise. You know you will have to be at your best for the trial, alert and ready for anything. It's no wonder you are feeling stressed out!

There are some things you can do to manage tension and rechannel stress to achieve positive results. The single best thing you can do to alleviate stress is to make sure you have prepared thoroughly. Use the worksheets and trial checklists throughout this book to help you organize your work. Checking items off the list as you complete them will give you a sense of control over the details. If you think of something in the middle of the night that you forgot to do, get up and write yourself a note, then try to relax. Once you have done all you can to prepare the case, you need to think about preparing yourself mentally and physically for the trial experience. The suggestions in § **6.6** will help you prepare to handle the pressure of being in trial.

§ 6.6 —Strategies for Handling Trial Stress

These are suggestions for coping with the stress associated with trials.

1. Learn to keep your composure. You have to behave in a professional manner, even when the people around you don't. Your ability to maintain control is especially important if your supervising attorney is the exasperating, "hyper" type. Two edgy, tense persons do not make a very good trial team. First of all, don't take it personally. Realize that the attorney is probably feeling the pressure, too. You can't control how the attorney acts, but you can control your own responses. Concentrate on balancing the hyper attorney's behavior with calm, controlled reactions of your own. In other words, try to stay just as calm as the attorney gets excited. If vague or unclear instructions are the source of the stress, ask smart questions (see § **1.29**) in a calm, regulated tone. You have every right to have your questions answered if you are to assist the attorney. Clearing up misunderstandings now helps to ensure that events will go smoothly in the courtroom. Persevere until you are satisfied that you understand what the attorney expects.

Your mental attitude has a lot to do with how well you handle pressure during trial preparation and the courtroom sessions. When the attorney's demands have you at the end of your rope, the last thing you want to do is panic. When you feel yourself getting rattled, practice this relaxation technique: Stop working for a minute. Shut the office door and lean back in your chair. Close your eyes and imagine a calm, peaceful setting (a sunny beach, a mountaintop, a cool, green forest, or whatever soothing scenario works best for you). Then take several deep breaths, straighten your shoulders, and resolve to stay in control. Mentally removing yourself from the tense situation for a moment can do wonders for your perspective.

2. Plan the clothes you will wear to court. The jurors will be watching you as well as the attorney in the courtroom. Knowing you look your best can go a long way toward reducing internal stress levels and increasing your confidence. At least one week in advance of the trial date, check your wardrobe. Assemble your most professional looking outfits, checking to make sure everything is clean, pressed, and in good repair. Keep accessories simple. Trial week is not the time to break in a brand new pair of shoes, especially if you will be walking to the courthouse each day. Wear comfortable shoes, but make sure they are polished and not run down at the heels.

3. Anticipate inclement weather. Dress sensibly for the weather in your area. It is difficult to maintain your poise and concentration when you have cold, wet feet, so wear warm boots in the winter and carry a pair of shoes to change into. Don't forget gloves, hat, earmuffs, and so on. If rain is in the forecast, be sure to carry an umbrella and raincoat.

4. Pack an emergency overnight bag. Prepare a small travel bag with a toothbrush and other essential toiletries (sample sizes are good for this), at least one extra set of undergarments, hosiery, and a shirt or blouse in a neutral color that will match any suit. Keep the bag handy in your office or car in case you spill coffee all over yourself or have to pull an "overnighter" on short notice. If you don't already have a miniature sewing kit in your office desk drawer, tuck one into the emergency bag.

5. Maintain your regular hairstyle. Save experimenting with a new look until after the trial. Two weeks in advance of the trial date, have your hair cut and styled. Don't make any drastic changes from your regular style. LADIES: Keep makeup subtle and simple. EVERYONE: Apply cologne or scent sparingly.

6. Remember to exercise. Regular exercise is always important, but it is especially so when dealing with trial stress. If you find your schedule is too hectic to make your aerobics class or racquetball game, at least take a short walk occasionally to get some fresh air. Your alertness will improve and you will feel better.

7. Try to get enough sleep. You may find you are keyed up from the hectic trial preparation process and you have difficulty sleeping. If you have been keeping late hours getting ready for the trial, you may not have had much time to sleep at all. Try to get sufficient sleep so that you can stay alert.

Set the alarm clock an hour early on the first morning of trial so you can arrive at work early in time to adjust your clothing, comb your hair, and so forth without having to rush. Remember to concentrate on staying calm.

8. Prepare your car. Make sure your gas tank is full before the morning of trial. You never know when you might be asked to pick up a witness at the airport or run some other last minute errand. If you have been having car trouble, it is a good idea to line up backup transportation (such as an associate in the office) in case your car doesn't start.

9. Carry a small amount of money. Have some petty cash available for unexpected small expenses, such as telephone calls, parking lot fees, or to cover a quick lunch at the corner hot dog stand.

10. Lock down your other obligations. You won't be able to do your best during the trial if you are distracted by responsibilities at home. You should plan on working long days during the trial. Make advance arrangements for someone to pick up your child from school or care for elderly relatives while you are in trial. Enlist support from family members to cover duties you normally handle at home.

§ 6.7 Assisting in Pretrial Courtroom Activities

Almost every case involves matters which must be worked out before the actual trial begins. These matters may include motions in limine (see **§ 5.9**; also see **§ 6.10**) rulings on deposition objections (see **§ 6.11**), and other procedural and evidentiary questions which the attorneys and the judge must discuss outside the hearing of the jury. This section discusses some other ways you can support the attorney by preparing and assisting with some of these pretrial considerations and activities.

§ 6.8 Learning about the Trial Judge

If a local judge will be presiding over your trial, you may already be familiar with the judge's attitudes and habits. However, if the judge is new or a visiting judge from another jurisdiction, the trial attorney may assign you the task of finding out as much as you can about the judge. The judge has absolute authority in the courtroom, so you want to do everything you can to avoid upsetting or annoying him or her. Any advance information you can discover about the judge's preferences and protocol for conducting trials will help you to anticipate problems and keep things going smoothly in the courtroom.

Try to find out how the judge feels about paralegals in the courtroom. Ask your colleagues and paralegals in other offices if they have ever assisted in cases before this judge. At the trial, it is a good idea for the attorney to introduce you to the judge or at least indicate to the judge who you are and that you will be assisting during the trial. Some judges will permit paralegals to sit at the counsel table provided there is enough room, but other judges do not allow anyone except the attorneys and clients to sit in front of the railing. (See § **6.12** on courtroom seating arrangements.)

§ 6.9 —Researching the Trial Judge

The following paragraphs list suggestions for learning more about your trial judge.

1. Check the Martindale-Hubbell™ directory for any information on the judge's age, background, education, and lawfirm affiliations.
2. Get to know the judge's bailiff, clerk, secretary, and other aides who have access to the judge. These people can be very helpful in working out logistical problems as they arise during the trial. You may be able to gather some advance information on how the judge normally conducts the voir dire process from these assistants (see § **6.19**).
3. Clarify the correct spelling of the judge's name, as well as the pronunciation if it is an unusual name. It may be helpful to write the name out phonetically if the pronunciation is especially difficult (or if your supervising attorney often has trouble with names).
4. If the judge is retired or visiting from another jurisdiction, obtain his or her correct mailing address for transmitting posttrial briefs and motions.
5. If you plan to use any unusual demonstrative evidence or special equipment in your trial presentation, find out how the judge feels about these techniques. Some judges have not fully accepted modern technology such as the VCR for use in the courtroom.
6. Run a search on Westlaw or LEXIS to see if the judge has made any previous rulings in other cases involving issues similar to those in your case.
7. If possible, sit in on someone else's trial with the judge to observe how he or she manages the courtroom. Notice the general daily schedule the judge follows, (the preferred morning starting time, the length of time normally allowed for the lunch break, and the time at which the judge normally adjourns for the day).
8. Early in the trial, usually in the pretrial conference, the judge will probably discuss any special scheduling problems which may arise during the trial, such as voting days or legal holidays that will affect the trial

scheduling or previous obligations, (such as a day set aside for criminal arraignments or a speaking engagement) which would necessitate suspension or early adjournment of the trial. Note these items on your trial planning form so that you can adjust the scheduled times for the trial witnesses.

§ 6.10 Tracking Pretrial Motion Rulings

If your case does involve pretrial motions by either side, you will need to pay careful attention during the pretrial session in which the court rules on these motions. This is important because the judge's rulings will help to "shape" the issues and procedures in the trial (see § **5.9** on motions in limine). The attorney may need to refer to your notes on the pretrial motions later on as he or she is preparing and refining the questions for each witness. To help you keep track of the court's rulings, prepare an outline of the various pretrial motions using the following form (see **Form 6–1**) or set up a similar page in your trial notes. As each motion is discussed and ruled upon, put a check mark in the appropriate column on the form.

§ 6.11 Recording the Court's Ruling on De Bene Esse Deposition Objections

De bene esse depositions are taken before a court reporter, and a judge is generally not present. However, counsel may enter objections to certain questions just as if they were before the judge at trial in order to preserve the objections for the record. The court's ruling on objections raised at the deposition will affect which portions of the testimony are heard by the jury. This can be especially important when the deposition testimony concerns a critical point or element in the case. Before a party can offer a witness's deposition testimony into the record at trial, the court must rule on the objections so that the transcript can be purged of any objectionable segments before it is read to the jury. (See § **3.40** *et seq.*, videotaping expert depositions in lieu of live testimony; see also § **5.53** on de bene esse depositions and § **5.56** *et seq.* on handling videotaped depositions.)

This procedure generally takes place shortly before the trial begins in a session with the attorneys and the judge, either in the courtroom or in the judge's chambers, out of the hearing of the jury. The discussion, including arguments of counsel relative to each objection, is usually recorded by a court reporter and becomes part of the record of the trial. You may be asked to follow this pretrial discussion and take note of the court's ruling on the objections in the transcript.

FORM 6–1
PRETRIAL MOTION RULINGS

PRETRIAL MOTION RULINGS

NO.	PLAINTIFF'S MOTIONS IN LIMINE	GRANTED	DENIED	TABLED	COMMENTS
1.					
2.					
3.					
4.					
5.					
6.					
7.					
8.					
9.					
10.					
11.					
12.					

NO.	DEFENDANT'S MOTIONS IN LIMINE	GRANTED	DENIED	TABLED	COMMENTS
1.					
2.					
3.					
4.					
5.					
6.					
7.					
8.					
9.					
10.					
11.					
12.					

Preparing for the Pretrial Objection Ruling Session

The following steps will help you prepare for a pretrial objection ruling session:

1. Prepare a spiral-bound copy of the deposition transcript.

2. Read through the transcript and use a highlighter pen to designate the lines containing each question to which an objection was made, the answer of the witness, and any discussion between counsel related to the particular objection.

3. If there are numerous objections, or if the transcript is lengthy and the objections are scattered throughout, you can assist the attorney in locating each transcript page which contains an objection by preparing a Transcript Objection Index (see **Form 6–2**). Use this form as a handy way to keep track of the court's ruling on each objection so that you can correctly edit the transcript for use at trial (see below).
Note: If you use a computerized program to summarize or abstract the deposition transcript, you may wish to prepare an Objection Index at the same time (see **Chapter 8**).

As the court considers each objection at the pretrial session, follow along in your copy of the transcript and note the judge's rulings on your corresponding Transcript Objection Index form, as follows:

- **Sustained**—If the judge sustains an objection, indicate this by writing an "S" in the margin of your transcript and putting a checkmark in the appropriate column on the form. Generally, when an objection is sustained, both the question and the answer, if any, must be stricken from the transcript. Use a pencil to clearly mark through the lines of the transcript that are to be omitted, including the entire question, the objection, any incidental comments or discussion related to the objection, and the answer. If the question-objection-answer series takes up a large block of lines or even a whole page of the transcript, do not take the time to pencil through each line. Instead, make a diagonal slash or an "X" across the entire page or segment of the transcript which is to be omitted.
- **Overruled**—If the judge overrules the objection, write in "overruled" (or the abbreviation "O/R") in the margin of the transcript and check the column on your form. Cross through the lines in the transcript which contain the objection, leaving the question and the corresponding answer intact.

FORM 6–2
TRANSCRIPT OBJECTION INDEX

TRANSCRIPT OBJECTION INDEX

CASE ID: ______________________________

WITNESS: ______________________________

PAGE	LINES	BASIS FOR OBJECTION	RULING			TRANS EDITED
			S	O/R	W/D	

- **Withdrawn**—In some instances, the attorney who made the objection at the deposition may decide to withdraw the objection, thus making a ruling by the court unnecessary. (The attorney may have changed his or her mind about the relevance of the question or the basis for the objection may have been removed.) If the objection is withdrawn, indicate this by writing "W/D" in the margin of your transcript and on your Index form. Then cross out only the transcript lines containing the objection, in the same manner as described above for an "Overruled" objection.

If the attorney and a witness on the stand are to read the transcript into the record at the trial, the reading will go much more smoothly if the readers have clearly marked edited copies of the transcript. Make sure all copies of the transcript are conformed and marked the same way so there is no confusion. If a portion to be omitted runs for several pages, staple together the top right corners of the pages to be skipped, so the witness will not have to leaf through numerous pages to find the next place he or she is to begin reading. In most trials, rather than have the court stenographer duplicate the deposition testimony, the transcript itself can be submitted to the court stenographer to be made part of the trial record. Make sure to have an extra edited copy of the transcript available to give to the court reporter.

If the deposition is on videotape, a written transcript must be submitted to the judge so he or she can rule on the objections. Once the judge has ruled on the objections, a copy of the corrected transcript must be given to the video operator so that the tape can be edited accordingly. (See § **5.56** on requesting rulings on videotape deposition objections.)

§ 6.12 Handling Courtroom Logistics

In the context of the courtroom where the drama of the trial takes place, the trial paralegal often assumes the role of the stage manager, whose job it is to keep the trial proceedings flowing smoothly. This means making sure that the witnesses, equipment, and exhibits are in the right place at the right time, that is, when the trial attorney needs them! A minor fumble or two may not lose the case for you, but a well-orchestrated presentation will certainly enhance the trial team's efforts and help to make a positive impression on the jury. Naturally, real life trials will not always go as smoothly as they do on television shows, but by thinking ahead and planning your courtroom presentation carefully, you can help to avoid embarrassing glitches which could distract the jurors' attention away from the content of the trial and affect the attorney's credibility.

Unexpected things always happen at trial. You can never anticipate *all* the problems that will arise. But the more details you can work out ahead of time, the easier it will be to pull it all together when it counts in the courtroom. Careful planning and attention to detail will reduce stress and allow you to concentrate on the developments at trial. Moreover, a polished trial presentation with no annoying distractions and delays makes it easier for the jurors to focus on evaluating the merits of the case.

§ 6.13 —Surveying the Courtroom

Courthouses can be found in a wide variety of architectural styles, and individual courtrooms come in various shapes and sizes. If at all possible, make an advance visit to the courtroom in which your trial will be held to familiarize yourself with the physical layout and features of the courtroom.

Make a rough sketch of the courtroom layout, noting the location and relative placement of the following:

- Judge's bench
- Jury box
- Witness stand
- Court stenographer's table
- Bailiff's desk
- Counsel tables
- "Bar" and swinging gate, if any
- Spectators' gallery
- Doorways/aisles

An advance look at the courtroom is especially useful when you will be using any type of demonstrative exhibits or audio-visual equipment, or if you must accommodate any special requirements of your clients or witnesses. (See **§ 6.15.**) You will be better able to prepare your clients for what they can expect in the courtroom.

You should be able to adapt your trial presentation to almost any courtroom facility. As you survey the courtroom, use the following checklist as a guide to other factors you may need to consider, depending on your specific case. Jot down any ideas or potential problems which occur to you relative to handling equipment or exhibits. Discuss these items with the trial attorney and get his or her input in one of your trial preparation meetings (see **§ 2.9**).

Checklist: Surveying the Courtroom

____ 1. Shape and size of the courtroom (oblong, square, oval? large or small?)

____ How much floor space is available for displaying blowups or charts on easels?

____ How large must visual aids be in order to be seen across the room?

____ Where could you set up other equipment? (a slide projector and screen, an overhead projector, a VCR and television set.)

____ 2. Acoustics

____ Is the courtroom small enough that the witness can be heard across the room without difficulty?

____ If the courtroom is large, is there a microphone wired to the witness stand? If so, does it work?

____ 3. Lighting

____ Type of artificial lighting and location of the light switches or controls.

____ Number of windows and type of covering (blinds, shades, draperies, and so forth)

____ Will you need to dim the light in the courtroom for viewing slides or overhead transparencies? Can this be done easily?

____ 4. Location of electrical outlets

____ This is very important if you will be using any equipment which must be plugged in, such as a projector or VCR. Courtrooms in new or renovated buildings will usually have plenty of outlets, but access could pose a problem in older buildings.

____ Think about where you could position your equipment to access the outlets with a minimum of cords strung out to reduce the chance of someone tripping.

____ Be sure to include a heavy duty extension cord in your courtroom equipment.

____ If you will need several outlets, consider using an outlet strip with multiple plugs.

____ 5. Equipment available in the courtroom

____ Is there a chalkboard or an easel already stationed in the courtroom? Will these items be available for you to use at trial?

____ Include your own chalk and marker pens in your courtroom equipment.

____ 6. Handicapped access

____ This will be a factor if your client or a witness is handicapped. (See § **6.14** for more information.)

____ If the judge's permission is needed for some special arrangement, remind the attorney to clear the matter with the judge ahead of time outside the hearing of the jury.

____ 7. Storage space

____ If you will have to leave any materials or equipment at the courthouse overnight, look in or near the courtroom for a room or closet where you might be able to safely leave your equipment. You or the attorney will have to clear any storage arrangements with the judge or the judge's bailiff or assistant.

____ 8. Seating arrangements

Some judges allow paralegals to sit at the counsel table if there are enough seats. Other courts do not allow anyone except the actual trial participants and the jury to sit in front of the "bar." I prefer to sit on the first or second row of the gallery, on the side nearest to the trial attorneys with whom I am working. (It is customary for the plaintiffs and their counsel to sit at the table or on the side of the table closest to the jury, while the defendants sit at the other table or on the opposite side of the center table, but check your local practices.)

One advantage of sitting in the gallery is that you are out of the direct line of sight of the jury. This allows you to observe the jurors and take notes unobtrusively, while still being close enough to the action to see and hear the attorneys, the witnesses, and the judge. I like to have plenty of room to arrange my notes and materials, so I usually spread them out on the second bench, hidden from the direct view of the jurors. Sitting in the gallery also gives you the flexibility to move around if you need to

- ____ leave the courtroom to make a telephone call
- ____ intercept deliveries from your office
- ____ hand materials or exhibits to the attorney
- ____ set up demonstrative exhibits or equipment
- ____ call witnesses in from the hallway.

____ 9. Location of attorney's materials and exhibits

Some attorneys like to have a separate table at the end of the counsel table on which to organize notes and papers during witness examinations. This works particularly well if the table is lectern height so the attorney can reach his or her notes without having to bend or stoop over the counsel table. Other attorneys like to leave their notes at their seat and move around in the courtroom. Be guided by the preferences of the attorney with whom you are working.

If you have several folders or several boxes of exhibit documents, decide where these will be located in the courtroom. Does the attorney want to keep the exhibits near the counsel table, or does he or she want you to keep them?

____ 10. Placement of demonstrative exhibits and visual aids

A common problem in courtroom layouts is placing visual aids so that they can be seen equally well by the witnesses, the judge, the jury, and the opposing counsel. The placement will depend on what equipment you plan to use in your presentation and the space available in the courtroom. Think through the testimony of each witness. Visualize how the attorney will interact with the witness on the stand. What exhibits will be used? What equipment will be needed? Some of the items you may need to provide are

- ____ Easel with or without pad; multiple easels
- ____ Chalkboard or magnetic board
- ____ Presentation boards
- ____ Model or miniature
- ____ Aerial map
- ____ Videotape equipment—VCR and television monitor
- ____ Overhead projector with transparencies
- ____ Slide projector and screen

§ 6.14 —Practical Courtroom Logistics: Problems and Solutions

Problem: A witness (especially an expert witness) may need to step down from the witness box during his testimony to point out something on a demonstrative evidence chart or to write calculations or figures on an easel pad or chalkboard.

Solution: When you are deciding on the placement of visual aids or equipment, allow room for the witness to get down from the stand gracefully. If a chart is displayed on an easel or tripod near the witness stand, make sure there is enough room for the witness to step up to the chart without tripping over the legs of the easel. Provide a pointer stick so the witness can point at the chart without blocking the jury's view.

If the witness will be asked to leave the stand for any portion of his testimony for the purpose of interacting in some fashion with a visual aid, the attorney should explain this to the witness during the trial preparation conference. The attorney may want to stage a practice session with the witness to ensure that the timing and utilization of the visual aid can be smoothly integrated into the witness testimony. During the practice session, you may want to remind the witness not to turn away from the jury or to speak while his back is turned any more than absolutely necessary.

Problem: The witness will be asked to testify about multiple exhibit documents which are contained in several heavy exhibit notebooks.

Solution: Arrange to have a table, ledge, or platform situated next to the witness stand for the exhibit notebooks to rest on. (See also § **6.65** on managing exhibits in the courtroom.)

This may require physically moving a table or shelf from elsewhere in the courtroom. (Check with the judge or the court bailiff before making any drastic changes.) It may also be helpful to use binders of contrasting colors to designate plaintiff's and defendant's exhibits, so the witness will not pick up the wrong book.

Problem: The witness is elderly or infirm, making it difficult to turn pages or to lift heavy exhibit notebooks.

Solution: Alert the attorney to the problem so that either you or the attorney can assist the witness by locating the proper page in the exhibit notebook for her. Another possibility would be for the attorney to remove individual exhibits from the notebooks temporarily and hand them to the witness one at a time. (Be sure the exhibits are replaced in the proper order in the notebooks.)

Problem: The witness is confined to a wheelchair, or is otherwise handicapped in such a way that it would be impossible for him to actually sit in the witness stand.

Solution: If the witness is the injured plaintiff in your case, you must evaluate the potential dramatic impact of the witness appearing before the jury in a wheelchair (or with a walker, crutches, cane, orthotic brace, and so forth) It may be quite effective and appropriate to your case to demonstrate the witness's physical limitations if they are related to the injuries at issue in the case, but you must weigh this against the risk of appearing melodramatic or embarrassing the witness.

The situation is a little different if the handicapped witness is not the injured party and his or her physical condition is completely unrelated to the case. For example, suppose the best eyewitness to an accident was a fellow in a wheelchair who just happened to be sitting in his yard at the time the accident occurred. You don't want the jurors to be distracted by something unrelated to the case.

There is nothing magical about the actual witness box. Very often it is just a regular chair which is placed inside a paneled enclosure. If the witness is unable to sit in the actual witness box, perhaps, because of a wheelchair, the judge will probably allow the witness to testify from the wheelchair which has been wheeled to a spot near the witness stand.

Check on general handicapped access within the courthouse (elevators, ramps, width of doorways, and so forth) as well as the actual aisle space available inside the courtroom. If it would be difficult or impossible to maneuver a wheelchair along the usual course (from the hallway outside, into the bar enclosure, around the counsel table, and up to the stand) it may be possible for the witness to enter the courtroom through another door (such as from the judge's chambers or through the jury room) with more direct access to the area near the witness stand. Make sure the witness is still facing the jury, oriented in basically the same direction as he would be on the stand.

If a nonparty witness is very self-conscious about a serious limp or having to use a walker, the judge may let the witness take the stand before the jurors enter the courtroom. Making witnesses uncomfortable has a decidedly negative impact on the jurors, so you want to work out a way for the witness to enter and exit the courtroom with a minimum of disruption.

§ 6.15 Arranging for a Jury View

In some trials it is advantageous to have the jury view the actual scene of the incident that gave rise to the lawsuit. This is particularly true when a picture or a diagram cannot adequately convey the scene to the jurors. In a case involving an automobile accident, the scene might be a particular intersection or curve in a road. In a property dispute, it might be the lot, field, or building involved. In an industrial accident, the site could be a factory or a particular piece of machinery which is too large to bring to the courtroom. The jury may need to see the site to properly understand perspective or depth. Having the jury view the actual place where the incident occurred helps the attorney to lay the foundation for the presentation of the case. Before the presentation of opening statements in a case, the attorney will file a request or motion with the court to allow a jury view of the site.

You may be asked to draft this request or motion. The request should contain a concise statement of why counsel believes a jury view is necessary. The exact reason, of course, will vary depending on the circumstances of the case (see **Form 6–3**). If the judge grants the request, you may have to coordinate with the court bailiff or deputy to make the arrangements for the van or bus to transport the jurors to their destination. If the attorney desiring the jury view represents the factory, manufacturer, or institution involved, you may have to contact the person in charge to alert them to the pending jurors' visit and to arrange for any necessary security clearance, work scheduling, and so forth.

Once the visit is under way, the bailiff will direct the jurors' attention to various items of importance. You and the attorneys may be allowed to accompany the jurors but you will not be permitted to talk with them. However, you may be able to listen to conversations between jurors and get an idea of the impact (favorable or not) of the view upon them. This information can then be relayed to the attorney (out of earshot of the jurors, of course) to assist him or her in playing up a favorable impression or toning down an unfavorable one in the presentation of the case. It will also be necessary to calculate the time the jury view roundtrip will take in the context of scheduling for the remaining trial activities (see **§ 6.61** on trial scheduling).

FORM 6–3
SAMPLE REQUEST FOR JURY VIEW

UNITED STATES DISTRICT COURT
NORTHERN DISTRICT OF OHIO, EASTERN DIVISION

THE XYZ PAINT COMPANY,	:	CIVIL ACTION NO. ________
	:	
Plaintiff,	:	JUDGE ABLE
	:	
vs.	:	
	:	
MARY L. LAMB,	:	REQUEST FOR JURY VIEW
	:	
Defendant.	:	

Now comes the Plaintiff, XYZ PAINT COMPANY, and respectfully requests the Court to permit the jurors empaneled in this case to travel to the premises located at 725 Main Circle, Akron, Ohio before the commencement of Plaintiff's case in chief in the trial of this matter.

This request is made upon the belief that, in order for justice to be fully and properly served, the jurors should have the opportunity to personally view the site of the activity which gave rise to Plaintiff's cause of action in this case. The issues in this trial concern certain large pieces of machinery that are located within the building which houses Plaintiff's business. It is impossible for Plaintiff to produce said machinery in the courtroom for examination by this panel, and photographs cannot convey the true size and complexity of the machinery in question. Therefore, in order for the jurors to fully comprehend and evaluate the testimony which will be presented in this matter, justice requires that the jurors be allowed to go to the above-mentioned premises and view the machinery prior to the start of trial.

____
Jane P. Smith
[address]
[city, state, zip]
[phone]
ATTORNEYS FOR PLAINTIFF,
THE XYZ PAINT COMPANY

§ 6.16 Assisting the Attorney in Voir Dire

In a jury trial, the success of a case may depend on the trial team's accurate assessment of jurors. The trial attorney bases the evaluation of a potential juror on a combination of factors: (1) the type of juror desired for a particular case; (2) the background information obtained about the juror; (3) the juror's verbal answers to voir dire questions; (4) the clues ascertained from the juror's non-verbal behavior; and (5) instinct or gut-level feeling about the juror.

While there is no perfectly reliable method of predicting juror behavior, one thing is certain: careful planning for voir dire is an important part of trial preparation. You can assist the attorney in preparing for and conducting the voir dire examination in the following ways:

1. Analyze the case to determine the juror characteristics you want (and also those you don't want) for that case.
2. Investigate and compile advance information on jurors.
3. Frame voir dire questions designed to elicit relevant information from the jurors.

4. Observe the jurors during voir dire questioning.
5. Provide input to the attorney based on your observations of the jurors.

§ 6.17 Understanding Voir Dire Purpose and Procedures

Our legal system guarantees a litigant the right to a jury composed of impartial jurors. The courts are responsible for providing each party an opportunity to examine prospective jurors to ascertain prejudice or bias. In a jury trial, the attorney must try to seat a jury composed of persons who are able to make fair judgments on the issues in the case. The main purpose of voir dire is to allow the trial team to evaluate the qualifications of potential jurors. In addition, since it is usually the first contact between the jurors and counsel, the process also gives the lawyer a chance to establish rapport with the jurors and inform them about the background of the case, thus setting the stage for presentation of the case.

Voir dire is commonly referred to as jury selection, but it is actually more a process of "de-selection" because it is a method of eliminating jurors considered least likely to be favorable to the case. The attorney's objective is to empanel jurors that he or she feels are capable of rendering an impartial decision, and where possible, to choose those jurors who will identify with his or her client and be the most sympathetic to the client's point of view. Therefore it is important to determine whether any jurors hold a bias or prejudice which would work against the attorney's case and to attempt to eliminate those persons from the panel. Through the questioning process, the attorney gains insight as to how a particular juror will perform, and he or she can then intelligently decide whether to challenge any prospective jury member.

Voir dire procedure varies greatly among different courts. Sometimes the trial judge allows the attorneys to conduct the whole voir dire process. With federal court judges in particular, there is a trend toward the trial judges taking more control over the process. In some jurisdictions, the judge will conduct the entire voir dire examination, allowing counsel to submit written questions to the court which the judge will then ask the prospective jurors. Usually, however, the procedure is a combination of questioning by the judge and the attorneys. The judge will ask the preliminary questions and the attorneys are then given the chance to follow up on particular areas of questioning.

Find out the specific procedure the trial judge will use for the jury selection in your case. This is especially important if the trial will be held in an unfamiliar forum, for example, a different county from your local jurisdiction. Call the judge's bailiff or clerk and ask how the trial judge will conduct the voir dire process. Know what will be expected so you can help the attorney prepare thoroughly for voir dire.

§ 6.18 Developing the "Ideal Juror" Profile

In your trial preparation agenda sessions (see § **2.9**), discuss with the attorney his or her thoughts on the type of juror which would be best for your case. The desired juror characteristics will vary depending on the type of case being tried and whether you represent the plaintiff or the defendant. Use the Juror Profile Worksheet (see **Form 6–4**) and follow these steps to help the attorney assess the prospective jurors:

1. Consider the characteristics (age, sex, education, occupation, economic status) of your client to determine the type of juror who could best identify with and sympathize with your client.

2. Clarify the key issues in your case and analyze the legal elements you have to prove.

3. Confront the negative aspects or weaknesses of your case to decide the factors which could be most damaging to your case. This will help you determine the type of persons you don't want as jurors.

For example, in a medical malpractice case against a doctor or a hospital, the plaintiff would want to keep a juror who has had a bad experience with a hospital, or one who has had a complaint against a doctor. Plaintiff would want to remove a juror who is a doctor or nurse, or is in any other way associated with the medical health care field, because that person would be likely to sympathize with the defendant.

§ 6.19 Conducting the Juror Investigation

In order to evaluate the individuals on the jury panel properly, the attorney needs as much advance information about them as possible. You can assist the attorney and save much valuable courtroom time during voir dire by investigating some general facts about the potential jurors and compiling the available information prior to the trial. This background information can give you a preliminary idea of which jurors you want to keep or reject.

§ 6.20 —Obtaining a List of Potential Jurors

Request a list of the jury pool from the jury commissioner or other court officer in charge of the jury roster. It is usually possible to obtain this list a week to several days before the trial. Many times this list will give only the names and addresses of potential jurors, but some jurisdictions provide additional information such as age, sex, and occupation of the individuals in the jury

FORM 6–4
JUROR PROFILE WORKSHEET

JUROR PROFILE WORKSHEET		
	Type of Persons Who WOULD Identify w/Client	Type of Persons Who WOULD NOT Identify w/Client
CLIENT CHARACTERISTICS:		
Age:		
Sex:		
Education:		
Occupation:		
Economic Status:		
LEGAL ISSUES/ ELEMENTS TO PROVE		
WEAKNESSES/ NEGATIVE ASPECTS		

pool. You should become familiar with the procedures followed by your local courts and include the task of obtaining the jury list in your final trial preparation agenda (see § **2.9**).

If the trial is to be held in an unfamiliar locale, check with the jury commissioner well in advance of the trial date to determine the procedure used. Also check periodically with the court officer to make sure the jury pool list is current, noting whether certain jurors have been eliminated or excused from the list due to illness or other reasons.

§ 6.21 —Obtaining General Background Information

In major cities, professional jury services can provide certain background information and records of previous jury service by individuals. The jury commissions in some counties keep records on jurors as to how many times they have served and the types of trials on which they have served. This is, of course, only a surface investigation. The amount of detail you go into in gathering biographical information depends on (1) the nature and complexity of the issues in the case; (2) the desirable variables determined by your "juror profile" (see § **6.18**); (3) the time available; (4) the ability to obtain the jury list ahead of time; and (5) the number of names on the list. In obtaining background information, never contact prospective jurors directly.

§ 6.22 —Searching Public Records

You can unearth a surprising amount of information quickly and inexpensively by examining records available to the public. Use the resources available at your public library and public offices.

City directories give residence, spouse's name, occupation, and length of time at the current residence. Checking the address can tell you if a juror lives in the same neighborhood as a client, attorney, or witness in the case. You can usually tell whether the address is an apartment building or a single-family dwelling. The listings arranged by street name can tell you whether the area is primarily commercial or residential. The type of neighborhood can be important if your juror profile involves placing the juror in a specific social or economic category.

Telephone books and criss-cross directories allow you to cross-check the juror's address and confirm that he or she has a telephone. Libraries usually have a wide selection of current telephone directories for various communities. A listing in the business section or the Yellow Pages may reveal a juror's occupation and whether he or she owns or runs a business. This can be significant if one of the parties in your case is a company or corporation. The type of business owned by a juror could also affect your evaluation. For example, a gun shop owner would probably have some strong opinions in a criminal case involving a handgun.

Voter registration records are available to the public and can help in locating basic relevant information such as name, address, sex, race, age, date of birth, place of birth, date registered, and political party affiliation. This would be significant if a party to the case is a well-known politician or government official.

County Auditor/Real Estate Tax Department records can identify homeowners, marital status, length of residence, and the value of the home or property. Jurors who are homeowners are usually gainfully employed and tend to be concerned as citizens about issues involving the community. Large real estate holdings would very likely indicate a high economic level, and here again, you can infer economic status from the neighborhood in which a juror lives.

Bureau of Vital Statistics records can reveal the date of birth and place of birth. This would be useful if your juror profile targets a particular age group or ethnic group.

§ 6.23 —Checking Various Court Records

A check of local courthouse records (federal, county/superior/common pleas, municipal, probate, and bankruptcy courts) can turn up information on previous litigation involving potential jurors, as well as any judgments, garnishments, or liens filed against those individuals. An attorney seeking a large money verdict would probably want to avoid a juror who had previously had a large judgment assessed against him or her.

§ 6.24 —Checking Other Possible Sources

If you work in a large firm or company, it may be helpful to circulate the list of potential jurors to the lawyers and paralegals in the firm to see if any of them have personal knowledge of anyone on the list.

§ 6.25 Preparing a Jury Information Grid

Once you have collected the information on the prospective jurors, you need to present it to the attorney in a concise format for courtroom use. This can be done by filling in the pertinent information about each juror on a composite data grid (see **Form 6–5**). The data grid provides the attorney with a

FORM 6–5
JURY INFORMATION GRID

JURY INFORMATION GRID

PROSPECTIVE JUROR	JUROR #____	JUROR #____	JUROR #____	JUROR #____	JUROR #____	JUROR #____
1. NAME						
2. ADDRESS						
3. AGE						
4. OCCUPATION						
5. ESTIMATED INCOME						
6. EMPLOYER						
7. EDUCATION						
8. MARITAL STATUS						
9. SPOUSE'S OCCUPATION						
10. SPOUSE'S EMPLOYER						
11. CHILDREN						
12.						
13.						
14.						
15.						
16.						
17.						
18.						
19.						
20.						
21.						

thumbnail sketch of each juror for use in formulating questions, while also enabling the attorney to see the information on all the jurors at the same time. For example, if a search of the case indexes in the office of the court clerk reveals that a juror has been a defendant in a previous lawsuit, the attorney will want to question that juror about the type of suit, whether it was a jury trial, the resulting verdict, and so on. Include notations of any comments made by colleagues who know the juror, as well as notes on specific additional questions that should be asked.

Even when it is not possible to obtain the jury list beforehand (the attorney is simply handed the list on the morning the trial begins) you can help the attorney on the day of trial by filling in an information grid with the names, occupations, and so on as soon as you receive the court's jury panel list. As the attorney asks the potential jurors questions as to occupation, marital status, children, and so forth take notes and fill in the relevant information on the chart.

Preparing the Jury Information Grid

Lines 1 through 11 on the grid are labeled to accommodate standard juror data. Customize the grid by using the remaining blank lines for other relevant information tailored to your case. Use the points on the following checklist as you prepare the jury information grid (see **Form 6–5**).

____ 1. Names of the parties, the attorneys, and the judge should be typed at the top.

____ 2. Use abbreviations which the attorney will be able to read easily.

____ 3. Type information on the form, if possible, to conserve space.

____ 4. Keep the overall size small (no larger than the size of a legal pad) so the attorney can refer to it unobtrusively in the courtroom.

____ 5. Use a transparent highlighter pen to draw the attorney's attention to an item worth particular note.

____ 6. Leave room for the attorney to add notes.

____ 7. Provide phonetic spellings of difficult names, if possible.

§ 6.26 Outlining Voir Dire Questions

The attorney will probably have a list of standard questions which he or she routinely asks potential jurors. Most courts allow the attorney a broad scope of voir dire questions. There will be additional specific questions tailored to the type of case at issue, and still others arising from specific information learned during the voir dire process. Keep a file of the questions the attorney routinely asks during voir dire and work with the attorney to develop specific questions for each case.

In planning voir dire questions, review the facts and issues involved in your case. Isolate the main themes of the case and the legal elements you need to prove at trial. Address any problems or negative aspects of your case. Every voir dire question should have a specific purpose and you should know the answers you want. The best voir dire questions are open-ended ones which encourage the jurors to talk about themselves.

Organize the voir dire questions around the following areas of inquiry:

1. Juror's Personal Background—These are standard questions which will be asked in nearly every case to fill in any data not discovered in the advance investigation.
2. Juror's Acquaintance with Trial Participants—Use to rule out prejudice or bias arising from a juror's personal association with any party, witness, attorney, firm, or judge.
3. Past Experience as Juror, Witness, or Litigant—Use to discover previous courtroom experience, and favorable or unfavorable effects on the juror's attitude.
4. Juror's Willingness and Ability to Be Fair and Objective—Use to weed out the "know-it-all" or the maverick who has his own ideas about the law.
5. Juror's Familiarity with the Case Subject Matter—Use in a case which has received extensive publicity or involves a public figure and also to discover a juror's expertise in a particular technical field.
6. Juror Attitudes on Specific Issues—Tailor these questions to the specific issues in your case (see §§ **6.27–6.43**).

§ 6.27 —Sample Questions: Juror's Personal Background

These are standard questions which will be asked in nearly every case to fill in any data not discovered in the advance investigation.

1. What is your occupation?
2. (If retired) What was your former occupation?
3. Are you involved in law enforcement?
4. Are you married?
5. Is your spouse employed?
6. Do you have any children?

7. Have you always lived in this community? If not, where else have you lived?
8. Have you served in the military?
9. Have you ever been convicted of a crime?

§ 6.28 —Sample Questions: Juror's Acquaintance with Trial Participants

Use to rule out prejudice or bias arising from a juror's personal association with any party, witness, attorney, firm, or judge.

1. Do any of you know any of the trial participants?
2. Do you have any relationships—business, social, or family—with any of these persons?
3. (Introduce counsel) Have you ever had any professional, business, or social relationships with the attorney (or the attorney's firm) representing the opposing party?
4. (Name lawfirms) Are you acquainted with any of the attorneys in these firms, or with any employees or other person affiliated with these offices or any members of their families?

§ 6.29 —Sample Questions: Past Experience as Juror, Witness, or Litigant

Use to discover previous courtroom experience, and favorable or unfavorable effects on the juror's attitude.

1. Have any of you ever served on a jury before?
2. If yes: Was it a criminal or civil case? Was a verdict reached? For plaintiff or defendant? What kind of case?
3. Can you disregard your previous experience or involvement for the purpose of deciding this case?
4. Have any of you testified as a witness in any case? If yes: For plaintiff or defendant? What kind of case?
5. Have any of you ever been plaintiffs or defendants in a lawsuit? Have you ever sued anyone? Have you ever been sued by someone else? What kind of case?

§ 6.30 —Sample Questions: Juror's Willingness and Ability to Be Fair and Objective

Use to weed out the "know-it-all" or the maverick who has his own ideas about the law.

1. The court will instruct you that (anticipated instruction of the court on application of the law). If the court tells you to do so, will you follow that instruction?
2. (Explain reading depositions into evidence or showing videotaped depositions). Can you weigh such testimony equally with that of the live witnesses?
3. Do you feel you can give my client the same consideration that you give the opposing party in judging this case?
4. Will you be able to follow the law as the court gives it to you, even if you have a personal opinion or belief to the contrary?
5. Do any of you have personal problems at home which would prevent you from giving your full attention to the case?
6. Do any of you have any physical, mental, or other disabilities (such as vision or hearing problems) that would prevent you from sitting and hearing the case?
7. Is there anything I have failed to ask you, or anything else which you think should be disclosed which would affect your sitting on this case?

§ 6.31 —Sample Questions: Juror's Familiarity with the Case Subject Matter

Use in a case which has received extensive publicity or involves a public figure and also to discover a juror's expertise in a particular technical field.

1. Have you heard or read anything about this case?
2. Do any of you have an interest in the outcome of this lawsuit?
3. You will be sworn by the court to try the case upon the facts presented in the courtroom and nothing else. Can you lay aside any misinformation or preconceptions which you may receive from any other source and try the case solely on the facts and the testimony you hear from the witnesses?
4. If the case involves a claim against a member of a particular profession, (physician, engineer, and so forth): Do you have any training or expertise in this area?

§ 6.32 Juror Attitudes on Specific Issues

Tailor these questions to the specific issues in your case.

The following sections contain sample questions for the following types of cases:

§ 6.33	Automobile Accident;
§ 6.34	Accident/Injury/Wrongful Death;
§ 6.35	Medical or Pharmacy Malpractice;
§ 6.36	Insurance;
§ 6.37	Corporate/Company Identification; Corporate (Defendant);
§ 6.38	Monetary Awards;
§ 6.39	Real Estate/Landlord-Tenant;
§ 6.40	Will or Trust (Probate);
§ 6.41	Banking;
§ 6.42	Defense;
§ 6.43	Products Liability.

§ 6.33 —Sample Questions: Automobile Accident

1. Do you drive a car? Have you ever been cited for a traffic violation? Do you have points on your license? Any restrictions? Ever had license suspended or revoked?

2. Have you ever been involved in an auto accident?

3. Have you ever witnessed an automobile accident?

4. Are you familiar with the location of the incident (accident)?

5. (Feeling about company car): Is a company responsible for people who drive its company vehicles? Should a company be held responsible if it allows an unfit person to drive its vehicles?

6. Do you have elderly relatives? How would you feel about telling them not to drive or preventing them from driving? What is your position on the issue of elderly drivers?

7. Are you involved with automobile maintenance or repair?

8. Do you wear your seatbelt when you drive?

9. How do you feel about the use of alcohol? (Some people are so completely prejudiced against the use of alcohol that if one of the parties is drinking, they will find against that party even when the alcohol had no bearing on the accident.)

§ 6.34 —Sample Questions: Accident/Injury/Wrongful Death

1. Have you or anyone in your family (or anyone close to you) ever been in an automobile (or other type) of accident? Slip and fall?
2. Have you ever had a loved one injured or killed in an accident?
3. Have you suffered any psychological injuries or neuroses (trauma) resulting from an accident? Have you ever had to seek professional help for psychological injuries?
4. Any preexisting injuries? Aggravated by a later trauma?
5. Do you have any feeling against suits brought to recover compensation for personal injuries caused by the fault of another?
6. Do you believe you can listen to medical testimony and that of other persons regarding the effect of the injuries upon [party] and translate that fairly into a monetary verdict?
7. Have you ever had to care for an injured or disabled person?
8. Have you ever been hospitalized?
9. (Sympathy—widowed spouse and children): Have you been widowed or orphaned?

§ 6.35 —Sample Questions: Medical or Pharmacy Malpractice

1. How do you feel about doctors in general? Any complaints about doctors? Pharmacies? Hospitals?
2. Are you related to any persons who are physicians or other health care providers? (Nurses, dentists, pharmacists) Medical health field? Pharmaceutical industry? Do you own stock in any drug companies?
3. Have you ever been treated by Dr. _______ or his/her associates (or at ____ hospital)?
4. Have you ever filed a claim or suit against a pharmacy or a doctor (or a hospital)?
5. (Pharmacy): Are you on any medication (for example, Valium)?
6. Have you ever had prescriptions filled at a pharmacy?

§ 6.36 —Sample Questions: Insurance

1. Have you ever worked for an insurance company?
2. Are you related to or do you have friends who are insurance adjusters or work for an insurance company?

3. Do you own stock in an insurance company?
4. Have you ever made a large claim against an insurance company? If so, what were the circumstances?

§ 6.37 —Sample Questions: Corporate/Company Identification

1. Are you involved in a family business?

   (Corporate Defendant):
2. Does anyone feel that big corporations have greater rights than individuals?
3. Will the fact that the ______ company is not an individual person but a company affect your ability to treat it in this case just as you would the (plaintiff/defendant)?
4. People have a natural tendency to feel automatic sympathy for a person who has been injured, especially when the defendant is a company instead of an individual. Can you put aside your feelings of sympathy in listening to the evidence, and in reaching your verdict treat both the plaintiff and the defendant equally?
5. Have you ever done business with [company]? If so, were you pleased with the service received? Was there a complaint about the service/product? Was it resolved to your satisfaction? Even if not, can you treat both parties equally for the purpose of deciding this case?
6. Have you ever owned stock in [company]? Do you own stock in any corporation?

§ 6.38 —Sample Questions: Monetary Awards

1. Is a person entitled to compensation just because they filed a lawsuit and it goes to court?
2. How do you feel about a person being compensated for pain from an injury? Can you return a verdict for a monetary amount?
3. The claim on behalf of [party] for serious injuries is in the amount of $__________. This may seem to be a large amount, and it is within the jury's power to return a verdict in any smaller amount or even a greater amount if it finds for the plaintiff. Do you understand that the question of the amount of compensation is for the jury to determine?
4. If you find that [plaintiff's] injuries are serious enough to require a verdict for the full amount which he/she seeks, are you willing to return a verdict for the full amount of compensation which you find the plaintiff should receive?

5. If you find from the greater weight of the evidence and the court's instructions that the verdict for [plaintiff] should be $_________ or more (high amount), will you willingly sign a verdict for that amount?
6. Are you willing to assess the amount of compensation for intangible losses such as suffering, limitation of ordinary activities and other non-financial injuries, as well as for out-of-pocket expenses?

§ 6.39 —Sample Questions: Real Estate/Landlord-Tenant

1. Are you familiar with the locations of the properties involved in this lawsuit?
2. Have you ever sold or bought real estate? Do you have any experience in managing real estate, or familiarity with appraisal of real estate and market value?
3. Have you ever rented a house or apartment? Did you have any involvement with landlord/tenant problems?
4. What is a listing agreement? What does it mean if a property is listed and can't be sold?

§ 6.40 —Sample Questions: Will or Trust (Probate)

1. Do you have a will? What is your understanding of the legal effect of that will?
2. Do you know what a trust is?
3. Have you ever been beneficiary of a will or trust?
4. Have you ever been executor or administrator of an estate or trust?

§ 6.41 —Sample Questions: Banking

1. Are you related to bank examiners or anyone who works in a bank?
2. Do you bank at [name of bank]? Have you ever been refused credit or a loan? Have you ever been sued by a bank?
3. What do you think about banks in general? Any complaints about banks?
4. If a bank is a defendant, do you think that because they have a lot of money they should pay something, whether or not they did anything wrong?
5. If a bank is sued, would you be able to return a verdict in favor of the bank?

§ 6.42 —Sample Questions: Defense

1. Are you willing to require the plaintiff to prove that my client was the wrongdoer?
2. If you determine that the plaintiff was injured of her own doing, will you return a verdict for my client?
3. If you determine that the plaintiff knew or should have known of the condition which she claims caused her injury and still persisted in her conduct which caused her injury, will you return a verdict for my client?
4. Do any of you believe that every injury should be compensated regardless of how the injury occurred?

§ 6.43 —Sample Questions: Products Liability

1. Have you ever used [the product]?
2. Have you bought other products from that manufacturer?
3. Have you ever returned a defective product under warranty?
4. Have you ever been injured by a product that did not work properly?

§ 6.44 Helping the Attorney Evaluate Potential Jurors

Voir dire is the first chance for communication between the attorney and the jurors. The attorney will elicit answers from the jurors which indicate how they are likely to behave in deciding the case. In the courtroom, two kinds of communication take place. Besides giving verbal answers to the questions, the jurors will convey information about themselves through nonverbal communication. Keen observation of the jurors' appearance and body language can reveal important clues about their personalities and attitudes.

§ 6.45 —Observing the Jurors

You can help the attorney observe the jurors as they enter the courtroom and as they react and respond to questioning during voir dire. The attorney will be concentrating on the questioning process, usually focusing on one juror at a time, and so may not be able to discern the subtle clues conveyed by the jurors' nonverbal behavior. A second observer can greatly assist in picking up on other jurors' reactions to a particular question or response. The old saying "Two heads are better than one" is particularly true in visual assessment of the jurors.

As the jurors come into the courtroom, certain obvious characteristics will be readily apparent, such as:

- Race
- Gender
- Approximate age
- A limp or other obvious physical handicap
- A cast or bandage indicating an injury
- A hearing aid or thick glasses.

Watch the way the jurors walk, stand, and sit. A straight, upright posture indicates a confident person, while a slouched posture may reveal a submissive or nervous person.

Note the way they are dressed. The quality and type of clothing a person wears conveys significant nonverbal messages. The same is true for jewelry, accessories, and hair styling. For example, a juror wearing an expensive suit is likely to be a professional person and thus could be expected to be fairly sophisticated. Extremely casual clothing may indicate that this person does not take this obligation very seriously.

During the voir dire questioning, pay attention to the body language exhibited by each juror. A person who sits facing forward with arms relaxed and feet on the floor is conveying an interested, open attitude, but one who sits with head or shoulders turned sideways and with crossed arms or tightly clasped hands tends to convey tension or fear. Note whether they are paying attention, whether they appear to be interested or bored, whether they are sleeping, whether they are willing to make eye contact with the attorneys, and so on. Nodding in agreement with another juror's comment or frowning in disagreement or confusion are behaviors which are readily observable. Certain nervous mannerisms such as tapping fingers, clasping and unclasping hands, and crossing arms or legs can tell you something about the juror's level of comfort or discomfort with a particular question.

Some aspects of the jurors' personalities and qualifications can be determined only through their spoken responses to specific questions posed by the attorneys. However, you may be able to pick up clues based upon the person's voice: a heavy accent may indicate geographic background; a very soft voice may indicate shyness; an extremely loud voice may indicate an overbearing person, and so on. When verbal and nonverbal responses send mixed signals, the nonverbal communication is usually more reliable because it is subconscious behavior.

Note any characteristics of this type on the jury information grid, along with particularly relevant answers to the voir dire questions. These observations can provide valuable input to the attorney in his or her overall evaluation of the jurors.

§ 6.46 —Taking Notes During Voir Dire

During voir dire, check off questions as they are asked by other counsel, so that questioning doesn't get repetitious. Fill in information on the grid as the jurors answer questions, either singly or in groups. While the attorney is questioning the jurors, observe and take notes unobtrusively. Sit where you can see the faces of the jurors. (See § **6.12** on courtroom logistics; see also § **6.51** *et seq.* on taking notes at trial.)

§ 6.47 —Deciding Which Jurors to Eliminate

When the questioning and observation process is concluded, the attorney must decide whether to exercise the right to challenge any juror. Provide the attorney with your input based on observations of the jurors during voir dire. The decision on which jurors to eliminate from the panel depends on the type of case, the side of the controversy you represent, and the attorney's preferences.

§ 6.48 —Keeping Track of Challenges

There are two types of challenges the attorney may use to eliminate jurors who appear unsympathetic or biased: (1) challenges for cause, and (2) peremptory challenges.

A juror may be challenged for cause when responses elicited in the questioning process reveal that the juror is clearly prejudiced or biased, and it is obvious that he is unable to render a fair and impartial verdict. These types of challenges are unlimited in number. Statutory grounds for challenge for cause include, among others

- Jurors who have an interest in the outcome of the particular case;
- Jurors who have a business, family, or professional relationship to any party, attorney, or witness in the case; and
- Jurors whose answers disclose they are not willing to follow the law of the case.

Peremptory challenges, which are usually limited in number, may be exercised without stating a reason or explanation. The attorney uses this type of challenge to eliminate a juror who, for whatever reason, the attorney thinks would not be sympathetic to his case.

As each side exercises challenges, keep track of the jurors eliminated, whether through challenges for cause or peremptory challenge, and cross through the names of those jurors on your data grid.

§ 6.49 —Preparing a Jury Box Diagram

Once the jurors have been selected, prepare a chart of the jury box with the names of the jurors, and any particularly pertinent information about them. The final composition of the jury panel lets the attorney know the general nature of his or her audience and allows him or her to incorporate this knowledge into the trial presentation strategy.

As the trial proceeds, continue to observe the jurors and note their nonverbal reactions to various activities in the courtroom. In a trial which lasts several days, your observations can assist the attorney in gauging the impact, either positive or negative, of certain testimony. He or she can then defuse any particularly damaging evidence by confronting it in his closing argument; likewise, he or she can emphasize favorable evidence.

§ 6.50 Using an Expert to Assist in Jury Selection

You may be involved in trials in which the issues are so complex or the subject matter so volatile that choosing a jury requires the assistance of an expert trained in psychology. The attorney may ask you to prepare an outline of the issues in the case for the expert to analyze. The expert can assist the trial team in determining the characteristics of the ideal juror for the case and in developing specific questions to elicit the desired information from jurors. The expert may be allowed to sit in the courtroom and observe the voir dire procedure and subsequently give feedback to the attorney before the challenges are made.

You may be asked to perform the following tasks:

- Locate the expert
- Coordinate pretrial meetings with the expert
- Compile a narrative of the case issues
- Generally act as liaison between the expert and the attorney

- In the courtroom, you may have to relay the expert's opinions to the attorney as to the qualifications of individual jurors.

(See § **3.19** *et seq.* on working with experts.)

§ 6.51 Observing and Documenting the Trial

As a trial paralegal, you are in a unique position to observe the jurors, witnesses, judge, and opposing counsel. While the attorney is occupied with his or her responsibilities, you will have an opportunity to watch the reactions of the jurors and the opposing counsel as the attorney presents the case. By staying alert and observing the trial activities, you may be able to give the attorney valuable feedback for more effective presentation of the case. For example, suppose the jurors seem to be having trouble hearing the attorney or the witness. The attorney may be concentrating so hard on the witness that he or she does not notice this. The jurors cannot decide a case properly if they do not hear all the testimony, so you should let the attorney know if you think the jurors cannot hear what is being said. Likewise, you may be able to gauge the jurors' reactions to some particularly damaging testimony from the witness stand. Sit where you can see and hear everything in the courtroom (see § **6.13** on courtroom seating arrangements).

One of the most valuable ways you can support the attorney in the courtroom is by observing, taking notes, and documenting events as they actually occur during the trial. An accurate record of the trial events can be enormously helpful in reconstructing the case for posttrial work or analysis. Your daily trial record, which functions as a comprehensive outline or diary of the case proceedings, will basically consist of

- Your notes
- Scheduling block sheets
- Daily exhibit logs
- Other logs and forms you use to record and organize the trial information.

In any trial lasting more than two or three days, the events will seem to run together, and you can easily become confused when you try to remember exactly what took place. As the attorney plans oral or written arguments in the later stages of the trial, he or she will need to know the dates and the exact order of the events earlier in the trial. As in the voir dire process, the attorney will be busy handling the trial questioning and may only have time to take a few brief notes, if any. In some very large trials daily transcripts will be available from the court reporter, but this is not usually the case. In the majority of cases, in order to review what has transpired during the day's trial proceedings, attorneys must rely on their memories and, of course, on notes and documentation kept by a capable legal assistant.

Your comprehensive trial documentation helps the attorney assess exactly what the jury has heard during the trial presentation. Before the close of your case, review your notes with the attorney to make sure that all of the evidence has been presented and that he or she has not inadvertently left out some important piece of information. Your notes can also help the attorney to study the overall picture of the opponent's case as it was presented to the jury. Many times a seemingly insignificant event during the trial turns out to be important in retrospect, especially when preparing for

- Rebuttal
- Closing arguments
- Posttrial briefs
- Appeal.

§ 6.52 —Taking Good Trial Notes

Use these suggestions to help you develop your notetaking skills.

1. Keep all your trial notes on the same tablet, pad, or notebook. Always carry extra tablets in case you fill up the first one. Leave one or two blank pages at the front of the pad to cover your notes when you have to leave them unattended. Use the type of paper you prefer, but be sure to have a rigid backing to support your writing surface, especially if you are not able to sit at a table but have to balance the tablet in your lap while you write. Use a clipboard to give you a firm writing surface.
2. Always date your notes and indicate the starting and ending time of each segment, including time taken for breaks or for lunch. Mark the date and time on each page. On a busy trial day when several witnesses testify, having the times in your notes will help you reconstruct the day's proceedings.
3. Use paper with a vertical rule down the page (like the standard yellow legal pad) for notes on witness testimony. Use a question and answer format similar to a page of deposition transcript. Write your notes on the right-hand side of the rule and use the left column to note such things as times, dates, exhibit numbers, objections, and so forth. When you review your notes, insert categories, main topics, and key words into the left-hand column. By doing this type of "diagramming," you give your notes instant clarification and make it easier to locate a note on any specific topic.

4. You can incorporate a bit of color-coding into your notetaking (see § 2.85). Use two contrasting colored pens and switch pens each time the proceedings change from direct to cross-examination, for example. Or, use a red pen to highlight objections or other significant notations.
5. Write as legibly as possible. Always have extra pens available in case yours runs out of ink.
6. Unless you are a whiz at shorthand (most of us are not) it is virtually impossible to take verbatim notes on every word spoken in the courtroom. You must listen carefully and be a selective note taker. Use consistent abbreviations for plaintiff, defendant, lengthy company names, and so forth. Develop your own set of "shorthand" notations.
7. Note any questions interjected by the court and the responses to those questions by the witness.
8. Note when any exhibits are marked or referred to by the witness.
9. Review your notes at the end of each trial day, while the testimony is still fresh in your mind. If anything is unclear, go back through your notes and fill out any sketchy areas. Highlight any items or admissions by the witness you think are particularly significant.
10. If the attorney takes any trial notes, date them, number the pages, and staple them together so they will stay in order. Review them to determine any important points the attorney noted. Keep all the trial notes together in a labeled folder so they will be handy whenever the attorney needs to review them.

§ 6.53 Opening Statements

Listen carefully to each party's opening statement. The purpose of the opening statement is to briefly introduce the facts and communicate the main theme of the case to the jury. The opening statement should be a concise account of the facts and issues involved in the case. Counsel will have already learned much about the opposing party's case during the discovery phase. However, the precise elements which the opposing counsel chooses to include in the opening statement will give some indication of the strategy he or she intends to use. By noting the major points covered by each party in the opening statements, you will be able to informally outline the case to be presented. Use the following checklist as a guide to what you should look for in opening statements.

Checklist: Opening Statements: Important Things to Look For

____ 1. Primacy.

Pay attention to the order in which the main points are mentioned in the opening statement. It is usually significant which points the attorney chooses to present first and last, since these are the items juries are the most likely to remember.

____ 2. What the parties will prove.

Listen for statements indicating what each party intends to prove. These statements may be prefaced by phrases such as "The evidence will show . . ." or "You will hear testimony which will prove . . ." or "We will prove . . . ." Learn to recognize such phrases as promises of evidence which counsel intends to produce to prove the client's case. If a party says something in the opening statement which he fails to prove during the presentation of his case, the opposing attorney will want to mention that deficiency in his or her closing argument. Use your opening statement notes as a check to see if each party accomplished what it promised to prove.

____ 3. Witnesses.

Listen as each attorney mentions the witnesses he or she will call and the subjects about which each witness will testify. The attorney's characterization of his or her client or a witness may give some insight as to how the attorney wants the jury to see that client or witness. Take particular note of any mention of expert witnesses and the description of the points the expert's testimony will support.

____ 4. Exhibits or physical evidence.

Note any specific evidence or exhibits the attorney promises he or she will produce to support the case.

____ 5. Damages.

Listen for mention of monetary damages, especially exact dollar figures. Note any itemization of the components of damages (money, expenses, pain and suffering) and any mention of the method by which the damages are being calculated.

____ 6. Weaknesses or negative aspects.

Counsel for a party whose case has negative aspects or weaknesses will often admit those problems to the jury in the opening statement with the intention of lessening the impact of those negative facts later on in the trial. (These areas may also have been brought out during the voir dire procedure.) Note particularly any problem areas discussed by your adversary as these may be the points your side will want to emphasize during your trial presentation.

____ 7. Omissions.

Note any glaring omissions of major facts. Such an omission could possibly be an oversight, but it might also give a clue as to the theory or strategy of the opposing counsel. What the opponents leave out could be as significant as what they leave in.

Practice Tip: Get a transcript of the opening statements. Make arrangements early in the trial to have the court reporter transcribe the opening statements of both parties. Being able to review the actual transcript can give you a tactical advantage as the case develops, especially in preparing for closing arguments. Let the court reporter know shortly after the beginning of the trial that you need these transcripts. If the court reporter can transcribe the opening statements at his or her convenience, you can avoid paying for expedited transcription service.

§ 6.54 Witness Testimony

Start a new page of notes for each witness. Put the name of the witness, the date, and the start time at the time of the sheet. The time is important because the attorney may want to know later exactly how long the witness was on the stand. Mark the time on your scheduling block sheet as well (see § **6.61**).

Most direct examinations begin with a few general background questions to identify the witness, where he resides, what he does for a living, and so on. The examining attorney will then go on to develop one or more areas specifically pertaining to the facts of the case. The examining attorney may also introduce exhibits or documents about which he or she will ask the witness.

Observe the body language and mannerisms of the witness. Does the witness look directly at the jurors when he answers? Does he make eye contact with the attorney? Does he seem nervous? Does he appear to be telling the truth? Do the responses seem spontaneous, or do they seem forced, as if the witness has been coached? Try to evaluate the impression the witness is making on the jury. Are the jurors paying attention? Do they seem to like this witness? Do they nod in sympathy or understanding? Note any remarks made by the witness which seem to particularly affect the jurors, such as those which evoke a verbal response (gasp, chuckle) or a nonverbal response (raised eyebrows, smirks, tears).

If the person testifying is your party's witness, you will probably have a general idea of the questions the attorney intends to ask. The attorney may have prepared an outline or plan for developing the witness examination, although he or she may not adhere strictly to the outline throughout the testimony. If you have an outline or witness sheet (see § **5.83**) follow the examination and check off questions as the attorney asks them. Be prepared to hand the attorney any exhibits for this witness at the appropriate time.

Listen closely to the cross-examination questions. If the person testifying is the opposing party's witness, try to determine what information the attorney is trying to elicit. You may be familiar with interrogatory answers or deposition testimony given by the witness during discovery. Listen for any answers which are inconsistent with the ones given in discovery. If a cross-examining attorney uses a discovery document (such as an excerpt from a deposition transcript or an interrogatory answer) to impeach a witness, note the page and line number or question number of the discovery item in your trial notes.

§ 6.55 —Expert Witness Testimony

Pay close attention to technical explanations by the expert witness, as well as conclusions and opinions expressed. Note the various materials the expert reviewed and the factors he or she considered in arriving at those opinions.

§ 6.56 Noting Counsel's Objections

Note the objections made by counsel for either side, the basis for the objection, and the judge's ruling on each. Counsel will make objections to preserve them for the record, and these could be very significant if the case is appealed.

§ 6.57 Noting Depositions Read into Evidence

If any depositions are read into the record in lieu of live testimony, note the deponent's name, pages, and lines read. If possible, highlight a copy of the deposition transcript to indicate the portions read into the record.

§ 6.58 Keeping Track of Exhibits

Keep a daily log of exhibits introduced into evidence. Note the name of the witness, the exhibit designation, and a brief description of the exhibit on the exhibit index or log. Note when any exhibit is mentioned or discussed by any witness, even if that witness was not the person who initially authenticated the exhibit. At the close of each party's case, use the index to keep track of which exhibits are admitted into evidence (see **§ 6.65** *et seq.* on managing trial exhibits).

§ 6.59 Preparing for Closing Arguments

The closing argument or summation is the attorneys' last chance to reinforce impressions about the evidence upon the minds of the jurors before they deliberate. The closing will be shaped to some degree by the opening statements and the way the evidence is developed during the presentation of the case. The closing is a summary and review of the evidence presented during the course of the trial.

During the trial, your supervising attorney may mention certain documents, key points, key statements in testimony, which should be included in the closing. Whenever the attorney mentions something like this, put a note or a copy of the document in a folder marked "Closing Argument." The attorney may want some last minute blowups of key documents or excerpts of the testimony to use as demonstrative exhibits in the closing. Arrange to have the opening statements transcribed for the attorney's review in preparing the closing argument (see § **6.53,** Practice Tip).

§ 6.60 Working with the Court Reporter at Trial

These are some things you can do to make the court reporter's life easier:

1. Compare your daily list of exhibits with the court reporter's list. The court reporter will generally keep all documents and exhibits which have already been introduced in the trial.

2. Wherever portions of deposition transcripts are read into the record, provide the court reporter with an extra copy of the transcript, clearly marked with the portions read, so that he or she will not have to record it but can merely insert it into the record. (This is assuming a stipulation and consent by the judge that the reporter does not have to reenter the portions read.)

3. Assist the court reporter with the correct spellings of names, technical terms, and so forth, to help the reporter in preparing an accurate record of the trial.

4. Be as specific as possible when requesting transcripts of portions of the trial proceedings. Tell the court reporter the name of the witness, the exact date and time the testimony took place, and so on. Give the court reporter as much lead time as possible to prepare the transcripts, and make sure the bill is paid promptly.

§ 6.61 Planning and Scheduling Trial Witnesses

Use this simple chart (see **Form 6–6**) to help you visualize and plan the approximate order and scheduling for your trial witnesses. You can also use this form during the trial to track the actual progress of the trial as part of your documentation (see § **6.51** *et seq.*).

Some of the scheduling will be beyond your control because it is set by the court (holidays, voting days, and so forth, when there is no court in session). You have to schedule your trial presentation around these dates. Other scheduling is flexible, depending on the trial team's presentation strategy. To use the scheduling form:

1. Fill in calendar dates (Oct. 11, 12, 13, and so forth)
2. Block off holidays, voting days, judge's scheduled call days, and so forth when no court will be in session.
3. Number the remaining trial days (Trial Day #1, #2, #3, and so forth)
4. Block in the approximate hours for each day (usually 9:00 A.M.–4:30 P.M.). Include time for a lunch break, and morning and afternoon recesses.
5. Plan blocks of time for the various stages of the trial:
   - Pretrial activities (motions, and so forth)
   - Voir dire (1/2 day to ???)
   - Opening statements
   - Plaintiff's case—direct and cross-exam of individual witnesses (number varies with each case)
   - Defendant's case—direct and cross-exam of individual witnesses
   - Rebuttal, if any
   - Closing arguments
   - Jury charge
6. Fit the remaining available time as closely as possible to the witnesses you plan to call. Use the list of points to discuss with the attorney to determine the approximate time you will need for each witness (see § **6.62** on scheduling considerations for trial witnesses).

Witness scheduling never goes exactly as planned. Some witnesses will take more time than expected and others will take less. Leave some room for flexibility and be prepared to adjust the scheduling as the trial progresses. Assess your progress at the end of each trial day and plan for the next day's witnesses. After the conclusion of the trial, it is always interesting to compare the planned schedule with your notes on what actually happened during the trial.

FORM 6–6
TRIAL SCHEDULING & PLANNING SHEET

TRIAL SCHEDULING & PLANNING SHEET

CASE: ____________ COURT: ____________ TRIAL DATE: ____________

MONDAY	TUESDAY	WEDNESDAY	THURSDAY	FRIDAY	SATURDAY
A.M.	A.M.	A.M.	A.M.	A.M.	A.M.
P.M.	P.M.	P.M.	P.M.	P.M.	P.M.

Within the strategic framework of the trial presentation, your goal in scheduling witnesses should be to fill up the right amount of court time each day without going too long past the normal daily adjournment time. This means a balance between having enough witnesses ready to testify without making witnesses wait all afternoon only to tell them they have to come back in the morning. If you have to choose, err on the side of having the witnesses ready and waiting. Few things are more embarrassing to the trial attorney than lamely telling the judge at 2:15, "That's all we had planned for today, your honor"; or "The witness isn't here yet" for a witness you scheduled at 3:30.

Try not to keep witnesses waiting to testify any longer than necessary, and hold them over to the next day only if absolutely necessary (see §§ **5.10,** *et seq.* on preparing trial subpoenas). If you have to bring a witness back for a second day of testimony, try to break for the afternoon at a logical place in the testimony. If possible, it is best to stop for the day on a dramatic note or at a high point in the testimony that you want the jurors to remember. An exception to the previous admonition is that you may WANT to break up long, dry, complex testimony for the benefit of the jury and the witness. Spreading the testimony over two days could be beneficial if you want to review, reiterate, or reinforce the previous day's testimony at the start of the second day.

Try not to introduce critical complex technical testimony at the end of the day. After the lunch break, some jurors may have a tendency to nod off and they do not give the testimony their full attention. Late in the afternoon, everyone is tired and anxious to go home for the day. Jurors are generally rested and more alert in the morning, so they are better able to absorb complex information early in the day.

Practice Tip: It is important to vary the pacing of the trial testimony to keep the jurors interested:

- Video depositions (you know the exact amount of time the playback will take)
- Reading deposition excerpts (estimate amount of time). Deposition reading is usually very dull and monotonous to the jurors. Keep it to a minimum; break them up (read them on different days) if you are using more than one. Prepare the materials and readers for the best reading.
- Depositions can be used to fill in time if the witness testimony did not take as long as expected.

§ 6.62 —Scheduling Considerations for Trial Witnesses

Discuss the points on this checklist with the trial attorney at one of your trial preparation agenda meetings (see § **2.9**) to determine the approximate amount of time you will need for your trial witnesses.

1. Review the points to be covered in testimony for each witness. Consider what the witness will add to the case. (See § **3.3** on evaluating trial witnesses.)
2. Estimate time needed to cover direct examination.
3. Add estimated time for cross-examination.
4. Determine who is flexible, who is locked in. (Be considerate of work schedules, school schedules, and so forth, for witnesses, as much as possible.)
5. You may have to schedule expert witnesses for a specific date (to work around other trial commitments, speaking engagements, and so forth)
6. Allow travel time for out of town witnesses. Local witnesses are generally available on short notice.
7. Consider whether any testimony will be presented via depositions (either regular or videotape). You can make a fairly accurate estimate of how long it will take to read the deposition or play the videotape.
8. Will you need to set up any visual aids or equipment for the witness? If so, try to schedule the witness at the beginning of the day or just after a break so you will have a chance to set up when the courtroom is empty.

§ 6.63 When Your Client Is a Witness

The strategic considerations for when to call your client as a witness will vary with different types of cases. It is best in some cases to present the client's testimony early in the trial, and then establish support for the client's testimony through corroboration and amplification by expert witnesses, family members, and friends. A very nervous client may be happy to get his or her testimony out of the way early, or the client may prefer to become acclimated to the courtroom before he or she testifies. Some trial presentation strategies will save the client's testimony for last in order to make a final strong impact on the jury. It may be necessary to take the client's testimony slightly out of the planned order if you need to fill in a time gap. The clients are present during the whole trial, so they are always available in a pinch, but if you have a choice, try to take the client's wishes into account.

§ 6.64 Dramatic Impact: Scheduling Strategies

These are some strategies to consider in planning the scheduling and order for your trial witnesses.

1. Bookending. A technique often recommended by trial experts is what I think of as "bookending;" that is, you begin and end the testimony with strong witnesses and put the others in between. This strategy is based on the theory that jurors retain the best recollection of the first and last testimony they hear. This technique works especially well when you have two good expert witnesses and you can schedule them first and last. Bookending also lends a sense of symmetry to the trial presentation, and can work to your advantage if you need to offset other less effective witnesses.

2. Stairstep. Another approach is to start with a routine background witness, then use successively stronger witnesses to build the case, finishing with your strongest witness who will make an important impression on the jury.

3. Stage setting. Start with a strong first witness to set the stage, and then use the other witnesses to support or fill in essential details. Some cases may require that a certain witness testify first to lay a foundation for the jury to understand the testimony of subsequent witnesses. With this approach, you should still try to finish with a fairly strong and likeable witness to create an effective and favorable last impression on the jury.

4. Showcasing. Another technique which works with some cases is to showcase a star witness in the middle of the trial, flanked by support and supplementary witnesses before and after. However, this approach is risky unless the witnesses after the star are able to keep the jury's interest and attention.

5. Chronological Framework. Some cases lend themselves to a strictly sequential presentation of the facts. For example, you might have a situation where a series of witnesses have all held the same job over different periods of time, or where one witness has deep background or historical knowledge and other witnesses can bring the information up to the present date.

§ 6.65 Managing Exhibits in the Courtroom

An important function of the trial paralegal is assisting the attorney in managing the trial exhibits in the courtroom. The trial attorney needs to have ready access to all the case documents and exhibits. A trial attorney's nightmare might include a scenario where the judge and jury are waiting impatiently while the attorney fumbles through folders or boxes trying to find a crucial document or item. Such a situation in a real courtroom is not only disruptive to the flow of the trial, but it can actually hurt the attorney's credibility with the jury. You can be invaluable to the attorney in the courtroom if you are familiar with the system by which the exhibits are organized.

A good system of organization incorporating detailed indexing and cross-referencing (see §§ **2.75–2.79**) is essential to the successful management of trial exhibits, but there is no single best method for organizing and controlling trial exhibits. Every case is different, and the system you use must be tailored to the requirements of the individual case. Here are a few pointers to keep in mind:

- The person who organized the system should be present in the courtroom to assist the attorney in locating exhibits for use at the proper time.
- The system must be flexible to accommodate the unexpected at trial.
- You must have sufficient copies of document exhibits for distribution in the courtroom (see § **5.65**).
- You must have a backup system for locating exhibits in case something gets mixed up or misfiled.

The method by which you organize and contain the exhibits for ease of handling and retrieval in the courtroom depends on several factors:

- What type of exhibits you have
- How many exhibits you have
- Your strategy in presenting the case
- What auxiliary equipment is required (such as an easel or an overhead projector).

§ 6.66 Methods of Physical Organization of Exhibits

This section will discuss handling paper exhibits (documents) in cases with a few hundred to a few thousand documents. (See § **5.58** *et seq.* on preparing exhibits for trial; see also § **6.78** for tips on handling nondocument exhibits.) These are some suggestions for various ways to physically organize the trial exhibits. These methods can be used either alone or in combination, depending on the needs of your case:

- By witness
- By date
- By issue or subject
- By type of document
- By sequence of use

§ 6.67 —Organizing Exhibits by Witness

This method works best when there are numerous witnesses and a limited number of documents.

1. Use a separate folder for each witness, clearly labeled with the name of the witness.
2. Use either binders or folders (manila or expanding) to contain the documents. The size of the container depends on the number of documents which will be used with that witness.
3. Arrange the exhibit documents within each folder or binder in roughly the order you anticipate they will be used at trial. It may not be possible to put the exhibits into exact order, but refer to the attorney's outline or schedule for the order of witnesses to help you determine the approximate sequence of use for the exhibits. (See § **6.61;** see also § **5.63** on assigning exhibit designations.)
4. If an exhibit is to be used with more than one witness, place a copy of that exhibit in the folder or binder for each witness. (See § **5.8** on preparing files for the courtroom.)
5. Binders, folders, or labels could be color-coded (see § **2.85** on color-coding) to designate the following categories:
   —Plaintiff and Defendant Witnesses
   —Direct and Cross-examination
   —Expert or Lay Witnesses
   —Liability or Damage Witnesses
6. Arrange the folders or binders alphabetically by the last name of the witness.
7. Set aside any documents which are unrelated to a specific witness in a separate folder designated for general reference.

§ 6.68 —Organizing Exhibits by Date

This method is useful when the case lends itself to chronological presentation, tracing a series of events or transactions over a period of time.

1. The number of guides or divisions will depend on how many documents there are and how long a time span is represented (see § **2.1**).
2. Divide by year, by quarter (three-month period), by month, by week, or by day, if applicable
3. Use a separate folder for each time increment, clearly labeled with the beginning and ending dates included in the time increment.
4. Use either binders or the appropriate size folders, depending on how many documents are included in the individual time increment.
5. Color-coded labels can be used to designate the divisions between time increments, such as, one color for each year or one color for each month. (See § **2.85** on color-coding.)
6. Gather any undated documents into a separate folder and place it at the front of the exhibit folders.

(See also § **6.72** on preparing a chronological backup set of exhibits.)

§ 6.69 —Organizing Exhibits by Issue or Subject Matter

This technique works best when there are only a few witnesses but many exhibit documents.

1. Organize the exhibits into folders corresponding to the major case issues they support. Confer with the trial attorney if you are unsure about the individual issues.
2. This method requires some indication (on an index or a cross-reference list) of which witnesses are expected to testify about each subject or issue.
3. Defense tip: This type of organization can be useful when you are not sure which documents are going to be important in cross-examination of the plaintiff's witnesses.

§ 6.70 —Organizing Exhibits by Document Type

This method can be useful in a case where the documents naturally fall into logical groupings, for example, a series of contracts or amendments to contracts; batches of sequentially numbered forms, purchase orders, transaction slips, receipts, and so forth.

- Group similar documents together, and place them in folders labeled with the document type.
- Arrange each group numerically or chronologically within its folder.

§ 6.71 —Organizing Exhibits by Sequence of Use

Use this method, in which the documents are arranged in the approximate order you expect to use them during the trial, when the attorney plans to introduce a number of documents in the opening statement, or when the attorney has a clear plan for which documents will be used for direct and cross-examination of the witnesses.

- Make separate files or folders for each stage of the trial:
  —Opening Statement
  —Direct Examination (by witness)
  —Cross-Examination (by witness)
  —Rebuttal (by witness)
  —Closing Argument
- The folder labels could be color-coded, using a different color label for each stage of the trial. (See § **2.85** for more on color-coding.)

§ 6.72 —Organizing Master Exhibit Backup Sets

Backups By Number. No matter how carefully you organize the trial exhibits, you can never depend on the order of exhibits going exactly the way you planned it. You should always have a backup set or index to help you locate a particular exhibit in the event the witness testimony and the accompanying exhibits occur out of turn. The most useful backup set is one arranged by exhibit number or letter, or by document number, if you have consistently number stamped all the case documents as they were received. (See § **2.80** on numbering documents generally and § **5.63** on assigning trial exhibit designations.)

Backups By Date. Depending on the individual case, it is sometimes useful to have a set of exhibits arranged in strict chronological order, making it easy to find any particular exhibit if you know only the date of the document. (See also § **6.68.**)

§ 6.73 —Organizing Supplementary Exhibit Indexes, Lists, and Subsets

Supplementary Indexes, Cross-References, and Lists. Make up indexes or lists of various subsets, even if you do not physically arrange the documents into subsets. A computerized system (using either simple word processing or more complex database technology) can be invaluable in preparing indexes and cross-reference lists according to various criteria. (See **Chapter 8** on using computers in trial work.)

Supplementary Physical Subsets. If you have a reasonably small number of documents (less than 100), consider making multiple copies of the documents, then arranging one set by document number, one by witness, one by date, one by subject, one by type of document, and so on. This can be expensive for copies, but it ensures that the document can be found in any of the logical places you might look for it. Whether this is feasible will depend on how many documents you have. Supplementary lists and cross-reference indexes may have to suffice if the number of documents is very large. (See § **2.75** *et seq.* on indexing techniques; see also § **6.74** on handling large numbers of exhibits.)

§ 6.74 —Containing and Storing Exhibits During Trial

Once you have selected the trial exhibits and assigned identifying number or letter designations, you will need to decide upon the best way to contain and store the exhibits during the trial. There are two factors which will determine what type of container or containers you use to hold the exhibits: (1) the number of exhibits; and (2) the type of exhibits. These factors have to be considered together.

If you have a relatively small number of exhibits (one to 300) they can probably be contained in looseleaf binders, expanding folders, or a small number of boxes. However, document counts over a few hundred will require expanded storage space. Consider using cardboard storage drawers or sets of two-drawer cabinets made of corrugated cardboard, which come in either legal or letter size, to contain and transport your documents.

The trial attorney will need a reference set of exhibits at the office to use in preparing witnesses, preparing cross-examination, and so forth. It is always best to have a complete set of copies both in the courtroom and back at the office. This means you have to either carry the entire set of exhibits back and forth between your office and the courtroom, or make a duplicate set of trial exhibits (both plaintiff and defendant). If the exhibits can be contained in notebooks (even if there are several volumes), prepare a duplicate set of exhibits to keep at the office for reference purposes. You can then safely leave one set of exhibits in the courtroom overnight during the trial. (See § **5.74** on preparing trial exhibit notebooks.)

Label each set of exhibits clearly to indicate that one is the office copy, to remain in the trial preparation room at the office, and the other is the courtroom set, to be left in the courtroom. Note: Be sure to update both sets whenever new exhibits are added during the courtroom sessions. (See § **6.77,** Updating Exhibit Notebooks During Trial.)

§ 6.75 —Tips for Managing Large Volumes of Documents

If there are simply too many documents to duplicate easily or to cart back and forth daily, the judge may allow you to store the documents in boxes, file drawers, or cabinets in a room adjacent to the courtroom. However, a disadvantage with this system is that you may not be able to get to the documents after business hours, should you need them during the evening for witness preparation, and so on.

Questions about special exhibit storage requirements should be worked out with the judge and opposing counsel as part of the pretrial agenda. (See § **6.7** *et seq.* on handling pretrial matters.)

If the documents are stored in numerous boxes, file drawers, or cabinets, you must have an accurate index of what is contained in each and how they are arranged (alphabetical, numerical, chronological) so that you can locate any specific document within a few minutes' time.

§ 6.76 Tracking and Cross-Referencing the Opponent's Exhibits

In document-intensive cases, the opposing party's exhibits may include some of the same documents you have on your exhibit list. As soon as you receive a set of proposed trial exhibits from the opposing party, compare them with your set of exhibits in order to identify any duplicate exhibits. Use the index description as a guide for the preliminary comparison, but carefully examine each actual exhibit document in the opponent's set to determine whether it is exactly the same as your version. Watch out for small but significant differences in the documents, such as the following:

- Marginalia
- Missing pages
- Attachments or enclosures (either additional or missing ones)
- Signed or unsigned version (the same letter may have been in the files of several witnesses)
- Reduced or excerpted version of a full-size original document
- Clearer (or muddier) copy of the same original document.

If the opposing party's exhibit is identical to your exhibit, simply note the duplicate by writing in the opponent's equivalent exhibit designation on your cross-referencing index. If the exhibit presented by the opposing party is not exactly the same as the corresponding document on your list, note the differences on your cross-referencing index; for example, ("Same as Plaintiff's Ex. 12, except missing enclosures.") Slight differences between versions of the exhibit document may or may not be significant. Point them out so the attorney can decide whether to use the document from your set of exhibits or go with the opposing party's exhibit.

It is also useful to make a copy of the opposing party's exhibit index and indicate your corresponding exhibit designation in a column beside the opponent's exhibit designation. This way you have a cross-reference to duplicate exhibits on both exhibit indexes.

Unless the number of exhibits is prohibitive, make a duplicate of the opposing party's exhibit book to keep at the office for reference during the trial. This will reduce the load of items you have to transport back and forth from your office to the courtroom. Be sure to update the office reference set if any new exhibits are added during the course of the trial. (See § **6.77** on updating exhibit notebooks during trial.)

If each side has approximately the same number of exhibit documents, the parties may agree ahead of time to exchange two sets of exhibit notebooks so that each party has an office set and a courtroom set. If the parties have exchanged sets of exhibits before trial, just keep a list of documents used by opposing party. If not, keep a separate folder containing a copy of each exhibit document introduced by the opponent.

§ 6.77 Updating Exhibit Notebooks During Trial

It is an important part of the trial paralegal's job to keep the exhibit books and indexes updated (both plaintiff and defendant) as the trial progresses. Generally, the parties will exchange sets of proposed exhibits before the trial starts, but under certain circumstances (such as, oversight, stipulation that all deposition exhibit documents may be eligible as exhibits, different version of the same document, rebuttal exhibits, and so forth), exhibits may be added during the course of trial. The party introducing the additional exhibits should present them to opposing counsel (together with corresponding tabs and an updated index) the first thing in the morning on the day the exhibits will be used, or as soon as possible after the determination to add exhibits has been made. Take particular care to update all the notebooks or sets when new exhibits are added.

Use the grid form (see **Form 6–7**) as a checklist to make sure all the notebook sets are conformed. (See § **5.74** *et seq.* on exhibit notebooks.) List all the

FORM 6–7
EXHIBIT NOTEBOOK UPDATE TRACKING GRID

#	EXHIBITS ADDED	ATTORNEY'S SET 1.	OPPOSING COUNSEL'S SET 2.	JUDGE'S SET 3.	WITNESS SET 4.	COURT REPORTER'S SET 5.	CLIENT'S SET 6.	TRIAL PARALEGAL'S SET 7.	OFFICE REFERENCE SET 8.	9.	10.	11.	12.	13.	14.	15.

sets of exhibits in the spaces at the top of the form, then check off each one as you add the new exhibits. (See also § **5.58** on preparing exhibits for trial.)

§ 6.78 Labeling and Handling Nondocument Exhibits

The ideas previously covered pertain mainly to paper exhibits (documents). Additional handling, labeling, and storage problems can arise when your case involves exhibit items (three-dimensional objects) which are not standard-sized paper documents. It may take some imagination and creativity to handle these unusual exhibits, which could include the following:

- Small items (or sets of items)
- Very fragile items
- Large or oversized items
- Odd-shaped, very heavy, or bulky items
- "One-of-a-Kind" items.

The following are general goals and considerations in handling nondocument exhibits:

- Protect from loss or damage.
- Protect from light, heat, and moisture.
- Protect from breakage (glass) or spillage.
- Protect from dirt and fingerprints.
- Preserve to prevent deterioration.
- Preserve for specific effect (original container).
- Keep a set of items together.
- Aid in ease of transportation to the courtroom.
- Present a neatly organized appearance or display.
- Securely label for trial identification.

§ 6.79 —Guidelines for Special Exhibit Containers

1. Secure but Accessible. You will not want to seal the containers permanently for most exhibits because the witness may need to remove the object from its container to examine it. Therefore, make sure that the exhibit container can be securely closed, but can still be opened easily when necessary.

2. Size, Strength, and Weight Commensurate with Contents. The box, bag, or other container you choose to contain the exhibit must be sturdy enough to hold the weight of the physical evidence, but the container should not add any more weight or bulk of its own than is absolutely necessary. In other words, use the lightest weight and most streamlined container that will do the job.

3. Easily Identifiable. If your office uses standard transfer boxes or the brown "banker's boxes" for storage of regular case files, documents, and paper exhibits, choose a box for your special exhibit which is different in appearance from the other storage boxes in the case. Also, make sure that the special exhibit box is clearly labeled with the appropriate trial information so that it is not inadvertently thrown in the dumpster or otherwise mislaid by some well-meaning office mate or maintenance worker (see § **2.92** on labeling).

4. Neat Appearance. Do not use ratty looking boxes or dog-eared envelopes to contain your special exhibits. It is relatively inexpensive to purchase clean boxes or envelopes, and the effect on the jury in the courtroom will be one of organization and efficiency. **Caveat:** The original container could be effective in enhancing the item's authenticity during the witness examination. ("Are these the actual containers in which you kept the specimens?") In this situation, you would want to leave the exhibits in their original containers.

§ 6.80 —Tips for Containing Small Objects

- Small plastic bags with a reclosable strip at the top:
  Supplier/brand: "Handi-loc"™ bags made by
  The Angler's Group, Ltd.
  45-25 162nd Street
  Flushing, New York 11358-3157
  (718) 961-7744

  These thin, strong, transparent, resealable storage bags are watertight and dustproof and they have a white panel for writing on or affixing a label to identify the contents. They come in a wide variety of sizes to accommodate small items from 2 by 3 inches to 8 by 10 inches.

  Various sizes of plastic bags (such as, Glad "Zip-loc"™ storage bags) are available at the grocery store. These may not have the write-on panel, but you could substitute a self-adhesive label. (See § **2.92** on labeling.) Some of the bags made specially for freezer use do have write-on panels for labeling. Note: These little bags are also handy for storing some of the small items in your "Traveling Office Supplies" kit which you will take with you to trial (see § **5.89**).

- Multidrawer Organizer Cabinet

  If you have a number of very small objects, such as small tools or machine parts or fittings, consider getting a small cabinet with plastic drawers (such as the ones you might use in a home workshop) and place one item in each drawer. Then label the drawers so that you can easily identify their contents. If the parts or pieces look similar enough to each other that they could easily get mixed up, also attach a string-tag label to the actual item and clearly label both the tag and the drawer so that you are sure to replace the item in the correct drawer.

- Set of Small Tools or Other Items (where it is important to display the pieces of the set all together)

  —Use a piece of pegboard (or substitute foam-core board if the items are fairly lightweight) and attach by means of covered elastic cord threaded through the holes. Draw the shape of the tool (or label the board) so it is easy to put the item back in the correct place.

  —Attach a pocketed carpenter's apron to a sturdy piece of foam-core board. Put the items in the individual pockets.

§ 6.81 —Tips for Containing Medium-Sized Objects

- Labeled Box

  The storage box could be of an opaque material, such as corrugated cardboard, or of clear plastic, like the boxes you might buy to organize the shoes or sweaters in your clothes closet, depending on the desired effect. Depending on strategy, the trial attorney may want to keep the exhibit concealed until a certain point in the trial, or he or she may wish to have it in a transparent container so that it is in full view of the jury during the entire trial. It could be to your advantage to use a brightly colored box to draw attention to the contents of a particular box or to arouse the curiosity of the jurors. ("What's in that big red box?")

- Cardboard Shoe Organizer

  For exhibits which are long and narrow or cylindrical and which also may be fragile (such as glass jars or bottles, ceramic vases), corrugated cardboard shoe organizers are usually sold in discount stores or department stores. A bit of simple assembly is required. Turn the box on its back so the slots are at the top, and stand the items up in the slots.

- Plastic Bins or Baskets

  These inexpensive plastic organizers can be found in most discount and department stores. Many have handles for easy carrying and some styles come with matching lids. Use these bins "as is" for sturdy exhibits, or fit them with plastic or foam dividers to protect fragile exhibits.

§ 6.82 —Tips for Containing Oversized Exhibit Items

- Large, Flat Paper Items (such as plat maps, architect's drawings, or blueprints)
  —Roll up and place in cardboard mailing tubes.
  —Roll up, put a rubber band around the roll, and place in long, clear plastic bags (available at drafting supply stores).
  —Fold neatly and insert into plastic page protector which can be clipped into a three-ring binder.

Note: Label the outside or the back of the document and roll or fold it so that the label shows when it is rolled up. Label both sides of the documents if you have several which tend to look alike. (See also § **4.14** on copying oversized documents.)

- Illustration Boards or Charts
  —Wrap in brown mailing paper and tape or string.
  —Place two charts face-to-face and clip together with binder clips.
  —Use an artist's zippered vinyl portfolio with a handle for easy carrying.
  —Some office supply and art supply stores sell large paper portfolio envelopes with cord handles.

§ 6.83 Miscellaneous Exhibits

- X-ray Films or Photographic Enlargements
  —Protect in a large manila envelope or jacket
  —Use an artist's portfolio
  —Some office supply and art supply stores sell large paper portfolio envelopes with cord handles

- Automobile or Motorcycle Tire
  —Place in a large plastic trash bag to keep it from getting dirt on whoever has to carry it
  —Wrap in dry cleaning plastic

- Roll of Plastic Tubing (unwieldy item)
  —Roll into loops and fasten with plastic twist ties (the kind that come with trash bags)
  —Put in a clear plastic trash bag

- Very Bulky or Very Heavy Items
  —Use a dolly or similar wheeled cart to make transportation easier

- Storing Photographic Slides (see also § **4.44** on using photographic slides in trial work)
  —Use a "carousel" or a rectangular holder with slots designed to hold standard 3-by-3-inch slides. (Check photography or camera supply stores.)
  —Plastic sheet designed for a photo album page with slots to display standard slides.
  —Photo-mount corners attached to a lightweight cardboard sheet (inexpensive idea)

- Laboratory Slides (Glass or Plexi-glass™)
  —Use a small box (either matchbox-slide type or regular box with lid). Fit with a piece of styrofoam with slots cut to hold the slides.
  —Science and hobby shops have little cases designed specifically to hold lab slides and specimens.

- Test Tubes from Laboratory Tests (water samples, soil samples, and so forth)
  —Use a rack with holes slightly larger than the diameter of the vials so they will stand up and be held at the top. Check at a science or hobby store.
  —Put styrofoam strips or bubble packing between the vials so they do not clink together and break during transport.

- Glass (framed document or photograph)
  —Put in a box slightly larger than the frame; pad the box with bubble packing or a piece of foam-core board cut to fit the box.
  —Securely clip or fasten with rubber bands between two sheets of foam core board.

- Fragile Instrument (assembled or parts)

  Buy an inexpensive suitcase or briefcase. Fit with a double layer of thick foam rubber with cutouts to accommodate the various pieces (like a microscope or telescope carrying case.)

- Aerial Map with Acetate Overlays
  Custom built carrying crate with removable screws. Open with latches or a screwdriver; very sturdy.

- One-of-a-Kind Items (ankle brace or back corset brace)
  If the item is cloth or plaster, regular exhibit labels may not stick to it. Use an oak-tag label (looks like a pricetag with a string attached) and place the exhibit sticker on the tag. Use the string to tie the label onto the object.

§ 6.84 Daily Maintenance of Exhibits and Equipment

Use the daily trial exhibit log (see **Form 6–8**) to make a record of the trial exhibits introduced each day. (See § **6.58** on keeping track of exhibits.) This form will also help you record the court's rulings on admission of the various exhibits (see § **6.85**). Replace any unused exhibits back into their folders or boxes. Check with the court reporter at the conclusion of each trial day to make sure your list comports.

Keep track of all the equipment and other materials. Be sure to retrieve all equipment and materials from the courtroom if you have to change courtrooms during the trial (see § **2.92** on labeling trial equipment; § **4.64** on monitoring trial equipment). It may be helpful to inventory everything you brought to the courthouse: exhibit boards, portfolio, easels, boxes, exhibit books, briefcases, and so on, and check the actual equipment and materials against the inventory list each day. (See also § **6.12** on courtroom logistics.)

§ 6.85 Tracking the Court's Ruling on Exhibits

At the end of each party's case in chief, before the party rests its case, the court will rule on the admissibility of each exhibit offered into evidence. Some exhibits may have been listed on the original exhibit list but not actually used, so follow your daily exhibit log when the court considers the question of admissibility for the trial exhibits. Note the offer of the exhibit, any objection raised, and the court's ruling on whether the exhibit is admitted or denied (see **Form 6–8**).

After the court has completed its rulings, revise the index for your side's exhibits accordingly to omit any exhibits which were denied. If your index is on word processing equipment or on a database, simply edit the document or database report and reprint it. If the exhibit index is not on computer, use

FORM 6–8
TRIAL EXHIBIT LOG

TRIAL EXHIBIT LOG

Exhibit I.D.	Description	Offered	Admitted	Denied	Witness

correction tape or the cut-and-paste method to block out the description of any exhibits which the court denied, then copy the revised index. Before submitting the exhibit books to the jury for examination, compare the updated index to the actual exhibit notebooks and remove any exhibit documents not admitted, then insert a copy of the updated index into the front of the notebook.

§ 6.86 Tips to Facilitate Smoother Exhibit Handling

- If possible, obtain a stipulation with opposing counsel to use copies of exhibit documents. Leave the originals at the office for safekeeping, unless for some reason the original is absolutely required in court.
- If the trial witnesses will have to refer to or compare several thick documents (such as various drafts of a multipage contract) from the exhibit notebooks, prepare a separate set of loose (securely bound or stapled, however so they won't come apart) copies for the attorney to hand to the witness, so the witness will not have to fumble with large, bulky exhibit notebooks.
- If the witness will have to shift between heavy exhibit notebooks, try to place a table or platform next to the witness stand for the books to rest on. (See § **6.12** on courtroom logistics.)
- When the attorney uses blowups or document excerpts to emphasize specific wording (for example, changes in language from one draft of a contract to another), place a small copy of the document in the attorney's trial notebook with the language changes highlighted for easy reference. (See also § **5.77** on preparing the attorney's trial notebook.)
- Prepare and carry extra exhibit stickers (for both plaintiff and defendant) in case the attorney needs to add or change an exhibit designation.

CHAPTER 7

ASSISTING THE ATTORNEY IN POSTTRIAL ACTIVITIES

§ 7.1 Handling Posttrial Activities

Whether the trial concludes with a settlement, judgment, or verdict, a trial paralegal's job is not automatically finished at the conclusion of the courtroom proceedings. There are always arrangements and details that require attention after the trial, and in many cases there will be some type of formal posttrial activity such as motions or appeals. The checklist in **§ 7.2** outlines a timetable for posttrial activities.

§ 7.2 —Posttrial Activities

The following activities should be undertaken after trial.

____ Immediately After the Trial (Same Day):

- ____ Make sure the clients understand what occurred in the courtroom. Rejoice with them (if you won) or sympathize with them (if you lost). Either way, listen to them talk about how they are feeling and make sure they get the answers to their questions either from you or from the attorney.
- ____ Verbally thank any witnesses and support personnel at the courthouse or the office for their contributions to the trial.
- ____ Fill in details about the final day(s) of the trial activities on your indexes, charts, and forms while the events are still fresh in your mind.
- ____ Absorb the immediate comments and observations in your discussions with office colleagues about the outcome of the trial.
- ____ Talk to the attorney. Even if it's a brief conversation at this point (everyone will be tired), you need to touch base with the attorney about what posttrial activity, if any, you will pursue.

____ Within One to Five Days After Trial:

- ____ Collect all trial materials from the attorney's office before they get scattered.
- ____ Arrange for the return of rented or borrowed equipment.
- ____ Vacate the war room (see **§ 5.3**).
- ____ Stow case and trial preparation files in interim storage.
- ____ Take a short break to recharge your energy (see **§ 7.5**).
- ____ Continue to record thoughts and observations about the trial as they occur to you.

____ Within One to Two Weeks After Trial:

- ____ Discuss the trial with the attorney.
- ____ Prepare and file posttrial motions (see **§ 7.6**).
- ____ Send letters or notes of appreciation to experts, witnesses, and others who helped in the trial presentation. Don't forget clerks, secretaries, and other office personnel who pitched in to help you.

 ____ Conduct the posttrial jury inquiry (see § **7.58**).
 ____ Pay the bills (see § **7.35**).
 ____ Report trial results to jury research data services.

____ Three to Four Weeks After Trial (and sometimes later, depending on posttrial activity):

 ____ Process the appropriate accounting paperwork for your office and the court clerk (see § **7.34**).
 ____ Analyze the trial results (see § **7.57**).
 ____ Prepare and file the appeal, if any (see § **7.16**).
 ____ Close and store the files (see § **7.39**).
 ____ Archive samples of work product (see § **7.45**).

§ 7.3 Preserving Momentum When the Trial Is Continued

If you work as a trial paralegal for any length of time, you are bound to experience the frustration that occurs when you have all the materials ready, the arrangements made, the witnesses standing by and ready to go forward—and then the trial is suddenly continued to a later date! Last minute continuances can happen for a variety of reasons. Perhaps your civil case was bumped by a criminal case that took precedence on the court's calendar, or perhaps one of the parties or a key expert witness fell severely ill just before the trial was scheduled to begin. These things happen in the unpredictable world of litigation, and if you want to survive as a trial paralegal, you have to learn to turn an unexpected trial continuance into a positive experience.

Regardless of the subject matter of the litigation or the amount of work devoted to a trial's preparation, you will almost always feel like there just wasn't *quite* enough time to finish everything you had planned to accomplish before the courtroom presentation. When a trial is continued to a later date, consider it a reprieve that allows you a bit of extra time to complete those last few tasks on your "To Do" list.

It is important to keep up the momentum of the trial preparation, even if you felt you were completely prepared before the continuance was announced. Although the working pace will naturally slow down a bit, you cannot afford to let the trial team relax too much. At the very least, you will have to reschedule witnesses and other arrangements around the later trial date. Given a little more time, the case issues often will develop or change slightly. The trial team will have time to refine the trial strategy and further develop the good ideas generated during planning sessions the first time around. Other trial preparation tasks will crop up if more time is available, so there will still be plenty to do to get ready.

A continuation is merely a postponement, not a cancellation, and therefore it is very important to preserve the trial preparation work done so far on the case. A key part of your job in assisting the attorney is to control the trial materials and keep the trial plans and preparations intact so that your team will not have to start over when the trial is revived.

These are some actions you can take to preserve the integrity of the trial preparations and keep the witnesses and other persons standing by until they are needed again:

1. Update your trial preparation agendas, indexes, planning sheets, and notes and keep them all together in a master file so you will have an accurate and complete record to refresh your memory when you renew the trial preparation efforts later. If you have not taken the time to prepare these helpful sheets, do it now.
2. If the trial preparation has been a team effort, team members are likely to have various portions of the file in their possession. Collect the materials so that they do not get scattered throughout the office, misfiled, or lost. Clearly label any such materials and incorporate them into the trial files. Keep the team members informed of the changing case status so that they will be aware of the new trial date.
3. Ascertain the status of projects assigned to other trial team members (most assignments should be near completion). Write up summary memoranda and place them in the various project files so that team members can refresh their memories about small details of the assignments when the new trial date comes around.
4. Promptly inform your expert witnesses of the continuation so that they can free their calendars for other cases and work. If you know the new trial date, tell the expert witnesses now so that they can schedule around it.
5. Inform all interested persons as soon as possible that the trial date has been rescheduled. You or the attorney should take the time to explain the rescheduling to the clients and witnesses, many of whom may have made arrangements to take off work or changed other plans to accommodate the original trial date. It is especially important to contact anyone planning to travel from out of town so that they can reschedule their travel arrangements.
6. Discuss with your supervising attorney whether the original trial subpoenas for the lay witnesses will still be enforceable at a later date, or if the subpoenas will have to be issued and served again for the new trial. Either way, save your witness subpoena file and master index for future use.
7. Remember to contact anyone you may have lined up to render service specifically in connection with the trial (video technician, court

reporter, subpoena servers, graphic artists), especially when something has been ordered on an expedited basis. Be considerate of their schedules and avoid incurring extra charges for rush projects if you end up having extra time to prepare before the trial.

§ 7.4 Handling Settlement of the Case

Another phenomenon in trial work is that negotiations which have been stalled for months before the trial may suddenly experience a major breakthrough and the parties agree to a settlement, obviating the need to go forward with the trial. It is natural to feel a little disappointed when the case settles just before the trial is set to begin (or in some instances, after the trial has started). You may find it quite discouraging to have devoted all your energies to completing an enormous amount of trial preparation work, only to be deprived of the chance to use it. However, keep in mind that the fact that your trial team was prepared and ready to try the case was probably instrumental in settling the case. You can still learn a lot from a case that settles. If nothing else, you gained valuable experience in preparing for trial and working with a trial team.

Your work is not finished just because a settlement offer is accepted. You will still have responsibilities related to the case following a settlement, such as:

- notifying the court clerk of the settlement
- drawing up the settlement documents and releases
- paying the case expenses (see § **7.34**)
- thanking the witnesses and others who contributed
- archiving work product samples
- preparing the case file for closing and storage (see § **7.39**).

A word of caution: Everyone involved in the case and others who know about it will be curious about the settlement terms and amounts. Be very discreet about divulging the terms of the settlement unless the attorney specifically authorizes you to relay this information. Remember that you have an ongoing obligation to protect your client's confidentiality.

§ 7.5 Dealing with Posttrial Letdown (Win or Lose)

Trial work is both an exhilarating and exhausting business, especially during the final stages of preparation and courtroom presentation. During the weeks before trial, the trial team concentrates its collective energies on matters related to the trial preparation. Everyone is "psyched up" for the trial. Then, at the actual trial, your full attention is riveted on the courtroom events as they unfold. You will be immersed in overseeing the daily details and logistics of presenting the trial in the courtroom. Regardless of the size of the case or the subject matter, there will always be at least a few days during which you are required to operate at a frenzied, hectic pace.

Several days or weeks of the intense concentration required to present a courtroom trial can take a lot out of you! Don't be surprised if you feel a mental and physical letdown once the case is over. You might expect this feeling if the outcome of the trial is unfavorable to your client, but it is likely to occur even if your side prevails. You may find the transition back to your regular office schedule and your normal caseload after the excitement of the trial somewhat difficult.

You will need to find a way to recharge after the trial, especially if the case has been a lengthy, grueling one. If you can arrange it, after you have the immediate wrap-up tasks out of the way (see **§ 7.1**), take a little time to rest and relax away from the pressures of the office. Spend a few hours at whatever leisure time activities you enjoy, especially those which give you some exercise and help you to get back in touch with your family, friends, and events in the rest of the world. If your side won the case, treat yourself to some small reward for a job well done. If the result was not favorable to your client, give yourself a treat anyway and consider it consolation and therapy. Even if you can only take an afternoon off, getting away will replenish your energy and help you regain your perspective.

Of course, the case may not really be finished if there are posttrial motions or appeals (see **§ 7.6** and **§ 7.16**), but taking a short break will give you a chance to switch gears. When you return to your office you will be able to think more clearly and the details of the trial will actually be sharper if you have had a chance to rest. (Continue to jot down additional details, comments, or questions as they occur to you during your rest break so you will not forget to check up on them.) When you return to work you will be refreshed and ready to tackle the analysis of the results of the case, begin posttrial activities, and attend to whatever else has been piling up on your desk during the trial.

§ 7.6 Handling Posttrial Motions

Whether the case is a jury trial or a bench trial, Rule 58 of the Federal Rules of Civil Procedure sets out the usual method for entering the official judgment once the matter has been decided. When a jury has returned a general verdict or when the judge has decided that a party is either entitled to recover a certain amount of money or is not entitled to recover anything, Rule 58 directs the court clerk to prepare and enter a judgment accordingly, without waiting for further instructions from the court. In more complicated cases, such as when the judge grants a party something other than a money judgment, or when a jury returns a special verdict or a general verdict accompanied by answers to interrogatories, the judge must approve the form of the judgment before the clerk enters it into the record. A judge may ask counsel to prepare the final order or entry, but unless the case issues are unusually complicated, it is generally more expeditious for the clerk to prepare and enter the judgment.

In most courts, the judgment entry will not be finalized until a few days after the conclusion of the trial. The filing date of the final judgment entry starts the time period within which any party may appeal the judgment or file posttrial motions, if appropriate. An important thing to remember about posttrial motions is that the filing of certain motions will suspend the normal running time for filing an appeal (see **§ 7.16**) until the judge makes a ruling on the motion. The posttrial motions a party files will depend upon the type of trial and the issues involved. The following sections briefly review some of the posttrial motions allowed under federal court rules. (State courts may allow other types and forms of posttrial motions. Always check the local rules for your jurisdiction.)

§ 7.7 —Assisting the Attorney in Preparing Posttrial Motions

You will not generally have a full transcript of the trial before preparing postjudgment motions, both because of the short time period allowed for filing and because of the expense involved. Therefore, in developing the supporting arguments for posttrial motions, the attorney will rely on your memory of the trial and your impressions of what transpired, bolstered by your notes and other documentation of the trial. Your ideas and insights can be quite useful to the attorney because *you were there.* You worked on the trial preparation and sat in on the strategy sessions. You were present during the courtroom activities, taking notes, paying attention, observing the jury and the witnesses, discussing each day's events with the trial team. You heard the testimony, the attorneys' arguments, and the judge's rulings on objections. You have had time to digest what you saw and heard and to reflect on how the proceedings went. (They almost never go exactly as planned!) You are as well informed as anyone about how the actual events unfolded in the courtroom, and the wise trial attorney will welcome your ability to apply logical reasoning, common sense, and perspective to the posttrial proceedings.

You can help the attorney to clarify the supporting arguments and illustrate the points in the posttrial motions by providing concrete examples from the trial proceedings. The exact items you will look for will depend on the basis for the posttrial motion. Review the available trial documentation and focus on the portions related to the specific error or deficiency that is the basis for your motion. For example, if your motion involves error related to the jury in some way, review your copies of the requested jury instructions, the court's instructions or charge to the jury, any notes related to the jury panel, and so forth.

Trial notes (yours, the attorney's, and those of other trial team members, if any) taken in the courtroom can be invaluable in refreshing your recollections of what occurred during the trial. In addition to the notes, you will find that reviewing the other documentation of the trial (your lists, schedules, indexes, and so on) will help to jog your memory and put the courtroom events in context. You may also want to review the trial briefs and the transcripts of counsel's opening statements if you have them (see § **6.53**) to ascertain what facts the other side said they would prove, what evidence and testimony they promised to present, and so on. Compare these statements with your notes and recollections and see if the opposing party did accomplish what they said they would. Discrepancies between promises made and what was actually presented can sometimes be used to augment points set out in posttrial motions.

The attorney will also appreciate your assistance in the mechanics of preparing and assembling the posttrial motion papers. The attorney will probably draft the motion and supporting arguments, but you can help to improve the final product by careful attention to detail, meticulous proofreading, and judicious editing. The following checklist covers some specific ways you can help the attorney in preparing these documents.

§ 7.8 —Preparing Posttrial Motion Papers

This checklist identifies some particular concerns of the posttrial motion process.

____ 1. Aim for a concise statement of the situation written in a clear, persuasive style. Avoid confusing language, jargon, and legalese whenever possible. Include sufficient detail and explanation, but try to omit any extraneous information which tends to clutter or distract from the argument presented.

____ 2. Clearly identify the parties mentioned in the motion, especially in cases with multiple plaintiffs or defendants. Use the actual names rather than just referring to "the defendant" or "the plaintiff."

____ 3. Check the accuracy of the facts (names, figures, dates, and so forth) cited in the motion.

____ 4. Cite-check references to supporting case law (see § **5.40**).

____ 5. Assemble and label documents that may be attached as exhibits to the motion. Make sure that the labels on the attachments correctly correspond to the references in the motion.

____ 6. Check for any pertinent local rules, procedures, or preferred forms that apply to your motion.

____ 7. Stay alert to the relevant time periods for filing the posttrial motions. Make sure the motions are timely filed and properly served.

____ 8. Set up a separate file folder or jacket to contain posttrial motions and the supporting research and documentation.

§ 7.9 Motion for Judgment as a Matter of Law—FRCP 50(a)

Rule 50(a) of the Federal Rules of Civil Procedure, revised effective December 1, 1991, eliminates the language of the previous Rule 50(a) concerning motions for a directed verdict. Instead, new Rule 50 allows a party to move for judgment "as a matter of law" when the evidence presented does not sufficiently support the claims made by the opposing party. The Motion for Judgment as a Matter of Law under revised FRCP 50 is similar in many respects to a Motion for Summary Judgment (FRCP 56), which also concerns a party's entitlement to judgment "as a matter of law." In a jury trial, when a party believes that the opposing party has not presented sufficient proof to support a claim on a particular issue, the moving party may petition the court for a ruling as a matter of law on those claims or issues.

The Motion for Judgment as a Matter of Law may be filed only in cases tried before a jury, and the motion must be filed before the case is submitted to the jury for deliberation. This allows the opposing party the opportunity to correct any inadvertent deficiencies in the evidence presented before the jury begins its consideration of the case. The Motion for Judgment as a Matter of Law must clearly articulate "the judgment sought and the law and the facts on which the moving party is entitled to the judgment" under FRCP 50(a)(2). This supporting information may incorporate specific references to the testimony, exhibits, and argument presented at trial. You can help the attorney by reviewing the trial materials and assembling the appropriate documentation to support your arguments (see § **7.7**).

§ 7.10 Renewal of Motion for Judgment as a Matter of Law after Trial—FRCP 50(b)

Rule 50(b) of the Federal Rules of Civil Procedure, also revised effective December 1, 1991, provides that when a party has moved for Judgment as a Matter of Law (see **§ 7.9**) at the close of the evidence and the court either denies the motion or reserves ruling on it, the party may renew the Motion for Judgment as a Matter of Law within 10 days after the filing of the final judgment entry in the case (see **§ 7.6**). (**Note:** You may be more familiar with the terminology of previous Rule 50(b) which provided for Judgment NOV, an abbreviation for the Latin phrase *non obstante veredicto* meaning "notwithstanding the verdict.")

The essence of Rule 50(b) is that the court may grant a judgment in favor of the moving party even though a verdict was returned in favor of the opposing party, if such a ruling is proper according to the controlling law on the issues involved. For example, suppose the plaintiff in a negligence action failed to present any evidence at trial on one of the elements required for a prima facie negligence case (the duty of the defendant, the failure of the defendant to carry out the required duty, a causal connection between the defendant's actions and the injury suffered by the plaintiff, and actual damage or loss to the plaintiff). If the jury returned a verdict for the plaintiff in spite of this clear lack of proof, the defendant would be entitled to a judgment as a matter of law.

The renewal of a Motion for Judgment as a Matter of Law must be based on the same grounds as the preverdict motion. The renewed motion may be combined with a Motion for New Trial according to FRCP 59 (see **§ 7.11**), or the Motion for Judgment as a Matter of Law may request a new trial in the event the court denies the renewed Motion for Judgment as a Matter of Law. If the Motion for Judgment as a Matter of Law is renewed, the court can allow the original judgment to stand, reopen the judgment and order a new trial, or direct the entry of judgment as a matter of law. FRCP 50(c)(2) also provides that if the court grants the motion and directs judgment as a matter of law in favor of the moving party, the opposing party may then move for a new trial within 10 days of the entry of the judgment.

§ 7.11 Motion for New Trial—FRCP 59

Federal Rule of Civil Procedure 59 provides that any party may move for a new trial on any or all of the issues in a case tried with or without a jury. The Motion for New Trial under FRCP 59 may be combined with a Motion for Judgment as a Matter of Law under FRCP 50 (see **§ 7.9** and **§ 7.10**). Rule

59(d) also provides that the court can order a new trial on its own initiative or for a reason not stated in a party's motion, providing that the court gives the parties "notice and an opportunity to be heard on the matter." In either case, the court must state the grounds upon which it is ordering a new trial. In addition, Rule 59(e) provides that a party may file a Motion to Alter or Amend a Judgment.

FRCP 59 does not specifically list the grounds for a Motion for New Trial, but instead allows such a motion "for any of the reasons for which new trials have heretofore been granted in actions at law in the courts of the United States." Most state court rules give a more concise definition of the grounds for a new trial motion. Depending on the jurisdiction, these grounds might include:

- misconduct of the jury
- misconduct of the prevailing party
- judgment not sustained by the weight of the evidence
- judgment contrary to law
- excessive or inadequate damages in certain circumstances
- error of law at trial, brought to the attention of the trial court by the party filing the Motion for New Trial
- newly discovered evidence that could not reasonably have been discovered before the trial.

In most federal cases, a Motion for New Trial (or to Amend a Judgment) must be made within 10 days after the entry of the final judgment in the case. If the Motion for New Trial is based on information that is not included in the trial record, that information must be presented in the form of an affidavit which is served along with the motion. The opposing party then has 10 days to serve opposing affidavits, although this time period may be extended by order of the court or by stipulation between the parties. (Note: Some state courts allow a slightly longer time period, usually 14 days, for the filing of a Motion for New Trial and for filing affidavits. Always check the local rules for your area for the applicable filing deadlines.)

§ 7.12 Motion for Relief from Judgment—FRCP 60

Rule 60(a) of the Federal Rules of Civil Procedure provides that a party may file a motion for the correction of clerical mistakes in judgments or other parts of the record which would be prejudicial to the moving party. The court itself may also order necessary clerical corrections. If there is an appeal in the case, any clerical errors may be corrected before the appeal is docketed in the appellate court, or after docketing if the appellate court orders such a correction.

FRCP 60(b) allows a party to move for relief from a judgment under certain circumstances, including: mistake, inadvertence, surprise, or excusable neglect; new evidence that could not reasonably have been discovered in time to move for a new trial under Rule 59(b); fraud or misconduct of an adverse party; satisfaction, release, or discharge of the judgment. Rule 60(b) states that a motion for relief from judgment must be made "within a reasonable time" after the judgment, and that motions filed on certain grounds, such as fraud or newly discovered evidence, may in some circumstances be filed up to a year after the judgment. **Caution: A Rule 60(b) motion does not generally suspend the running of the time for appeal.**

§ 7.13 Motion for Amendment of Court's Findings—FRCP 52(b)

Rule 52(b) of the Federal Rules of Civil Procedure allows a party in a nonjury trial to move for amendment of the court's findings or for additional findings within 10 days after entry of a judgment. A motion for amended findings under Rule 52(b) may be combined with a Motion for New Trial according to Rule 59 (see **§ 7.11**). Under the federal rules, a Rule 52 motion generally does suspend the running of the appeal time, but check the rules governing your jurisdiction for specific procedures related to this type of posttrial motion.

§ 7.14 Motion to Charge Costs—FRCP 37(c)(2)

The text of Federal Rule of Civil Procedure 37(c)(2), revised effective December 1, 1993, reads as follows:

> If a party fails to admit the genuineness of any document or the truth of any matter as requested under Rule 36, and if the party requesting the admissions thereafter proves the genuineness of the document or the truth of the matter, the requesting party may apply to the court for an order requiring the other party to pay the reasonable expenses incurred in making that proof, including reasonable attorney's fees. The court shall make the order unless it finds that (A) the request was held objectionable pursuant to Rule 36(a), or (B) the admission sought was of no substantial importance, or (C) the party failing to admit had reasonable ground to believe that the party might prevail on the matter, or (D) there was other good reason for the failure to admit.

A posttrial motion under FRCP 37(c)(2) is usually related to a pretrial discovery Request for Admission that was denied by an opposing party, but was proved to be true at trial. When this occurs, and when the party who propounded the request prevails at trial, that party may be entitled to recoup the cost associated with proving the fact which the opposing party failed to admit in discovery, even if that party later stipulates to the fact at trial.

For example, suppose the Request for Admissions served by the plaintiff on the defendant included a request to admit that plaintiff was the lawful owner of the automobile she was driving at the time of the accident. The original title was given to the towing company to which plaintiff sold the car, and that company had since gone out of business. The plaintiff had not kept a photocopy of the car title, although she did have a receipt for the sale of the car to the towing company. The defendants had no reason to doubt that the automobile involved in the accident belonged to the plaintiff, but for some reason the defendants failed to admit the fact that plaintiff was the owner of the car when they responded to her Request for Admissions. The plaintiff was then obliged to incur expenses in obtaining an official "Certified Title History" in lieu of the car title (on an expedited schedule that included express mail charges) from the archives of the state Bureau of Motor Vehicles in order to present evidence of ownership as an exhibit at trial. At the conclusion of the trial, the jury granted a verdict for the plaintiff. Believing that she was entitled to recover the costs of providing evidence of ownership, plaintiff's counsel filed a motion requesting the court to order the defendant to pay these costs. The following **Form 7–1** illustrates a basic form for a Motion to Charge Costs. (To properly support this motion, insert applicable case law references for your jurisdiction.)

FORM 7–1
SAMPLE MOTION TO CHARGE COSTS—FRCP 37(C)(2)

IN THE _____ DISTRICT COURT
FOR THE _____ DISTRICT OF _____

____________________	)	CASE No. __________
Plaintiff	)	
v.	)	
____________________	)	MOTION TO CHARGE COSTS
Defendant	)	TO DEFENDANT

The Plaintiff, [Name], by and through counsel, hereby respectfully moves this Court for an Order pursuant to FRCP 37(c)(2) allowing certain trial expenses incurred by the Plaintiff in this litigation (as set forth in the attached schedule) to be charged to and included in the court costs to be paid by the Defendant, [Name], in the above-entitled action.

The trial of this case began on [date] on a lawsuit brought by [Plaintiff] against [Defendant], for damages resulting from a collision between Plaintiff's automobile and the vehicle driven by Defendant. Before trial, Plaintiff served certain Request for Admissions pursuant to FRCP Rule 36. Defendant filed responses denying certain Requests for Admission. A copy of those Requests and Defendant's response is attached hereto and by reference incorporated herein.

On [date], the jury returned a verdict in favor of the Plaintiff in the amount of [amount]. Plaintiff now requests the Court to order that certain trial expenses be charged to the Defendant in this case.

Plaintiff's counsel obtained documentary evidence for trial to prove that [Plaintiff] was the owner of the subject automobile. The towing company to whom [Plaintiff] sold the car had subsequently gone out of business, and therefore a copy of the title or a record of the title transfer was not readily available. In lieu of the actual automobile title, Plaintiff's counsel obtained a "Certified Title History" on the subject automobile from the [state] Bureau of Motor Vehicles. This document was designated as Exhibit F on Plaintiff's list of trial exhibits.

Defendants had no reason to doubt that Plaintiff was the owner of the automobile, yet the denial of Plaintiff's Request for Admission No. 3 caused Plaintiff to incur expenses in obtaining documentary proof of ownership for trial. Plaintiff was the prevailing party at trial, and Rule 37(c)(2) provides that the prevailing party is entitled to reasonable expenses in making proof of a fact denied upon request for admission.

[Insert appropriate supporting case law in your jurisdiction] In the instant case, the costs expended by Plaintiff in proving the ownership of the automobile should properly be assessed against Defendants.

[attorney signature]
[address and telephone number]

§ 7.15 Processing Appeals

When the final judgment or order has been entered on the posttrial motions, if any, in your case, you may begin preparing for an appeal of the decision (from your side if you lost, from the opposing side if you won). This section provides a brief overview of the steps involved in an appeal, based on the Federal Rules of Appellate Procedure (FRAP). It is not meant to be a comprehensive study of appellate procedure. **Caution:** These are general guidelines only, and the discussion is limited to appeals as of right from courts of record in civil cases. Always check your state's appellate procedures and your appellate court's local rules, which supplement the formal rules, for additional information.

If you assist the attorney with appeals in numerous cases, you will find it helpful to prepare the following reference lists and add them to your master reference notebook (see **§ 1.60**):

- Appellate court addresses in your state
- Names and addresses of appellate court judges
- Addresses and telephone numbers of appellate court clerks
- Map of appellate districts in your state
- Samples of special forms required by your court.

Separate the appeals paperwork from the trial files. Start a new expanding file folder for the materials and documents that will accumulate as you work through the steps of the appeal. Use the Appeals Checklist Log (**Form 7–2**) as a guide.

§ 7.16 —Questions to Ask About Appellate Procedure

The following checklist of questions will help you determine the requirements that apply in your appellate jurisdiction. Once you have determined the answers to these questions, use **Form 7–2** to record the information and dates pertinent to your appeal. This will help you in tracking the matter through the various steps of the appeal. Be sure to enter the critical filing dates on your calendar and office docket system, and arrange to send a reminder to the attorney well in advance of these deadlines.

____ 1. When must the Notice of Appeal be filed?
(Usually within 30 days of the date of the entry of the judgment or order appealed from.)

____ 2. How much is the filing fee?
How should the check be made out?

____ 3. Does the court of appeals require a docketing statement? If so, when should it be filed and what form must be used?

____ 4. When is the record due?
____ days after filing of the Notice of Appeal

____ 5. What is the procedure for obtaining an extension of time for transmitting the record?

____ 6. What arrangements must be made for transfer or storage of the trial exhibits?

____ 7. Is there a maximum length for the briefs?

FORM 7–2
APPEALS CHECKLIST LOG

APPEALS CHECKLIST LOG				
CLIENT:			FILE No.:	
CASE CAPTION: Appellant v. Appellees			ATTORNEYS:	
APPEAL TO:			COURT OF APPEALS	
CLERK (or contact):			PHONE:	
TRIAL COURT:				
CASE No.:			JUDGE:	
DATE OF ORDER OR JUDGMENT ENTRY BEING APPEALED:				
DEADLINE FOR FILING NOTICE OF APPEAL:			DOCKETED:	

OPPOSING PARTIES	COUNSEL	ADDRESS/PHONE

NOTICE OF APPEAL (30 days after order or judgment entry)			Due:	Filed:
	By Atty.	By Clerk	Filing Fee:	
Filed with Trial Court				
Served on Opposing Counsel				
Copy to Court Reporter				
Copy to Court of Appeals				
Praecipe for Transcript (or Docketing Statement)			Due:	Filed:
Filed with Trial Court Clerk			Deposit Paid:	
Served on Opposing Counsel				
Copy to Court Reporter		Reporter Name/Phone:		
Transmittal of Record (40 days after Notice)			Due:	Filed:
Notice of Transmittal issued by Trial Court Clerk:				Filed:
Brief of Appellant (20 days after transmittal of record)			Due:	Filed:
Extension obtained to:			Due:	Filed:
Copies to Opposing Counsel			Date:	
Brief of Appellee (20 days after Appellant's Brief)			Due:	Filed:
Extension obtained to:			Due:	Filed:
Copies to Opposing Counsel			Date:	
Reply Brief (10 days after Appellee's Brief)			Due:	Filed:
Copies to Opposing Counsel			Date:	
Oral Argument			Date set:	

- Appellant's Brief: ____ pages
- Appellee's Brief: ____ pages
- Reply Brief: ____ pages

____ 8. How many copies of briefs must be filed and served -
- with the Clerk of the Appeals Court? ____ copies
- on counsel for each opposing party? ____ copies

____ 9. How many copies of the appendix must be filed and served
- with the Clerk of the Appeals Court? ____ copies
- on counsel for each opposing party? ____ copies

____ 10. When is the appellant's brief due?
____ days after the filing of the record

____ 11. When is the appellee's brief due?
____ days after service of the appellant's brief.

____ 12. When is the reply brief due?
____ days after service of the appellee's brief.

____ 13. What is the procedure for obtaining an extension of time to file briefs?

____ 14. Is a Corporate Disclosure Statement required when one of the parties to the appeal is a corporation?

____ 15. How much time is scheduled for oral argument?
____ minutes per side

§ 7.17 Preparing the Notice of Appeal

To initiate an appeal of a final judgment entry or order by the trial court, the party wishing to appeal (the appellant) files a Notice of Appeal with the clerk of the trial court before the expiration of the period allowed for appeals. Important Note: Failure to file the Notice of Appeal within the proper time period is grounds for *dismissal* of the appeal. The purpose of the Notice of Appeal is simply to *notify* the trial court, the appeals court, and the opposing party of the intent to appeal. The federal rules do not require a detailed explanation of the basis for the appeal in the notice, so the Notice of Appeal is a pretty basic document in most jurisdictions (see **Form 7–3,** Sample Notice of Appeal). FRAP 3(c) states that the Notice of Appeal must

- clearly identify the party or parties making the appeal
- specify the judgment or order being appealed
- include the date the order or judgment was filed and the case number in the trial court
- indicate the appellate court to which the appeal is being made.

Always consult the local rules governing your case for any additional information that your jurisdiction may require to perfect the Notice of Appeal. The caption of the Notice of Appeal is the same at this point as captions in the trial court pleadings, except for the addition of the designation "appellant" to the name of the party filing the appeal and "appellee" for the opposing party. (The appellee is called the respondent in some jurisdictions.) Most of the subsequent appeal filings will bear the caption and case number of the appeals court.

If a party files a Notice of Appeal within the proper time limit, any other party may file its own Notice of Appeal within 14 days after the date the first Notice of Appeal was filed. When two or more parties are entitled to appeal from the same judgment and the parties have substantially similar interests in the issues on appeal, they may file a joint appeal. These parties may also consolidate their appeals after filing separately, handling their joint interests as a single appeal after that point. The court may order consolidation of the appeals, or the appealing parties may move for or stipulate to consolidation of the appeals.

FORM 7–3
SAMPLE NOTICE OF APPEAL (BY DEFENDANT)

IN THE UNITED STATES DISTRICT COURT
FOR THE ______ DISTRICT OF [STATE]

__________________________,) CASE NO. ____________
)
Plaintiff-Appellee,) JUDGE ______________
v.)
)
__________________________,)
)
Defendant-Appellant.) NOTICE OF APPEAL

Notice is hereby given that [NAME OF PARTY], defendant in the captioned case, hereby appeals to the _____ District Court of Appeals for the _____ District of [State] from the [final judgment/decree/order] entered in this action on the _____ day of _________, 19___.

Dated: ____________________

____
[Attorney]
[Address & telephone]
Counsel for Defendant

§ 7.18 Computing Time for Filing the Appeal

In most civil cases, the Notice of Appeal must be filed within 30 days from the filing date of the final order or judgment entry being appealed. However, in cases in which the United States or an officer or agency of the United States is a party, the time for filing the notice of appeal is generally extended to within 60 days after the judgment entry or order being appealed. In computing time periods for any filing under the Federal Rules of Appellate Procedure, the day from which the time period begins (the day the final order being appealed is filed) is NOT COUNTED. The last day of the period IS COUNTED, unless it falls on a Saturday, Sunday, or a legal holiday, or a day on which the clerk's office is closed or inaccessible for some reason (such as, extremely inclement weather, fire, flood, earthquake). Saturdays, Sundays, and legal holidays **do count** as days in the computation, except when the time period you are calculating is less than seven days. **Note: There is no provision in civil cases for extension of the time for filing the initial notice of appeal. Failure to file the notice of appeal on time can cause the appeal to be dismissed.**

If a party files a timely motion with the trial court for certain posttrial rulings, the 30-day appeal period is suspended and does not begin to run until the date of the final order disposing of the posttrial motion (see **§ 7.6** on posttrial motions). Rule 4 of the Federal Rules of Appellate Procedure, amended effective December 1, 1993, contains the guidelines for calculating the time for appeals under various conditions. FRAP 4(a)(4) contains an important provision concerning appeals and posttrial motions in civil cases:

> If any party makes a timely motion of a type specified immediately below, the time for appeal for all parties runs <u>from the entry of the order disposing of the last such motion outstanding</u>. This provision applies to a timely motion under the Federal Rules of Civil Procedure:
>
> (A) for judgment under Rule 50(b);
>
> (B) to amend or make additional findings of fact under Rule 52(b), whether or not granting the motion would alter the judgment;
>
> (C) to alter or amend the judgment under Rule 59;
>
> (D) for attorney's fees under Rule 54 if a district court under Rule 58 extends the time for appeal;
>
> (E) for a new trial under Rule 59; or
>
> (F) for relief under Rule 60 if the motion is served within 10 days after the entry of judgment.
>
> A notice of appeal filed after announcement or entry of the judgment but <u>before</u> disposition of any of the above motions <u>is ineffective</u> to appeal from the judgment or order, or part thereof, specified in the notice of appeal, until the date of the entry of the order disposing of the last such motion outstanding. Appellate review of an order disposing of any of the above motions requires the party, in compliance with Appellate Rule 3(c), to <u>amend a previously filed notice of appeal</u>. A party intending to challenge an alteration or amendment of the judgment shall file an amended notice of appeal within the time prescribed by this Rule 4 measured from the entry of the order disposing of the last such motion outstanding. No additional fees will be required for filing an amended notice [emphasis added].

In practical terms, this means that if you have filed a Notice of Appeal on a judgment before the trial court makes its final ruling on certain types of posttrial motions in the case, you may have to file an amended Notice of Appeal in order to preserve your client's right to appeal. If your case involves posttrial motions, discuss this with your supervising attorney to make sure that you have filed a valid Notice of Appeal (or Amended Notice of Appeal) before the appeal period expires. I strongly recommend that you read the Advisory Committee Notes accompanying Appellate Rules 3 and 4 for a better understanding of the time calculations and the provisions in the 1993 amendment to these rules.

§ 7.19 —Serving the Notice of Appeal

The clerk of the trial court serves the Notice of Appeal along with a copy of the docketing statement, if any (see **§ 7.21**) by mail on the opposing parties or their counsel of record. The trial court clerk also serves a copy of the Notice of Appeal on the clerk of the appellate court named in the notice. Some courts require a praecipe giving the trial court clerk instructions for serving the Notice of Appeal. The praecipe may be included on the same document as the Notice of Appeal, or it may be set up as a separate filing (see **Form 7–4,** Sample Praecipe for Service of Notice of Appeal). Serving the Notice of Appeal is the clerk's responsibility, but it is common practice in many states for the attorney to also serve a copy of the notice on opposing counsel to ensure that they are promptly notified of the appeal. (**Note:** If the attorney serves the Notice of Appeal to the opposing counsel, add a certificate of service at the end of the Notice of Appeal.)

FORM 7–4
SAMPLE PRAECIPE FOR SERVICE OF NOTICE OF APPEAL

IN THE UNITED STATES DISTRICT COURT
FOR THE ______ DISTRICT OF [STATE]

______________________,	)	CASE NO. ____________
	)	
Plaintiff-Appellee,	)	JUDGE ______________
v.	)	
	)	
	)	
______________________,	)	
	)	PRAECIPE FOR SERVICE
Defendant-Appellant.	)	OF NOTICE OF APPEAL

TO THE CLERK OF COURTS:

You are hereby requested to serve a time-stamped copy of the Notice of Appeal filed herein by regular United States Mail upon each of the following:

[List names and addresses of the persons to serve]

Dated: ____________________ ____________________________
[Attorney]
[Address & telephone]
Counsel for _________

§ 7.20 —Paying the Costs Deposit

Generally, courts require the appellant to pay a costs deposit to commence the appeal. Failure to pay the required deposit could result in the clerk's refusal to file the Notice of Appeal. Some courts require payment of fees to both the trial court and the appeals court clerks. Find out what your local courts require, and make sure the Notice of Appeal is accompanied by a check in the proper amount in order to avoid any last minute filing problems. FRAP Rule 4(a)(4) cited in **§ 7.18** specifies that no additional fees are required for an Amended Notice of Appeal.

§ 7.21 —Handling the Docketing Statement

Appeals courts in some areas have implemented an accelerated calendar system to aid in the efficient disposition of certain cases that require less than the usual amount of time. For example, a case might be assigned to the accelerated calendar when no transcript is required, when the transcript is very short and can be prepared quickly, or when the parties submit an agreed statement of proceedings in lieu of the record. In some instances the court may transfer a case to the accelerated calendar from the regular calendar. (Local rules may designate other specific types of cases for the accelerated calendar. Check the local rules for your court.) To enable the clerk to determine whether to assign a case to the regular calendar or to the accelerated calendar, the party filing the appeal provides information on a form called a "docketing statement" (see **Form 7–5,** Sample Docketing Statement), which is filed along with the Notice of Appeal. Most courts have their own docketing statement forms with blanks to fill in or boxes to check to provide the information pertinent to the appeal being filed. If your court uses an accelerated calendar system, the attorney may ask you to obtain the appropriate forms and prepare the docketing statement for filing along with the Notice of Appeal.

FORM 7-5
SAMPLE DOCKETING STATEMENT

IN THE ________ DISTRICT COURT OF APPEALS
________ COUNTY, {STATE}

____________________________	)	TRIAL COURT CASE NO. ____
	)	
Plaintiffs,	)	DATE OF PRAECIPE
	)	________, 19___
v.	)	
	)	DATE OF DOCKETING STATEMENT
____________________________	)	________, 19___
	)	
Defendants.	)	<u>DOCKETING STATEMENT</u>

1. This appeal should be assigned to:
   - ☐ The regular calendar.
   - ☐ The accelerated calendar.

   Assigned to the accelerated calendar for the reason checked (see Local Rules).
   - ☐ 1. Transcript consists of one hundred (100) or fewer pages.
   - ☐ 2. Agreed statement submitted in lieu of record within twenty (20) days.
   - ☐ 3. Administrative hearing record was filed with the trial court.
   - ☐ 4. All parties to appeal agree to an assignment to the accelerated calendar.

   Assigned to the regular calendar with full briefing for reason checked.
   - ☐ 1. Transcript is more than one hundred (100) pages.
   - ☐ 2. Brief in excess of fifteen (15) pages is necessary to argue the issues adequately.
   - ☐ 3. Appeal concerns unique issue of law which will be of substantial precedential value in the determination of similar cases.
   - ☐ 4. Other:

2. WAIVER OF ORAL ARGUMENT:
   - ☐ The undersigned party waives oral argument.
   - ☐ The undersigned party waives oral argument, if all adverse parties waive.
   - ☐ The undersigned party will waive oral argument or advise the court later if oral argument is preferred.

3. Did the judgment or order dispose of all claims by and against all parties?
   ☐ Yes ☐ No.

If the answer is no, does the judgment or order include an express determination that there is "no just reason for delay"? See Civ.R. 54(B).
☐ Yes ☐ No.

4. Nature of Case:

☐ Administrative Appeal	☐ Domestic Relations	☐ Personal Injury
☐ Contract	☐ Juvenile	☐ Probate
☐ Declaratory Judgment	☐ Medical Malpractice	☐ Other (Describe)

5. Has counsel for appellant changed on appeal?
☐ Yes ☐ No.

6. Do you know of other case(s) pending before this court which rase the same issue or issues?
☐ Yes ☐ No. If yes, please cite case(s): ____________________
____

7. Does the appeal turn on an interpretation or application of a particular cases(s) or statute(s)?
☐ Yes ☐ No. If yes, please cite case(s) or statute(s): __________
____

8. How would you characterize the extent of your settlement discussions prior to judgment?
☐ None ☐ Minimal ☐ Moderate ☐ Extensive.

9. Have settlement discussions taken place since the judgment or order appealed from was entered?
☐ Yes ☐ No.

10. Would a prehearing conference be of any assistance to the resolution of this matter?
☐ Yes ☐ No ☐ Maybe.
Please explain: ________________________________

11. Briefly summarize the assignments of error anticipated to be raised on appeal.

____
{Address}
{Phone}
Attorney for __________

§ 7.22 Transmitting the Record

The judges in the appeals court must be able to review documentation—the "record"—of what has previously transpired in the case before they can evaluate and rule on the issues raised in the appeal. The party bringing the appeal (the appellant) is responsible for seeing that the record is properly transmitted to the clerk of the appeals court within the appropriate time period, usually 40 days after the Notice of Appeal is filed. The appellant must also make sure that the official record includes all the documents and key materials necessary for the appeals court judges to decide the case. For purposes of appeal, the official record has three main components:

1. The original papers (pleadings, documents, exhibits) filed with the trial court throughout the case
2. A certified copy of the docket entries prepared by the clerk of the trial court
3. A transcript of the trial proceedings (see **§ 7.23**).

In some trial courts, the clerk will automatically begin to prepare the necessary portions of the record upon receipt of the Notice of Appeal. However, some jurisdictions require the appellant to file a written praecipe directing the trial court clerk to prepare the original pleadings and a certified copy of the docket entries of the trial court for transmittal to the court of appeals. (The original papers are usually returned to the trial court at the conclusion of the appeal.) The transcript of proceedings, if any, is ordered separately from the court reporter (see **§ 7.23** and **§ 7.24**). If no transcript is available or if the parties prefer to save the time and expense involved in the preparation of a transcript, they may submit an agreed statement of the proceedings in lieu of the transcript. The statement of the case, which all parties must approve, must describe the proceedings in the trial court and show how the issues in the appeal arose in enough detail to allow the judges of the appeals court to make a decision on the appeal. The following sample praecipe (**Form 7–6**) applies to a case in which no transcript of proceedings is required.

FORM 7–6
SAMPLE PRAECIPE TO CLERK TO PREPARE THE RECORD
(NO TRANSCRIPT REQUIRED)

IN THE UNITED STATES DISTRICT COURT
FOR THE ______ DISTRICT OF [STATE]

______________________,	)	CASE NO. ____________
	)	
Plaintiff-Appellee,	)	JUDGE ______________
v.	)	
	)	
______________________,	)	
	)	PRAECIPE TO PREPARE
Defendant-Appellant.	)	THE RECORD

TO THE CLERK OF COURTS:

Please assemble the original pleadings and a certified copy of the docket entries in the above case and transmit the Record for filing to the Clerk of the Court of Appeals for the _____ District of ____, in Case No. CA_____. No transcript will be necessary in this case.

Dated: ____________________

____
[Attorney]
[Address & telephone]
Counsel for _________

CERTIFICATE OF SERVICE

§ 7.23 —Ordering the Transcript of Proceedings

The party filing the appeal is responsible for obtaining the transcript of the trial proceedings from the court reporter or stenographer who recorded them. The appellant is also responsible for paying the court reporter for the cost of the transcription. The appellant must present a written request to the court reporter ordering a transcript of the trial proceedings (see **Form 7–7**), and a copy of the order for transcript must also be filed with the clerk of the trial court. The order for transcript is usually filed at the same time the Notice of Appeal is filed, but the federal rules specify that the appellant *must* order the transcript within 10 days of filing the Notice of Appeal.

When a court reporter receives an order for transcript, he or she will sign and date the order to acknowledge receipt and fill in the approximate date on which the reporter expects to have the transcript completed, usually within

30 days from the date of the order for transcript. This endorsed order is then forwarded to the clerk of the court of appeals.

The court reporter will prepare the written transcript of the trial proceedings in a fashion resembling a deposition transcript, usually in a bound booklet with sequentially numbered pages and lines. The transcript will generally be indexed according to parts of the trial (voir dire, opening statements, testimony of each witness, and so forth). When the requested transcript of proceedings is completed, the court reporter will file it with the clerk of the trial court and notify the clerk of the appellate court that the transcript has been completed and filed.

FORM 7–7
SAMPLE REQUEST FOR TRANSCRIPT OF PROCEEDINGS

IN THE UNITED STATES DISTRICT COURT
FOR THE ______ DISTRICT OF [STATE]

________________________,	)	CASE NO. ____________
	)	
Plaintiff-Appellee,	)	JUDGE _______________
v.	)	
	)	
________________________,	)	
	)	REQUEST FOR TRANSCRIPT
Defendant-Appellant.	)	OF PROCEEDINGS

TO: Court Reporter Name
Address

Please be advised that a Notice of Appeal in the above matter has been filed with the Clerk of the [Trial Court] by the Defendant-Appellant, and that said Defendant-Appellant hereby requests a complete transcript of the proceedings together with all exhibits for the purpose of transmitting the same to the Court of Appeals for the _____ District of _________.

Dated: ____________________

____
[Attorney]
[Address & telephone]
Counsel for _________

CERTIFICATE OF SERVICE

§ 7.24 —Ordering a Partial Transcript

In most instances, the court reporter will transcribe the entire trial, but the appellant may request to have only certain portions of the trial proceedings transcribed. (The customary procedures for this vary from state to state.) The appellant must specify the portions of the transcript requested in the order to the court reporter (see **Form 7–8,** Sample Request for Partial Transcript).

When the appellant intends to use less than the entire transcript of proceedings, the appellant must file and serve on the appellee a description of the portions to be included in the record, along with a statement outlining the issues the appellant intends to present on appeal (see **Form 7–9,** Sample Notice of Intent to Use Less Than Complete Transcript). If the appellee believes that other portions of the transcript are relevant and necessary to the determination of the issues involved in the appeal, the appellee has the right, within 10 days after receiving the appellant's statement, to order additional portions of the transcript from the court reporter, who will include them in the record. The appellee must then file and serve on the appellant a description of the additional portions of the transcript to be included in the record.

FORM 7–8
SAMPLE REQUEST FOR
PARTIAL TRANSCRIPT OF PROCEEDINGS

IN THE UNITED STATES DISTRICT COURT
FOR THE ______ DISTRICT OF [STATE]

________________________,	)	CASE NO. ____________
	)	
Plaintiff-Appellee,	)	JUDGE ______________
v.	)	
	)	
________________________,	)	
	)	REQUEST FOR PARTIAL
Defendant-Appellant.	)	TRANSCRIPT OF PROCEEDINGS

TO: Court Reporter Name
Address

Please be advised that a Notice of Appeal in the above matter has been filed with the Clerk of the [Trial Court] by the Defendant-Appellant, and that said Defendant-Appellant hereby requests a partial transcript of the proceedings together with all exhibits pertinent to the parts ordered for the purpose of transmitting the same to the Court of Appeals for the _____ District of _________.

The partial transcript is to include the following portions of the proceedings:

[List parts to be included]

1.
2.
3.

Dated: ____________________

____
[Attorney]
[Address & telephone]
Counsel for _________

CERTIFICATE OF SERVICE

FORM 7–9
SAMPLE NOTICE OF INTENT TO USE LESS THAN COMPLETE TRANSCRIPT

(Description of Parts of Transcript to be Included in Record and Issues to be Presented on Appeal)

IN THE UNITED STATES DISTRICT COURT
FOR THE ______ DISTRICT OF [STATE]

______________________,	)	CASE NO. ____________
	)	
Plaintiff-Appellee,	)	JUDGE _______________
v.	)	
	)	
______________________,	)	NOTICE OF INTENT TO USE
	)	LESS THAN COMPLETE
Defendant-Appellant.	)	TRANSCRIPT OF PROCEEDINGS

To: [Counsel for Appellee]

Please take notice that Appellant intends to include in the record on appeal the following portions of the transcript of the proceedings: [list parts to be included]

1.
2.
3.

Appellant intends to present the following issues on appeal:

[list issues to be presented on appeal]

1.
2.
3.

Dated: ____________________ ____________________

[Attorney]
[Address & telephone]
Counsel for Defendant

CERTIFICATE OF SERVICE

§ 7.25 —Extending Time for Transmittal of the Record

Although it is the appellant's duty to oversee proper and timely transmittal of the record, the appellant really has no control over the exact time that this occurs. Once the appellant has ordered the assembly of the record (and the transcript, if any) the next phase of the process is up to the clerk of the trial court and the court reporter.

If the court reporter cannot produce the requested transcript within the time allotted (duc to the length of the proceedings, other commitments, and so forth) the court reporter must apply to the court of appeals for an extension of time for transmitting the record. The court clerk then notifies the parties to the appeal of the requested extension. In some courts, the appellant must file a motion (actually on behalf of the court reporter) requesting extension of the time to transmit the record. This type of request for extension is granted routinely in most jurisdictions. See **Form 7–10,** Sample Motion and Order.

FORM 7–10
SAMPLE MOTION AND ORDER TO
EXTEND TIME TO TRANSMIT THE RECORD

IN THE _____ COURT OF APPEALS
FOR THE ______ DISTRICT OF [STATE]

____________________,	)	C.A. NO. _________
	)	
Plaintiff-Appellee,	)	
v.	)	
	)	
	)	
____________________,	)	
	)	MOTION TO EXTEND TIME TO
Defendant-Appellant.	)	TRANSMIT THE RECORD

Appellant, [Name], filed a notice of appeal to the Court of Appeals of [Court] in this action on [date]. Appellant, [Name], ordered a transcript of the proceedings in this case from the court reporter on [date]. The court reporter will be unable to complete the preparation of the transcript within the original time allowed due to [state reason]. Appellant moves the court to extend the time for transmitting the record on appeal in this case to and including [date].

Dated: ____________________ ____________________

[Attorney]
[Address & telephone]
Counsel for Appellant

CERTIFICATE OF SERVICE

IN THE _____ COURT OF APPEALS
FOR THE ______ DISTRICT OF [STATE]

____________________,) C.A. NO. __________
)
Plaintiff-Appellee,)
v.)
)
____________________,)
) ORDER EXTENDING TIME TO
Defendant-Appellant.) TRANSMIT THE RECORD

Upon motion of the Appellant, [Name], for good cause shown, it is hereby ordered that the time for transmitting the record on appeal to the Court of Appeals for _________ is extended to and including _________, 19___.

Dated: ____________________ ____________________

Judge

§ 7.26 —Handling the Trial Exhibits on Appeal

Local rules vary concerning the location of the documentary trial exhibits during the appeals process. In some jurisdictions, the trial exhibits remain with the clerk of the trial court until they are needed by the appellate judges. In other jurisdictions, the court reporter receives the exhibits for safekeeping as they are offered at the trial, in which case the court reporter will index and attach the exhibits to the completed transcript of proceedings.

If the trial involved oversized exhibits (enlarged documents, charts, diagrams, and so forth) or physical objects (nondocument exhibits), and if those items are pertinent to the issues on appeal, you may have to make special arrangements with the court clerks for the transmittal and storage of those items. Generally, the clerk of the trial court is not required to transmit exhibits of unusual size or bulk unless specifically ordered to do so by the appellate court. Check your local clerk's retention procedures pertaining to trial exhibits to ascertain how much time you will have after the trial to claim the exhibits or make special arrangements with the clerk if you want to have them returned to you at the conclusion of the case.

§ 7.27 —Docketing the Appeal

When the clerk of the court of appeals receives the Notice of Appeal from the trial court clerk, the appeals clerk will enter the Notice of Appeal on the court docket and assign an appellate case number to the matter. Upon receipt of the completed record (comprised of the original pleadings, the certified docket entries, and the transcript, if any) from the trial court clerk, the appeals clerk will file the record and notify the parties of the date it was filed. This date is very important because it triggers the deadline for filing the appellant's brief (see **§ 7.28**).

§ 7.28 Preparing Appellate Court Briefs

The purpose of the appellate briefs is to present the court with the necessary background, supporting data, and legal arguments to enable the judges to decide the issues on appeal. In consolidated appeals, the parties can file a joint brief if their interests in the case are substantially similar. It is important to file and serve appellate briefs within the time periods allowed because if the appellant fails to file a brief within the proper time period, the appellee can move for dismissal of the appeal. If the appellee fails to properly file a brief, counsel may not be allowed to be heard in oral argument.

The appellant's brief must be filed within a certain number of days after the clerk notifies the parties of the completed transmittal of the record from the trial court. This filing deadline is 40 days according to the federal rules, but within 20 or fewer days under many state appellate rules. The time period may be shortened for cases in courts that have adopted accelerated calendar procedures (see **§ 7.21**). The date for filing the appellee's brief is determined by the date the appellant's brief is filed and served, and the date for the reply brief is determined by the date the appellee's brief is filed and served. Deadlines for filing appellate briefs may be extended when the party files a proper motion with the court and the court grants extra time to file (see **Form 7–11,** Sample Motion to Extend Time to File Brief and corresponding Order). Consult your local rules for the applicable filing deadlines and the procedures for obtaining extensions of filing dates for briefs in your court.

The attorney may ask you to assist in drafting the factual portions of the brief, researching the issues, proofreading, cite checking, and overseeing assembly of the brief. You should be familiar with the mechanics of producing a brief and make sure the brief meets all the rules for formatting and content required by your court. If you are assisting with an appellate brief for the first time, it is a good idea to ask another paralegal or an attorney in your office for a good specimen brief from another case to which you can refer for examples of format and arrangement of the contents.

FORM 7–11
SAMPLE MOTION AND ORDER
TO EXTEND TIME TO FILE BRIEF

IN THE ____ COURT OF APPEALS
FOR THE ______ DISTRICT OF [STATE]

________________________,	)	C.A. NO. __________
	)	
Plaintiff-Appellee,	)	
v.	)	
	)	
________________________,	)	
	)	MOTION TO EXTEND TIME
Defendant-Appellant.	)	TO FILE BRIEF

Defendant-Appellant, [Name], by its counsel, moves this Court for an Order extending the time within which it may file its Brief to and including the ____ day of __________, 19___. Defendant-Appellant states that this motion is not made for purposes of delay and that no previous extension of time has been obtained from the adverse party or granted by this court.

Dated: ____________________

____
[Attorney]
[Address & telephone]
Counsel for Appellant

CERTIFICATE OF SERVICE

IN THE ____ COURT OF APPEALS
FOR THE ______ DISTRICT OF [STATE]

______________________,	)	C.A. NO. _________
	)	
Plaintiff-Appellee,	)	
v.	)	
	)	
______________________,	)	
	)	ORDER EXTENDING TIME TO
Defendant-Appellant.	)	FILE BRIEF

Defendant-Appellant, [Name], having moved the court to extend the time within which it may file its Brief, and it appearing to the Court that the motion is for good cause shown, it is, therefore, ordered that the time for the Defendant-Appellant to file its brief be extended to and including [date].

Dated: ____________________ ________________________
Judge

§ 7.29 —Parts of the Appellate Brief

The following is an outline of the main sections usually included in the appellant's brief. (**Note:** The sample forms (**Forms 7–12, 7–13,** and **7–14**) in **§ 7.31** illustrate one way to set up the cover page, table of contents, and outline for an appellate brief. The preferred arrangement and titles of the sections may be different in your court. Consult your local rules.)

1. Table of Contents. List the titles of the main divisions and subdivisions of the brief along with the page number of the brief where each begins (see **§ 7.31**).

2. Table of Cases and Authorities. List all the cases referred to or cited in the body of the brief, arranged alphabetically by case name, and separately list additional statutes and other authorities with the page references in the brief where they are cited or mentioned.

3. Statement of Subject and Appellate Jurisdiction. State the subject matter of the case and identify the courts involved; include statements as to the relevant filing dates (such as the dates of the order appealed and the Notice of Appeal), the timeliness of the appeal. State that the appeal is from a final appealable order.

4. Assignments of Error. Describe the erroneous rulings or incorrect decisions the appellant believes the trial judge made during the trial.

5. Issues Presented for Review. Separately state the legal issues presented for review to the appellate court.

6. Statement of the Case. Briefly summarize the nature of the dispute, the relevant factual background, the course of the trial proceedings, and the disposition of the case in the trial court.

7. Statement of Facts Relevant to the Assignments of Error. Describe how the facts brought out at trial support the appellant's position that errors were made by the trial court.

8. Law and Argument. State the appellant's position regarding the issues presented and the legal and factual reasons the court should decide in the appellant's favor, supported by citations to the relevant authorities, statutes, and parts of the record. The arguments in this section are generally organized in the same order as the issues presented to make it easy for the judges to refer back and forth from the issues to the arguments that support them.

9. Conclusion. A concise statement of the relief sought.

10. Certificate of Service. Include a standard certification that the brief was served on opposing counsel.

11. Appendix. (Optional; may be a separate volume). The appendix contains excerpts and key materials from the record for the convenience of the judges (see **§ 7.32**).

The appellee's (or respondent's) brief follows the same general guidelines for content as the appellant's brief, except that the statement of jurisdiction and issues presented is not necessary unless the appellee disagrees with the appellant's statements or determines that the appellant's statements are not complete. The appellant may also file a reply brief, if appropriate, following the same basic format (including a table of contents with page references). Local court rules generally limit the length of reply briefs, and the content of reply briefs is usually restricted to arguments in rebuttal of the appellee's brief. No further briefs are allowed without the court's permission.

§ 7.30 —Corporate Disclosure Statement

Rule 26.1 of the Federal Rules of Appellate Procedure (added April 25, 1989, effective December 1, 1989, and amended April 30, 1991, effective December 1, 1991) requires that a corporation which is a party in an appeal must file a disclosure statement identifying all parent companies, subsidiaries (excluding wholly owned subsidiaries), and affiliates that have issued shares of stock to the public. The purpose of the disclosure is to assist the appellate judges in determining whether they have any interests in the party's related entities that would disqualify them from hearing the appeal. A copy of the Corporate Disclosure Statement must be included in front of the table of contents in the party's main brief, even if the statement was previously filed separately from the brief. A local court can request the parties to supply additional information as needed to make a proper determination.

§ 7.31 —Tips for Preparing Appellate Briefs

Note: These are general guidelines and are not meant to be all-inclusive. Use the sample forms following this list for reference, but check your local rules for specific requirements for formatting briefs in your court.

1. Briefs must be typed or printed in crisp, clear, black letters. Use at least 11-point type (10 or fewer characters per inch) and opaque white paper that is not shiny or glossy in a size no larger than 8.5 by 11 inches. Keep typed or printed text within margins of 6.5 by 9.5 inches. Copies may be reproduced by any means that yields a clear black image on white paper. All typed or printed text should be double-spaced, except quoted matter which may be single-spaced.
2. Follow the preferred format for the cover page of the brief. Most courts require the front cover of the brief to contain the following information:

- the name of the court
- the case number
- the title of the case
- the name of the trial court
- the title of the document (for example, Brief of Appellant); and
- names and addresses of counsel for the parties.

3. Most courts require briefs to be bound into booklet form, using standard binding techniques (spiral comb or heat binding). Courts may also

require a specific type of cover and backing sheets for briefs, perhaps color-coded to designate which party submitted the brief. For example:

Color Key for Appellate Briefs
(Check your local rules)

Appellant	Blue
Appellee	Red
Amicus Curiae	Green
Reply Brief	Gray
Appendix (if separate volume)	White

If your local court has similar requirements and your cases often include appellate work, ask your office supply manager to order a supply of the cover stock you need. If your office does not have binding machines or you deal with appeals only occasionally, your local copy services can do both copying and binding jobs quickly and inexpensively, and they probably stock the booklet covers you need for the briefs.

4. Use the actual names of the parties or other descriptive labels in the body of the brief for clarity. Too many references to "appellant" or "appellee" can be hard to follow.

5. Reproduce the text of statutes, rules, regulations, ordinances, constitutional provisions, etc. referred to in the brief in an addendum or appendix (see **§ 7.32**). FRAP 28(e) sets out the rules for numbering the pages in the addendum or appendix.

6. Courts may dictate a maximum length for briefs. For example, the federal rules (FRCP 28(g)) limit briefs to no more than 50 pages, and the reply brief to no more than 25 pages, not counting the corporate disclosure statement, table of contents, table of authorities, or appendix. Check your local appellate rules for similar length limitations on briefs.

7. Prepare the appropriate number of copies to be filed with the court, served on opposing party, and retained for your records. Check your local rules for this requirement.

8. All references to the record in the brief must include the appropriate volume and page numbers where the referenced materials can be found. Case citations must include the volume number, page number, and the particular page numbers relevant to the point of law for which the case is cited (sometimes called "locus pages" or "pinpoint cites").

FORM 7–12
SAMPLE TABLE OF CONTENTS FOR APPELLATE BRIEF

TABLE OF CONTENTS

Page

FORM 7–13
SAMPLE OUTLINE OF
APPELLATE BRIEF SECTION HEADINGS

TABLE OF CONTENTS

TABLE OF AUTHORITIES

STATEMENT OF SUBJECT
AND APPELLATE JURISDICTION

ASSIGNMENTS OF ERROR

ISSUES PRESENTED FOR REVIEW

A. First Issue
B. Second Issue
C. Third Issue

STATEMENT OF THE CASE

STATEMENT OF FACTS
RELEVANT TO ASSIGNMENTS OF ERROR

LAW AND ARGUMENT

I. Summary of Argument

II. ______________________________

III. ______________________________

IV. ______________________________

CONCLUSION

Respectfully submitted,

____

CERTIFICATE OF SERVICE

APPENDIX

FORM 7–14
SAMPLE COVER PAGE FOR APPELLATE BRIEF

IN THE COURT OF APPEALS
FOR THE NINTH JUDICIAL DISTRICT
SUMMIT COUNTY, OHIO

ANYBIG INSURANCE COMPANY,	)	CASE NO. CA 00000
	)	
Plaintiff-Appellant,	)	
	)	
v.	)	
	)	
BYTE COMPUTER CORPORATION,	)	
	)	
Defendant-Appellee.	)	

BRIEF OF APPELLANT, ANYBIG INSURANCE COMPANY

Attorney Name (ID# 999999)
FIRM NAME
Address
City, State, Zip
Telephone
Counsel for Appellant,
Anybig Insurance Company

Attorney Name
FIRM NAME
Address
City, State, Zip
Telephone
Counsel for Appellee,
Byte Computer Corporation

§ 7.32 Preparing the Appendix to the Appellate Brief

The appellant is responsible for preparing the appendix, which is usually filed simultaneously with the appellant's brief, although under certain circumstances it may be filed later. The appendix is not the record, but rather contains key excerpts of materials selected from the record for the convenience of the judges. The contents of the appendix could include legibly reproduced copies of:

- the judgment, order, or decision being appealed;
- the Notice of Appeal (or Amended Notice of Appeal, as appropriate);
- relevant findings of fact, conclusions of law, or judicial opinions;
- statutes, rules, regulations, ordinances, and constitutional provisions cited in the brief;
- unofficially published opinions and unpublished opinions (subject to applicable restrictions); and
- other portions of the record to which the appellant wants to direct the court's attention.

The parties are supposed to agree on the contents of the appendix, but if they cannot reach an agreement, the appellant must serve on the appellee a description of the contents he or she intends to include in the appendix. The appellee then has 10 days to file a request to have additional items included if they are essential to a determination of the issues. This is similar to the procedure for designating the portions of the transcript to be included in the record (see § **7.24**). The appellant usually pays the cost of producing the appendix, but if the appellee has requested that additional materials be included, the appellee may have to share the cost.

Federal court rules require the appendix to be in a separate volume, but state courts may allow the appendix to be bound with the brief. The appendix must have a table of contents at the front listing what is included in the order it appears, with page references to the page of the appendix where each part begins. Any excerpts from the transcript of proceedings that are included in the appendix may be numbered as pages in the appendix, but they must also indicate in brackets [ ] the page number in the actual transcript where the excerpt may be found. Indicate omissions of text from the transcript by asterisks (***).

File the appropriate number of copies of the appendix with the clerk and serve one copy on each opposing counsel. The exact number of copies required is determined by the court. Consult your local rules.

§ 7.33 Preparing for Oral Argument

The oral argument is the last chance for the attorney to direct the attention of the judges to specific arguments set out in the brief and attempt to persuade the panel to decide the issues in favor of the attorney's client. Each side is allowed only a limited amount of time for the oral argument, so the wise attorney will concentrate on the one or two most important points and briefly mention the other issues discussed in the brief. Although the material presented in the briefs is really the foundation for the decision of the appellate judges, a compelling oral argument may tip the scale in a close case. Oral arguments are generally allowed by appeals courts unless the parties waive them or the judges decide oral argument is not necessary for them to decide the case.

Ask your supervising attorney what you can do to help in preparing for oral argument. Even experienced attorneys view oral argument in appellate court as a high stress duty. It is easy to understand how an attorney might be nervous about arguing the appeal before an imposing and inquisitive panel of judges. Here are some suggestions for ways you may be able to assist:

1. The appeals court clerk notifies the parties of the date and time the oral arguments are scheduled. Keep the attorney apprised of any postponements or changes to the date and time.
2. A common complaint from appeals court judges is that attorneys are not adequately prepared to answer impromptu questions from the panel. The attorney must be familiar with the entire record and able to quickly locate materials in it. You can help by making sure the attorney has a good index of the materials related to the appeal issues. Clearly tab and highlight sections that the attorney will need to find quickly.
3. While preparing for the oral argument, the attorney may ask you to do some informal research on the judges. Knowing something about their personalities and their past decisions in similar cases may help the attorney anticipate questions and tailor the oral argument to the judges who will be the audience. See § **6.9** for tips on gathering information about judges.
4. If the attorney plans to use any documents or demonstrative exhibits from the case during the oral argument, you may be asked to oversee setting up the materials in the courtroom before court convenes and removing them after the session adjourns.

§ 7.34 Preparing the Final Accounting

Regardless of the outcome of the trial, certain financial housekeeping details will require attention at the conclusion of the case. The trial paralegal will often be assigned the task of overseeing the administrative paperwork necessary to close out the case. Your level of involvement in this aspect of posttrial operations will depend on your experience, the size of your office, and the attorney's preferences. The following sections discuss some areas that a trial paralegal typically handles, but the procedures for processing the final case accounting vary widely from office to office. Talk to your supervising attorney and the bookkeeper or accountant to ascertain the correct procedures in your office.

§ 7.35 Paying All the Bills

Your office probably advanced certain expenses on the client's behalf at various times during the case. Some expenses incurred early in the case may have already been paid, but the bills for expenses directly related to the trial preparation may not come in until days or weeks after the conclusion of the trial. The trial expenses might include charges for:

- Demonstrative evidence preparation (enlargements of documents, reprints of photographs, and so forth)
- Charges for certified records obtained from hospitals, government agencies, courts, and so forth
- Deposition transcripts and court reporter fees
- Video technician's fees for filming a video deposition and for video playback in the courtroom at trial
- Expert witnesses (travel and lodging, expert report fees, preparation time, witness testimony hourly expenses)
- Lay witnesses (witness fees and mileage served with trial subpoenas)
- Outside investigators and related charges
- Mileage and parking (for clerks who had to run errands, deliveries, pickups)
- Westlaw, LEXIS and other on-line research conducted to prepare the case for trial
- Long distance telephone charges
- FAX or telecopier charges
- Overnight or express mail charges
- Photocopying expenses

Track these expenditures diligently. You will need to provide the client with an itemization of all the case-related expenses (see **§ 7.37**). Collect the bills for the trial expenses in one folder or envelope as you receive them. You may want use a chart or worksheet like the one shown (see **Form 7–15**) to track the bills as they are paid. If your case information is on computer, you may prefer to enter this data on your spreadsheet or database program (see **Chapter 8**).

Find out what paperwork your office requires to requisition checks and make sure that all the trial bills are paid promptly. Send a cover letter enclosing the check for payment and a copy of the bill or invoice for reference. Be sure to thank anyone who gave you especially good service. Keep copies of this correspondence and note any questions or follow-up activity. You may need to get receipts for large amounts.

FORM 7–15
TRIAL EXPENSES WORKSHEET

TRIAL EXPENSES WORKSHEET

CASE ID ____________________ CLIENT/FILE No. ____________

Item No.	Description	Bill Type	Date Received	Amount	Date Paid	Check No.
				$		
				$		
				$		
				$		
				$		
				$		
				$		
				$		
				$		
				$		
				$		
				$		
				$		
				$		
				$		
				$		

§ 7.36 Paying Subrogated Medical Expenses

When you represent the plaintiff in a case involving injuries that required medical treatment, and you obtained a recovery for your client via verdict or settlement, there may be subrogated claims for medical expenses. These amounts must be reimbursed to the health care providers or insurance company for outstanding medical bills that the attorney guaranteed would be paid from the proceeds of any verdict, judgment, or settlement. Normally, your client will want your office to take care of paying the subrogated expenses as part of the final accounting at the close of the case. This relieves the client of the task and ensures that you will have accurate documentation of the payments. Review the file to locate any subrogation agreements and attorney guaranty or protection letters the attorney may have sent during the course of the case. Consult your supervising attorney on any questions about the procedures in your office for handling these payments.

When you are ready to disburse the funds, verify the correct balance due to each doctor, hospital, or other medical care provider (your client may have made some interim payments you were not aware of). You may want to use the Medical Expenses Worksheet (see **§ 2.67**) to help you track the subrogated amounts. Remember that by the time a personal injury case gets to trial, some of the medical bills your client incurred may be three or four years old. If any of the bills have been referred to collection agencies, you will probably find correspondence from collectors in the file.

Send a cover letter briefly explaining the origin of the payment and thanking the health care provider or collection agency for their patience and cooperation (see **Form 7–16**). Be sure to include sufficient information in the letter to enable the health care provider to identify the bill and properly credit the payment on your client's behalf. Clearly identify the health care provider's account number or other reference code from the bill in your letter.

You will need to itemize the subrogation payments made on behalf of your client as part of the final accounting. It is a good idea to get a receipt acknowledging payment in full from each health care provider so that you will have complete documentation of the payments. Send the following enclosures along with the letter: the check; a copy of the bill or invoice; the receipt; and an addressed, stamped return envelope.

The following sample (**Form 7–17**) is a model cover letter and receipt form to accompany payment of subrogated expenses to the health care provider. If your word processing program accommodates mail-merge letters, subrogation letters are a good use for that capability (see **§ 8.14**) since you probably have the information stored on a computer database or word processing program. The sample letter and receipt indicate the location of the variable data fields you will need to fill in to generate the letters and receipts using a word processing program's merge codes feature. Format the data in your merge records according to these fields:

{FIELD 1} Name
{FIELD 2} Company
{FIELD 3} Address
{FIELD 4} City, State, Zip
{FIELD 5} Account No.
{FIELD 6} Date of Services
{FIELD 7} Balance
{FIELD 8} Salutation
{FIELD 9} Check No.

FORM 7–16
SAMPLE LETTER TO SUBROGATED HEALTH CARE PROVIDER

[Date]

{FIELD 1} Name
{FIELD 2} Company
{FIELD 3} Address
{FIELD 4} City, State, Zip

Re: Patient: [Client Name]
Responsible Party: [Parent if client is a minor]
Account #: {FIELD 5}
Date of Services: {FIELD 6}
Balance: {FIELD 7} Amount

Dear {FIELD 8} Salutation:

This office represents the above-named client in litigation and settlement negotiations arising from injuries received in a motor vehicle accident which occurred on [accident date]. We have now reached a settlement of this matter, and we are happy to enclose our disbursement Check No. {FIELD 9} in the amount of {FIELD 7} in full payment of the balance due on the account indicated above.

We would appreciate it if you would acknowledge payment of this account in full by signing the enclosed receipt and returning it to us for our records in the envelope provided.

Thank you on behalf of our client for your patience and cooperation in withholding collection proceedings on this account. If you should have any questions regarding the enclosed payment, please contact the undersigned.

Very truly yours,

Name
Title

Enclosures

FORM 7–17
SAMPLE RECEIPT FOR SUBROGATED EXPENSE

RECEIPT

In the matter of [Client Name/Case Identification]

To: {FIELD 1} Name
{FIELD 2} Company
{FIELD 3} Address
{FIELD 4} City, State, Zip

Re: Patient: [Client Name]
Responsible Party: [Parent if Client is a Minor]
Account #: {FIELD 5}
Date of Services: {FIELD 6}
Balance: $ {FIELD 7}

The undersigned representative of {FIELD 1} Name or {FIELD 2} Company hereby acknowledges receipt of Check No. {FIELD 9} in the amount of {FIELD 7} from [Attorney or Firm Name] as PAYMENT IN FULL of the above-referenced account balance on behalf of [Client Name].

Dated: ____________________ ____________________________

§ 7.37 Preparing the Final Disbursement Statement

In cases that settle or end in a judgment or verdict awarding money damages, and in which there is no appeal, there will normally be a brief time lag between the date of the settlement or judgment and the date the check is actually in hand. The check will usually be made payable to both the attorney and the client(s), so you will have to arrange a brief meeting with the clients to get their signatures before you can deposit the check. In most law offices, the check will be deposited into an escrow or trust account where it is held pending final disbursement. Verify the exact procedures for your office with your company's bookkeeper or accounting department.

If the case is based on a contingent fee agreement, review the original fee contract or signed letter of representation carefully to determine the percentage of recovery to be allocated to legal fees and provisions for payment of the expenses advanced. Make sure that all the bills for trial-related items and subrogated medical expenses have been paid (see **§ 7.35** and **§ 7.36**). If you can, use a computer spreadsheet or database to help you easily track and update these expenses.

The client is entitled to know exactly what advances were paid. Be prepared to produce supporting documentation of expenses as necessary to answer the client's questions. Use the suggestions in the following checklist to help you in preparing this final accounting for the client.

Checklist: Preparing the Disbursement Statement

____ 1. Request an account summary or billing statement (or the equivalent in your office) from the bookkeeper or accounting department.

____ 2. Examine the account summary or billing statement to make sure that all items charged to the account do belong there. (Even the best accounting departments occasionally duplicate expenses or charge them to the wrong account. Check this carefully before you prepare the Final Disbursement Statement.)

____ 3. Review the account records for any previous or partial payments made by clients on legal fees or the expenses advanced, and be sure these payments are properly credited to the client's account.

____ 4. Examine the account summary or billing statement to make sure you can clearly identify the various advances listed (such as, court reporting and transcription expenses for a specific witness). Refer to your Expenses and Receipts file for assistance in identifying items by date or amount (see § **2.67**).

____ 5. Group the various expenses into logical categories and list them on the Final Disbursement Statement. A computer spreadsheet can help here. **Form 7–18** illustrates a typical disbursement statement itemizing the advances.

____ 6. Proofread the disbursement sheet carefully and run a calculator tape to double-check the figures. If you are using a computer spreadsheet, make sure the formulas and amounts are entered correctly.

____ 7. Print two original disbursement sheets, and have the supervising attorney sign both originals.

____ 8. Arrange a conference with the clients to review and sign the disbursement sheet. Give the clients one of the signed originals along with the settlement check.

FORM 7–18
SAMPLE FINAL DISBURSEMENT STATEMENT

FINAL DISBURSEMENT STATEMENT

In the matter of [Client Name/Case Identification]

Amount of Judgment [or Settlement] received from [Defendant or Insurance Company]		$ xxx,xxx.xx
Legal fees to [Attorney or Firm Name] per fee agreement of [date]	-	$ xx,xxx.xx
		=========
		$xxx,xxx.xx
Less expenses advanced (Itemized Below)	-	$ xx,xxx.xx
		=========
Less reimbursement/payment to health care		$ xx,xxx.xx
providers for subrogated amounts	-	$ xx,xxx.xx
		=========
Net Disbursement to [Client Name]:		$xxx,xxx.xx

ITEMIZATION OF EXPENSES ADVANCED:

• Expert Witnesses	$ xx,xxx.xx
• Court Reporters/Transcripts)	$
• Computer Research (Lexis, Westlaw)	$
• Medical Records and Reports	$
• Outside Investigation and Reports	$
• Court Filing Fees	$
• Long distance telephone	$
• Telecopier (FAX)	$
• Photocopies	$
• Postage (Express Mail, etc.)	$
• Mileage	$
	=========
Total Expenses Advanced:	$ xx,xxx.xx

I(we), the undersigned client(s), hereby agree to indemnify and hold harmless the firm of [name] and its employees or representatives for any and all subrogation claims not heretofore disclosed and paid with respect to the above-captioned litigation, and I(we) further certify that I(we) have notified said firm of all subrogation interests pertaining to this action.

Dated: _________, 19___ ____________________
[Client Name]

Dated: _________, 19___ ____________________
[Attorney Name]

§ 7.38 Handling Releases

The settlement or verdict check will usually be accompanied by a release of claims that must be signed by your clients and returned to the opposing attorney or insurance company. The release may be a typed document or a printed form; some releases are more elaborate than others, depending on the issuing company. You will need to arrange a brief meeting with the clients to execute the release. If the attorney asks you to handle this meeting, be prepared to briefly explain the release and disbursements to the clients. Make sure the clients understand that by signing the release they agree, in exchange for receipt of the money, they will never again sue these same defendants for the claims, injuries, or other losses arising out of the incident that was the subject of the lawsuit. If the release requires that the signatures be witnessed or notarized, be sure to have the appropriate witnesses present. The original release is normally returned to the insurance company or its attorney. Give the client a copy of the signed release and keep one copy with your other closing records on the case.

§ 7.39 Closing out the Case Files

The trial paralegal often supervises the task of preparing the materials in the case files for closing and storage. At the conclusion of the trial, the case files may be unceremoniously dumped in your office. You may be inclined to want to bury the case and never think about it again, but your job is not finished. Each office has procedures for closing, storing, and archiving the files when a case is completed. Of course, you can't really close out the file for storage until you are certain that all the proceedings are completed. This means at least 30 days past the date of the judgment entry or order confirming the judgment or jury verdict, and longer if there are any posttrial proceedings or appeals. However, you can perform some cleanup chores immediately after trial while the materials are still familiar and your memory is fresh about how the materials are arranged. This interim cleanup helps to organize the file for posttrial motions (see **§ 7.6**) or appeals proceedings (see **§ 7.15**) or for conducting the posttrial research and analysis (see **§ 7.57**).

As soon as possible following the conclusion of the trial, empty the trial briefcases and collect any trial materials that the attorneys or other trial team members may have in their possession. Regardless of how conscientious you are during the trial about returning items to their proper places each day, at the conclusion of the trial there will still be miscellaneous materials that need a home in the file. Go through any materials that have accumulated during the trial but which you have not had a chance to put away. Replace these materials into their proper original files, or make new folders or files to accommodate items that do not fit with previously labeled files.

§ 7.40 —Preparing the Synopsis or Case ID Sheet

Write a case synopsis stating the basic facts and issues in the case along with pertinent identifying data: client name, file number, case number, judge, opposing parties, and counsel, trial date, notes of special exhibits used, special problems in the case, experts used, and the result or disposition of the file. Place copies of both the synopsis and the closed file index (see **§ 7.41**) in your master reference notebook (see **§ 1.61**). If you have previously prepared a synopsis of the case, you may only need to add the information on the results of the trial. You may want to start a computer database to store the file closing information (see **Chapter 8**).

§ 7.41 —Preparing the Closed File Index

The best way to ensure that you will be able to easily retrieve all or part of a case file in the future is to prepare an accurate closing index, a detailed listing of the file contents before the materials go to storage. Use the initial file diagram outline you created when you first organized the file (see **Chapter 2**) as a starting guide. If you have not already done so, update the file diagram to include the sections, folders, and new divisions of materials that you created specifically for trial (see **§ 5.8**). Place copies of both the closed file index and the case synopsis (see **§ 7.40**) in your master reference notebook (see **§ 1.61**).

§ 7.42 Returning Items to Their Owners

Return all personal materials and records to your client or the witness who provided them. The client's personal property could include such items as diaries, calendars, datebooks, awards, photographs, mementos, tax returns and financial documents, and original records or certificates (such as, marriage, birth, or death certificates). Be sure to return all official records or other original reference materials to expert witnesses who provided them during the trial preparation.

§ 7.43 —Preserving Local Rules and Procedures

If the trial was conducted in a forum other than the jurisdiction in which you usually practice, you will have accumulated certain materials specific to the foreign venue (see **Chapter 1**). The materials on out-of-town courts might include:

- Local court rules
- Schedule of local filing fees
- Local judge's standing trial orders
- Directions/maps/diagrams of courthouse and facilities
- Names of local counsel, court reporters, and so forth

Consult your supervising attorney on whether these materials should be stored with the file, or whether they should be added to your library of practice aids. If the local court rules are substantially different from your own, place a copy of the rules and the schedule of court costs in your master reference notebook under the section for information on out-of-town courts (see § **1.61**).

§ 7.44 Preparing Pleadings for Storage

Assemble a *complete* master set of pleadings that were generated during the case, including the documents that were filed just before or during the actual trial proceedings. Of course, you will have already kept your substantive pleadings index up to date as a matter of good file maintenance (see **Chapter 2**) until those last few days just before trial when the preparation pace got really hectic.

Collect a time-stamped copy of each item filed during the trial, add them to the pleadings binder, and update your index to reflect the additions. Be sure to include any pleadings filed by the opposing parties as well as those filed by your office. A particularly important item to log in the pleadings index is the court's final order or entry reciting the judgment or verdict rendered in the case. The filing date on this order or entry triggers the date for posttrial motions and appeal (see § **7.6** and § **7.15**). Other trial filings might include:

- Trial briefs/bench briefs
- Motions in limine and supporting memoranda
- Requests for jury charge
- Proposed jury instructions (from both sides)
- Actual jury charge (given by the judge at trial)
- Jury interrogatories
- Jury verdict forms.

The court clerk will have a complete set of pleadings in the official records of the case, but an accurate set in your file is a convenient reference. A complete set of pleadings can be useful whether or not there is any posttrial activity. If the case does involve posttrial activity, such as a motion for new trial or an appeal, the attorney will need to refer to the pleadings filed during the case in order to prepare the posttrial documents. If there is no posttrial activity, you will have a complete set of the case pleadings to use for examples in future cases. Make sure all binders in a multivolume set are clearly labeled.

If the case involved posttrial activities, consider creating a separate volume or index binder to keep these records segregated from the main bulk of the file pleadings. This serves two purposes: it keeps the appeals papers all together (they will have a different case number from the trial court pleadings) and you or the attorney can easily transport or access the appeals pleadings only without having to dig through the whole pleadings file. See **Chapter 2** for more information on organizing and indexing pleadings.

§ 7.45 —Archiving Work Product

The attorney may want to refer to work product from the trial file in future cases dealing with similar issues, and you must be able to quickly locate and retrieve the desired documents. If you have saved selected trial materials in archive sample files, indexed and organized by type, you may be able to produce the example the attorney wants without retrieving the entire closed case file. If you are new to trial work and you aren't sure what to save, or if you are working with an attorney whose preferences you do not know well, ask for input on what types of materials from the trial files might be useful in future cases. You may also want to collect the computer word processing files for documents generated by your office in an automated brief bank. Consider building sample files for routine trial documents, such as:

- Motions in limine
- Trial briefs
- Voir dire questions (both general and case-specific)
- Jury instructions
- Jury interrogatories
- Memoranda and briefs on points of law.

As you compile the master set of pleadings during the file cleanup (see § **7.44**), you are likely to find duplicates in the file. Conserve paper by adding these duplicates to your bank of samples instead of making additional photocopies. Use three-ring binders or sturdy folders with top-edge fasteners to contain your sample files, and prepare an index for each binder (see § **2.75**). As you complete work on each new trial, add examples from the case to your sample files. Samples of trial pleadings prepared in other cases can be really useful drafting aids, especially if you ever train new paralegals or assist novice attorneys.

§ 7.46 —Handling Special Packets of Pleadings

As you review the case files, you will undoubtedly find discrete packets of pleadings and discovery materials that were assembled for specific purposes (for example, a last minute deposition of an expert just before trial). You will have to decide whether a particular collection of materials should be preserved. Most of the materials may be duplicates of original documents already in the file, but some packets may consist of documents, notes, and related materials compiled as supporting information for certain calculations, opinions, proposals, or positions, so it may be wise to keep these packets together so that the materials can be viewed in context.

If you decide the set of materials should stay together, put them in their own clearly labeled folder, envelope, or binder. You probably will want to create separate files or binders to contain sets of materials from other types of organized proceedings, such as arbitration, mediation, and summary jury trial proceedings used in some federal courts (see **§ 2.18**).

§ 7.47 Preserving Research and Resource Materials

When you initially organized the case file, you probably designated one or more sections to contain research and reference information. As you prepare to close out the case, you must determine the appropriate disposition for various types of resource materials that have accumulated in the files. Talk with the attorney about materials he or she would like to retain for future reference. The following sections contain some suggestions for preserving and storing legal and factual research.

§ 7.48 —Preserving Legal Research Materials

The file may have accumulated a large amount of legal research on various evidentiary issues during the life of the case (see **Chapter 2**). In addition, the trial team may have conducted legal research in the last few days before trial to support the client's position on specific issues for motions in limine, proposed jury instructions, and so forth. Some of this research may be useful in preparing motions and briefs, if the case involves any posttrial activity or if there is an appeal. Saving key legal research materials may enable you to avoid additional photocopying later.

If the amount of legal research is relatively small, you may decide to simply two-hole punch the documents, fasten them into a manila folder, and then file them away with the other general case materials. If a large amount of research has been compiled on an important issue, prepare an index of the supporting cases (see § **2.75** *et seq.*) Punch the indexed cases and place them into a clearly labeled folder or binder for easy retrieval when a similar issue arises in another case. Try to match up photocopied cases from the West Reporters and/or Westlaw and LEXIS printouts with the specific motion, instruction, memorandum, and so forth the cases support and staple them to a copy of the document they support. If this is not possible, at least make labeled subfiles, for example, "Legal Research–Motions in Limine" to contain these groups of supplemental research. Depending on the issues in the case, the amount of materials collected on each issue, and what other file materials already exist, you may want to file legal and factual research materials separately.

§ 7.49 —Preserving Factual Research Materials

If you have compiled a large amount of factual research materials, such as background articles and texts on a specific medical condition, consider whether these materials could be relevant to other cases in the future, particularly if you routinely handle cases involving similar issues (such as, automobile accidents or medical malpractice cases). Do not file these resource materials with the case files that will be sent to storage. Instead, set up a library or bank of these materials, indexed by subject matter, for reference in future cases. This is a great project for a simple database if you have access to a computer (see **Chapter 8**). If the research includes substantive sections from books or treatises, prepare an index and have the materials bound or place them into a ring binder to retain for future reference. If your in-house library has a "clippings file," this may be the appropriate place to deposit some of the materials for storage and retrieval.

§ 7.50 Storing Specific Types of Materials

Just as you considered specific categories of materials when you initially organized the file (see § **2.61**), you must also think about the best way to permanently store these materials.

§ 7.51 —Storing Depositions and Deposition Exhibits

As you sort out the file for closing, compile a set of all the depositions in the case. Update your manual or automated Master Deposition Index (see § **5.49**) to include data on any depositions that were taken in the last few days before trial. Include in the master index descriptions of transcripts and audio or video cassette tapes, if any, of taped depositions taken in the case.

The deposition file should include clearly marked copies of any deposition testimony read into the record at trial. Keep a marked copy of video or conventional deposition objection transcripts (see § **6.11**) in case of appeal. In addition, your supervising attorney may want to place a copy of a particular expert's deposition transcript in the expert's reference folder (see § **3.27**).

Place any deposition abstracts or summaries you have created in the folders or binders with their respective depositions. Also attach a complete set of exhibits to each deposition so that a person reading the deposition at some future date would have the exhibits mentioned in the deposition readily available without having to dig through the file to find them. For additional information on organizing and categorizing depositions, refer to **Chapter 2** and § **5.42** *et seq.*

§ 7.52 —Consolidating the Trial Materials File

As you return materials to their proper places in the files, try to keep a set of all the materials actually used for trial intact. Assemble the actual trial materials into a binder or expanding folder to form a concise record of what transpired at the trial for anyone who refers to the file in future years. The trial materials file should include the following:

1. Schedule and Index Sheets. Complete your scheduling block sheets, exhibit indexes, worksheets, and so forth, so that you have a record of the sequence of events during the last couple of days of trial (see §§ **6.61, 6.79**).
2. Subpoenas File. Save one filed copy of each subpoena, along with these supporting documents:
   - Trial witness subpoena index (see § **5.31**)
   - Copy of completed service return
   - Copy of motion and order designating persons to serve subpoenas
   - Copy of witness fee checks (return any unused or uncashed checks to your accounting department to be credited to the client's account of expenses advanced; see § **7.37**).

3. Attorney's Trial Notebook (see § **5.77**)
4. Jury and Voir Dire Materials (see § **6.16** *et seq.*)
   - Jury profile sheets
   - Jury panel investigation and jury research
   - Voir dire outlines and questions to add to your bank of sample forms (see § **7.45**)
   - Posttrial juror questionnaire, if any (see § **7.58**)
5. Expert Witnesses. Put materials related to the expert witness in the expert's reference file (see **Chapter 2,** § **3.27**). Label these materials in sufficient detail to identify the case they came from (client name, case name, file number, trial date, court, judge, and so forth). Materials for the expert's reference file could include:
   - Curriculum vitae (make sure it is dated)
   - Description or background on expert's business or company
   - Outline of specific questions used to qualify the expert
   - Copy of deposition transcript for future reference
6. Trial Notes. Make a folder (if you have not already done so) for all trial notes taken by either you or the attorney. Be sure to date and label these, and securely staple them together. Your trial notes will be particularly important if the attorney plans posttrial motions and an official transcript has not yet been prepared by the court reporter. The important points and quotes you recorded in your notes will assist the attorney in outlining arguments for posttrial motions and appeal. Also insert a copy of your trial scheduling sheet (see § **6.61**) into this file so that the attorney can recall the exact order in which the witnesses testified, the date and time each phase of the trial occurred, and so forth. This is especially helpful if the trial lasted more than two or three days.
7. Trial Exhibits. Compile a complete set of all the exhibits used at trial and fasten them to a completed exhibit index. Catalog and store any reusable demonstrative exhibits (such as anatomical charts) with your other reference materials and trial supplies. You will probably want to dispose of all the customized oversize exhibits or demonstrative evidence, but check with the client before you pitch these items. The client paid for these exhibits and occasionally a client will want to keep certain exhibits for some reason. If the client doesn't want the oversized exhibits, check with the artist or illustrator who created them. The artist may want exhibits for her portfolio of work. If you decide not to keep oversized artwork, file a photograph of the exhibit or at least a detailed description of it with the closed file materials so that if someone years later needs to use the file for a reference, they will know what the exhibit looked like.

§ 7.53 Preparing Files for Storage

Storage space for inactive files is expensive. Your case will have generated a lot of paper that is not necessarily best kept in long-term storage. In order to save storage space, you need to consolidate the file materials, remove duplicates and other extraneous materials, and recycle any reusable materials gleaned from the file.

§ 7.54 —Consolidating Files and Removing Duplicates

When you get ready to store the closed files, make the file contents as compact as possible. Check first with your supervising attorney about retention policies for important client records to find out what materials and files you absolutely should keep. For other noncritical files, remove any extraneous materials to reduce the bulk of the file. There is no reason to store multiple photocopies of documents just because they ended up in the case files file. Keep one (or two at the most) labeled copies (time-stamped, certified) and pitch the duplicates. Examine any apparent duplicates of a document to make sure that they are identical to the original. For example, some transcripts may have the same cover sheet, but one may be a corrected copy or a preparation or briefing copy with highlighted portions or marginal notations. Consider keeping this type of working copies of documents, especially if they seem to belong in with a special packet of materials (see § **7.49**). Save the extra exact duplicates only until you have completed preparing the file for storage, in case you decide that a copy belongs in context elsewhere in the file. If you have to choose between keeping the original and keeping a copy of a record or document, keep the original unless it should be returned to its rightful owner (see § **7.42**).

Generally, there is no need to keep drafts of major pleadings (see also § **7.44**, Preparing Pleadings for Storage). Documents such as trial briefs often go through several revisions before the final version. The attorneys may have kept each draft just in case they need to compare versions or refer back to the original document. Usually, the final version of a pleading is the only one that matters, but **check with your supervising attorney about this before you pitch them!**

§ 7.55 —Recycling Reusable Materials

Try to recycle any reusable materials from the file, especially bulky items like expensive vinyl notebooks that take up valuable storage space.

Yellow Legal Pads

If your supervising attorneys are like most, they will have used a dozen or so different legal pads for notes, outlines, lists, and so forth during the trial preparation and presentation. (There seems to be a pervasive unwritten policy among trial attorneys that compels them to use a fresh legal pad each time they begin a work session.) You will usually find that only the top few pages of the tablets have been written on, leaving most of a tablet of clean, unused sheets. A single partly used legal pad in the files may not amount to much, but several pads can take up valuable inches of long-term storage space.

When you encounter partly used legal pads as you weed out the files, neatly tear off the used sheets from each tablet and firmly staple the sheets together at the top. Add a label, if necessary, to indicate the type or subject matter of the notations, the approximate date(s) they were made, and by whom, and then file the stapled packet in the appropriate place in your case files. Combine all sequential trial notes into a reference file. You can then use the remaining partial pads for future notes and everyday projects. When the tablets are finally used up, I also salvage the cardboard backings to use as stabilizers for packets of loose papers and materials (see **Chapter 2**). (**Note:** Yellow legal paper is not recyclable. You may want to suggest that your attorneys switch to buff or white tablets.)

Manila Folders and Jackets

If you have previously created folders to contain specific subjects or divisions of trial materials, try to reuse these to store some portion of the case file. If you need to change the label to reflect the new contents, first cross out the old label with a heavy marker, then add a new adhesive label over the old one. You can also turn manila folders inside out and use the clean side of the tab for a new label.

Extra Supplies

Except in very large cases, you probably will not use the whole package of labels, stickers, color-coding dots, art supplies, brief covers, or other supplies ordered specifically for the case. Stockpile these in your paralegal trial supply closet for use in future projects and cases.

§ 7.56 —Labeling Files for Storage

Contain any remaining loose papers in the files. Staple related items together and remove any paper clips. Fasten papers into files, or punch holes and insert papers into sturdy folders or jackets. Label file folders, pockets, jackets (whatever you use) and make sure that the labels are securely affixed. Pack the files away in storage boxes or files, depending on the size of the file and the preferred procedures in your office. Index and label multiple boxes or folders as "Box 1 of 3, Box 2 of 3, Box 3 of 3" or "File 1 of 12, File 2 of 12, File 3 of 12" and so forth. See also **Chapter 2** on organizing file materials.

§ 7.57 Learning from Trial Experience

I have always felt that each trial has its own sort of flavor or personality comprised of high and low points, successes and difficulties, sometimes moments of humor or pathos. A trial's unique characteristics come readily to mind even years later when someone mentions the case or the client. (Listen to any group of litigators informally discussing their work. Trial attorneys always have favorite war stories about long-ago trials that they recall as clearly as yesterday!) The issues in a lawsuit may be similar to issues in other cases, but the exact combination of participants (clients, attorneys, experts, judge, jurors), facts, timing, and results will be unique for each trial. Developing trial skills is a cumulative process, and each trial is a learning experience precisely because of its unique features. As a trial paralegal, you will benefit from reviewing and analyzing each trial to learn more about the litigation process, improve your skills, and refine your trial preparation techniques. Learning and improving with each case will quickly increase your value to the trial attorney.

§ 7.58 Conducting Posttrial Jury Interviews

Interviewing the jurors after the trial can yield valuable information for trial team members. Whether the verdict was favorable or unfavorable to your client, the attorneys will wonder how the jurors arrived at their decision, what factors affected their decision the most, whether they understood the presentation, and so forth. The jurors are not obliged to talk with you, but in most jurisdictions they *may* discuss the case if they want to. When you objectively analyze their responses, the collective insight and wisdom of the jurors can help the trial team hone their skills.

See what your supervising attorney thinks about juror interviews. Under no circumstances should you attempt to contact the jurors unless you have first cleared the plan with the trial attorney! If the attorney wants to survey the jurors after the trial, he or she may prefer to conduct interviews either in person or by telephone, or may ask you to prepare a survey questionnaire to mail to the jurors. **Form 7–19** illustrates a cover letter and a model jury questionnaire, which contains a number of different questions you can adapt to create either a telephone interview guide or a written questionnaire. Choose the questions that apply to your case and add any others the attorney feels are appropriate. Keep these points in mind as you prepare the jury survey questionnaire and cover letter:

1. Keep the questionnaire as brief as possible so the jurors will not feel the survey is burdensome to answer. Try to structure the questions in a way that will elicit additional thoughts and comments from the jurors.
2. Send the questionnaires (or contact the jurors by telephone) soon after the trial while the evidence and testimony are still fresh in their minds.
3. Provide space after each question for the jurors to write in their answers. Indicate that they can use the back of the page or attach extra sheets if they need more space to complete their answers.
4. Insert the names of the parties and the attorneys in place of "plaintiff" or "defendant" or "counsel" to help the jurors recall which party was which.
5. The responses may be more candid when you give the jurors the option of remaining anonymous. Do not require a signature or other identification on the survey response form. (**Note:** If you want to keep track of which jurors return answers, put an unobtrusive code number or letter somewhere on the form or on the return envelope and check these off as the questionnaires are returned.)
6. Use the mail-merge function in your computer word processing or database software (see **§ 8.14**) to insert the individual juror's name and address to personalize the form cover letter. The trial attorney should sign the letters, because the jurors will remember the attorney from the courtroom proceedings. Although a typed envelope is usually preferred for business letters, try addressing the juror letters by hand. People tend to open hand-addressed mail first because it doesn't look like junk mail or bills.
7. Enclose a return envelope stamped with sufficient postage to make it easy for the jurors to return the questionnaire.

Not all the jurors will take the time to respond, but a few of them usually will. The jurors' responses to the survey will help you to view the case from the jurors' perspective. Jurors often pick up on seemingly insignificant details in the courtroom, and some of the factors that influenced their decision may surprise you. Comments from the jurors will typically reveal information on such points as:

- Whether your witnesses were perceived as truthful
- Whether the expert witness was effective and credible on the stand (useful data if you plan to use the expert again)

- Whether the trial attorney seemed organized and prepared
- Whether the jurors like the opposing attorney or client
- Whether the demonstrative evidence helped the jurors understand the testimony
- Whether any aspect of the trial offended, troubled, confused, or amused the jurors.

FORM 7–19
SAMPLE COVER LETTER ENCLOSING JUROR SURVEY QUESTIONNAIRE

Re: [case identification]

Dear [Juror Name]:

Thank you for serving recently on the jury panel in the [court name and location]. I represented [client name] at that trial. I am requesting that you answer the questionnaire enclosed with this letter and return it to me in the envelope provided. Your answers will help me improve my skills as a trial lawyer and enhance my ability to see the case from a juror's point of view.

(OPTIONAL PARAGRAPH)

After you have had a chance to read through this questionnaire and think about your answers, please contact me to discuss the case. If you prefer, [state other options for action, depending on what the attorney wants to do].

You are not required to respond at all, but I would very much like to hear from you as I believe your comments about this case would be valuable to me. If you are willing to discuss this case with me, please call me next week at XXX-XXXX. If I am away from the office when you call, please speak with my legal assistant, [name].

Very truly yours,

Trial Attorney

SAMPLE POSTTRIAL JUROR SURVEY QUESTIONNAIRE

QUESTIONNAIRE TO JURORS

Re: [case identification]

1. Was there any single fact or factor that decided the case for you? Please explain.

2. Please comment or give your opinion on the following aspects of Plaintiff's case:

   A. Most effective part of Plaintiff's case.
   B. Least effective part of Plaintiff's case.
   C. Most effective witness for Plaintiff.
   D. Least effective witness for Plaintiff.

3. Please comment on or give your opinion of the following factors in Defendant's case:

   A. Most effective part of Defendant's case.
   B. Least effective part of Defendant's case.
   C. Most effective witness for Defendant.
   D. Least effective witness for Defendant.

4. Please state whether there was anything about Plaintiff's counsel's manner of speaking, dress, or presentation that

   A. You felt helped Plaintiff's case;
   B. You felt weakened Plaintiff's case;
   C. You found personally offensive.

5. Did the Plaintiff's calling ______ as a witness affect your decision in any manner? Please explain.

[OR]

Did Plaintiff not calling ______ as a witness affect your decision in any manner? Please explain how.

6. For each of the expert witnesses listed below, please tell us:

   A. Your impression of the witness's credibility; and
   B. Whether you think the witness helped or hurt Plaintiff's case.
   [List experts and field of expertise]

7. If you could give one recommendation to Plaintiff's counsel to aid in future trial presentations, what would that recommendation be? Please elaborate.

8. Was there any part of Plaintiff's case that you did not understand or that was confusing to you? Please explain.

9. Was there any part of Defendant's case that you did not understand or that was confusing to you? Please explain.

10. Were you embarrassed or offended by any questions that Plaintiff's counsel or Defendant's counsel asked the jury panel during voir dire? If so, please state the question and explain why it embarrassed you.

11. What additional evidence or testimony, if any, do you feel would have been necessary for you to vote for a verdict in favor of ________?

12. Was there any evidence that was NOT presented by either side in the case that you would have liked to hear or see to aid you in deciding the case?

13. Do you feel that the visual aids presented by Plaintiff's counsel were helpful in understanding the testimony? Do you have any suggestions for making such visual aids more effective?

14. If Plaintiffs had proved their case to you on the liability issue, what money compensation would you have awarded for pain and suffering?

15. Please feel free to add any other comments, questions, or suggestions not covered by the above questions.

§ 7.59 Studying the Attorney's Work Style

Open communication between the attorney and the trial paralegal is vital to effective trial preparation. After the trial, building on that rapport is important to your future working relationship with the trial attorney. Look for an appropriate time and setting shortly after the trial to talk with the attorney about the case. If you have difficulty starting the discussion, consider using the jury questionnaire and responses (see **§ 7.58**) as a springboard for topics to discuss. Listen for comments that indicate the attorney's preferences and priorities. Get the attorney's perspective on what the problems were and what could have been done better.

Ask questions about events at trial that were unexpected or that you didn't completely understand. Listen to the attorney's explanation and try to determine why events unfolded the way they did. The attorney's assessment can help you grasp the issues on posttrial motions and appeal. In addition to scrutinizing your team's case presentation, evaluate the tactics and strategies the opposing attorney used and try to figure out why those methods succeeded or failed.

Working with multiple attorneys on the trial team (see **§ 1.20**), gives you the opportunity to study the similarities and contrasts in their work styles. How did you work as a team? Did the attorneys communicate well with each other and with you? Were there any mixed or missed signals about what the attorneys expected from you? Did they give you explicit instructions, or did they expect you to read their minds? Discuss how you might have handled the situation differently and ways to avoid similar problems in the future. Resolve to sharpen your communication skills for the next case you handle.

Try to get feedback from the attorney about the positive aspects of the trial, what went well, what exhibit organization worked best, how successful the visual aids were, and so on. You will be able to repeat and build on these successful techniques in future trials.

This type of candid discussion will enable you to better assist the attorney the next time you prepare for trial. You will be more familiar with the attorney's trial style after working through an entire case. Express interest and willingness to learn and perfect your skills. This can go a long way toward gaining the attorney's confidence and respect for the next case. See also the suggestions in **Chapter 1** on learning to work with trial attorneys.

If you work on a trial with an attorney you do not know well, you can learn something about the attorney's preferences and work style by examining how the attorney organizes and uses trial information. Take a look at the attorney's trial notebook after the trial. Study the way the attorney arranged and used the various sections of the trial notebook. Were some of the tabbed sections left empty? Did the attorney insert any materials in the notebook that you had not anticipated? If so, include tabs for these sections in the next trial notebook you prepare for that attorney.

§ 7.60 Planning for Next Time

The purpose of posttrial analysis and critique is not to fix blame or make excuses, but rather to determine how you can improve your skills as a trial paralegal. A key to learning from mistakes is the ability to accept constructive criticism gracefully and apply the lessons learned. We can all learn from experience, and this is especially true in trial work. Reflect on how the actual courtroom presentation was different from the one you planned in your strategy sessions. Consider what worked and what didn't. No trial presentation is problem-free. That wouldn't be a challenge! Things rarely go exactly the way we plan. Analyzing the trial is worthwhile even if you won a favorable ruling in the case, because, no matter how good your team is, there will always be some things that you could have managed better. There is no guarantee that the same problems won't crop up again in a future trial, but planning for foreseeable problems gives you the confidence to manage other emergencies as they arise. (Some new glitch *will* come up the next time!)

These are some areas to consider:

1. How could you have been better prepared? If you ran out of time, examine why. Were you punching holes in the exhibit photocopies and assembling the exhibit binders at 11 P.M. on the night before trial?

Could some of the copying and punching have been done earlier when you had some help? Perhaps you could schedule extra workers to help you next time, or send the copying out to a service. You may also want to consider getting some training in time management and delegation skills. See **Chapter 1.**

2. Were your exhibit folders and notebooks easy to locate and retrieve? If not, try to identify the problem. Were the labels too small to read? Was your index helpful? Were you able to keep the documents organized? Did you have too many or too few copies of exhibits? Did the attorney ask you for information or materials you did not have readily available? Look around for useful office supplies and bone up on paperwork management techniques. See **Chapter 2** and **Chapter 5.**
3. Did you need equipment that you didn't have on hand? Could your office possibly purchase this equipment? Did you take the right supplies and accessories to the courtroom? Did you run out of anything? Notice what items you used from or added to your tool kit and adjust your checklist accordingly for the next time you prepare for trial. Acquire duplicates of inexpensive, useful items like pocket-cutters and highlighter pens. Build up a reserve of small portable supplies so your tool kit is always stocked and ready to go. See **Chapter 6.**
4. Review the forms, lists, and indexes you prepared and used throughout the trial. Did you need more space for notes in some columns? Were there extra spaces or columns you didn't use? You can tailor forms to suit your cases. Study how you actually used the forms and then refine the form design to better fit your style of information recording. See **Chapters 1** and **2.**
5. Did you deal with outside vendors? Did you know whom to call? Did they give you good service? Keep up your contacts with service company personnel, video technicians, court reporters, subpoena servers, and investigators. You may need to call on these services again for future trials.
6. Did you use a computer to prepare the trial documents and indexes? Did you have trouble keeping track of key information? Resolve to develop your computer skills and learn more about automated litigation support techniques.

Working through a trial to conclusion gives you a good opportunity to observe the judge. Each judge has a different style. The next time you have a case before that judge, you will know more about what to expect (scheduling, general demeanor, preferences, and so forth) and how to handle trial support in his or her court. Studying a trial's flaws and problems gives you insight into the areas where you need to strengthen your knowledge and gain experience. See **Chapter 1** for suggestions and tips on developing and enhancing your professional skills.

Does it get easier? Yes, after about 10 or 15 trials! If you are just starting out, don't be discouraged. Managing trial preparation is challenging work. Winning a good result for your client is very satisfying. Hearing trial attorneys say they couldn't have done the job without your help makes the hard work and stress worthwhile. And of course, they are absolutely right!

CHAPTER 8

INTEGRATING COMPUTERS INTO TRIAL WORK

§ 8.1 Using Computer Power in Trial Preparation

Disclaimer: This chapter offers some ideas and suggestions for ways to apply computer power to many of the trial preparation activities discussed throughout this book. It is beyond the scope of this chapter to teach you how to use the computer or to endorse any particular type or brand of software. You should always determine for yourself whether any particular hardware or software is suited to your needs before you buy. The descriptions of automation products in this chapter and throughout this book do not constitute endorsement of any product. *Paralegal Trial Handbook* assumes no responsibility for your choice or use of any product discussed and disclaims all warranties and representations.

§ 8.2 Using Computers to Stay Competitive

Today's law practice is more competitive than ever before. As the law business changes, attorneys and paralegals must change with it. Businesses and workers who don't adapt to new technology will be left behind. A recent Pitney Bowes Management Services poll of 101 chief administrators from among the 400 largest law firms in the United States reported that 87 percent of the respondents agreed with the statement that "the way firms provide legal services probably will change more in the next 10 years than it has in the past 50." Many large firms have already modified the way they operate, and updating technology is a major factor in those modifications. (Source: "Firms Re-engineer," *ABA Journal* p. 24, June 1994.) A computer won't win the case for you, but computers can really help you do a better job if you learn how to use them in preparing a case for trial. In addition to augmenting your ability to efficiently accomplish routine case work, automation technology has opened exciting and imaginative new possibilities for producing demonstrative aids, transmitting documents electronically, and communicating in the courtroom.

In the early days of computers, only very large cases could justify the expense of automated litigation support. We have progressed in a very short time from room-size computers to compact desktop units that are many times faster, more powerful, and less expensive. In today's trial practice, reliable computers and sophisticated, powerful software programs are readily available and affordable. This means that you can effectively and economically use some form of computer application in even the smallest cases, regardless of the size of your firm or law office.

§ 8.3 The Small Firm Perspective

Automation is essential to the small firm or law office. Lawyers and paralegals from small offices sometimes think that computerizing would be too expensive. I believe that small firms can't afford NOT to acquire some level of computerization. Clients expect their lawyers to keep up with the times. Lawyers have an ethical duty to use the best tools available to get the job done. These days, that means using computers to handle work efficiently. Technology saves time and money by allowing you to work in a more cost-effective way. At the same time competition is increasing in the legal business, clients as legal consumers are looking more closely at the costs of hiring an attorney. Insurance companies and corporations are carefully scrutinizing services and fees of outside counsel. Some are finding it more economical to move counsel in-house. Businesses that continue to retain their outside attorneys are reexamining the concept of the billable hour, and some have moved to alternative billing arrangements. This competition and client scrutiny means that firms have to work as efficiently as possible. Firms that do not streamline their procedures and reduce their costs will be unable to survive, much less compete in today's market. Firms that implement effective automated systems enhance the ability of attorneys and paralegals to provide cost-effective legal services to clients. The current business climate demands that lawfirms make effective use of technology to improve client communications and to better control witnesses and documents. Computers have been called the great equalizers of small firms and large firms for good reason. Small law offices have to do more with less in order to compete with larger firms. Computers can help small offices accomplish this by putting them on a more equal footing with the capabilities of large law offices.

§ 8.4 Getting Started with Computer Technology

Are you reluctant to plunge in and learn about computers? The first hurdle in your quest for computer literacy may be overcoming fear (both your own and the attorneys') of the new and unknown. Granted, the plethora of new products and choices available today can be very confusing, but software and hardware keep improving, getting less expensive and easier to use. Don't be intimidated by the rapid advances in technology and the mystique surrounding computers. You really don't have to know very much about the technical aspects to start putting the computer to work for you. Computers are vital tools for productivity and efficiency in the law office. Smart paralegals keep up on technological developments, and are at least aware of the types of programs and equipment available and what can be done with them. Trial attorneys and their paralegals should realize that resisting computerization may place them at an extreme disadvantage in cases where the opponent employs automated techniques. Your role in supporting trial attorneys includes taking the lead in learning to use your computer to help you achieve greater efficiency and higher productivity in the work of preparing cases for trial.

If you are just beginning to use computers, start out slowly. Don't try to learn everything at once. Allow time for a "learning curve" to become comfortable with a new program and its capabilities. Read the manual that comes with the software and work through the program's on-line tutorial to learn the basic functions. Take training courses or seminars that are offered by the software manufacturer and by many vocational and community colleges. (If attorneys can learn to use a new program in a few hours, you can, too!) Ask experienced users of the program for help. After you have mastered the basics, keep exploring additional features and more advanced functions of the program. Document your progress by keeping a notebook of ideas, tips, and instructions that you figure out for one project, and apply these ideas to the next project or case. You'll learn a little more about how to use your computer with each project.

Learn to use the software programs that are installed on your office computer. You will be at a disadvantage if you don't know how to use the programs your company has available. The skills you learn using one program will usually transfer to other programs as you gain experience with computers. Continue to read articles on new and prevailing software and technology. Join user groups or bar association committees dealing with computers and technology issues. The paralegal is a liaison for the attorney on computer interpretation and applications. With so many training programs, user groups, tutorials, books, and magazines available to help you learn, there is really no good excuse not to explore the possibilities of enhancing your work with computers.

§ 8.5 Handling the Transition from Manual to Automated Systems

Very few offices still manage with entirely manual procedures, nor are most offices completely automated, although projections indicate that 90 percent of law offices expect to be automated by the year 2000. Instead, most law offices are somewhere along the continuum between manual and automated methods. In other words, most offices use a combination of manual and automated systems, tools, and techniques to do their work. There is nothing magical about automated systems. They simply enhance your speed and efficiency in recording and retrieving information, making it possible to complete tasks much faster than you could in the past. Before converting to an automated system, take a close look at the manual systems you have in place. Are records being kept on paper forms? Are the forms easy to read and follow? The information on these records can probably be transferred successfully to a computerized database. A well-designed manual system greatly increases the chances of a successful transition to computer, but virtually any manual task you can think of can use some form of automated assistance.

Computers have had and will continue to have a profound effect on how we handle information in the law office. Trial paralegals, along with many other professionals, are "information workers," because processing information is a vital component of the activities we refer to as litigation support. Think about how you work with the information in your cases: You record information about clients or witnesses by taking notes or filling out forms. You assemble similar or related documents and store them in file folders or binders. You refer to the records as needed to refresh your memory, or perhaps to incorporate portions of the information into a letter, pleading, or other document. Sometimes you add to the basic stored information, updating or correcting it as new facts surface. And finally, you locate and retrieve the stored information related to a specific topic when the attorney requests it. Computers can help you do all these same tasks, only more accurately, quickly, and efficiently than you could ever do it manually. You can get the required information to the attorney sooner, and you have more time free to analyze and really USE the information rather than just maintaining files and documents.

§ 8.6 Evaluating Computer Software

Paralegals in law offices across the country use computers in many different ways. Your skill level and the equipment you have available will partially determine how you use the computer in trial preparation. However, computer applications in trial practice are really only limited by the imagination and creativity of the user. Many different types of software are available to perform a variety of trial preparation functions. Some programs are specifically designed to accommodate legal and trial-related information and others are generic business programs that you can adapt and customize to the requirements of your trial practice. Most paralegals do not rely on a single type of software program, but rather use a combination of several programs to achieve the desired results. Some offices have *integrated* software packages, meaning that several different programs work together and can exchange and share the same information. The most common uses for computers in law offices are:

- Document Preparation (Word Processing)
- Accounting and Billing
- Docketing and Scheduling
- Conflict Checking
- Information Storage and Retrieval (Databases)
- Financial Calculations (Spreadsheets)
- Communications
- Specific Practice Applications.

What Kinds of Programs Should You Use?

Word processing and billing are probably the two most familiar uses for computers in the law office. Surveys show that most lawfirms have hardware and software to perform these routine tasks. Modern accounting programs do much more than generate client bills. These programs can allow a firm's financial personnel to track expenses charged to a case, balances in trust accounts, accounts payable, and general ledger functions. Most lawyers and paralegals now have computers on their desks. In addition to billing, attorneys and paralegals use programs primarily for word processing, spreadsheets, and database functions. Once they have the basic system components in place, however, the most savvy lawyers and paralegals continue to explore new ways to use technology to help them do their work. In evaluating software programs to try out in your office, ask the attorney what the expectations are for automating a process. What information do you want to keep track of? How will you use the information? What end results do you want? What kinds of questions will you need to answer based upon the information in the computer? As you develop your skills on the software and equipment in your office, you will find it easier to evaluate new products. If you are interested in learning about new programs, many manufacturers can provide a demonstration disk for little or no cost so you can get a sample of what their programs can do, and some will allow you to order a program on 30-day approval. Other software vendors will be happy to set up a demonstration session in your office to show you how their products operate and what sort of work you can do with them.

What Makes a Program Easy to Use?

The most "user-friendly" software programs are *menu-driven;* that is, at almost every step of the program, the computer displays a menu, or list of choices to pick from. You can generally tell what you are supposed to do next because the options are shown right on the screen in front of you. Each option is an item on the menu. To tell the computer your choice from the list, you press the number or letter key that corresponds to your selection. The computer then activates the program, function, or other activity that the menu choice represents. In many programs, you can also use the arrow keys on the computer keyboard to move the cursor (a little blinking square that shows you where you are on the screen) to the choice, and then press the {Enter} key. Some programs and computers require you to move a pointer that you control with a handheld device known as a "mouse" to the choice and then pressing the button on the mouse. This is known as "clicking" on the menu choice. A helpful menu means you don't have to remember very much to actually use the program, regardless of whether you use the program every day or once a month. You don't have to type in a long string of characters to move around in the program. The list of options to pick from is displayed right in front of you. Menus may be displayed constantly at the bottom, top, or down one side of the screen, or you may have to press one key (usually the F1, F2, or F3 key in most programs) to display the list. When you have picked from the list, the menu disappears from the screen. Sometimes a second, different menu appears, and you make another choice from that list to indicate what you want the computer to do. Menu-driven software makes it easy for even casual computer users to figure out what they are supposed to do next, because the users don't have to remember what buttons to push. Reliable software programs should have documentation that is easy to read and understand, but many of them do not. Menu-driven programs are so easy to understand that the user doesn't need to refer to the manual all the time. When you start learning a software programs, you will quickly get to the point where you remember the most used commands or choices, but it is always comforting to know the menu is there if you need to refer to it.

If you have been exposed to computers at all, you are doubtless aware of the ongoing debate among computer users who prefer the familiar DOS™ programs and others who like Windows™ programs. How is Windows™ different? Windows™ uses something called a "GUI" in computer parlance. GUI (pronounced gōō-ee) is an acronym that stands for *graphical user interface,* meaning that instead of only using words and text characters for the menus, the programs use little pictures or symbols (graphics) called icons to represent the choices. The icons are usually arranged within a frame or box on the screen. In Windows™ programs, you indicate your choice from the row of icons by using the mouse to move the pointer arrow to your choice and pressing ("clicking") the button on the mouse. The GUI started with the Apple Macintosh™ computer developers to make software programs easier to use. GUIs were once considered useful only for playing games on the computer, but that is definitely changing. Just a few years ago, it seemed that very few lawyers and paralegals used Windows™. New programs that make IBM-type computers more like the Macintosh have encouraged many legal professionals to start using computers because they find the programs easy to use. More software developers are focusing on the Windows™ environment, and it is likely that the trend will continue as software becomes more sophisticated and computers become more powerful.

§ 8.7 Evaluating Computer Hardware

Computer hardware is the equipment, or the actual machine, that uses instructions in the software programs to process information. Usually, an individual computer workstation (a personal computer, or PC) is comprised of the main computer box or central processing unit (CPU), a monitor or video display terminal (VDT) that looks like a television screen, and a keyboard. Hardware can also refer to other equipment known as peripherals because they are accessories to the main computer. Peripherals include printers, modems, external tape drives, optical scanners, and other accessories. Experts recommend that you figure out what software you would like to use, and then select hardware that can run the programs. Computers and related products are becoming less expensive all the time. Surveys indicate that lawyers and paralegals tend to prefer the IBM environment over Macintosh, with the vast majority using IBM PCs or clones. Law offices generally do not need the most expensive hardware available, but you should avoid buying computer equipment simply because it comes at bargain prices. Buy hardware from a reputable vendor who will be able to provide service and replacement parts when you need them. Some lawyers delay making the investment in computers because the technology is developing so rapidly that they are afraid their system will be outdated before they can learn to use it. Computer consultants recommend that you not consider a hardware purchase a one-time only cost, but that you buy the prevailing standard in hardware that you can add to or upgrade when your needs dictate. A computer purchase now should serve your needs for at least three to five years, especially if you are just starting out with automation. The key is to have computer hardware that is powerful enough to run the software programs you want to use.

§ 8.8 Computers in Communications

Technology has had an enormous effect not only on the way we process information in our work, but also on the ways in which we transmit that information to and communicate with other people. One example is cellular telephone technology that has made it possible to communicate with your client or your secretary from just about any location, including your car and the courtroom. Calls can be forwarded from your office telephone, allowing you to make good use of travel time if you have a long commute to work or to court. This section will examine some of the other ways that technology has made it possible to communicate more quickly and efficiently than ever before.

§ 8.9 Advantages of a Computer Network

In a computer network, a series of computers are linked together. Each computer can operate alone, but they can also share data with other computers, share printers, and draw from a central pool of stored documents. If the linked computers are within the same office or building, they form a local area network or LAN. If the network includes a computer outside the building that is connected by a modem/telephone line, the system may be called a wide area network, or WAN. The individual computer terminals or workstations may be directly linked in a peer to peer fashion, or they may be connected to a central file server that houses the software which runs the network operating system. While networking equipment in the law office was once considered an option or a luxury, it has now become almost essential and is reasonably priced. There are many good reasons to connect the computers in your office. Networks allow you to:

- do group calendar checks and meeting scheduling
- consistently and reliably back up your files from the central file server
- access the lawfirm's document library or brief bank
- share a fast laser printer or modem
- have access to on-line research sources right at your desk
- exchange electronic mail on your in-house network or with lawyers in distant offices.

§ 8.10 E-Mail

Technology enhances a law office's ability to communicate both internally and with outside clients. Using electronic mail (E-mail) as a means of sending messages back and forth is rapidly becoming standard practice in some law offices. Attorneys and paralegals who become proficient at E-mail like the convenience of it. Firms that establish some form of computerized telephone link are finding that their clients really like it, because many clients have modems in their offices and homes. E-mail via modem is easy and cheap enough for even small offices. It is a means of quickly getting messages to busy clients, adjusters, experts, and others outside the office and communicating with coworkers and support staff inside. Printing E-mail messages is also an easy way to create a permanent record of the conversation, and E-mail can be useful for transmitting documents electronically. E-mail provides a quick and easy alternative to telephone calls and written memoranda for communicating with your supervising attorneys and other paralegals in your office. Most E-mail systems also allow you to send the same message to multiple recipients simultaneously. If E-mail is available in your office, take advantage of it to quickly update trial team members on developments in the trial preparation, advise of meeting dates, or send questions about the case that they can answer at their convenience.

§ 8.11 On-Line Information

A vast array of information is available through the use of a modem, a device that links your computer to a telephone line allowing you to connect to a number of commercial databases. The most familiar use for the modem in the law office is for performing legal research and instant cite checking through the Westlaw and LEXIS/NEXIS systems. These excellent automated legal research systems enable you to perform computerized searches on case law, as well as permitting access to an enormous database of statutes, regulations, and administrative codes. Both LEXIS/NEXIS and Westlaw add more databases every month. The on-line world holds important information for every trial paralegal. Both the Westlaw and LEXIS networks provide access to extensive resources for a variety of uses, including:

- conducting factual research or obtaining background information (see § **1.57**)
- locating expert witnesses in various fields (see § **3.20**)
- researching previous rulings by the trial court judge (see § **6.9**)
- following the activity of your competitors or opposing counsel's clients
- tracking press coverage about your client or your firm
- checking company financial statements.

Courses and training programs are available to help you learn to use these valuable services. If your office does not have access to these research services, you may be able to use the facilities at your law library, or a time-sharing program may be available through your local bar association. Members of the Association of Trial Lawyers of America (ATLA) are entitled to a group rate for LEXIS. Call 1-800-356-6548 for information.

In addition to the legal databases, a number of public information databases are available on a subscription basis to facilitate your factual research tasks (e.g., Dialog, ABAnet, NewsNet, Infosearch, Dow Jones News/Retrieval, and so on). A modem can connect you with public access bulletin boards such as CompuServe and Prodigy. Counsel Connect is an on-line bulletin board that allows attorneys to communicate by computer, send nationwide requests for information, and consult experts and leaders in specialty fields. ATLA's Exchange also allows lawyers from any size of firm to communicate about cases and share resources with other lawyers across the country.

§ 8.12 CD-ROM Technology

As CD-ROM (Compact Disk–Read Only Memory) products continue to proliferate and reliable CD-ROM disk drives become less expensive, law offices of all sizes are increasing their use of CD-ROM technology. In a 1994 survey conducted by the American Bar Association, large firms reported their use of CDs (information storage disks) increased from 45 percent in 1992 to 60 percent in 1993. That survey also indicated that 35.2 percent of small firms use CDs, and another 59 percent say they expect to use them in 1994. The Martindale-Hubbell legal directory is available on CD-ROM, and many other databases of case law and state statutes are becoming readily available in the CD-ROM format. For example, in Illinois lawyers can get case law back to the mid-1950s on CD-ROM disks for a one-time cost of about $500, plus $40 per month for update disks.

§ 8.13 Fax Technology

Fax technology has successfully enhanced the office's most reliable communication tool, the telephone. Fax machines are standard fixtures in most law offices and businesses. In fact, fax technology has been called the worldwide communications method of choice. Busy trial paralegals in large and small offices appreciate the value of being able to conveniently transmit a document to a client or another law office anywhere in the country (or the world) within seconds. Even the court system is recognizing the utility of this technology, as some courts now permit fax filings of legal pleadings and documents. *Office Systems 94* magazine reported in its July 1994 issue on a recent Gallup survey, conducted on behalf of Pitney Bowes, that found that American businesses continue to increase their use of fax technology. A majority of Fortune 500 companies and Dun & Bradstreet midsize companies reported that their fax usage had increased over the past 12 months (from July 1993 to July 1994). The survey also reported that 84 percent of the Fortune 500 and 89 percent of the mid-size company fax users said they have never been trained to operate a fax machine! If you don't already know how to operate the fax machine in your office, make it a high priority to learn. There will be times during trial preparation that you'll need to transmit a document to a client or opposing attorney's office after the clerks and secretaries have gone home for the day. Don't be caught unprepared.

§ 8.14 Using Word Processing in Trial Preparation

A large part of the law business involves processing written information to create documents. We read information, write it, convert it from one form to another, add to it, use it to fill in forms, and print it out for other people to read. This preoccupation with written information probably explains why computerized word processing is the most familiar type of automated litigation support. Nearly all law offices today have some form of computer-assisted word processing. The term *word processing* basically means the ability to create, store, retrieve, and edit text (letters, numbers, and punctuation) to generate documents (pleadings, memoranda, correspondence, briefs, lists, indexes). The major significance of modern word processing over the old fashioned typewriter is the ability to easily copy, edit, and reuse information *without having to retype it.*

Word processing makes corrections and revisions extremely easy to do. (Some legal secretaries would argue that revisions are too easy. Attorneys think nothing of making numerous document revisions because they know how easy it is to make changes!) Specifically, word processing in trial preparation (or any type of legal work) has the following advantages:

- Saves time by eliminating repetitive typing;
- Lowers the risk of errors caused by retyping, thus ensuring accuracy and consistency;
- Allows you to format the same information in different ways for different uses (reuse the same information in a different document or format); and
- Lets you easily store the information and recall it for later use.

Modern word processing using powerful computers has almost completely replaced the conventional typewriter in most offices. Of course, instead of typing a pleading or report, now we create a document, but the principles are the same. Word processing equipment has a number of fundamental advantages over the typewriter. With a computer monitor, you can see the characters on the screen as you type. On most machines the keyboard position is flexible for maximum comfort. Computerized word processing not only reduces retyping, but sometimes eliminates typing altogether. Documents or legal research that are transmitted electronically via modem hookup or transferred from a floppy disk requires no typing. Court reporting companies can provide deposition transcripts on disk to make summarizing and annotating tasks much easier (see § **8.24**). Today's powerful, inexpensive computers combined with increasingly sophisticated OCR (Optical Character Recognition) software packages have made scanning affordable for even very small law offices. Scanning technology allows users to scan documents from outside sources into the computer to create editable text files (see § **8.25**). This can be big help in preparing interrogatory answers and other discovery responses.

Word processing used to be a separate function, but it is now integrated with other types of information processing and computer functions, resulting in a blending of what once were strictly clerical office functions. In some law offices paralegals and attorneys use word processors to do team writing, combining the efforts of several writers on different parts of the same brief or legal memorandum. Even if your secretary does most of the document preparation with the word processing equipment, you should be familiar with the capabilities and limitations of the system so that you can communicate your instructions clearly, with reasonable expectations of what your assistant can accomplish. If you have access to a computer, I strongly recommend that you take the time to learn one of the leading word processing programs that have become standard fixtures in today's law offices, such as WordPerfect™ or Microsoft Word™. (Recent surveys indicate that a majority of large and small firms alike use some version of WordPerfect.) In addition to creating documents, you can use word processing to help you organize the case files and materials following the step-by-step procedures described in § **2.34.** Putting the file headings on computer makes it easy to rearrange the file listings to create labels for the files and a comprehensive diagram index for the trial file (see §§ **2.36–2.43**). You will find many other creative uses for word processing applications as your trial preparation progresses.

You will quickly realize the value and convenience of entering your notes and ideas directly into electronic form, and of being able to revise a document when your secretary has gone home for the day. Whenever you can, type your ideas directly into a computer. Move text around to combine ideas, separate them into distinct elements, and classify or combine notes from various sources. You can always go back later and edit your work, because you have captured key ideas electronically. Use the computer to collect lists, ideas, and random thoughts electronically—the first time you think of them. You can then combine the information with other data, move, copy, save, file, and store it for later use. This can be particularly useful if you have access to a portable computer (see § **8.40**) so you can record ideas when you are away from your office computer.

A word processing outlining function is a great drafting tool. It helps you organize your document by assigning a priority level to each fact or piece of information as you write. You can rearrange the information into a logical order, grouping like topics together and creating points and subpoints (just like you learned in school). The software will automatically renumber the topics with the correct outline sequence each time you move a topic from one place to another in the outline. Learn to use the other features in your word processing program, such as the thesaurus, dictionary, and spell check capabilities to improve your writing.

Develop Protocols and Procedures

Work with your secretary to adapt manual procedures and develop efficient new approaches to trial preparation tasks involving word processing. Develop a standard protocol for assigning computer file names so that you can find the documents your secretary stores on the computer. Set up a log of the standard forms and documents produced for each case you prepare for trial. This is particularly useful when you have to recruit supplementary staff members to help in an emergency. The substitute word processing typist will easily be able to locate the correct caption, certificate of service, client names and addresses, and so on, enabling him or her to quickly produce documents even if he or she is unfamiliar with the actual trial file. Ask your secretary to maintain the log in a looseleaf binder containing copies of your standard forms bearing the reference initials or codes under which the documents are stored in the computer system (see **Form 8–1**). You may also want to store detailed instructions for various procedures such as preparing and filing trial subpoenas. The procedures sheet should set out instructions on which document or form is prepared first, what attachments must accompany it, the amount of fees required to file it, and so forth. Use the following checklist as a starting point to compiling your most frequently used trial documents and forms.

§ 8.15 —Word Processing Applications in Trial Preparation

The following checklist suggests a number of uses for word processing applications in trial preparation.

____ 1. Court Filings: Pleadings and Notices

Set up standard caption (court, case number, judge, parties, and so forth); signature block for the attorney, firm name, address, phone; and proof of service

FORM 8–1
COMPUTER FILE NAME LOG

COMPUTER FILE NAME LOG

#	DOCUMENT FILE ID	DESCRIPTION	DATE

- ____ Motion and order pro hac vice (see § **1.17**)
- ____ Notice of de bene esse video deposition (see § **3.42**)
- ____ "Cleanup" interrogatories and document requests (see § **5.6**)
- ____ Request for admissions (see § **5.7**)
- ____ Motions in limine (see § **5.9**)
- ____ Praecipe for subpoena duces tecum (see § **5.12**)
- ____ Motion and order appointing persons to serve subpoenas (see § **5.26**)
- ____ Notice of filing depositions (see § **5.55**)
- ____ Request for ruling on objections (see § **5.52**)
- ____ Outline for trial brief (see § **5.34**)
- ____ Request for jury view (see § **6.15**)

____ 2. Correspondence: Form and model letters

- ____ Witness letters (see § **3.10**)
- ____ Expert witness engagement letter (see § **3.25**)
- ____ Expert witness trial notice (see § **3.35**)
- ____ Request for official photographs (see § **4.31**)
- ____ Reminder letters
- ____ Continuation of trial date
- ____ Letters of appreciation

____ 3. Trial preparation agenda (see § **2.14**)

____ 4. File organization:

- ____ File contents diagram (see § **2.36**)
- ____ File and folder label text (see § **2.42**)
- ____ Color-coding key (see § **2.85**)

____ 5. Lists and indexes:

- ____ Master reference notebook data (see § **2.9**)
- ____ Indexes for various types of materials (see § **2.45** *et seq.*)
- ____ Hospital records index (see § **2.63**)
- ____ Supplies and equipment inventory (see § **4.63**)
- ____ Attorney trial notebook index (see § **5.77**)
- ____ Exhibit lists (see §§ **5.60, 5.71**)

____ 6. Hospital records certification affidavit (see § **2.74**)

____ 7. Witness materials:

- ____ Witness documents index (see § **3.10**)
- ____ Pretrial interview notes (see § **3.5**)
- ____ Testimony summaries (see § **5.42**)

____ 8. Depositions:

  ____ Digests and summaries

  ____ Master deposition index (see § **5.49**)

  ____ Deposition exhibit index (see § **5.49**)

____ 9. Tabular charts for demonstrative exhibits (see § **4.16;** see also § **8.21,** spreadsheet/graphics applications)

____ 10. Federal court summary timetable (see § **2.16**)

____ 11. Indexes of expert witness materials (see §§ **3.47–3.51**)

____ 12. Client trial reminders (see § **3.14**)

____ 13. Glossary of relevant terms (see §§ **2.71, 3.32**)

____ 14. Cite-checking slips for trial brief authorities (see § **5.41**)

____ 15. Voir dire questions (see § **6.26**)

____ 16. Index sheets for various trial information

____ 17. Forms for database coding (see § **8.19**)

§ 8.16 Harnessing the Power of Macros

Macros are frequently used terms, phrases, and blocks of text that you store in the computer, and then call up with a keystroke or two and insert into a document without retyping. You can combine macros with word processing techniques to produce standardized sections of text that are then assembled into pleadings. For example, you could create macros that would automatically insert the case caption, attorney's signature block, and the certificate of service into a pleading. You can also use macros with standard form letters to produce customized correspondence to witnesses or clients. Macros can be used for any blocks of text that you or your secretary type over and over, such as addresses of opposing counsel. You can also record a macro for a standard set of page format settings (margins, tabs, font, and so forth) so that your documents are all set up the same way. Macros are great timesavers, but they don't help you if you forget what keys you stored them under on your word processing program. Keep a list of macros as you add them on a log sheet. See **Form 8–2,** Macro Log. Other text blocks you might want to assign to macros could include:

- Case Caption—Listing all parties
- Case Caption—Abbreviated
- Signature blocks—Attorneys, yours
- Certificate of Service
- Standard Page Format Settings for Letters
- Standard Page Format Settings for Pleadings

FORM 8–2
MACRO LOG

MACRO LOG MACRO FILE STORED AS:			
ALT	CTRL	DESCRIPTION	DATE
A			
B			
C			
D			
E			
F			
G			
H			
I			
J			
K			
L			
M			
N			
O			
P			
Q			
R			
S			
T			
U			
V			
W			
X			
Y			
Z			

§ 8.17 Document Assembly

Many law offices use a specialized type of advanced word processing program called document assembly software to develop legal documents. Document assembly programs may either be purchased or developed inhouse. *Document assembly* is an automated way of pulling the components of a text document together. Some programs use templates, which are similar to fill in the blank forms for the computer, merging standard paragraphs of information into finished documents. Many legal applications are perfect for document assembly techniques that involve inserting variable information into a boilerplate language template. Other specialized, more complex document assembly software asks the user a series of conditions or questions to obtain the necessary information, and then, on the basis of the answers, generates the appropriate document.

§ 8.18 Redlining Software

Paralegals in most law offices draft (and redraft) documents and pleadings, such as trial briefs. The finished product sometimes bears little resemblance to the original draft document. It may be important to know exactly what material was inserted and deleted from a document, especially when parties must agree on jointly drafted documents, such as stipulations, or the agreed discovery plan called for in amended Rule 26 of the Federal Rules of Civil Procedure (see **§ 2.29**). The manual procedure called "redlining" refers to comparing different versions of a document line by line, and indicating (usually by underlining in red) the changes, additions, and deletions from the previous version. The process of comparing documents is a tedious and time-consuming chore, but software programs are available to help you perform redlining functions with only a few keystrokes. Some word processing packages offer built-in redlining capabilities. There are also software programs whose sole purpose is to simplify the process of comparing documents. Generally, programs devoted specifically to redlining provide more detailed specific information on the changes made to a document. Many programs use a vertical line in the margin to indicate which sections of a document have been affected by additions, deletions, replacements, or moves. They may use an underline to show new text. (You may be able to customize how you want revisions to appear: select bold, italics, or double underlining to indicate additions.) Some programs allow you to redline a document as you are making revisions, rather than comparing the finished version to the previous one. Deletions may appear as strike-through text, or indicated by brackets at the beginning and end of the deleted passage. Some programs prepare a third composite document showing the differences in the first two, while others may show the changes in the second document only from the first one. Some programs can also give you a list that summarizes the changes line by line. You can then review the comparison results either on the screen, in a saved document, or by printing them. The program may split the screen into two windows to show the comparison of Document A to Document B, with the revisions marked. This allows you to see both versions of the document at once, and how each has been revised.

Basic Steps in Using Redlining Software

1. Create two documents to compare.
   You must first create two documents to compare. The most practical approach is to copy an original document, and make subsequent revisions to the copy. Clearly name these documents. Tell the program the names of the two documents to be compared and the name of the third output document showing the composite.
2. Tell the program what word processing program was used to draft the documents. Most comparison programs recognize the most common formats: WordPerfect, ASCII, Microsoft Word, and so forth.
3. Indicate how you want the marked revisions to appear. Usually, additions are underlined and deletions are shown by strike-through text, but many programs give you the option to change these parameters.
4. Give the program the OK to compare. This is usually very fast. An intermediate screen may appear to track the progress of the comparison.
5. Once the document comparison is generated, you can then view the composite document either on-screen or print it out.

§ 8.19 Using Databases to Prepare for Trial

The first question you might ask is, "What exactly is a *database?*" *Data* is information (dates, facts, figures, and so on). A *base* is a foundation or support; a fundamental structure. Therefore DATA + BASE = DATABASE. The computer draws from a pool or base of information or data that you have compiled. A computer database is a set of electronic records containing specific elements of information arranged in a structured format. A common example of a database you use every day is the telephone directory. Each entry or record is structured the same way, listing the person's (or company's) name, address, and telephone number, and the entries are generally arranged in alphabetical order.

You use much of the same data repeatedly throughout the life of a case. In the context of litigation work, a database is a group of records containing uniform sets of specific items of information (data fields), that can be searched, sorted, listed, and reported in a variety of ways. Database software lends itself to a broad range of applications in trial preparation tasks, primarily those related to indexing functions (see §§ **2.75–2.79**). Database software sometimes overlaps and combines with word processing or spreadsheet functions, merging database name and address listings with a word processing form to create customized witness letters. If you are in the process of converting from manual to automated litigation support, remember that any information that can be captured and recorded on an index card or a fill in the blanks form can probably be successfully transferred to a database record/field format. In fact, one technique for building a database is to use a paper coding sheet with blanks to initially collect and record the appropriate information on each item. These are some ways that databases can help you in your work:

- A database allows you to use and reuse the same elements of information in different ways, simply by arranging them in a different order, without having to retype the information.
- A database helps you organize and recall information in a variety of ways specifically suited to your needs (arranged alphabetically, numerically, or chronologically).
- A database organizes and stores your information efficiently, making it easy for you to recall the information later.
- A database allows you to edit and update the information in the records.

There is no mystery to computerized databases. The steps involved in organizing the materials and planning the data fields in the database are basically the same as planning the components of a manual index (see § **2.76**), but the computer helps you do things more efficiently. If you have ever filled out a form (and who hasn't?), you have created a paper record containing specific data. A very simple example of a form would be a coupon for a raffle or drawing. An example of a complex form might be a tax return for the Internal Revenue Service. The purpose of a paper form is to collect certain pieces of information in a uniform way. A database does the same thing, but in electronic format. It lets you see common elements between records, or consider more than one record at a time. In a conversion from manual systems to computerized systems, the form blanks become the information "fields" in a database. The beauty of a database is that it lets you instantly organize and reorganize data in a variety of ways, resulting in the ability to locate information much faster than you could by conventional manual methods. Thus you can find multiple uses for the same basic set of data by selecting, sorting, and printing it in different formats.

The computer does basically the same type of searching and sorting a human would do, only the computer can do it much faster. For example, it is conceivable that you could search through several thousand documents for common references to a specific subject, but it would be a tedious job and it would take you at least a few hours to do it. By contrast, a computer database containing descriptions of several thousand documents can search, locate, and report on any subject contained in the documents within a few seconds! The database search tells you almost instantly the numbers of the documents that fit the criteria you are looking for, and you can then easily locate the documents in a master file where the documents are arranged numerically.

You can use database applications in many aspects of trial preparation. For example, you might build a database of information on your trial exhibits. You would include the exhibit number, date, type of document, witness who will testify about the exhibit, and so on. With this information you could accomplish the following:

- Append or incorporate listings of trial exhibits into the text of the trial brief (see § **5.39**).
- Prepare a list by exhibit number as a table of contents for trial exhibit notebooks (see §§ **5.71–5.72**).
- Cross-reference any duplicate exhibits introduced by the opposing side (see § **6.76**).

You could build another useful database containing information on the trial witnesses. This database would include witness names, addresses, phone numbers, subjects about which they will testify, date scheduled to testify, exhibits they will authenticate, and so on. With this database you could do the following:

- Produce an alphabetical listing of witnesses with home and work telephone numbers for the front of your trial notebook (see § **5.88**).
- Prepare an index of witnesses who will receive subpoenas, tracking method of service, amount of witness fees, and so on (see § **5.31**).
- Prepare a list of witness names with corresponding exhibits for exhibit or witness folders (see § **6.66**).
- Incorporate a report listing trial witnesses and brief synopsis of their testimony into trial brief (see § **5.38**).
- Compile a witness list in the order they are scheduled to testify (see § **6.61**) for witness preparation conferences or to include in the attorney's trial notebook (see § **5.77**).
- Use the name and address data in a "mail-merge" to issue letters of thanks to witnesses after the trial.

Checklist: Database Applications in Trial Preparation

These are suggestions for other ways you can put databases to work in preparing for trial.

____ 1. Tracking multiple uses of documents produced in discovery throughout the litigation and trial (see § **5.51**)

____ 2. Listing and tracking trial exhibits (see §§ **5.58, 6.65**)

____ 3. Compiling witness information (see §§ **3.8, 5.34**)

____ 4. Trial witness subpoena data (see § **5.31**)

____ 5. Deposition master index (see § **5.49**)

____ 6. Brief bank of in-house work product

____ 7. Juror selection database (see § **6.16**)

____ 8. Daily time records (see § **1.40**)

____ 9. Expert witness reference by field of expertise (see § **3.20**)

____ 10. Master reference notebook data (see § **1.61**)

____ 11. Research articles database (see § **3.31**)

____ 12. Glossary of terms (see § **3.32**)

____ 13. Correspondence index (see § **2.46**)

____ 14. Date sorting for tabular chronology or timeline (see § **4.16** *et seq.*)

____ 15. Generating sequential indexes of numbered documents (see §§ **2.80, 2.83**)

§ 8.20 Building a Database

Building a database requires an initial time investment for planning and input. (How much time depends on how many pieces of information you collect on each record and how many records or documents you have.) The time you spend up front capturing the information pays off later when the data is readily available and can be reached and used quickly for various purposes in the litigation, for example, for quickly assembling a list of trial exhibits. You can learn a lot about database techniques by taking take training classes and seminars, studying the manuals that come with database software, and reading articles in computer magazines. Truths about building a database:

- Collecting data is painstaking
- Updating data is routine
- Searching and sorting data is easy
- Analyzing data for patterns and connections is FUN and produces results!

Preliminary Considerations in Designing a Database

1. Plan the project. Decide what you want to accomplish with a database. How do you want to use the information you capture? What is the desired end result for the information? (There will probably be more than one.) If you want to print out specific reports, sketch out on paper how you want the reports to look and what information should be included in each. This will give you a start on what elements or fields of information should be recorded in the database. For example, a useful project in trial preparation would be a simple database to track the case documents that could potentially be used as trial exhibits. Your goals or desired end results might be to:

- Produce a list of the privileged documents.
- Prepare an index for the court and opposing counsel of your trial exhibits, listing exhibit number (or letter) in order, the date of the document, and a brief description of the document.
- Compile a list for the attorney of which exhibits will be used by which witnesses.
- List of the exhibits in chronological order.

2. Design the Form and Data Entry Screen. How much information do you need to keep track of? What information should be captured? What will you need to know about each document? How many documents are you planning to track? See § **8.25** for a discussion of large document management projects. In the above example, the specific elements of information you would want to record about a set of case documents would include:

- A number or letter (exhibit ID)
- Bates Number
- The date
- Who wrote or prepared the document?
- Who received it? (Is it important to know if someone received a copy?)
- Brief description of what the document says
- What type of document it is (letter, report, tax return, invoice, and so forth)
- Where the document came from (where your attorney got it)
- Which witness(es) will testify about it?
- A summary of what the document says

3. Decide how you will capture the important information about each document. What resources are available (hardware, software, people to do the data input?)

Who will do the input? (You? Your secretary? Temporary workers? Interns?) Will the coders work directly from the documents, or will they use coding forms? Using forms as a way to organize the raw data can help you delegate part of the work of building a database. A form gives a standard layout to help document reviewers structure the information, putting it into a usable form that is later transferred to the computer. You create order by the methodical collection of data in a structured format. Coding forms make it easy for people to fill in the correct information about each document. Coders may not be able to fill in all the blanks on a form, but you are likely to get more complete information in the blanks than if you provided just a blank sheet of paper with no discernible structure. People have a tendency to fill in the blanks with the requested information.

4. Lay out the form design on the screen. In the context of trial work, a database is a tool you can use to impose order on chaos.

Just as you use paper forms to capture information in a structured format, the database screen design "frames" the information as you enter it into the computer. A database screen design will look very similar to the layout of a paper form. In fact, experts recommend that you sketch your design out on paper first, using blanks or boxes to indicate certain standard pieces of information that you want to record. The following figure shows the typical fields or data elements you might want to collect for a trial exhibit database.

These individual pieces of information are the FIELDS in the database (or the blanks in the form or paper record). They contain the information you have decided to collect about a document. A label tells what kind of information goes in the blank that follows it. The label and the information blank together make a FIELD. A value is what you type into a field. A form design (or template) is a collection of fields arranged in a particular way on the screen. A filled out record is a profile or abstract. A database is the collection of filled-out forms that have the same design and are stored together.

Database fields are one of two types: objective and subjective. Objective fields contain information that is readily apparent on the face of the document, document number, date, type, author, and so forth. These pieces of information speak for themselves. They can be determined reviewer with only superficial knowledge about the case. Subjective fields are those which call for an interpretation or summary of the meaning or significance of the document, such as the information typically found in the "Summary" or "Description" field in a database. Subjective coding requires higher levels of knowledge, skill, and judgment than objective coding.

Tips for database screen design:

- Put the fields in logical order (the order you would expect to find most of the information on the documents you are coding.)

- Use meaningful labels instead of abbreviations for field names wherever possible. For example, "Doc. No." or "Document #" will be easier to understand than a cryptic "DN."
- Make the form design look pleasing on the screen, to make it easy on the data entry personnel.

  Leave enough room for the information that goes in the blank. For example, a telephone number will need only 12 spaces (three for the area code, one space, eight for the number)
- Put any instructions at the top of the form.

5. Assign information types to the fields. Some fields will contain text, some (at least one) will contain dates, others may contain numbers, dollar amounts, Yes/No, and so forth. Most database programs will allow you to specify if only certain answers are acceptable in a field. This helps to validate your data entry by making it more difficult for someone to enter the wrong data in a field.

6. Fill in the forms or records. This could mean either displaying blank forms and typing information into the fields or adding new records to an existing database. Fill out one form (or record) for each document. Documentation is the key to making automated database building work. Create a manual of your procedures and conventions, tailored to fit the project. Include a copy of the paper form that the coders are filling out.

7. Searching and Retrieving. This means telling the database what forms (records) you want to see, and in what order you want to see them. You give the program the parameters for the records you want to see. For example, if you wanted to see only the documents that were written by Mark Wise, you would type "Wise, Mark" into the author field. The database software will look at each record and then show you the records where that name appears in the author field.

You might also ask the computer to sort the entries in a particular way. Why would you want to sort? Assigning sequential numbers to raw database entries lets you view the information in numerical or sequential order. Each document will have a number, so that number goes into the first field (or blank). But the order in which the records were numbered might not always be meaningful to you. After you develop profiles or abstracts representing the documents, you can look at common patterns to determine relationships between the documents, for example, determining when each document was written. It could be useful to sort chronologically or alphabetically. A date order sort is usually the most useful.

8. Create a Report. You will usually want to obtain a printout of information taken from the forms in the database. Creating a report means telling the program what fields of information you want to see, and in what order you want the columns to appear on the page. **Form 8–3** is an example of a report taken from data records in the database in **Figure 8–1.**

FORM 8–3
SAMPLE REPORT FROM DATABASE

Bates #	DATE	DOCUMENT TYPE	AUTHOR	RECIPIENT
--------	-----------	---------------	---------------	---------------
00001	12/1/89	Schedule	Unger	Sellers
00004	5/4/90	Memo	Faulkner, R.	Dexter, D.
00006	1/1/94	Vita	Maxwell, S.	
00011	1/27/95	Memo	Maxwell, S.	Trout, K.
00015	8/30/90	Schedule		
00022	4/9/93	Letter	Asher, L.	Maxwell, S.
00143	5/18/83	Letter	Shook, S.	Perth, R
00381	11/28/90	Notes	Unger	
00396	11/21/88	Memo	Newberry, D.	Adler, T.

(Type all names like this: Last Name, First Name, Middle Initial)

Exhibit ID:	**Document Bates #:**
Document Date:	**Document Type:**

Author:

Recipient:

Source:
Witnesses:

Figure 8–1.

§ 8.21 Using Spreadsheet and Graphics Programs

Spreadsheets are most useful for projects involving numerical or statistical data and related formulas or calculations, such as medical expenses and insurance payments in a personal injury case. Most spreadsheets can also perform database-type functions, allowing the user to select and sort data according to various criteria (see also **§ 8.19** on databases) and some basic text search and formating functions. In computer spreadsheet programs (such as Lotus 1-2-3™ and Excel™), what you see on the screen resembles an accounting ledger sheet, with rows across and columns down the page. Of course, computer spreadsheets contain many more columns and rows than would fit on printed ledger paper. In a blank spreadsheet, the columns are labeled with letters across the top (A,B,C) and the rows are labeled with numbers (1,2,3) down the left-hand side. The box where a column and row intersect is called a *cell*—identified by a column letter and a row number. For example, cell A1 is the square in the upper left corner of the spreadsheet, cell B1 is the first cell in the second column, cell A2 is the box in the first column, second row, and so forth.

You can type information or numbers into any cell in a spreadsheet, such as:

1. Text—a column heading or row description

2. Amounts; or

3. Mathematical formulas to automatically calculate amounts.

Another way you can use spreadsheets is to create graphs based on designated data in the spreadsheet. The graphs can be enhanced with titles, legends, labels, and scale grids and automatically displayed on the screen or printed to the printer. Most spreadsheet programs can produce bar graphs, stacked-bar graphs, line graphs, and pie graphs, that can be used as is or as a guide for preparing an enlarged chart (see **§ 4.16**). The following checklist describes a number of trial applications for spreadsheet and graphics programs.

Checklist: Spreadsheet/Graphics Trial Applications

____ 1. Prepare or check calculations of any numerical data

____ 2. Itemize and calculate component elements of damages (medical expenses, lost wages, property damage, and so forth)

____ 3. Apply a formula to calculate witness fees and mileage for trial subpoenas (see **§ 5.28**)

____ 4. Prepare a summary or analysis of costs or damages based on numerical data taken from case records and documents (see **§ 5.61**)

____ 5. Calculate hypothetical figures based upon selected variables to support the testimony of an expert witness such as an economist or accountant (see § **3.47**)

____ 6. Plan the layout of tables and charts to be used as demonstrative evidence (see § **4.16**)

____ 7. Combine with graphics feature to graph tabular data in various ways to determine which type of graph is most effective (see § **4.16**)

____ 8. Plan the layout of a timeline or chronology for a demonstrative exhibit (see § **4.26**)

____ 9. Track trial preparation expenses.

§ 8.22 Docket Management and Utility Programs

Docket management software is a specialized type of program that can help you record and easily update "address and telephone book" data, and assist with calendaring, planning, and scheduling activities. Docket management systems help you calculate and enter court dates, filing deadlines, and meeting dates, and then let your print daily or weekly schedules and listings of work to be done for yourself and other trial team members. Docketing or calendar software can help avoid missed filing deadlines or statute of limitations dates. Utility programs assist with your computer "housekeeping" chores, such as tracking your computer filenames, deleting outdated files, facilitating backup procedures, copying and renaming tasks, and so forth.

Checklist: Trial Applications for Docketing Software

____ 1. Print reference lists of clients, witnesses, opposing counsel, etc. (name, address, telephone numbers)

____ 2. Master reference notebook data (see § **1.61**)

____ 3. Listing parties and counsel (combine with word processing functions for proof of service information)

____ 4. Preparing trial calendars and daily "To Do" lists

____ 5. Coordinating calendars and scheduling preparation meetings for trial team members (see § **2.7**)

____ 6. Scheduling witness preparation conferences or client meetings (see § **3.10**)

____ 7. Scheduling conference rooms

____ 8. Planning proposed order of witnesses and related trial scheduling (see § **6.61**)

____ 9. Tracking account numbers, price quotes, and so forth, for various outside vendors and services

____ 10. Keeping time and billing records (see § **1.40**)

____ 11. Preparing summary of federal court due dates (see § **2.18**)

§ 8.23 Comprehensive Case Management Software

A comprehensive case management program may be a good choice if you are new at using computers in trial work, because these programs guide you step by step through the standard case information you need to compile for most trials. Case management software also helps you track the progress of work on the case, as well as develop data on evidence, witness statements, and documents according to specific case issues. In addition, most case management software programs have a calendaring feature to assist you in calculating and flagging case due dates and deadlines. Case management software is usually most effective if it is used consistently from the very beginning of the case. A number of case management software programs are tailored specifically to cases involving personal injuries, but other programs can be used in any type of litigation. Keeping client case data on personal information manager software (case tracking) can enable you or the lawyer to answer a client's question immediately without having to go pull the actual case file. This not only helps you keep the clients informed but also provides personal details about the clients, such as when their son or daughter is graduating from high school or where they like to go on vacation. You might ask them how their children are doing in school or other appropriate personal information. Clients love this sort of personal touch and happy clients are good for your business.

Case management software may have some limitations, however. For example, the predetermined report formats may be too structured and may not be flexible enough to suit your case needs. The indexing and tracking needs in a very large case may exceed the capacity of some case management software programs, and a small case may not require all the cross-references and other features provided. Beware of case management software programs tailored to specific state laws. If you practice in a different state from the one for which the program is set up, some of the forms and date calculations may not comport with your local court rules and procedures. If you work on lots of the same types of cases, case management software could be all you need to keep track of data on witnesses, clients, testimony, facts, and documents.

§ 8.24 Deposition Summary Software

One of the biggest changes in the way paralegals prepare cases is reflected in the use of deposition summary software. A number of good deposition summary software packages are available to assist you in searching, analyzing, and summarizing deposition transcripts. These specialized programs combine the flexibility of word processing functions with sophisticated database searching and indexing functions. The major difference between deposition summary software and standard database programs is that deposition software is based on full-text retrieval rather than the selected and abstracted criteria in a database. Most court reporters can provide computer-aided transcription (CAT), which means they can give you a computer diskette containing the text of the deposition transcript in addition to the conventional paper copy of the transcript. Many of the functions performed by deposition summary software can be done with standard word processing software, but deposition summary software is tailored to the way you use deposition transcripts in preparing for trial. You can create standard page/line deposition summaries using word processing software. You can search these manually by reading through them, or on the word processing program by using the search key (F2 on WordPerfect). The word processing program generally cannot sort, group, or rearrange the entries. Programs like Summation™ can still print the traditional summaries, but you can also search quickly through multiple transcripts for references to a certain issue, document, date, or witness, and compile those references for comparison and contrast.

A software program such as Summation is an integrated database, which is a powerful tool because it allows you to cross-reference deposition testimony, notes, and document summaries in one program file. This type of software allows you to search deposition transcripts quickly for names, topics, or issues. Deposition summary software makes it easy to collect sections of the deposition transcript for printing to paper or storing in a computer file. For example, you might want to compile all the testimony about a certain topic or document. You can also print testimony to a word processing file and include it in a memorandum, brief, or motion. This saves you or your secretary retyping.

Deposition summary software gives you some additional abilities. For example, if you are reading a transcript and you want to make a note of a key piece of testimony, you press the menu choice for "Notes"—the program records the page and line number of the testimony and any notes or thoughts you add to it. You can type in a note, copy part of the transcript and add issue codes or dates. You can easily print the notes, with or without the transcript sections they refer to. If you have assigned issues or dates to the notes, you can sort them into groups according to issues or in chronological order. The notes become a separate (but related) database, allowing you to collect notes and testimony from all the deposition witnesses, sorted by the issues that are important to your case.

Deposition summary software makes it very easy and fast to do the following:

- Assign key subject and issue headings to portions of the transcript
- Prepare deposition exhibit indexes
- Prepare an objection transcript for tracking the court's rulings on objections (see § **6.10**)
- Determine and locate key words, issues, and terms to facilitate preparation of testimony outlines; and
- Isolate and excerpt specific portions of deposition testimony verbatim for use with the witness, either as a review of points to cover in preparation or as ammunition for impeachment during courtroom testimony.

Deposition summary software has particular utility in a case with multiple depositions. For example, when you wish to summarize the testimony from all the various witnesses on a particular subject, the deposition summary program makes it easy to search for key terms across the depositions of several witnesses to quickly locate the relevant testimony and prepare a report listing page and line number references. This process can be done manually (the old cut-and-paste method), but deposition summary software lets you do it with much greater accuracy and speed.

Deposition summary software tends to be a relatively expensive type of program, so investigate and evaluate the options carefully before you invest in a deposition summary program. Many software manufacturers will provide a demonstration diskette or let you try out the program for a trial period (usually 30 days) before you purchase it. Contact your legal software representative to find out more about this type of litigation support software. Make sure the software you choose is compatible with your computer equipment and that of the court reporters in your area. Other considerations in choosing deposition summary software include the following:

- Ease of learning the program and ease of use
- Substance and organization of the documentation
- Availability of special features, such as a spelling checker, glossary, and page and line number referencing
- Flexibility in formatting and printing reports and summaries based on the indexing capabilities; and
- Availability of customer technical support from the manufacturer, including advice on upgrades to the system.

§ 8.25 Using Technology in Litigation Support

Controlling the information from the beginning of the case enables your trial team to stay on top of case developments and streamline the trial preparation and presentation. We have seen how database techniques (see **§ 8.19**) can help you track and retrieve critical information in a number of ways. There is no question that an automated database is an essential tool for managing and using the information in the documents. The trial team that does not use database technology can find itself at a tactical disadvantage, particularly if the opponents have built databases to control their documents. Despite advances in automation, the main way most of us exchange information in cases is still by producing paper documents. A complex business case can easily generate hundreds or thousands of documents. In fact, review, assembly, and storage of paper documents is typically the largest ongoing expense in a complex litigation. Paralegals spend a lot of time organizing and maintaining paper files and records.

Cases that generate millions of pages require technology beyond the basic database and manual paper handling techniques. A computer database that incorporates imaging technology is an even more powerful tool for litigators by enhancing the ability to quickly retrieve and review documents. Optical imaging is the most effective way to reduce both the time and expense associated with document management. Imaging allows: (1) an almost instantaneous retrieval rate of seconds as opposed to hours; (2) the ability to review documents on screen before printing to narrow down the number of documents selected for printing; (3) sorting into chronological order (or other desired categories and sequences) before printing. Attorneys will have much quicker access to any set of documents, allowing them to begin their analysis sooner without having to wait for document retrieval. The faster retrieval rate with imaging saves the client money because it saves you and the attorneys time. Imaging allows you to quickly respond to discovery requests and generate subsets of documents for depositions, settlement negotiations, witness books, trial exhibits, and so on. The following sections discuss techniques for planning and implementing a large document management and database coding project and how imaging technology can help you to prepare for trial and facilitate faster resolution of the matter at a lower overall cost to the client.

§ 8.26 Planning a Document Management Project

1. Determine the desired results. Has this scenario ever happened to you? The attorney shows you a shipment of 100 boxes of paper and says, "I need you to put this on the computer. Tell me how long it will take and how much it will cost." In attorney language, "put it on the computer" usually means that the attorney wants you to construct a database. In order to do this, you will need to get answers to some questions first. Carefully planning a document project helps you avoid duplicating efforts and make sure that the results are what the attorney expects. Careful implementation of the plans will help to ensure that the resulting database is an accurate and useful tool. Insist that the attorney sit down with you and think through the project. Ask the attorney: "If you could ask any question about the documents in this box, what would you ask?" Try to get the attorney to think about what he or she wants as the end result of the "computerization." A general list of what is in the boxes? A detailed analysis of the information on each document? How do you want to use the information? What kinds of work do you want to be able to do when the database is completed?

In federal court cases, you may also have to comply with the court's Case Management Order in the case (see § **2.16**). A Case Management Order typically requires each side to:

- sequentially number documents;
- produce nonprivileged documents to opposing counsel;
- compile a log of the documents being withheld on the basis of privilege; and
- compile a log to identify those documents produced, but redacted on the basis of privilege.

2. Determine the time availablc and chart critical deadlines. One of the most important questions to ask the attorney is, "When do we need this?" You need to know how long you have to complete the project. Consider both formal and informal deadlines and projections for other activities in the case. Also consider how long you will use the information. If you are at the start of a case that may last five years, you are likely to get a lot of return on a document management project. However, if the case is going to trial in two weeks, you may not have time to build the database or realize the returns from the work. Consult the court's case management order or scheduling order for dates and deadlines that apply to various stages of discovery in the case.

3. Determine the budget and resources for the project. You need to know if it will be possible to purchase additional equipment, hire additional personnel, contract with outside sources, etc. Determine the resources you have available. Will you need to trade information with clients or other law offices (co-counsel, opposing counsel, the court or judge)? Can your system convert a client's old fashioned data into a compatible format? Do you need E-mail or fax links to the client's facility?

An important initial determination is whether to do the project in-house or employ an outside litigation support vendor. Some extremely large cases require the services of an outside vendor. If the job must be done very quickly (rush) you may have no choice. **Section 8.38** discusses considerations in dealing with outside vendors. If you plan to do automated litigation support work in-house as opposed to hiring an outside service bureau, you must have someone in-house who thoroughly understands the problems and what needs to be done. If you decide to do the work in-house, your primary goals in a document management project should be:

1. To determine appropriate and effective methods for building a database and managing the document repository in a manner that is both cost-efficient to the client and suitable for the requirements of the litigation;

2. To ensure that the end result is an accurate, usable database that is compatible with equipment and software used by both the client and the law office. The law office personnel should also be allowed adequate access to the document repository.

3. To use available personnel, equipment, and resources to the fullest extent possible.

4. Develop a work flow plan. You will need to formulate a comprehensive plan for managing and processing the document repository in any litigation with a large number of documents. Analyzing the document work flow means examining what happens to the paper at each stage of the project. Envision how the system will actually work, step by step. The following checklist gives are the work-flow steps that typically occur in a large-scale database project. Each step is described in more detail in the sections that follow.

Checklist: Steps in the Work Flow Process

____ 1. Identify document sources

____ 2. Estimate the volume of paper.

____ 3. Gather the documents.

____ 4. Log the documents.

____ 5. Arrange numbering and copying (if necessary)

____ 6. Develop protocols and documentation

____ 7. Design document coding forms and screens

____ 8. Perform data input—coders

____ 9. Conduct quality control

____ 10. Apply imaging/OCR conversion (optional)

____ 11. Produce and track documents

____ 12. Create privilege log/redaction log

§ 8.27 Steps in the Work Flow Process

1. Identify document sources. Ask the attorney to list potential sources of documents that will need to be catalogued. Use the Source Summary Chart (see **Form 8–4**) to record the potential sources. Begin by making a chart of the known sources of documents. For example, if your client is a paint manufacturer, there might be documents from various production facilities, from plants, corporate offices, distribution points, and other sources. Examples of document sources:

- Materials produced by opposing party or parties
- Expert consultant or witness
- Public records
- Records and materials from related cases (e.g., bankruptcy)

FORM 8–4
SUMMARY OF POTENTIAL DOCUMENT SOURCES
IN PARTY A VERSUS PARTY B LITIGATION

SUMMARY OF POTENTIAL DOCUMENT SOURCES IN {PARTY A} vs. {PARTY B} LITIGATION			
SOURCES		PAGES[1]	DOCUMENTS (3:1 ratio)

[1] Insert page count figures as soon as this information becomes available.

- Documents from previous counsel's files
- Client's personal files
- Client's business files. The client may already have numerous documents from various sources. Don't overlook closed files related to the litigation. You may identify other sources as the litigation proceeds.

2. Estimate the volume of paper. You need some idea of how many pages of documents you have. In large-scale litigation cases, responses to discovery and production requests will typically generate a substantial number of documents. A volume estimate in the scenario mentioned above, assuming the 100 boxes comprise the total collection. For most cases, however, you probably will not have exact figures on the number of documents expected from each source at the initial planning stage. The best you can do is determine where the documents are likely to come from and how many sources you have. Try to get an estimate from each source of the number of documents they have.

- How many boxes? (A standard banker's box will hold about 2,000 to 2,500 pages.)
- How many file drawers?
- How many file pockets? (redropes)

If you can get any information on the volume of documents, ascertain whether the total indicates DOCUMENTS or PAGES. The industry standard usually figures an average of three to four pages per document, although this can vary widely, depending on the type of documents involved. For example, a case involving a company that generates long contracts versus a more typical file of one-, two-, or three-page letters and memoranda. Be sure you know whether the estimate refers to documents or pages. Some litigators use these terms interchangeably.

3. Gather the documents. The next step is to gather the documents from all the potential sources. Plan a place for the document repository. Allow for expansion. Make arrangements to ship documents to the repository. Use the Source Summary Chart form as a starting framework for organizing your efforts to locate and retrieve the documents.

4. Log the documents. Log in all documents by source and volume, and label the boxes as you receive them. Decide who will log in boxes as they arrive at the office or repository. Assign each box a sequential number and note the source of the box on a Log-in Chart (see **Form 8–5,** Log-in Chart).

FORM 8–5
SAMPLE LOG IN CHART FORM

NUMBER SERIES ASSIGNMENT			SOURCE FILE IDENTIFICATION
	to		
	to		
	to		
	to		
	to		
	to		
	to		
	to		
	to		
	to		

DOCUMENT TYPES LOG		NAMES LOG	
CODE	DOC. TYPE	NAME	COMPANY

5. Arrange numbering and copying. The first principle of good document management is that every page of every document receives a unique number. Number the documents at the beginning of the project, before any photocopies are made. The court's Case Management Order will almost certainly require sequential document numbers containing a prefix to identify the documents each party produces, both for production and for the privilege and redaction logs. Document numbers can be applied either by the copier at the time the documents are copied or imaged, or number labels can be generated and then hand-placed on the documents (see **§ 2.80**). (**Note:** If you have opted for imaging program, the vendor may be able to number the documents for you. Discuss this with the project manager.)

6. Develop documentation and screening protocols. The documents must be screened before they are processed further. The purpose of the attorney review before coding, imaging, or any other processing step is to determine the category of privilege that should apply to each document, and at the same time to indicate which documents in the collection are not privileged and can therefore be produced to the opposing side in the litigation. Work with your supervising attorney to develop a review protocol that sets out guidelines for the review and privilege determination on the documents. You need to understand what constitutes a privileged document and how to recognize privileged documents, even if attorneys do the actual privilege review. The privilege review takes time, regardless of what automated litigation support techniques are used. An experienced reviewer can get through approximately 250 pages, or about 80 to 85 documents per hour on a typical box of documents (assuming a 3:1 page-to-document ratio). The pace may be somewhat slower for very complex documents.

For the privileged documents, the reviewing attorneys will indicate the type(s) of privilege that apply. The document reviewer should also indicate documents to be stamped "confidential" and those that require redaction of some portion before they can be produced.

- **Relevance/Responsiveness**—Reviewers determine which documents are responsive to the discovery requests, or otherwise relevant, according to a predetermined protocol for responsiveness.
- **Privilege**—For those documents deemed responsive and/or relevant, reviewers determine which are privileged (to be withheld) and which are nonprivileged (and may be produced). For the privileged documents, reviewers indicate the type(s) of privilege that apply (attorney-client, work product, joint defense). Draft a privilege review protocol setting out guidelines for the review and privilege determinations on the documents. You will need to develop this protocol to include a comprehensive list of counsel names.

- **Confidential/Trade Secret**—Reviewers identify documents that should be stamped "confidential" and/or those that contain trade secret or otherwise sensitive information. A review protocol must be developed for this determination.
- **Redaction**—Reviewers identify documents that require redaction of some portion before they can be produced. The Case Management Order typically requires redacted documents to bear a stamp indicating the fact of redaction. You will also need to retain a control set of documents showing both the original and redacted versions of such documents for your records.

Once the privilege determinations have been made, all of the documents will be imaged and coded, and a log of the privileged documents will be prepared and produced. The optimum procedure is to complete the database coding **before** the nonprivileged documents are produced, but this is not always a realistic option. The attorneys may want to proceed with the privilege review before the documents are coded in order to produce photocopies of the non-privileged documents at the earliest possible date.

One way for the reviewing attorneys to mark the documents is by using a tape flag system. After reviewing the documents according to the reviewing protocol, the attorneys indicate these designations by applying colored self-adhesive tags to the top right-hand edge of the document page, with each color having a different significance. For example, use RED for attorney-client; GREEN for work product; BLUE for joint defense; YELLOW to indicate confidential; and PURPLE to indicate redactions. Note that these are the one-inch plastic indicator flags, not regular paper notes. These plastic flags are self-adhesive and, while they are designed to be removable, they stick quite well, even when the papers are handled repeatedly.

You could also use self-inking stamps to place the appropriate designation right on the face of the document, but consider the following disadvantages to this method:

- The attorney may have reservations about adding ANYTHING to the face of the document other than the required Bates number and the CONFIDENTIAL stamp, if applicable.
- Self-inking stamps are an improvement over the old rubber stamp and inkpad method, but they are still somewhat messy and the ink tends to smear. There could also be a problem with making a sharp, clear impression when a stamp is used repeatedly during a reviewing work session.
- The stamped impression would be more difficult to change if a mistake is made or a decision is changed. You need to have the flexibility to change the initial privilege designations, because when the attorneys review their work on a particular group of documents, they sometimes change their initial

decisions. Even though reviewing attorneys are diligent in their attempts to be consistent, they still typically make numerous changes when they proofread the draft privilege log. After the privilege log is completed and produced, there will be challenges from the opponents. Ultimately, some percentage of the documents will be declassified.

You will also need to develop a training and coding manual, to give the coders some background on the case to help them understand the issues and get a better sense of what information may be important to capture from the documents. The manual should also include coding conventions you want the coders to use, such as standard abbreviations, key words, and so forth.

7. Design document coding forms and screens. This process is discussed in **§ 8.19.**

The only way to adequately gain control of the information in a large document collection is to build a computerized database. Coding documents into the database is the foundation of any information project. "Coding" means reviewing each document, extracting certain elements of information from document (document number, date, type, author, recipient, and so forth), and typing this information into fields in database. These records then represent the actual documents in the database, and the records can be sorted, and listed in various ways. You must code in order to construct a database, regardless of equipment or technology you use. There is no substitute for coding, nor is there any instant way to do it. Coding work is labor-intensive and represents the bulk of the cost in building any database.

Objective and Subjective Fields

Database coding fields are one of two types: objective and subjective. Objective fields contain information that is readily apparent on the face of the document (document number, date, type, author, and so forth.) These pieces of information speak for themselves. They can be determined and entered by a reviewer with only superficial knowledge about the case. The objective fields in a typical document database could include:

Objective Fields

Document Number—Beginning

Document Number—Ending

Reviewer Initials

Document Date

Document Type

Document Title

Document Source

Author Name(s)

Recipient Name(s)

Copyee Name(s)

Names Within the Document

Keywords (from a predetermined list)

Document Numbers of Attachments

Document Characteristics (illegible, marginalia, etc.)

Subjective fields call for an interpretation or summary of the meaning or significance of the document, such as the information typically found in the "Summary" or "Description" field in a database. Subjective coding requires higher levels of knowledge, skill, and judgment than objective coding. Examples of subjective fields would be:

Subjective Fields

Privilege Basis (determined by reviewers according to protocol)

Confidential/Trade Secret (determined by reviewers according to protocol)

Redacted (determined by reviewers according to protocol)

Short Summary (This field may only be entered for privileged and redacted documents. It is a brief description sufficient to identify the document for the public privilege and redaction logs.)

Detailed Summary

Attorney Comments

Hot Documents (particularly helpful or harmful concerning coverage issues)

8. Perform data input—Coders. The information from the control forms must be entered into the appropriate fields on a computer database system. Decide what database system the data will be entered and who will do the actual keying into the system. In a large case for a client with an in-house legal department, a cost-effective technique is to use the client's staff personnel (management information systems (MIS) director or typists under his or her direction) to enter the data into the database from the coding forms. Other cases may require outsourcing to a vendor. The attorneys should commit to taking some training on the system so that they will be able to use the database. Decide whether the coders will work from coding sheets or enter data directly into the computer.

Coding sheet method: The coder fills out a form for each document, indicating relevant data concerning the document. Make this process as easy and efficient as possible for the reviewers by structuring the form to contain blanks or boxes for the information you need to capture in the database. A typist later transfers the information from the coding sheet to the database fields. You may need to use this method if you do not have enough computers for everyone to work at once.

Direct entry method: Coders may also enter data directly into the database from the keyboard. This eliminates a step in the process. The coders must each have a computer and be proficient at the keyboard and familiar with the database software.

Vendor coding: You may decide to have a vendor code the objective fields for the database. Once the objective coding is completed by the vendor, the database can be loaded onto the system at your office, where paralegals can code the subjective fields.

9. Quality control. The quality control step is very important to ensure accuracy and reliability of the data entered into the database. Ideally, someone other than the input typist will proof the data input. Run test reports.

10. Imaging/OCR conversion (optional). Scanning and OCR by a litigation support vendor can be done either on-site at the client's facility or at the imaging vendor's facility, and stored on optical disks or on CD-ROM. A discussion of the advantages of imaging technology may be found in § **8.28** *et seq.*

11. Document production/tracking. Once the database is constructed, nonprivileged documents that are responsive to various discovery requests will be copied (or printed, if imaging is employed) and shipped to opposing counsel. After production, database records must be updated to indicate which documents were produced. The mechanics of physically producing the nonprivileged documents will differ, depending on whether you employ imaging technology or rely on the hard copy paper document repository. If you use the hard copy repository, you will have to generate a list of the documents destined for production, manually pull the documents from the boxes, copy the documents, and then refile them in their proper places. If the documents are imaged, they can be printed directly from the database for production, thus eliminating the need to handle the hard copy repository documents (see the discussion of imaging in § **8.28** *et seq.*).

12. Privilege log/redaction log. Print draft reports listing the privileged documents and the redacted documents from the database for review and proofreading. Make corrections as needed. The final privilege log and redaction log with all corrections made can then be printed, copied, and produced to opposing counsel.

§ 8.28 Imaging Technology

Document image processing, first developed in 1975, is currently experiencing explosive growth in many different industries. Imaging technology will dramatically change the way we do our work. Imaging allows you to link the database directly to the case documents, which are the trial attorney's main focus.

§ 8.29 —How Imaging Works

Imaging uses an image scanning device to take an electronic picture of a document, but instead of reproducing it on paper, the computer stores the image as an electronic or computer graphics file in its original, unalterable form. Imaging is somewhat similar to fax technology, because it works by scanning the dark and light areas on a page (the dark typed or printed words on the white paper background), converting it to dots (or pixels) that are captured by the computer. Note: You do not have to understand how this works technically to use the end product, any more than you have to know the inner workings of a fax machine before you can send a document to an office across town. Special software links the images to the records in the database, allowing the attorney or paralegal to view a picture of the document on screen at the same time the database record is displayed, as opposed to having to manually retrieve a paper copy of the document from a file box or drawer or from microfilm. The on-screen images can be enlarged, reduced, rotated, panned, and annotated. In sophisticated systems, the documents can be placed together in a new order, such as for a trial exhibit notebook. Documents can also be forwarded to others (electronically) for viewing or sent to a remote fax machine. If you want a hard copy on paper, you can print a "blowback" of the image on your printer.

§ 8.30 —Storage Media

Typical image processing systems use mass storage media. Floppy disks and hard drives are not enough, because each image page takes 60kb of storage versus 2kb for text. Currently, there are three basic types of storage media for images:

1. Rewritable optical platter (also called a magnetic disk or optical disk) has a magnetic surface that allows it to be reused. Optical platters are fast, but have lower storage capacity and cost more per image. They are best for temporary storage of images before permanent storage.
2. WORM (Write Once Read Many) disks cannot be reused because the images are physically "burned" into the platter surface. A WORM disk

holds about 20,000 images, equal to up to 10 document boxes or two standard four-drawer filing cabinets.

3. CD-ROM also are not reusable. CDs are generally preferred because the hardware and media are less expensive. The CD-ROM platters are similar to the CDs you use in your stereo to play music. Imaged files can be stored on CD-ROM just like word processing file are stored on the floppy disk or hard disk in your computer. The difference is that specialized equipment is needed to store (or "burn") the images onto the disk, and the images cannot be altered. A standard CD-ROM platter holds over 15,000 images (about 10,000 to 20,000 pages or 5–10 bankers boxes). A CD "jukebox" is a CD-ROM changer unit that holds more than one compact disk player. By using a CD jukebox, the computer can access multiple disks.

§ 8.31 —Economic Advantages

Some experts believe imaging will fundamentally change the way attorneys view and use litigation support. Firms that implement imaging technology will have a strategic advantage over those that ignore it, because imaging provides a dramatic savings of time, copying costs, and labor spent in organizing and retrieving documents and exhibits. The increased level of efficiency in retrieving and printing documents for use in depositions and settlement negotiations will make a difference in the overall time required to process the case. In a typical conventional deposition preparation scenario, a paralegal is given a list (generated from the database) of potentially relevant documents to be pulled from boxes or files of paper documents. The "pull rate" for hard copy documents from boxes is about 85 documents per hour. A typical document "pull list" for a witness deposition could contain 3,000 to 4,000 documents. This means that a single request list could take a paralegal from five to eight working days to just to pull the documents, which must then be sent out for photocopying. Often, the photocopies must then be rearranged (put in chronological order) to be usable to the attorney. In addition, with hard copies, the documents have to be refiled in the boxes or drawers after copying. This takes additional time and there is always the risk of losing documents or misfiling them when they are returned to storage.

§ 8.32 —Paper Costs

Lawyers are reluctant to give up their paper. The Association for Information and Image Management (AIIM), an industry trade group, reports that 90 percent of corporate information resides on paper. But it is expensive for law offices to store and manage paper documents. The costs include:

- Paying employees to process, file, retrieve, photocopy, refile, and forward paper documents
- Equipment costs for filing cabinets, shelving; file folders, binders, notebooks, labels; photocopy machines, supplies, and paper itself
- Phone bills for clients kept on hold or called back after retrieving documents
- Office space to store documents in file cabinets and people to manage them.
- Time employees spend looking for documents they need.

In complex, document-intensive cases, it is not unusual for a paralegal to spend an hour or more a day simply locating documents the attorneys request, having the documents photocopied, and replacing them in the files. The attorneys often request the same document more than once (they always manage to lose the first one). When several attorneys are working on the file, the requests multiply accordingly. At $60 per hour, one hour per day × 5-day week = $300 minimum per week. At 50 weeks per year, the paralegal spends $15,000 worth of valuable billable time just to pull, copy, and replace documents in the files, in addition to the photocopying charges. Certain problems are inherent in the storage of paper documents:

1. Most stored paper documents are not on a computer system because they originated outside the office: transcripts, pleadings, letters, contracts, interrogatories.
2. Paper cannot be safeguarded from human error. If a document cannot be found in a file, the document is either lost, misfiled, or being used by someone else.
3. Paper cannot be protected from fire, theft, intrusion, or malicious destruction.
4. Paper documents have to be laboriously unstapled and then rearranged in order to be presented in a useable format different from the original.

§ 8.33 —Microfilm

The typical retrieval rate is even lower for documents that are retrieved and printed from microfilm. For each document on the list, the microfilm reel containing the desired document number must be located, the tape loaded onto the machine, the particular frame brought up, the document printed, and the tape reel rewound and replaced in its holder. Microfilm printers can print only about four documents per minute. This could potentially translate into hundreds of paralegal hours to locate documents and print copies from microfilm for a pull list like the one described above. This retrieval procedure is typically repeated many times in the course of deposition preparation, motion responses, and so forth during the life of the case, amounting to an enormous amount of time invested in the tasks of retrieving and maintaining the documents. It is likely that scanning products and services will eventually replace microfilming as the primary means of storing and retrieving image data.

These are some other benefits of imaging and electronic document storage over hard copies or microfilm:

- All documents (on CD-ROM or optical platters) can be stored and accessed at both your office and at the client's offices, if desired.
- More than one attorney can access the image database simultaneously. There is no waiting for someone else to finish reviewing the file before work can be started.
- Images can be viewed and culled before they are selected for printing. This reduces photocopying costs and saves paper.
- Print quality from images exceeds that of microfilm prints.
- Documents cannot be lost, misfiled, or altered once they are imaged.
- Paper handling is reduced; images can be sorted in any order (before printing) for review and there is no worry about replacing pages in correct order.
- Storage and shipping costs for paper are reduced because documents are stored on CDs. One CD can hold 18,000 to 20,000 pages (8 to 10 boxes).
- An imaged set becomes a portable document collection that can be taken to the courtroom with a laptop computer. This allows the attorney access to all the documents without having to physically transport them.
- Document coding can be updated to reflect the history of the use of the documents as deposition exhibits, produced, etc. Also, attorney comments about the document can be recorded and captured the first time through, and will thereafter travel with the document for reference.

Image Processing Advantages

1. Provides great savings over paper in storage space, office supplies, administrative handling, and input cost (except for database coding)
2. Integrated into existing computer systems
3. Captures typed and handwritten text and graphics—no operator translation or interpretation
4. Image is identical to the original (except perhaps a tad smaller)
5. Image databases can import information from or be integrated with other databases
6. Image processing systems have multilevel security features.

7. Image processing systems have electronic annotation, image forwarding by fax, and transaction tracking features to receive or review, process, reorder, emphasize, and forward docs to other users.
8. Document images are not alterable; may be more likely to be admitted as evidence
9. Immediate access; multiple users at the same time; images can be compared easily

Image Processing Disadvantages

1. More expensive (than OCR)
2. Images cannot be imported into ASCII applications without OCR
3. Text searching not possible; only done within the database created to go with document
4. Image storage takes more computer space than OCR

Checklist: What to look for in selecting an imaging system

____ 1. Integration with existing hardware and operating system software. The system should work on your office's computer environment. Windows is essential.

____ 2. Vendor's reputation in service, product, training, and support. The product should have been extensively tested and used in law applications before you buy it.

____ 3. Ease of use. The average attorney or paralegal should be able to use the system and work with it at his or her desk.

____ 4. Customization. Can the system be customized to your firm's specific needs?

____ 5. Does the system allow for easy expansion without a loss of initial hardware or software investment?

____ 6. Does the system adhere to industry standards (for future compatibility)?

____ 7. Are there strong system security and disaster recovery features?

____ 8. Does the vendor provide full cost and savings analysis?

§ 8.34 —Optical Character Recognition (OCR)

OCR (Optical Character Recognition) development began in the early 1970s, but it has only recently become easy and affordable. Documents can be converted into OCR format to allow text-based searching as a supplement to the database. Using an image scanner as the input device, OCR software analyzes the individual dots that make up the text on a page to interpret what characters (letters, numbers, punctuation) are represented. The interpretation is then stored in computer readable format (generally ASCII) as a text file that can be edited, searched, or used in a word processing document. Searching on OCR text is not perfect, because even the most advanced OCR software cannot decipher every word on a given page due to variations in type style and condition of the documents. It is possible to remedy this deficiency through costly cleanup editing of the OCR text, but this editing is labor-intensive and generally quite expensive (OCR cleanup can add as much as $10 per page to the cost of processing a document.) Even in unedited form (about 75 to 80 percent accuracy), annexing the OCR data adds a very powerful capability to the database, allowing for retrieval of an enormous amount of information from the documents, such as an unlimited number of key words. The OCR text is a supplement to the search capability of the imaged and coded database. Scanned images cannot be full-text searched until they have been read through the OCR software. The OCR process does not have to be applied to all the documents. You might want to apply OCR to only a selected subset of the most substantive documents. Also, the OCR step does not have to be done right away. It can be completed at any point in the process after the image scanning is done.

OCR limitations include the following:

1. Electronic data can be altered easily; originals must still be retained.
2. OCR equipment cannot read marginal handwriting, photos, letterhead, number stamps, seals, and signatures.
3. OCR equipment cannot read poor resolution text or unusual fonts.
4. Data requires manual intervention to separate text from graphics and interpret illegible characters.
5. The text arrangement is rarely identical to the original.

OCR advantages include the following:

1. It provides quick and cheap input.
2. The data can easily be integrated into existing systems and other software.
3. Paper received from outside can be scanned in.
4. Scanned information can be altered and annotated.

§ 8.35 Outsourcing to Litigation Support Vendors

When cases are too large or complex to handle in-house, you may need to employ the services of an outside litigation support vendor. This section discusses some of the factors you will need to consider in evaluating and selecting vendors.

§ 8.36 —Estimating Vendor Coding Time versus In-house Coding Time

In order to analyze the feasibility of vendor coding, one must first estimate how much time it would take for paralegals to do full coding in-house. The chart below indicates the approximate number of weeks required for full coding on projects of various sizes. For example, using the industry standard page-to-document ratio of 3:1 (average of three pages per document) a project containing 200,000 pages would yield approximately 66,666 documents to be coded. In a typical document collection, a paralegal can do full coding at a *maximum* rate of about 10 documents per hour (this rate decreases somewhat if the documents are complex or highly technical in nature), so a 66,666-document project would require about 6,666 hours of coding time. The maximum time that one paralegal could realistically devote to coding is 35 hours per week (7 hours per day × 5 days per week), assuming that the coder works on this project full-time, with no interruptions or holidays. In this example, a project consisting of 200,000 pages would take a staff of six full-time paralegals 31.7 weeks, or 7 to 8 months to complete the coding. A 300,000-page project would take a team of six coders 47.6 weeks (nearly a year) to complete. The law office would have to employ a staff of 25 to 30 coders in order to achieve the turnaround time you can expect from the coding vendor. This is not feasible for most offices. The coding vendor has the capability to assign many more coders to a project (in multiple shifts, if necessary) with a realistic expectation of completing the objective coding within a time frame of weeks instead of months.

§ 8.37 —Comparing Vendor Coding Costs to In-house Coding Costs

Litigation support vendors generally quote a flat per-page rate for coding work. In order to present a valid comparison, you have to calculate a paralegal's per-page coding cost. For example:

A paralegal billing at $55 per hour costs $.92 per minute. Based on the fields required for this type of database, the *maximum* rate for full coding (both objective and subjective fields) is 10 documents (or 30 pages) per hour. This means about six minutes per document or two minutes per page to code and proofread, resulting in a cost of $1.84 per page [$.92/min. × 2 = $1.84]. To express it another way, at $55 per hour, coding 10 documents per hour costs $5.50 per document (or about $1.84 per page for the average three-page document). Even experienced coders agree that a coder would have to work at a very fast pace to actually do 10 documents an hour, and this could only be accomplished consistently if the documents were all fairly simple and straightforward. If the coding takes more than two minutes per page (not unusual with complex or highly technical documents), or if the paralegal's billing rate is higher than $60 per hour, the per-page cost could easily increase to $2.00 to $3.00 or more. The calculations for in-house full-coding in **Table 8–1** are expressed as a range, from a low of $1.84 per page to a high of $3.00 per page. **Table 8–2** shows a comparison of vendor coding costs versus in-house coding costs.

Determine an approximate cost for subjective coding only. Experienced document coders and various vendors estimate that the portion of the full-coding time that would normally be devoted to the more substantive subjective fields is about one-third of the coder's time. You can calculate costs for subjective coding based upon one-third of the full-coding costs. The vendor prices shown here reflect a composite of quotes by vendors on document database projects. You would need to solicit quotes for your particular project.

Table 8–1

ESTIMATED MINIMUM TIME TO COMPLETE FULL CODING IN-HOUSE

PROJECT SIZE:		100,000 pages (33,333 docs)	200,000 pages (66,666 docs)	300,000 pages (100,000 docs)	400,000 pages (133,333 docs)
No. of Coders	Hours per Week	Estimate 3,333 coding hours	Estimate 6,666 coding hours	Estimate 10,000 coding hours	Estimate 13,333 coding hours
1	35	95.2 weeks	190.5 weeks	285.7 weeks	380.9 weeks
2	70	47.6 weeks	95.2 weeks	142.9 weeks	190.5 weeks
3	105	31.8 weeks	63.5 weeks	95.2 weeks	126.9 weeks
4	140	23.8 weeks	47.6 weeks	71.4 weeks	95.2 weeks
5	175	19.1 weeks	38.1 weeks	57.1 weeks	76.2 weeks
6	210	15.9 weeks	31.7 weeks	47.6 weeks	63.5 weeks
7	245	13.6 weeks	27.2 weeks	40.8 weeks	54.4 weeks
8	280	11.9 weeks	23.8 weeks	35.7 weeks	47.6 weeks
9	315	10.6 weeks	21.2 weeks	31.7 weeks	42.3 weeks
10	350	9.5 weeks	19.0 weeks	28.6 weeks	38.1 weeks
12	420	7.9 weeks	15.9 weeks	23.8 weeks	31.7 weeks
20	700	4.8 weeks	9.5 weeks	14.3 weeks	19.1 weeks
30	1050	3.2 weeks	6.3 weeks	9.5 weeks	12.7 weeks

Table 8–2

COMPARISON OF VENDOR CODING COSTS versus IN-HOUSE CODING COSTS

PROJECT SIZE:	100,000 pages	200,000 pages	300,000 pages	400,000 pages
I. Paralegal full coding—objective and subjective fields [$1.84–$3.00/pg]	$184,000–$300,000	$368,000–$600,000	$552,000–$900,000	$736,000–$1,200,000
II. Paralegal objective coding [about 2/3 of full coding cost]	$122,660–$200,000	$245,340–$400,000	$368,000–$600,000	$490,000–$800,000
III. Paralegal subjective coding only [about 1/3 of full coding cost]	$61,333–$100,000	$122,670–$200,000	$184,000–$300,000	$245,333–$400,000
IV. Vendor objective coding [$.89–$1.17/pg]	$89,000–$117,000	$178,000–$234,000	$267,000–$351,000	$356,000–$468,000
III and **IV** Combined:	$150,333–$217,000	$300,670–$434,000	$451,000–$651,000	$601,333–$868,000
Savings over paralegal full-coding cost: [18%–28%]	$33,667–$83,000	$67,330–$166,000	$101,000–$249,000	$134,667–$332,000

Note: All figures are estimates based on the assumptions described herein and are presented here for purposes of illustration only. Estimates would be subject to change should the project parameters change. These figures should not be construed as authoritative quotes.

Advantages of vendor coding for the objective fields include

Less Expensive: A vendor can do objective coding for $.89–$1.17 per page. The comparable in-house cost would be at least $1.22 to $2.00 per page. In addition, a vendor's per-page price for objective coding generally decreases when the total number of pages increases, resulting in a further cost savings to the client for large coding projects.

Faster: Paralegals can construct the remainder of the document database (the subjective fields) in less time if the objective fields are coded by the vendor. The vendor can put on three coder shifts, if necessary, to return the objective database to the law office for further processing in a matter of weeks instead of months.

High Quality: A reliable vendor can bring experience, efficiency, and high quality skills to the objective coding. The vendor will code according to your precise specifications, and quality control to ensure input accuracy should be included in the vendor pricing.

Resource Use: Trained paralegals can concentrate their efforts on the subjective coding, substantive analysis, and research required to produce the privilege log and redaction log.

Vendor coding for the objective fields is usually cost-effective for the client. As illustrated in the above table, the combination of vendor objective coding and paralegal subjective coding results in a savings to the client of 18 to 28 percent over in-house full-coding costs. The client may also have paralegals on its corporate staff who may be assigned to portions of the project. To the extent that the client utilizes its staff paralegals, you would need to adjust the cost projections accordingly.

§ 8.38 —Considerations in Selecting an Outside Vendor

The information in this section is a guide to evaluating vendors for your project. The procedures described here may not be the best for your project. The attorney will want to get the client's cooperation and approval of any plan to apply outside vendor coding and/or imaging to the project. It is usually a good idea to request quotes from several imaging and coding vendors on your project. Comparing the pricing schedules from various vendors can be difficult, because vendor submit their quotes in a variety of formats. You can make your job easier by submitting a Request for Proposal specifying the services you require. After selecting a vendor, the next step in the process is to hold a project design and planning meeting with the vendors to discuss the specific details of the project. The vendor will formulate a Statement of Services for the precise steps involved in executing the project.

There are several different kinds of vendors:

- Litigation Support Vendors—coding is their profit center. Don't buy into a system that ties you exclusively to a particular vendor's system. Aim for maximum flexibility. Be on guard against computer hardware (and software) sales personnel who are more interested in selling you lots of hardware than in solving your litigation support problem. Avoid proprietary systems and aim for "open architecture" systems.

- Value Added Resellers (VARs) often hook up with technology companies to sell specific products. Watch out for proprietary system components, a lack of sophistication concerning your needs for litigation support, and a desire by sales force to sell you the most expensive equipment and products they have.
- Proprietary Imaging Vendors and Consulting Groups—Their primary business is imaging. They sell total imaging systems comprised of hardware and software components. These systems are usually pretty sleek, because firms usually spend a lot of up-front time tailoring a system to meet your specific needs. (This also adds considerably to the cost.)

Look closely at the systems vendors try to sell you. Be very cautious about investing in any system built on a company's proprietary architecture. To qualify as an objective consultant, a company shouldn't manufacture or resell any particular imaging systems. Before you buy, view other imaging systems the vendor has installed in an actual user environment. Check out systems in lawfirms as well as other industries, such as law enforcement, medical, insurance, and airlines.

A strict cost comparison among vendors does not tell the whole story, however. Before recommending a particular vendor, examine the literature and proposals from several different vendors and talk with them about their ideas for handling your project. Only after you complete this research will you be in a position to recommend that your clients authorize your office to contract on their behalf with outside vendors to perform the coding and imaging services. The following is a list of questions to consider concerning vendors.

1. Are the vendor representatives responsive and informative?
2. Are they willing to educate you about the imaging and coding process?
3. What imaging software do they use?
4. What are their quality control procedures?
5. What is their reputation?
6. Can they provide references? Have references been pleased with the performance and service?
7. Do you feel comfortable that the vendor could handle the job the way you want to see it done?
8. How do their prices compare with other vendors?
9. Do you plan to obtain and install at your premises the work stations and peripheral equipment compatible with the vendor's software product?
10. Does this vendor offer some capability that others do not?
11. Does the company specialize in large imaging and coding projects?
12. Will the vendor do the scanning on-site, if necessary?

13. Does on-site imaging involve additional costs?
14. Do the vendor's services and prices appear to be in line with those of other vendors?
15. Is the vendor a full-service litigation support company?
16. Does the vendor convey enthusiasm and a high level of knowledge about the requirements of project similar to yours?
17. Does the vendor use a proprietary online input system?
18. Does the vendor offer a document repository service for storage and management of paper records in huge multiparty litigation cases?
19. Does the vendor have the ability to put on a large enough staff to carry out the project?
20. How long has the company offered image-based services?

Avoid the following

1. Vendors who want to press you into fitting your case to their methods, rather than developing solutions that would suit the needs of your situation
2. Vendors who lack the depth of expertise that other companies exhibit
3. Vendors whose cost proposals contain vague cost items which they are evasive about explaining or hidden costs that would add to the overall per-page cost
4. Vendors who make misleading claims
5. Vendors whose documents are poorly written and full of grammatical and/or typographical errors
6. Vendors whose prices are generally too high in comparison to others
7. Vendors who seem eager to promise things you feel they could not deliver.

§ 8.39 Portable Computers (Notebooks and Laptops)

The shrinking size of computer technology has seen the advent of powerful, reliable computers that are portable enough to be carried into the courtroom. This development has important ramifications in trial work. The paralegal or attorney who takes a portable computer to trial can gain a considerable advantage over the uncomputerized opposition. Although you try to anticipate all the information that will be needed at trial, the potential for surprises is always present. A portable computer enables the trial team to have instant access to an enormous variety of critical data on the spot in the courtroom. The first truly portable personal computers became available around 1983, and the quality, power, and speed of portable computers has improved at a remarkable rate ever since. Most of the major computer manufacturers now market smaller, lightweight, portable versions of their computers. Best of all, the prices have dropped dramatically, making portable computers readily affordable for even small law offices. High quality portable computers are available at reasonable prices from a number of computer manufacturers.

Portable personal computers are often referred to as "laptop" or "notebook" computers. The main difference between the two designations is their weight. Portable computers that weigh around seven pounds or less are generally referred to as notebooks, and those that weigh over seven pounds are laptops. The average notebook computer weighs five to seven pounds and can operate on batteries for two to four hours without a recharge. Generally, a portable computer should be as thin and lightweight as possible. Most models provide the option of using either battery power or AC adapter cables (see § **8.40** for more on battery considerations).

Both laptop and notebook computers take up much less room than a standard desktop PC. Many notebook computers are small enough to be folded into a briefcase! Portability in a computer (defined as a combination of weight, bulk, and handle design) gives you the freedom and flexibility to work while traveling or in remote locations, or to take new software home with you to practice or learn it away from the distractions of the office. A portable computer can be easily folded and stored out of sight or carried to meetings, depositions, and into the courtroom.

A number of extra features are available on various models of portable computers. For example, some portables come with built-in modems that enable you to access computerized on-line research services such as LEXIS and Westlaw from remote locations. A portable computer can also be connected via modem to your office network for electronic mail messages, document transfers, and calendaring uses. Laptops with add-on boards can even provide fax capability. Some portable computers allow you to use an external monitor or projector at the same time as the internal monitor. This capability enables the attorney to project text or graphics on a large screen for presenting information in the courtroom. Some other ways the trial team can use a portable computer outfitted with the appropriate software at trial include the following:

- Track and cross-reference trial exhibits or deposition testimony with database software
- Search database for exhibits or previous testimony that could be used to impeach a witness on cross-examination
- Record notes during voir dire or witness testimony
- Review transcripts of daily trial testimony recorded by CAT (computer-aided transcription) by the court stenographer

- Use waiting time productively by updating calendar entries, drafting correspondence and memoranda, or reviewing outlines of trial examinations
- Use RAM-resident time and billing software to write timeslips or post expenses on the road.

Just as you should have backups for other types of equipment used in the trial presentation, you need to have a contingency plan in case your portable computer refuses to work for some reason. If possible, you should have access to a replacement portable computer loaded with the same information that is on your laptop in case something happens to your machine. It is also useful to have a backup copy of the programs and information on tape or floppy disk that could be quickly loaded into a substitute computer, as well as printed copies of trial outlines, deposition summaries, witness notes and other critical documents you plan to use at trial.

§ 8.40 —Considerations in Choosing a Portable Computer

When you are looking for a notebook or laptop that will be right for you, do some research and ask plenty of questions. It is important to try out a computer that is outfitted with the software programs you normally use before you decide. The combination of the monitor, keyboard, and other features of the computer should suit the way you plan to employ them in typical daily use. The following checklist covers some of the main points to keep in mind when evaluating portable computers.

1. Compatibility
Be sure the portable is compatible with your office computer system. It should be easy to transfer data between the portable unit and your desktop PC.

2. Disk Drives
Most notebooks come with a built-in floppy disk drive, but some require an external floppy drive that must be hooked up to the portable unit. The standard floppy drive laptop disk is the 3 1/2 inch microfloppy, but some units can accommodate the larger 5 1/4 disks. Make sure the built-in floppy disk drive is conveniently located and protected from the elements.

For serious business use, a hard disk drive is essential on a portable computer. Fortunately, the prices of hard disks have come down dramatically and most portables come equipped with a substantial chunk of hard disk memory (anywhere from 40 to 120 megabytes is not unusual). The amount of disk space required will depend on the programs you plan to run and how you plan to use the portable computer.

3. Speed
The speed of the portable computer's central processor will greatly affect the response time if you plan to run database software or other complex programs. A minimum of a 386SX processor is desirable, especially if you use Windows™ software. For larger databases or more sophisticated programs, a 486SX processor can make a big difference in operating speed.

4. Price
Most portable computers have list prices in the $2000 to $3000 dollar range, depending on the size and speed of the hard drive and the other options. However, it pays to shop around because discounts and sale prices are readily available in this highly competitive market.

5. Monitors
The quality of the display and the size of the monitor vary among different designs of portable computers. The monitor display should be bright, easy to read under various lighting conditions, and free from excess glare or reflection. Look for a portable that has contrast adjustment and brightness controls. Other desirable monitor features are the ability to alter the palette (the choice of gray shades displayed on screen) and the ability to turn off the backlighting from the keyboard.

The second important consideration with portable computer monitors is size. A courtroom laptop or notebook computer should display at least the full standard 25 lines and 80 columns that a regular desktop computer monitor can show. Some models compress the letters to shorten the screen, while others stretch the characters to fill a squarer screen. Graphics tend to show up best on the screens that are more nearly square-shaped. The notebook computer you choose should have a monitor that is easy to read and look at for extended periods of time. Also, make sure the frame holds the monitor securely at a comfortable angle without flopping over.

6. Keyboard
The size of the individual keys and the touch of the keyboard are important factors in selecting a notebook or laptop computer. Some portables are so small that they have to squeeze the size of the screen and the keyboard. The keyboard should feel solid and be comfortable to type on and the keys should operate smoothly and quietly without making a clacking sound that could be disturbing in the courtroom. Make sure the angle of the keyboard is comfortable for you. Some models have rear feet that snap down to create an angled keyboard surface.

Study the size and placement of individual keys, especially the directional or function keys that you use most often with your software programs, as these will affect your long-term satisfaction with the keyboard. For example, on some notebook computers the cursor arrow keys and the "Home," "End," "PageUp," and "PageDown" keys are quite small or very close together. Make sure the "Enter," "Shift," and Function keys are conveniently sized and correctly placed for the way you use the keyboard. Some models have an embedded numeric keypad while others require a separate add-on keypad, which will be an important consideration if you use the portable computer for extensive number crunching work.

7. Quiet Operation
For courtroom use, a portable computer must be not only small but also quiet so that it is unobtrusive. In addition to the keyboard noise, notebook computers normally emit various beeps when they are first started up, when the battery power is getting low, and sometimes when the computer case is shut while it is still on. In addition, some backlit screens emit a hum or buzz that could be distracting in a quiet room. These noises can be annoying and distracting in the courtroom, and can cause the judge to order that the computer be turned off. Check to see if the notebook computer you are considering has a switch to turn off the sound.

8. Battery Life
Reliable battery power is important if you plan to use a portable computer at trial. You might not always be able to use an extension cord in the courtroom, either because no electrical outlet is available or because the judge objects to stringing an extension cord out through the room. If you do have to rely on battery power, look for a portable computer that efficiently manages its power usage. Some models shut down certain components when not in use and conserve battery power by operating in a standby mode. A notebook computer that will be used all day in the courtroom should allow you to adjust the power saving settings to extend the life of the battery.

Find out how long the portable computer will operate on a normal battery charge and the amount of time required for the battery to recharge. Some notebook computers can be recharged while they are being used, but others have to be turned off. Some units are equipped with a handy light that indicates the battery is charging. Also check on the availability of a spare battery pack that is easy to insert. Watch out for built-in batteries that are not removable, because these units don't allow you to use extra battery pack if you must work away from an AC outlet for a long period of time.

9. Mouse
If you use a mouse (for example, for Windows™ applications), the portable computer you choose needs to have either a built-in mouse or a port to attach one. A growing number of machines are coming with a built-in trackball device, while others have a clip-on trackball which attaches to a port at the front or side of the computer case.

10. Durability
Make sure the portable computer is sturdy and durable, as it will have to stand up to a lot of abuse. Look for solid construction and protective slots or doors over the various ports and connectors. A protective carrying case is an essential feature if you plan to do much traveling with the machine.

§ 8.41 The Automated Courtroom

Imagine having access to all the documents and exhibits in a case, but NOT having to prepare exhibit binders! No blowups! Instant transcripts! No special equipment arrangements for videotaped depositions! A dream? Maybe, but it describes the courtroom of the (very near) future. We hear a lot about what could be done with computers in the courtroom, but relatively few paralegals have real experience with the technology. This is changing gradually. The legal profession tends to be slow to change established habits and routines. Until recently, the way in which lawyers conducted trials was not very different from the way they did it 200 years ago. Before the advent of computers, the stenographic machine (invented in 1911) was the last big technological advance to reach the courtroom. But these days, even the most conservative law offices agree that courtroom presentation methods have to change, especially in complex cases, because it is simply physically impossible to manage cases involving literally millions of pages of documents without the use of computers. As a trial paralegal, you can make yourself very valuable by helping your supervising attorney keep up with and eventually make use of new techniques necessary to present cases in the automated courtroom.

Computers can be extremely effective tools for presenting a case to a jury, especially in cases with highly technical subject or ones involving many documents. A computerized courtroom system can provide the following benefits to trial teams:

- Computer monitors allow trial attorneys to present a complex case in an understandable fashion, at a lower cost to the parties involved than traditional trial presentations.
- Computers can help court reporters be faster and more accurate in their recording and transcription of the trial testimony.
- Computers enable the judge to conduct the trial smoothly, and provide additional benefits for the judge's staff.

A typical computerized courtroom system might include a computer and nine or ten large monitors, each about the size of a large television screen. The monitors would be placed strategically throughout the courtroom, on the judge's bench, the bailiff's desk, the witness stand, each counsel table, and three or four in front of the jury box. (The number of monitors for the jurors can vary. One recent Cincinnati, Ohio, trial courtroom used three monitors for nine jurors.)

When a witness is testifying on the stand, the attorney directs a computer operator (perhaps a paralegal or the judge's bailiff) to display a certain document on the monitor. The operator types a code number into the computer that corresponds with the exhibit number the attorney wishes to display. The image of the document appears initially on the screens in front of the judge, the witness, and the trial attorneys for both parties. After the witness identifies a document, the attorney moves for it to be admitted as an exhibit. Once the judge admits the document, the document image is immediately displayed on the monitors in front of the jury. The jury can then see and read the document on the monitor as the witness testifies about it.

While still a relatively expensive undertaking, an image scanning system can be cheaper than producing multiple sets of bulky exhibit notebooks. The judge and jurors don't have to struggle with huge binders or fumble through stacks of documents. Computers help trials go more quickly and smoothly. The process of passing a document from juror to juror can take up many precious minutes of court time if each juror reads the document carefully. Displaying a document on screen can solve this problem. The jurors can all see and read the document at the same time with no delay to the trial. In addition, each party's documents appear in the same format on the video monitors, so there is no disadvantage for the party who does not have the resources to produce fancy tabbed exhibit binders.

Computer assisted exhibits eliminate the paper clutter that occurs when you have thousands of pages of paper documents. Attorneys and their paralegals can streamline and organize the evidence presentation. When necessary, they can quickly display a series of related documents on the screen, eliminating the need for jurors to thumb through exhibit books and the time it takes to make sure everyone is on the same page.

Computer monitors can make complex information less confusing and more interesting for the jury. People are accustomed to seeing information on a television screen, and jurors are comfortable with it. Jurors have reported that they like computerized techniques because it helps them understand the testimony. Jurors tend to prefer watching the computer monitors over reading paper copies of documents. The testimony moves quickly, even when the witnesses are questioned about numerous documents. Best of all, a computerized display eliminates the need for a hard working trial paralegal to perform the tedious process of assembling hard copy exhibit notebooks.

An automated system can reduce distractions and confusion in the courtroom when a document has to be located unexpectedly. Typically, you won't use all of the case documents in the courtroom, but the attorney will want to have them available just in case. Traditionally, this meant that trial paralegals were responsible for transporting multiple boxes of documents to the courtroom and figuring out how to organize and store them there. Any experienced trial paralegal knows how nerve-wracking it can be to search for a particular document in a bank of file boxes or cabinets at the back of the courtroom while the judge, jury, attorneys, and witnesses wait. A computerized system can reduce the contents of those boxes to a small stack of computer disks and make any document in the case available at the touch of a key.

The computer also allows additional flexibility in displaying documents that conventional blowups cannot provide. The trial attorney can highlight or enlarge a word, phrase, or specific portion of a document, or zoom in on a paragraph, a date, or a signature. Focusing the jury's attention on a particular image helps to ensure that everyone is looking at the same document or specific portion of a document at the same time.

Computers will not completely eliminate the need for paper in the courtroom. You will want to have a single hard copy of each exhibit for the bailiff or court reporter to file for the appellate record. You may also want to give the jurors paper copies of certain official documents so that they can see that the computer documents are accurate replicas of the original documents.

Using automated courtroom systems requires advance preparation that is somewhat different from the traditional trial preparation duties. The exhibit documents must be scanned into the imaging system and a database constructed to index the documents (see § **8.25** *et seq.* for more on this topic). The attorneys can display any scanned document immediately. If a question arises on a document that has not been previously scanned in, the scanning can be done in a few seconds if the courtroom is equipped with a scanner. The judge does not have to waste precious time waiting for a trial paralegal to make copies of a document.

Software for image scanning and display creates and labels an image of each document page that can then be called up on the screen or printed out on a laser printer. The key to successful image search and retrieval is using good indexing and database software. You create a database of exhibit summary records, then press a key to display the corresponding document on the screen in a window or overlay (or side by side). The system can handle everything from one-page documents to documents of 100 or more pages. You may want to index individual pages of longer documents to make it easier to quickly locate the correct portion of a lengthy document. (Jump from the first page of a document to the key portion on page 40 with no delay.) The system can locate and display particular pages within a large document. Moving from one exhibit to the next is fast and precise.

You will need at least two sets of the images: one for the courtroom use and the other for office use to prepare witness examinations in the evenings or on weekends. The court needs a system and each lawyer's office needs one also. The attorneys need to have their own computer to build their databases, with security codes to protect privileged and confidential work product and information. The attorneys should not be limited by not having the tools in the courtroom to search, and organize their data.

Other advantages to automated courtrooms include:

1. There is no time delay for setting up the equipment for playing videotaped depositions in the courtroom. The equipment is already in place. Jurors are much more likely to pay attention to videotaped deposition testimony than to the deadly practice of reading it on the stand. (The least satisfactory way to present testimony is by reading from a transcript.) The jurors can watch video depositions on their monitors. Computer monitors can be wired to a VCR to show videotaped depositions or demonstrative exhibits.
2. Transcripts of previous deposition or trial testimony can be displayed for the jury to read during impeachment. The attorneys can do key word searches if questions come up about what a witness said in previous deposition testimony. The courtroom stenographer can instantly translate the testimony into transcript that the judge or jury can review. Courtroom computers can make the court stenographer's job easier, too. The chances of misspelling technical terms or names are reduced when the court reporter can see the document on screen. and reduces editing time during the preparation of the transcript. Some court reporters now use real-time reporting. The keystrokes from the court reporter's stenographic machine are instantly translated into English by the computer and displayed on the courtroom monitors. The court reporter does not have to read back a question off the paper strip. The judge can quickly find the precise wording of a question or statement to rule on an objection. Printed trial transcripts (or computer disks) can be available at the end of the trial day for the attorneys to review in preparing for the next day's testimony. A real-time system also helps hearing impaired persons to participate in trials as jurors, witnesses, and litigants. (Courts can thereby comply with the Americans with Disabilities Act, which became effective in January 1992.)
3. One of the trial judge's most important duties is to keep the testimony as clear and coherent as possible. Jurors are more likely to pay attention to what is displayed on the monitors. It is easy for them to see the document to which the attorney and the witness are referring. The court can also use it to prepare orders or findings. The judge also has immediate access to all the case documents on computer without the need for heavy notebooks or stacks of paper documents. The judge can conduct research from the bench if necessary. In some courts, jury instructions are accessible on the court's computer network, so the judge can look

them up quickly if needed. This facilitates the preparation of the jury charge.

4. The courtroom deputy can use the computer to prepare reports, check calendars, or issue judicial notices of hearings and trial dates. A computer on the judge's clerk's desk enables the clerk to do research on LEXIS or Westlaw on the spot, retrieve information from court docket sheets, or refer to the judge's previous opinions. The court also can keep its calendar on the system. The staff can use the computer to assign cases for trial and hearing dates, generate pretrial orders, (dates for discovery cutoff, final pretrial conference, and trial date). This ensures that each party is notified of the trial month 10 to 12 months in advance. Court orders, calendars, etc. can be issued directly to a fax machine from the computer.

INDEX

WHAT'S NEW?

Recent developments included in this supplement:

- Advice on planning effective and interesting trial presentations for juries in the 1990s
- Tips on improving videotaped depositions of expert witnesses, along with other suggestions for using videotape in trial preparation and presentation
- Update on conventional forms of demonstrative evidence, such as enlargements and photographs
- A new section on planning and using computer-generated animation as demonstrative evidence at trial
- Tips on evaluating and working with demonstrative evidence vendors
- A new section on planning, conducting, and using mock trials and jury focus groups as trial preparation tools
- Information on updated courtroom technology, including tips on effectively using computerized court transcripts

PARALEGAL TRIAL HANDBOOK
SECOND EDITION

1997 Cumulative Supplement Current through January 1, 1997

BEVERLY K. HUTSON

*****HERE'S WHAT'S NEW INSIDE*****

- Obtain advice on planning effective and interesting trial preparations for juries, see page 29.
- Find valuable examples on improving videotaped depositions of expert witnesses, along with other suggestions for using videotape in trial preparation and presentation, see page 33.
- You receive a completely new section on planning and using computer-generated animation as demonstrative evidence at trial, see page 10.
- Also provided is a new section on planning, conducting and using mock trials and jury focus groups as trial preparation tools, see page 15.
- and more, see page i for details.

Insert in the pocket in the back inside cover of the bound book. Discard previous 1996 Cumulative Supplement.

Wiley Law Publications
JOHN WILEY & SONS, INC.
New York • Chichester • Weinheim • Brisbane • Singapore • Toronto

HUTSON/TRIAL HANDBOOK 2E 97S
ISBN 0-471-18534-5

This text is printed on acid-free paper.

Library of Congress Cataloging in Publication Data:

ISBN 0-471-12167-3
ISBN 0-471-18534-5 (supplement)

Printed in the United States of America

10 9 8 7 6 5 4 3 2 1

PREFACE

This supplement to *Paralegal Trial Handbook* discusses ideas and techniques to help readers update their professional skills in the late 1990s era of technology. The advice in the main volume remains valid. Paralegals still have to coordinate the basic components of trial preparation—witnesses, written materials, exhibits, and courtroom logistics. They still must take the initiative to communicate with and provide support for their attorneys. As always, paralegals must make effective use of all the tools available to accomplish the tasks involved in trial preparation. Today's trial paralegals also have a responsibility to keep up on developments in technology.

There can be no doubt that technology has profoundly affected the practice of law. Computers have become indispensable tools in law offices and corporate legal departments. Internet usage continues to grow at a phenomenal rate. Courtrooms are being updated to accommodate portable computers and other electronic equipment. Court clerks' offices in many jurisdictions are installing automated systems to make it easier to locate and retrieve information. Recent advances in technology have resulted in tools and techniques that did not exist a few years ago. The material in this supplement discusses new approaches to conventional trial preparation tasks. Updated courtroom technology is also discussed, including tips on effectively using computerized court transcripts.

This supplement includes some new ideas on planning effective trial presentations for juries in the 1990s. Supplemental material to **§ 3.40** offers tips on improving the (typically) dull videotaped depositions of expert witnesses, along with other suggestions for using videotape in trial preparation and presentation. **Section 4.66** discusses computer-generated animation, and **§ 4.1B** updates conventional demonstrative exhibits such as enlargements and photographs.

Another type of tool in trial preparation is the services and products provided by consultants and outside vendors. Vendors can provide needed equipment and expertise in virtually any size of case. Outsourcing to vendors can simplify trial preparation and save your time for other important tasks. **Section 4.1A** offers advice on evaluating and working with outside vendors to produce demonstrative exhibits.

Paralegals recognize the value of knowledgable, early preparation for trial. While some tasks cannot be completed until the last few days before the trial date, the more you can anticipate and handle ahead of time, the easier it is to cope with the last-minute flurry of activity that always accompanies a trial. Section 5A of this supplement expands the discussion in § **5.2** on pretrial research tools such as mock trials and jury focus groups that provide the trial team with *advance* information when it really counts—during trial preparation. Naturally, most books and articles on pretrial research discuss the advantages to the attorney. This supplement emphasizes the value of mock trials and focus groups from the paralegal's perspective and explains why you should welcome and encourage pretrial research as a technique to give you a head start on preparation for the real trial.

Your comments, questions, and suggestions for future supplemental topics are most welcome. Contact me by telephone at (330) 336-3026, by mail at 415 Kaser Drive, Wadsworth, Ohio 44281, or by E-mail at either bhutson@lx.netcom.com.

Cleveland, Ohio
April 1997

BEVERLY K. HUTSON

NEW IN THIS SUPPLEMENT

Note to the Reader: Materials that appear only in the supplement and not in the main volume are listed below.

* CHAPTER 3

PREPARING TRIAL WITNESSES

§ 3.40 Videotaping Expert Depositions

Page 270, add at end of section:

Today's jurors are accustomed to receiving information from television and computer screens, and they tend to pay close attention to what's shown on video monitors in the courtroom. As a result, television monitors and videotape are playing an expanded role in today's trial presentations. The low cost and accessibility of video technology have inspired new uses for videotape in the courtroom.

Improving Videotaped Depositions

Videotape is a relatively new development in the context of trial presentations. In the days before "America's Funniest Home Videos" and video rental stores on every block, videotaped depositions were rare and still considered a novelty. Attorneys generally had to obtain the court's permission to take a videotape deposition, and only a few court reporters had the proper recording equipment. We knew things were changing in 1980 when Federal Rule of Civil Procedure (FRCP) 30(b)(4) was amended to authorize taking videotaped depositions as a matter of course.

Trial attorneys have long recognized that videotaped deposition testimony is generally more interesting to jurors than listening to attorneys read the transcript into the record (see **§§ 3.40–3.41**). But jurors get bored quickly with typical videotaped depositions that drone on and on (sometimes for hours), focusing only on the "talking head" of the witness with no change in scenery. It's not surprising that jurors tend to doze off—most video depositions are quite dull! FRCP 30(b)(4) states in part, "The appearance or demeanor of deponents or attorneys shall not be distorted through camera or sound-recording techniques." Apparently, many trial attorneys and court reporters interpret this to mean that a video deposition should be a cure for insomnia!

The doctor or other expert witness may have some dynamite testimony, but their remarks could be totally wasted if the jurors are not paying attention to the videotape. Attorneys are not video producers, and they may not realize that they can do some subtle things to make a videotaped deposition more watchable. (There is no law against making your expert look as good as possible.) If you plan to use a videotaped deposition at trial, consider some of the following techniques:

- Select a court reporter/videographer with the necessary skills and equipment to produce an attractive videotape. Talk with the videographer about what you can do to make the presentation more interesting (within the Rules of Evidence, of course).
- Use a neutral background. (Light blue or navy works well; stark white does not.) Make sure no logos or distracting patterns are in the background. Adequate lighting is essential to a nice-looking videotape. The videographer can add external lights, if necessary.
- Try to capture the jury's attention by breaking up the plain talking head as much as possible. Injecting some movement into the deposition is much more effective than a stationary shot. Movement draws the eye to the screen and helps to keep the jurors' attention. Consider using two cameras to convey movement by changing the camera angle every so often.
- Make sure you have some visual aids ready for the deposition. When the witness refers to a document, have the camera zoom in for a closeup of the document itself. Use demonstrative evidence (models, graphs, charts, and so forth) on the video, and have the videographer focus on the visual aid while the witness explains it. If you plan to use computer-generated exhibits with the witness, show the graphic or video animation while the witness talks about it. Use graphic labels and overlays (arrows, color, dotted lines) to emphasize specific details and add to the impact of the witness testimony.

"Day in the Life" Videos

"Day in the life" videos are sometimes used in personal injury and medical cases to show the client's abilities and disabilities or to support claims for the high cost of custodial care. Videotape can be edited relatively quickly, is less expensive than motion picture film, and allows overdubbing of narration and graphic titles to introduce various segments. The admission requirements are the same as for other videotape: the tape must be an accurate depiction of the person's regular activities on a typical day. It must not be misleading or inflammatory. The purpose of this type of video is certainly to persuade the jurors on an emotional level, but it can backfire. Day in the life videos that appear staged or contrived can offend the jury.

View of Premises

Some cases involve events that occurred in locations where a jury view is simply not feasible. A videotaped survey of the location can be effective in orienting the jurors to the scene of the events. A video camera can be used to record a property inspection, especially when conditions are likely to change or there would be difficulty returning to the property.

Video Collage

Excerpts from other previously admitted videotaped testimony can be transferred to videotape for use in closing arguments. The segments would summarize the testimony of the various witnesses and highlight the strong points of the case for the jury.

Split-Screen Video Techniques

Side-by-side screens allow you to display portions from a videotaped deposition on one side and display enlarged exhibit documents on the other side simultaneously. This helps the jury keep track of what documents the person on the videotape is talking about. You can also display photographs on either screen to help the jury identify the person being talked about in the video. Alternating between the split and full screens whenever the witness refers to a document adds an element of movement that will keep jurors interested.

Other Uses for Videotape—Outside the Courtroom

Inexpensive and accessible, videotape is routinely used in various aspects of trial preparation. Most law offices now have a television and VCR. Many seminars and training materials are available in video format. Attorneys often show "witness how-to" videos to their clients as part of their preparation for deposition or trial testimony. Libraries have videos that can provide factual and background information on subject matter related to the case. Video presentations are also used in mock trials and focus group research before the trial.

* CHAPTER 4

PREPARING VISUAL AIDS AND DEMONSTRATIVE EVIDENCE

§ 4.1A Working with Demonstrative Evidence Vendors (New)

Should you produce graphics in-house or hire an outside graphics firm to do the work? The answer to this question depends on many factors. Consider the following questions as a starting point to determine whether in-house production is cost effective for your situation:

- Do you already have the equipment in-house, or would you have to buy it? Figure out how much you would have to invest in computer hardware, graphics or presentation software, and a high quality printer. (Normally, the equipment expense can be amortized over several cases.) Remember to include the cost of supplies (ribbons, film, pens, paper, toner) and service contracts for the equipment.
- Do you have the skills in-house? If you have someone on staff who is trained to use computers and graphics software, fine. If not, estimate the training time and costs required for staff to learn to use the computer and graphic software. (Multiply the number of training hours by the hourly wage of the employee.) You might have the skills in-house, but the software is still relatively expensive.
- How many graphics would you need in an average year? Estimate the number of graphics you normally will need in a year. If you have many cases that require graphics, the fixed cost per case decreases. On the other hand, in-house production may not be cost-effective for firms that need only a few graphics per year.
- An outside graphics firm brings technical expertise and creative ideas to the project. Your in-house efforts may be limited by the

computer operator's creativity and your system's software capabilities.

- In-house capability allows quick revisions, and graphics can be produced on short deadlines. However, your in-house computer system could malfunction, shutting down graphics production until the problem is solved.

You may well have the ability to produce adequate two-dimensional static graphics in house. But in cases involving large dollar amounts or that require high-end technology, use an outside company. Once you have decided to use an outside firm, you have to find one. There is no magic formula for selecting a good demonstrative evidence firm. It's important to interview several companies and do some comparison shopping, especially in cases where the stakes are very high. Look for a balance of technical expertise, artistic eye, and knowledge of legal admissibility standards. The best graphics companies indicate an understanding of the overall visual strategy behind the presentation. They must be able to communicate with engineers, physicians, and other professionals to gather the necessary technical information. (See also **§ 8.38** on imaging vendor outsourcing. Many of the same considerations apply to visual evidence firms.) The following is a list of factors to consider in evaluating outside graphics firms:

- Experience in litigation and legal graphics
- Appropriate technology for high-end graphics
- Ability and willingness to work with your expert
- Quality and responsiveness (quick turn-around is critical)
- Competitive pricing
- Multiple services
- Qualified personnel and professional staff
- Check confidentiality; conflicts checks
- Obtain and check references thoroughly
- Discounts for volume or retainer work

§ 4.1B Demonstrative Evidence Presentation Techniques Update (New)

In 1989, when the main volume was written, courtroom visuals were pretty much limited; document and photograph blowups, blackboards and flip charts, or hand-drawn diagrams and graphs were the norm. Back then, overhead transparencies and slides were considered innovative. I recall using an expensive slide show illustrating pharmacy labeling as part of the demonstrative evidence in one of my first trials. Some of the jurors we interviewed after the trial thought the slide presentation was excessive for the images it displayed. Slide shows are now conventional. Courtroom presentation techniques have evolved significantly in the last two decades. An update on demonstrative evidence is in order to discuss new forms of demonstrative evidence and the ways in which technology has updated conventional techniques.

Blowups

Sections 4.6–4.15 discuss conventional document enlargements, or "blowups," which have become commonplace in the courtroom. Attorneys are accustomed to using blowups, and courts readily accept them as demonstrative evidence. Blowups are quick to produce at the last minute, and they are still relatively inexpensive. Indeed, blowups may still be the best choice in cases with only a few key documents or modest budgets. However, blowups do pose some practical problems.

Too many important documents. At a recent seminar I presented on trial preparation to paralegals in Cleveland, Ohio, one paralegal asked me, "What do you do if your attorney tells you to have 50 document blowups made?" My response was, "Don't make 50 blowups! That's too many!" Some cases involve many key documents that the jury needs to see, but the attorney must be selective. Blowups lose their impact when *everything* is enlarged.

Too many oversized boards can be a logistical nightmare in the courtroom. The attorney has to lift the unwieldy boards on and off the easel, which can be awkward in a small courtroom. (In the O.J. Simpson criminal trial, jurors were inadvertently bumped by large boards as the boards were being placed in view.) Court reporters and clerks often do not have adequate storage space for large exhibit boards. Mounted blowups weigh about a pound apiece, so multiple boards quickly become quite heavy to carry. Fifty boards would weigh more than three of the heaviest bowling balls!

Black and white document blowups all tend to look alike. A popular use for blowups is enlarged pages or excerpts from actual deposition transcripts that impeach or reinforce a witness's live testimony. But standard black and white blowups of transcript pages are pretty boring. When you have dozens of them, it's hard to grab the right one quickly because they all tend to look alike. Also, the standard 12-point type on transcript pages usually does not come out large enough to do much good, anyway. The page may be larger, but the actual type is only about 1/2 inch high, which most people cannot read from more than a few feet away.

Blowups are inexpensive, but the cost adds up. It's true that blowups are a relatively inexpensive type of visual aid. In the Cleveland area, standard 30 x 40 inch enlargements cost about $60 to $80 each. This is fine if you only need a few. But 50 documents at $60 each would cost $3,000! If your case budget allows that much, you should consider using another technique as an alternative to document blowups. For example, you could use projected images in lieu of multiple enlargement boards. Documents and transcript pages can be scanned and stored on a compact disk, and the images projected on a large screen or on monitors in the courtroom. Everyone can see the document at the same time, but the attorney doesn't have to fumble with large boards.

Photographs

Courts have accepted traditional still photographs as admissible evidence for decades (see §§ **4.29–4.44**), but photo enlargements continued to be controversial until the 1950s because people feared they would be prejudicial to the jury. Opponents raised concerns over accuracy until technology made it feasible to tell whether a photo had been tampered with. We seem to have come full circle on this score. Although photographic enlargements are extremely common and well-accepted in courtrooms today, technology has raised new questions about tampering. Technology makes it possible to modify and enhance photographs so that it is again very difficult to tell whether they have been altered.

Methods of preparing photo enlargements have changed. Years ago, you had to either supply a negative of the photograph or have one made before the photo could be enlarged (see § **4.39**). Now digital technology enables a color scanner to quickly scan, enlarge, and print photographs with high-quality resolution. Color copiers can often produce copies of photographs that are adequate for most purposes. We also have the technology to capture still images from videotape.

§ 4.2 Determining the Purpose of the Visual Aid

Page 293, add at end of section:

A big part of your responsibility as a trial paralegal is helping the attorney plan the most compelling format available for presenting the information in your case. Let's face it—a lot of what goes on in a typical trial is just plain boring! Jurors must pay attention to evidence in order to understand it; they must understand the evidence before they will remember it; and they must remember the evidence before they will be persuaded by it. You can't change the facts of a case. You have to work with the people, exhibits, and events involved. But you can increase your chances of success by presenting the trial in a polished and persuasive package that will hold the jurors' interest and attention.

Audiences typically display a high level of attention for only 15 to 20 minutes at a time, and juries are no exception. Throughout history, speakers and performers have known that short presentations were easier for audiences to understand and remember than long ones. (Typical sermons in U.S. churches last no more than 15 to 25 minutes. Vaudeville acts were usually only about 12 minutes long. Lincoln delivered his famous Gettysburg address in about three minutes!) The most successful trials present accurate information to the jury in small, easy to digest segments (a concept sometimes referred to as "chunking").

Research shows that an average juror watches television seven hours a day. Jurors not only want to receive information quickly and in small segments, but they also expect to be entertained or at least engaged by the presentation. Extensive televised coverage of high-profile trials and programs like *Court TV* and *LA Law* have increased the public's awareness of what happens inside the courtroom. Jurors expect trials to have the pacing and production values that they see on television and in films.

Attorneys have long recognized that jurors understand and remember information better when they see it as well as hear it. Research has shown that audiences remember only about 10 to 15 percent of the information they hear, but they are likely to retain six to eight times as much of the information they both hear *and* see. It's important to give the jurors something to look at while they listen to testimony. A good trial presentation conveys the client's story to the jurors accurately, clearly, and convincingly. The attorney imparts information to the jury through witness testimony and documentary exhibits. Visual aids help jurors to understand and remember the information. Attorneys have long used charts, graphs, and blowups to enhance a witness's testimony and help the jurors to understand the information. Improved technology gives attorneys many more options and makes preparation and presentation faster and easier.

§ 4.66 Computer-Generated Animation (New)

Computer animation has been used in court since the late 1970s, but the production techniques were so expensive that only catastrophic cases with high damages such as airplane crashes could justify the cost. Computer animation is becoming more common in courtroom applications. Attorneys and courts have started to realize how useful animations can be in depicting events that would be impossible to show any other way. Animations are gaining greater acceptance by courts. The technology has improved so much that realistic and affordable animations can now be used in medium-sized cases.

Most people are familiar with "animation" in connection with entertainment: cartoons on television, children's films, and movie special effects. Before the current advances in computer technology, animation in films such as the classics produced by Walt Disney Studios was created the old-fashioned way. Artists painstakingly hand-painted thousands of individual frames or "cels." Each succeeding cel moved the action forward by a small increment. The series of cels was transferred to film and played back at high speed (30 frames per second), creating the illusion of continuous motion. This laborious process was time-consuming and very expensive.

Computerized animation uses the same principle of creating thousands of individual images, except that the individual cels are created electronically instead of by hand and the images are stored on a computer. The series of images is transferred to videotape and played back at high speed to create the illusion of movement, just as in conventional animation.

Three-dimensional computer graphics originated in the scientific field. Computer technology advances enabled scientists and engineers to perform complex analysis which generated vast amounts of numerical data. They turned to three-dimensional graphic representations to help them visualize the data.

Computer animation in legal applications generally takes one of three forms: tutorials, reconstructions or recreations, and simulations. It is important to distinguish among these three types because they are used for different purposes in the courtroom. The terms *reconstruction, recreation,* and *simulation* are sometimes used interchangeably in the literature. However, they are not necessarily the same thing.

Tutorial animations educate the jury about some aspect of the case. Tutorials do not depict the actual events in the case. Instead, they are teaching tools that provide the jurors with certain background information to help them understand other testimony and evidence. Tutorials are particularly useful in cases involving highly technical or complex subjects, such as an airplane crash case in which jurors need to understand the basic principles of aerodynamics. The tutorial provides a foundation or framework to help the jurors comprehend other testimony in the case. Expert witness testimony will make a lot more sense to the jury if they have a basic understanding of the principles involved.

An *animated reconstruction* depicts what happened in a specific event, such as an accident or an explosion, based on known data and facts from the accident investigation. For example, an accident reconstruction expert might use data such as skid marks, distances traveled, coefficients of friction, and vehicle weights to illustrate the events in an automobile accident.

Animated simulations are different from reconstructions. Rather than depicting what actually happened, a simulation (sometimes called "scientific animation") illustrates an expert's opinion of what could or should have happened under different conditions. Simulations use sophisticated computer software to predict the behavior of physical objects, based on established and accepted scientific principles and mathematical formulas. Generally, an expert witness must sponsor a simulation for it to be admitted into evidence.

Animation will not be appropriate for every case. For example, if you only needed to show "before and after" views of something (such as how a person looked before and after an accident), still pictures may suffice. Generally, animation is most useful in cases where it would be impossible to physically demonstrate something to the jury, especially when movement is involved. For example, a products liability case involving the malfunction of a large piece of machinery could use animation to illustrate how the machinery works, how the various parts move and interact, and so forth. Animation is also useful to illustrate events over elapsed time. For example, in a construction dispute case, animation could show the gradual erosion of a building's foundation over a period of years. Other applications for animation could include:

- Events that would be too dangerous or expensive to physically replicate, such as explosions or aircraft accidents.
- Visualizing something that would be impossible to actually see. For example, criminal trials sometimes use animations to help juries visualize a crime scene that has been altered or no longer exists.
- When real-time motion is critical to issues in the case, such as the events in automobile or railway accidents.
- Simplifying complex concepts or procedures. For example, a medical malpractice case involving a botched operation could use animation to teach the jury basic information about anatomy and explain how the operation is normally performed.

Animation complements and augments traditional forms of demonstrative evidence (photographs, diagrams, charts, models, and so forth) because animation offers presentation techniques that are not available in conventional visual aids.

Movement. The element of motion is the key factor that distinguishes animation from other types of graphic illustration. Animation can depict how objects move and interact with each other. Action can be shown in slow motion so that jurors can understand what occurred. This would be particularly important in cases where the timing of events is critical, such as an automobile accident or an elevator failure. Changes that took place over a long time period can be condensed into a few minutes to help the jury grasp what happened.

Perspective. A still image captures a moment in time from a particular view, but animation can illustrate an object or scene from different vantage points. For example, in the products liability example above, animation could show the machine from the top, side, or bottom views. Another example would be an automobile accident where the animation could show the action from both the driver's and the pedestrian's points of view.

Detailing. Detailing directs the jury's attention to specific areas of an object by using graphic labels, arrows, directional lines, and so on to point out details. The animation can add color to highlight important features or zoom in to give a closeup view of a particular section.

Dissolves. Dissolves or cutaways remove visual obstructions to allow the jury to see inside or underneath the surface of an object. For example, animation could illustrate how the internal parts of a machine work and fit together. Animated dissolves make it possible to view areas that would be physically impossible to see with a normal camera.

Good animation shares many characteristics with conventional forms of demonstrative evidence. It should be short and get to the point quickly. It is streamlined, including the essential details but omitting any unnecessary details that could detract from the content. A good animation should simplify the subject and make good use of labels and directional lines to clarify the images and avoid confusing the jurors. Animation communicates a lot of information quickly, holding the jurors' attention. Animation can help the attorney focus on the key information, and may well enhance subject matter that is otherwise dry or boring.

A computer animation (or any other visual aid, for that matter) cannot make a good case out of bad facts. Using animation to illustrate evidence does not make the evidence any more accurate or reliable. The old computer adage "Garbage in, garbage out" applies to animation as well. An animation is only as good as the data upon which it is based.

The cost of producing computer animation has come down considerably. Animations were once justified only in cases with large damages, but advances in computer technology have made animation feasible in moderate-sized cases. However, animation is still more expensive than most other types of visual aids.

Preparation time is essential for animations. Animations that once would have taken months to create can now be generated in a few weeks, but animation still requires extensive and meticulous advance planning early in the trial preparation. It simply cannot be done at the last minute.

I know of a recent case where the attorney had worked with a demonstrative evidence firm to prepare an animation of an industrial accident. When it came time to play the animation in the courtroom, the judge would not allow it, saying that he didn't want any "cartoons" in his courtroom. The attorney had not notified the judge or opposing counsel ahead of time, and therefore was not allowed to use the animation at trial.

If you and your supervising attorney decide that computer animation is the best format for your case, you must make sure you can use it in court. Most animations are used as demonstrative evidence, which must meet certain foundational standards before the court will allow you to use it. You have to convince the judge that any demonstrative evidence is related to the case, is accurate and complete, helps the jury understand testimony or other evidence, and is fair and not misleading to the jury. The concern about unfair prejudice is particularly important in considering computer animations. Improved technology could enable the attorney to prepare a high quality animation that is so lifelike that the jurors could subconsciously accept it as actual recorded reality rather than as counsel's version of the events. The attorney must make it clear to the jury that the animation is meant for purposes of illustration only.

Advances in technology have raised many new questions, and the law is still developing concerning guidelines for admissibility of computer-generated evidence. A thorough discussion of the rules on evidence and admissibility is beyond the scope of this book. Consult your supervising attorney for details.

* CHAPTER 5A (NEW)

MOCK TRIALS

§ 5A.1 Pretrial Research

The field of jury research, which was still something of a novelty just a few years ago, has expanded and evolved. Trial teams in most of the highly publicized cases over the last decade have undertaken extensive pretrial research in conjunction with jury experts to help in formulating their trial strategies. Attorneys have come to respect the results obtained by expert trial consultants using research tools like focus groups and mock trials to gather advance intelligence on probable outcomes and jury reactions to the evidence in a case. This supplement section will expand the discussion in § **5.2** on using mock trials in trial preparation.

Trial attorneys and paralegals know that posttrial juror interviews and questionnaires (see § **7.58**) can yield valuable feedback about a trial from the jury's perspective. Attorneys analyze information from posttrial juror interviews to help them improve their techniques in future trials. However, posttrial insights on aspects of the trial (what jurors did and did not understand; which witnesses they liked or disliked; what they thought was missing from the case presentation) are just that—posttrial. The attorney can apply what he or she learns to future trials, but the information does not help in the trial that has just concluded. Pretrial research tools like mock trials and focus groups give attorneys the advantage of advance information that can help them when it really counts—during trial preparation.

§ 5A.2 Definitions

Focus groups and mock trials are two primary tools in pretrial feedback research. Attorneys use the two terms almost interchangeably (some attorneys also use the terms "jury simulation" and "surrogate jury") to describe pretrial research. No matter what you call it, the purpose of pretrial research is to gain advance information that will help the trial team do a better job in presenting the actual trial. In both focus groups and mock trials, the attorney presents information about the case to a group, and then monitors the group's discussions to gain a better understanding of how jurors are likely to react to the case. This section will discuss some of the similarities and differences between the focus group and mock trial formats.

The term *focus group* may refer to any short presentation, usually made by one person, to a small group of individuals who discuss and give immediate feedback on what they have heard and seen. Focus group research originated with marketing analysts who used small groups of consumers to provide businesses with valuable feedback about products and services. Focus groups in legal practice generally involve interactive round-table discussion by a group of objective lay people whose comments and observations help trial attorneys see the case from a juror's perspective. A focus group presentation is short (about three hours for one or two issues) and tends to be fairly narrow in scope, such as a summary of facts about a particular issue. However, focus groups can also resemble an abbreviated version of the trial, complete with witness testimony and exhibits. Some attorneys do not use testimony at all for focus groups, but instead merely summarize the case for each side and get the group's reaction through open discussion of the issues in the case.

A *mock trial* is usually a more extensive and elaborate presentation than in a focus group. Mock trials take the form of an abbreviated version of the real trial, presenting both plaintiff's and defendant's cases. Objective outsiders acting as mock jurors first view the presentation, which may be live or videotaped, and then actually deliberate and decide issues much like a real jury would. Usually, the mock jurors also participate in a debriefing session (led by the attorney, consultant, or other facilitator) where they can offer candid comments and observations, just as focus groups do. Although a mock trial usually takes more time than a focus group (mock trials can take a whole day), it is still a short exercise compared to the actual trial. The brief time frame forces the trial team to distill the case to its essential elements.

Focus groups and mock trials are relatively inexpensive to produce, and either format may be presented through live witnesses or on videotape. Group discussions in both formats should be videotaped for further evaluation by the trial team. Because the formats are similar and the definitions often overlap, the comments in the following discussion apply to both focus groups and mock trial research projects. The key factor in pretrial research is that attorneys get to listen to the deliberations by the group of mock jurors. Attorneys don't get to hear the mysterious process of jury deliberations in real trials, which may account for the fact that the reasoning juries adopt in reaching their decisions sometimes simply confounds the trial team. (A favorite trial attorney and mentor of mine used to say that "juries are fickle," usually right after the jury had voted against us in a case that we thought was a winner.) Focus groups and mock trials afford attorneys a rare opportunity to observe and listen to the deliberation process and discussion that lead to a jury's decision on a case.

You may also encounter the term *shadow jury* in connection with feedback research tools. In contrast to focus groups and mock trials, which are conducted well before the trial date, a shadow jury is used *during* the actual trial. Essentially, a shadow jury is a small group of persons who attend the trial and observe the proceedings from the spectators' gallery. At the end of each day, trial consultants interview these individuals for feedback on the day's events. Because the shadow jurors see exactly the same presentation as the actual jurors, they can give the trial attorneys valuable daily feedback that would not be possible to obtain from the real jurors until the posttrial juror interviews. Like pretrial research participants, shadow jurors usually do not know which side hired them, and this enables them to be candid and objective in their observations and comments.

§ 5A.3 Benefits of Pretrial Research

Both mock trials and focus groups use jury questionnaires to ascertain jurors' background information and opinions related to specific issues. The attorneys review the questionnaires and decide which jurors they would strike from the panel in the real trial. No one is actually excused from the research project, but the exercise gives the attorneys practice in quickly evaluating the juror information just as they have to do during actual voir dire. Observing the behavior and influence of those individuals throughout the discussion provides insight on the type of jurors that would be desirable and potential problem jurors for the real trial.

Many books and articles directed to trial attorneys recommend developing one or two central themes around which to organize the trial preparation. Strong themes that are repeated throughout the trial help jurors remember key ideas. Focus group and mock trial research can give feedback on the validity of possible themes. The trial themes to be tested in pretrial research groups should be short, catchy, and limited to no more than three.

Focus group research also enables the attorney to explore alternate theories or techniques for presenting specific evidence. For example, an attorney who is unsure about the most positive way to present evidence that is damaging to his client's case can gauge potential juror reactions to various approaches by trying them out on a focus group. He can then adapt the most successful approach to include in the trial presentation.

Attorneys often work on large cases for several years before the trial, and they sometimes get so involved in a case that they lose their objectivity. They get so bogged down with presenting their own case that they forget to analyze the opponent's case. Mock trial research helps the trial team get a fresh look at the strengths and weaknesses of both sides of a case. Presenting a sufficiently strong rendition of the other side's case is key to ensuring the validity of the research. Outlining the opponent's best case is important because a research presentation that is skewed toward your client's case could yield misleading feedback from the mock jurors, causing the attorney to underestimate the strength of the opponent's case. Identifying weaknesses in the opponent's case also helps the attorney in planning effective cross-examination to exploit the opponent's weaknesses.

Jurors have to understand information before they can be expected to remember it and make informed judgments about the evidence. Some cases involve exceedingly complex subjects that are very difficult for jurors to comprehend. Some examples would include principles of aerodynamics or physics; complex accounting procedures or financial transactions; and highly technical engineering or manufacturing processes. Trial attorneys often enlist the help of expert witnesses to educate the jury about the subjects, but not all experts are good teachers. (Also, some subjects are so complicated that even an excellent teacher-witness has a difficult time getting jurors to understand.) Pretrial research can alert the attorney to what the jurors did and did not understand about the case. Based on input from focus groups, the attorney can work out ways to simplify and streamline the presentation to make sure the information can be easily grasped and quickly assimilated by the real jurors.

Mock trials provide the attorney a chance for a "dress rehearsal" before presenting a jury trial in the courtroom. Even experienced trial attorneys can benefit from practice. Pretrial research provides a low-risk method for inexperienced attorneys to work out ways to present difficult or novel issues to a jury.

Focus groups and mock trials can elicit feedback from the jurors on whether a witness is likeable and credible. If the mock jurors don't respond well to the witness, the real jurors probably won't either. Witnesses and clients, especially those with no previous experience in testifying, get a chance to become accustomed to the rhythm of the question and answer format. Practice testimony by witnesses enables the attorney or trial consultant to spot and correct nervous habits that could prove distracting or annoying to jurors. For example, we once dealt with a very knowledgeable key witness who tended to unconsciously rock or swivel his chair from side to side whenever he answered a question from the attorney. Not only did the swiveling make him appear to be squirming in discomfort at the question (body language that could be interpreted as shifty or dishonest), but the side to side movement also caused fluctuations in the sound level picked up by the microphone. We showed the witness the videotape of his practice testimony and coached him on keeping the chair still. He complied, and the effect of this small change was immediate and dramatic. He answered the same questions as before, but he appeared much more trustworthy and in control when he stopped swiveling the chair. Likewise, attorneys can observe and coach other witnesses on distracting nervous habits or body language that could affect jury responses.

Focus group research is also extremely useful when the case relies heavily on testimony from one or more expert witnesses. An expert witness's testimony may be essential to the case, but an expert who does not come across well to the jury is of limited value to the case presentation. If focus group research reveals that a brilliant expert is a terrible witness, the attorney can work with the expert to improve the expert's testimony skills. Failing that, the attorney may decide to hire a different expert or work out another way to present the critical information.

Likewise, if the opposing side has retained a top-notch expert who could potentially undermine your case, you may want to include segments of the opposing expert's videotaped deposition testimony in order to see how well he or she comes across to a jury. We once used a focus group to test the impact of an opposition expert who we felt came across as arrogant and condescending. We were sure that his manner would offend jurors and diminish the effectiveness of his testimony. The mock jury surprised us by responding quite well to the expert, indicating that they believed his testimony was knowledgeable and credible. They did not seem to mind or even notice his pompous manner. The jury's reaction let us know that we needed to prepare a strong counter-attack to the expert's testimony because the real jury was apt to believe him also.

Unfortunately, one of the last things that many trial attorneys plan is the demonstrative evidence for the case. The shortened format of mock trials and focus groups compels attorneys to use visual aids to convey information quickly and simply. Charts, tables, and other graphics can help the research participants grasp information quickly and accurately. Even if the demonstrative evidence for the actual trial is not finalized, pretrial research can use mockups of visual aids. Graphics and visual evidence companies frequently provide preliminary "proof" versions of visuals for early research. Advance research is particularly valuable when the case is suitable for high tech computer graphics or animations (see **§ 4.66**). Visual evidence firms are accustomed to working under extremely tight deadlines because attorneys request changes right up to the last possible moment, but high tech demonstrative evidence such as computer animations must be planned well ahead of time. They simply cannot be executed at the last minute. Pretrial research projects are the ideal place for testing the impact of custom computer graphics and animations. Focus group and mock trial feedback allows attorneys and graphic designers adequate lead time to refine and modify the preliminary visual aids so they will be more effective at trial. Early feedback can save money, too, because changes can be made before the final printing or production steps are completed.

Wise trial attorneys encourage the client to get involved in focus group and mock trial research because these tools can help clients evaluate their position and recognize problems with their case. For example, if focus group members are not convinced that your client is not at fault, the client will have a clearer understanding of the problems in proving liability that you would face at trial. The research can also be a reality check for clients who refuse to discuss settlement or who are set on recovering a certain dollar amount. A client's expectations as to the amount of damages a jury is likely to award should be more realistic after the research. Focus groups can be useful in determining the real value of a case and helping the client to realistically evaluate settlement offers.

An added benefit to client involvement is that pretrial research gives the client an idea of what is involved in the trial process and can increase the client's confidence in the attorney. Clients are typically fascinated by the research process, and their involvement in the behind-the-scenes preparation allows them a closeup look at the work the attorney does on their behalf.

§ 5A.4 Setting Up Pretrial Research

Generally, the larger the expected verdict in the case, the more time, money, and resources can be devoted to pretrial research. However, mock trials and focus groups are not limited to very large litigation. They can also be cost-effective in medium and small cases as well. A single focus group costing about $500 can prove to be a good investment for smaller cases. **Figure 5A.1** lists various elements of expense involved in mock trials and focus groups. Naturally, not all cost items will apply in all cases. For example, if you use your office conference room for the research instead of renting a meeting room, no costs would be associated with facility rental. However, you would still need to plan for food service or catering needs. Use the worksheet as a guide to the various costs involved in pretrial research. Fill in the worksheet items that apply in your case to help you evaluate cost-effectiveness and track expenses of pretrial research in your case.

Attorneys can conduct in-house focus groups that provide some benefits of group feedback at a modest cost appropriate for smaller cases. (**Section 5.2** of the main volume discusses a simple mock trial, conducted in a law firm conference room, with no jury consultant, using office staff as mock jurors.) Some attorneys use a paralegal or associate as a facilitator and support staff to help with the logistics. In-house focus groups can be done for as little as $500 depending on the number of participants and other factors.

Some attorneys use jury research consultants to organize and moderate focus group and mock trial research. Expert analysis of the research results can increase the value of the research dramatically. Naturally, engaging a professional consultant also adds considerably to the cost of the research project. A professionally conducted full-scale mock trial project could cost $20,000 to $30,000. The consultant's detailed written report and analysis of the research results could add another $2,000 to $10,000 to this cost. Not every case can justify these costs, but the benefits of the consultant's expertise can easily offset the expense in cases involving very high potential damages. Consultants work with the trial team to prepare the videotape presentation and moderate the research sessions. In addition, consultants may also handle the logistics of screening the mock trial participants, preparing questionnaires, and arranging the location, food, and audio-visual equip-

RESEARCH SITE	Facility rental	$ ___
	Catering/food service	$ ___
MOCK JURORS (or FOCUS GROUP PARTICIPANTS)	Advertisement or employment agency	$ ___
	Answering service	$ ___
	Juror incentives (payment for participants)	$ ___
RESEARCH CONSULTANT	Consultation fee	$ ___
	Juror screening	$ ___
	Travel & accommodations	$ ___
	Conducting research session	$ ___
	Analysis & report	$ ___
VIDEO SERVICES	Producing presentation tape (include equipment rental, editing, retakes, etc.)	$ ___
	Video playback & monitoring equipment at site	$ ___
	Videotaping discussions at site	$ ___
	Duplicating tapes	$ ___
VISUAL AIDS	Consultation with graphics company	$ ___
	Production	$ ___
MATERIALS	Supplies (pens, pads, nametags, etc.)	$ ___
	Juror exhibit notebooks (binding, covers, etc.)	$ ___
TRIAL TEAM	Accommodations (if needed)	$ ___
	Time	$ ___
MISCELLANEOUS	Photocopies	$ ___
	Telephone & fax	$ ___
	Other	$ ___
	TOTAL	$ ___

Figure 5A.1 Costs Worksheet for Mock Trial and Focus Group Research

ment. A consulting firm may also be able to provide the facilities and arrangements for viewing and recording the research project.

Focus group research offers the most benefit when it is used early in the case. In fact, attorneys sometimes use focus group feedback before the litigation is even filed to determine such factors as what theories of liability to include, whether a case can be won in the jurisdiction, which defendants are most likely to be held liable, and whether undertaking a case is economically feasible. After the initial discovery is completed, focus groups can provide valuable comments on the best way to proceed in developing the case. For example, the attorney may need help on determining the best way to present difficult liability issues or controversial subject matter. Regardless of the matters being tested, legal practitioners agree that focus groups are most useful early in the case while the attorney still has many options available about the direction the case should take.

Mock trials generally produce the best results after the case issues are fully formulated and trial preparation is under way. Mock trials present a condensed version of the trial, using specific evidence, exhibits, witness testimony, and arguments. The best timing for mock trial research will vary with individual cases, but some experts recommend conducting a mock trial at least three months before the actual trial date. If the research results are not favorable to the client, the attorney will have time to amend pleadings, conduct additional discovery, or hire new experts. Either type of research should be done early enough (well before the actual trial) to allow for adjustments based upon the feedback received from the group.

Although most experts advise against it, some attorneys prefer to conduct the research in a conference room at or near their law offices. In addition to being economical in smaller cases with tight budgets, holding the research project at the attorney's office is convenient for the trial team members. They have easy access to case materials and supplies, no travel is involved, and the on-site location provides a measure of protection from discovery by the opposing side.

On the other hand, holding the research session on-site could make it difficult to conceal which side is conducting the project, and this could potentially cause the participants to respond less candidly than they would in a neutral setting. In addition, the trial team may find it hard to avoid the inevitable distractions of the office environment, and law office conference rooms may not be set up to accommodate the necessary audio visual equipment needed for research and observation by the trial team.

Experts in the jury research field recommend holding focus groups and mock trials at a neutral site, such as a hotel conference room. Hotel meeting rooms come in all sizes and are usually equipped with adequate outlets and wiring for the necessary audio-visual equipment. Ideally, a hotel or convention facility can provide two or three adjacent rooms: one for the presentation; a second for deliberations by the trial participants; and a third for the trial team to use as an observation room. In addition, a hotel can easily arrange food service for a large group. A neutral location away from the lawyer's office helps to ensure that the participants cannot tell which side is conducting the research, and the trial team gets some practice in the logistics of transporting equipment and materials before the trial. If you are working with a jury research consultant, his or her office may prefer to make the site arrangements. Discuss this with the attorney to clarify who is responsible for reserving the research site.

Regardless of the location you choose for the research session, it is important to make arrangements to capture the entire research session and jury discussions on videotape. While you will get a lot of information from watching the live action, you need the ability to replay the tape to review the discussions and get a closer look at the expressions and body language exhibited by the jurors as they watch the presentation and deliberate. Reviewing the tape will reveal details you did not catch during the actual research session. The videotapes can be replayed, reviewed, and studied multiple times, as needed, for later evaluation by attorneys, consultants, and clients.

§ 5A.5 Recruiting the Jurors

The goal in recruiting participants for either a focus group or a mock trial is to assemble a group which mirrors the makeup of the jury pool in the actual trial as closely as possible. The attorney or consultant must determine the appropriate demographics (gender, age, race, education, occupation, and so forth) for the research group. The sample demographics chart (see **Figure 5A.2**) illustrates the characteristics for a proposed focus group of 20 people, based upon the jury pool that an attorney could expect in the Cleveland, Ohio area. The sample demographics chart is based on a hypothetical case and is meant for demonstration purposes only. The demographics for your jurisdiction could be quite different.

Experienced lawyers and researchers feel that a group of 8 to 10 persons is the ideal size for a focus group. A mock trial may require 8 to 12 jurors. I worked on a recent mock trial where we recruited 20

PROPOSED DEMOGRAPHICS FOR 20 FOCUS GROUP PARTICIPANTS

CHARACTERISTIC	BREAKDOWN	No.
SEX	Male	10
	Female	10
AGE	21 - 29	4
	30 - 39	4
	40 - 49	4
	50 - 59	4
	60 +	4
RACE	White	10
	Black	8
	Hispanic	2
EMPLOYMENT	White collar	4
	Blue collar	6
	Unemployed/homemaker	4
	Retired	6
INCOME	Under $20,000	6
	$20,000 - $40,000	8
	$40,000 - $60,000	4
	Over $60,000	2
EDUCATION	High school or less	8
	Some college, trade, or vocational school	6
	College degree	4
	Advanced degree	2
POLITICAL SLANT	Conservative	10
	Moderate	6
	Liberal	4

Note: These demographics were prepared for a hypothetical case in the Cleveland, Ohio area. They are presented here as an example only, and should not be construed as appropriate for other cases.

Figure 5A.2 Sample: Proposed Demographics.

participants, who were split into two groups for separate discussions. Typically, you will need to solicit about 10 times as many initial response calls as the number of participants you want. For example, a project requires about 110 responses to yield a group of 8 to 10 persons who fit the appropriate jury characteristics. The 20-person group mentioned above required about 250 responses to get 20 appropriate jurors. It's a good idea to recruit a few more persons than you actually need to allow for emergencies or no-shows. For example, enlist 25 prospective jurors to ensure that 20 or 21 of them actually show up.

Focus groups or mock trial juries like the one described in § **5.2** may include friends, family, office staff, and co-workers who can provide some feedback on various issues. However, experts believe that paid outsiders who are not familiar with the case or the trial team are more likely to offer objective and candid feedback on the presentation. Recruit jurors from the same city or county in which the real trial will be held. A jury consultant will usually screen and select the research group, but you may be responsible for soliciting calls from prospective participants. Following are some ideas for finding qualified individuals.

A temporary employment agency can recruit prospects with the appropriate mix of educational and occupational backgrounds. Specify the number of persons and the demographics needed.

Another suggestion I have heard for locating a good cross-section of participants is to use old jury lists from the court in your jurisdiction. Jurors who have been called for jury duty usually cannot serve again for a certain period of time, so there is little likelihood of contacting someone that would be in the actual jury pool for your trial. Check with your supervising attorney about the feasibility of this technique in your jurisdiction.

You can also locate participants through a classified advertisement in the newspaper. Run the ad for three or four days, including a weekend. Keep the ad very simple and do not identify who is conducting the jury research. Even a simple ad like the one in **Figure 5A.3** usually attracts many more callers than you actually need for the research.

Hire an answering service on a short-term contract to take the calls, collect the basic information from the callers, and then relay this information to the jury consultant or to whomever will be screening the responses. Give the answering service specific instructions on what information they need to get from the callers (name, address, telephone number, age, race, and occupation) and how they should answer

JURY RESEARCH
PARTICIPANTS NEEDED
$100/1 DAY ONLY
CALL 555-0000

Note: The telephone number in the ad will be the number for the answering service. DO NOT put your law office's number in the ad.

Figure 5A.3 Sample advertisement for jury research participants.

questions from respondents curious about the project. In the interest of protecting confidentiality, the less information the answering service operators know about the project, the better. The answering service should simply inform callers that someone from the research service will contact them shortly. Tell the answering service the dates the advertisement will run and how long the answering service number should remain active. Take care not to turn off the answering service number before the newspaper ad is finished running, even if you already have enough responses to choose from. Callers tend to get upset when they can't get through to a telephone number listed in the newspaper, which is apt to provoke a call from the newspaper's classified editor to ascertain the problem. (I know because it happened to me.) Remember to calculate the cost of the advertisement and the answering service contract into the costs for the research project.

Ideally, a jury research consultant will screen and select the jurors who will participate in the research project. In the screening process, consultants first review the basic information provided by the initial respondents to select persons who fit the jury profile. The consultant's staff then contacts the prospective participants to conduct further screening. In addition to representing a cross-section of the population that is similar to the actual jury pool, the individuals selected must be willing and able to attend on the day and time in question and stay for the entire time allotted. They should also be able to articulate their opinions and willing to speak up to give comments or ask questions.

Either you or the jury consultant should send the selected participants a reminder postcard about a week before the date of the research project. In addition to the date, time, and place, include a map or directions to the research site, if necessary. If the attorney does not want to do a mailing, arrange for someone to call each participant to remind them.

§ 5A.6 Planning the Presentation Content

The hardest part of preparing a mock trial presentation is compressing the facts of a whole case into a two or three-hour time frame. Boiling a case down to its essential points and ideas is difficult enough in simple cases, but cases with extremely complex fact patterns present a real challenge to the trial attorney. In planning a videotaped presentation, the attorney has to extract the critical information and figure out how to assemble witness testimony into short timed segments.

Jury consultants feel that the most effective case presentations are those that convey factual information in a straightforward story form, with a beginning, middle, and end. Experts caution against presenting arguments to the jury, because you want the results to be based on the facts, not on emotional or persuasive appeals by the attorneys. The attorneys will have to work hard to extract only the vital elements of the case, but the work pays off handsomely in terms of organizing the trial preparation and formulating strategy.

Presenting the opposing side's best case is essential to deriving the most value from the research project. Attorneys are trained advocates who can argue either side of an issue, but they sometimes become so focused on presenting their own case that they forget to examine the other side's position. Outlining a strong presentation for the other side forces the attorney to examine strengths and weaknesses of the opponent's case. (This exercise helps the attorney clarify what needs to be accomplished in cross-examination, even without the jury research.)

Of course, someone must portray the opposing counsel and witnesses in the presentation tape. Normally, the attorney on the trial team who is most knowledgeable about the case should present the opposition's case. Segments of videotaped testimony from the opponent's expert witnesses can be edited into the presentation tape at the appropriate points. If the opposing side's witnesses are not available on videotape, the attorney may need someone to act the role as convincingly as possible. In some instances, another attorney, paralegal, or staff member could play the role, but some attorneys prefer to hire professional actors. (This adds to the cost, of course.) The attorney must script the answers for the actor-witness so that the testimony is accurate.

It's also important to use documentary exhibits and visual aids for both sides of the presentation, both to give the jurors something to look at besides witnesses and to convey the maximum amount of information quickly. The attorneys will probably take most of the responsibility for preparing the content of the research presentation tape, but you may be asked to assemble transcripts, documents, and other materials from the case file.

§ 5A.7 Juror Exhibit Notebooks

Juror exhibit notebooks are critical to the success of the research, because they enable the jurors to closely study the exhibits mentioned during the presentation. The exhibit booklets you prepare for a mock trial should contain the following materials:

- table of contents
- chart identifying principal names in the case
- timeline of significant dates
- exhibit documents for each side
- demonstrative aids for each side
- jury instructions
- verdict forms

Aim for a maximum of ten exhibits per side. Any more than this gets confusing and overloads the jurors with information. (Narrowing down the exhibit selection seems to be difficult for attorneys, who typically want to add documents right up to the last minute. You will have to keep after them to finalize their exhibits before the taping deadline.) Include copies of any visual aids the attorneys will use in the juror notebooks, if possible. I offer the following tips for producing juror notebooks for a mock trial.

The cover page should say "Juror Exhibit Notebook" with no indication of attorney or firm names. Use the full-page, 8.5 x 11 exhibit indexes with graduated side tabs that are easy to read from either the front or back of the notebook. You can use either lettered or numbered tabs (depending on the case and the attorney's preference), along with dividers to indicate which exhibits are plaintiff's and which are defendant's. I recommend using spiral bound booklets instead of looseleaf ring binders for the juror notebooks because they are lightweight, they open flat, and the pages are less likely to fall out.

(Unlike trial exhibit binders, you don't want anyone to easily remove or rearrange these documents.)

The attorneys and witnesses who appear in the taped presentation should use exactly the same notebooks that the mock jurors have before them at the research session. Prepare at least two or three exhibit notebooks for the attorneys before the videotaping begins so they can refer to the exhibits by tab number. (Label the exhibit documents with their corresponding tab numbers as well.) The attorneys and witnesses should take care to refer to the correct exhibit tab numbers in the presentation tape. Jurors who are trying to follow the presentation are easily confused when an attorney inadvertently refers to an incorrect exhibit number. They will end up searching through their notebooks or asking their neighbor about which page they should be looking at, meanwhile missing what's being said about the exhibit. The first time I prepared a mock trial, we did not have the tabbed notebooks ready when we made the videotape. The attorneys just worked with loose copies of the exhibit documents, and they were not consistent about references to the tab numbers. The jurors watching the tape got confused about which exhibit they were supposed to look at.

As the attorneys tape the presentation, keep track of the exhibits they refer to. If a proposed exhibit document is not actually used, do not rearrange or change the numbers of the remaining exhibits! Remove the unused documents from the notebooks and replace them with a page stating that "This page was left blank intentionally. Exhibit No. 9 was removed." Also, be sure to revise the table of contents to reflect the missing exhibit.

You will need a notebook for each mock juror, but you'll also want to make plenty of extra copies. Each attorney, client, and witness who is observing the research will want their own notebook. Keep one (or two) for yourself, of course. You may also need to give the videographer a notebook as a reference to the exhibits on the tape. The jury consultant will need one or two for his file, and it doesn't hurt to have a couple of extras for the case file. Follow the same procedure you would use to assemble trial exhibits (see § **5.66**): Start with the best unmarked copies you can find to ensure clean photocopying. Make sure the documents are straight on the page and that both sides of any double-sided documents are copied. Keep the set of unbound, unmarked originals together and put them away in a safe place, just in case you need to make additional copies. Write the initials of the attorneys, experts, and clients on their respective copies. In addition to copies of the notebook contents, remember that you will need the same number of tab sets, exhibit stickers, cover stock, and spiral binding supplies for whatever number of copies you decide to make.

Highlight relevant portions of the exhibits to make it easy for jurors to quickly locate pertinent information on each document. Sit down with the attorneys and decide what portions to highlight on each exhibit. (Use a different color for each party.) Create a master notebook with highlighted pages, and conform the highlighting on all the copies. (This is a task you may be able to delegate to an assistant.)

§ 5A.8 Visual Aids

Visual aids serve the same functions in pretrial research as they do in an actual trial. We know that jurors retain much more information when the attorneys use visual aids to reinforce the spoken words (see § **4.2**). Visual aids are particularly critical in the condensed format of focus group and mock trial research where the attorney must convey a lot of information quickly to jurors.

Two simple but effective demonstrative tools can be useful in any type of case: a name chart to identify the key players in the case; and a timeline to quickly orient the jurors to significant dates. If the case preparation is advanced, you should already have compiled most of the information you'll need for both documents. If not, work with the attorneys to develop lists of names and key dates. If you have the capability to produce charts and timelines in the office, you can probably prepare adequate versions of these documents yourself. If not, you can at least provide your graphics vendor with a draft of the information. (Remember to prepare and insert letter-size copies of these documents in the juror notebooks.) Use attractive and colorful visual aids for both sides of the presentation. On the tape, have the videographer zoom in for a tight shot on the demonstrative aid or exhibit long enough for the jurors to absorb it.

You can also use the focus group or mock trial formats to test demonstrative evidence and give the attorneys practice using it before the trial. If a research group does not understand a diagram or the attorney is not comfortable with a chart, you will want to revise it or make adjustments before the actual trial. Sometimes, just the process of preparing for the mock trial can point out adjustments that you need to make before the trial. For example, for one mock trial our graphics firm prepared a pie chart with removable pieces to represent segments of a sum of money (a "where the money went" illustration). The chart was cut out of 3/8" foam core board and fit onto a deeper background board (similar to a child's wooden puzzle) so the pieces could be placed one at a time to build the pie. However, the attorney found that fumbling with the individual pieces was just too cumbersome to accomplish smoothly in front of jurors (or a camera). We decided just to insert color photocopies of the chart in the juror notebooks for the videotape presentation, knowing that later we'd have to figure out another way to present the information at the trial.

§ 5A.9 Making the Presentation Videotape

Jury consultants usually recommend preparing a videotaped presentation rather than using live witnesses for a research project, for several reasons. The segments can be timed to fit into the desired schedule for the research project (see the sample schedule in **§ 5A.10**). The expert can critique the taped presentation ahead of time and the attorneys can make corrections or retape segments, if necessary. The trial team and the jury expert will know exactly what the mock jurors are going to see, and the experiment can be replicated with another mock trial or focus group, if needed. Segments from videotaped deposition testimony can easily be edited into the presentation. The presentation tape can be replayed multiple times, as needed, for later evaluation.

Unless you are a trained videographer, do not attempt to tape the mock trial presentation yourself. Hire a qualified professional videographer who has the equipment (cameras, lighting, microphones, editing capability, and so forth) and expertise necessary to produce a high quality tape at a reasonable price. *I repeat—do not try this yourself.* You will have plenty of other work to do to coordinate the preparation and taping. If you employ a jury consultant, he or she may want to discuss the project with the videographer before the taping begins.

You may know a professional video company from other work you have done or through a referral by a colleague. Some very large law firms have a professional videographer on staff who could do the job. However, if you have no existing leads, start with the Yellow Pages in your telephone directory. Look at the advertisements and services offered. Call a few video companies and briefly describe the project, but be careful not to reveal the names of clients or witnesses. It's a good idea to prepare a list of questions to ask (see below) so that you can easily compare responses from different companies. If possible, talk directly to the videographer, not to the assistant or receptionist.

Some companies will give informal price quotes over the telephone, but many companies are reluctant to do so, and I have found that no two video companies quote exactly the same way. You may want to request a proposal (if time permits) and then compare pricing. Studying proposals will indicate whether a company's prices are way out of line (either high or low) with the others. (Remember that charges will be higher if the videographers have to set up multiple times or do expedited editing.) See **Fig. 5A.4**.

LIVE PRESENTATION		VIDEOTAPED PRESENTATION	
PRO	**CON**	**PRO**	**CON**
Less expensive than videotaping	Attorneys must present, can't watch jurors	Attorneys can watch juror reactions	Adds to cost of research
	Unpredictable time Unpredictable content (if someone goofs, you're stuck with it)	Predictable time Predictable, editable content	
Can be revised at the last minute			Must plan and make tape in advance
	Difficulty scheduling all parties for the same date and time	Segments can be taped on different days and edited into the final tape	
		Taping with editing can ensure a polished, concise presentation	
	The exact presentation cannot be replicated	Tape can be replayed to clients or viewed later for analysis	
	No labels for segments	Segments can be labeled to avoid confusion	

Figure 5A.4 Live vs. Videotaped Research Presentations.

In comparing video companies, ask these questions:

Do they have experience with legal projects?
Can they do it within the time frame and deadlines you require?
Can they provide references?
Are they local? (Travel time and mileage add to the cost.)
Do they sound like they can handle the project?
Beware of hidden charges (Ask about charges for setup, travel, special equipment, etc.).
Do they have a space you can use for the taping, or will they come to your office?
If you need two cameras, can they provide them?
Do they have background backdrop screens, lights, microphones, and so on?
Can they do editing and copying of the final tapes quickly?

There is a direct correlation between the quality of the tape and the quality of the feedback from the research group, so it is important to make the best presentation tape you can. While the tape need not look like a Hollywood production, neither should it look like an amateur home video. Production values (particularly lighting and sound levels) are very important to the success of the research. If you shoot the video in a conference room, make sure the lighting is adequate. Have the videographer bring external lights, if necessary. The attorneys and witnesses should be equipped with external microphones to ensure adequate sound quality.

You will need a neutral background behind the attorneys and witnesses. Consult with the videographer about the proper background, lighting, and sound equipment for the room in which you will be taping. Watch out for stark white conference room walls and large expanses of white on visual aids and charts. White can wreak havoc with the videographer's white balance.

Choose a room for the taping that is relatively quiet. (You'll want to post "Quiet, Please. Taping in Progress" signs as well.) Disable the telephone in the room so it can't ring during the taping. Make sure the room has adequate electrical outlets for the videographer's equipment. If the videographer must run extension cords to electrical outlets outside the room, be sure to tape these down securely so no one will trip over them.

Naturally, the lawyers should dress for the videotape in the same clothing they would wear in court. If retaping is necessary, make sure the lawyers wear exactly the same clothing on the second day as they did for the first taping.

The attorneys should not stand behind a lectern, but they will need some sort of table to hold their documents and notes. Try to position the table out of camera range, but check that the attorneys do not have to look down too much when they refer to the notes. Looking down diverts the speaker's eyes from the camera and can affect the sound quality from the microphone. (Also, some jurors think that attorneys who look down too much seem unprepared and slightly "shifty.") The attorneys should not read their statements or questions. They should try to look straight into the camera and deliver their presentations in a natural, conversational fashion. Witnesses on camera may be seated, especially if they have to review documents as part of their testimony. Go over all these details with the attorneys, and listen to the videographer's suggestions on getting the best tape you can. The videographer should be prepared to take closeup shots of exhibit documents and demonstrative aids. During the taping, you or the videographer will need to time the segments and signal the attorneys as to how much time is left. Bring a reliable clock or watch (a stopwatch is even better) and make cardboard cuecards to let the speakers know when time is running out.

Have the videographer put a caption on the tape before each segment of the presentation to orient the jurors to what they will be seeing. For example, before the Plaintiff's Opening Statement the caption should read: "Plaintiff's Opening Statement [12 minutes, 10 seconds]" Likewise, the other segments would be captioned accordingly [Defendant's Opening Statement; Plaintiff's Case in Chief; Defendant's Case in Chief, and so on].

Ask the videographer to put each segment on a separate tape (the project described here took five tapes) and to label and sequentially number the tapes. This makes it easy for the person who does the video playback to play the tapes in correct sequence (even if it's a different video company from the one who produced the tape). Separate tapes also ensure that the presentation pauses to allow for evaluations at the proper points. If the tape should accidentally run past the end of the segment, the mock jurors would only see blank tape. Once the tapes are in final form, have the videographer make a duplicate backup set, and guard them with your life.

§ 5A.10 Conducting the Research Session

The following section describes a typical mock trial presentation conducted with the assistance of a jury research consultant. Focus group presentations would be shorter and less formal than the mock trial described here, but focus group activities would be conducted in a similar manner.

A proposed schedule for a day-long mock trial presentation might look like this:

7:30–8:45	Participants arrive and fill out questionnaires
8:45–9:00	Introduction and explanation by moderator
9:00–9:15	Presentation tape: Plaintiff's Opening Statement
9:15–9:30	Evaluation Form
9:30–9:45	Presentation tape: Defendant's Opening Statement
9:45–10:00	Evaluation Form
10:00–10:15	Break
10:15–11:00	Presentation tape: Plaintiff's Case in Chief
11:00–11:15	Evaluation Form
11:15–12:30	Presentation tape: Defendant's Case in Chief
12:30–12:45	Evaluation Form
12:45–1:45	Lunch
1:45–2:00	Presentation tape: Plaintiff's Rebuttal
2:00–2:15	Evaluation Form
2:15–2:45	Jury Charge
2:45–3:00	Break
3:00–5:30	Deliberations
5:30–6:30	Debriefing

Jury research participants behave much like real jurors in that some of them invariably arrive as much as 30 minutes before the stated time. This means, for example, if you told them to be at the site at 7:30, at least a few will arrive shortly after 7:00. Plan for this and make sure that someone is present at the registration table to greet the early arrivals. Assign each participant a juror number and have them sign in as they arrive at the research site. Give each participant a note pad (the small 5 x 8 legal pads work well for this), a pen or pencil, and a name tag. You can either prepare the name tags ahead of time, or let each participant print his or her first name in large letters. Also prepare place cards with each person's first name to place on the tables in front of the jurors. Prominent nametags and placecards make it easier for the jurors to address each other by name during the discussion and help the lawyers associate names with the faces on the questionnaires and videotapes.

Each participant should fill out a jury questionnaire covering basic identification and background data and opinions on the civil justice system generally, as well as questions designed specifically to reveal any biases concerning the specific issues in the case. Ask the participants to fill out the questionnaires completely and honestly. On the questionnaire and all the other forms, put a blank at the top for the jurors to write in their juror number. This enables you to make sure you have all the forms and to match the responses with the correct juror profile. Each juror should sign a statement agreeing to keep all information confidential.

Once the participants have arrived, the facilitator or moderator (which may be a professional consultant or one of the trial team members) should introduce the project to the jurors. Our jury consultants explain that this is a research project and that the group's input is very important to their research. They tell the group that the information in the presentation may or may not be based on a real case, and reiterate that candid comments and opinions are welcomed and valued. The moderator should explain that the video camera will be running throughout the day, recording the project as a way to assist the researchers later and to document the research. (Jurors may be a little wary of the camera at first, but they tend to get used to it throughout the day and forget about it.)

The moderator then explains the format and timetable for the presentations. He tells the group that they are not free to leave the research room until the moderator releases them. This is to prevent jurors from roaming the halls and inadvertently encountering one of the trial team. The moderator will then pass out the juror exhibit notebooks.

At the end of each segment of the presentation, the moderator passes out evaluation forms which the jurors fill out. The trial team will need to prepare evaluation forms for each segment: plaintiff's opening statement, defendant's opening statement, plaintiff's case in chief, defendant's case in chief, and plaintiff's rebuttal.

You will gain feedback not only from the jurors. You will also hear the lawyers (and consultants, if you use them) brainstorm ideas throughout the day. Make a note of anything the attorney says like, "We should have (whatever) at the trial." "I should have said (this) instead of (that)." "Remind me to include that document next time." "We need a chart to show these numbers instead of just talking about them." The attorneys may mention additional witnesses who are not on your list or other documents that should be included in the trial exhibits. In one focus group we did, the jury consultant listed random thoughts and ideas on a flip chart as they occurred to him throughout the day. He also drew rough diagrams of ideas for better visual aids and demonstrative evidence that we could develop for trial.

Jurors in a mock trial are given jury instructions similar to those that a real jury would receive. After the presentation and before the discussion or deliberations, the moderator reads the jury instructions to the jurors, just as the judge does in court. The jury instructions include general instructions as well as case-specific instructions. The attorney is usually responsible for preparing the jury instructions and verdict forms, often in consultation with the jury consultant. You can help by proofreading the document thoroughly, carefully checking question numbers and page numbers. Make the language as clear as possible, especially when one question refers to another.

After the participants have seen the presentation, filled out evaluation forms for each segment, and received the jury instructions, they are asked to discuss what they have seen (in focus groups) or to deliberate and reach a verdict, much as a real jury would do (in mock trials). Jurors are encouraged to ask questions about anything they did not understand. One technique that I have seen is to give the presentation to the whole group, then divide the group in half and have each conduct separate deliberations or discussions. At least one of the groups is likely to be representative of the probable composition of the real jury. Comments from both groups will prove valuable. The trial team will watch the discussions on closed-circuit monitors. Watching jurors struggle with the language contained in the jury instructions is enlightening (terms like "negligence" and "proximate cause" often give jurors a lot of trouble). Observing what troubles mock jurors can help the attorney do a better job of explaining these concepts to the real jurors during the actual trial. Pay attention to which exhibits and demonstrative evidence the jurors use to refresh their memories and figure out answers to the questions on the verdict forms. Observing the jury discussion can enlighten and surprise the trial team. Issues that were of particular concern to the attorney may not trouble the jury, while other points may generate lively discussion among the jurors.

At the conclusion of the deliberation or discussion, the facilitator may direct a round-table discussion involving all the group members (and sometimes the lawyers, although generally the attorneys remain concealed from the jurors). If the participants have split into two groups, the moderator may either debrief the groups separately, or he may prefer to bring them back together for the debriefing. The moderator guides the debriefing discussion to probe further into the reasoning process the jury groups used to reach their decisions. If the jurors were unable to come to a unanimous decision or to answer questions on the verdict form, the moderator will inquire about the factors that prevented them from reaching a decision. This also yields valuable feedback for the trial attorneys, who can then see what information the actual jurors would need to overcome these questions. The moderator may ask the jurors additional questions from the attorneys. (The jurors don't know that the attorneys posed the questions, because they are in a note delivered to the moderator by an assistant.) The trial team watches all this interaction via closed-circuit video cameras from a separate conference room.

At the conclusion of the debriefing and questions, the moderator pays each juror for his or her services. After thanking the jurors for their attention and input and reminding them that the research is confidential, the moderator releases the jurors.

After the jurors leave, collect all materials, tapes, notebooks, notepads, forms, and so on from the conference rooms. Make sure you do not leave anything behind. Arrange payment of all the bills for the hotel, catering, video technicians, and so on.

§ 5A.11 Protecting the Confidentiality of the Research

Attorneys on either side of a case can benefit from pretrial research, but the research is usually a closely guarded secret from the opposing counsel. There is nothing dishonest or unethical about focus groups or mock trials, but the attorneys for one side generally do not want the other side to know that they have the advantage of the information gained from the research. Such research is usually considered protected under the work product doctrine, but the other side could attempt to discover the results if they found out about it. In any event, it is prudent to take reasonable precautions to keep the project confidential and prevent accidental discovery by the opposing side.

- The research location should be disclosed only to the final participants selected. Do not indicate the site in the advertisement or other solicitation.
- The project moderator should stress the confidential nature of the research and ask all participants to sign a confidentiality agreement. Jurors must not be allowed to take any materials with them (notes, exhibit books, forms, and so on) away from the research site. After the project is completed, pick up any leftover or discarded materials and take them back to your office.
- Redact the names of the attorneys, partics, and firms from the materials. Use plain boxes, folders, note pads, and pencils that do not contain any firm identification.
- Make sure the answering service, videographer, hotel personnel, and any other outside services understand the need for confidentiality about the project. Ask the videographer to return all materials from the project to you.

At the research site, it is critical to the integrity of the research that the jurors do not see the lawyers or witnesses who appear on the videotape. The jurors should remain completely unaware that they are being watched live. The trial team should assemble in the observation room well before the stated arrival time for the jurors. (Remember that a few jurors always arrive early.) The team should stay in the observation room until all jurors are seated and accounted for in the presentation room. The success of the research relies on candid comments from the participants, who might not be so frank if they know the attorneys are listening. At the conclusion of the session, make certain that all the jurors have left the premises before the attorneys venture into the hallway. (Don't forget to check the restaurant or lounge for jurors who may have decided to stop for dinner.)

§ 5A.12 Improving Pretrial Research Preparation

Pretrial research results are only a tool in trial preparation. Information and insight gained from the research may be valuable, but it is certainly not foolproof and there are no guarantees. The trial team should not rely entirely on research results, because the real jury could easily reach a totally different decision, even when multiple focus groups have been consistent in their judgments.

In preparing and conducting a pretrial research project, as in the actual trial, you learn more from your mistakes from things that went right. You have to think on your feet and be prepared to improvise solutions to problems. You can correct small errors (yours and others') to make things go more smoothly the next time. Just a couple of examples:

- Make sure you go to the correct conference room. In one mock trial project, the consultants switched the hotel conference rooms that were to be used for the presentation and observation. Nobody told me about the change, and I blithely walked into the room I had originally been told. Fortunately, no jurors were present yet so it didn't matter, but I could have blown our cover.
- The video technicians forgot to bring enough blank tapes, so we had to send someone out to buy them, which delayed the presentation schedule for a few minutes. I immediately added extra videotapes to my list of supplies to have on hand.
- The consultant asked me to have the questionnaires and evaluation forms copied and collated, which I did. I found out later that he wanted a stack of each form, not a set of forms for each juror. I wasn't in the room at the time, so the attorneys spent a few fun minutes separating the sets into individual stacks. No one was upset and this glitch didn't cause a big problem, but I was

embarrassed that I had misunderstood the consultant's instructions. Clarify instructions carefully with the trial consultant or the attorney.

- In the first full-scale mock trial project that I worked on, we discovered (too late) an error in the date of a meeting on a document listed in the table of contents. Also, there was a misspelling in one of the witness names on the chart of the players, and a couple of the exhibit notebooks had pages missing for some reason. Again, these weren't major problems, but the lesson is: Proofread all materials carefully and check the exhibit notebooks to make sure all the pages are present and in the correct order.

§ 5A.13 The Paralegal's Perspective

Ideally, the whole trial team should participate in the highly educational exercise of preparing a focus group or mock trial presentation. In addition to providing benefits to attorneys and clients, pretrial research projects are also excellent learning opportunities for the paralegals involved in the case.

Trial paralegals should welcome and encourage pretrial research because the preparation required for the project gives them a head start on preparation for the real trial. The number one complaint from litigation paralegals is that attorneys tend to procrastinate until the last minute before deciding about many of the elements of trial preparation. (See **§ 1.12** for a discussion on attorney procrastination.) Unfortunately, the attorney's last-minute decisions usually involve the very elements that paralegals handle at trial, adding to the normal pressure caused by tight trial preparation deadlines. Probably the greatest benefit of focus group and mock trial research to the trial paralegal is that the attorney has to prepare at least part of the case ahead of time.

For trial paralegals, even a little advance knowledge is a wonderful thing. The nature of jury research projects demands that the attorney make early decisions about fact witnesses, experts, exhibits, demonstrative evidence, and so forth. The shortened format of a mock trial allows only enough time for testimony from a few key witnesses. The attorney therefore has to decide which testimony is pivotal to the case. The exercise of cutting an expert witness's testimony down to a 15-minute segment requires both the attorney and the expert to focus on the most crucial points.

Likewise, preparing the juror exhibit notebooks for a mock trial forces the attorney to narrow the exhibits down to the few documents that are really vital to the jurors' understanding of the case. A trial paralegal can be pretty sure that most of the key witnesses and exhibits that make it into the research presentation will also be significant in the actual trial. Logistically, a mock trial gives you a chance to do a practice run transporting equipment and materials before the real trial. All these factors enable a paralegal to better anticipate what will be required at the actual trial and determine what else needs to be prepared.

If you have just been assigned to an unfamiliar case, focus group and mock trial research can quickly give you a feel for the key issues, exhibits, and witnesses that will be important in the real trial. Preparing a mock trial presentation can also give you a better idea of what to expect from attorneys whose work styles you do not already know. If you pick up a case at a point after pretrial research is completed, a review of the materials and research results can bring you up to speed on the case issues.

In addition to the benefits of early preparation, you can learn a lot during the research project itself. Feedback from the research may remind the attorney of additional items, documents, exhibits, or witnesses that could be useful at trial. You will gain a better understanding of the legal issues and theories in the case by listening to the attorney's discussions with the trial consultant. Pretrial research tools like focus groups and mock trials give you a preview of some problems and issues you may encounter in the actual trial before the trial, while you still have time to adjust and refine the presentation.

You can always do a better job on something when you get a second chance. If you have ever worked on a second trial of the same case (for example, after the case is remanded to the trial court following an appeal) you know that it was easier to organize and prepare the case the second time around, because you had the opportunity to improve the case presentation to correct mistakes that were made by both sides. This is why I recommend analyzing what went right and what went wrong in the trial (see **§ 7.57**) so that you can learn from it. Pretrial research can help you do a better job in preparing for trial by virtually giving you a second chance to get it right.

§ 5A.14 Forms Checklist

This checklist is a guide to the written materials you will need to prepare for mock trials and focus groups. Additional forms may apply in your cases.

Jury Sign-in Sheet ____
Jury Questionnaire ____
Confidentiality Agreement ____
Juror Receipt ____
Evaluation Forms:
  —Plaintiff's Opening Statement ____
  —Defendant's Opening Statement ____
  —Plaintiff's Case in Chief ____
  —Defendant's Case in Chief ____
  —Plaintiff's Rebuttal ____
Jury Instructions ____
Verdict Forms ____
Juror Exhibit Notebooks ____
Chart of Names ____
Timeline of Significant Dates ____

§ 5A.15 Materials and Supplies Checklist

This checklist is a guide to the materials and supplies you will need to assemble for a mock trial or focus group.

Forms (see § **4A.14**) ____
Labeled folders for forms ____
Juror exhibit notebooks ____
Schedule of timed videotaped segments ____
Supplies:
Nametags ____
Place cards ____
Seating diagrams ____

Notepads ____
Pens or pencils ____
Sticky notes ____
Highlighters and markers ____
Extra blank videotapes ____
Easel and blank tablet ____
Binder clips ____
Boxes to transport materials ____
Juror payment and plain envelopes ____
Checks to pay hotel, video technicians, etc. ____

§ 5A.16 Preparation Checklist for Mock Trials and Focus Groups

Many of the preparation tasks for mock trials and focus groups are the same as for an actual trial. Pretrial presentations are abbreviated, however, and some tasks are specifically for the research. Use this checklist as a guide to preparing a pretrial research project.

Decide on the appropriate format for your presentation(s)
____ Focus group
____ Mock trial
____ Combination
Decide the issues or topics to be evaluated
Meet with jury research consultant, if applicable
Work out the timing and schedule a date for the research
Decide where to hold the research session
____ On-site (your office or nearby conference room)
____ Off-site (hotel or convention facility)
____ Make arrangements to reserve the site
____ Arrange food and beverage service as appropriate
Recruit the "jurors"
____ Determine the demographics of the real jury
____ Advertise or contact agency
____ Hire answering service

§ 5A.16 PREPARATION CHECKLIST

____ Locate prospective jurors
____ Screen
____ Finalize selections
Plan the case presentation content
____ Decide on format (live or videotape)
____ Engage a videographer
____ Determine the players
—Attorneys
—Witnesses
—Experts
—Clients
—Others
____ Write the script
Prepare juror exhibit notebooks
Plan and execute visual aids
Shoot the video
Reshoot the video if needed
Prepare written materials
____ Jury questionnaire
____ Confidentiality agreement
____ Evaluation forms
____ Jury instructions
____ Verdict forms
Plan and schedule the audiovisual equipment
Secure supplies
Assemble forms and materials
Make travel and hotel accommodations for jury research consultant and others, as needed
Conduct the research sessions
Debrief the mock jurors
Analyze the results
Decide how to apply the results to trial preparation

CHAPTER 7

ASSISTING THE ATTORNEY IN POSTTRIAL ACTIVITIES

§ 7.6 Handling Posttrial Motions

Page 533, insert before first paragraph:

The end of the trial does not always mean the end of the pleadings work in the case. At the very least, the judge prepares and signs a judgment or order finalizing the trial results for the record. The trial may result in a verdict (in jury trial cases) or a judicial decision (in bench trials). In most courts, the actual judgment entry document is not finalized until a few days after the conclusion of the trial. The filing date of the final judgment entry is important because it starts the time period within which the parties to the case can file posttrial motions or appeals.

Federal Rules of Civil Procedure 50–63 contain the rules for entering judgments and filing posttrial motions in both jury and bench trials. Minor stylistic changes in the language of these rules took effect on December 1, 1995. The remarks in the following sections are based on the proposed 1996 Federal Rules of Civil Procedure, effective December 1, 1995 (absent contrary Congressional action).

§ 7.9 Motion for Judgment as a Matter of Law—FRCP 50(a)

Page 536, insert before first paragraph:

The rule title and text of FRCP 50 language were modified slightly in the amendment that became effective December 1, 1995 (absent Congressional action). Previous revisions in 1991 to FRCP 50(a) eliminated the language of an older version concerning motions for "directed verdict," but the amendment was not intended to change the existing standards under which a court could grant directed verdicts.

Page 536, add to first paragraph:

Rule 50(a)(1) allows the court to grant a motion for judgment as a matter of law when the judge determines that the evidence presented at trial does not sufficiently support the opposing party's claims.

§ 7.10 Renewal of Motion for Judgment as a Matter of Law after Trial – FRCP 50(b)

Page 537, insert before first paragraph:

Rule 50(b) of the Federal Rules of Civil Procedure (language modified effective December 1, 1995) provides for filing a post-verdict motion as a "renewal of an earlier motion made at the close of the evidence."

§ 7.11 Motion for New Trial – FRCP 59

Page 537, replace first sentence of first paragraph with:

Federal Rule of Civil Procedure 59 (language revised effective December 1, 1995) provides that any party may move for a new trial on any or all of the issues in a case (either a jury trial or a bench trial).

Page 538, replace last sentence of first paragraph with:

In addition, Rule 59(e) provides that a party may file a motion to alter or amend a judgment, and the motion must be filed no later than 10 days after the judgment is entered.

CHAPTER 8

INTEGRATING COMPUTERS INTO TRIAL WORK

*

§ 8.4 Getting Started with Computer Technology

Page 598, add at beginning of section:

The electronic age has arrived. Predictions made at the beginning of the decade have proven true: legal professionals have embraced technology in a big way. Legal publications abound with articles on computers, software applications, automation, and many other related topics. Seminars and continuing education courses routinely offer training on computer topics for attorneys and paralegals. Internet usage has become widespread, with more and more lawyers joining the network every week. Many law offices, research facilities, resource clearinghouses, and legal service vendors have home pages on the World Wide Web. Experts predict this popular trend will continue well into the next century. Advances in computer technology, combined with the increased availability and lower costs of hardware and sophisticated software, have had an enormous impact on litigation and trial practice, particularly in the areas of court information access and retrieval and courtroom evidence presentation techniques.

§ 8.9 Using Networking Technology to Enhance Trial Teamwork (New title)

Page 603, add at end of section:

As we have discussed throughout this book, preparing a case for trial is a team activity. Lawyers, paralegals, and other team members collaborate and pool their efforts to get witnesses and exhibits ready for the courtroom presentation. This work often includes such tasks as reviewing documents, extracting key information, and indexing and storing notes on the key information for later use. A computer network can enhance the ways in which trial teams do this sort of work. A networked system in the law office, particularly one that incorporates document imaging (see § **8.28**, *et seq.*), opens new channels of communication among the team members and provides new ways for lawyers and paralegals to enrich the on-screen information and collaborate in a team effort.

E-mail Electronic mail makes it easy to alert trial team members to new developments, changes in meeting dates, and questions that must be answered quickly. When the law office's network is also connected to the client's computer, the client becomes a more involved member of the trial team. Questions and requests for information can be handled quickly.

Team members can bring key documents to the attention of the lead attorney. Some systems let the user drag an icon representing a document to the E-mail address of the receiving person. Attorneys can review documents instantly, with no delay. A network is useful for multiple attorneys from the same office, multiple attorneys from distant offices, co-counsel, and in-house counsel because it's faster to transmit documents electronically than by routing paper drafts around the office. Several attorneys can have documents on their respective screens at the same time (see also § **8.10**).

Documents Document imaging should be incorporated into the work flow, and not regarded as merely an auxiliary function. Advances in imaging technology have made it easy for law offices to store a case document collection electronically on computer instead of on paper. Lawyers and paralegals can still create on paper hard copies of the documents whenever they wish.

- *Compiling document annotations*: A networked system can help the trial team in compiling document annotations. Each team member can record his or her thoughts about the significant parts of documents for others to see. This way, instead of each team member hoarding their little stacks of paper documents with notes attached, everybody adds to a central document so that the other team members can see their work. Work product (good ideas, links to other documents or witnesses, potential strategy considerations) is not lost and time is not wasted because the thoughts are captured the first time through and preserved for later use. Senior attorneys can review notes made by junior associates and paralegals instantly by calling the document image to the screen. The senior attorney can supervise the team's efforts more effectively to make sure everyone is consistent in classification and treatment of the various documents.

- *Tracking document usage*: Electronic storage of the central document repository makes it easier for team members to track the usage history of a document. Each time a document is produced, used as a deposition exhibit, appended to a brief, and so on, you update the database record for that document accordingly. Anyone looking up that document on computer can instantly tell whether it's been marked as a deposition exhibit, produced to the opposing party, withheld as privileged or confidential, and so on. You can also track various waves of production, versions of the documents, and so forth.
- *Replicating document sets*: Whenever you assemble a set of documents for a particular witness or issue, it is easy to recreate the set electronically. You can also track various combinations of documents used as appendices, reviewed by experts, and so on.
- *Eliminating duplicates*: You can reduce the volume of documents by eliminating the true duplicates, and still keep track of the same document going to multiple recipients or from their files, but you need to access the image only once when the documents are stored electronically.
- *Linking and cross-referencing*: The same document can be grouped with more than one compilation and cross-referenced in the database accordingly. You can insert electronic links in the annotations that will indicate the document is related to another document elsewhere in the collection and that the two documents should always be considered together. You can add links and cross-references to electronic deposition transcripts to indicate exhibit documents referred to in the testimony. Any team member who reviews the transcript or its summary needs only to click on the link icon to display the image of the exhibit document. You can also record annotations or links to background research or

other supporting materials that the attorney may wish to review. You can compare the testimony of different witnesses on the same issues, and team members can add to a centrally stored cumulative timeline of events in developing the case.

- *Flagging potential exhibits*: Whenever a team member reviews a document that might be a potential trial exhibit, he or she adds an electronic note to the database that travels with the document thereafter. This facilitates compiling the preliminary list of trial exhibits.

(See also §§ **1.8; 1.10–1.19; 2.7–2.15; 3.4; 3.7; 3.29; 4.6; 5.39; 5.58,** *et seq.*; and **6.65,** *et seq.*)

§ 8.27 Steps in the Work Flow Process

Page 633, change heading of item 6 to:

6. General Guidelines for Identifying Privileged and Protected Documents and Developing a Document Screening Protocol.

Page 635, add after first full paragraph:

The main volume provides an extensive discussion of the mandatory pretrial disclosure provisions included in Rule 26 of the Federal Rules of Civil Procedure (see § **2.29**). Rule 26 requires each party to produce voluntarily its nonprivileged documents early in the case. For documents not produced, parties must provide a brief description of the documents, or a privilege log. This section discusses some key considerations involved in screening the document collection to classify protected documents.

Although the attorney must approve the final decisions, paralegals often arrange for the initial document collection and inventory in preparation for the attorney's review. Your goal in document production is to disclose fairly to the opposing party documents that support your client's claims while at the same time protecting documents that may contain privileged or confidential information. Whenever you set up a document production, always be aware of certain categories of documents that are protected, because you generally are *not* required to produce protected documents to the opposing side. A careful screening of the documents is the only way to determine which ones may be subject to protection.

The following material outlines sample review guidelines for identifying privileged and protected documents in your client's files. Using these as a starting point, work with your supervising attorney to develop similar guidelines, or protocols, that you can put in writing for document reviewers to follow. Of course, an attorney should make the final decision on privileged and protected documents, but a printed protocol helps to ensure that document reviewers are accurate and consistent in their preliminary determinations of which documents may be protected. A written protocol may also prove useful as a reference if any discovery disputes should arise later in the litigation.

Note: These are general guidelines only. They are meant to illustrate basic screening protocols in a sample case, and should not be construed to represent "black-letter" law or its application to the documents involved in your cases. Your case may have different parameters or additional considerations that will determine which documents are classified as privileged. Discuss the criteria that apply to your particular case with your supervising attorney.

Keep the following litigation support tips in mind as you prepare the documents for attorney review:

1. Number *all* the documents *before* you separate them. This is the only way I have ever found to absolutely preserve the documents' original context. (See §§ **2.80–2.84** on document numbering techniques.) No matter how carefully you note where documents originated, it's almost impossible to reconstruct them later without sequential numbers.
2. Haste leads to mistakes. Try to identify the types of materials most likely to contain sensitive information early in the inventory process. Ask the attorney what kinds of materials might be considered "hot" or potentially damaging to your client's case. Continue to be on the lookout for these types of materials throughout the project.
3. Make reference lists. List the names of persons from the client's business who handle sensitive and confidential information. Focus on identifying key names and topics. Update the list as you identify new names and categories.

4. Follow a pattern if you can. Ask the attorney for a sample privileged document list or review protocol from a similar case, if one exists. This will give you some idea of where to start in developing the protocol instructions.

Relevancy review. In a typical document production, you will first assemble all the documents that appear to respond to the other party's Requests for Production. The first determination you must make in reviewing potentially responsive documents is whether they are *relevant*. Relevant documents concern events or transactions that are at issue in the case. A document is *not* relevant if it clearly concerns an event or issue other than the issues in the case. For example, the Request for Production may specify a certain time frame for documents. Documents dated before or after the specified dates may not be relevant and therefore you may not have to produce them. Prepare a list of the specific claims, issues, and events that are involved in the case. Document reviewers can then compare a document against that list to determine whether the document appears to relate to one of the items listed.

The relevancy review will result in a subset of documents that appear to be both responsive and relevant. Next, you will determine whether any of the documents should be withheld because they meet one or more of these criteria:

Privileged
Attorney or litigation work product
Confidential or secret information.

1. **Privilege Review.** The general rule is that any communications between a client and an attorney for the purpose of seeking or giving legal advice are privileged communications that should not be disclosed. In document review protocols, it's a good idea to define your terms. For example:

- **Client:** The *client* in your case may be an individual, a business entity or an organization. If the client is a business (a company, a corporation, and so forth) any of its employees, agents, representatives, subsidiaries, divisions, and operating units may also be considered to be the client for document review purposes. Clarify this with your supervising attorney to make sure you understand who is included in the "client" definition.

- **Agent:** A client's *agent* is someone operating on behalf of a client, such as an employee, an outside expert, or a consultant who is working for the client. Communications between a client's agents and the client's attorney may be privileged and should not be disclosed.
- **Third-party communications:** A *third party* is an individual or entity other than the client, the client's agent, or the client's attorney. A document that a client sends to, or receives from, a third party generally is *not* privileged.

Generally, the attorney-client privilege applies to any material that consists of communication (1) from client to attorney; (2) from attorney to client; and/or (3) between client's agents or personnel, referring to attorney advice. Your screening protocol could include the following categories for possible attorney-client-privileged documents:

- Documents sent between employees of a client corporation that name the client's attorneys or refer to legal advice that was sought or given;
- Documents that discuss or refer to legal advice, even when the attorney is not named specifically;
- Documents that contain any annotations, comments, or marginal notes written by an attorney. (Note: If an otherwise non-privileged document contains attorney notes, you should produce any "clean" copies of that document, that is, documents without any annotations);
- Documents and materials that were designated as privileged in related litigation should generally also be withheld in the current case.

2. **Work Product Review.** Generally, any document that reflects an attorney's thought processes, strategies, or mental impressions is considered protected. In addition, the work product protection generally covers documents prepared by an attorney or other persons in anticipation of litigation (or in connection with litigation after it is filed). These documents would include special materials the attorney had asked the client to prepare or

compile, as opposed to routine business records normally kept by the client. Such materials are generally protected, unless the opposing side can convince the judge that (1) the information is crucial to its case preparation, and (2) it cannot obtain the equivalent information any other way without incurring undue hardship (see discussion of FRCP 26(b)(3) at § **2.29**). Work product materials might also include:

- Otherwise unprotected documents containing any annotations, comments, or marginal notes written by an attorney. As with privileged documents, you may be able to produce other versions of the documents that do not contain attorney notes.
- Documents and materials protected under the work product category in similar or related litigation. This material should generally be withheld in the current case as well.
- Documents prepared by a client's agent at the attorney's request to assist in rendering legal advice (for example, an expert's evaluation of damages prepared for the attorney's review).
- Documents obtained (by the attorney or paralegal) during investigation of government files. Such documents may also be protected as work product if:
  - (a) they are not from the client's records;
  - (b) they were compiled specifically in connection with the pending litigation; and
  - (c) they are public records, equally available to opposing counsel.

3. **Confidentiality Review.** Confidential documents might include materials containing trade secrets and proprietary information (for example, chemical formulas); investment records and other financial data; sensitive personnel records, and so on. Develop a list for the document reviewers of specific types of records that contain potentially confidential information in your case. If documents combine nonprotected relevant information with sensitive portions, you may be required to redact (block out before copying) certain segments and produce the redacted versions. The Case Management Order generally specifies how confidential and redacted documents should be stamped or labeled (see § **2.17**; also see § **8.27**, item 6). As with attorney-client privilege and work product documents, any

materials classified as "confidential" in related cases should maintain that designation in the current case. Do everything you can to preserve the integrity of a document's previous privilege designations.

Caution: The attorney should always make the ultimate decision on whether to produce or withhold documents. Consult the attorney about any documents that reviewers are unsure how to classify. If an otherwise unprotected document contains potentially damaging information, show it to the supervising attorney for a determination on whether there is an appropriate basis for withholding the document. Finally, when in doubt, withhold the document until the attorney can review it. Holding a document back temporarily causes no harm, but inadvertently producing privileged information might damage your client's case. It's easier to replace a document in the "to-be-produced" box than to retrieve it after opposing counsel gets the shipment.

Replace §§ **8.39** *and* **8.40** *with the following:*

§ 8.39 Portable Computers (Notebook Computers) (New)

Advances in technology have generated compact, powerful, and reliable computers that are easily portable for attorneys and paralegals to take into the courtroom. The development of today's popular *notebook* computer (which descended from the older laptop and heavier portable machines) has important ramifications in trial work. The attorney or paralegal who takes a computer to trial can gain a considerable advantage over the uncomputerized opposition. Although you try to anticipate all the information that will be needed at trial, the potential for surprises is always present. A portable computer enables the trial team to have instant access to an enormous variety of critical data on the spot in the courtroom.

Since the first truly portable personal computers became available around 1983, the quality, power, and speed of notebook computers have continued to improve at a remarkable rate. In its September 1995 issue, *Consumer Reports* magazine lists as significant recent improvements in notebook computers: better screen display; faster processors; larger hard drive; longer battery life; easier-to-use keyboard and pointing device; fax/modem capability; multimedia capability; and pre-installed software. Most of the major computer manufacturers now market smaller, lightweight versions of their desktop computers. Best of all, the prices have dropped dramatically, making notebook computers readily affordable for even small law offices. High-quality notebook computers are available at reasonable prices from a number of computer manufacturers.

The primary advantage of notebook computers is that they are lightweight and take up much less space than a standard desktop PC. Some notebook computers are small enough to be folded into a briefcase! Portability in a computer (defined as a combination of weight, bulk, and handle design) gives you the freedom and flexibility to work while traveling or in remote locations, or to take new software home with you to practice on or learn to use it, away from the distractions of the office. A notebook computer can be easily folded and stored out of sight or carried to meetings, depositions, and into the courtroom.

Numerous extra features are available on various new models of notebook computers. For example, some notebooks come with built-in modems that enable you to access the Internet and computerized on-line research services such as LEXIS and WESTLAW from remote locations. A notebook computer can also be connected via modem to your office network for electronic mail messages, document transfers, and calendaring uses. Some notebook computers allow you to use an external monitor or projector simultaneously with the internal monitor. This capability enables the attorney to project text or graphics on a large screen for presenting information in the courtroom.

Some other ways the trial team can use a portable computer outfitted with the appropriate software at trial include the following:

- Track and cross-reference trial exhibits or deposition testimony with database software;
- Search database for exhibits or previous testimony that could be used to impeach a witness on cross-examination;
- Record notes during voir dire or witness testimony;
- Review transcripts of daily trial testimony recorded by computer-aided transcription (CAT) by the court stenographer;

- Use waiting time productively by updating calendar entries, drafting correspondence and memoranda, or reviewing outlines of trial examinations; and
- Use RAM-resident time and billing software to write timeslips or post expenses on the road.

Just as you should have backups for other types of equipment used in the trial presentation, you need to have a contingency plan in case your notebook computer refuses to work for some reason. If possible, you should have access to a replacement machine loaded with the same information that is on your laptop. It is also useful to have a backup copy of the programs and information on tape or floppy disk that can be quickly loaded into a substitute computer, as well as printed copies of trial outlines, deposition summaries, witness notes, and other critical documents you plan to use at trial.

§ 8.40 Considerations in Choosing a Notebook Computer (New)

When you are looking for a notebook computer that will be right for you, do some research and ask plenty of questions. Try out a computer that is outfitted with the software programs you normally use before you decide. The combination of the monitor, keyboard, and other features should suit the way in which you plan to employ them in typical daily use and in the courtroom.

Here are some features to keep in mind when evaluating notebook computers:

1. **Compatibility.** Be sure the notebook is compatible with your office computer system. It should be easy to transfer data between the portable unit and your desktop PC.
2. **Disk drives.** Most current notebook models include a floppy disk drive as a standard feature. Make sure the built-in floppy disk drive is conveniently located and protected from the elements. For serious business use, a hard-disk drive is essential on a notebook computer. Fortunately, hard disk prices have dropped dramatically and notebooks now routinely come equipped with large capacity hard-disk drives. The amount of

disk space you need will depend on the programs you plan to run and how you plan to use the portable computer. The larger the hard-disk drive, the more programs you can run on your notebook computer.

Your computer may also need a port to connect a CD-ROM drive if you plan to use software or multimedia reference works that are stored on CDs with your notebook. Check with your hardware vendor about available CD-ROM options.

3. **Microprocessor speed.** The speed of the notebook computer's central processor will greatly affect the response time if you plan to run database software or other complex programs. Notebook computers may not have the fastest processor chip on the market, because new processors generally appear on desktop models first, then filter down to notebooks as the technology is adapted to the smaller size. This means that notebooks are typically a step behind desktop computers in processor speed. Today's notebooks are still very fast, however. A 486 processor is currently standard on notebook computers from most manufacturers.
4. **Price.** Notebook computers are much less expensive now than when they first appeared on the market. At the end of 1995, moderately priced notebook computers ranged from $2,500 to $3,500, depending on the size and speed of the hard drive and other options. The prices on current models are likely to keep dropping as new technology from desktop computers filters down. Compare prices carefully, and be on the lookout for discounts and sale prices that manufacturers frequently offer in this highly competitive market.
5. **Monitor display.** The quality of the display and the size of the monitor vary among different designs of notebook computers. The monitor display should be bright, easy to read under various lighting conditions, and free from excess glare or reflection. Current notebook computers typically feature liquid crystal display (LCD) screens. Early monitors that used reflective LCD screens to produce a display similar to that found on digital watches were sometimes difficult to read in dim light. Today's notebook computers, especially those in the higher price ranges, offer very crisp, bright color monitors. Although the notebook

displays are still not as good as desktop models, screen display technology continues to develop. Expect this trend to continue.

The second important consideration with notebook computer monitors is size. A courtroom notebook computer should display at least the full standard 25 lines and 80 columns that a regular desktop monitor can show. Some models compress the letters to shorten the screen, while others stretch the characters to fill a squarer screen. Graphics tend to show up best on screens that are more nearly square in shape. The notebook computer you choose should have a monitor that is easy to read and look at for extended periods of time. Look for adjustable brightness and contrast controls. Also, make sure the frame holds the monitor securely at a comfortable angle without flopping over. Test notebook models from several manufacturers to make sure you will be comfortable with the screen display.

6. **Keyboard.** The size of individual keys and the "touch" of the keyboard are important factors in selecting a notebook computer. The keyboard should feel solid and be comfortable to type on, and the keys should operate smoothly and quietly without making a clacking sound that might be disruptive in the courtroom. Make sure the angle of the keyboard is comfortable for you. Some models have rear "feet" that snap down to create an angled keyboard surface.

   Study the size and placement of individual keys, especially the directional or function keys that you use most often with your software programs, as these will affect your long-term satisfaction with the keyboard. For example, on some notebook computers the cursor arrow keys and the HOME, END, PAGEUP, and PAGEDOWN keys are quite small or very close together. Make sure the ENTER, SHIFT, and function keys are conveniently sized and correctly placed for the way you use the keyboard. Some models have an embedded numeric keypad while others require a separate add-on keypad, which will be an important consideration if you use the notebook computer for extensive "number-crunching" work.

7. **Quiet operation.** For courtroom use, a portable computer must be not only small but also quiet so that it is unobtrusive. In addition to the keyboard noise, notebook computers sometimes emit various beeps when they are first started up, when the

battery power is getting low, and when the computer case is shut while it is still on. In addition, some monitor screens emit a hum or buzz that might be distracting in a quiet room. These noises can be annoying in the courtroom, and can cause the judge to order that the computer be turned off. Check to see if the notebook computer you are considering has a switch to turn off the sound.

8. **Battery life.** Reliable battery power is important if you plan to use a portable computer at trial. You might not be able to use an extension cord in the courtroom, either because no electrical outlet is available or because the judge objects to stringing an extension cord out through the room. If you do have to rely on battery power, look for a portable computer that efficiently manages its power usage. Fortunately, new developments in battery chemistries have produced strong batteries that can run from 1½ to 3 hours, depending on what is being powered. Some models shut down certain components when not in use and conserve battery power by operating in a "standby" mode. A notebook computer that will be used all day in the courtroom should allow you to adjust the power-saving settings to extend the life of the battery.

   Find out how long the portable computer will operate on a normal battery charge and the amount of time required for the battery to recharge. Some notebook computers can be recharged while they are being used, but others have to be turned off to be recharged. Some units are equipped with a handy light that indicates the battery is charging. Also check on the availability of a spare battery pack that is easy to insert. Watch out for built-in batteries that are not removable, because these units do not allow you to use an extra battery pack if you must work away from an AC outlet for a long period of time.

9. **Mouse.** You will need a pointing device (commonly known as a *mouse*) in order to run the popular point-and-click software programs on your notebook computer. The portable notebook computer you choose needs to have either a built-in mouse or a port to attach one. Most standard notebook computers now are equipped with one of three types of built-in pointing devices: a trackball, a trackstick, or a trackpad. Try all three to see which type of pointing device you like best before you buy.

10. **Durability.** Make sure the portable computer is sturdy and durable, as it will have to stand up to a lot of abuse. Look for solid construction and protective slots or doors over the various ports and connectors. A protective carrying case is a useful feature to have if you plan to do much traveling with the unit.

*

§ 8.41A Court Information Access and Retrieval (New)

Technology's effect on trial practice is reflected by changes in the actual court buildings and offices. Court clerks' offices are gradually updating their systems to keep pace with attorneys and others who have embraced computer technology. Many court clerks' offices have plans to install computerized systems to track court scheduling and docketing information. Some courts now allow attorneys to transmit and file documents electronically, via fax or e-mail. It is likely that courts will eventually make dockets available on-line so that attorneys and paralegals can monitor filings in a case right from their desks.

Historically, courts have needed to store enormous amounts of paper. Many courts are considering electronic filing and imaging systems that can alleviate file storage problems and make court documents easier to locate and retrieve. Naturally, the project of converting a court's manual procedures to automated systems is an enormous undertaking, requiring months of detailed analysis and meticulous planning. After the conversion, however, case information is easy to update, fast to locate, and accessible.

Judges now routinely use portable computers on the bench to give them instant access to case law, statutes, and regulations as well as scheduling information. Older courtrooms have been retrofitted with adequate wiring for electronic equipment. New courtrooms are being built to accommodate automation and multimedia trial presentations by installing adequate wiring and equipment such as large monitors and projection screens.

*

§ 8.41B Computerized Transcripts (New)

Computerized court reporting, also called "real-time" reporting (see **§ 8.41**) has been available for several years, but courts now use it routinely. Real-time reporting eliminates the wait for the court reporter to prepare a conventional transcript of the trial proceedings. Instead, the computer uses special software to convert the court reporter's stenography symbols into English text. The resulting transcript is displayed almost immediately on computer monitors in the courtroom. The transcript is in rough form until the court reporter can edit it, particularly when the case involves technical terms or long names with difficult spellings, but most common words will already be in the court reporter's personal dictionary and will convert cleanly. The instantaneous transcript display has obvious advantages for hearing-impaired trial participants, but trial teams can also take advantage of real time transcripts in the following ways:

- Cross-examination. Immediate access to the transcript gives the trial attorneys instant recall of precisely what the witness said. The attorney can use the displayed transcript to quickly impeach a witness who gives different answers on cross-examination. Access to the previous testimony helps the attorney to make sure he or she has covered all the important points in cross-examination.
- Objections. The judge and lawyers can immediately review the remarks that prompted an objection. Judges like this because it helps them to be consistent in their rulings and avoid potentially prejudicial errors that could result in appeals.
- Exhibits. The trial team has a reliable daily record of which exhibits were introduced with each witness. This can be an enormous help in organizing exhibit notebooks and updating exhibit lists.
- Appeals. Real-time reporting technology allows judges and counsel to make confidential electronic annotations on the transcript. For example, when something happens during the trial that the attorney believes may be a basis for appeal, the instant transcript allows him or her to immediately place a marker or note on the transcript at that point. This makes it easy for the trial team later to review the transcript for potential appealable issues. (The electronic annotations are confidential for each attorney and for

the judge, who may also wish to mark a segment for further research or consideration.)

- Planning, review, and follow-up. The trial team can review the real-time transcript at the end of each day to clarify which witness said what and to prepare for the next day's testimony. Computerized court testimony can easily be printed out into a conventional or condensed-format transcript. It can also be telecommunicated (faxed or sent as an e-mail document), stored on CD-ROM or other computer media for later use, and integrated with a videotape to be used in closing arguments.

§ 8.42 Introduction to the Internet (New)

This supplement to *Paralegal Trial Handbook* provides what I hope is a simple explanation of the basic elements of a very complex subject, namely the Internet. I will not attempt to explain all the technical aspects of the Internet; that topic would far exceed the scope of this book. You do not need an in-depth knowledge of computer networking to use the Internet, any more than you have to know auto mechanics to drive a car. It is not necessary to understand how the Internet works, so long as you can get the job done. But some knowledge of the Internet's basic concepts and terminology will prove helpful in understanding how to accomplish specific tasks you encounter on the job. This material is intended to introduce you to some of the terminology and concepts involved in the fascinating world of the Internet and to give you some suggestions for ways you can use Internet resources in trial work. To assist you in understanding some of these concepts, I have created a diagram "model" of the Internet (see **Figure 8–1**). This is not at all scientific (you can't actually *see* the Internet). Rather, it's my conception of what the Internet might look like if you *could* see it.

I have also provided a selected bibliography of resource materials I came upon in my research, but don't stop there. You will find dozens of good Internet primers at any library or bookstore. Be cautioned, however, that this information changes almost daily, and that anything in print can become outdated quickly. Use the information provided here only as a starting point to understanding this strange new information frontier, and learn all you can from other sources as well. To summarize:

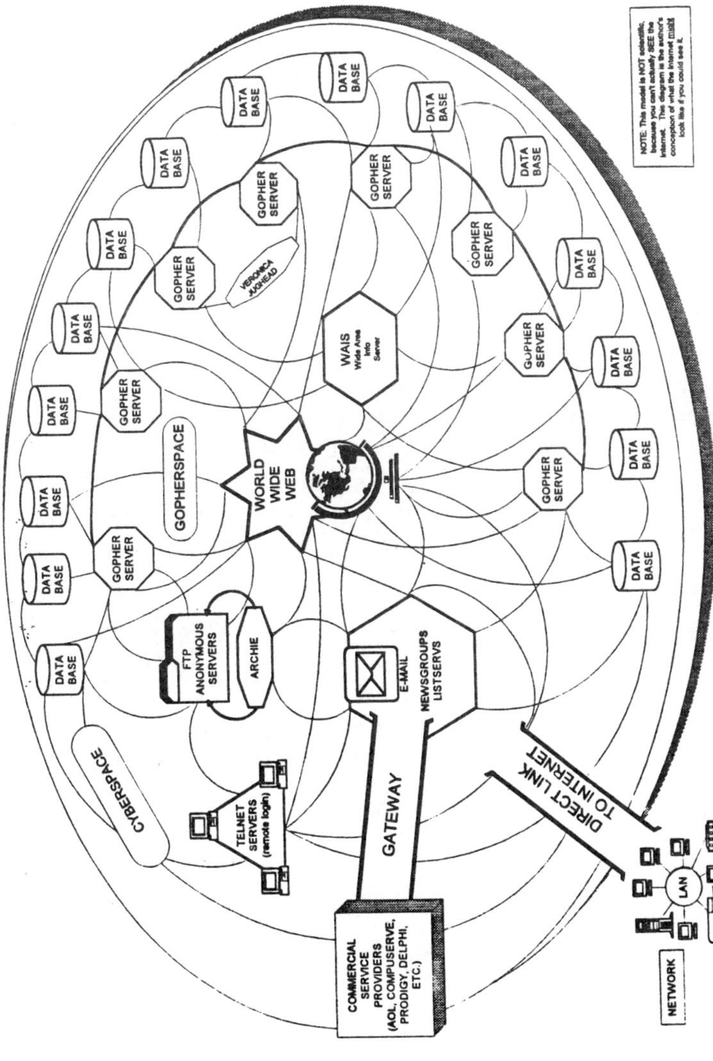

Figure 8–1. Internet Model.

- Read everything you can about the Internet.
- Join computer user groups and technology committees.
- Ask questions.
- Talk to experts.
- Take courses or seminars.
- Watch demonstrations.
- Experiment on your own.

§ 8.43 —The Internet: The Future Is Now (New)

Unless you have been living on another planet, you cannot have escaped hearing about the Internet, the main thoroughfare of the information superhighway. The Internet has been hailed as the "wave of the future" in communications technology. I submit that it's not so futuristic. The Internet is here *now*. Evidence of the Internet's growing presence bombards us at every turn. People everywhere talk about "surfing the Net," peppering their speech with strange-sounding terms and phrases that did not exist in everyday conversation 10 years ago. Every magazine seems to contain an article about the World Wide Web or a notice of information that is now available online. Popular news and entertainment magazines (*Time*, *Newsweek*, *U.S. News & World Report*, *Entertainment Weekly*, to name just a few) have added regular sections featuring news on technology and various "cyber" topics. Television news, science, and entertainment programs routinely announce the addresses of World Wide Web "home pages" where viewers can get more information about the programs or sponsors. The Internet excitement has caught on with businesses and services worldwide. Make no mistake about it, the Internet is here *today* and is growing at a phenomenal rate. Anyone who doesn't learn about it is going to be left behind.

§ 8.44 —Why the Internet Matters: Communication/Information (New)

You may be wondering what all this Internet talk has to do with trial preparation work. The main function of the Internet is to make information readily available to anyone who seeks it. Information exchange is precisely why the Internet was created. As discussed in other sections of the main book, two primary components in the law business are information and communication, which means paralegals have become "information workers" in the truest sense. Regardless of where we are along the technology continuum, our work entails a constant process of gathering, assembling, and analyzing all sorts of information; this is why the ability to index and retrieve information is a key skill for trial paralegals. The Internet gives us virtually unlimited access to vast libraries of information that we can use in our work, all at the touch of a few computer keys. For example, Internet access can assist trial paralegals in key parts of their work, such as conducting factual research (see § **1.57**); getting information and making arrangements for out-of-town trials (see § **1.18**); conducting juror investigations (see § **6.19**); performing various types of online research (see § **8.39**); and locating expert witnesses on virtually any topic (see § **3.21**).

Of course, the information we gather is useless until we *use* it. One way we use information is by conveying (communicating) the information to other people (clients, witnesses, opposing counsel, courts, government, and so on) for various reasons. Sometimes we communicate by speaking in person or on the telephone. Much of our information is put into written form (letters, memoranda, pleadings) and sent to others by mail, courier, or fax. Many of us now use computers, those excellent information-processing tools, to help us compile information and produce documents. The Internet's worldwide E-mail capabilities take communications to an unprecedented new level.

Imagine for a moment how a law office functioned before telephone service was in common use. Clients went to see the attorney to discuss their cases. Law office personnel created memoranda, files, and other records to document the client's case. A lawyer who wished to schedule a conference with another lawyer had to write out the request on paper, have the paper delivered to another law office across town, and wait for a reply—a slow process. The telephone provided a fast, easy way to contact someone in another office, and quickly became an essential office tool for spoken communications. But documents still had to be sent through the mail or delivered by messenger until the advent of facsimile (fax) technology. Readers old enough to remember when fax machines first came out will recall how strange it seemed to send documents electronically, *over the telephone lines*. Fax machines, once considered a novelty, are now commonplace office tools. I predict that employees of the future will view the Internet just as casually.

Legal professionals have a responsibility to learn to use new technology and to incorporate new ways of communicating into their repertoire of working skills. Computers have already changed the way we work, and Internet access will have a profound effect on the way people do their work in all businesses, including the legal business. Thousands of lawyers and paralegals around the country are already using the Internet to get key information from government and university databases, and many court systems are actively considering projects to computerize at least some part of their court records. As more and more information becomes available, the Internet will become an essential tool for paralegals, lawyers, and others in the legal profession.

In a recent CNN program about the proliferation of the Internet, a businessman said that customers expect you to have an E-mail address and a Web home page. If you're not on the Internet today, you may appear old-fashioned. Be assured that this technology is not going away. It is here to stay, and growing all the time. I encourage you to embrace this technology. Dig in and learn it, take the challenge, and welcome to the Net!

§ 8.45 —The Small Office Advantage (New)

A primary underlying premise of the Internet is making information widely available to anyone who seeks it. This feature has especially important ramifications for small law offices that must compete in an increasingly competitive environment. According to the American Bar Association's 1995 "Survey of Automation in Smaller Law Firms," which tabulated responses from 2,000 individual lawyers and nearly 2,000 small firms, an overwhelming majority (87 percent) reported that they plan to enhance their communications capability by adding electronic mail, online services, CD-ROM technology, and computerized research. The survey found that computer usage in small law offices increased 4 percent from 1994 to 1995, and nearly 30 percent since the results were first tabulated in 1990. (Source: *Office Systems95*, October 1995).

§ 8.46 What Is the Internet? (New)

Basically, the Internet is a massive, complex computer network that links many other computer network systems of various sizes around the world. The Internet is everywhere, and its size is fluid, changing constantly. The Internet includes a wide range of services with various purposes, and information is delivered in a variety of ways. Internet users can send electronic (computerized) messages to each other, and they can also get enormous amounts of information on thousands of topics from computer databases around the world. According to current estimates, more than 35 million people already use the Internet, and the number of users grows daily. Experts predict that more than 100 million people will be connected to the Internet by 1998.

§ 8.47 —Evolution of the Internet: A Brief History (New)

It may seem that the Internet appeared suddenly, out of nowhere, because many of us are just now becoming aware of it. However, the Internet actually began nearly 30 years ago. The following timeline briefly highlights the major events that lead to the evolution of today's Internet. For a more complete history of the development of Internet technology, *see* Daniel P. Dern, *The Internet Guide for New Users* (New York, 1994).

The U.S. Department of Defense (DoD) created the forerunner of the Internet in the late 1960s, when the DoD began investigating the feasibility of connecting various types of computers over a wide geographic area. The first large-scale computer network, called ARPAnet (Advanced Research Projects Agency Network), was an experimental network initially designed to support military-industrial research and development. The goal of the project was to enable scientists and engineers in distant locations to work together by exchanging and sharing information resources over a computer network.

In 1972, at the International Conference on Computers in Washington D.C., ARPAnet's developers demonstrated to the public what networking power could accomplish, and the computing community began to take the new technology seriously. By the mid-1970s ARPAnet had grown into a fully operational computer network, linking thousands of engineers, scientists, and researchers over a wide geographic area.

By 1980, most major universities and research centers had connections to the network. ARPAnet contracted with the computer science departments of several large universities to develop communications standards, or "protocols," that would allow various types of computers to use the new network. The result was a standard set of communications rules for computers, known as TCP/IP (Transmission Control Protocol/Internet Protocol). Numerous books and articles about the Internet have dubbed TCP/IP as the "glue" that holds the Internet together. The Internet allows users to connect all types of different computers with many different operating systems (IBM, Macintosh, Unix, Amiga, and others). However, in order for a computer to be able to communicate with any other computer on the Internet, both must use the TCP/IP standard language. You don't have to remember what TCP/IP means (although if you do, you'll sound like an expert compared to most people). Just be aware that a standard IP (Internet Protocol) exists that lets different types of computers talk to each other over the Internet. TCP/IP makes it possible to do basic computer tasks, such as sending and receiving E-mail messages, transferring files, and accessing files on a remote computer.

The DoD provided funding for the Berkeley UNIX development group to incorporate TCP/IP protocols into the UNIX operating system environment, and many of the standards established for ARPAnet were later adopted for use by the current Internet. The TCP/IP protocols developed in the early 1980s to manage communication between diverse types of computers with different operating systems are still used to support the Internet's common functions (file transfer, E-mail, and remote log-in).

In 1984, the National Science Foundation (NSF) enlarged the scope of the project to cover a much broader area by setting up several supercomputing centers across the United States. These centers were linked by a high-speed network called NSFnet, which remains one of the largest components of the current Internet. NSFnet eventually incorporated linked networks at the national, regional, and campus levels. When the DoD discontinued ARPAnet in 1990, the NSFnet and a few other large networks became the primary backbone networks supporting the functions of the Internet.

In the early 1990s, the U.S. government began a program known as National Research and Education Network (NREN) for use by government agencies. NREN was part of the High Performance Computing Act (proposed by then-Sen. Albert Gore) to provide technologically advanced networking facilities for the research and education communities. In late 1992, the NSFnet backbone was upgraded to support faster data transmission to keep up with increased traffic on the Internet, and the system continued to grow rapidly. In 1993, the number of Internet host computers reached the one-million mark.

Throughout its first two decades of growth, the Internet functioned primarily as a research tool for governments, universities, and large corporations. Computer science departments developed much of the Internet software and made it available to Internet users either as *freeware* at no cost or as *shareware* with a nominal registration fee. In 1994–95 the National Center for Supercomputing Applications developed the landmark software known as Mosaic. Whereas previously the network had required fairly sophisticated computer skills, Mosaic provided an easy-to-understand graphical user interface for getting around the Internet. Netscape Communications began freely distributing The Navigator, a commercial Web browser. These programs made it extremely easy and intuitive for computer users to find their way around the Internet's many resources. As the Internet became more popular and computer equipment became less expensive and readily accessible, commercial entities began offering Internet access to the general public. At the same time, companies began realizing the potential for reaching a global market for goods and services over the Internet. The size and scope of the Internet have exploded from there, and will undoubtedly continue to grow.

§ 8.48 —Why the Internet Seems So Confusing (New)

Grasping the concept of a global information network can be somewhat overwhelming. There is so much to know! Also, the Internet is continually growing and changing. About the time you think you have figured something out, there will be new things to learn. But you have to start somewhere. Everyone seems to know something about the Internet, but few people can describe it precisely. The sheer volume of information is a bit mind-boggling. The Internet is constantly developing and changing and the whole concept seems somewhat unstable. Here are some reasons why it's all so confusing:

- The Internet is not currently owned, monitored, or organized by any individual, agency, or centralized system of management, yet it is available to everyone.
- The format and content of the information vary with each source. Information from some sources is changed or updated frequently. Information is often provided in multiple forms, so that it's available to many different users with various levels of electronic (computer) capabilities. Efforts are being made to establish worldwide standards, but the proliferating number of information repositories makes this task all but impossible.
- No definitive index to the Internet exists now. There is so much information from so many different sources that no single service has been able to catalog it all. However, some fairly comprehensive listings have been compiled (see **§ 8.72, Useful Internet Sites for Readers**), and new services are being developed continually to focus on resource-searching technologies (programs that help you figure out what's hiding where).
- The original Internet was not particularly "user-friendly." In its early days, the Internet was something of an exclusive club, because a person could connect to the Internet only if he or she was (1) involved in research or academia *and* (2) a computer technology buff. The Internet was developed using commands based on the UNIX operating system commands. Unless you are a computer wizard, UNIX commands tend to be very confusing and obscure, with no nice graphics to help you in making selections. Fortunately, a number of excellent windows-based programs exist today that make the Internet much easier to use. There are easy-to-use tools to help you find information on the Internet.
- No set prices for Internet services exist, and there are different types of connections to the Internet. You may have access to all the Internet services or only part of them, depending on what type

of connection you have and who your service provider is. The price for connecting to the Internet varies from free (in the case of community- or library-sponsored networks) to very expensive (where a company installs a dedicated telephone line for unlimited direct access). Fortunately for individuals and small companies, many service providers offer reasonably priced access to all the services available on the Internet.

- Many people erroneously use the terms "Internet" and "World Wide Web" interchangeably. They are not the same thing. Rather, the World Wide Web is a navigational tool for getting around the Internet (see § **8.62**, *et seq.*).

You don't have to be an expert to use the Internet, but you do need a basic understanding of the Internet's basic functions and the various ways a computer user can acquire an Internet connection so that you can properly evaluate the various packages offered by Internet service providers. As of late 1995, the Internet's functions included the following services: E-mail; file transfer; remote log-on; information "browsing"; and keyword searching (in some databases). You have to know a few basics about these various services to get started. These concepts and functions are discussed in more detail in the following sections.

§ 8.49 Requirements to Use the Internet (New)

You need three things in order to use the Internet:

1. A computer that is connected to a modem.
2. An Internet account (sometimes called *access*). If you work in an office with a network that has an account, you may not have to be concerned with this. Be aware, however, that there are several different types of Internet accounts. (See § **8.53**.)
3. Telecommunications software that lets your computer "talk" to other computers.

§ 8.50 —Client/Server Model (New)

Two terms you may encounter in reference to the Internet are *client* and *server.* Two computers connected to each other via the Internet operate in a structure known as the *client/server* relationship. A client computer requests information over the network from a remote host computer, the server. Both computers must use the TCP/IP standards as the medium by which they communicate over the network. When you log on, you establish a connection with the remote host, or server computer. The host computer accepts your request, services it, then sends the results back to the client computer (you).

§ 8.51 —Modems (New)

The term *modem* is a combination of the words MOdulator and DEModulator. A modem is a small device (not much larger than a pack of index cards) that connects your computer to a telephone line. A modem converts (modulates) the computer's digital signals into electrical signals that can travel over the telephone lines. The modem on the computer at the other end converts (demodulates) the electrical signals, translating them back into digital signals that the computer can understand. (See **Figure 8–2.**)

Modems come in different transmission speeds, expressed as bits per second (bps). Buy the fastest modem you can afford. At a minimum, you need a 14,400-bps modem to get around on the Internet. A slower modem will work, but the transfer time will be longer (this is very tedious). Currently, the 28,800-bps modem is recommended if you plan to do a lot of work on the Internet. A modem must be compatible with the computer attached to it, so that the computer's software can give the modem the appropriate commands to pick up, dial, hang up, and so on. Make sure the modem you buy is *Hayes-compatible,* that is, compatible with the Hayes standard developed by Hayes Microcomputer Products. If the box doesn't say "Hayes-compatible," don't buy it. A modem may be internal (installed inside the box of the CPU) or external, in a separate box connected to the computer by a separate power cord. Modems are relatively inexpensive computer components. As of late 1995, a standard 14,400-bps internal modem cost less than $50; a

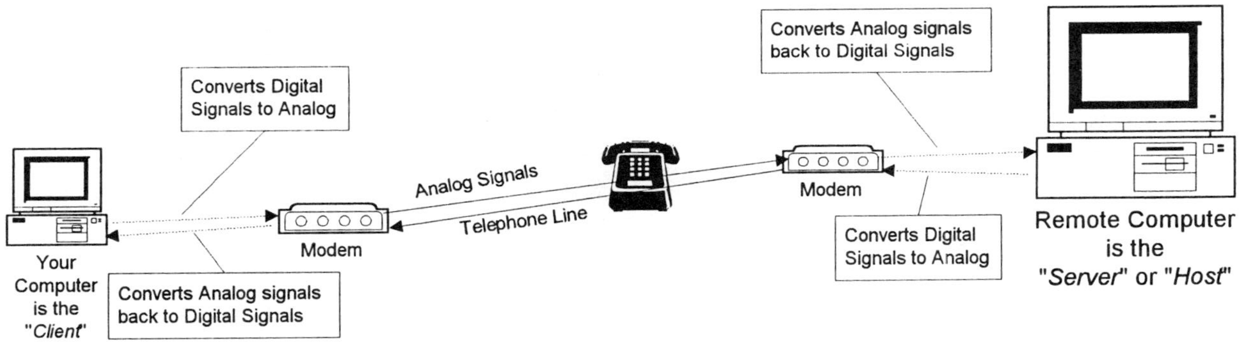

A modem converts (MOdulates) the client computer's digital signals into electrical (or analog) signals that can travel over the telephone lines. The modem on the remote computer at the other end converts (DEModulates) the signals back into digital signals the computer can understand. The process is done in reverse for communications from the remote server computer to the client computer.

Figure 8–2. How a Modem Works.

faster 28,800-bps modem cost about $150. By the time you read this, the prices will probably be lower, and even faster modems may be available.

§ 8.52 Internet Connections (New)

There really is no "typical" Internet connection. Every computer that can reach Internet resources does so over different channels and through varying types of services. However, the general process for all users is similar. Many users connect to the Internet through their work or campus network. More recently, numerous independent service providers have started offering access to individual home computers through dial-up facilities. These Internet access providers are private companies that sell access to users. You need to know something about the levels of connections in order to:

- decide what type of account you need;
- compare vendors and commercial service providers; and
- understand how the various services fit together.

§ 8.53 —Internet Accounts (New)

There are four grades of Internet accounts to consider.

1. **Gateway connection.** Popular online service companies such as America OnLine, CompuServe, Delphi, Prodigy, and others offer accounts known as *gateway* connections. Although they provide the easiest way to connect to the Internet, these companies may not offer complete access to all the Internet functions. Subscribers to these services may have only limited access to the Internet, depending on the services the provider offers (e.g., E-mail, USENET news groups, and basic file transfer capability). (NOTE: This may change in the near future.)
2. **Internet service provider (ISP) shell account.** Hundreds of service providers offer a *shell account,* which is the least expensive type of Internet access. (There are also some government-funded local "FreeNet" systems that provide free access to users.) With a shell account, the service provider's computer is

actually the one on the Internet. You dial into the service provider's machine to use whatever Internet programs and options the service provider has made available. To access the Internet functions, you may have to type in certain codes (based on the UNIX command-line system or the service provider's proprietary system), although some services offer attractive-looking graphical user interfaces. Either way, you are limited to the tools the service provider makes available to you.

3. **Direct Link.** Internet service providers may also offer a direct link using a class of software known as *SLIP* or *PPP* connection. This type of account combines a base of TCP/IP communication software with a set of Internet utilities for navigating and searching the Internet. This connection joins your PC directly with the Internet, and may be more expensive than the shell accounts because you have increased access to all the Internet services. The easiest way to acquire this type of account is to buy an all-in-one package that incorporates both the TCP/IP and navigational software. Commercial Internet service providers, such as NETCOM or InterAccess (in the Chicago area), send you the software, and then typically supply you with an E-mail address, a password, and a telephone number for your modem to dial to enter the Internet.
4. **Dedicated Link.** Large corporations and law firms with local area networks (LANs) may connect directly to the Internet. The entire company LAN becomes part of the Internet with the installation of TCP/IP software, then a hookup to the Internet via a high-speed dedicated telephone link. This is the most expensive type of account, but it gives users complete and unlimited access to all the Internet functions and services (see **Figure 8–3**).

§ 8.54 —Cost (New)

Government agencies, corporations, and universities may buy large blocks of long-distance telephone time at a discounted monthly fee. Internet access providers (private companies that sell access to users) and commercial services buy telephone time in bulk and resell it to subscribers at rates ranging from $2 to $5 per hour. Some services let

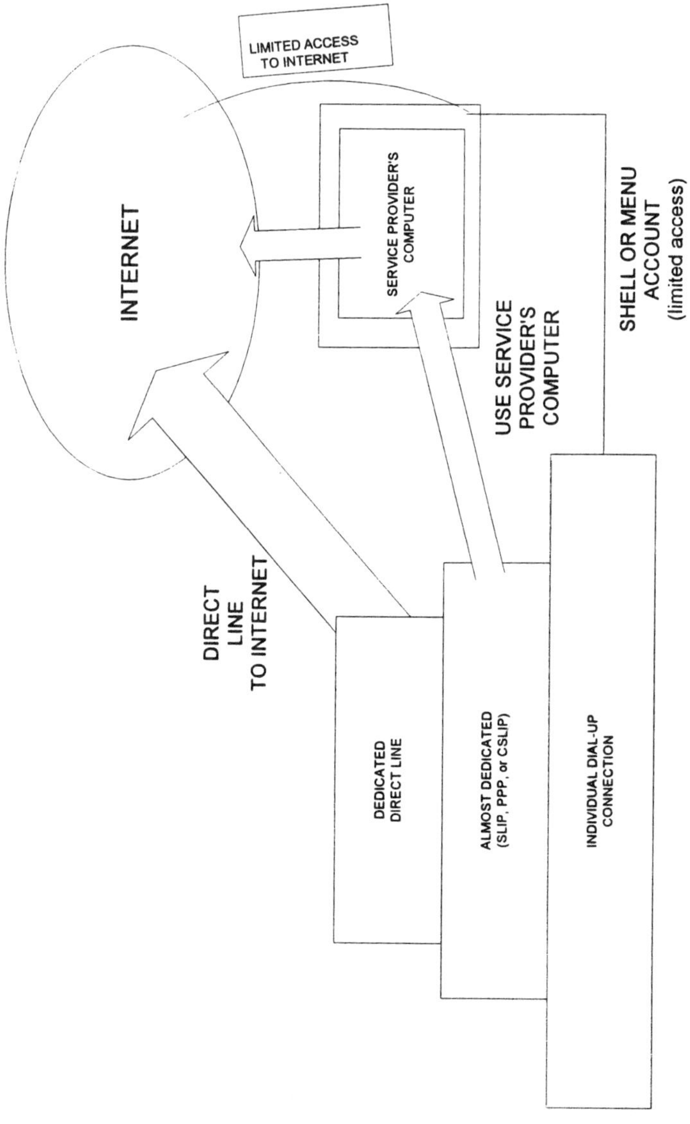

Figure 8–3. Different Types of Internet Accounts.

subscribers pay a monthly fee for unlimited time on the network. The cost is low enough that small businesses and individuals can participate. (By late 1995 there were no standard or fixed prices for Internet services.) Different service providers offer different fee structures and supply you with whatever services they decide upon. Consequently, provider service charges and quality vary greatly. Prices to get connected range from absolutely free (via public-access networks such as Cleveland Free-Net, Peoria Free-Net, and similar community or library-based networks) to very expensive; the charges are not necessarily related to the level of service you receive. Spend some time looking around and asking questions before you choose a service provider.

§ 8.55 —Checklist: Evaluating Internet Service Providers (New)

Use the following as a starting point in evaluating the characteristics of service providers under consideration:

- What is the service typically used for?
- Does the provider offer all the basic Internet services?
- What type of accounts does the service offer?
- What are the initial sign-up fees?
- What is the basic monthly service charge?
- How does the service bill hourly connection charges?
- Does the provider have a local telephone number (to avoid long-distance telephone charges)?
- Does the service require special software?
- What are the telecommunication charges to connect to the service provider?
- Is the service's user interface a windows-type "point-and-click" program or plain text? (The *user interface* is the software program that comes up automatically on the computer screen when you log on.)
- How much storage space are you allotted for files and E-mail on the provider's system?

- Does the service provide technical and customer support lines?
- Are there any hidden costs?

§ 8.56 Basic Internet Functions (New)

A trial paralegal should have a basic understanding of the various services that make up the Internet. You need to understand what types of things you can do and how you can do them. The following sections give a brief overview of the Internet's "big three" basic functions: E-mail, remote log-in, and file transfer.

§ 8.57 —E-mail (New)

Most new Internet users begin their journey to the networking world by experimenting with electronic mail (E-mail), one of the main communication devices on the Internet. E-mail is easy, convenient, fast, inexpensive, useful, and fun—no wonder it's the Internet's most popular function!

If you have a computer with a modem, an E-mail program, and access to the Internet (an account), you can send E-mail messages to anyone else on the Internet, virtually anywhere in the world. Most commercial online services provide access to Internet E-mail, even if you do not have access to all the other Internet services. If the computers in your office are on a local area network (LAN), chances are you have already used E-mail to send or reply to messages from colleagues (see **§ 8.10**). Office E-mail is a great way to quickly notify individuals or groups within the office of updated information about the case. Office administrators can use E-mail to advise all employees at once of urgent announcements, upcoming meetings, and so forth. The Internet expands this concept, making it possible for you to communicate with persons outside your local network.

Communication is an extremely important component of the legal business, and E-mail provides a new way to communicate with clients, witnesses, and colleagues. Lawyers are finding that many client businesses and organizations are adding E-mail capability to their offices (see **§ 8.10**). When your office network is connected to the Internet, you can send messages to clients, experts, witnesses, investigators, and others in the case (see **Figure 8–4**).

E-mail addresses are appearing on business cards and stationery, in print and television advertisements, and under the signatures of letters to the editor in many periodicals (see **§ 8.68** on understanding Internet addresses). This is similar to the way businesses began adding fax numbers to their postal address information a few years ago, a practice that is now commonplace. E-mail usage is becoming increasingly widespread among legal professionals. The *Martindale-Hubbell Law Directory* (May 1995) added electronic mail addresses to its index listings for over 800,000 attorneys. The identification number next to each attorney's name also serves as an E-mail address accessible through the Internet. The directory's new E-mail address feature is a joint project with LEXIS Counsel Connect, the legal online service company that provides the E-mail addresses (Daniel B. Kennedy, "E-Mail Expansion," *ABA Journal* at 41, June 1995).

You will find many uses for E-mail, both inside your organization and outside via the Internet. E-mail will probably never completely replace other types of communications; in-person meetings will continue to be important. But E-mail can make communicating quick and convenient in numerous ways:

- E-mail provides a means to communicate in addition to the telephone. E-mail can help you avoid some of the inevitable "telephone tag" that occurs in legal work. E-mail capability helps with scheduling. Users can dial into the system to pick up their messages at their convenience, from home or office computers or from portable computers. This feature is handy for spanning time zones if you work with attorneys who practice international law (unlike telephone communications, which require people to be at each end of the conversation).
- Paralegals and lawyers can exchange messages and files with clients and colleagues. This ability is especially helpful to trial teams from firms or corporations that have multiple offices in scattered locations. Exchanging documents electronically lets each person review documents and type in comments at their convenience, and avoids the delays that usually occur in routing paper drafts.

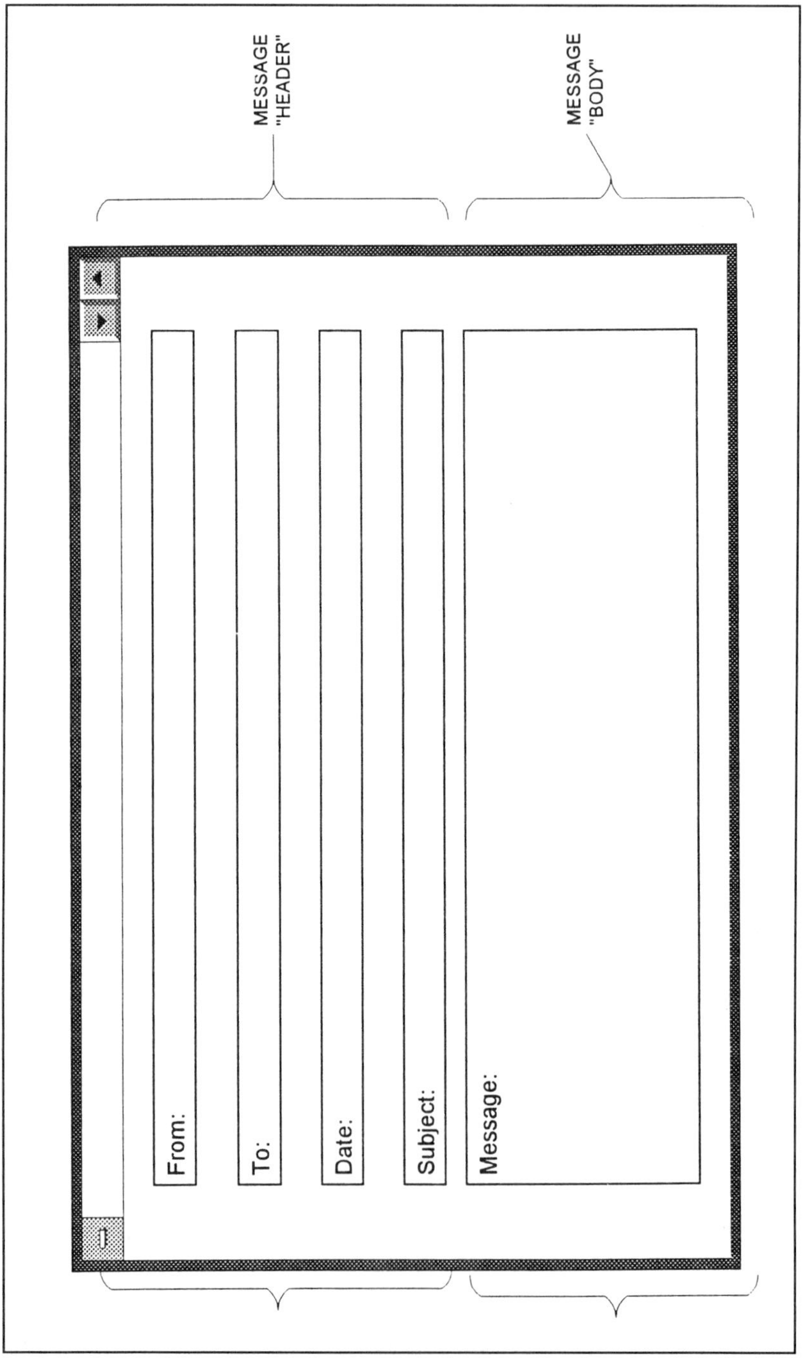

Figure 8–4. Sample E-mail Screen.

- E-mail provides a convenient way to schedule trial team meetings and send updates to trial team members on developments in the case.
- Exchanging documents via E-mail makes it easy for the attorney or paralegal to redraft or revise documents or briefs sent by corporate in-house counsel or other co-counsel.
- E-mail can be used to quickly communicate ideas, trial strategies, local court rules, or other information to out-of-town co-counsel during trial preparation.
- Internet electronic bulletin boards or Listserv mailing lists help keep you up to date on developing technology or current legal issues.
- E-mail enables you to contact other trial paralegals around the country who can help with problem-solving ideas. Someone who has faced a problem like yours may provide a solution—or at least some guidance on where to look for additional information.
- Using E-mail, you can locate and communicate with expert witnesses, many of whom are at universities that already have E-mail connections through campus network systems.
- Some courts already permit electronic filing of motions and briefs, and many court systems across the country are considering putting some portion of their records online.

§ 8.58 ——E-mail Etiquette ("Netiquette") (New)

Certain conventions and rules apply to conducting E-mail conversations, whether inside or outside the office:

1. Keep messages brief and to the point.
2. Stay with the topic being discussed when responding to a posting. Make sure the "Subject" header accurately describes what you are writing in the message.
3. Avoid using uppercase letters. All uppercase is considered SHOUTING and is more difficult to read on screen than text using mixed uppercase and lowercase. To emphasize a word, bracket it with **asterisks**.

4. Type flush to the left margin; make the right margin 80 maximum; and use single spacing. Start paragraphs with either an indent or a line space, but not both.
5. Avoid typographical errors and misspellings in your postings. Proofread your messages carefully.
6. Avoid "flaming." Heated replies to newsgroup postings are referred to as *flames,* and they can get pretty rude. Don't be tempted to spout off in a public forum.
7. Be courteous. Think before you post. Take care with sarcastic remarks; they don't always translate well in print. In short, don't put anything in an E-mail message that you wouldn't want published in a family newspaper!
8. Remember that E-mail postings may be read by persons other than the addressee. When composing messages, be mindful of your duty to the client to maintain confidentiality.
9. For discussion groups, read the FAQ (frequently-asked-questions) file to bring you up to date on the discussion.
10. Learn E-mail shorthand abbreviations (see **Table 8-3**).
11. Print out and save copies of important messages.

§ 8.59 ——Online Discussions: LISTSERVS and Newsgroups (New)

For one-on-one E-mail messages, you need only to type in the other person's E-mail address. Most E-mail systems allow you to define a group of recipients for the messages; when you send E-mail to a group of people on a related subject, you have created a rudimentary distribution list (similar to a mailing list). E-mail is the basic means of conducting online discussions and discussion groups. Two Internet services address this role directly: *LISTSERVs* and *newsgroups*.

LISTSERVs

LISTSERVs are special-interest-group electronic mailing lists managed by automated distribution list handlers. You join a discussion group on a particular topic by sending an E-mail message to the list handler at a sponsoring host computer. (*Hosts* are large computers that store central

Table 8-3

E-MAIL SHORTHAND ABBREVIATIONS

ADN	Any day now	NOYL	Not on your life
AFAIK	As far as I know	OIC	Oh, I see
BBS	Bulletin Board System	OTOH	On the other hand
BCNY	Be seein' you	PITN	Pain in the neck
BTDT	Been there, done that	POV	Point of view
BTW	By the way	ROTFL	Rolling on the floor, laughing
CON	Come on now		
CUL	See you later	RSN	Real soon now
FWIW	For what it's worth	SLCUL	So long, catch you later
FYI	For your information	SYSOP	System operator
IANAL	I am not a lawyer	TIA	Thanks in advance
IC	I see	TPTB	The powers that be
ICBYS	I can't believe you're serious	TTBOMK	To the best of my knowledge
IMHO	In my humble opinion	TTFN	Ta-Ta for now
IOW	In other words	TTUL	Talk to you later
IRL	In real life	WRT	With regard to
LBJ	Light bulb joke	WYSIWYG	What you see is what you get
LOL	Laughing out loud		

information that can be used by thousands of individuals.) The list handler puts you on the distribution list for the discussions, and your messages are automatically forwarded to everyone on the list. Messages from other people are automatically forwarded to your E-mail in-box, and the entire discussion shows up in your own E-mail system. LISTSERVs may be moderated; that is, someone is in charge of tailoring what information goes out to the persons on the distribution list. Some systems let people choose whether to receive each individual message or to have them consolidated into a digest. Most LISTSERVs allow anyone on the Internet who has an E-mail address to join, although the list manager can control membership in some cases. LISTSERVs generate a huge amount of E-mail traffic. If a list on a single host computer has a thousand subscribers, the LISTSERV will distribute 1,000 separate copies of each message posted to the group. A single LISTSERV subscriber could receive hundreds of E-mail messages each week. To alleviate this problem, the early developers of Internet services developed an alternative way to distribute messages, via newsgroups (see next section). There are LISTSERVs on thousands of topics on the Internet. LISTSERVs are relatively easy to set up, and discussion topics tend to come and go fairly quickly. Currently, LISTSERVs are not centrally registered and can be difficult to keep track of. Lyonette Louis-Jacques at the University of Chicago focuses on LISTSERV discussion groups and maintains one of the most comprehensive indexes of LISTSERVs related to legal topics. Participating in discussion groups for legal professionals is an information resource and networking opportunity.

Newsgroups

Newsgroups (also called forums, conferences, and roundtables) are the Internet equivalent of a public bulletin board system: you log on, scan through the messages, and post replies that everyone in the Newsgroup will see. The discussions on various topics are organized under a set of broad headings called newsgroups and may have several discussions going on simultaneously. Each section may have a library of useful documents, records of previous online discussions, software resource lists, resumes, and so on. Each newsgroup host computer keeps just one copy of each message; participants browse through the stored discussions, using special "newsreader" software to read through the messages at their convenience and to post replies if they wish. Host computers in the background handle the task of distributing individual postings to all of the other participating host computers. Some newsgroups, such as "newsfeeds" from major wire services, involve a fee (the people who run the host computer must pay a fee for receiving those newsgroups). Not every host computer subscribes to every newsgroup. The collective process of exchanging newsgroup postings is often referred to as USENET.

Newsgroup designations are organized with the broadest grouping first in the name, followed by an arbitrary number of subgroupings in descending order of specificity. The name of each group is separated from its "parent" and subgroupings by a period (.). In a newsgroup address, the main topic classification appears first, followed by subtopics, separated by periods. For example a newsgroup labeled

rec.sports.baseball

would be under the "recreation" classification, covering sports, and specifically baseball. Seven of the top-level newsgroups have been in existence for a long time. These are indicated by boldface type in **Table 8–4**. Also included are some additional specialized newsgroup classifications you may encounter.

Most LISTSERVs and newsgroups ask newcomers to review the group's FAQ file before filling the discussion with basic questions. Usually, you will need File Transfer Protocol (FTP) or some other file exchange capability to get the FAQ files, which may also be labeled README files. These information files usually contain basic helpful introductory information. If you're new to a newsgroup, reading the FAQ of a newsgroup will help you get up to speed about the basic elements of the group. Remember that newsgroups are public forums. Everything you post becomes readable by anyone who cares to do so. Think before you post!

Table 8-4

NEWSGROUP CLASSIFICATIONS

alt	Alternative newsgroups about various subjects and topics
bionet	Newsgroups of interest to biologists, about biological sciences
bit	The most popular BITNET LISTSERV discussion groups
biz	Commercial and business-related topics, advertisements
clari	ClariNet newsgroups
comp	Computer-related topics, including software sources and information on hardware and software systems
courts	Law-related topics, legal issues
eunet	European newsgroups
info	Newsgroups "gatewayed" from mailing lists
misc	Topics that don't fit into other categories or that fit into several categories
news	Information on network news and USENET
rec	Hobbies, sports, recreational activities, and the arts
relcom	Newsgroups from the former Soviet Union
sci	Scientific research and applications, established scientific and engineering disciplines
soc	Social and cultural issues
talk	Forum for debating controversial topics (politics, religion, etc.)

§ 8.60 —Telnet (New)

Two other functions besides E-mail that are important to the Internet are Telnet and FTP. *Telnet* (telnet://) is an Internet basic utility or "protocol" for remote log-on or log-in that allows you to connect to another networked computer and use its functions. In other words, you sit at a keyboard connected to your desktop computer and log on to a remote computer elsewhere on the network through a telephone line. (The other computer may be in the same building, on the same campus, in a distant city, or even in a foreign country.) A process known as *terminal emulation* makes your computer act as if it were directly connected to the remote computer. You can then use the services and programs that are on the remote computer. Each remote computer's system may look different, because the screen setup depends on the preferences of the computer owner and the exact software being used. Telnet is used to view files and search online resources, such as public databases and library card catalogs.

§ 8.61 —File Transfer Protocol (New)

File Transfer Protocol, or FTP (ftp://) is a basic utility program that lets users send and receive files across the Internet. In other words, the FTP's function is to copy files from one computer to another. Your communications software must include FTP for you to get data files from another computer on the Internet. Fortunately, nearly everyone connected to the Internet has FTP, and most major service providers include it with their packages.

Once you know how to exchange computer messages with other E-mail users, the next logical step is to include information you found in an Internet database in a report or document you are creating on your computer. With only E-mail capability, you could read what was on the screen, but that information would be lost as soon as it scrolled off the screen or you exited the file. FTP, a tool for copying a file from a remote system to your local computer, can be used to transfer software programs and other types of files, such as word processing, spreadsheet, and graphics files. FTP is most useful for retrieving files from public archives that are scattered around the Internet.

FTP is an economical way for businesses and other organizations to distribute files containing information such as catalogs, price lists, schedules, and so on. Some of the most useful collections of information on the Internet are kept on public FTP servers, known as *anonymous FTP sites.* The term "anonymous" means that this is a generic account that anyone can use to log on to an FTP server, using "anonymous" as the user identification, and to transfer (or *download*) programs and other files to the user's own computer at no charge (some restrictions may apply for security reasons).

Caution: Some FTP files are quite large and may take several minutes or even hours to download to your PC.

§ 8.62 Basic Tools for Navigating the Internet (New)

You will need to know about the basic tools available for finding resources on the vast network that is the Internet. There are two main types of resource-finding tools: *browsers,* whereby a person does the search by choosing items from lists; and *searchers,* whereby a computer does the search in response to a keyword query from the computer user. This section is not a technical explanation of how to use these tools, but the following sections will introduce you to some of the major navigational tools and related terms you are likely to encounter on the Internet.

§ 8.63 —Archie (New)

The file transfer protocol (FTP), described in **§ 8.61**, is used to copy files from other computers; however, the programs on the remote computer do not always display a friendly-looking list of files from which to choose. You need a way to determine which files you want to see. *Archie* (a play on the word "archive") is a popular search utility program that looks for key words in the titles of files on remote computers. Archie serves as a limited directory to anonymous FTP files (by name or category). Archie allows you to search indexes to locate files that are available on public file servers (archives). You type in key words for topics you want to see, and Archie returns a list of file names that contain the key words, along with the locations of the files. You ask Archie to find file names containing certain key words, or to suggest files whose descriptions contain a certain word. Archie returns the actual file names that meet the search criteria and the name(s) of the servers containing those files. Once you decide which of the files is most likely to meet your needs, you can easily copy the file to your computer with FTP.

The Archie creators run a program once a month that scans the more than 1,200 FTP file servers and builds a directory of all the files on each server. There are many Archie servers scattered across the Internet; each server builds an index of the FTP archives close to itself, and then the servers share the information. All the Archie servers have the same data. You care only about picking the server that will answer your queries the most quickly, probably the one that is closest to you geographically. (Ask your service provider for a recommendation.) To use Archie, you must have access to a version of the Archie software and database, or you need to log onto one of the several Archie servers (usually using Telnet). Archie can be accessed in multiple ways. There are several Archie servers, all of which are equivalent, and more Archie servers are being added all the time.

§ 8.64 —Gopher (New)

Gopher (gopher://) is a basic utility for browsing through information on the Internet. Often available at government and educational facilities, Gopher is a search tool popular with Internet users because it is easy to access and use, and it contains powerful search-and-retrieval features. Gopher is generally best for broad searches. With a few quick menu choices, you may be able to jump around to different host computers throughout the world in less than a minute. Gopher lets you browse through the Internet by selecting resources from menus. A search brings up another menu on another computer. When you choose a topic you want to view from one of the resource lists, Gopher automatically gets the file for you to look at. (It doesn't really matter where the material you want is located, as long as it is part of the Gopher system.)

The Gopher system was invented by computer programmers at the University of Minnesota in response to a need for a campus-wide information retrieval service. (The system name refers to the Golden

Gophers of the University of Minnesota, and also to the system's ability to "go fer" information.) Gopher sites on the Internet contain lists of files as well as hierarchical lists of resources like searchable databases, graphics files, and Telnet sites that you can immediately connect to and use. The first graphical approach to searching the Internet, Gopher allows users to search via key words; it also retrieves and displays documents from other computers (servers) throughout the Internet. Gopher displays simple text menus from which the user makes choices. Some menu choices may lead to documents stored on host computers, to local searching programs (like WAIS), or to other Gopher sites on other host computers. The hundreds of Gopher sites are referred to collectively as "Gopherspace." You may find hypertext links in other documents that take you to Gopher sites, or you can connect to a Gopher site directly if you know its URL address (see **§ 8.70**). Once you have found a useful title, you can "bookmark" your spot to save the location information so that your local Gopher server can easily re-establish the link when you need it.

§ 8.65 — —Veronica and Jughead (New)

Two Gopher-specific resource discovery services, "Veronica" and "Jughead," provide limited searchable directories of Gopher listings. Most of the Veronica and Jughead services are accessible through either Telnet or Gopher. Developed at the University of Nevada, *Veronica* (an acronym for very easy rodent-oriented netwide index to computerized archives) is a software utility that helps you navigate through Gopherspace and allows key word searches on Gopher menu items. (*Note:* Veronica searches menu titles only, not the contents of documents or files.) The program takes your key words and searches all available Gopher server menus for matches, then returns a menu list to you of those matches.

Jughead is another search tool closely linked with Gopher. A Jughead server maintains a searchable database of the menu items at a particular Gopher site. It allows the user to refine a search by specifying limitations on the type and number of files to be retrieved. A Jughead program installed at a Gopher site allows the user to search all the Gopher's menu titles at once.

§ 8.66 —WAIS (New)

WAIS (wais://) is an acronym for Wide Area Information Server. This is a relatively simple information retrieval system for full-text key word searching Internet collections of databases using simple English queries. A WAIS provider establishes a database to which any Internet user can send queries. The WAIS system conducts a search and gives a response that not only evaluates exact matches but also tries to list the responses in order of relevancy for the matches found. WAIS lets you search through Internet archives for articles containing groups of key words. WAIS is also a tool for conducting text searches in large databases. Like Gopher, WAIS allows you to find and access resources on the network without regard to where the resources reside, similar to searching in a library devoted to a specific topic. WAIS databases may be not the primary part of a service, but users can usually get to WAIS databases through Telnet or Gopher. As of late 1995, most access providers did not offer WAIS as part of their packages as they do for browsers like Gopher and the Web, but this may change as more publishers begin using WAIS servers to distribute their work online.

§ 8.67 —World Wide Web (New)

Undoubtedly, the World Wide Web (also known as WWW, W3, or, simply, the Web) is one of the most significant and fast-growing Internet browsing tools. (*Note:* The Internet and the World Wide Web are *not* synonymous.) The quickly expanding Web, with its "user-friendly" graphical user interface, facilitates the task of locating information on the Internet. When people talk about the Web, they are often referring to HTML (hypertext markup language) documents located on the Internet. HTML documents, also referred to as *home pages*, attractively display information (text and graphics) and allow easy access to other documents across the Internet. (See **Figure 8–5**.) Internet users typically use a "browser" program that runs on their computers to access Web servers and other types of Internet servers such as FTP or Gopher. A *browser* is a program that searches through hypertext files. Mosaic is one popular browser program.

The Web's popularity can be attributed to how easy it is to use. Instead of entering search queries for key words or phrases, you follow

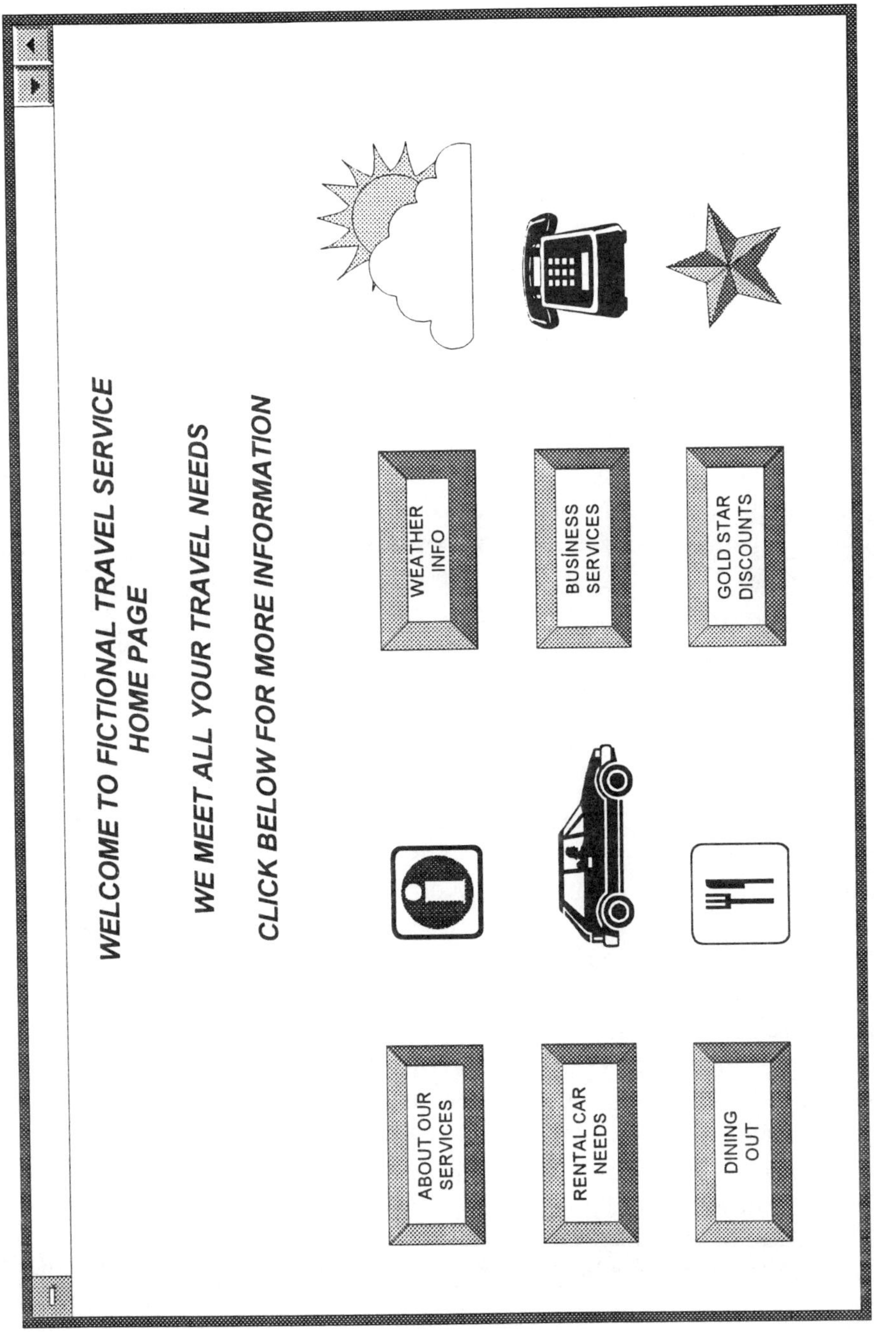

Figure 8–5. Sample Home Page.

a "trail" of linked words. You select a topic that interests you from a Web home page, and the screen displays information on that topic, with listings of hypertext links or markers pointing to sources of related information. From that list, you select a link to another topic that interests you, and information on that topic is then displayed. You move from one topic to another, and you can easily retrace your steps. The Web adds two significant features to browsing on the Internet, embedded hypertext links and multimedia capability.

Hypertext links are what make the Web easy to use. The hypertext technology that forms the foundation for the Web is called Hypertext Transport Protocol (or http). A Web document is a text document created using the HTML, a coding system for making hypertext links and sending formatted text and graphics from Web servers to Web browsers. Browsers, used to scan through sources of information on the network, are usually connected with an ability to retrieve the information you've found, such as FTP for file exchange. Most Web documents contain hypertext "links" (also referred to as *hyperlinks*) that allow you to jump to other documents and resources on related subjects. (See **Figure 8–6**.) The author of a Web document sets up certain words, phrases, or graphics in a document, using HTML to indicate push-button links to another document, a definition, or a site on another host computer that gives additional information about the highlighted term. This type of instant cross-referencing to get additional details may prove to be perfectly suited for the types of factual research that trial paralegals perform.

Hypertext links are based on a standard addressing scheme called *universal resource locator* (URL) (see **§ 8.70**). The *home page* is the base address (starting point) of any Web site, and it contains links to the content material that is stored at the site. A constantly growing number of Web sites, or home pages, comprise the Web, which was designed to incorporate all sorts of interlinked resources in an easy-to-browse manner. Some home pages are jazzy, polished presentations, incorporating fancy logos and graphics. They present information in an attractive display or design that reflects the personality and flair of the company. Other home pages are plain text and appear somewhat primitive by contrast. They may offer a plain table of contents (menu) of choices.

Once you are in a home page, a simple mouse click takes you to information about topics listed on the home page. Linked references within a Web document become the jumping-off points to help you find

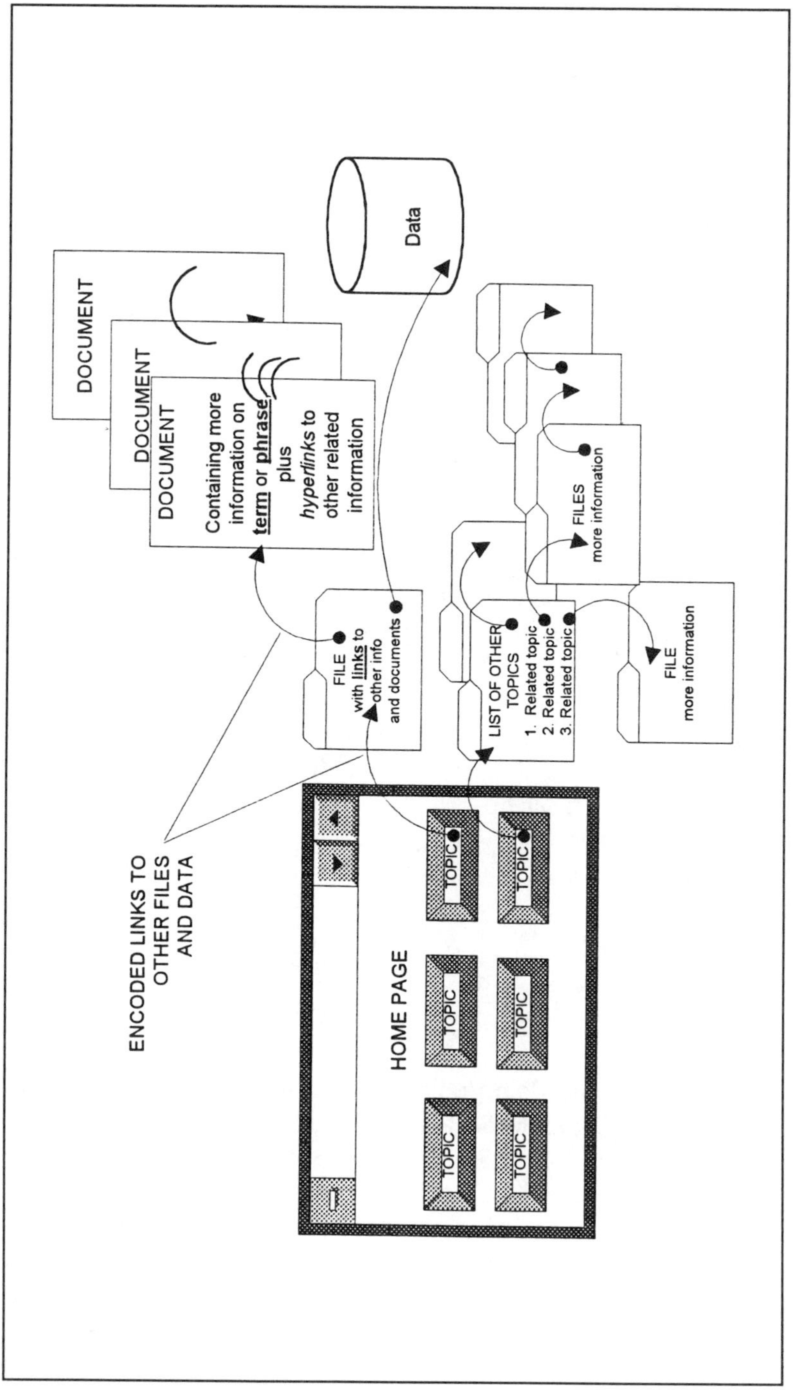

Figure 8–6. World Wide Web Hyperlinks.

other documents, lists, and resources. Depending on what software you use, the linked topics may be indicated by text in a different color or font, or by text underlining or highlighting. Once you're in the Web, all of the Internet's Web sites (home pages) are accessible. Jumping from one site to another resembles surfing, resulting in the popular expression "surfing the Net." World Wide Web locations are like addresses for the tables of contents displayed on the home pages. Typically, the home page lists numerous topics, documents, and other menus that are behind the opening screen and linked to additional information about the topic you select. Some home pages also feature searchable indices and "forms" capability (you can enter comments during an online session by filling out the fields in an onscreen form). Be aware that many Web sites are new and still under development. Some newer Web sites may not have much substantive information available yet, and they may display a note telling you to check back soon for further developments.

Multimedia capability is made possible by the Web to create multimedia sites by incorporating graphics, images, pictures, diagrams, video, music, and sound. Instead of typing in text, issuing commands, or even selecting from menus, users click on pictures, text buttons, and graphics to get from place to place. The Web gives the Internet a colorful and very compelling look, similar to what you get from multimedia CD-ROMs. Many Web sites feature attractive color photographs, and some even play sounds and display video clips, although downloading video with a standard modem can be very time-consuming. By late 1995, a new language called "Java" was being developed that will enable Web developers to incorporate full-motion video into Web home pages.

§ 8.68 Understanding Internet Addresses (New)

Just as you need to know a postal address in order to send a letter, you need to know a computer's address to send or receive information over the Internet. The TCP/IP standards (see § **8.47**) define Internet addresses. Each computer is defined by a unique IP address, four sets of numbers separated by periods: 123.45.6.789. The leftmost is your network, the next is a subnetwork, followed by the specific host or computer number. But numbers are difficult to remember and easy to mistype, so the current Internet provides automatic conversion of most addresses into something a little more user-friendly.

§ 8.69 —E-mail Addresses (New)

An Internet user's E-mail address usually consists of the user's name and the host computer used by that person, separated by an @ symbol: **username@hostname**. The E-mail address may also include a domain name designation.

Example 1: The E-mail address for someone named Beverly Hutson at the law firm of Brouse & McDowell might be:

bhutson@brouse.com

In this example, "bhutson" is the computer user's name, "brouse" is the name of the computer, and ".com" is the domain name designation signifying a company.

Example 2: The E-mail address for the National Organization of Paralegal Associations (NFPA) is:

info@paralegals.org

The mail recipient is called "info," "paralegals" is the computer name, and ".org" is the domain name designation for a not-for-profit organization.

§ 8.70 —Uniform Resource Locator (New)

The World Wide Web uses a standard address notation called a *Uniform Resource Locator* (URL) to assign a unique location to files, databases, and other kinds of resources. URLs typically provide information about three components of the resource:

- Service type;
- Host computer location and domain; and
- Path directory, subdirectory, and specific file name.

URL notation structures the addresses like this:

service://host computer location.domain/directory/subdirectory.filename

- *Service type* indicates the type of computer server that houses the resource. A URL always starts with a service type, which designates the Internet tool or protocol to be used to get to the document or file so that you can read or retrieve it. Service types are identified by a particular shorthand notation and separated from the rest of the site name by a colon and a double slash:

://

For example, the format for a Gopher URL is:

gopher://gopher.filename.com

A file with the prefix "http" is always a World Wide Web address. **Table 8–5** shows various service types you may see in Internet addresses. (See **Figure 8–7** for a diagram of a typical Web address.)

Table 8-5

Service Types Used in Internet Addresses

ftp://	File transfer protocol
gopher://	Gopher sites
http://	Hypertext transport protocol. The http:// prefix always means the file is located at a World Wide Web site
mailto://	Mail transfer protocol (E-mail)
telnet://	Telnet server (remote log-on)
wais://	Wide-area information server

- *Location.Domain* indicates the name of the host computer where the file is maintained, along with a domain name. The right-hand side of the URL (after the double slashes) indicates the host computer (a name or set of names separated with periods) that is connected to the Internet and the subdirectory, if any, where the file is stored. Many Web sites designate their host computer as "www" or "web."

§ 8.71 —Domain Name System (New)

The Internet uses a scheme of addresses known as the *domain name system* (DNS), that identifies the name and type of organization that owns the service. A domain name is usually assigned when a user opens

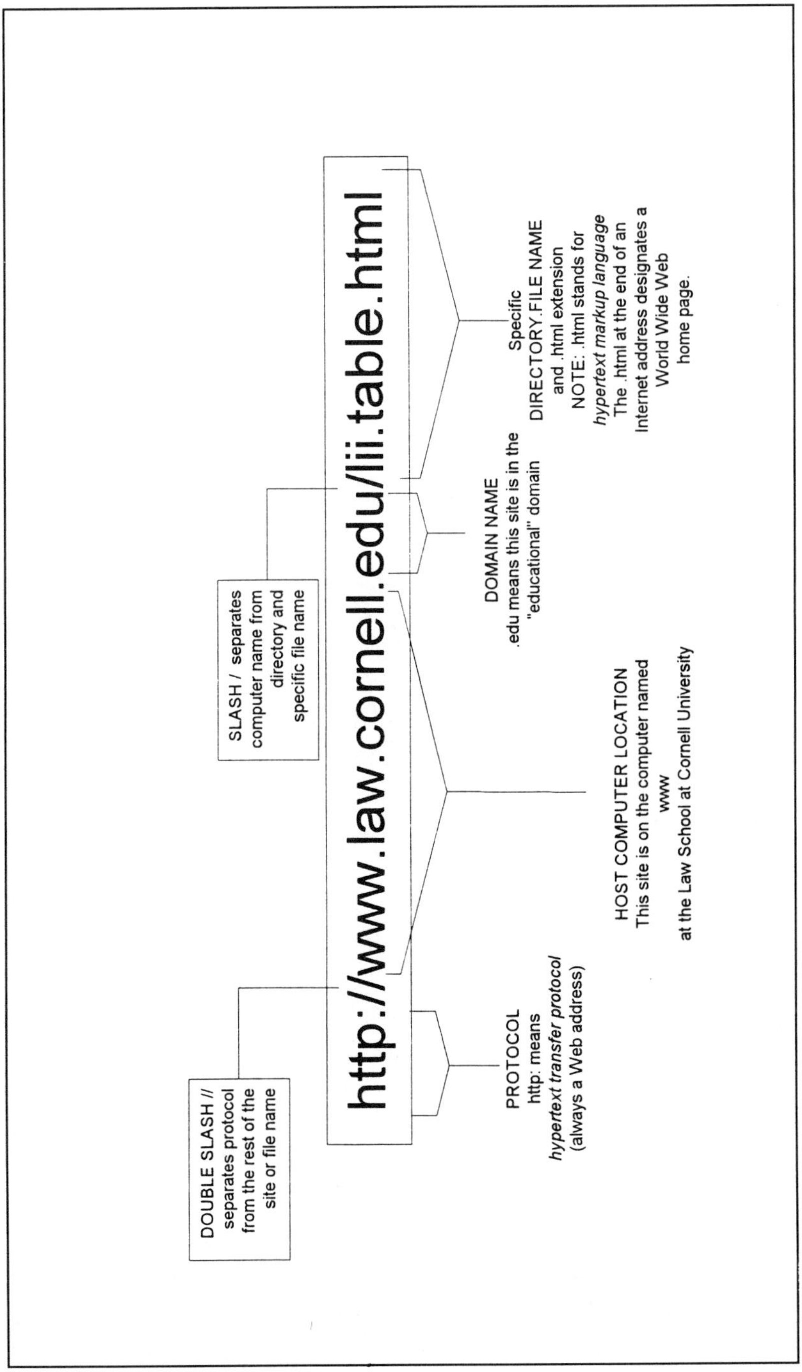

Figure 8–7. Uniform Resource Locator.

an Internet account, and domain names are registered. An Internet user must establish an account and register his or her domain name with an organization called InterNIC. Domain names are organized from left to right with the most specific (the individual computer) name at the left, and the most general (or domain) designation at the right. The top-level domains on the Internet are:

.com	commercial and industrial entities
.edu	education (universities and other educational organizations)
.gov	government (non-military)
.mil	military or defense organizations
.net	network operation and service organizations
.org	nonprofit and research organizations

NOTE: Sometimes the domain name is also a geographical designation. For example, the domain name for the United States is **.us**, and Great Britain's designation is **.uk**.

- *Path* indicates the directory, subdirectories, and file name. There can be one or more slash delimeters (/) to indicate the directory "path" to the desired Web page. For example, NFPA's Internet Web site is:

  http://www.paralegals.org

  or, to reach NFPA's home page specifically

  http://www.paralegals.org/home.html

  (The .html extension means "hypertext markup language," indicating that this is a World Wide Web home page.) Notice that the URL addresses tend to be somewhat lengthy compared to the eight-letter file names most DOS users are accustomed to seeing. This is partly due to the Internet's origins in the UNIX operating system, which uses long but cryptic file names.

Internet technology enables you to see connections (or links) between ideas and facts that you might never have seen. You can do more research and fact-gathering with the Internet than you ever could have done manually, and much faster. This is key, because in our business, time is money. (Billing practices are changing, but most of us still bill our time to clients by the hour. Paralegals have to make the best use of time in order to get everything done.) Clients are our customers, and they pay us well. Clients expect us to use the best tools available to do our work on their behalf. It is incumbent upon us to keep up with what's going on in the rest of the world.

The Internet will be useful to trial paralegals in conducting background research on various topics, such as:

- Industry practices and standards
- Professional associations
- Statistics and demographics
- Government regulations and agencies
- Quotes or cultural references
- Surveys
- Newspaper articles
- Magazine articles
- Professional and trade journals
- CLE seminars and workshops
- Places to find legal information

Research on the Internet may not get you exhaustive results. For the time being, you should verify information from other sources. But Internet resources can give you some idea of what's out there (things you never knew about) and where to look further for supplemental or more detailed information (some sources offer to send you documents via E-mail for further information). The Internet may also lead you to people who know about various topics, which could be very handy for locating potential expert witnesses. Some services let you send queries via E-mail and receive replies or lists of further resources by return E-mail, so that you can have the service (such as WAIS) conduct the search for you. The information on the Internet is not complete and will not be for a long time. Many sites are still under construction. They invite you to check back soon on work in progress.

§ 8.72 Useful Internet Sites for Readers (New)

The following is a list of abstracts describing some of the Internet legal resource sites that may be of interest to paralegals. This is by no means a complete listing; it would be impossible to list all the sites that contain legal information (new sites are added daily, and existing sites may change), but these will help to get you started.

- American Bar Association (ABA)
  http://www.abanet.org
  The ABA established its World Wide Web page on the Internet in late March of 1995. The ABA Web site offers general legal information and law resources, news of ABA meetings and events, and information on continuing legal education and seminars. In addition, Internet users can read parts of the *ABA Journal* online and order legal publications and videotapes.

- American National Standards Institute (ANSI)
  http://www.ansi.org/
  This site will give you background and current news about the ANSI federation, a catalog of published American National Standards, a directory of people to contact at ANSI, and much additional information on standards. The ANSI Reference Library lets you read information online or have it sent to your E-mail address.

- Central Intelligence Agency Server (CIA)
  http://www.odci.gov/cia/

- United States Intelligence Community (IC)
  http://www.odci.gov/ic
  Both of these sites contain lists of public information available from the CIA and the IC, as well as links to other related information elsewhere on the Internet.

- Colorado Legal Alliance—Law on the Net
  http://www.usa.net/cololaw/index.htm
  The Colorado Legal Alliance focuses on Colorado laws, statutes, rules, cases, and government information, with source links to federal sources and similar compilations for other states. This site includes an extensive index to Colorado lawyers, firms, and law schools, plus references to many other legal resources on the Internet. Additional references at this site include: a directory of businesses serving the Colorado legal community; a local

perspective on law office technology; a list of Legal Gems and pointers to other sites of general interest.

- Cornell University Legal Information Institute (LII)
  http://www.law.cornell.edu/
  The Legal Information Institute (LII) holds one of the Internet's most extensive compilations of law-related information, including research links to state, federal, and international legal information; includes a topical index and a source index.

- The Center for Corporate Law (CCL)
  University of Cincinnati College of Law
  http://www.law.uc.edu/CCL/
  This site specializes in compiling electronic data to assist lawyers in corporate and securities law practice. The CCL contains the text of the federal securities laws and their accompanying rules and forms.

- Cyberweb Business Resources
  http://www.bookmasters.com/cyberweb/resource.htm
  - AT&T 800 Number Directory (toll-free 800 numbers)
  - Currency Converter (pending)
  - Commerce Net
  - Internet Business Center
  - EDGAR Mutual Funds
  - NETworth
  - Strategy Web

- The Dorsai Embassy—Full Access Internet Site
  http://www.dorsai.org/p-law/index.htm
  This site offers information on the services and programs of The Dorsai Embassy, Inc., a New York not-for-profit corporation that provides computer hardware, software, consulting, and training to other not-for-profit organizations, community service groups, youth, the disabled, and the general public. Dorsai's services and operations include: The Dorsai Challengers, an access program for the differently abled; The Dorsai Youth Computer-centered activities and training for "at-risk" youth; Operation Renew; Operation Literacy; and Trial Access—Internet Practice.

- Federal Express

  http://www.fedex.com

  The Federal Express customer service web site allows you to electronically track the delivery status of FedEx packages.

- Federal Publications—Federal Judicial Center

  http://www.fjc.gov/pubs.html

  Publications available online from FJC include all sorts of information, such as evidence and litigation reference manuals, sentencing guidelines, reports on arbitrations in district courts, and much more.

- The Forms Room—'lectric Law Library

  http://www.inter-law.com/form.html

  This site claims to have "the Net's biggest collection of legal forms," classified into two broad categories: General Business and Law Practice. The General Business section includes dozens of standard forms for assignments, agreements, certificates, contracts, demands, deeds, notices, promissory notes, releases, trusts, and wills. This section also offers checklists for incorporation and purchase of real estate. The Law Practice section contains forms for standard affidavits, applications, declarations, demands, fee agreements, notices, orders, statements, and stipulations.

- LawTalk—Indiana University

  http://www.law.indiana.edu/law/lawtalk.html

  LawTalk is a service provided by Indiana University. Each segment deals with some aspect of Law or Legal Studies and is authored by a faculty member from either the IU School of Law in Bloomington or the IU School of Law in Indianapolis. The segment titles include: LawTalk Titles Arranged by Subject; Amendments to the US Constitution; Business and Personal Finance Law; Criminal Law; Civil Law; Miscellaneous.

- LAWCOPEDIA—WWW Virtual Law Library

  http://www.inter-law.com/ref.html

  This is an encyclopedia of legal terms and phrases, arranged alphabetically and grouped into about 25 topic areas. Some descriptions include supplemental explanatory material and case citations. As of late 1995, this site was still under development. By the time you read this, it should be well under way.

- Lawlink—A Comprehensive Guide to Internet Law Resources
  http://www.kentlaw.edu/lawlinks/outlines.html
  This site offers searchable subject-oriented lists on a variety of subjects, including: Business Issues, Caselaw, Computer Law, Constitutional Issues, Environmental Issues, Family Issues, Foreign Law & Information, Federal and State Government, Health, Human Rights, Intellectual Property, International Law, Law-related Companies, Legal Domain Network, Political Action Groups, Real Property Issues, Tax Issues, Tort Issues, U.N. Sources, and Workplace Issues.

- Lawyers Cooperative Publishing
  http://www.lcp.com
  Information on books and publications from Lawyers Cooperative.

- Law Office Technology Homepage
  http://starbase.ingress.com/tsw/ds/ds.html
  Law Office Technology Homepage is sponsored by Dana Shultz & Associates, a technology consulting firm. The site provides articles on various current technology topics and products. The site promises that new articles will appear on a regular basis.

- Inter-law's 'lectric Law Library
  http://www.inter-law.com
  Extensive repository for all sorts of material, including a legal dictionary/encyclopedia, court rules, case transcripts, National Judicial College information, legal humor, and much more.

- The Legal Domain Network—Chicago-Kent College of Law
  http://www.kentlaw.edu/lawnet/lawnet.html
  This is a good source for finding Internet mailing lists and discussion groups on topics related to the legal profession.

- The Legal List Internet Desk Reference
  http://www.lcp.com/
  Erik Heels, attorney in Eliot, Maine, maintains the Legal List, a compilation of useful Internet resources for the legal community. The Legal List, which contains hundreds of entries arranged alphabetically, is available via an E-mail LISTSERV, or you can buy a printed hardbound version.

- The Legal Professional's Lounge ('lectric Law Library)
  http://www.inter-law.com/pro.html
  Information on various paralegal (and attorney) professional issues; legal support products and directories.

- LERN—Legal Research Network
  http://witness.net
  LERN, a forum for legal professionals, is the online service of the Legal Research Network of Holden, Massachusetts. LERN is currently building one of the largest databases of expert witness resumes on the Internet. You can contact any listed expert directly, and all referrals are free of charge. You can subscribe to the LERN service, or you can join LERN's electronic mailing list to receive their newsletter. LERN maintains a list of files available to the public via E-mail, as well as numerous links to other World Wide Web pages and a catalog of products of interest to legal and expert witness professionals.

- Library of Congress
  http://lcweb.loc.gov/homepage/lchp.html
  Invaluable reference for book searching; contains lots of other information in searchable format.

- LII's Supreme Court Web Server
  http://www.law.cornell.edu/supct/
  This subdirectory features the text of U.S. Supreme Court decisions from 1991 and other Supreme Court update information.

- Lycos, Inc.—"The Catalog of the Internet"
  http://lycos.cs.cmu.edu
  Lycos is a large search engine that searches Uniform Resource Locator addresses and documents in some databases. Lycos gives you different ways to search and provides links to all sorts of World Wide Web references, from business, education, and government to sports, travel, and weather, with a whole section devoted to Legal Information. Lycos links can take you to press releases, reference works, survey results, plus slides, conference papers, and other archives. Read through Lycos' Frequently Asked Questions (FAQ) file for more information on using Lycos.

- MEDMarket "Virtual Industrial Park"
  http://www.medmarket.com
  This site provides information on a number of associations and companies related to the healthcare manufacturing industry. It includes links to various types of data from manufacturers of medical devices and electromedical products, human resources consultants, and laboratory and research concerns. MEDMarket's offerings also include a document library containing publications of interest from the FDA and other sources.

- National Federation of Paralegal Associations (NFPA)
  http://www.paralegals.org
  Loads of information on paralegal and legal assistant issues, plus discussion groups and links to many other legal resource sites on the Internet.

- National Institutes of Health Servers
  http://www.nih.gov/
  This site compiles a vast repository of information on health issues, particularly those associated with various types of cancer.

- National Technology Transfer Center Servers
  http://iridium.nttc.edu/nttc.html
  This web site operated by NTTC offers information on federal laboratories and technologies developed at federal laboratories, and much more. Congress established the NTTC to link federal labs with companies that can turn research results into commercial products.

- NIH Gopher CancerNet Menu
  http://text.nlm.nih.gov/
  The CancerNet offers a searchable index of all sorts of cancer-related documents and links to medical and scientific resources maintained by the National Library of Medicine.

- Nolo Home Page
  http://gnn.digital.com/gnn/bus/nolo
  Nolo Press publishes easy-to-use books and software on consumer law subjects such as wills, small claims court, divorce, and debt problems. Nolo also provides excellent legal information to small business, including help with incorporation, partnerships, employment law, patents, and trademarks. In addition, Nolo's GNN Business Pages organize information about commercial

resources on the Internet. Currently under development, watch for this site's Business Pages to grow in coverage as well as services. Note: The GNN Business Pages are funded by the organizations and professionals who appear there.

- Nolo Press Lawyer Jokes
  http://gnn.digital.com/gnne-2a.gnn.com/gnn/bus/nolo/graphics/jokes
  Nolo Press offers a frequently updated list of favorite lawyer jokes and quotes.

- P-Law Legal Resource Locator
  http://www.dorsai.org/p-law/
  This site contains a good outline for navigating the Internet for substantive research. This is a good starting point for locating various types of research facilities and legal resources. The items are divided into major topics such as: legislative and government information; universities and international groups (such as the United Nations); specific legal areas (advertising, corporate law, anti-trust law, and so forth); various reference and statistical information sites; and articles of current interest. You can visit the guest book and register your e-mail address to receive additional information; site maintained by New York Atty. Kenneth M. Perry.

- Rice University servers
  http://www.riceinfo.rice.edu
  Links to hundreds of other locations containing federal, state, and local government information.

- St. Olaf Travel Advisories
  http://www.stolaf.edu/network/travel-advisories.html
  Travel advisories from the State Department for every country in the world.

- Securities & Exchange Commission
  http://www.sec.gov/edgarhp.htm
  This is a large SEC filings database.

- Small Business Administration
  http://www.sbaonline.sba.gov/
  This site contains a wealth of information on starting, financing, and expanding small businesses; the site also offers a list of Frequently Asked Questions (FAQ) and a menu of information on

legal aspects of small business ownership, along with links to related government and commercial resources.

- Smithsonian Institution
  http://www.si.edu
  The Smithsonian, the world's largest museum and research complex, adds information daily to this enormous repository of research and scholastic information.

- Social Security Administration (SSA)
  http://www.ssa.gov/SSA_Home.html
  This site contains information about the SSA.

- Technical Assistance Bureau (TAB)
  http://www.intr.net/tab
  This service is a good starting point for locating expert witnesses in medical malpractice, and all fields of science, engineering, commerce, industry, sports, and recreation. TAB offers an E-mail newsletter containing articles of interest to trial lawyers.

- U.S. Bureau of Mines
  http://www.usbm.gov/
  This site contains general background information on the USBM, technical information about the mining industry, health and safety issues, minerals information, and pollution prevention and control. The USBM home page also features many links to related information from the USGS and other resources.

- U.S. Census Bureau Servers
  http://www.census.gov/
  This site contains various types of information from the Federal Census Bureau.

- U.S. Consumer Product Safety Commission (CPSC)
  http://www.cpsc.com
  This repository includes press releases (from 1990 on) and statistical information concerning incidents where consumer products caused death or injury; information for manufacturers, retailers, and distributors; a public calendar of CPSC events; and access to the U. S. Government Printing Office. The CPSC also offers a listserv distribution list for automatically receiving information from the CPSC via E-mail.

- U.S. Department of Transportation (DOT)
  http://www.dot.gov/
  This site is still under development, but it holds lots of DOT information, plus numerous links to other government information and databases.

- U.S. Environmental Protection Agency (EPA) Servers
  http://www.epa.gov/epa.home/index.html
  Searchable indexes of documents, regulations, etc. from the EPA.

- U.S. Food and Drug Administration (FDA)
  Electronic Bulletin Board
  http://www.fda.gov/
  This site contains good links to lots of information on the FDA. Most of the information maintained by the FDA is full-text searchable. When you visit this site, you may be asked for a Log-in and Password. Type **bbs** for both.

- U.S. General Services Administration (GSA) Server
  http://www.gsa.gov/
  Numerous free government publications on many topics.

- U.S. House of Representatives Internet Law Library
  http://www.pls.com:8001/
  Includes information on U.S. federal laws (arranged by agency and by original source) plus additional information on international laws and treaties, law school library catalogues, law book reviews, and legal profession directories.

- U.S. House of Representatives Servers
  http://www.house.gov/
  This site compiles a wealth of legislative information, data about members, committees, and schedules, plus links to other government databases and resources.

- U.S. Patent and Trademark Office (USPTO)
  http://www.uspto.gov/
  The USPTO offers loads of information on patents and trademarks, including a subject index of contacts, downloadable USPTO forms, and a listing of patent attorneys and agents registered to practice before the USPTO.

- Universities Water Information Network (UWIN)
  http://uwin.siu.edu
  Joint project of U.S. Geological Survey and Universities Council on Water Resources.

- University of Illinois Weather Machine
  http://www.atmos.uiuc.edu
  Detailed weather information for all 50 states, etc. Operated by Department of Atmospheric Sciences at the University of Illinois.

- Useful Internet Sites—WWW sites
  http://www.dot.gov/useful.html
  Descriptions and links to various legal resources on the Internet.

- The VCILP Legal Web
  http://ming.law.vill.edu/legalweb.html
  The Villanova Center for Information Law and Policy is another good archive collection, with numerous links to assist you in locating various types of legal information.

- Wiley & Sons Publishing
  http://www.wiley.com
  A variety of information on the Wiley organization and its various publications.

- World Wide Web Virtual Law Library
  http://www.law.indiana.edu/law/lawindex.html
  This site, managed by the Indiana University School of Law at Bloomington, compiles extensive Web-based listings of many types of law-related references, from law firms to state agencies.

- Yahoo
  http://www.yahoo.com
  Stanford University maintains Yahoo, an impressive World Wide Web searchable "card catalog" containing tons of law-related materials and pointers to other Internet locations.

§ 8.73 Internet Glossary (New)

The following glossary lists some terms and phrases you will encounter when you venture onto the Internet.

analog signals: The type of tones normally transmitted over standard telephone lines. A modem converts the digital signals generated by your PC into analog tones during an on-line session.

anonymous FTP: Internet sites containing archive files that are open to the public (see § **8.61**).

ANSI: American National Standards Institute

Archie: A program that indexes and catalogs files on Internet host computers. (The name is a play on the word "archive.") Archie helps users search for and locate anonymous FTP files (publicly available document files) on computers around the Internet (see § **8.63**).

ARPAnet: Advanced Research Projects Agency Network; the prototype for and ancestor of the Internet (see § **8.47**).

ASCII: American Standard Code for Information Interchange. A standard plain-text format that includes no coding, widely used in the computer industry.

bandwidth: Refers to the size of the data pipeline that carries electronic information over the Internet; the higher the bandwidth, the faster the information can be transmitted.

baud: A unit of speed in data transmission, indicating how fast a modem can transfer information. The higher the rate, the faster the transfer.

BBS: Computer Bulletin Board System. A computer system that you can connect to using a modem. BBS usually refers to small E-mail systems and discussion conferences, maintained either as a hobby or for business purposes.

BITNET: Because It's Time Network. A worldwide academic network of mailing lists connecting more than 1000 universities, colleges, and research organizations in the United States, Canada, and Europe, with gateways to the Internet, Usenet, and other networks. BITNET uses a communications protocol different from the Internet.

bits per second (bps): The speed at which bits of information are sent over communication lines.

ClariNet: A commercial service that offers news and features to newsgroups.

click: To point the mouse pointer at a word or icon on the screen, press the button, and then release quickly; usually used to select an item or activate a program feature.

client: A computer program that requests or uses services from another computer (called a server) (see § **8.50**).

compression: Squeezing data so that computer files take up less disk storage space.

CPU: Central Processing Unit; the main computing part of the computer.

CWIS: Campus-Wide Information Systems; networks that provide college and university campuses with information such as directories, news items, and library connections.

cyberspace: A term sometimes used to refer to the collection of linked computer systems that make up the Internet; a world in which computers and people coexist; the term was coined by author William Gibson in his science fiction novel *Necromancer.*

directory: A menu or list of resources or files available at an Internet site.

domain name: Part of an Internet address that describes what type of entity the information or message comes from, such as .edu for a university or college, .com for commercial entities, and so on (see § **8.71**).

DOS: Disk Operating System. The basic system software that controls the computer and gives it instructions on using other software programs.

download: To copy a file from a remote computer to your computer; opposite of *upload.*

electronic bulletin board: Computer that maintains a central list of messages so computer users on the system can post and read public messages.

Electronic mail or **E-mail:** Electronic messages (text) composed on one computer and sent to another person's computer. E-mail usually refers to private messages; bulletin board usually refers to public messages (see § **8.57**).

FAQ File: Frequently Asked Questions. A sort of HELP file, generally provided for new users of LISTSERVs and Newsgroups to answer basic questions about the service, so that new users do not clutter up the discussion with elementary questions.

finger: A utility program used to locate basic information about users at some federal information sites on the Internet.

flame: An angry or heated response to a message posted on a discussion or Newsgroup system.

Free-net: A community-based organization that provides free Internet access to computer users in certain areas, such as public libraries.

freeware: Software programs that computer users can use free of charge.

front-end software: A program designed to simplify certain online services for users. Many front-end programs have graphical interfaces, simplified menus, help screens, and so on.

FTP: File Transfer Protocol. A tool for transferring files between computers (see § **8.61**).

gateway: A connection between two computer networks, such as between an E-mail service and the Internet. A gateway connection lets you move from one computer system to another.

GIF: Graphics Interchange Format. A popular format for compressing and storing computer pictures, or graphics. A computer file with a .gif extension is a picture file.

Gopher: A menu-based program developed at the University of Minnesota to make it easier to find Internet resources. Gopher organizes Internet files into levels of menus that the user can choose from; a popular way to access the Internet (see § **8.64**).

graphics: A computer's ability to plot individual pixels on the screen, instead of just displaying alphanumeric text characters.

header: The top part of an electronic mail (E-mail) message that identifies the sender, date, and subject matter (see § **8.57**).

home page: The first page of a World Wide Web site; serves as a master table of contents to the groups of computer files connected with a site; home pages are linked by hypertext links to other information files (see § **8.67**).

host computers: Large machines directly connected to the Internet. Host computers store information that thousands of individuals can look up and use.

hostname: The name of a computer that is linked to the Internet. System administrators can assign whatever name they wish.

html: HyperText Markup Language; a coded language used to compose World Wide Web documents (see § **8.67**).

http: HyperText Transfer Protocol; a prefix that indicates a World Wide Web file (example: http://www.paralegals.org).

hypertext links or **hyperlinks:** Specially coded terms or phrases within a World Wide Web document; selecting a link automatically leads to one or more related documents or files (see **§ 8.67**).

icon: A small on-screen picture or graphic that represents a software function or feature.

information superhighway: A futuristic metaphor for a world linked entirely by telecommunications; aka the mature Internet.

interface: How the user's computer screen looks.

Internet: A world-wide system of linked computer networks.

Internet Service Provider (ISP): A company that offers Internet access accounts for sale to users.

InterNIC: Internet Network Information Center.

ISDN: Integrated Services Digital Networks. A scheme for converting the telephone system to digital technology.

jpeg: A compressed-file format for image or picture files (see GIF).

Jughead: A program for searching Gopher files (see **§ 8.65**).

knowbots: Programs that search through networks locating specific information; robotic "librarians."

LAN: Local Area Network; usually refers to a business office system of computers connected to a central server computer.

LISTSERV: A program that manages electronic mailing lists; automatically distributes information to a list of E-mail recipients.

log off: Issue instructions for the computer to terminate a modem connection, thus ending an online session.

log on or **log in:** The process of connecting to a computer network system at the start of a session. Usually entails providing some kind of account name and a password.

macro: A simple program that plays back a series of recorded keystrokes to automate a repetitive chore or task on the computer.

megabyte: A term representing about one million (1,049,576) bytes or characters. Also written as MB, Mb, Mbyte, M-byte and meg.

menu: An on-screen list of computer file names or program options for the user to choose from.

microprocessor: the electronic chip that is the central processing unit (CPU) on a computer; it controls what happens inside the CPU.

modem: An abbreviation that combines the terms MOdulate and DEModulate; a modem is a device that converts digital computer data into electronic signals that can be sent or exchanged over standard telephone lines (it then converts the signals back into digital form so they can be read by the computer at the receiving end) (see § **8.51**).

Mosaic: A graphical interface program designed to access Internet information in a point-and-click fashion; Mosaic was the original freeware program for accessing the WWW hypertext system.

mouse: A hand-held pointing device that moves the cursor on a computer screen with great precision.

multimedia: Files containing multiple kinds of data, such as text, video, sound, and graphics.

NCSA: National Center for Supercomputing Applications; managed by the University of Illinois, NCSA is the home of Mosaic and many large computers containing vast collections of information.

newbies: A popular slang term for new users of the Internet.

NREN: National Research and Education Network. Funded by Vice President Albert Gore's High Performance Computing Act of 1991; a high-performance computer research and development network, targeted for completion in 1996. Will allow faster data transmission and connect (via ISDN and fiberoptics) rural locations and schools to the major universities and research centers in the United States.

online: Communicating with another computer on a network.

password: A code word used to gain access to some Internet sites.

path: The route you follow to reach a certain piece of information on a computer or a network.

pixel: Short for "picture element," a single dot on a computer's display screen.

posting: An article or message sent to a USENET newsgroup.

PPP: Point-to-point protocol; a kind of connection that links a computer to the Internet with a standard telephone line and a high-speed modem.

protocol: A standard set of rules or procedures that two computers must follow in order to correctly exchange and interpret messages or information.

public domain: Refers to free software programs not protected by copyright; public domain software is available to users of a computer network and may be duplicated at will.

RAM: Random Access Memory; the working memory portion of the computer where software programs are loaded and used.

remote access: The ability to use another computer from a distance, usually through a modem and telephone lines.

ROM: Read-Only Memory; the permanently programmed part of a computer's memory that cannot be changed by the user.

server: An Internet computer that has files available to other computers. When you "visit" an Internet site, you are connecting to a server.

session: The time between log-on and log-off that a computer user spends working on a computer system.

service provider: See Internet Service Provider.

shareware: Computer software programs that can be copied and distributed so users can try them out before deciding whether to buy them.

site: A computer network compilation of data; many sites have information on multiple topics; many are still being developed.

Telnet: An Internet protocol that lets you connect to another computer and use it as if it were on your desk (see § **8.60**).

upload: To send or copy a file from your computer to another computer; opposite of *download.*

URL: Uniform Resource Locator. A standard method of "addressing" locations on the Internet (see § **8.70**).

USENET: A worldwide, public-access network of Newsgroups on the Internet; used for electronic mail and special-interest groups.

USENET Newsgroups: Discussion groups where users exchange messages about specific topics.

user: A person who uses a computer on the Internet.

user interface: The features of a computer program that determine how the program looks on the screen to the person using the computer.

Veronica: A service that helps the user search Gopher menus for key words (see § **8.65**).

WAIS: Wide Area Information Server. A powerful system for full-text searching in databases or libraries on the Internet (see § **8.66**).

World Wide Web, WWW, W3, or **the Web:** A hypertext system for browsing through Internet resources; WWW documents contain hypertext links to other related files on the Internet (see § **8.67**).

§ 8.74 Selected Bibliography (New)

For readers seeking more information about the Internet and related topics, I recommend the following resources.

G. Burgess Allison, "A Bestiary of INTERNET Services," *Law Practice Management* (March 1995).

David Angell & Brent Heslop, *The Internet Business Companion* (Addison-Wesley, 1995).

Paul Bernstein, "Making Connections on the Internet," *TRIAL* (Jan. 1995).

Judith Broadhurst, "Use Technology to Get Help Online," *Executive Female* (July/Aug. 1994).

Elizabeth Powell Crowe, *The Electronic Traveller: Exploring Alternative Online Systems* (Windcrest/McGraw-Hill, 1994).

Frank J. Derfler, Jr. & Les Freed, *How Networks Work* (Ziff-Davis Press, 1993).

Daniel P. Dern, *The Internet Guide for New Users* (McGraw-Hill 1994).

Paul Gilster, *Finding It on the Internet: The Essential Guide to Archie, Veronica, Gopher, WAIS, WWW (Including Mosaic) and Other Search and Browsing Tools* (John Wiley & Sons, 1994).

Brent Heslop & David Angell, *The Instant Internet Guide* (Addison-Wesley, 1994).

Daniel B. Kennedy, "E-Mail Expansion," *ABA Journal* (June 1995).

Peter Kent, *The Complete Idiot's Guide to the Internet* (McMillan, 1994).

Ed Krol, *The Whole Internet User's Guide & Catalog* (O'Reilly & Associates, 1994).

Lawrence Magid, "New software untangles access to Web sites," *Business First* (March 20, 1995).

§ 8.74 SELECTED BIOGRAPHY

Bruce Maxwell, "How to Access the Federal Government on the INTERNET," *Congressional Quarterly* (1995).

Gregory Miller, "Getting Primed for the Internet: An Introductory Roadmap," *National Paralegal Reporter* (Summer 1995).

Javed Mostafa, *The Easy Internet Handbook* (Hi Willow Research & Publishing, 1994).

Jack Nimersheim, *The First Book of Modem Communications* (SAMS, 1991).

Eric Persson, *NetPower: Resource Guide to Online Computer Services* (Fox Chapel, 1993).

Steve Rimmer, *Planet Internet* (Windcrest/McGraw-Hill, 1995).

Charles Seiter, *The Internet for MACS for Dummies* (IDG Books, 1994).

Donald D. Spencer, Ph.D., *Personal Computer Dictionary* (Camelot, 1995).

David P. Vandagriff, "Hanging Ten on the Internet," *ABA Journal* (Feb. 1995).

Tracy Weidner, "Using the Internet for Substantive Research," *National Paralegal Reporter (Fall 1995).*

Lamont Wood, *Get On-Line* (John Wiley & Sons, 1993).

INDEX

ISBN 0-471-18534-5